The
PRAETORIUS ORGAN

By
PAUL G. BUNJES

Doctoral dissertation
issued by permission of the
Graduate Research Committee
of the Eastman School
of Music of the University
of Rochester, Rochester,
New York

Concordia Publishing House

St. Louis   London

PREFACE

The present study on <u>The Praetorius Organ</u> concerns
itself with an area of learning which has been inaccessible
to many for a very long time. Inasmuch as modern theoreticians and technicians are seeking to develop a theory of
the organ for our time, it is both natural and rewarding
that a lively interest should have become evident in the
principles and practices of the Baroque with respect to the
instrument. To the writer's knowledge no comprehensive effort has thus far been undertaken to explain, organize, and
summarize the theories presented by M. Praetorius in his
<u>De Organographia</u> and illustrated in his <u>Theatrum Instrumen-</u>
<u>torum</u>. Published in 1619 and 1620 respectively, these
treatises appeared at a most appropriate time and may be
considered an excellent primary record of the ideals which
moved the artisans of the early baroque period and of the
theories which guided their efforts. It is in the hope of
bringing these studies back to life that the present work
was undertaken.

The <u>Praetorius Organ</u> concerns itself with three major areas of investigation. It seeks, first of all, to
gather together, summarize, organize, and develop a useful
terminology for, the concepts which prevail today in western

ii

Europe and in America, and which seem to control the development of the tonal resource of the organ and its systematic incorporation. It seeks, secondly, to explore, analyze, and extract the principles which governed the creation of the organ as a musical instrument during the period of the Early Baroque. M. Praetorius in the _De Organographia_ and, together with E. Compenius, in the _Orgeln Verdingnis_, painstakingly outlines and discusses the art of the organ as he envisioned it and as it was realized in the surviving records of noteworthy instruments of the time. Many specifications and annotations concerning instruments constructed by such builders as E. and H. Compenius, G. Fritzsche, H. Scherer, D. Beck, H. Henke, and others have found their way into these writings. It seeks, finally, to relate the theories of our time to those of the Early Baroque with a view toward discovering a surviving legacy, recognizing similarities and differences, and rediscovering useful concepts which may have been lost in the intervening time.

Within the proposed scope of the present study certain outcomes were sought to be realized. First of all, an effort was made to reconstitute, as far as possible, the mechanical and pneumatic disposition of the early baroque instruments, from which an insight could be gained as to their operation and control. From such a study a fairly accurate appraisal can be made which, in turn, may hopefully prove useful for further research into this or related areas.

iii

Without such knowledge and insight, the surviving records of tonal dispositions are hardly intelligible to the modern scholar. It is only through a thorough investigation of the engineering capabilities of the time that many of the symptoms described by the theoreticians can be properly diagnosed. From such diagnoses the principles which underlie the work of these early builders can be effectively rediscovered.

Secondly, it was sought, wherever possible, to develop the tonal resource of the time into quantitative measure, so that the governing principles can be accurately defined and related to present-day theory. In order to make such comparisons meaningful, it became necessary to summarize and organize the prevailing concepts of the organ as they have emerged in our time. Such concepts are, unfortunately, scattered widely throughout the contemporary literature and are not directly accessible to the student or the technician. It became equally necessary to set all current quantitative measures into the framework of American technology and shop practice, based upon units of measure commonly used or possible of use in our country.

Thirdly, it was hoped that by a careful analysis, quantitative definition, and comparative relation, certain concepts of the time which may have been lost during the intervening years, might be rediscovered to contribute toward the re-establishment of a useful set of principles for the instrument of our time.

Finally, it was considered a legitimate burden of the present thesis to re-examine the early concepts and their realization from unimpeachable primary sources, so that misconceptions which have come down through the subsequent literature might be resolved. From time to time it seemed appropriate also to indicate areas of study in the field which could bear further investigation.

In order to present the rather large amount of material demanded by the scope of the present study, in a clear and useful format, the present work is organized into four major parts, each of which comprises a single volume.

The first part contains seven chapters and is subtitled, "Basic Concepts of the Organ." It deals with the requisite mechanical, pneumatic, and acoustical foundations of the instrument as expounded by such contemporary theoreticians as Mahrenholz, Supper, Smets, Elis, and Ellerhorst. It also draws in supplementary information from the classical literary monuments of modern times by such theoreticians as Werckmeister, Dom Bedos, Adlung, Toepfer, Hopkins, and Audsley. Within it are developed basic concepts dealing with the chest mechanism, the harness, and the application of the wind. A taxonomy of the tonal resource of the organ based upon the factors which differentiate the classifications is undertaken here and designed to reflect and enlarge the groundwork initiated by others. All tables and illustrative charts are predicated upon American Standard Pitch and are presented in metric values, occasionally extended to include British equivalents.

The second part comprises four chapters and is subtitled, "The Early Baroque Organ: Mechanics and Pneumatics." It deals with a systematic investigation of the manner in which the chest mechanisms and harness systems were laid out by the early baroque builders. The whole concept of permanent coupling and transmission is here explored to as full an extent as the record of Praetorius and Compenius will allow. A detailed study of the wind systems employed by the early builders contributes supplementary insights into the influential effect of pneumatics upon the concept of the organ. In order to rest the study upon a secure footing, extensive quotations from the primary sources have been presented and parallel translations subjoined, so that the interested scholar may continuously check the present author's discussions and conclusions.

The third part comprises four chapters and is subtitled, "The Early Baroque Organ: The Tonal Resource." Here an effort is made to discover in a quantitative way, the organ registers which constitute the tonal repertoire of the Early Baroque. Praetorius is the only writer of the time who provides a comprehensive insight into this important area of activity. A careful study of his record can provide the modern scholar with an encyclopedic summation of his tonal concepts and their implementation by his contemporaries.

Whenever possible, findings in this area are compared and related to the current theories concerning the tonal resource.

The fourth part gathers together useful material in the form of supplementary appendices, charts, and plates, and is subtitled, "Atlas: Appendices, Bibliographies, Charts, and Plates." It was felt that a separation of these items from the text would permit a clear and unencumbered presentation of the cursive discussion and provide a handy study tool to expedite references made to this material in the ongoing presentations of the text.

The entire project comprised a period of eleven years from its inception until its conclusion (_i.e._ 1954-1965), and the writer wishes publicly to acknowledge and gratefully thank certain individuals for specialized assistance he received in the pursuit of this study. Mr. Herman Schlicker, president of the organ firm that bears his name, undertook the fabrication of all of the labial pipes shown in the De Organographia and in its accompanying atlas, the Theatrum Instrumentorum. Mr. Benjamin W. Woodward prepared the electronic apparatus required to secure frequency readings from the fabricated pipes, and assisted in the actual registration of the frequencies. Prof. Theodore Klammer translated the several Latin segments of the original source. Prof. Richard Lange was of incalculable assistance in verifying the mathematical propositions which underlie certain portions of this study. The author's wife, Barbara, typed the entire manuscript in its initial and final forms. Much encouragement and assistance were graciously supplied by Dr. Allen Irvine McHose, Associate Director, and by Dr. Wayne Barlow, Associate Dean for Graduate Research Studies and director of the present thesis, both of the faculty of the Eastman School of Music of the University of Rochester.

The entire thesis is submitted in the hope that it may be helpful in the quest for a clear understanding of the Praetorius organ in its mechanical, pneumatic, and tonal aspects.

June 1, 1965   Paul G. Bunjes
                               Chairman: Division of Music
                               Concordia Teachers College
                               River Forest, Illinois

TABLE OF CONTENTS

PART I. BASIC CONCEPTS OF THE ORGAN

Chapter

TABLE OF CONTENTS--Continued

LIST OF TABLES

LIST OF TABLES--Continued

LIST OF TABLES--Continued

LIST OF APPENDICES

LIST OF CHARTS--<u>Continued</u>

PART I

BASIC CONCEPTS OF THE ORGAN

CHAPTER I

THE TRACKER ORGAN: MECHANICAL
AND PNEUMATIC DISPOSITION

Of paramount importance in the pursuit of Praetorius'
theory of the organ[1] is a thorough knowledge of the basic
concepts underlying the functioning of the old mechanical or
tracker organ. It is, therefore, desirable to lay out and
establish, first of all, a frame of reference to which all
the theoretical concepts that may emerge in the work of
Praetorius and his contemporaries can be compared, similarities and differences noted, and departures and extensions
analyzed. Upon such a foundation, a comprehensive and meaningful theory of the organ as Praetorius practiced it and
as it is reflected in the instruments of his day can be
built up, step by step.

Such a frame of reference must concern itself with
the three general areas that comprise the functional unity
of the organ; namely, the mechanical disposition, the system
of wind supply, and the concepts governing the registers.

The Mechanical Layout

The mechanical layout of the tracker organ divides
itself into four distinct areas. These are:

2

1. The chest itself with its internal disposition

2. The tracker action as such, comprising the
machinery between the key and the chest

3. The stop action, comprising the machinery
between the drawknob and the slider in the chest

4. The coupling system

The Chest Itself

The slider chest is the type which was used almost
exclusively by Praetorius and the builders of his time.
This chest is of a rectangular shape, divided latitudinally
into as many partitions as the keyboard which controls it
has keys. These partitions are channels and are equipped
with openings below to receive the pressure wind from the
pallet box by means of pallet valves, operated by the keys.[2]
Above the channels are openings in the form of round holes
for the purpose of expending the wind into the pipes.

Below the chest, but firmly attached to it, is another rectangular compartment which is as long as, but only
partly as wide as, the chest. This compartment holds the
wind under pressure, and contains as many movable valves as
the chest has channels. These valves are in the upper part
of this compartment and are seated against the lower openings
of the chest above. They are attached to the keys and serve
to admit wind into the channels whenever a key is depressed.

The top of the chest comprises a superstructure which contains, among other things, the <u>sliders</u> (from which designation the chest derives its name) which can be shifted longitudinally to an "on" or "off" position. When "on," the slider permits the wind from the channel to enter the pipe; when "off," it will check the flow of the wind.

This meager description gives but the barest outline of the chest and its function. A somewhat closer inspection of this type of chest will serve to refine the concepts. The Atlas presents correlated plan, elevation, section, and perspective drawings of a typical tracker chest layout, including the customary English terms for the various parts and mechanisms attached to it. The following discussion refers to these drawings. See Plates I, II, III, IV, V, VI, and VII.

Whenever the bellows are operated, the pallet box $\underline{B}$ is supplied with wind under pressure. The tracker $\underline{E}$ together with the pull-down $\underline{C}$ is connected with the appropriate manual or pedal key. When the key is depressed, the corresponding pallet valve $\underline{A}$ is pulled away from its seat and the wind is admitted into the appropriate channel $\underline{G}$, which, running latitudinally across the whole chest, is able to communicate with any or every pipe of the corresponding note on the chest. A slider $\underline{K}$ is provided for each set of pipes. When the register is drawn, the holes in the slider

correspond to the holes in the table J and upper board L.
Accordingly, whenever wind is admitted to the channel G, it
will immediately be admitted to the appropriate note or pipe
of every register on the chest whose slider is in the "on"
position. The wind thus admitted excites the pipe. When
the slider K is in the "off" position, its holes will not
correspond with those in the table J and upper board L, and
so no wind is admitted from the channel G to the pipe O of
the register thus turned "off." Upon releasing the key the
pallet A returns, by action of the spring D to its position
of rest, thus cutting off the wind to the channel G and
thereby also to the pipe O, causing the same to remain silent.

The Tracker Action

The action of the tracker organ comprises the machinery needed to transmit the motion of the key to the pallet. The key, pivoting on a rail, transmits its motion to
the pallet by means of squares, backfalls, stickers, rollers,
and trackers, all properly aligned and levered to combine a
maximum of motion with a minimum of friction. The effort is
to secure the greatest possible efficiency of action.

The manual key is usually pivoted near its center in
the form of a first class lever, so that the initial motion
of the key is inverted and reacts in a contrary direction.
See Plate VIII, 1. A downward motion at D is transmitted as

an upward motion at $\underline{E}$.

The pedal key is usually pivoted near one end after the manner of a third class lever, so that its motion is not inverted but remains direct. See Plate VIII, 2. A downward motion at $\underline{D}$ reacts as a similar motion at $\underline{E}$.

Stickers are rigid rods of wood which are employed to transmit a pushing force. See Plate VIII, 3. The motion at $\underline{E}$ is transmitted as a similar motion at $\underline{G}$.

Trackers are flexible bands of wood attached by means of leather buttons (nuts) and employed to transmit a pulling force. See Plate VIII, 4. The motion at $\underline{E}$ is transmitted as a similar motion at $\underline{G}$.

Squares are pivoted right angles of wood which are employed to change direction of motion, as for example, from vertical to horizontal. See Plate IX, 1. The upward motion at $\underline{E}$ is converted to a horizontal motion at $\underline{G}$.

Depending upon how the square is positioned, it can achieve a variety of directional changes. See Plate IX, 2. All of the horizontal motions at $\underline{E}$ are changed to vertical motions at $\underline{G}$.

A combination of squares, properly positioned, permits a multiple change of direction. See Plate X, 1. The upward motion at $\underline{E}$ is converted to a horizontal motion and thence to a downward motion at $\underline{G}$.

A backfall is a thin, but fairly rigid strip of

wood, pivoted in the center and employed to change direction of motion (in effect, it is a 90° square extended to 180°). See Plate X, 2. The upward motion at E is converted to a downward motion at G.

A combination of backfall and square is known as a T-square, and permits change of motion into two different directions. See Plate XI, 1. The upward motion at E is changed to a downward motion at G_1 and a horizontal motion at G_2.

A roller is employed to shift motion from one plane into another. See Plate XI, 2. The upward motion at E is eventually converted to a downward motion at G, but in a different plane from that of the original.

A gang of rollers mounted on a frame known as a roller board is used not only to shift motions into different planes, but also to re-space the original planes. See Plate XII, 1 and 2. The motions at E are shifted to different planes at G.

A combination of all of the mechanical devices is sufficient to display the working action of a complete system from key to pallet. See Plate XIII.

The Stop Action

The stop action of the tracker organ comprises the mechanism needed to transmit motion from the draw knob to the slider, in order to shift it into or out of position.

When shifted into registration ("on"), its bores will correspond exactly with the appropriate bores in the table and upper board; when shifted out of registration ("off"), its bores will not correspond. No other mechanical devices, other than those already illustrated and discussed, are needed to effect this action. The devices are, to be sure, more sturdily and rigidly constructed in order to withstand the greater resistance offered by the various parts of the mechanism. Certain items are often fabricated of iron rather than of wood, in order to resist the greater force placed upon them when operated. Alternate labels are employed for the mechanical devices: drawknob, drawpull, trundle, trace, etc. See Plate XIV. The sketch is in perspective and shows one stop in registration ("on"). When the drawknob A is drawn outward, its drawpull B acts upon the trundle arm C_1 and trundle D_1 by turning the same in a counterclockwise direction. Trundle arm C_2 acts upon trace F which, in turn, rotates trundle D_2 through trundle arm C_3 in a clockwise direction, causing its right-angled trundle arm C_4 to draw out slider E and place it into registration ("on"), thereby aligning the bores. The effect of the key action is thereupon capable of being consummated, since the wind is able to reach and excite the appropriate pipe. When the drawknob A is pushed inward or cancelled, the motion is contrary throughout the system, and the slider is shifted out of registration ("off"), so that its bores will not correspond with the ones in the table and upper board. In this case, the effect of the key action will reach the slider, but the slider will serve as a check to prevent the wind in the channel from reaching and exciting the pipe.

The Coupler System

The purpose of the coupler system is to make it possible to play registers from another or from several other different chests upon a given keyboard. Basically, there exist two methods of implementing this purpose:

1. The keyboards themselves may be coupled

    a. By shifting the keyboard into and out of position, thereby engaging or disengaging the coupling action

    b. By shifting the coupler mechanism instead, in order to achieve the same effect

2. The action may be coupled

    a. By shifting the keyboards into and out of position, thereby engaging or disengaging the coupler mechanism

    b. By shifting the coupler mechanism, in order to achieve the same effect

To be sure, many diverse methods and devices have been historically employed to realize all of these functions, but it will be sufficient to present one schematic illustration for each of the four basic dispositions enumerated above.

For Case 1a, the keyboards are coupled by shifting the manuals. See Plate XV, 1. In this case, coupling is effected by pulling the upper keyboard a certain distance out toward the player. By this shift the upper manual is coupled to the lower. When playing on the lower keyboard while the coupler is engaged, the keys of the upper manual are visibly affected, moving in the same direction as the lower keys.

For Case 1b, the keyboards are coupled by shifting the coupler mechanism. See Plate XV, 2. In this case, the keyboards are not shifted, but remain stationary at all times. Instead, the gang of coupler jacks is shifted into or out of position in order to engage or disengage the coupling mechanism. As in the previous case, the upper manual is coupled to the lower, so that when playing on the lower keyboard, the upper is visibly affected.

For Case 2a, the mechanical action is coupled by shifting a keyboard. See Plate XVI. In this case, coupling is effected by pushing the lower keyboard a certain distance away from the player. By this device, the upper manual is coupled to the lower. When playing on the lower keyboard while the coupler is engaged, the keys of the upper manual are not visibly affected.

For Case 2b, the mechanical action is coupled by shifting the coupler mechanism. See Plate XVII. In this case, the keyboards are not shifted, but remain stationary at all times. Instead, the gang of backfalls is shifted into or out of position in order to engage or disengage the coupling mechanism. As in the previous case, the upper manual is coupled to the lower, so that when playing on the lower keyboard while the coupler is engaged, the upper keys are not visibly affected.

The System of Wind Supply

In order to bring the organ to life, a continuous and controlled supply of pressure wind is required. In connection with the wind supply for the organ, three areas require delineation:

1. The machinery and method for capturing, storing, and controlling the wind

2. The machinery and method for conducting or transporting the wind; devices for disturbing it

3. Methods of measuring the wind pressure

Capturing, Storing, and Controlling
the Wind

The starting point for any wind system in the organ is a mechanism designed to capture a portion of the atmosphere, hold it in confinement, compress it, and expend it into the pallet boxes of the chests while registering a pressure beyond that of the surrounding atmosphere. For this purpose the tracker organ had recourse to a pneumatic device known as a bellows. Two forms of bellows seem to have been in common use at various times. The older form featured a series of ribs inserted between two panels which were hinged to form a wedge and could be folded and unfolded. So constructed, the device may be termed a multiple fold bellows. Its skeleton consisted of a top panel, a bottom panel, and a system of triangular and trapezoidal ribs, all hinged at one end (the "front" of the bellows) and free at the other end (the "rear"). See Plate XVIII, 1. To seal the bellows, the joints of the ribs and the hinge were overlaid with strips and gussets of leather, in order to create an air-tight compartment. See Plate XVIII, 2.

In order to capture air and compress it, certain appurtenances were required. There had to be intake openings covered with movable valves which were generally positioned on the bottom panel. These were constructed and fitted, so that they would open to admit air when the bellows were unfolded, and close, in order to confine air, when the bellows were folded. See Plate XIX, 1. The intake valves were most often in the form of hinged panels of wood, attached so as to operate over the appropriate openings of the bottom panel. They were mounted on the inside and toward the rear of the bellows. The valves themselves

were frequently shaped in the form of prisms and underlaid
with leather, which was extended beyond the edge to serve
as a hinge. See Plate XIX, 2. When positioned, four valves
were placed back to back in pairs, freely hinged, and provided with bumpers to prevent their opening farther than
necessary. See Plate XIX, 3.

Whenever the top panel was raised by unfolding the
bellows, the freely hinged valves would open to admit a
portion of air into the bellows compartment. When, however,
the top panel was forced downward by folding the bellows,
the captured air within the compartment, seeking to escape
through the intake openings, would press the valves firmly
against these openings and cut off its own escape. Confined
within the compartment, the air was compressed and held cap-
tive.

However, an escape route was provided elsewhere for
the compressed air. It was exhausted into the canal which
fed it through the wind trunk and the subsidiary conductors
into the pallet boxes of the various chests. For this purpose exhaust openings were cut into the bottom panel of the
bellows toward the front. These were connected directly to
the wind canal of the organ. See Plate XX, 1. The entire
working assembly, drawn in longitudinal section, appeared as
shown on Plate XX, 2. The bottom panel B was rigidly af-
fixed to a supporting beam K at the roar end of the bellows,

and to the throat I at the front end. When the top panel A
was lifted by means of the handle L, the ribs C unfolded.
The valves F, freely hinged, opened to admit air into the
bellows compartment through the intake openings E. Concomitantly, an exhaust check valve located in the throat I and
subsequently to be described, closed, thus denying the bellows any intake through its own exhaust openings H. As soon
as the motion of the top panel A was reversed and the bellows made to fold, the air within the compartment forced
the intake valves F to close immediately, while the air, in
the process of being compressed, could and would escape only
through the exhaust openings H and enter the canal through
the throat I. Through each cycle of the bellows action, the
compartment took in air, compressed it, and expended it.

The more recent single fold type of bellows operated, in nearly all respects, exactly as the multiple fold
type and was equipped with the same appurtenances. It differed from the preceding in that its top panel and bottom
panel were hinged together by a single set of ribs; it presented, therefore, a single rather than a multiple fold.
See Plate XXI, 1.

Whereas the multiple fold type of bellows could be
constructed only in a moderate size, the single fold type
permitted much larger construction and could capture, compress, and expend a much greater volume of wind in one cycle.

Both forms of bellows could be mounted, so that the bottom
panel lay either in a horizontal plane or on an incline,
with the front resting higher than the rear. See Plate
XXI, 2.

The bellows were usually operated indirectly; the
top panel A was weighted with stones, bricks, or heavy
plates of iron or lead. In operating the bellows, the operator merely raised the top panel A to unfold the bellows
and capture a quantity of air; the bellows were "cocked."
In the reverse phase of the cycle, the inert mass of the
weights served to compress the air within the bellows and
deliver it through the exhaust openings into the canal.

One illustration will serve to show how the bellows
were disposed for indirect operation. See Plate XXII. The
cocking took place in front of the bellows. By means of
the lever P, the bellows were cocked by hand, one at a time,
in order to capture air. While the second one was being
cocked, the first one compressed its air by means of the
surmounted weights Q, and delivered it under pressure into
the canal.

Although the organs of the late sixteenth and early
seventeenth centuries displayed no additional basic devices
for developing wind in the organ, the most important single
advance in the mechanism concerned with the wind supply will
serve to show how the lack of this additional equipment in

the early organs presented grave difficulties to the builders in their efforts to secure a steady wind for the instrument. This improved mechanism was in the form of the so-
called compound bellows. Audsley points to its invention
and first application: "The compound bellows was invented
about the year 1762 by an English clock-maker by the name of
Cumming. It was put to practical test for the first time in
an organ constructed for the Earl of Brute in 1787."[3] The
compound bellows, in effect, was an intermediary storage
compartment known as a receiver or, less aptly, a reservoir
inserted into the wind supply system between the moving
diagonal bellows and the wind canal; it comprised, actually,
both mechanisms. Audsley describes it thus:[4]

> The compound bellows comprises two chief por-
> tions -- the feeder or feeders and the receiver. The
> feeders collect the air and inject it into the re-
> ceiver, where it is compressed to the required degree
> under the action of weights or springs. It passes
> thence either directly, through wind trunks to the
> wind chests, or is distributed to the intermediate
> reservoirs.

See Plate XXIII. The feeders R, in the form of the
single fold, diagonal bellows described earlier and occurring here in two pairs, were mounted on the under side of
the receiver S in an upside down position. They were provided with intake valves which communicated with the atmosphere, and exhaust valves which communicated with the receiver S immediately above. The exhaust valves of the feed-

ers served also as intake valves for the receiver. To the
trunk band T of the receiver, were attached the wind trunks,
forming exhaust openings for it. The wind trunks contained
the necessary exhaust valves which opened whenever the pressure in the receiver was greater than in the trunk, and
closed whenever the reverse was true. In action, the pulsa-
tions occurred in the feeders while the receiver merely rose
or fell to maintain a consistent density of the air stored
within it. The contribution toward a steady and plentiful
wind supply which the compound bellows made, was vast; its
omission points up the inadequacy and unsteadiness of the
wind supply in the earlier organs here under investigation.

Conducting, Transporting, and

Disturbing the Wind

The compressed wind, upon leaving the bellows
through its exhaust openings, entered the system provided
for conveying it to the various parts of the organ, culminating eventually in the pallet boxes of the various chests.
Basically, the conveyances were of four types, all connected:

1. The throats, which were firmly attached to
the exhaust openings of the bellows and conveyed the
wind into the canal

2. The canal, which communicated with all the
throats and delivered the wind into the common wind

trunk

3. The wind trunk, which led from the canal into the appropriate area of the instrument where the wind needed to be distributed

4. The wind conductors, which were branches in the form of diminutive trunks and were used to distribute the wind from the common trunk into the various pallet boxes. See Plate XXIV, 1.

The throat was attached to the front of the bellows. In the case of the multiple fold bellows, it extended into the bellows compartment through the exhaust opening. A sketch in longitudinal section will serve to illustrate the method of mounting as well as show the general disposition of the exhaust valve. See Plate XXIV, 2. The exhaust valve E was freely hinged and opened whenever the pressure in the bellows exceeded that in the canal E; it closed when the opposite condition occurred. It actually performed a double function: it served as an exhaust valve for the bellows and as an intake valve for the canal.

In the case of the single fold bellows, the throat was attached to the exterior of the exhaust opening, extending from there into the wind trunk. Often the exhaust valve was made in smaller units as shown on Plate XXV, 1.

The wind trunk was normally constructed of wood in a shape either square or rectangular in cross section. One end of it was joined to the canal which gathered the pressure wind from the series of bellows throats, and the other end was joined to the various conductors required to distribute the wind to the several pallet boxes. The wind conductors were always of less area in their cross sections than the wind trunk which fed them. Joined to the wind trunk, they proceeded by the shortest possible route to the pallet boxes which they supplied with wind whenever the bellows were operated. It will be noted that any mechanical or pneumatic contrivances introduced into the wind trunk affected the whole instrument, while those introduced into the conductors affected only those chests with which they communicated.

Certain devices associated with the wind trunk and its conductors occurred in the older organs, and their use constituted an important element of registration. Of these devices, two were very much in evidence; these were the wind trunk ventils and the tremulants.

Wind trunk ventils were check valves which, when closed, cut off the supply of wind. When placed into the main wind trunk, such a ventil shut off the wind to any chests or pneumatic mechanisms lying farther from the bellows than itself. In short, the whole organ could be silenced by engaging such a ventil. Those ventils which were introduced into the subsidiary conductors affected only

those chests and pneumatic mechanisms which the respective
conductor normally supplied with wind. Depending upon how
ventils were introduced into the wind trunk and conductors
of an organ, it was possible to silence one or another division or possibly the entire organ by engaging the requisite
draw knob to open or shut one or another of these ventils.
Plate XXV, 2 presents a schematic diagram of a wind trunk
ventil.

Of the tremulants, two types were distinguishable.
One was the tremblant doux or mild tremulant, the other,
the tremblant fort or strong tremulant. Both were intended
to impart to the wind some pulsating effect which could
affect the speech of the pipes. It was reflected there either mildly or boldly, depending upon which type of tremulant was in operation.

The tremblant doux was a counterbalanced gate in the
main wind trunk which was confined entirely within it and
had no communication with the outer atmosphere. See Plate
XXVI, 1. The mechanism was placed in a somewhat enlarged
segment of the wind trunk, so that the opening for the tremulant ventil M would not be any less in cross section than
the area of the entering wind trunk itself. When disengaged, the lever L held the tremulant ventil M open and stationary, allowing the wind free and unaffected egress to
the wind conductor K. When engaged, the lever L dropped

the tremulant ventil M over its opening, so that the wind
from the trunk B could act upon it. The wind approaching
the ventil would open it and thereby upset the equilibrium
of the spring weight N which would react and close the ventil M; thereupon the cycle thus established, repeated periodically, provided the spring weight N was adjusted to and
in balance with the wind acting upon the ventil M. This
type of tremulant had a very mild effect since no wind was
taken out of the trunk; it was merely propagated in undu-
lating waves.

The tremblant fort or Bock tremulant as the Germans
were apt to call it, was a more elaborate mechanism, lying
partly within and partly outside the wind trunk. It permitted the wind trunk to communicate with the outer atmosphere. See Plate XXVI, 2. When disengaged, the tremulant
mechanism occupied the positions shown, permitting the wind
in the trunk B to pursue its normal course unaffected, since
the opening was fully closed. When engaged, the coil spring
C, by action of the draw rod J, opened the inner ventil F,
permitting the pressure wind to enter the ventil box I.
Since the pressure in the box was thereupon greater than
atmosphere, the outer ventil G opened to permit a segment
of wind to escape to atmosphere. While opening, the outer
ventil G exhausted the ventil box I, causing the pressure
wind in trunk B, together with the tension of V-spring E,

to close the inner ventil F. Thereupon, the outer ventil G
would fall, and its momentary impulse upon the air in ventil
box I was sufficient to allow the coil spring C to overcome
the force of V-spring E and reopen the inner ventil F.
Thereupon, the cycle thus established repeated periodically.
As in the previous case, the various springs and weights
had to be neatly adjusted and in perfect balance. This type
of tremulant had a much stronger effect upon the wind, since
it actually discharged segments of it to the atmosphere.
Audsley describes the effect as follows: "The puffs of air,
which this appliance permitted to escape at regular intervals, communicated a pulsation to the wind of the organ, and
caused the speech of the pipe-work to tremble."[5]

Measuring the Wind

There are two basic methods of measuring the pressure of the wind in the organ. One is by means of the
single-column manometer, the other by means of the double-
column manometer. Both manometers are of the open type, and
in either case water is used as the inert mass. The intake
nozzle of the gauge is attached to the wind conductor or to
the pipe bore in the chest; the pressure of the wind will be
the same at any of these connecting points.

Dom Bedos illustrates the single-column manometer.[6]
See Plate XXVII, 1. The container A is filled with water
through the bung D up to the initial water level E. The

bung D is then corked and the nozzle B is attached to the
wind conductor by means of a rubber hose. The pressure of
the wind, acting upon the initial water level E in the nozzle B, forces it downward. The displaced water seeks escape through the glass tube C, rising therein to the final
water level F. In doing so, the level of the water in the
container recedes, lowering, therefore, also the initial
zero point of the water level in the tube C. Since the
tube is calibrated in some agreeable units of measurement,
the wind pressure can be read off directly by comparing the
final level of the water in the tube C with the calibration
on the tube. If the water level in the tube C rises one
inch, the pressure will be read off as one inch of wind but
will, in effect, be somewhat greater, since the initial zero
point will have receded somewhat.

Toepfer illustrates the double-column manometer.[7]
See Plate XXVII, 2. The glass tube C is filled halfway with
water which, seeking its own level, will rise to an equal
level in tube G. The nozzle B is attached to the wind conductor. The pressure of the wind, acting upon the water in
tube G, forces it downward in this segment of the tube and
upward an equal amount in segment C. Since the tubes are
calibrated in agreeable units of measurement on gauge H,
the wind pressure is read off directly as the difference
between the levels in the two tubes. If the water level in

tube <u>C</u> rises <u>one</u> inch, the pressure will be read off as <u>two</u> inches of wind.

Accordingly, the single-column manometer registers somewhat less than half the pressure of the double-column manometer; conversely, the double-column manometer registers somewhat more than twice the pressure of the single-column type. For example, a given pressure which registers one inch on the single-column manometer will register in excess of two inches on the double-column manometer; a given pressure which registers one inch on the double-column manometer will register less than one-half inch on the single-column manometer.

CHAPTER II

THE MODERN ORGAN: ORDERS AND

FAMILIES OF REGISTERS

With respect to the mechanical disposition and wind
supply of the organ, chapter i examined the earliest intelligible and comprehensive sources, in order to establish
the concepts of a functional system which could serve as a
legitimate frame of reference for the pursuit of the Praetorius organ. With respect to the voices and tonal structures of the organ, however, the basic concepts had best be
developed out of present day theory and practice, because
the concepts concerning the tonal resources of the modern
organ are predicated upon and seek to revivify the theory
that underlay the work of the Early and High Baroque builders, the former of which form the major burden of the present study.

Modern theory with respect to the voices of the
organ finds its most noteworthy and systematic expression
in the writings of Christhard Mahrenholz,[1] Hans Henny Jahnn,[2]
Walter Supper,[3] Winfred Ellerhorst,[4] and Paul Smets.[5] A
composite theory. concisely outlined and summarized from
these writings and coupled with the current practice of our

most significant builders, will serve to provide the necessary foundation and reference against which the tonal concepts of the Praetorius organ can be compared and contrasted.

The Designation of Pitch

The modern system of pitch designation for the voices
of the organ has developed somewhat consistently over a period of several centuries. It expresses the pitch of organ
voices in terms of foot lengths; thus, 8', 4', 2 2/3', 2',
etc. The relation of the foot designation to the physical
length of a pipe has a rather loose basis, largely caused by
the following conditions:

1. Different species of feet have been used for
reference in different times and places, as for example, the Rhenish, the Brunswick, the Weimar, the
English foot, etc.

2. Standard pitches have varied from time to
time

3. The lower limits of the keyboard have not
always been the same

4. The reference, in any case, has always been
merely approximate to the physical length of the corpus of a Great C open cylindrical pipe of moderate
scale

The first point of reference is the designation, 8'
pitch. This is what is known as aequal pitch or the pitch

whose frequency agrees with the notation. By using the
American Standard pitch as reference, an organ voice which
vibrates at 440 cycles per second when a' is played upon
the keyboard, is said to be of aequal or 8' pitch. See
Appendix A. The same is true of any voice which vibrates
at 261.63 cycles per second when c' is played. The designation, 4' pitch, describes that pitch whose frequency is
twice that of the notation; hence, an octave above aequal
pitch. The 4' voice will vibrate at 880 cycles per second
at a' or at 523.25 cycles per second at c'. The designation, 2 2/3' pitch, describes that pitch whose frequency is
three times that of the notation; thus, the 2 2/3' voice
will vibrate at 1318.51 cycles per second at a' or at 783.99
cycles per second at c'.[6]

Theoretically expressed, the pitch designation of
an organ voice is equal to the ratio of the aequal pitch
and the harmonic partial at which it vibrates; thus, D =
A/P, where D is the designation, A the aequal pitch, and P
the serial number of the partial. A segment of the Harmonic Series will serve as a basis for these relationships.
The various partials are integral ratios of the fundamental,
such as 2/1, 3/1, 4/1, 5/1, etc. When predicated upon C of
64 cycles per second, the partial structure distributes
itself as shown in Table 1 and in Appendix P.

By assuming that the key C is played in each case,

TABLE 1

RELATIVE FREQUENCIES OF THE FIRST SIXTEEN
PARTIALS OF THE HARMONIC SERIES
($\underline{C}$ = 64 CYCLES PER SECOND)

Partial	Note, if $\underline{1}$ is $\underline{C}$	Frequency in Just Intonation[a]
1	$\underline{C}$	64
2	$\underline{c}$	128
3	$\underline{g}$	192
4	$\underline{c}'$	256
5	$\underline{e}'$	320
6	$\underline{g}'$	384
7	$\underline{a\sharp}'$	448 ($\underline{a\sharp}'$- $\underline{bb}'$)
8	$\underline{c}''$	512
9	$\underline{d}''$	576
10	$\underline{e}''$	640
11	$\underline{f\sharp}''$	704 ($\underline{f}''$- $\underline{f\sharp}''$)
12	$\underline{g}''$	768
13	$\underline{ab}''$	832 ($\underline{ab}''$- $\underline{a}''$)
14	$\underline{a\sharp}''$	896 ($\underline{a\sharp}''$- $\underline{bb}''$)
15	$\underline{b}''$	960
16	$\underline{c}'''$	1024

[a]See Appendix B for the values conventionally adopted for keyboard use.

the pitch designation for the organ voice sounding a partial note can be determined from Table 2.

A terminology more descriptive than the foot designation is current among organ builders and organists. The
terms used are chiefly English, but at times Italian. The

TABLE 2

DERIVATION OF PITCH DESIGNATION
FROM AN AEQUAL BASIS

Key Playing	Note Sounding	Partial Sounding	Ratio A/P[a]	Pitch Designation
c	c	1st	8/1	8'
c	c	2nd	8/2	4'
c	g	3rd	8/3	2 2/3'
c	c'	4th	8/4	2'
c	e'	5th	8/5	1 3/5'
c	g'	6th	8/6	1 1/3'
c	a♯'	7th	8/7	1 1/7'
c	c''	8th	8/8	1'

[a]Aequal pitch / serial number of partial.

designations are based upon the serial numbers of the diatonic steps of the scale. The aequal or 8' pitch is called
the unison or principale; the 4' pitch, eight diatonic
notes higher than the unison, is called the octave or otta-
va; the 2 2/3' pitch, twelve diatonic notes higher than the
unison, is called the twelfth or duodecima, etc. Accordingly, the partials are designated by the serial numbers of
the diatonic notes whose frequencies they represent, the
unison serving as number 1. See Table 3.

It is, of course, possible to reckon these designations from a pitch basis other than aequal or 8' pitch. If
reckoned from a 4' pitch basis, all the designations would

TABLE 3

ENGLISH AND ITALIAN PITCH DESIGNATIONS
RECKONED FROM AN AEQUAL BASIS[a]

Partial	Foot Designation	English Terms	Italian Terms
1st	8'	Unison	Principale
2nd	4'	Octave	Ottava
3rd	2 2/3'	Twelfth	Duodecima
4th	2'	Fifteenth	Decimaquinta
5th	1 3/5'	Seventeenth	Decimasettima
6th	1 1/3'	Nineteenth	Decimanona
7th	1 1/7'	Twenty-first	Vigesimaprima
8th	1'	Twenty-second	Vigesimaseconda

[a]See Appendix C for a more complete catalog.

describe pitches an octave higher than previously; if reckoned from a 16' pitch basis, all the designations would describe pitches an octave lower. See Table 4.

In either case, the foot designation is derived as before, except that the desired pitch basis must be inserted for the aequal pitch; thus, D = B/P, where D is the foot designation, B the pitch basis used for reckoning, and P the serial number of the partial.

The Orders of Pipes

The pipes, which represent the sound producing portion of the organ, are generally grouped into larger and smaller classifications. The first division concerns itself

TABLE 4

ENGLISH AND ITALIAN PITCH DESIGNATIONS
RECKONED FROM VARIOUS BASES[a]

Pitch Basis	Partial	Foot Designation	English Terms	Italian Terms
4'	1st	4'	Unison	Principale
4'	2nd	2'	Octave	Ottava
4'	3rd	1 1/3'	Twelfth	Duodecima
4'	4th	1'	Fifteenth	Decimaquinta
4'	5th	4/5'	Seventeenth	Decimasettima
4'	6th	2/3'	Nineteenth	Decimanona
4'	7th	4/7'	Twenty-first	Vigesimaprima
4'	8th	1/2'	Twenty-second	Vigesimaseconda
16'	1st	16'	Unison	Principale
16'	2nd	8'	Octave	Ottava
16'	3rd	5 1/3'	Twelfth	Duodecima
16'	4th	4'	Fifteenth	Decimaquinta
16'	5th	3 1/5'	Seventeenth	Decimasettima
16'	6th	2 2/3'	Nineteenth	Decimanona
16'	7th	2 2/7'	Twenty-first	Vigesimaprima
16'	8th	2'	Twenty-second	Vigesimaseconda

[a]See Appendix C for a more complete catalog.

with the method of exciting the air column in the pipe. Two
orders of pipes are apparent:

1. Labial pipes, or those whose air columns are
excited by means of edge tones. These pipes have no
moving parts and constitute the largest number of

voices in the organ

    2. Lingual pipes, or those whose air columns are excited by means of striking metal reeds

    Labial pipes are generally fabricated of metal or wood. Plate XXVIII, 1 and 2 identifies the various parts of the pipe by the customary terms.

    In the case of the labial pipe, the organ wind enters the foot B through the bore in the toe C and escapes in the form of a wind sheet through the windway E. Striking against the upper lip J, the wind produces an edge tone which, in turn, excites the air column in the corpus A, setting it into vibration. Basically, the length of the corpus enclosing the air column determines the pitch of the sound. All other factors constant, the longer the corpus, the lower the pitch; the shorter, the higher.

    The lingual pipe exhibits a more complex structure. Plate XXIX, 1, 2, and 3 identifies the various parts of the pipe and its appurtenances by the customary terms.

    In the case of the lingual pipe, the wind enters the boot B through the bore in the toe C and escapes through the orifice in the face of the shallot G. In doing so, the reed tongue H is set into vibration which, in turn, excites the air column in the resonator A, setting it into vibration. The pitch of the sound is determined by the mass of the reed tongue and by the length of the air column enclosed in the resonator. All other factors constant, the longer the reed, the lower the pitch; the shorter, the higher. The air column in the resonator reacts as in labial pipes. A composite influence is, therefore, exerted upon the resultant pitch: that of the tongue and that of the resonator.

The Families of Pipes: Labial

Both orders of pipes, labial and lingual, are further subdivided into families. These are differentiated from each other by the length and shape of the vibrating air column which they enclose. They may be classified as follows:

1. Open cylindrical pipes
2. Open conical pipes
3. Fully covered pipes
4. Partly covered pipes
5. Pipes with cylindrical resonators
6. Pipes with conical resonators
7. Regals of various kinds

Open Cylindrical Pipes

The corpora of pipes in the open cylindrical family are of a constant diameter and are open at the mouth and end of the pipe. See Plate XXX.

The theoretical physical length of the pipe body in this family is equal to one-half of the wave length. The wave length λ, in turn, is equal to the ratio of the velocity $\underline{V}$ to the frequency $\underline{f}$; thus, $\lambda = V/f$. If, then, the length is to be one-half of λ, the equation must read, L = V/2f. Hence, if the wave length is, for example, 16', the corpus needs to be about 8' long. Since in actual practice the pipe body needs to be a little shorter than the equation would permit, the physical length of an open cylindrical pipe body at $\underline{C}$ is, therefore, only approximately equal to the foot designation.

In general, it should be observed that the requisite length of the corpus is influenced by several factors. To maintain a given pitch or frequency in an open cylindrical pipe:

The length
must vary
$\begin{cases} \text{directly} \\ \text{as the} \end{cases}$ $\begin{cases} \text{mouth width} \\ \text{quantity of wind} \\ \text{pressure of wind} \\ \text{cutup} \end{cases}$

$\begin{cases} \text{inversely} \\ \text{as the} \end{cases}$ $\{ \text{diameter}$

A catalog of values which proposes to represent the requisite theoretical lengths of open cylindrical pipes must consider the reference pitch (for example, $\underline{a}'$ = 440 cycles per second, American Standard) and the temperature (for example, 20° Centigrade or 68° Fahrenheit, a convenient standard for tuning). Accordingly, the numerical values for $\underline{f}$ may be derived from a frequency table of Equal Temperament (see Appendix A), while the numerical values for V must be calculated from the usual temperature level at which these values are given in scientific tables.[7] The velocity of sound in dry air at $0°$ Centigrade is equal to 331.57 meters per second;[8] thus, V_o = 331.57 m. The increase in velocity is equal to .607 meters per second per degree Centigrade rise in temperature;[9] thus, $V_t = V_o + .607t$, where V_o is the velocity at $0°$ Centigrade, V_t the velocity at any desired temperature in plus or minus Centigrade values, and t the temperature in degrees Centigrade. Table 5 presents a catalog of the theoretical lengths of open cylindrical pipes as calculated from a pitch reference of a' = 440 cycles per second, and for a temperature of 20° Centigrade or 68° Fahrenheit.

Because of the phenomenon known as end correction, according to which the air column vibrates beyond the edge of the pipe (spilling over, as it were), the theoretical lengths derived from the formula, $L = V/2f$, are too great and must be reduced by a certain amount in order to arrive more closely at the actual, useful length. Empirical formulas (chiefly "rule of thumb") have been developed by organ builders to arrive more nearly at the real length of the corpus. For open cylindrical pipes the formula reads, $l = L - 3D/2$, where l is the actual length of the corpus, L the theoretical length, and D the diameter of the

TABLE 5

THEORETICAL LENGTHS OF OPEN CYLINDRICAL PIPES[a]

(VALUES IN CENTIMETERS)

Note	16'	8'	4'	2'	1'	1/2'	1/4'	1/8'
C	525.55	262.78	131.39	65.69	32.85	16.42	8.21	4.11
C#	495.98	247.99	124.00	62.00	31.00	15.50	7.75	3.87
D	468.14	234.07	117.04	58.52	29.26	14.63	7.31	3.66
D#	441.90	220.95	110.48	55.24	27.62	13.81	6.90	3.45
E	417.12	208.56	104.28	52.14	26.07	13.04	6.52	3.26
F	393.71	196.86	98.43	49.21	24.61	12.30	6.15	3.08
F#	371.58	185.79	92.90	46.45	23.22	11.61	5.81	2.90
G	350.72	175.36	87.68	43.84	21.92	10.96	5.48	2.74
G#	331.06	165.53	82.77	41.38	20.69	10.35	5.17	2.59
A	312.47	156.24	78.12	39.06[b]	19.53	9.76	4.88	2.44
A#	294.93	147.47	73.73	36.87	18.43	9.22	4.61	2.30
B	278.35	139.18	69.59	34.79	17.40	8.70	4.35	2.17

[a]Valid only for a reference pitch of a' = 440 cycles per second, American Standard; temperature at 20° Centigrade or 68° Fahrenheit.

[b]Calculation for a': $L = \dfrac{V_t}{2f} = \dfrac{V_o + 60.7t}{2f} = \dfrac{33157 + (60.7 \times 20)}{2(440)} = 39.06$ cm.

orpus.[10] By using the diameters of the <u>Normprincipal</u>, the values for the lengths of the various <u>C</u>'s appear as shown in Table 6. See also Appendix D, 2.

TABLE 6

ACTUAL LENGTHS FOR <u>C</u> PIPES OF THE
OPEN CYLINDRICAL FAMILY[a]

Pipe	Theoretical Length (L) in Centimeters	Theoretical Length (L) in British Feet	Diameter (D) in Centimeters	Actual Length (1) in Centimeters	Actual Length (1) in British Feet
<u>C</u> 16'	525.55	17.24	25.93	486.66	15.97
<u>C</u> 8'	262.78	8.62	15.42	239.65[b]	7.86[b]
<u>C</u> 4'	131.39	4.31	9.17	117.64	3.86
<u>C</u> 2'	65.69	2.15	5.45	57.52	1.88
<u>C</u> 1'	32.85	1.08	3.24	27.99	.92
<u>C</u> 1/2'	16.42	.54	1.93	13.53	.44
<u>C</u> 1/4'	8.21	.27	1.15	6.49	.21
<u>C</u> 1/8'	4.11	.13	.68	3.09	.10

[a]The table is valid only for a reference pitch of a' = 440 cycles per second; temperature at 20° Centigrade or 68° Fahrenheit; diameters of Normprincipal.

[b]Calculation for <u>C</u> 8':

$$1 = L - \frac{3D}{2} = 262.78 - \frac{3(15.42)}{2} = 239.65 \text{ cm. or } 7.86 \text{ British feet.}$$

The acoustic spectrum (i.e., the profile of the partial structure) of an open cylindrical pipe reveals the presence of a consecutive system of partials. The pipe can be overblown to sound the second, third, fourth partial, etc. In organ parlance it is said to overblow "at the octave." In practice this is accomplished by doubling the length of the corpus (8' length for 4' pitch) and winding the pipe to overblow into the second partial. See Chart 1 for the acoustic spectrum of the note c' (261.6 cycles per second) of an open cylindrical pipe (Geigendprincipal).

Open Conical Pipes

The corpora of pipes in this family are of graduated diameters, so that the pipes present the shape of a cone or pyramid, either upright or inverted. The pipes are open at the mouth and end. See Plate XXXI.

The degree of conicity or taper is generally expressed as the ratio of the diameter at the top to the diameter at the mouth; thus, T = d/D, where T is the degree of taper, d the diameter at the top, and D the diameter at the mouth. If the diameter at the top is three inches, and at the mouth four inches, then the taper is expressed as 3/4. Note that a ratio of 1/4 displays a greater degree of conicity or taper than a ratio of 3/4.

The physical length of the pipe body is less than that of open cylindrical pipes. The requisite length is

nfluenced by certain factors. To maintain a given pitch
 r frequency in an open, upright conical pipe:

The length
must vary
 directly
as the
 — mouth width
quantity of wind
pressure of wind
cutup

 inversely
as the
 — diameter
degree of taper

To determine the actual lengths of the pipes, the
theoretical lengths of open cylindrical pipes are used as
the point of departure. See Appendix E. These values are
then reduced by a "rule of thumb" formula for open, upright
conical pipes; thus, $l = L - (2D + d/2)$, where $\underline{l}$ is the actual, usable length of the corpus, $\underline{L}$ the theoretical length
of open cylindrical pipes, $\underline{D}$ the larger diameter (at the
mouth) and $\underline{d}$ the smaller diameter (at the end of the corpus).[11] By using the diameters of the Normprincipal, the
values for the lengths of the various $\underline{C}$'s appear as shown
in Table 7. See also Appendix D, 2.

To determine the actual lengths of invert conical
or pyramidal pipes, the theoretical lengths of open cylindrical pipes are used as the point of departure. See Appendix E. These values are then reduced by this, likewise
"rule of thumb", formula for open, invert conical or pyramidal pipes; thus, $l = L - (D/2 + d/2)$, where $\underline{l}$ is the actual,
usable length, $\underline{L}$ the theoretical length for open cylindrical

TABLE 7

ACTUAL LENGTHS FOR C PIPES OF THE OPEN, UPRIGHT CONICAL OR PYRAMIDAL FAMILY[a]

Pipe	Theoretical Length (L) in Centimeters	Theoretical Length (L) in British Feet	Diameter at Mouth (D) in Centimeters	Diameter at Top (d) in Centimeters	Actual Length (l) in Centimeters	Actual Length (l) in British Feet
C 16'	525.55	17.24	25.93	8.64	469.37	15.40
C 8'	262.78	8.62	15.42	5.14	229.37[b]	7.53[b]
C 4'	131.39	4.31	9.17	3.06	111.52	3.66
C 2'	65.69	2.15	5.45	1.82	53.88	1.77
C 1'	32.85	1.08	3.24	1.08	25.83	.85
C 1/2'	16.42	.54	1.93	.64	12.24	.40
C 1/4'	8.21	.27	1.15	.38	5.72	.19
C 1/8'	4.11	.13	.68	.23	2.64	.09

[a]The table is valid only for a reference pitch of a' = 440 cycles per second; temperature at 20° Centigrade or 68° Fahrenheit; diameters of Normprincipal at mouth; 1/3 taper.

[b]Calculation for C 8':

$$1 = L - (2D + d/2) = 262.78 - (2 \times 15.42 + \frac{5.14}{2}) =$$

229.37 cm. or 7.53 British feet.

pipes, D the greater diameter (at the top) and d the lesser diameter (at the mouth).[12] By using the diameters of the Normprincipal, the values for the lengths of the various C's appear as shown in Table 8. See also Appendix D, 2.

TABLE 8

ACTUAL LENGTHS FOR C̲ PIPES OF THE OPEN, INVERT
CONICAL OR PYRAMIDAL FAMILY[a]

Pipe	Theoretical Length (L) in Centimeters	Theoretical Length (L) in British Feet	Diameter at Top (D) in Centimeters	Diameter at Mouth (d) in Centimeters	Actual Length (1) in Centimeters	Actual Length (1) in British Feet
C̲ 16'	525.55	17.24	34.57	25.93	495.31	16.25
C̲ 8'	262.78	8.62	20.56	15.42	244.79[b]	8.03[b]
C̲ 4'	131.39	4.31	12.23	9.17	120.70	3.96
C̲ 2'	65.69	2.15	7.27	5.45	59.34	1.94
C̲ 1'	32.85	1.08	4.32	3.24	29.07	.95
C̲ ./2'	16.42	.54	2.57	1.93	14.18	.46
C̲ 1/4'	8.21	.27	1.53	1.15	6.88	.22
C̲ 1/8'	4.11	.13	.91	.68	3.32	.11

[a]The table is valid only for a reference pitch of
a' = 440 cycles per second; temperature at 20° Centigrade or
68° Fahrenheit; diameters of Normprincipal at mouth; 4/3
taper.

[b]Calculation for C̲ 8':

$$1 = L - (D/2 + d/2) = 262.78 - (\frac{20.56}{2} + \frac{15.42}{2}) = 244.79 \text{ cm.}$$

or 8.03 British feet.

As in the case of open cylindrical pipes, those of
the conical or pyramidal family, upright or inverted, reveal a similar partial or acoustic spectrum, i.e., all

partials are present. The pipes can be overblown to sound consecutive partials; hence, they are said to overblow "at the octave." Should this condition be desired, the pipes are made twice the actual speaking length and winded to overblow.

Fully Covered Pipes

In the family of fully covered pipes, the pipe bodies are of a cylindrical or conical shape. The pipes are open only at the mouth, being covered at the opposite end by means of plugs inserted into the ends of the pipes, or by caps surmounting them. See Plate XXXII.

The physical length of the pipe body is in the vicinity of one-half of the theoretical length of an open cylindrical pipe. See Appendix F. The requisite length of the corpus is again influenced by certain factors, but the relationships are slightly different than for open cylindrical pipes. To maintain a given pitch or frequency in a fully covered pipe:

The length } directly { diameter
must vary } as the { mouth width
{ quantity of wind
{ pressure of wind
{ cutup

The actual lengths vary, depending upon whether the pipes are cylindrical or conical. For covered cylindrical pipes the lengths are derived from the theoretical values for open cylindrical pipes by means of the following "rule of thumb" formula: $1 = L/2 - 3D/2$ (cap included), where $\underline{1}$ is the actual, usable length, $\underline{L}$ the theoretical length of open cylindrical pipes, and $\underline{D}$ the diameter of the pipe body.[13] By using the diameters of the Normprincipal, the values for the lengths of the various $\underline{C}$'s appear as shown in Table 9. See also Appendix D, 2.

The length of a covered cylindrical pipe is, very roughly, about one-half that of an open cylindrical pipe of the same pitch, or about one-fourth of the wave length. Contrary to the open cylindrical pipes, those of the covered cylindrical family reveal a partial or acoustic spectrum in which only the odd-numbered partials are present. The overtone structure is, therefore, considerably impoverished and causes the tone quality of these pipes to differ widely from that of open pipes. The pipes can be overblown to sound alternate partials, as the third, fifth, seventh, etc. and are, therefore, said to overblow "at the twelfth." The pipes must be made of three times their simple, actual length, in order to overblow into the third partial; hence, 6' length for 4' pitch, winded to overblow.

Research into the phenomena relating to covered conical pipes is inconclusive at present. Voices from this family appear, at times, in European instruments, but are extremely rare in America. Some basic observations are,

TABLE 9

ACTUAL LENGTHS FOR C PIPES OF THE
COVERED CYLINDRICAL FAMILY[a]

Pipe	Theoretical Length (L) of Open Cylindrical Pipes in Centimeters	Theoretical Length (L) of Open Cylindrical Pipes in British Feet	Diameter (D) in Centimeters	Actual Length (1) in Centimeters	Actual Length (1) in British Feet
C 16'	525.55	17.24	25.93	223.89	7.35
C 8'	262.78	8.62	15.42	108.26[b]	3.55[b]
C 4'	131.39	4.31	9.17	51.94	1.70
C 2'	65.69	2.15	5.45	24.71	.81
C 1'	32.85	1.08	3.24	11.58	.38
C 1/2'	16.42	.54	1.93	5.32	.17
C 1/4'	8.21	.27	1.15	2.40	.08
C 1/8'	4.11	.13	.68	1.03	.03

[a]The table is valid only for a reference pitch of a' = 440 cycles per second; temperature at 20° Centigrade or 68° Fahrenheit; diameters of Normprincipal; cap included.

[b]Calculation for C 8':

$$1 = \frac{L}{2} - \frac{3D}{2} = \frac{262.78}{2} - \frac{3(15.42)}{2} = 108.26 \text{ cm. or } 3.55 \text{ British feet.}$$

however, evident in a qualitative way. With respect to the

length of the corpus, it lies very nearly between the

lengths of open cylindrical and covered cylindrical pipes;
hence, about three-fourths of the length of correspondingly-
pitched open pipes or three-eighths of the wave length; thus,
6' length for 8' pitch. The values for the theoretical
lengths of the covered conical pipes can be computed as the
geometric mean of open cylindrical and covered cylindrical
pipes; thus, $L_3 = \sqrt{L_1 \times L_2}$, where L_3 is the theoretical
length of a covered conical pipe, L_1 the theoretical length
of a correspondingly-pitched open cylindrical pipe, and L_2
the theoretical length of a correspondingly-pitched covered
cylindrical pipe. See Appendices E and F. Table 10 gives
the values for the theoretical lengths of covered conical
pipes.

A second known phenomenon evident in covered conical
pipes has to do with the partial structure. Contrary to the
covered cylindrical pipes, the covered conical family presents a consecutive set of partials, precisely as in the
case of open cylindrical pipes. They overblow "at the octave." To achieve this condition, the pipes are constructed
of twice their simple length, in order to overblow into the
second partial; hence, six-fourths of the length of correspondingly-pitched open pipes or 6' length for 4' pitch.

Partly Covered Pipes

The corpora of pipes in this family are of a compound form of which the basic ingredient is the cylindrical

TABLE 10

THEORETICAL LENGTHS FOR COVERED CONICAL PIPES[a]

(VALUES IN CENTIMETERS)

Note	16'	8'	4'	2'	1'	1/2'	1/4'	1/8'
C	371.62	185.81[b]	92.91	46.45	23.23	11.61	5.80	2.90
C#	350.72	175.36	87.68	43.84	21.92	10.96	5.48	2.74
D	331.00	165.50	82.75	41.38	20.69	10.34	5.17	2.59
D#	312.48	156.24	78.12	39.06	19.53	9.77	4.88	2.44
E	294.96	147.48	73.74	36.87	18.44	9.22	4.61	2.30
F	278.39	139.19	69.60	34.80	17.40	8.70	4.35	2.17
F#	262.76	131.38	65.69	32.85	16.42	8.21	4.11	2.05
G	248.00	124.00	62.00	31.00	15.50	7.75	3.87	1.94
G#	234.08	117.04	58.52	29.26	14.63	7.32	3.66	1.83
A	220.96	110.48	55.24	27.62	13.81	6.90	3.45	1.72
A#	208.55	104.28	52.14	26.07	13.03	6.52	3.26	1.63
B	196.82	98.41	49.20	24.60	12.30	6.15	3.07	1.54

[a]The table is valid only for a reference pitch of a' = 440 cycles per second; temperature at 20° Centigrade or 68° Fahrenheit.

[b]Calculation for C 8':

$$L_3 = \sqrt{L_1 \times L_2} = \sqrt{262.78 \times 131.39} = 185.81 \text{ cm.}$$

corpus, to which is added a diminutive cylindrical or conical chimney or a full-sized cone or pyramid. The following
forms are employed:

    1. A cylindrical corpus covered with a cap sur-
mounted by a cylindrical chimney

    2. A cylindrical corpus covered with a cap sur-
mounted by a conical chimney

    3. A cylindrical corpus covered with an open
cone or pyramid

See Plate XXXIII.

In each case, the length of the basic cylindrical
portion of the corpus varies between that of a fully covered and fully open cylindrical pipe, the necessary length
of the corpus being materially affected by the length and
width of the chimney, cone, or pyramid. The prevailing conditions are so manifold and definitive research in this respect so meager and inconclusive, that at present it is
impossible to establish any laws governing the relationships
in a quantitative way. It is only possible to approach the
attendant phenomena of the partly covered pipes in a qualitative and descriptive way. It is generally agreed that a
compound wave materializes in the pipe and chimney but, inasmuch as they are in direct communication with each other,
cross modulation takes place and each one influences the
other.

Concerning the length of the corpus, it is in every case greater than that of the fully covered family of pipes. The length and cross-sectional area of the surmounting chimney exert an influence upon the requisite length of the corpus. The basic relationships were established by R. Gerhardt and are quoted by Mahrenholz:

Die Laenge des Rohrfloetenkoerpers ist auf jeden Fall groeszer als die eines Vollgedacktes, und zwar verursacht (nach Gerhardt) die Verlaengerung des Aufsatzroehrchens bei konstantem Querschnitt eine Verminderung der Tonerhoehung, die Vergroeszerung des Querschnittes des Aufsatzroehrchens bei konstanter Laenge eine Vergroeszerung der Tonerhoehung.[14]

The length of the Rohrfloete corpus is, in every case, greater than that of a fully covered pipe. (According to Gerhardt) the elongation of the chimney, while the cross-sectional area is held constant, causes a fall in pitch, while the enlargement of the cross-sectional area of the chimney, while the length is held constant, causes a rise in pitch. [Translation by the present author]

Accordingly, to maintain a given pitch or frequency in a partly covered pipe:

The length of the
corpus must vary
{
  directly
  as the   { diameter of
              the chimney

  inversely
  as the   { length of
              the chimney
}

Concerning the actual lengths of partly covered pipes, the necessary constants are presently not yet available in simple and intelligible formulas to permit computing them quantitatively from the theoretical lengths of open pipes. As stated, the lengths vary between those of fully covered and fully open pipes, being in every case greater than the actual lengths of the fully covered, and less than those of the fully open family.

The acoustic spectrum of the partly covered family of pipes is described by Mahrenholz:

Der Einflusz des Rohraufsatzes auf den Klang der Pfeife ist bereits im vorigen Jahrhundert Gegenstand einer eingehenden Untersuchung gewesen, die jedoch dem Nichtphysiker schwer verstaendlich ist. Es handelt sich hier im Wesentlichen um die Tatsache, dasz durch den Rohraufsatz eine Verschiebung der Teiltoene der Halbgedackte stattfindet, dasz also die Rohrfloete unharmonische Obertoene hat, die dem Grundton umso naeher liegen, je weiter und laenger der Rohraufsatz ist, vom Grundton aber umso entfernter sind, je enger und kuerzer man das Roehrchen gestaltet. So stehen die Rohrfloeten, wie Gerhardt richtig sagt, hinsichtlich ihres Obertonaufbaues in der Mitte zwischen den offenen und gedeckten Pfeifen. Die unharmonischen Beitoene verleihen dem Gesamtcharakter der Pfeife etwas Helles, Mixturartiges, weil dem Ohr unharmonische Obertoene eher auffallen, als solche, die in der normalen Obertonreihe stehen und zum Grundton konkludieren.[15]

The influence of the chimney upon the tone of the pipe has, already in the previous century, been the subject of a thorough investigation, the results of which, however, are hardly intelligible to the non-physicist. Basically, the problem resolves itself into the fact that, through the influence of the chimney, the partial tones of the partly covered pipes are redistributed, so that the Rohrfloete presents inharmonic overtones which lie close to the fundamental when the chimney is long and wide, but are farther removed from it when the chimney is short and narrow. It is for this reason, as Gerhardt correctly states, that with respect to their partial structure the Rohrfloetes occupy a position between that of open and fully covered pipes. The inharmonic overtones lend something bright and mixture-like to the tone color of the pipe, because they are more conspicuous to the ear than those which belong to the normal harmonic series by nature attached to the fundamental. [Translation by the present author]

The Families of Pipes: Lingual

Pipes with Cylindrical Resonators

The corpora of this family of lingual pipes present a variety of possible situations among which the following find application in practice:

1. A fully cylindrical resonator of constant diameter attached directly to the block

2. A preponderantly cylindrical resonator of constant diameter plus a diminutive cone inverted to serve as a connection between the resonator and block or inverted to serve as a bell

See Plates XXXIV and XXIX.

For the production of tone in reed pipes two factors are at work in a compound way. The first comprises the reed tongue itself. Activated by the wind, the tongue serves not only as the medium of excitation for the air column in the resonator, but also as a source of tone and pitch, both of which are controlled by its own natural period of vibration. Striking against the orifice of the shallot, the tongue and the wind acting upon it serve effectively to close the orifice; thereby, no compressions or rarefactions in the air column can be dissipated here; nodes only can be formed at this point. The air column resolves itself into a standing wave with a static node at the orifice of the shallot. It is for this reason that lingual pipes with open or partially

open (i.e., shaded) cylindrical resonators function acoustically as fully covered labial pipes; thus,

1. The cylindrical resonators, in normal length,
are approximately one-fourth of the wave length or
one-half of the pitch designation; hence, 4' resonators for 8' pitch

2. The acoustic spectrum, as in the case of
fully covered labial pipes, presents alternate partials; in fact, only the odd-numbered series: 1, 3,
5, 7, etc.

The theoretical lengths of the resonators for cylindrical lingual pipes are those of covered cylindrical labial
pipes. In each case, however, the length must be reckoned
from the tangential contact of the tuning wire and reed up
to the tuning device of the resonator. See Appendix F.

Compared to fully covered labial pipes, the cylindrical reeds are excited at the opposite end of the system.
Whereas in labial pipes the excitation takes place at the
open end of the air column, in reeds of this family it occurs at the closed end. One may visualize the resonator,
then, as an inverted covered cylindrical pipe. Since the
area of excitation presents, in effect, a closed end, the
opposite or top end of the resonator may never be fully
closed; it may be open, shaded, or pierced; should it be
completely sealed off, the pipe would become acoustically

unable to function; it would cease to speak.

Inasmuch as the pitch of the tone is influenced not only by the length of the resonator, but also by the natural period of vibration of the tongue itself, a double relationship is evident with respect to the pitch. To maintain a given pitch or frequency in a cylindrical reed:

The length of the resonator must vary }	inversely as the	{ length and mass of the tongue

It is desired, for example, to tune a given cylindrical reed pipe to c'; every time the tongue is lengthened to lower the pitch, the resonator must be shortened to raise the pitch proportionately. This double phenomenon operates, however, only within certain narrow limits; should this limit be exceeded, the pipe will overblow into one of its partials or cease to speak. Whenever the pitch of the pipe is thus controlled by two factors (the mass of the tongue and the length of the resonator), a concomitant phenomenon becomes evident; this is the effect such a manipulation has upon the resultant tone color. Suppose that the mass of the tongue and the length of the resonator are in a hypothetically desired relationship with the pitch at c' and the color "normal," a manipulation of either factor produces the following effects:

1. If the tongue is lengthened and the resona-

tor shortened within the operational limits described,
so that the pipe retains its pitch, the tone will become more free and aggressive; the overtone structure
will tend to predominate and the fundamental recede

2. If, on the contrary, the tongue is shortened
and the resonator lengthened, so that the pipe again
retains its pitch, the tone will become more choked
and constricted; the overtone structure will tend to
recede and the fundamental brought into prominence

Since the length of the resonator is only partly responsible for the pitch, it achieves a certain independence.
In fact the pipe, by virtue of the reed tongue, will speak
without any resonator at all. The resonator, therefore,
serves chiefly the purpose of reinforcing, by its own period
of vibration, selective partials in the overtone structure
of the reed tone. Of course, the most advantageous relationship is the one where the resonator reinforces the fundamental partial of the reed. When this condition is achieved
in cylindrical lingual pipes, the resonator will have what
is known as its normal length, $\underline{i}.\underline{e}.$, 4' length for 8' pitch.
Expressed mathematically, the relationship is as follows:
$R_1/T_p = P/2$, where $\underline{R}_1$ is the length of the resonator, $\underline{T}_p$ the
pitch of the reed tongue, and $\underline{P}$ the serial number of the
partial to be reinforced by the resonator. It is possible
to overblow such pipes also; for practical purposes over-

blowing takes place at the third partial (overblown) and at the fifth partial (doubly overblown) provided the pipes are winded to achieve this effect. Table 11 shows the necessary theoretical lengths of the resonators for various cases.

TABLE 11

THEORETICAL LENGTHS FOR RESONATORS OF OVERBLOWN
CYLINDRICAL LINGUAL PIPES

Pitch	Partial, when not Overblown	Requisite Normal Length	Partial, when Overblown	Requisite Length of Resonator	Partial, when Doubly Overblown	Requisite Length of Resonator
16'	1st	8'	3rd	24'	5th	40'
8'	1st	4'	3rd	12'[a]	5th	20'
4'	1st	2'	3rd	6'	5th	10'
2'	1st	1'	3rd	3'	5th	5'
1'	1st	1/2'	3rd	1 1/2'	5th	2 1/2'

[a]Calculation for 8' pitch overblown into the third partial:

$$\frac{R_1}{T_p} = \frac{P}{2} \text{ or } R_1 = \frac{T_p \times P}{2} = \frac{8 \times 3}{2} = 12'$$

Because the length of the resonator is not the sole determiner of pitch it is possible to use resonators shortened below normal length. In such cases the mass of the

reed tongue is, in effect, increased, the pitch is maintained, and the resonator serves to reinforce one of the
partials in preference to the fundamental. All that is necessary for the pipe to function effectively is that the period of vibration of the tongue is in some direct and integral ratio with that of the resonator. Instead of the
ratio being R_1/T_p = P/2, the relationships appear in alternate form; thus, R_1/T_p = 1/2P. When these relationships are
achieved, resonance coupling takes place and the resonator
is able to reinforce the frequency of the tongue at one of
its partials. Table 12 gives the requisite theoretical
lengths of the resonators depending upon which available
partial it is desired to reinforce.

Pipes with Conical Resonators

The corpora of the family of pipes with conical resonators vary in their shape, except that in every case a
substantial portion of the air column is enclosed in a conical resonator. The corpus may be simple or compound as
follows:

1. A single inverted cone, truncated and of a
constant degree of graduation

2. Double inverted cones, both truncated and
each with a different degree of graduation

3. Triple inverted cones, all truncated and
each with a different degree of graduation

TABLE 12

THEORETICAL LENGTHS FOR SHORTENED RESONATORS
OF CYLINDRICAL LINGUAL PIPES

Pitch	Partial to be Reinforced	Requisite Length of Resonator	Partial to be Reinforced	Requisite Length of Resonator	Partial to be Reinforced	Requisite Length of Resonator
16'	1st	8'	3rd	2 2/3'	5th	1 3/5'
8'	1st	4'	3rd	1 1/3'[a]	5th	4/5'
4'	1st	2'	3rd	2/3'	5th	2/5'
2'	1st	1'	3rd	1/3'	5th	1/5'
1'	1st	1/2'	3rd	1/6'	5th	1/10'

[a]Calculation for 8' pitch, the resonator shortened
to reinforce the third partial:

$$\frac{R_1}{T_p} = \frac{1}{2P} \text{ or } R_1 = \frac{T_p}{2P} = \frac{8}{2 \times 3} = 1 \text{ } 1/3'$$

4. A single inverted cone, flared at the end

5. Two inverted and one upright cone, all truncated and with various degrees of graduation

See Plate XXXV.

The conical lingual pipe (since the reed tongue and
the pressure of the wind at the orifice of the shallot serve
effectively to close the resonator at this point) must be
viewed as an inverted covered conical labial pipe, the exci-

tation taking place at the apex of the cone rather than at its base. For this reason, the acoustical phenomena of this family resemble those of covered conical labial pipes:

1. The theoretical normal length of the resonator is equal to three-eighths of the wave length or three-fourths of the pitch designation; hence, 6' length for 8' pitch

2. The partial or acoustic spectrum presents consecutive overtones, both the odd and the even-numbered series

In view of these conditions, the theoretical normal lengths, calculated from the tangential contact of reed and tuning wire to the tuning device in the resonator will be the same as those given for covered conical labial pipes in Appendix G.

Concerning the method of excitation, the influence and relationship between tongue and resonator on the pitch and tone color, and the various devices for shading the resonator, all function similarly in conical lingual pipes as in the cylindrical lingual family.

Inasmuch as the acoustic spectra of these pipes present a complete series of partials, the pipes are able to overblow "at the octave" and at further consecutive partials. The normal or natural length is the one where the resonator reinforces the fundamental partial of the reed.

When this condition is achieved in conical lingual pipes, the resonator will have what is known as its normal length, i.e., 6' length for 8' pitch. Expressed mathematically, the relationship is as follows: $R_1/T_p = 3P/4$, where $\underline{R}_1$ is the length of the resonator, $\underline{T}_p$ the pitch of the reed tongue, and $\underline{P}$ the serial number of the partial to be reinforced by the resonator. For practical purposes, overblowing takes place at the second partial (overblown) and at the third partial (doubly overblown) provided the pipes are winded to achieve this effect. Table 13 shows the necessary theoretical lengths of the resonators for various cases.

As in the case of the cylindrical family of reed pipes, it is possible to employ shortened resonators with conical reeds in order to reinforce a desired partial. The conditions and effects are similar to those discussed under cylindrical lingual pipes, except that both odd and even-numbered ratios will serve to effect resonance coupling. The reason for this greater versatility of the conical over against the cylindrical lingual family lies in the fact that the conical resonators are by nature able to deliver in their partial or acoustic spectrum a consecutive system of partials. Accordingly, the period of vibration of the tongue must be in some direct ratio with that of the resonator. Instead of the ratio being $R_1/T_p = 3P/4$, the relationships appear in alternate form; thus, $R_1/T_p = 3/4P$.

TABLE 13

THEORETICAL LENGTHS FOR RESONATORS OF OVERBLOWN
CONICAL LINGUAL PIPES

Pitch	Partial, when not Overblown	Requisite Normal Length	Partial, when Overblown	Requisite Length of Resonator	Partial, when Doubly Overblown	Requisite Length of Resonator
16'	1st	12'	2nd	24'	3rd	36'
8'	1st	6'	2nd	12'[a]	3rd	18'
4'	1st	3'	2nd	6'	3rd	9'
2'	1st	1 1/2'	2nd	3'	3rd	4 1/2'
1'	1st	3/4'	2nd	1 1/2'	3rd	2 1/4'

[a]Calculation for 8' pitch overblown into the second
partial:

$$\frac{R_1}{T_p} = \frac{3P}{4} \text{ or } R_1 = \frac{T_p \times 3P}{4} = \frac{8 \times 3 \times 2}{4} = 12'$$

Table 14 gives the requisite theoretical lengths of the resonators depending upon which available partial it is desired
to reinforce.

The Regal Family

The corpora of reeds in the Regal family may assume
a multitude of different shapes; occasionally these are simple, but more often, compound. They may be:

1. Preponderantly cylindrical

TABLE 14

THEORETICAL LENGTHS FOR SHORTENED RESONATORS
OF CONICAL LINGUAL PIPES

Pitch	Partial to be Reinforced	Requisite Length of Resonator	Partial to be Reinforced	Requisite Length of Resonator	Partial to be Reinforced	Requisite Length of Resonator
16'	1st	12'	2nd	6'	3rd	4'
8'	1st	6'	2nd	3'[a]	3rd	2'
4'	1st	3'	2nd	1 1/2'	3rd	1'
2'	1st	1 1/2'	2nd	3/4'	3rd	1/2'
1'	1st	3/4'	2nd	3/8'	3rd	1/4'

[a]Calculation for 8' pitch, the resonator shortened
to reinforce the second partial:

$$\frac{R_1}{T_p} = \frac{3}{4P} \quad \text{or} \quad R_1 = \frac{T_p \times 3}{4P} = \frac{8 \times 3}{4 \times 2} = 3'$$

2. Preponderantly conical

3. A combination of both shapes

See Plates XXXVI, XXXVII, and XXXVIII.

The resonator is usually less than the normal
length, but does not generally maintain its initial ratio
of length to pitch designation throughout the compass of the
voice. Accordingly, it may be of normal length or greater
than normal in the upper register. Mahrenholz describes the

historical practice in this respect as follows:

Bei der Bemessung der Laenge der Regalkoerper hat man sich allem Anschein nach an bestimmte Regeln, etwa in der Weise, dasz man die Laenge der Aufsaetze in ein festes Verhaeltnis zur Becherlaenge natuerlich langer Rohrwerke gesetzt haette, nicht gehalten. Zwar hat die groeszte Regalpfeife vielfach einen Becher, dessen Laenge 1/2, 1/3, 1/4, 1/5 oder dergl. der natuerlichen Laenge betraegt, aber diese Proportion wird nach oben hin nicht durchgefuehrt, weil dann die Becher wegen ihrer Kleinheit kaum mehr ausfuehrbar sind. Die Becherlaenge nimmt deshalb meistens nach einem kleineren Oktavenverhaeltnis als dem natuerlichen (1:2) ab, sodasz die Becher der hoechsten Oktave oft nicht nur natuerliche Laenge haben, sondern gelegentlich sogar als ueberlang angesprochen werden muessen.[16]

In determining the lengths of the Regal pipe bodies it seems, from all appearances, that no definite laws, in the manner that the lengths of the resonators be held in a firm relationship to that of normal length resonators, were maintained. Very often, certainly, the largest Regal pipe [of a given set] was given a resonator which comprised 1/2, 1/3, 1/4, 1/5, etc. of the normal length, but this ratio was not carried into the upper register, since the resonators became too small to construct. Therefore, the lengths of the resonators proceeded [in their diminution] generally more slowly than by the natural octave ratio (1:2), so that the resonators in the upper register often did not only approach the normal length, but occasionally also exceeded it and became overlong. [Translation by the present author]

It may, therefore, be maintained that the length of the corpus has no definite or direct relationship to the normal length or the pitch designation. Rather, the lengths and shapes, either simple or compound, are chosen to suppress or reinforce certain desired partials present in the vibrations of the reed tongue, in order to achieve a desired tone color. Mahrenholz describes the function of the resonator as follows:

Die Zunge allein entwick-
elt eine sehr grosze Anzahl
von Obertoenen und klingt
deshalb roh und ungeschlacht.
Ein wenn auch noch so kurzer
Aufsatz lenkt die Oberton-
bildung aber in bestimmte
Bahnen und gibt je nach der
Aufsatzform und -Laenge das
besondere Klanggepraege.[17]

The tongue alone develops
a very large number of overtones, and sounds, therefore,
crude and uncouth. A resonator, however short, forces
the formation of overtones into defined limits and develops, depending upon the shape
and length of the resonator,
a singular acoustic spectrum.
[Translation by the present
author]

CHAPTER III

THE MODERN ORGAN: GENERA OF REGISTERS

AS DETERMINED BY SCALE

A subdivision of the families results in the classification of genera. The genera are differentiated from
each other by the scale of the pipe and the treatment of
the mouth.

Scale in General

Under the term scale is understood the relative
"fatness" of the corpus; under mouth treatment are understood the width of the mouth, its cutup, and the disposition
of the windway and languid.[1] Certain of these factors influence the tone of the pipes as follows:

The scale			
The mouth width	influences chiefly	the extensity[2] the dynamic strength the tone color	
The cutup			

Expressed more descriptively, the greater the scale
of the corpus, the more extensive the tone; the greater the
width of the mouth, the louder the tone; the lower the cutup, the richer the tone.

63

The Octave Ratio

The scale of a pipe, then, refers to the ratio of its diameter to its length. Suppose, for example, that a diameter of 10 centimeters would produce a satisfactorily extensive tone in a pipe whose corpus had a length of 100 centimeters. The relation of the diameter to the length would then be expressed as a 1/10 ratio.[3] Theoretically, such a ratio can be used as a starting point for developing a series of pipes for a given voice. If it were maintained throughout the compass of the voice, the diameters of the successive octaves would be related to each other as 1/2, inasmuch as the octaves of the lengths are by nature subject to the diminution of that ratio.[4] In such a case, the ratio of the diameters would be wholly and rigidly dependent upon the progressive variation in the lengths of the corpora. In practice, this condition is undesirable since long experience has proven that such a ratio of diminution in the diameters materially affects the extensity and resultant tone color, the effect being that the pipes diminish much too rapidly in their diameters, thus prohibiting the maintenance of a consistent extensity and tone color in the successive pipes of the series. Accordingly, in the course of time, organ builders have sought to correct this discrepancy in various ways. No really satisfactory solution, however, was found until the ratio of diminution of the

diameters was completely divorced from that of the lengths.
Once this condition was established, each factor was able
to pursue its own ratio of diminution, independent of the
other; the term "scale" took on a different meaning. Instead of expressing the ratio of the diameter to the length
of the corpus, it now expressed the ratio of the diameter
or cross-sectional area of one octave to the same dimension
of the next higher or next lower octave. Obviously, the
lengths of the pipe bodies continued to proceed in the octave ratio of 1/2, while the cross-sectional areas ranged
between the extreme octave ratios of 1/2 and 1/4.

Toepfer was the first one to set the problem upon
an intelligible mathematical footing.[5] He proceeded empirically and found, by experiment, that the geometric mean between the two historic extremes provided a satisfactory octave ratio, in the framework of which the pipes in the series did maintain a very consistent extensity and tone col-
or.[6] His mean value for the ratio of the cross-sectional
areas amounted to the square root of the product of the extremes; thus, Mean = $1/\sqrt{2 \times 4} = 1/\sqrt{8}$. Since his time, this
value has proven to be a norm for the octave ratio of the
cross-sectional areas.[7] Expressed in terms of diameters,
the same octave ratio would be $1/\sqrt[4]{8}$, i.e., if the octave
ratio of the cross-sectional areas is $1/\sqrt{8}$ (a ratio of
planes), then the octave ratio of the respective diameters

is $1/\sqrt[4]{8}$ (a ratio of linear dimensions).[8]

The Step Ratio

Since there are twelve steps within the octave, the step ratio will be the twelfth root of the octave ratio;[9] thus, $1/\sqrt[12]{\sqrt[4]{8}} = 1/\sqrt[16]{2}$. This value bespeaks the step ratio of the diameters whenever $1/\sqrt[4]{8}$ relates the diameters of the octave.[10]

From the step ratio it is possible to compute which step in the series will arrive at the half measure when ascending or at the double measure when descending from a given reference note.[11] This will be found to be the sixteenth step in the series when the octave ratio of the diameters is $1/\sqrt[4]{8}$ and the step ratio is $1/\sqrt[16]{2}$. In organ parlance, a voice which, in its diameters, reveals a ratio of diminution equal to $1/\sqrt[4]{8}$ for its octaves or $1/\sqrt[16]{2}$ for its steps, is said to "halve on the sixteenth step or seventeenth pipe."

The Normprincipal

Inasmuch as the octave ratio, $1/\sqrt[4]{8}$ for the diameters or $1/\sqrt{8}$ for the cross-sectional areas, assures a high degree of consistency in extensity and tone color in a given series of pipes it has, since Toepfer's day, become a norm; a set of pipes predicated upon an agreeable basic diameter and progressing through the series in the octave ratio of

$1/\sqrt[4]{8}$ for the diameters is called a <u>Normprincipal</u>, <u>i.e.</u>, a
theoretical set of pipes which can serve as a norm or a
measure of reference, to which all other voices can in some
way be related. The history of this Normprincipal reveals
the following metamorphoses:

    1. Toepfer established a base value of 52.6 mm.
for the diameter of <u>c</u>', which is equivalent to a diameter of 148.9 mm. for <u>C</u>.[12] His normal ratio of
diminution was $1/\sqrt{8}$ for the cross-sectional areas or
$1/\sqrt[4]{8}$ for the diameters, which caused the half measure to fall on the sixteenth step or seventeenth pipe.
His reference pitch was International: <u>a</u>' = 435 cycles per second

    2. The <u>Freiberger Orgelkommission</u>, established
in 1927, shifted the base value one half-tone larger,
so that the diameter for <u>C</u> was taken at 155.5 mm.[13]
The ratio of diminution was retained at $1/\sqrt{8}$ for the
cross-sectional areas or $1/\sqrt[4]{8}$ for the diameters,
which caused the half measure to fall again on the
sixteenth step or seventeenth pipe. The reference
pitch was identical to Toepfer's; namely, International: <u>a</u>' = 435 cycles per second

    3. The Freiberg Normprincipal requires slight
adjustment in order to arrive at an American equivalent. All of the values for the various notes need

to be slightly less since the American Standard Pitch
at $\underline{a}' = 440$ cycles per second and requires, therefore, somewhat smaller diameters than International
Pitch at $\underline{a}' = 435$ cycles per second.[14] Accordingly,
the diameter for an equivalent $\underline{C} = 154.17$ mm. The
ratio of diminution and the consequent halving can be
retained

By using 154.17 mm. as the diameter for $\underline{C}$ of the
Normprincipal and computing the remaining values by means
of the step ratio $1/\sqrt[16]{2}$, a complete table giving numerical
values for all of the notes of the compass can be set up.[15]
Table 15 gives the equivalent American values for the diameters of the Freiberg Normprincipal.

The Normprincipal (NP) is, therefore, a table of
theoretical diameters which, for a given hypothetical series
of pipes, assures the greatest possible consistency of extensity in the resultant tone. In practice, it hardly ever occurs that a set of pipes is built according to these dimensions. Variations and departures from it are the rule today. The table is, therefore, a pedagogic abstraction, and
its value lies in its function as a rule of reference and
as a measuring device to which all other theoretical and actual realizations can be compared and related. It is occasionally referred to as the Normal Measure (NM).

The course of the Normprincipal can be charted on a

TABLE 15

VALUES FOR THE DIAMETERS OF THE AMERICAN EQUIVALENT OF THE FREIBERG NORMPRINCIPAL[a]

(VALUES IN MILLIMETERS)

Note	32'	16'	8'	4'	2'	1'	1/2'	1/4'	1/8'
C	436.06	259.28	154.17	91.67	54.51	32.41	19.27	11.46	6.81
C♯	417.57	248.29	147.63	87.78	52.20	31.04	18.45	10.97	6.52
D	399.87	237.76	141.36	84.06	49.98	29.72	17.67	10.51	6.25
D♯	382.91	227.68	135.38	80.50	47.86	28.46	16.92	10.06	5.98
E	366.68	218.03	129.64	77.09	45.83	27.25	16.21	9.64	5.73
F	351.13	208.78	124.14	73.82	43.89	26.10	15.52	9.23	5.49
F♯	336.25	199.93	118.88	70.68	42.03	24.99	14.86	8.84	5.25
G	322.00	191.46	113.84	67.69	40.25	23.93	14.23	8.46	5.03
G♯	308.35	183.34	109.01	64.82	38.54	22.92	13.63	8.10	4.82
A	295.27	175.57	104.39	62.07	36.91	21.95	13.05	7.76	4.61
A♯	282.73	168.12	99.97	59.44	35.34	21.02	12.50	7.43	4.42
B	270.76	160.99	95.73	56.92	33.84	20.12	11.97	7.12	4.23

[a]The table is predicated upon American Standard Pitch ($\underline{a}$' = 440 cycles per second), a base value of 154.17 mm. for $\underline{C}$ 8', and an octave ratio of diminution of 1:$\sqrt{8}$ for the cross-sectional areas or 1:$\sqrt[4]{8}$ for the diameters.

graph, in order to show its progress visually. Since the
frequencies of the notes proceed in the step ratio of $1/\sqrt[12]{2}$
and the diameters in the step ratio of $1/\sqrt[16]{2}$, the calibrations on both of the axes must be logarithmic. Upon the
abscissa (X-axis) are charted the successive steps of the
compass of the series (sixty steps). Upon the ordinate
(Y-axis) are charted the diameter dimensions in abstract
values, where 0 equals the base dimension; 1/2, the half
measure; $(1/2)^2$, the quarter measure; $(1/2)^3$, the eighth
measure; and $(1/2)^4$, the sixteenth measure. A secondary
logarithmic calibration on the Y-axis might be the diameter
dimensions of the successive half-tones. Inasmuch as the
diameters in the series show diminishing values as the steps
move forward, the line representing the Normprincipal must
appear as a descending diagonal and is, therefore, properly
charted as a function of the fourth quadrant.[16] See Chart
2. The disposition of the line representing the Normprincipal (NP) reveals two conditions:

1. It appears as a diagonal of -45° (or +315°)
from the horizontal; this condition indicates a halving on the sixteenth step which, in turn, results in
a fairly consistent extensity of tone throughout the
compass

2. The line is perfectly straight; this condition indicates a constant scale, i.e., a scale which

adheres to a non-varying ratio of diminution throughout the compass

If both of the conditions prevail, the scale is a
constant one, subject to a ratio of diminution equal to
$1/\sqrt[4]{8}$ for the diameters, and may be represented as ═══ ,
to indicate its non-varying character.

The Base Value and Ratio of Diminution

To establish the Normprincipal tabularly or graphically, a minimum of two values are required:

1. The base, or the value of the first diameter
in the series

2. The ratio of diminution for the series

In the case of the Normprincipal, the base value
chosen ($\underline{C}$ = 154.17 mm.) is charted at point $\underline{O}$ on the $\underline{Y}$-
axis;[17] the ratio of diminution of the diameters is $1/\sqrt[4]{8}$
for the octaves, the value halving on the sixteenth step or
seventeenth pipe.[18]

With the base value and octave ratio of diminution
for the Normprincipal thus established, it is possible to
relate other scales to it and show the deviations from it
graphically. These deviations may reveal one or both of the
following conditions:

1. They may be predicated upon different base
values

2. They may exhibit different ratios of

diminution

The base value at $\underline{0}$, having been established as
154.17 mm. for $\underline{C}$, it is possible to choose from the Normprincipal table (see Table 15 or Appendix D, 2), a value
for $\underline{C}$ equal to one half-tone (1 HT), two half-tones (2 HT),
three half-tones (3 HT), four half-tones (4 HT), five half-
tones (5 HT), etc. larger (+) than $\underline{0}$, the base value of the
Normprincipal.[19] Conversely, it is possible to choose $\underline{C}$-
values less than 0 HT or the Norm. In such cases the values
for $\underline{C}$ will be expressed as one half-tone (1 HT), two half-
tones (2 HT), three half-tones (3 HT), etc. smaller (-) than
$\underline{0}$, the base value of the Normprincipal.[20] Accordingly, the
designations + $\underline{x}$ HT or - $\underline{x}$ HT, relate the chosen base value
to the $\underline{C}$-diameter of the Normprincipal, plus-values (+) indicating greater dimensions, minus-values (-), lesser dimensions; all applicable base values, however, chosen from
the Normprincipal table.

The octave ratio of diminution, having been established at $1/\sqrt[4]{8}$ for the Normprincipal, other octave ratios
may be chosen to let the half measure fall earlier (faster
ratio: $\searrow$) or later (slower ratio: $\diagdown$) than on the
sixteenth step or seventeenth pipe. Table 16 shows the various octave ratios of diminution which let the half measure
fall on steps near the sixteenth.

TABLE 16

OCTAVE RATIOS OF DIMINUTION
FOR THE DIAMETERS[a]

| Half Measure on | | Octave Ratios | | Alternate Form of Ratio | Symbolization |
Step (1)	Pipe (2)	Raw (3)	Reduced (4)	(5)	(6)
12	13	$1/\ 2^{12/12}$	$1/\ 2$	$1/\ 2$	⟩
13	14	$1/\ 2^{12/13}$	$1/\ 2^{12/13}$	$1/\ \sqrt[13]{2^{12}}$	⟩
14	15	$1/\ 2^{12/14}$	$1/\ 2^{6/7}$	$1/\ \sqrt[7]{64}$	⟩
15	16	$1/\ 2^{12/15}$	$1/\ 2^{4/5}$	$1/\ \sqrt[5]{16}$	⟩
16	17	$1/\ 2^{12/16}$	$1/\ 2^{3/4}$	$1/\ \sqrt[4]{8}$	=
17	18	$1/\ 2^{12/17}$	$1/\ 2^{12/17}$	$1/\ \sqrt[17]{2^{12}}$	⟨
18	19	$1/\ 2^{12/18}$	$1/\ 2^{2/3}$	$1/\ \sqrt[3]{4}$	⟨
19	20	$1/\ 2^{12/19}$	$1/\ 2^{12/19}$	$1/\ \sqrt[19]{2^{12}}$	⟨
20	21	$1/\ 2^{12/20}$	$1/\ 2^{3/5}$	$1/\ \sqrt[5]{8}$	⟨
21	22	$1/\ 2^{12/21}$	$1/\ 2^{4/7}$	$1/\ \sqrt[7]{16}$	⟨
22	23	$1/\ 2^{12/22}$	$1/\ 2^{6/11}$	$1/\ \sqrt[11]{64}$	⟨

[a]It should be noted that if the octave ratio is expressed as an exponential function of 2, the half measure of the series can be read directly from the fractional exponents in column (3): the numerator gives the serial number of the octave step, the denominator, the serial number of the step of the half measure. Thus, in the octave ratio $1/\ 2^{12/16}$, the numerator 12 in the exponent establishes this as an octave ratio, the denominator 16, that the half measure falls on the sixteenth step.

Types of Scales

Any scale whose ratio of diminution, once chosen, does not vary throughout the compass of the voice is known as a constant scale. Of the constant scales, the following dispositions are possible:

1. Static constant scales, or those whose ratios of diminution maintain a consistent extensity in the tone of the several pipes of the series.[21] These are visually represented as ═══

2. Increasing constant scales, or those whose ratios of diminution are slower than for the static constant scales, and whose half measures, therefore, fall later than on the sixteenth step.[22] These are visually represented as ⊲

3. Decreasing constant scales, or those whose ratios of diminution are faster than for the static constant scales, and whose half measures, therefore, fall earlier than on the sixteenth step.[23] These are visually represented as ▷

Constant Scales

A sampling of various possible cases in graphic form will help to visualize the dispositions of constant scales and their relation to the Normprincipal. The following cases will be presented:

1. Identical ratios of diminution

    a. Static constant scale, originating at a positive base value

    b. Static constant scale, originating at a negative base value

2. Variant ratios of diminution

    a. Decreasing constant scale, originating at a normal base value

    b. Increasing constant scale, originating at a normal base value

3. Variant ratios of diminution

    a. Decreasing constant scale, originating at a positive base value

    b. Increasing constant scale, originating at a positive base value

4. Variant ratios of diminution

    a. Decreasing constant scale, originating at a positive base value

    b. Increasing constant scale, originating at a negative base value

Numerical quantities may be introduced for the base values and ratios of diminution, in order to develop concrete cases to exemplify the various dispositions enumerated above. Table 17 delineates appropriate courses for voices predicated upon definite base values and progressing through the compass by defined ratios of diminution.

TABLE 17

QUANTITATIVE DELINEATION OF A PROSPECTIVE
SERIES OF CONSTANT SCALES

Case	Scale Type	Base Value	Ratio of Diminution	Half Measure on	
				Step	Pipe
1a		+4 HT	$1/\sqrt[4]{8}$	16	17
b		-4 HT	$1/\sqrt[4]{8}$	16	17
2a		0 HT	$1/\sqrt[5]{16}$	15	16
b		0 HT	$1/\sqrt[17]{2^{12}}$	17	18
3a		+4 HT	$1/\sqrt[5]{16}$	15	16
b		+4 HT	$1/\sqrt[17]{2^{12}}$	17	18
4a		+5 HT	$1/\sqrt[7]{64}$	14	15
b		-5 HT	$1/\sqrt[3]{4}$	18	19

Cases 1a and 1b are static constant scales, 1a exhibiting a base value of +4 HT, 1b a base value of -4 HT.
See Chart 3. The broken line represents the graphic course
of the Normprincipal, introduced into the graph as a line of
reference. Cases 1a and 1b proceed parallel to it; this
condition indicates that their ratios of diminution are the
same as for the Normprincipal. Their relative positions,

higher or lower on the graph, are a reflection of their variant bases, whether larger (higher) or smaller (lower). At any point in the course of scale 1a, the difference between it and the NP is equal to +4 HT. At any point in the course of scale 1b, the difference between it and the NP is equal to -4 HT. Sample readings, taken at various steps, reveal the constant relationship to the NP scale. See Table 18.

TABLE 18

DIVERGENCE OF CONSTANT SCALES 1a AND 1b
FROM THE NORMPRINCIPAL COURSE

| Case | Scale Type | Divergence from Norm in ± HT | | | | |
		at Step 0	at Step 16	at Step 32	at Step 48	at Step 60
1a	════	+4	+4	+4	+4	+4
1b	════	-4	-4	-4	-4	-4

Both scales, 1a and 1b, retain throughout their compass a consistent extensity. Scale 1a is wider than the NP, hence somewhat fuller throughout its compass; scale 1b is narrower than the NP, hence somewhat keener throughout its compass.

Case 2a is a decreasing constant scale, while 2b is of an increasing constant type. Both exhibit identical base values of 0 HT. See Chart 4. The broken line represents

the graphic course of the Normprincipal, introduced into the
graph as a line of reference. Case 2a, beginning with the
same base value as the Normprincipal, proceeds away from the
Norm in a downward direction; this condition indicates that
the ratio of diminution is faster than for the NP, so that
the extensity in the course of the progression becomes less
and less full (or, more and more keen) than that of the Normprincipal. Such a scale is referred to as a decreasing constant scale: ⟩ . Case 2b, beginning with the same base
value as the Normprincipal, proceeds away from the Norm in
an upward direction; this condition indicates that the ratio
of diminution is slower than for the NP, so that the extensity in the course of the progression becomes more and more
full than that of the Normprincipal. Such a scale is referred to as an increasing constant scale: ⟨ . Sample
readings, taken at various steps, reveal the non-constant
relationship to the NP scale. See Table 19.

Both scales, 2a and 2b, move imperceptibly away from
the Normprincipal tone: Case 2a begins as Principal tone
but moves in the direction of String tone. Case 2b begins
also as Principal tone but moves in the direction of Flute
tone.[24]

Case 3a is a decreasing constant scale, while 3b is
of an increasing constant type. Both exhibit identical base
values of +4 HT. See Chart 5. The broken line represents

TABLE 19

DIVERGENCE OF CONSTANT SCALES 2a AND 2b
FROM THE NORMPRINCIPAL COURSE

Case	Scale Type	Divergence from Norm in $\pm$ HT				
		at Step 0	at Step 15	at Step 30	at Step 45	at Step 60
2a	$>$	0	-1	-2	-3	-4
		at Step 0	at Step 17	at Step 34	at Step 51	at Step 68
2b	$<$	0	+1	+2	+3	+4

the graphic course of the Normprincipal, introduced into the
graph as a line of reference. Case 3a, beginning with a
larger base value (+4 HT) than that of the Normprincipal,
proceeds toward the Norm in a downward (falling) direction;
this condition indicates that the ratio of diminution is
faster than for the NP, so that the original extensity, beginning with a more flutelike quality than the Norm, approaches, in the course of the progression, the extensity
of the Normprincipal. Such a scale is again referred to as
a decreasing constant scale: $>$. Case 3b, beginning
with a larger base value (+4 HT) than that of the Normprincipal, proceeds still farther away from the Norm in an upward (rising) direction; this condition indicates that the

ratio of diminution is slower than for the NP, so that the original extensity, beginning with a more flutelike quality than the Norm, becomes, in the course of the progression, still more flutelike. Such a scale is referred to as an increasing constant scale: ◁ . Sample readings, taken at various steps, reveal the non-constant relationship to the NP scale. See Table 20.

TABLE 20

DIVERGENCE OF CONSTANT SCALES 3a AND 3b
FROM THE NORMPRINCIPAL COURSE

Case	Scale Type	Divergence from Norm in $\pm$ HT				
		at Step 0	at Step 15	at Step 30	at Step 45	at Step 60
3a	▷	+4	+3	+2	+1	0
		at Step 0	at Step 17	at Step 34	at Step 51	at Step 68
3b	◁	+4	+5	+6	+7	+8

Case 4a is a decreasing constant scale predicated upon a base value of +5 HT, while 4b is of an increasing constant type predicated upon a base value of -5 HT. See Chart 6. The broken line represents the graphic course of the Normprincipal, introduced into the graph as a line of

reference. Case 4a, beginning with a large base value
(+5 HT) proceeds in a downward (falling) direction, crossing
the Norm at the thirty-fourth step. The ratio of diminution
is much faster than that for the NP, so that the original
extensity, beginning with a Flute tone, moves across the
Principal field in the direction of String tone. Such a
scale is again referred to as a decreasing constant scale:
⟩ . Case 4b proceeds in the very opposite direction;
beginning on the narrow side of the Principal field, it
crosses the Norm at about the forty-sixth step and proceeds
into the wide area of the Principal field. This scale is
referred to as an increasing constant scale: ⟨ . Sample readings, taken at various steps, reveal the non-constant relationship to the NP scale. See Table 21.

TABLE 21

DIVERGENCE OF CONSTANT SCALES 4a AND 4b
FROM THE NORMPRINCIPAL COURSE

Case	Scale Type	Divergence from Norm in ± HT				
		at Step 0	at Step 14	at Step 28	at Step 42	at Step 56
4a	⟩	+5	+3	+1	−1	−3
		at Step 0	at Step 18	at Step 36	at Step 54	at Step 72
4b	⟨	−5	−3	−1	+1	+3

Segmental Scales

Segmental scales are such as reveal more than one ratio of diminution in the course of their progression. For this reason they are not constant throughout the compass of a voice, but only for segments of the course. Depending upon how many different ratios are used and segments made, such scales may be bipartite if composed of two segments, tripartite if of three, quadripartite if of four, and multipartite if of more than that. They may be visually represented as, for example, ═══ ♯ ╱ : static constant scale from C to g♯', then increasing constant scale from g♯' to c'''' (bipartite). A tripartite example may be represented as ╲ e' ═══ g♯'' ╱ : decreasing constant scale from C to e', then static constant scale from e' to g♯'', then increasing constant scale from g♯'' to the upper limit of the compass.

In the main, two types of segmental scales are distinguishable:

1. Those whose segments meet; these may be called continuous segmental scales

2. Those whose segments do not meet but require to be bridged; these may be called broken segmental scales

A sampling of various possible cases in graphic form will help to visualize the dispositions of segmental scales

and their relation to the Normprincipal. The following
cases will be presented:

1. Continuous segmental scales--bipartite

    a. Originating at a negative base value
(-2 HT)

    b. Originating at a positive base value
(+4 HT)

    c. Originating at a negative base value
(-4 HT)

    d. Originating at a positive base value
(+6 HT)

2. Continuous segmental scales--tripartite

    a. Originating at a negative base value
(-2 HT)

    b. Originating at a negative base value
(-2 HT)

3. Broken segmental scales--tripartite

    a. Segments originating at various base
values

Numerical quantities may be introduced for the base
values and ratios of diminution, in order to develop concrete cases to exemplify the various dispositions enumerated above. Table 22 delineates appropriate courses for
voices predicated upon definite base values and progressing
through the compass by defined ratios of diminution.

TABLE 22

QUANTITATIVE DELINEATION OF A PROSPECTIVE
SERIES OF SEGMENTAL SCALES

Case	Scale Type	Base Value	Ratio of Diminution	Half Measure on	
				Step	Pipe
1a	$=\underline{\text{ǽ}}'<$	-2 HT	$1/\sqrt[4]{8}$	16	17
			$1/\sqrt[11]{64}$	22	23
1b	$=\underline{\text{ǽ}}'>$	+4 HT	$1/\sqrt[4]{8}$	16	17
			$1/\sqrt[7]{64}$	14	15
1c	$<\underline{e}''=$	-4 HT	$1/\sqrt[5]{8}$	20	21
			$1/\sqrt[4]{8}$	16	17
1d	$>\underline{e}'=$	+6 HT	$1/\sqrt[7]{64}$	14	15
			$1/\sqrt[4]{8}$	16	17
2a	$>\underline{e}'=\underline{\text{ǽ}}''<$	-2 HT	$1/\sqrt[7]{64}$	14	15
			$1/\sqrt[4]{8}$	16	17
			$1/\sqrt[11]{64}$	22	23
2b	$=\underline{e}>\underline{e}'<$	-2 HT	$1/\sqrt[4]{8}$	16	17
			$1/\,2$	12	13
			$1/\sqrt[13]{64}$	26	27
3a	$<\underline{\text{f}}'\ldots\underline{e}''<$	-6 HT	$1/\sqrt[5]{8}$	20	21
		bridge	$\ldots\ldots\ldots$	$\ldots$	$\ldots$
		+4 HT	$1/\sqrt[11]{64}$	22	23

Case la is a continuous segmental scale (bipartite)
exhibiting an initial base value of -2 HT. See Chart 7.
The broken line of the Normprincipal serves as a line of
reference. The scale la, beginning at -2 HT, proceeds parallel to the NP up to the thirty-second step. In the first
segment (a_1) the scale is constant and static; the original
extensity, slightly more meager than that of the NP, remains in this relationship. The second segment (a_2) begins
at -2 HT at the thirty-second step and increases six half-
tones to +4 HT at the fifty-fourth step, thus crossing the
NP scale. The course is made up of a static constant seg-
ment and an increasing constant segment: $\equiv g\sharp\mathllap{}\prime \;<$ (continuous, bipartite). Sample readings at various steps re-
veal the constant and non-constant relationship to the NP.
See Table 23.

TABLE 23

DIVERGENCE OF SEGMENTAL SCALE la FROM
THE NORMPRINCIPAL COURSE

Case	Scale Type	Divergence from Norm in $\pm$ HT				
		at Step 0	at Step 16	at Step 32	at Step 43	at Step 54
la	$\equiv g\sharp\mathllap{}\prime\;<$	-2	-2	-2	+2	+4

Case lb is a continuous segmental scale (bipartite)

exhibiting an initial base value of +4 HT. See Chart 8.
The broken line of the Normprincipal serves as a line of
reference. The scale 1b, beginning at +4 HT, proceeds parallel to the NP up to the thirty-second step. In the first
segment ($\underline{b}_1$) the scale is constant and static; the original
extensity, fuller than the NP, remains in this relationship.
The second segment ($\underline{b}_2$) begins at +4 HT at the thirty-second
step and decreases by four half-tones to 0 HT at the sixtieth step, arriving there at the extensity of the Normprincipal. The course is made up of a static constant segment
and a decreasing constant segment: $\equiv \underline{g}^{\sharp}\text{'} \gt$ (continuous,
bipartite). Sample readings at various steps reveal the
constant and non-constant relationship to the NP. See Table
24.

TABLE 24

DIVERGENCE OF SEGMENTAL SCALE 1b FROM
THE NORMPRINCIPAL COURSE

Case	Scale Type	Divergence from Norm in $\pm$ HT				
		at Step 0	at Step 16	at Step 32	at Step 46	at Step 60
1b	$\equiv \underline{g}^{\sharp}\text{'} \gt$	+4	+4	+4	+2	0

Case 1c is a continuous segmental scale (bipartite)
exhibiting an initial base value of -4 HT. See Chart 9.

The broken line of the Normprincipal serves as a line of
reference. The scale 1c, beginning at -4 HT, crosses the
line of the NP and arrives at +4 HT at the fortieth step.
In the first segment (c_1) the scale is of the increasing
constant type; the original extensity, beginning meager,
increases in fullness; its relationship to the NP is non-
constant. The second segment (c_2) begins at +4 HT at the
fortieth step and remains constant in this relationship to
the NP. The course is made up of an increasing constant
segment and a static constant segment: $\underset{\smile}{<}$ e'' $=$ (continuous, bipartite). Sample readings at various steps reveal the non-constant and constant relationship to the NP.
See Table 25.

TABLE 25

DIVERGENCE OF SEGMENTAL SCALE 1c FROM
THE NORMPRINCIPAL COURSE

Case	Scale Type	Divergence from Norm in $\pm$ HT				
		at Step 0	at Step 20	at Step 40	at Step 56	at Step 72
1c	$<$ e'' $=$	-4	0	+4	+4	+4

Case 1d is a continuous segmental scale (bipartite)
exhibiting an initial base value of +6 HT. See Chart 10.
The broken line of the Normprincipal serves as a line of

reference. The scale 1d, beginning at +6 HT, decreases by four half-tones to +2 HT at the twenty-eighth step. In the first segment ($\underline{d}_1$) the scale is of the decreasing constant type; the original extensity, beginning full, decreases in fullness throughout this portion of the course; its relationship to the NP is non-constant. The second segment ($\underline{d}_2$) begins at +2 HT at the twenty-eighth step and remains constant in this relationship to the NP. The course is made up of a decreasing constant segment and a static constant segment: $\succ$ $\underline{e}'$ $=$ (continuous, bipartite). Sample readings at various steps reveal this non-constant and constant relationship to the NP. See Table 26.

TABLE 26

DIVERGENCE OF SEGMENTAL SCALE 1d FROM
THE NORMPRINCIPAL COURSE

Case	Scale Type	Divergence from Norm in $\pm$ HT				
		at Step 0	at Step 14	at Step 28	at Step 44	at Step 60
1d	$\succ$ $\underline{e}'$ $=$	+6	+4	+2	+2	+2

Case 2a is a continuous segmental scale (tripartite) exhibiting an initial base value of -2 HT. See Chart 11. The broken line of the Normprincipal serves as a line of reference. The scale 2a, beginning at -2 HT decreases by

four half-tones to -6 HT at the twenty-eighth step. In the
first segment (a_1) the scale is of the decreasing constant
type; the original extensity, beginning meager, becomes
gradually more so; its relationship to the NP appears as
non-constant. The second segment (a_2) begins at -6 HT at
the twenty-eighth step and remains in this constant relationship to the NP up to the forty-fourth step; in this
segment the extensity established at the twenty-eighth step
remains unchanged, proceeding parallel to the NP. The
third segment (a_3) begins at -6 HT at the forty-fourth step
and increases by six half-tones to 0 HT at the sixty-sixth
step. In this segment, the extensity established at the
forty-fourth step increases in fullness. The course is made
up of a decreasing constant segment, a static constant seg-
ment, and an increasing constant segment: $> \underline{e}' = \underline{\text{\#}}'' <$
(continuous, tripartite). Sample readings at various steps
reveal the changing character in relation to the NP. See
Table 27.

TABLE 27

DIVERGENCE OF SEGMENTAL SCALE 2a FROM
THE NORMPRINCIPAL COURSE

Case	Scale Type	Divergence from Norm in $\pm$ HT				
		at Step 0	at Step 14	at Step 28	at Step 44	at Step 66
2a	$> \underline{e}' = \underline{\text{\#}}'' <$	-2	-4	-6	-6	0

Case 2b is a continuous segmental scale (tripartite) exhibiting an initial base value of -2 HT. ⸰ Chart 12. The broken line of the Normprincipal serves as a line of reference. The scale 2b, beginning at -2 HT, remains in a constant relationship to the Normprincipal up to the sixteenth step. In the first segment (b_1) the scale is of the static constant type; the original extensity, beginning moderately meager, remains so. The second segment (b_2) begins at -2 HT and decreases by four half-tones to -6 HT at the twenty-eighth step. In this segment the extensity moves still farther away from the NP in the direction of String tone. The third segment (b_3) is of the increasing constant type, moving rapidly across the NP to a value of +4 HT at the fifty-fourth step. The course is made up of a static constant segment, a decreasing constant segment, and an increasing constant segment: $\equiv \underline{e} > \underline{e}' <$ (continuous, tripartite). For sample readings at various steps see Table 28.

TABLE 28

DIVERGENCE OF SEGMENTAL SCALE 2b FROM
THE NORMPRINCIPAL COURSE

Case	Scale Type	Divergence from Norm in ± HT				
		at Step 0	at Step 16	at Step 28	at Step 41	at Step 54
2b	$\equiv \underline{e} > \underline{e}' <$	-2	-2	-6	-1	+4

Case 3a is a broken segmental scale (tripartite) exhibiting an initial base value of -6 HT. See Chart 13. The broken line of the Normprincipal serves as a line of reference. The scale 3a, beginning at -6 HT increases rapidly by six half-tones up to the thirtieth step, where it meets the course of the NP. At this point the scale is discontinued, and a new scale is begun at the fortieth step, starting at +4 HT and increasing gradually by six half-tones up to the sixty-second step, where it appears 10 HT larger than the NP. Since the two segments are disjointed, a broken scale results: $\prec$ f#'....e'' $\prec$ (broken, tripartite). The values for the steps of the bridge between the first and second segments must be interpolated. The terminal diameter of the first segment (t_1) and the primary diameter of the second segment (p_2) must be expressed as a ratio; thus, $D/d = t_1/p_2$, where D is the diameter of the larger (longer and wider) pipe, d the diameter of the smaller (shorter and narrower) pipe, t_1 the terminal value of the first segment, and p_2 the primary value of the second segment. Since the diameters for ten steps must be interpolated between t_1 and p_2, the formula $1/\sqrt[10]{t_1/p_2}$ will serve to represent the step ratio.[25] Accordingly, the values for the diameters of the bridge in Case 3a, are as given in Table 29, provided that the value for t_1 = 42.03 mm. and p_2 = 32.41 mm.

Sample readings from the entire scale at various

TABLE 29

DIAMETERS FOR THE BRIDGE OF
SEGMENTAL SCALE 3a

Step	Diameters in Milli-meters	Step	Diameters in Milli-meters
30th	42.03	36th	35.96
31st	40.95[a]	37th	35.04
32nd	39.90	38th	34.14
33rd	38.88	39th	33.26
34th	37.88	40th	32.41
35th	36.91		

[a]Calculation for the thirty-first step:

$$x = \frac{t_1}{\sqrt[10]{\dfrac{t_1}{P_2}}} = \frac{42.03}{\sqrt[10]{\dfrac{42.03}{32.41}}} = 40.95 \text{ mm.}$$

steps, show a continuously varying relationship to the Norm-principal. See Table 30.

Variable Scales

Variable scales are such as do not directly reveal a constant ratio of diminution in the course of their progression or in parts thereof. Two types are distinguishable:

1. Those which are set up entirely empirically

2. Those whose progressions are a composite of

TABLE 30

DIVERGENCE OF SEGMENTAL SCALE 3a FROM
THE NORMPRINCIPAL COURSE

Case	Scale Type	Divergence from Norm in $\pm$ HT					
		at Step 0	at Step 20	at Step 30	at Step 40	at Step 51	at Step 62
3a	$<$ f̲'...e̲'' $<$	-6	-2	0	+4	+7	+10

a constant ratio of diminution plus a positive or

negative arithmetic factor

The former are not subject to mathematical analysis

and can, therefore, not be illustrated here. Of the latter,

two scales will be developed to show the basic processes in-

volved in their generation:

    1. Composite variable scales

        a. Constant ratio of diminution plus posi-

        tive factor

        b. Constant ratio of diminution plus nega-

        tive factor

By introducing numerical quantities for the base

values, ratios of diminution, and arithmetic factors, Table

31 delineates the disposition of the graphs to follow.

By recording the values for the requisite $\underline{C}$'s from

Appendix D, 2 and adding the positive arithmetic factor, the

resultant values for the diameters in Case 1a are as shown

TABLE 31

QUANTITATIVE DELINEATION OF A PROSPECTIVE
SERIES OF VARIABLE SCALES

Case	Scale Type	Base Value	Ratio of Diminution	Arithmetic Factor
la	Variable	0 HT + factor	$1/\sqrt[4]{8}$	+5 mm.
lb	Variable	0 HT + factor[a]	$1/\sqrt[4]{8}$	-5 mm.

[a]Algebraic addition is implied.

in Table 32.

TABLE 32

DERIVATION OF VALUES FOR COMPOSITE
VARIABLE SCALE la

Note	Diameter of Normprincipal in Millimeters	Arithmetic Factor in Millimeters	Resultant Value in Millimeters	Divergence from Normprincipal (Approximate)
C	154.17	+5	159.17	+1 HT
c	91.67	+5	96.67	+1 HT
c'	54.51	+5	59.51	+2 HT
c''	32.41	+5	37.41	+3 1/2 HT
c'''	19.27	+5	24.27	+6 HT
c''''	11.46	+5	16.46	+8 1/2 HT

By plotting the resultant values on a graph with reference to the Normprincipal, a positive curve is obtained; this is the earmark of a variable scale with positive factor. See Chart 14. The broken line of the Normprincipal serves as a line of reference. The scale 1a, beginning at almost the same base value as the NP, accelerates its increase during the course of the progression, arriving at the sixtieth step with a diameter value 8 1/2 HT greater than that of the NP. The scale is variable, moving from Principal tone into Flute tone.

By recording the values for the requisite C's from Appendix D, 2 and adding the negative arithmetic factor, the resultant values for the diameters in Case 1b are as shown in Table 33.

By plotting the resultant values on a graph with reference to the Normprincipal, a negative curve is obtained; this is the earmark of a variable scale with negative factor. See Chart 15. The broken line of the Normprincipal serves as a line of reference. The scale 1b, beginning at almost the same base value as the NP, accelerates its decrease during the course of the progression, arriving at the sixtieth step with a diameter about thirteen halftones smaller than that of the NP. The scale is variable, moving from Principal tone into String tone.

The composite variable scales, as exemplified by

TABLE 33

DERIVATION OF VALUES FOR COMPOSITE
VARIABLE SCALE 1b

Note	Diameter of Normprincipal in Millimeters	Arithmetic Factor in Millimeters	Resultant Value in Millimeters	Divergence from Normprincipal (Approximate)
c	154.17	−5	149.17	−1 HT
c	91.67	−5	86.67	−1 HT
c'	54.51	−5	49.51	−2 HT
c''	32.41	−5	27.41	−4 HT
c'''	19.27	−5	14.27	−7 HT
c''''	11.46	−5	6.46	−13 HT

Cases 1a and 1b, present a bewildering array of possible
permutations, all characterized by a continuously changing
degree of extensity throughout the course of the compass;
the degree of change depends upon the following conditions:

    1. The initial base value chosen for the diame-
ters

    2. The ratio of diminution laid down as the
basis for the progression

    3. The value adopted for the arithmetic factor
Within the framework of the three basic types of

scales (constant, segmental, and variable), an infinite number of permutations are possible. The choice of various base values further multiplies the possibilities. Historically, all of these methods have been employed, the variable species early, and the constant and segmental ones in more recent time. In differentiating one genus of pipes from another it is customary to relate it to the Normprincipal by indicating usable base values and by showing the progress of the diminution by "rule of thumb" as ═══ , ◁ , or ▷ .

CHAPTER IV

THE MODERN ORGAN: GENERA OF REGISTERS
AS INFLUENCED BY THE MOUTH

Although the width of the mouth and its height are
not primary factors in establishing the classification of
registers into genera, their dispositions exert a secondary
influence and help to refine the classification.

The Mouth Width

In labial pipes, the width of the mouth is reckoned
as the horizontal or near-horizontal dimension of the upper
lip. See Plate XXXIX, 1, 2, 3, and 4.

The width of the mouth is one of the important factors that influence the tone of pipes. Its greatest influence lies in the control it exercises over the amplitude of
the vibrations or the dynamic strength of the tone. The
wider the mouth, the larger a segment of the air column in
the pipe will be directly excited, and, as a consequence,
the greater the amplitude of the resultant vibrations will
be. Succinctly stated:

The amplitude of the ⎱   directly   ⎰ the width of
  vibrations varies ⎰   as   ⎱   the mouth

98

Various methods of specifying mouth widths are in current use. The width may be expressed:

1. As the ratio of its dimension to the circumference of the corpus (dependent ratio)

2. As the tabular difference from an established norm, such as the Normprincipal (independent ratio)

The Dependent Ratio

In the first instance, the width of the mouth is given as the ratio of its dimension to the circumference of the corpus at the level of the mouth.[1] The factors are related by the ratio: $R_m = W/C$, where R_m is the ratio of the mouth, W its horizontal dimension, and C the circumference of the corpus at the mouth.[2] For example, a mouth, having a dimension of 25 millimeters in a circumference of 100 millimeters, is known as a 1/4 mouth.

When the mouth width is established as a dependent ratio of the circumference, its own ratio of diminution is chained to that of the circumference and will remain constant to that progression throughout the compass. For example, in the case of a 1/4 mouth, if the diameter and circumference proceed in an octave ratio of diminution equal to $1/\sqrt[4]{8}$, then the values for the mouth widths will also proceed in that same octave ratio of diminution throughout the compass. If this method is pursued, the designations for the mouth widths will appear as proper fractions: 1/4, 1/5, 1/6, etc. The range of mouth width ratios theoretically useful in practice may vary from a maximum unit ratio of 1/3 to a minimum unit ratio of about 1/7.[3] Set up in order from the widest to the narrowest, these ratios are (diminishing, left to right):

1/3   1/4   1/5   1/6   1/7

It is possible to interpolate one intermediate value between each of the unit ratios (diminishing, left to right):

1/3   1/4   1/5
(2/6)   2/7   (2/8)   2/9   (2/10)

              1/6   1/7
2/11   (2/12)   2/13   (2/14)

Should two intermediate values be interpolated between the unit ratios, the following values would result (diminishing, left to right):

1/3   1/4
(3/9)   3/10   3/11   (3/12)   3/13   3/14

1/5   1/6   1/7
(3/15)   3/16   3/17 (3/18)   3/19   3/20 (3/21)

Three intermediate values between each of the unit ratios gives the following divisions (diminishing, left to right):

1/3 (4/12)	4/13	2/7	4/15	1/4 (4/16)	4/17
2/9	4/19	1/5 (4/20)	4/21	2/11	4/23
1/6 (4/24)	4/25	2/13	4/27	1/7 (4/28)	

Four intermediate values between each of the unit ratios develops the following ratios (diminishing, left to right):

1/3 (5/15)	5/16	5/17	5/18	5/19
1/4 (5/20)	5/21	5/22	5/23	5/24
1/5 (5/25)	5/26	5/27	5/28	5/29
1/6 (5/30)	5/31	5/32	5/33	5/34

A composite of the ratios, gathering together the two-fold, three-fold, and four-fold interpolations, arranges them in the following order (diminishing, left to right):

1/3	5/16	4/13	3/10	5/17
2/7	5/18	3/11	4/15	5/19
1/4	5/21	4/17	3/13	5/22
2/9	5/23	3/14	4/19	5/24
1/5	5/26	4/21	3/16	5/27
2/11	5/28	3/17	4/23	5/29
1/6	5/31	4/25	3/19	5/32
2/13	5/33	3/20	4/27	5/34

Observe that the arrangement does not present equidistant
spacing between the values. See Appendix K, 1.

Further intermediate ratios can be interpolated between the unit ratios after the manner shown.

Most convenient for purposes of computation is a
table presenting nine interpolations between each of the
unit ratios, so that a ten-point division results, which is
particularly useful in making comparisons with unit ratios
which exhibit decimal divisions. See Appendix K, 2.

The effect of a dependent ratio, generally employed
in American organ building, should be noted. Since it has
been established that an octave ratio of $1/\sqrt[4]{8}$ for the diameters (or circumferences, for that matter) maintains a consistent extensity of tone, then a dependent mouth ratio associated with this progression will maintain, provided all
other factors are constant, a consistent dynamic strength
throughout the series. With a slower ratio of diminution
for the diameters as, for example, $1/\sqrt[3]{4}$ (half measure on
the eighteenth step), the pipes will exhibit not only an increase in extensity in their progress through the course,
but also a proportionate increase in dynamic strength. The
reason for such a concomitant phenomenon lies in the fact
that, by use of the dependent ratio, the mouth widths diminish at a slower rate as well. Conversely, with a faster
ratio of diminution as, for example, $1/\sqrt[7]{64}$ (half measure

n the fourteenth step), the results will be reversed; the
xtensity and the dynamic strength will diminish proportion-
tely.

The Independent Ratio

The entangling alliance of the dependent ratio,
hereby the progress of the extensity of the tone controls
lso the progress of the dynamic strength, has led theorists
nd practitioners to seek a method of determining mouth
idths that will relieve such a rigid association and per-
it the strength of the tone to be controlled somewhat inde-
endently of the extensity.

It was already established by Toepfer and is gener-
lly supported today, that a 1/4 mouth associated with an
ctave ratio of diminution for diameters equal to $1/\sqrt[4]{8}$
aintains a consistent dynamic strength throughout a series
f pipes. Accordingly, it has proved convenient to set up
n independent table for the mouth widths of the Normprin-
ipal which displays the following characteristics:

1. The mouth widths are equal to 1/4 of the circumferences of the Normprincipal; this is the base
value

2. The values for the mouth widths proceed from
this base value in an octave ratio of diminution equal
to $1/\sqrt[4]{8}$

3. The mouth widths assure a high degree of

consistency in the amplitude of the vibrations with-

in the pipes of the series

See Table 34 or Appendix I.

All of the dimensions for the mouth widths in the table, consequently, are equal to 1/4 of the circumferences of the Normprincipal. These widths are, therefore, considered as <u>normal</u> widths and presuppose a base value at <u>C</u> 8' of 121.09 millimeters and an octave ratio of diminution equal to $1/\sqrt[4]{8}$ for the diameters.

From the Normprincipal table of mouth widths it is possible to select a base value for a given set of pipes, which represents a mouth width equal to 1/4 of the circumference, provided that this base value is comparable to the base value chosen for the diameters. See Appendices D, 2 and J. For example, if the base value of the diameter is to be +2 HT, then the base value for the mouth must, likewise, be +2 HT.[4] Accordingly, there may not exist a tabular difference in half-tones (TD) between the diameters and the mouth widths if the 1/4 ratio is to result. Of course, it rarely occurs in practice that the mouth widths as well as the diameters are precisely those of the Normprincipal. A multitude of variations is possible from the following conditions:

1. The base value for the diameters, as previously shown, may be the same, greater, or smaller than

VALUES FOR THE MOUTH WIDTHS OF THE AMERICAN EQUIVALENT OF THE FREIBERG NORMPRINCIPAL[a]
(VALUES IN MILLIMETERS)

Note	32'	16'	8'	4'	2'	1'	1/2'	1/4'	1/8'
C	342.47	203.64	121.09[b]	72.00	42.81	25.45	15.14	9.00	5.35
C♯	327.95	195.00	115.95	68.94	40.99	24.37	14.49	8.62	5.12
D	314.07	186.74	111.02	66.02	39.26	23.34	13.88	8.25	4.91
D♯	300.75	178.82	106.33	63.22	37.59	22.35	13.29	7.90	4.70
E	288.00	171.23	101.82	60.54	36.00	21.40	12.73	7.57	4.50
F	275.77	163.98	97.50	57.97	34.47	20.50	12.19	7.25	4.31
F♯	264.08	157.03	93.37	55.51	33.01	19.63	11.67	6.94	4.13
G	252.90	150.37	89.41	53.16	31.61	18.80	11.18	6.65	3.95
G♯	242.17	144.00	85.62	50.91	30.27	18.00	10.70	6.36	3.78
A	231.90	137.88	81.99	48.75	28.99	17.24	10.25	6.09	3.62
A♯	222.05	132.04	78.52	46.68	27.76	16.51	9.81	5.84	3.47
B	212.65	126.45	75.19	44.70	26.58	15.81	9.40	5.59	3.32

[a] The table is valid only for $R_m = 1/4$; reference pitch of $\underline{a}' = 440$ cycles per second (American Standard Pitch); temperature at 20° Centigrade or 68° Fahrenheit.

[b] Calculation for $\underline{C}$ 8': If R_m is the ratio of the mouth, $\underline{W}$ the width of the mouth, $\underline{C}$ the circumference of the pipe, and $\underline{D}$ the diameter of the same, then $R_m = \frac{W}{C}$. Since $C = D\pi$, then $W = R_m \times D\pi$ or $\frac{1 \times 154.17 \times 3.1416}{4}$ or 121.09 mm.

the tabular value for the diameters of the Normprincipal

2. The base value for the mouth widths may also
be the same, greater, or smaller than the tabular value for the mouth widths of the Normprincipal

Accordingly, the two base values (one for the diameters, the other for the mouth widths) may be taken parallel, i.e., displaying no tabular difference; in this case,
the ratio of the mouth width is consistently 1/4 that of the
circumference. Conversely, the two base values (one for the
diameters, the other for the mouth widths) may be taken divergent, i.e., displaying a tabular difference of positive
or negative half-tones; in this case, the ratio of the mouth
width is never 1/4 that of the circumference. See Table 35.

Correlation of Dependent and Independent Ratios

It is desirable to be able to relate the second
method of specifying mouth widths (from a reference table)
with the first method (which establishes the mouth width as
a dependent ratio of the circumference). In order to make
the comparison visually effective, the two Normprincipal
tables (that of the diameters and that of the mouth widths)
must be brought into juxtaposition, so that the linear dimensions of the mouth widths lie in the same tabular positions as those of the diameters. The tables may then be
said to be in perfect registration, and the tabular differ-

TABLE 35

DERIVATION OF TABULAR DIFFERENCE BETWEEN
THE DIAMETER AND MOUTH WIDTH[a]

Tabular Position of Diameter (T_d)	Tabular Position of Mouth Width (T_w)	Tabular Difference ($T_w - T_d$)	Tabular Position of Diameter (T_d)	Tabular Position of Mouth Width (T_w)	Tabular Difference ($T_w - T_d$)
0 HT	0 HT	0 HT	+1 HT	0 HT	-1 HT
+1 HT	+1 HT	0 HT	+4 HT	+2 HT	-2 HT
+2 HT	+2 HT	0 HT	+5 HT	-1 HT	-6 HT
+3 HT	+3 HT	0 HT	-3 HT	+2 HT	+5 HT
-1 HT	-1 HT	0 HT	-4 HT	-1 HT	+3 HT
-5 HT	-5 HT	0 HT	0 HT	+2 HT	+2 HT

[a]The abbreviations used in the table represent the following concepts: T_d is the tabular position of the diameter, expressed as $\pm$ x HT; T_w is the tabular position of the mouth width, expressed similarly.

ences between the two tables can be read off directly. See Table 36.

The values for the mouth widths in the table are all equal to 1/4 of the corresponding circumferences and proceed, like the diameters, in an octave ratio of $1/\sqrt[4]{8}$, halving on the sixteenth step. In order to relate the two methods of expressing mouth widths from the compound table, it

TABLE 36

VALUES FOR THE DIAMETERS AND CORRESPONDING MOUTH WIDTHS OF THE AMERICAN EQUIVALENT OF THE FREIBERG NORMPRINCIPAL[a]
(VALUES IN MILLIMETERS)

Note	32'		16'		8'		4'	
	Diameter	Mouth Width	Diameter	Mouth Width	Diameter	Mouth Width	Diameter	Mouth Width
C	436.06	342.47	259.28	203.64	154.17	121.09	91.67	72.00
C♯	417.57	327.95	248.29	195.00	147.63	115.95	87.78	68.94
D	399.87	314.07	237.76	186.74	141.36	111.02	84.06	66.02
D♯	382.91	300.75	227.68	178.82	135.38	106.33	80.50	63.22
E	366.68	288.00	218.03	171.23	129.64	101.82	77.09	60.54
F	351.13	275.77	208.78	163.98	124.14	97.50	73.82	57.97
F♯	336.25	264.08	199.93	157.03	118.88	93.37	70.68	55.51
G	322.00	252.90	191.46	150.37	113.84	89.41	67.69	53.16
G♯	308.35	242.17	183.34	144.00	109.01	85.62	64.82	50.91
A	295.27	231.90	175.57	137.88	104.39	81.99	62.07	48.75
A♯	282.73	222.05	168.12	132.04	99.97	78.52	59.44	46.68
B	270.76	212.65	160.99	126.45	95.73	75.19	56.92	44.70

Continued on following page

[a]The table is predicated upon American Standard Pitch (a' = 440 cycles per second); temperature at 20° Centigrade or 68° Fahrenheit; diameters of the Normprincipal; mouth widths are 1/4 of the circumferences; octave ratio of diminution for all values equals $1:\sqrt[4]{8}$.

TABLE 36--Continued

Note	2' Diameter	2' Mouth Width	1' Diameter	1' Mouth Width	1/2' Diameter	1/2' Mouth Width	1/4' Diameter	1/4' Mouth Width	1/8' Diameter	1/8' Mouth Width
C	54.51	42.81	32.41	25.45	19.27	15.14	11.46	9.00	6.81	5.35
C♯	52.20	40.99	31.04	24.37	18.45	14.49	10.97	8.62	6.52	5.12
D	49.98	39.26	29.72	23.34	17.67	13.88	10.51	8.25	6.25	4.91
D♯	47.86	37.59	28.46	22.35	16.92	13.29	10.06	7.90	5.98	4.70
E	45.83	36.00	27.25	21.40	16.21	12.73	9.64	7.57	5.73	4.50
F	43.89	34.47	26.10	20.50	15.52	12.19	9.23	7.25	5.49	4.31
F♯	42.03	33.01	24.99	19.63	14.86	11.67	8.84	6.94	5.25	4.13
G	40.25	31.61	23.93	18.80	14.23	11.18	8.46	6.65	5.03	3.95
G♯	38.54	30.27	22.92	18.00	13.63	10.70	8.10	6.36	4.82	3.78
A	36.91	28.99	21.95	17.24	13.05	10.25	7.76	6.09	4.61	3.62
A♯	35.34	27.76	21.02	16.51	12.50	9.81	7.43	5.84	4.42	3.47
B	33.84	26.58	20.12	15.81	11.97	9.40	7.12	5.59	4.23	3.32

is necessary to discover the tabular difference (TD) in
half-tones between the mouth width (W) and the diameter (D).
The tabular difference will be equal to the difference between the tabular position of the mouth width (T_w) and the
tabular position of the diameter (T_d), both expressed as deviations in half-tones ($\pm$ HT) from the Normprincipal; thus,
TD = T_w - T_d. The following conditions are possible:

    1. The mouth width and the diameter may show a
tabular difference of 0 HT

    2. The mouth width may be x number of half-
tones smaller than the diameter (-x HT)

    3. The mouth width may be x number of half-
tones greater than the diameter (+x HT)

In Case 1, the ratio of the mouth width to the circumference
is equal to 1/4; in Case 2 it is less than 1/4; in Case 3 it
is more than 1/4.

    Table 37 shows the ratios as influenced by the tab-
ular difference in half-tones between the mouth widths and
the diameters; thereby the ratios of the mouth widths are
expressed as functions of the tabular differences.

    The ratios of Column (2) in Table 37, when plotted
upon a graph which combines the tabular differences with the
dependent ratios, will correlate the two methods (dependent
and independent) of delineating mouth widths. See Chart 16.

    From the graph can also be extracted the approximate

TABLE 37

RATIOS OF MOUTH WIDTHS AS INFLUENCED
BY TABULAR DIFFERENCE[a]

Tabular Difference $(T_w - T_d)$ (1)	Exact Ratio $(W/D\pi)$ (2)	Approximate Ratio (3)	Tabular Difference $(T_w - T_d)$ (1)	Exact Ratio $(W/D\pi)$ (2)	Approximate Ratio (3)
−13 HT	1/7.025	1/7	−3 HT	1/4.555	5/23
−12 HT	1/6.728[b]	10/67	−2 HT	1/4.362	5/22
−11 HT	1/6.442	5/32	−1 HT	1/4.177	5/21
−10 HT	1/6.169	5/31	0 HT	1/4.000	1/4
−9 HT	1/5.908	10/59	+1 HT	1/3.831	5/19
−8 HT	1/5.656	10/57	+2 HT	1/3.668	10/37
−7 HT	1/5.417	5/27	+3 HT	1/3.513	2/7
−6 HT	1/5.187	5/26	+4 HT	1/3.363	5/19
−5 HT	1/4.968	1/5	+5 HT	1/3.221	5/16
−4 HT	1/4.757	5/24	+6 HT	1/3.085	10/31

[a]Ratios of the mouth widths are expressed as functions of the tabular difference.

[b]Calculation for TD of −12 HT: If TD is the tabular difference, T_w the tabular position of the mouth width, and T_d the tabular position of the diameter, then, TD = $T_w - T_d$ or T_w = TD + T_d. If T_d = +10 HT and TD = −12 HT, then T_w = −12 + (+10) = −2 HT. Numerical values for the note C 8' are as follows: D at +10 HT = 237.76 mm. and W at −2 HT = 111.02 mm. To calculate the exact dependent

ratio of the mouth, it is necessary to use the original for-
mula for the ratio of the mouth width: $R_m = \frac{W}{C}$ or $\frac{W}{D\pi}$, where
R_m is the dependent ratio of the mouth, W the actual width
of the mouth, C the actual circumference of the corpus, and
D the actual diameter of the same. Since the ratio of the
mouth may also be expressed as $\frac{1}{x}$, then $\frac{1}{x} = \frac{W}{D\pi}$ or $x = \frac{D\pi}{W}$.
By substituting the appropriate numerical values for C 8':
$x = \frac{237.76 \times 3.1416}{111.02} = 6.728.$ If, then, $R_m = \frac{1}{x}$, $R_m = \frac{1}{6.728}$.

tabular differences necessary to achieve the commonly used

dependent ratios; thereby the tabular differences are ex-

pressed as functions of the dependent ratios of mouth widths.

See Table 38 or Appendix N.

Correlation of Mouth Width and Diameter

By thus divorcing the values of the mouth widths

from those of the diameters, it is possible to control the

extensity of the tone and the amplitude of the vibrations

separately and independently of each other. A number of

possibilities present themselves:

1. The mouth width and diameter may have the
same base values and the same ratios of diminution

2. The mouth width and diameter may have the
same base values but different ratios of diminution

3. The mouth width and diameter may have different base values but the same ratios of diminution

4. The mouth width and diameter may have

TABLE 38

TABULAR DIFFERENCES AS INFLUENCED BY DEPENDENT
RATIOS OF MOUTH WIDTHS[a]

Dependent Ratio $(W/D\pi)$	Approximate Tabular Difference between W and D $(T_w - T_d)$	Dependent Ratio $(W/D\pi)$	Approximate Tabular Difference between W and D $(T_w - T_d)$
1/3	+7 HT	5/26	-6 HT
5/16	+5 HT	5/27	-7 HT
5/17	+3 2/3 HT	2/11	-7 1/3 HT
2/7	+3 HT	5/28	-7 2/3 HT
5/18	+2 1/3 HT	5/29	-8 2/3 HT
5/19	+1 1/6 HT	1/6	-9 1/3 HT
1/4	0 HT	5/31	-10 1/6 HT
5/21	-1 1/6 HT	5/32	-10 5/6 HT
5/22	-2 1/6 HT	2/13	-11 1/6 HT
2/9	-2 2/3 HT	5/33	-11 1/2 HT
5/23	-3 1/6 HT	5/34	-12 1/3 HT
5/24	-4 1/6 HT	1/7	-13 HT
1/5	-5 1/6 HT		

[a]In this table, the tabular differences are expressed as functions of the dependent ratios. See Appendix N for a more complete catalog.

different base values and different ratios of diminution

In Cases 1 and 3, the extensity and amplitude

established at the beginning of the series do not vary from
each other during the course of the progression. As the extensity remains constant, increases, or decreases, so does
the amplitude of vibration: the progressions are parallel.
In Cases 2 and 4, the extensity and amplitude established at
the beginning of the series vary from each other during the
course of the progression. As the extensity remains constant, increases, or decreases, the amplitude of vibration
varies in a similar, oblique, or contrary progression: the
progressions are divergent.

A clear picture of the progression of the values of
the mouth widths and diameters can be gained by plotting the
courses of both progressions on the same graph. For this
purpose, the graphic layout used for the display of the diameters can be employed. See Chart 2. Since the ordinate
($\underline{Y}$-axis) of this graph does not represent numerical values
but only tabular positions, the line for the mouth widths
may occupy the same general area assigned to the diameters.
By using the dispositions established above as a basis, a
number of sample cases will be presented to help visualize
the parallel or divergent courses of the two values, diameter and mouth width. Table 39 presents quantitative values
for a prospective series of mouth widths.

Case 1a presents diameter and mouth width courses
which exhibit the same base values (0 HT) and the same

TABLE 39

QUANTITATIVE DELINEATION OF A PROSPECTIVE
SERIES OF MOUTH WIDTHS[a]

Case	Base Value of Diameter (D), Mouth Width (W)	Ratio of Diminution	Half Measure on Step	Symbol-ization
1a	D = 0 HT	$1/\sqrt[4]{8}$	16	≡
	W = 0 HT	$1/\sqrt[4]{8}$	16	≡
1b	D = +3 HT	$1/\sqrt[7]{64}$	14	>
	W = +3 HT	$1/\sqrt[7]{64}$	14	>
1c	D = -4 HT	$1/\sqrt[3]{4}$	18	<
	W = -4 HT	$1/\sqrt[3]{4}$	18	<
2a	D = 0 HT	$1/\sqrt[4]{8}$	16	≡
	W = 0 HT	$1/\sqrt[5]{16}$	15	>
2b	D = +3 HT	$1/\sqrt[5]{16}$	15	>
	W = +3 HT	$1/\sqrt[4]{8}$	16	≡
3a	D = +2 HT	$1/\sqrt[4]{8}$	16	≡
	W = 0 HT	$1/\sqrt[4]{8}$	16	≡

[a]The cases are purely hypothetical, designed only to show as effectively as possible, the parallel or divergent characters of the various progressions.

TABLE 39--Continued

Case	Base Value of Diameter (D), Mouth Width (W)	Ratio of Diminution	Half Measure on Step	Symbolization
3b	D = +4 HT	$1/\sqrt[5]{16}$	15	>
	W = -2 HT	$1/\sqrt[5]{16}$	15	>
4a	D = +2 HT	$1/\sqrt[5]{16}$	15	>
	W = -3 HT	$1/\sqrt[17]{2^{12}}$	17	<
4b	D = -2 HT	$1/\sqrt[3]{4}$	18	<
	W = +1 HT	$1/\sqrt[4]{8}$	16	=

ratios of diminution $(1/\sqrt[4]{8})$. See Chart 17. The solid line shows the course of the diameter values, while the broken line represents the values of the mouth widths. In fact, the graphic representation is precisely that of the Norm-principal for both courses. The diameters begin with a base value of 0 HT and proceed in an octave ratio of diminution of $1/\sqrt[4]{8}$, indicating a static and constant progression which displays the same degree of extensity throughout the series. The mouth widths, likewise, begin with a base value of 0 HT and proceed in an octave ratio of diminution of $1/\sqrt[4]{8}$, indicating a static and constant progression which displays the same degree of amplitude of vibration throughout the series.

By comparing the progressions of the diameters with those
of the mouth widths, it becomes apparent that as the extensity remains constant, so does the amplitude of vibration.
The two courses are parallel, each remaining static and constant: $\underline{D}$ ══ , $\underline{W}$ ══ . A usable Norm is thereby established. The tabular (or graphic) difference between the
mouth widths and diameters is equal to 0 HT throughout the
course. The dependent ratio, therefore, of W/C is equal to
1/4 for all members of the series. See Appendices M and N.

In the graphs following, the courses of the mouth
widths and diameters of the Normprincipal, here shown as a
broken and as a solid line respectively, will be combined
into one line; thus, ── o ── , to serve as a reference
to which the case values can be visually compared.

Case 1b presents diameter and mouth width courses
which exhibit the same base values (+4 HT) and the same ratios of diminution ($1/\sqrt[7]{64}$). See Chart 18. The mouth
widths and diameters of the Normprincipal are shown by one
line; thus, ── o ── . The diameters (solid line) of
Case 1b begin at +3 HT and end at about -5 1/2 HT, indicating a decreasing constant progression which displays great-
er extensity at $\underline{C}$ than at $\underline{c}''''$. The mouth widths (broken
line) begin at +3 HT and end at about -5 1/2 HT, indicating
a decreasing constant progression which displays a greater
amplitude of vibration at $\underline{C}$ than at $\underline{c}''''$. By comparing the

progressions of the diameters with those of the mouth widths,
it becomes apparent that as the extensity decreases, so does
the amplitude. The two courses are parallel, each one being
of a decreasing and constant type: $\underline{D} \searrow$, $\underline{W} \searrow$. The
tabular (or graphic) difference between the mouth widths and
diameters is equal to 0 HT throughout. The dependent ratio,
therefore, of W/C is equal to 1/4 for all members of the
series. See Appendices M and N.

Case 1c presents diameter and mouth width courses
which exhibit the same base values (-4 HT) and the same ratios of diminution $(1/\sqrt[3]{4})$. See Chart 19. The mouth widths
and diameters of the Normprincipal are shown by one line;
thus, ———— ° ———— . The diameters (solid line) of Case 1c
begin at -4 HT and end at +2 1/2 HT, indicating an increasing constant progression which displays greater extensity
at $\underline{c}''''$ than at $\underline{C}$. The mouth widths (broken line) begin,
likewise, at -4 HT and end at +2 1/2 HT, indicating an in-
creasing constant progression which displays a greater am-
plitude of vibration at $\underline{c}''''$ than at $\underline{C}$. By comparing the
progression of the diameters with those of the mouth widths,
it is clear that as the extensity increases, so does the amplitude. The two scales are parallel, each one being of an
increasing and constant type: $\underline{D} \lessdot$, $\underline{W} \lessdot$. The tabular (or graphic) difference between the mouth widths and
diameters is equal to 0 HT throughout. The dependent ratio,

therefore, of W/C is equal to 1/4 for all members of the
series. See Appendices M and N.

Case 2a presents diameter and mouth width courses
which exhibit the same base values (0 HT), but different
ratios of diminution (D = $1/\sqrt[4]{8}$, W = $1/\sqrt[5]{16}$). See Chart 20.
The mouth widths and diameters of the Normprincipal are
shown by one line; thus, ——— o ——— . The diameters (solid
line) of Case 2a begin at 0 HT and end at 0 HT, indicating
a static constant progression which displays the same degree of extensity throughout the series. The mouth widths
(broken line) begin at 0 HT and end at -4 HT, indicating a
decreasing constant progression which displays greater amplitude of vibration at C than at c''''. By comparing the
two progressions, it is evident that as the extensity remains constant, the amplitude decreases. The two scales are
divergent: that of the diameters being static and constant,
that of the mouth widths decreasing and constant: D ═══ ,
W ➤ . The tabular (or graphic) difference between the
mouth widths and diameters is equal to 0 HT at C and -4 HT
at c''''. The dependent ratio, therefore, of W/C at C is
equal to 1/4, decreasing to 1/4.757 (ca. 5/24) at c''''.
See Appendices M and N.

Case 2b presents diameter and mouth width courses
which exhibit the same base values (+3 HT), but different
ratios of diminution (D = $1/\sqrt[5]{16}$, W = $1/\sqrt[4]{8}$). See Chart 21.

The mouth widths and diameters of the Normprincipal are shown by one line; thus, —— ○ —— . The diameters (solid line) of Case 2b begin at +3 HT and end at 0 HT, indicating a decreasing constant progression which displays greater extensity at C than at c''''. The mouth widths (broken line) begin at +3 HT and end at +3 HT, indicating a static constant progression which displays the same degree of amplitude throughout the series. By comparing the two progressions, it is evident that as the extensity decreases, the amplitude remains constant. The two scales are divergent: that of the diameters decreasing and constant, that of the mouth widths, static and constant: D $>$, W $=$. The tabular (or graphic) difference between the mouth widths and diameters is equal to 0 HT at C and +3 HT at c''''. The dependent ratio, therefore, of W/C at C is equal to 1/4, increasing to 1/3.513 (ca. 2/7) at c''''. See Appendices M and N.

Case 3a presents diameter and mouth width courses which exhibit different base values (D = +2 HT, W = 0 HT), but the same ratios of diminution $(1/\sqrt[4]{8})$. See Chart 22. The mouth widths and diameters of the Normprincipal are shown by one line; thus, —— ○ —— . The diameters (solid line) of Case 3a begin at +2 HT and end at +2 HT, indicating a static constant progression which displays the same degree of extensity throughout the series. The mouth widths

(broken line) begin at 0 HT and end at 0 HT, indicating also
a static constant progression which displays the same degree
of amplitude throughout the series. By comparing the two
progressions, it becomes apparent that both the extensity
and amplitude are static and constant; the two scales are
parallel: $\underline{D} \rule{1cm}{0pt}$, $\underline{W} \rule{1cm}{0pt}$. The tabular (or graphic)
difference between the mouth widths and diameters is equal
to -2 HT throughout. The dependent ratio, therefore, of W/C
is equal to 1/4.362 (<u>ca</u>. 5/22). See Appendices M and N.

Case 3b presents diameter and mouth width courses
which exhibit different base values (D = +4 HT, W = -2 HT),
but the same ratios of diminution $(1/\sqrt[5]{16})$. See Chart 23.
The mouth widths and diameters of the Normprincipal are
shown by one line; thus, ——— ° ——— . The diameters (solid
line) begin at +4 HT and end at 0 HT, indicating a decreasing constant progression which displays greater extensity at
$\underline{C}$ than at $\underline{c}''''$. The mouth widths (broken line) begin at
-2 HT and end at -6 HT, indicating a decreasing constant pro-
gression which displays greater amplitude at $\underline{C}$ than at $\underline{c}''''$.
By comparing the two progressions, it is evident that both
the extensity and amplitude decrease. The two courses are
parallel: $\underline{D} \!>$, $\underline{W} \!>$. The tabular (or graphic)
difference between the mouth widths and diameters is equal
to -6 HT at $\underline{C}$ and -6 HT at $\underline{c}''''$. The dependent ratio,
therefore, of W/C is equal to 1/5.187 (<u>ca</u>. 5/26) throughout

the series. See Appendices M and N.

Case 4a presents diameter and mouth width courses
which exhibit different base values $(D = +2\ HT,\ W = -3\ HT)$
and different ratios of diminution $(D = 1/\sqrt[5]{16}\ W = 1/\sqrt[17]{2^{12}})$.
See Chart 24. The mouth widths and diameters of the Norm-
principal are shown by one line; thus, —— o —— . The
diameters (solid line) of Case 4a begin at +2 HT and end at
-2 HT, indicating a decreasing constant progression which
displays a greater extensity at $\underline{C}$ than at $\underline{c}''''$. The mouth
widths (broken line) begin at -3 HT and end at 0 HT, indi-
cating an increasing constant progression which displays a
greater amplitude at $\underline{c}''''$ than at $\underline{C}$. In comparison, the
extensity decreases while the amplitude increases. The two
scales are divergent: $\underline{D} \gg$, $\underline{W} \ll$. The tabular (or
graphic) difference between the mouth widths and diameters
is equal to -5 HT at $\underline{C}$ and +2 HT at $\underline{c}''''$. The dependent
ratio, therefore, of W/C is equal to 1/4.968 ($\underline{ca}$. 1/5), increasing to 1/3.668 ($\underline{ca}$. 10/37) at $\underline{c}''''$. See Appendices M
and N.

Case 4b presents diameter and mouth width courses
which exhibit different base values $(D = -2\ HT,\ W = +1\ HT)$
and different ratios of diminution $(D = 1/\sqrt[3]{4},\ W = 1/\sqrt[4]{8})$.
See Chart 25. The mouth widths and diameter of the Normprincipal are shown by one line; thus, —— o —— . The
diameters (solid line) of Case 4b begin at -2 HT and end at

+4 1/2 HT, indicating an increasing constant progression
which displays greater extensity at $\underline{c}$'''' than at $\underline{C}$. The
mouth widths (broken line) begin at +1 HT and end at +1 HT,
indicating a static constant progression which displays the
same amplitude throughout. In comparison, the extensity increases while the amplitude remains static. The two scales
are divergent: that of the diameters increasing and constant, that of the mouth widths static and constant:
$\underline{D}$ $<$, $\underline{W}$ $=$. The tabular (or graphic) difference between the mouth widths and diameters is equal to +3 HT at $\underline{C}$
and -3 1/2 HT at $\underline{c}$''''. The dependent ratio, therefore, of
W/C is equal to 1/3.513 ($\underline{ca}$. 2/7) at $\underline{C}$, which decreases to
1/4.656 ($\underline{ca}$. 10/47) at $\underline{c}$''''. See Appendices M and N.

Out of these basic methods of determining mouth
widths and relating them in various ways to the scales of
the diameters, a limitless number of cross modulations are
possible. The choice of various base values further multiplies the possibilities. Historically, the dependent ratios
held almost unchallenged sway during the nineteenth and
early twentieth centuries, while the independent ratios have
been developed more recently out of the various empirical
methods employed in earlier times. In the most recent practice (chiefly German and, selectively, American) the mouth
widths are differentiated by relating their base values to
those of the Normprincipal and then indicating the progress

of the diminution by "rule of thumb," as $=$, $>$, or $<$.

The Cutup

Under the term cutup is understood the distance of the upper lip from the lower, which gives, in effect, the height of the mouth opening. The cutup may be straight, arched, or angled. See Plate XXXIX, 5, 6, and 7.

The Ratio of the Cutup

The cutup is generally expressed in one of two ways:

1. Qualitatively, as "very low," "low," "medium," "normal," "high," or "very high"

2. Quantitatively, as the ratio of the vertical dimension of the mouth-opening (height) to the horizontal dimension of the same (width); thus, $R_c = H/W$, where R_c is the ratio of the cutup, H the height of the mouth, and W the width of the mouth

As a contributing factor toward the production of tone, the cutup influences chiefly and significantly the texture of the harmonic structure of the tone, thus controlling, to a marked extent, the resultant tone color of the voice. Briefly stated, the relationship appears as follows:

The richness of the acoustic spectrum varies } inversely as the { height of the mouth

Accordingly, a low cutup favors a richer, more high-ly developed tone; a high cutup, on the contrary, produces a more impoverished, less developed tone. Stated in anoth-er way, a low cutup exerts a positive influence upon the tone by bringing into greater prominence the elements which comprise the overtone structure; the fundamental, according-ly, seems relatively _less_ prominent. A high cutup, on the other hand, exerts a negative influence upon the tone by suppressing these elements; the fundamental, accordingly, seems relatively _more_ prominent. In this connection it must be understood that the cutup can reinforce or minimize only the harmonic structure which a given pipe inherently can produce; in the case of open or covered conical pipes, all partials; in the case of covered pipes, only the odd-numbered partials.

Range and Tendency of Modern Practice

The range of ratios generally used for quality work in modern organ building reaches from a maximum cutup ratio of 1/3 to a minimum of 1/6. A large number of values can be interpolated between these extremes to permit of fine gradations. The method of interpolation can be gathered from the discussion above, where the common ratios for the mouth widths were developed. The most important ratios for the cutup are the following, arranged in diminishing order from left to right; the most common reference values are bracketed:

[1/3]	5/16	4/13	3/10	5/17
[2/7]	5/18	3/11	4/15	5/19
[1/4]	5/21	4/17	3/13	5/22
[2/9]	5/23	3/14	4/19	5/24
[1/5]	5/26	4/21	3/16	5/27
[2/11]	5/28	3/17	4/23	5/29

The normal cutup is generally considered as the ratio 1/4. All ratios tending in the direction from 1/4 to 1/3 indicate a cutup higher than normal; all those tending in the direction from 1/4 to 1/6 indicate a cutup lower than normal. Table 40 relates the quantitative values and the qualitative descriptions often used for the height of the mouth.

There is no general agreement among organ builders and theorists as to which cutup ratio is most suitable for a given set of pipes. The nineteenth and early twentieth centuries employed relatively high cutups, still prevalent among many of our modern American builders. Earlier times and the present favor decidedly lower cutups, in order to achieve a greater richness of tone. Among significant modern writers on the subject of organ voices and their specific dimensions, Jahnn, Mahrenholz, and Ellerhorst prescribe cutups in most cases.[5] Sometimes their specifications for

TABLE 40

APPROXIMATE RATIOS OF THE QUALITATIVE
DESIGNATIONS FOR THE CUTUP

Qualitative Designation	Range of Ratios Used	List of Pertinent Ratios (Reference Values Bracketed)				
Very High	1/3 > 4/13	. . . . . . [1/3]	5/16	4/13		
High	3/10 > 3/11	3/10	5/17	[2/7]	5/18	3/11
Normal	4/15 > 4/17	4/15	5/19	[1/4]	5/21	4/17
Medium	3/13 > 3/14	3/13	5/22	[2/9]	5/23	3/14
Low	4/19 > 4/21	4/19	5/24	[1/5]	5/26	4/21
Very Low	3/16 > 1/6	3/16	5/27	[2/11]	5/28	3/17

the cutup are given as dependent ratios, occasionally as deviations from the Norm, and at times as qualitative descriptions. By careful cross reference between the several articles and books of each writer, it is possible to arrive at fairly accurate quantitative delineations, which may be helpful to define the frequently occurring qualitative descriptions. Table 41 summarizes and evaluates the recommendations of each writer.

It would appear from the survey that although the R_c = 1/4 is considered normal, the tendency is in the direction of as low a cutup as possible, the table indicating a considerable drift toward the area between 1/5 to 2/11 as perhaps the most often used ratios for the height of the

TABLE 41

RECOMMENDED RATIOS FOR THE
HEIGHT OF THE MOUTH[a]

Writer	Range of Ratios Recommended	Ratios Used Most Often	Mean Ratio	Qualitative Description
Jahnn	4/15 > 3/17	5/16 > 3/17	2/11	Very Low
Mahrenholz	3/10 > 3/17	4/19 > 4/21	1/5	Low
Ellerhorst	1/3 > 4/21	4/15 > 4/17	1/4	Normal

[a]This table is a summary of both quantitative and qualitative descriptions given by the respective writers. The correlations between the qualitative and quantitative delineations were, in some cases, made by the present author.

mouth.

The straight upper lip is overwhelmingly used today as in earlier times; the arched lip is becoming increasingly more rare. After all, the arched lip provides a means of cutting away the partial structure of the tone; it is a negative device, used to correct tonal deficiencies caused by injudicious attendant dimensions as, for example, the diameter, the mouth width, the quantity or pressure of wind, or the windway dimension.

CHAPTER V

THE MODERN ORGAN: GENERA OF REGISTERS, CRITICAL DIMENSIONS

The determinant factors of the scale and of the mouth treatment differentiate the registers of the several families from each other and result in the classification of the various genera. The following categories are identifiable:

1. Overly narrow-scaled pipes

2. Narrow-scaled pipes

3. Moderate-scaled pipes

4. Wide-scaled pipes

In each of the genera, certain species of registers are quite universally known, and their critical dimensions and tonal characteristics are reasonably well defined and recognized. These members of the various genera might well be considered as models. In order to develop the dimensions and characteristics of the genera in a logical way, the following model species, representing all families, may serve as a basis for discussion:

1. Overly narrow-scaled pipes

   a. Salicional

    b. Quintadena

    c. Zartgeige (echo form)

2. Narrow-scaled pipes

    a. Geigendprincipal

    b. Spitzgambe

    c. Gedacktpommer

    d. Spillpfeife

    e. Streichfloete (echo form)

    f. Gedackt-Zartfloete (echo form)

3. Moderate-scaled pipes

    a. Principal

    b. Spitzfloete

    c. Gedackt

    d. Rohrpfeife

    e. Floetenprincipal (echo form)

    f. Flûte douce (echo form)

    g. Lieblich Gedackt (echo form)

4. Wide-scaled pipes

    a. Nachthorn

    b. Gemshorn

    c. Gedacktfloete

    d. Rohrfloete

    e. Schwegel (echo form)

Overly Narrow-Scaled Pipes

Members of the overly narrow-scaled genus occur only

in the open cylindrical and the fully covered cylindrical
families of pipes. The genus is characterized by extremely
slim air columns; in the open cylindrical family the base
values range from about -5 HT to about -15 HT below the diameters of the Normprincipal; in the fully covered cylindrical family the base values range from -7 HT to -14 HT below
the Normprincipal. Inasmuch as the diameters are so extremely narrow, most members of this genus display ratios of
diminution resulting in static or increasing progressions,
seldom in decreasing ones. The mouth widths range, in general, from normal to medium ratios, depending upon the degree of strength desired from the voice. The cutups vary
from medium to very low, being largely controlled by the
available wind pressure and the tone color desired.

The tone of the overly narrow-scaled pipes is very
rich in overtones and meager in fundamental sound. The open
cylindrical ones possess an extremely keen and incisive
character, unyielding and unwilling to mix and blend with
other genera of tone. Voices from this genus are unsocial
and function best alone and unalloyed. For this reason,
they are generally looked upon and classified as Solo voices
(S). The fully covered cylindrical pipes have a highly developed overtone structure in the odd series of partials and
an extremely weak fundamental. In fact, the first and third
partials (unison and twelfth) are so equal in dynamic

strength that certain species from this genus give the impression of sounding the interval of a fifth. The tone is not as incisive as in the open cylindrical family, since these pipes deliver only half as rich a partial spectrum, but becomes, in turn, highly ambiguous both with respect to pitch and dynamic level.

Basic Forms: Overly Narrow Scale

A model voice from the overly narrow-scaled genus of the open cylindrical family is the Salicional. It possesses the tonal characteristics of its genus to a marked degree. To the listener, the tone is often perceived as String tone because of its keen edge and incisive character.

The best examples of the modern Salicional are predicated upon a base value of -5 HT to -8 HT below the Normprincipal, although in extreme cases, a base value as narrow as -16 HT is employed. The scale is either of a static ($=$) or increasing ($<$) type; frequently it is compounded of both, so that the ratios of diminution throughout the course or for segments of it permit the half measure to fall on the sixteenth step or later. The mouth widths vary from a maximum ratio of 1/4 to a minimum one of 4/19, the average ratio being about 2/9 which is, qualitatively expressed, a medium mouth. See Appendix L. The cutup dwells in the vicinity of a normal ratio. See Appendix O, 2.

The voice occurs chiefly at 8' pitch, occasionally

at 4' pitch, and very seldom at 16' or at 2' pitch. See
Plate XL which relates C 8' of the Salicional to the corresponding note of the Normprincipal.

A model voice from the overly narrow-scaled genus of
the fully covered cylindrical family is the _Quintadena_. Being covered, the voice is able to present only the odd series of partials. Its extremely narrow scale favors a
strong development of its overtones and suppresses the fundamental to such an extent that the third partial appears at
nearly equal strength to the fundamental, giving the voice a
"quinting" character and a pronounced ambiguity of pitch; in
fact, the voice is almost fully overblown. It is this characteristic which gives the voice its name, _quinta et una_
(fifth and unison), from which, by corruption, is derived
the term "Quintadena." The tone is extraordinarily dry and
glassy, somewhat recessive, suggestive of mild String tone,
and has the unusual ability of giving the aural illusion of
a variety of dynamic levels depending upon the influential
effect of other voices with which it may be combined in registration.

The scale of the modern Quintadena ranges from a
base value of -7 HT to -14 HT below the Normprincipal. The
scale is usually of a static ($\equiv$) or increasing ($<$)
type; frequently it is compounded of a combination of both,
so that the ratios of diminution either throughout the

course or for segments of it display a half measure on the
sixteenth step or later. The mouth widths are generally of
a normal dimension and vary from a maximum ratio of 3/11 to
a minimum of 3/13, depending upon the dynamic strength desired. See Appendix L. The cutup is variable, ranging all
the way from medium to low. See Appendix O, 2.

The voice occurs pre-eminently at 16' and 8' pitches;
the 4' pitch is possible in the Pedal, inasmuch as the compass there is only one-half that of the manuals. See Plate
XLI which relates the C 8' of the Quintadena to the corresponding note of the Normprincipal.

Echo Forms: Overly Narrow Scale

Most labial voices in the organ are functional,
working registers, built and voiced to contribute materially and effectively to the total tonal texture. Such voices
are conveniently differentiated as masculine or feminine.
If of a masculine or aggressive character, they are classified as Group I; if of a feminine or yielding character,
they are classified as Group II. Both classifications comprise, however, only the full-throated or "parent" voices
which make up the color palette of the organ.

There exists, however, a further group of voices
with representatives in each genus, whose quantitative contribution to the total tonal resources of the organ is extremely meager. Because the tone of these voices is so soft

and gentle, they are called <u>echo</u> voices. They are not working registers, but their use provides, at times, a welcome
relief from the full-throated parent voices. In fact, all
echo voices are built and voiced to reflect in miniature
some parent voice, and it is quite possible to construct an
acceptable echo form for each working register of the organ.
In practice this does not occur. Most organ builders and
organists are content to have available one or two echo
forms within each genus of pipes. Such echo voices are
built so as to reflect, in an average way, the general tonal characteristics of all of the parent members of the genus.

In order to achieve an echo form, the shape of the
corpus native to the genus and family is retained. The
scale, however, is taken much smaller, the mouth is made
somewhat narrower, and the voice is then lightly winded when
brought to speech.

A model voice from the overly narrow-scaled genus
of the open cylindrical family is the <u>Zartgeige</u>. It possesses a very soft, quiet, and relaxed string tone.

The best examples of this voice employ a base value
of -13 HT to -15 HT below the Normprincipal. The scale is
usually of the static (≡≡≡) type, although at times the
course is segmental, increasing in fullness toward the middle of the compass; in such cases, at least a bipartite

scale compounded of an increasing and a decreasing segment

is required ( ). The half measure falls on the

sixteenth step or somewhat later; it seldom falls earlier.

A variety of mouth widths is available for this

voice, ranging from a maximum ratio of 5/21 to a minimum of

2/9. Such a range permits the voice to be constructed to

serve as an echo form for a number of different parent

voices in the genus. An average ratio might be 3/13. The

cutup is generally low. See Appendices L and O, 2.

As in the case of almost all echo voices, the Zart-

geige is hardly ever constructed in a pitch other than 8';

it might occur in the Pedal at 16' pitch, although echo

voices are relatively expensive members at such grave pitch-

es in the Pedal. See Plate XLII which relates the C 8' of

the Zartgeige to the corresponding note of the Normprincipal.

Narrow-Scaled Pipes

A large and comprehensive array of organ voices,

representing every family of pipes, is available in the nar-

row-scaled genus. The group is a highly significant one for

purposes of disposition and registration, providing func-

tional and working voices as well as a respectable selection

of echo forms.

The members of this genus approach, in their tonal

effect, the group of organ voices known as Group I, which

indicates the fact that these voices are masculine in

character, aggressive in function, and desirous of occupying
a foreground position when associated with voices of other
genera. The tone of the narrow-scaled pipes lies somewhat
between that of Strings and Principals; it is, therefore,
frequently designated as occupying a place between the Solo
voices and those of Group I. A voice leaning toward String
tone would be classified as S; one leaning more in the direction of Principal tone would be classified as I; those
midway between are classified as S/I.

The voices of this genus are more social than those
of the overly narrow-scaled group and are capable of mixing
quite well with other registers of wider scale. In such as-
sociations these voices strive for eminence; they tend to
govern, control, and steer the combination.

The entire partial spectrum in each family is highly developed, giving these voices a very bright and rich
complex of tone; the fundamental provides a moderately
strong basis and there exists a better balance between it
and its overtones than in the case of the overly narrow-
scaled genus. However, the overtone structure still pre-
dominates, although not so emphatically as before.

Voices from this group, in whatever family they may
occur, are found at 16', 8', 4', and, more seldom, at 2'
pitches.

The base values for these voices range from about

-2 HT to -10 HT, overlapping, to some extent, voices from
the overly narrow-scaled group on the one hand and those
from the moderate-scaled one on the other. The line of demarcation between genera cannot be sharply defined, since
other determining factors beside the base value influence
the final production and function of the tone. A good, average base value figure would appear to be between -4 HT and
-6 HT below the Normprincipal. The ratios of diminution are
of all types: static ($=$), increasing ($<$), and decreasing ($>$), depending upon the specific function of
the particular voice in the total tonal ensemble of the organ. The voices are frequently modulated in their scale
progression, so that one often finds segmental scales of bipartite, tripartite, or multipartite character; at times a
constant progression is adequate. Among the parent voices
in this genus, the mouth widths range chiefly from normal to
medium. To favor the production of a rich and significant
complex of overtones, the cutups lie mainly in the normal,
medium, low, and very low ratios.

Basic Forms: Narrow Scale

A model voice from the open cylindrical family is
the Geigendprincipal. This voice occupies, both structurally and tonally, a middle position between the Salicional
and the true Principal; it develops a sharp, clear tone,
which possesses a good measure of the fullness and character

of the Principal together with the keenness and incisiveness of the Salicional. Its name, "Violining Principal," bespeaks its hybrid character. The voice is much used and occurs at 8', 4', and 2' pitches, and, on occasion, also at 16' pitch.

The best examples of this voice range, in their diameters, from a base value of -2 HT to -6 HT below the Normprincipal; the choice is influenced by the position the voice is expected to occupy in the ensemble, and by the size and acoustical properties of the building it is intended to serve. All types of scales are useful: static (══), increasing (◁), decreasing (▷), and combinations of these by segments. The half measure, accordingly, falls on the sixteenth step, slightly earlier, or slightly later. The mouth widths are usually of normal dimensions, ranging from 3/11 to 1/4, with a good average width being 4/15. See Appendix L. The cutups are kept medium and low, in order to assist the pipe in producing a very rich complex of overtones, fully developed. See Appendix O, 2. Plate XLIII relates C 8' of the Geigendprincipal to the corresponding note of the Normprincipal.

A typical voice from the open conical family is the Spitzgambe. Its tone approaches that of the Salicional, being of String character and fairly incisive in its effect; however, the blending character of the Gemshorn is vaguely evident within it also. It is generally classified as a hybrid register, lying somewhere between the Solo Group and Group I (S/I). The tone is clear, fairly thin, and rich in overtones; the fundamental is definitely perceptible but not prominent.

The base values chosen for this voice vary between -4 HT and -6 HT below the Normprincipal, lying thus squarely in the center of the narrow-scaled genus among the open conical pipes. The scale types suited to the development of this voice are static ($\equiv$), increasing ($\lessgtr$), or a combination of these. Accordingly, half measures fall on the sixteenth step or later, but hardly earlier. The mouth widths are normal to medium, using ratios between 5/21 and 5/22, an average width being about 3/13. The upper lip is cut very low. See Appendices L and O, 2. The upper diameter of the corpus varies between 1/3 to 1/2 that of the diameter at the mouth (d/D = 1/3 - 1/2). See Plate XLIV which relates C 8' of the Spitzgambe to the corresponding note of the Normprincipal.

From the fully covered family of pipes, the Gedacktpommer presents the chief characteristics of the narrow-scaled genus. In its construction and tonal function it lies between the Quintadena and the normal Gedackt. Its tone is slightly heavier than that of the former; in fact, in large buildings it often supplants the Quintadena. From its odd set of partials, the overtones are well developed; the fundamental, in turn, appears less prominent. Its characteristics establish it as a voice belonging to Group I. Usable chiefly at 16' and 8' pitches, it appears, at times, also at 32', 4' and 2' pitches.

The base values lie between -3 HT and -10 HT below the Normprincipal; -5 HT to -7 HT serve as good, average dimensions. Scale types employed for it are usually constant, either static (▭) or increasing (◁); occasionally the register is compounded of segments, in which case the decreasing (▷) type appears also. Half measures fall on the sixteenth step or later. Mouth widths are usually of normal dimensions; their ratios range from 4/15 to 4/17, with 1/4 as an average. The cutup tends to be medium, low, or very low. See Appendices L and O, 2. Plate XLV relates the C 8' of the Gedacktpommer to the corresponding note of the Normprincipal.

From the partly covered family, the Spillpfeife may serve as a model for the narrow-scaled genus. It has a compound corpus, partly cylindrical and partly conical; the ratio between the lengths of the two portions (cone/cylinder) is 1/1 or 3/4 with the intervening ratios possible. The diameter of the cone at the top lies between 1/3 and 2/3 of the diameter at the base (d/D = 1/3 - 2/3).

The tone is fairly bright, presenting a combination

of qualities normally associated with covered and with open conical pipes: full, clear, and with good blending qualities. The voice displays characteristics native to Group I.

Base values range between 0 HT and -5 HT below the Normprincipal, an average being -2 HT to -3 HT. The ratios of diminution are usually of the static ($\equiv$) or increasing ($\diagdown$) type; seldom do segmental scales occur. Mouth widths are generally med. or moderately narrow; the ratios range from 2/9 to 1/5, an average value being about 4/19. The cutup is best at a medium or low ratio. See Appendices L and O, 2.

The voice occurs at 8', 4', and 2' pitches and occasionally at 16' and 1'. See Plate XLVI which relates the C 8' of the Spillpfeife to the corresponding note of the Normprincipal.

Echo Forms: Narrow Scale

Within the open cylindrical family, no separate echo form appears from the narrow-scaled genus; normally, the Zartgeige, an echo voice from the overly narrow-scaled genus, serves for the narrow-scaled group as well; minor adjustments in the scale and mouth treatment provide an acceptable example.

In the open conical family, the Streichfloete serves as an echo form for the genus. The tone of this voice is mild and gentle; it presents a clearly perceptible String tone embedded upon a delicate, flute-colored background. The organ tone is analagous to the tone color of the lower muted strings of the violin when bowed gently.

Base values for this voice vary between -6 HT and -9 HT below the Normprincipal. The scale type is usually static ($\equiv$) and constant. The mouth widths are narrow and cluster around the ratio of 2/9. The cutup is very low. See Appendices L and O, 2.

The Gedackt-Zartfloete, an echo form from the fully covered family, occurs rarely, inasmuch as the parent voices themselves tend to be moderately quiet in their tonal effect. The voice appears as a diminutive form of the Gedacktpommer and similar registers. It presents a covered Flute tone, very delicate and fragile, yet clear and distinct.

The base values lie in the vicinity of -15 HT below the Normprincipal. The mouth widths center around a 1/5 ratio and the cutup is normal. See Appendices L and O, 2. Plate XLVII relates the C 8' of the Streichfloete and the Gedackt-Zartfloete to the corresponding note of the Normprincipal.

Moderate-Scaled Pipes

The voices of the moderate-scaled genus comprise the core or central color palette of organ tone. All other genera, such as narrow-scaled or wide-scaled, are considered as departures in one or another direction from this central position. It is within this family that the true, unimitative organ tone is developed. Every family has significant, noteworthy representatives in it; among them are the Principal, the Spitzfloete, the Gedackt, and the Rohrpfeife. Beside those, there exist within the genus many variant forms of the basic ones mentioned, so that a large selection of organ voices is available from it.

The tone of the voices within this genus is well balanced, a healthy relationship existing between the fundamental and its overtones; the composite tone is very satisfying, rich, full, and highly versatile in registration. The voices are aggressively social, mixing well into cohesive bouquets of tone color when combined with voices from the same genus or from others. The tone is masculine and essentially unyielding; these qualities establish the voices from the moderate-scaled genus as possessing the determining characteristics of Group I.

Members from this group appear at all usable pitch levels, from 32' up through the acute pitches of mixtures, such as 1/4', 1/8', and the like. They appear rather frequently also in the non-unison pitches, such as 5 1/3', 2 2/3', 1 3/5', etc.

In texture or plenum registrations, members of this group are indispensible throughout the pitch ranges required; in background and solo registrations they serve admirably for the foundational members of the combinations.[1]

The base values for the diameters of the moderate-scaled pipes range from -4 HT to +3 HT from the Normprincipal. They overlap to a small extent the base values adopted for some narrow-scaled pipes, and, on the other hand, also some of the values used for wide-scaled pipes. The line of demarcation between the genera cannot be drawn too sharply, since several factors beyond the base value influence the functional grouping of a register. The courses appear as constant, segmental, or variable. The ratios of diminution used for these voices run the full range of possibilities, including static ($\equiv$), increasing ($\lessdot$), and decreasing ($\gtrdot$) types. Mouth widths exhibit normal, medium, and, more rarely, moderately narrow ratios. The cutup is generally normal, medium, or low.

Basic Forms: Moderate Scale

The most typical voice from the open cylindrical family is the Principal. Because of its eminent position in the galaxy of organ voices--being certainly the most unique and native tone the organ possesses--it deserves this appellation. The voice should be placed into every organ, in fact, into every division of the instrument, and is often featured in the display of the case. Frequently, the voice appears at several pitches on the same division; in such cases, the lowest-pitched one establishes the Principalbasis

for the division, and is properly termed Principal. All
others derive their names from the pitch levels they occupy;
the higher octaves are generally called Octave, while the
off-unisons are named Quint or Terz, as the case may be.
Table 42 relates the use of the various terms.

TABLE 42

THE PRINCIPALBASIS AND DERIVATIVE APPELLATIONS

Pitch Level	The Principalbasis			
	16'	8'	4'	2'
1'	Octave	Octave	Octave	Octave
1 1/3'	Quint	Quint	Quint	. . . . . .
1 3/5'	Terz	Terz	. . . . . .	. . . . . .
2'	Octave	Octave	Octave	Principal
2 2/3'	Quint	Quint	. . . . . .	. . . . . .
3 1/5'	Terz	. . . . . .	. . . . . .	. . . . . .
4'	Octave	Octave	Principal	. . . . . .
5 1/3'	Quint	. . . . . .	. . . . . .	. . . . . .
6 2/5'	. . . . . .	. . . . . .	. . . . . .	. . . . . .
8'	Octave	Principal	. . . . . .	. . . . . .
10 2/3'	. . . . . .	. . . . . .	. . . . . .	. . . . . .
16'	Principal	. . . . .	. . . . . .	. . . . . .

The Principal is available and used at all unison
and mutation pitches: 32', 16', 10 2/3', 8', 5 1/3', 4',
2 2/3', 2', 1 3/5', 1 1/3', 1', 4/5', 2/3', 1/2', 2/5', 1/3',
1/4', etc.[2] The tone of the true Principal is bright, rich,
and well balanced between fullness and keenness, neither

quality existing in impoverished or extreme measure. It possesses a significant and comprehensive spectrum of partials, the fundamental and its overtones being well represented. A successful Principal presents a fine, singing quality of tone, neither too smooth nor too rounded. Among the voices of the organ, the Principals are definitely the workhorses, providing foundation, fullness, and brilliance in all combinations in which they properly occur. Their registrational functions lie within the domain of plenum or texture registrations; here they must occupy all pitches needed, or when combined with other species, they must appear in the superior positions. When so used, they control the color of the combination, giving it unmistakably plenum character.

Base values for the Principals lie between -4 HT and +2 HT from the Normprincipal, depending upon the pitch level they are to serve and the volume and acoustical properties of the building into which they are to be placed. All types of scales are employed: static (=====), increasing (<), and decreasing (>), in progressions that are constant, segmental, or variable. The mouth widths cluster around the ratio of 1/4, whereby this ratio has come to be looked upon as "normal." The cutup is generally normal, medium, or low. See Appendices L and O, 2. Plate XLVIII relates the C 8' of the Principal to the corresponding note of the Normprincipal.

From the open conical family, the Spitzfloete

represents the moderate-scaled genus in an admirable way.
The pipes have a considerable taper, the upper diameter varying between 1/3 and 1/4 of the lower, the average being
about 2/7. Accordingly, the pipes present a rather pointed
appearance. Because of this considerable graduation in the
diameter, the voice possesses characteristics of both moderate and narrow-scaled pipes; the tone has a certain re-
straint in its aggressiveness coupled with a suggestion of
String quality in its composite effect. It has a rich and
rather fully developed complement of partials which make the
tone bright and clear; it is less brilliant and full than
the cylindrical Principal, but more aggressive than the Gemshorn. The fundamental is less in evidence than in cylindrical pipes of this genus; prominence is given to the octave
or second partial. The taper has the effect of partially
closing the pipe, making the tone somewhat softer and more
yielding.

The voice occurs frequently at 8' and 4' pitches;
more seldom at 16', 2', and 1'. In registration, the voice
is very useful at foundational (8', 4', 2') pitches in plenum combinations; as the grave foundational (8', 4') pitches
in background registrations; and as fundamental (8') or
foundational (8', 4', 2') pitches in solo combinations. The
voice belongs to Group I.

Base values cluster around the dimensions of the

Normprincipal, +3 HT to O HT. All scale types, such as static ($\equiv$), increasing ($\prec$), or decreasing ($\succ$)
find application in the development of the register. Often
the types are combined to develop a single course. Mouth
widths are usually taken at 1/4 or nearly so. The cutup is
normal or medium. See Appendices L and O, 2. Plate IL relates the C 8' of the Spitzfloete to the corresponding note
of the Normprincipal.

The moderate-scaled Gedackt serves as representative
from the fully covered family. As noted earlier, the Gedackt is able to produce only the odd-numbered partials in
the composition of its overtone structure. Because of this
impoverished spectrum, the tone always sounds somewhat hollow, no matter of what diameter the pipe is constructed.
Inasmuch as a very wide range of diameters is used for this
voice, the tone possesses an equally wide range of characteristics reaching all the way from masculine to feminine
qualities. Whenever the voice is built of moderate dimensions, however, the tone functions chiefly as Group I, presenting masculine character. Whenever the voice is planned
for 16' or 8' pitch, its dimensions should not be too great,
but should lean toward the moderate. The Gedackt has a full
tone of considerable extensity, capable of filling sizable
acoustical volumes in a satisfactory manner. The more moderate or narrow the basic scale becomes, the more edge the

tone will develop; in fact, a well-dimensioned Gedackt in moderate scale presents a suggestion of Principal tone in its composite effect. Never can the voice be said to possess brilliance, but because of its impoverished partial structure, it has a propensity for mixing well with other voices; the cohesion is unusually firm. By analogy, the Gedackt has attributes of a sponge; it can "soak" up and hold firmly other organ voices with which it might be combined.

The voice functions well at foundational pitches, particularly the lower ones, such as 16', 8', and 4'; occasionally it appears at 32' and at 2' pitch. The upper ranges of the higher pitched registers must be supplanted by open pipes (often conical), since the covered pipes become too small to construct.

Base values range from 0 HT to -4 HT from the Normprincipal. Scale types are usually static ($\equiv$) or increasing ($\blacktriangleleft$); progressions are generally constant, although occasionally segmental or variable ones do occur. Mouth widths appear in normal, medium, or moderately narrow ratios (1/4, 2/9, 1/5), 1/4 being most common. The cutup dwells among medium, normal, or high ratios. See Appendices L and O, 2. Plate L relates C 8' of the Gedackt to the corresponding note of the Normprincipal.

The Rohrpfeife is the moderate-scaled voice from the partly covered family. It is a compound pipe composed of a covered corpus surmounted by a long and wide cylindrical open chimney of slightly shorter length than the main corpus. The voice possesses characteristics of both closed and open pipes. The chimney encourages the pipe to develop inharmonic overtones of considerable strength, which lend the tone an unusually bright, even coarse, character not usually found in covered pipes. Beside a quality of generous extensity, the tone is also very clear and distinct and somewhat lighter than that of the Gedackt; it displays a definite tonal kinship to the Principal and bespeaks the characteristics of Group I.

The voice occurs at 8', 4', and 2' pitches, the latter one especially for the Pedal. It serves as a basis for moderate plenum registrations, is usable in the grave pitches for background effects, and can be properly used for the foundational (8', 4', or 2') members of solo combinations.

Base values range from 0 HT to -4 HT from the Normprincipal. The chimney is relatively long and wide. Scale types are usually static ($\equiv$) or increasing ($\diagdown$), in constant or segmental progressions. The mouth widths dwell in the medium or moderately narrow ratios (2/9, 1/5), and the cutup is medium or low. See Appendices L and O, 2. Plate LI relates C 8' of the Rohrpfeife to the corresponding note of the Normprincipal.

Echo Forms: Moderate Scale

The following model voices will serve to illustrate
the echo forms from the various families:

1. Floetenprincipal from the open cylindrical
family

2. Flûte douce from the open conical family

3. Lieblich Gedackt from the fully covered
family

As with echo forms in general, these voices must not
be looked upon as working members, but rather as miniature
reflections of the parent voices in each family. They possess, therefore, no real group function, occur chiefly at 8'
pitch, and are not effective when combined with the working
voices of the organ. Their best use is either alone or combined with other echo voices, preferably at other pitches.

The Floetenprincipal uses base values varying between -3 HT and -6 HT from the Normprincipal; the scale is
usually of a static ($\equiv$) type, but occasionally increasing ($\diagdown$) or decreasing ($\diagup$) types find application.
The mouth width is generally medium (2/9) and the cutup,
normal, medium, or low. See Appendices L and O, 2.

The Flûte douce serves as an echo form for all members of the open conical family. The taper is from 3/5 to
4/5; hence, very slight. Base values range from -5 HT to

-8 HT below the Normprincipal. The scale is usually static
($\equiv$) and constant. The mouths are medium or moderately
narrow (2/9, 5/24), and the cutup, medium. See Appendices
L and O, 2.

The Lieblich Gedackt, more often than not, is executed in rectangular form in wood, but metal is eminently
possible for it. Base values range from -8 HT to -12 HT below the Normprincipal and the scales are usually of a static
($\equiv$) or increasing ($\prec$) type. The mouth is normal
(1/4), and the cutup, medium or low. See Appendices L and
O, 2. Plate LII relates C 8' of the Floetenprincipal, Flûte
douce, and Lieblich Gedackt to the corresponding note of the
Normprincipal.

Wide-Scaled Pipes

The wide-scaled genus comprises the real domain of
Group II registers. They are so classified because they
differ materially from those of Group I. The latter display
aggressive, relatively incisive, and masculine characteristics, while the former are much more yielding, relatively
round, and full-bodied in their tonal effect. A large representation of voices from each of the families is available; structurally they are of generous diameters but present
relatively narrow mouths. While the voices of Group I tend
to be full-throated, those of Group II are more full-cheeked
in their effect.

Their function in the tonal resources of the organ
is to provide fullness and body wherever needed, without adding much loudness or sharpness. They blend extremely well
with moderate or narrow-scaled pipes, especially when they
occupy a pitch position superior to these. It is for this
reason that they are most frequently found at 4' pitch and
above, particularly in the mutation pitches. A wide-scaled
voice, properly dimensioned, will when combined at a superi-
or pitch with narrower-scaled pipes, lose its identity,
serve materially to color the combination, and yield its eminence to the total compound tonal effect. Consequently,
the wide-scaled voices are indispensible as superior pitches
(both unison and mutation) in all solo registrations. Their
receding character befits them also for background registrations in the grave foundational pitches. In plenum or texture registrations their function is least noteworthy; they
merely add fullness without brilliance; if overused they
tend to thicken and blunt the total effect.

Diameters for this genus range in base values from
about +2 HT to +14 HT above the Normprincipal. Among the
fully covered family a few half-tones narrower find occasional use. At times, static constant scales are used for
progressions through the compass of the voice. More often,
the scales are segmental or variable with the ratios of diminution so arranged, that the pipes diminish in relative

diameters as one or both extremes of the compass are reached;
thus,

1. Static and decreasing (═══ ▷)

2. Increasing and decreasing (◁ ▷)

3. Increasing and static (◁ ═══)

When a constant scale is employed, it is either static
(═══) or decreasing (▷). Mouth widths are minimum,
very narrow, narrow, moderately narrow, and, at times, medium. The unusually narrow mouth is one of the cardinal features of wide-scaled pipes. It is apparent that, as the diameter enlarges beyond moderate dimensions, the mouth narrows
down proportionately. The cutups are kept in the very low,
low, medium, and, more rarely, normal ratios.

Basic Forms: Wide Scale

The Nachthorn, from the open cylindrical family, represents the widest-scaled pipe used in the organ. Because
of its wide scale and very narrow mouth, its tone is singularly voluminous without being loud. The voice is a magnificent filler, lending substantial body to any combination in
which it occurs. The tone, provided a very narrow mouth is
constructed for the pipe, is by no means dull; on the contrary, a clear and strongly fundamental sound develops. Because of the relatively great size of the pipes and the manner in which they function tonally, the voice is usually
placed at the higher unison and mutation pitches, such as

4', 2 2/3', 2', 1 3/5', 1 1/3', and 1'. The voice belongs
outspokenly to Group II and functions particularly well in
solo combinations, where it serves as one of the superior
pitches. In background registrations its yielding and feminine character gives great fullness without any trace of aggressiveness, especially when it occupies the superior pitch
level.

The base values for the Nachthorn range from +8 HT
to +14 HT above the Normprincipal; these values make the
pipe in the vicinity of an octave larger than the Norm.
Scale types are either static, when constant; or decreasing, as one or both extremes of the compass are approached,
when segmental ($\prec\!\!=\;=\!=\;=\!\!\succ$). The mouth widths are
of narrow and minimum dimensions; ratios from 1/6 to 1/7 are
generally adopted in quality work; 2/13 may be considered a
good average. The cutup is kept as low as possible. See
Appendices L and O, 2. The narrow mouth, coupled with the
generous diameter of the pipe, bespeaks in the fullest sense
the analogy that the wide-scaled pipes appear, both visually
and aurally, as full-cheeked voices. See Plate LIII, which
relates C 8' of the Nachthorn to the corresponding note of
the Normprincipal.

The Gemshorn represents the open conical family in
the genus of wide-scaled pipes. Because of the upright conical shape of the air column, the pipe presents a graduated

diameter which, at its greatest dimension (mouth), is of wide scale, and at its minimum dimension (top), is of narrow scale. The degree of taper may vary from 1/3 to 3/8. Accordingly, the pipe delivers a tone which presents characteristics of several genera of voices (wide, moderate, narrow) and gives, for this reason, the impression of complexity and ambiguity. This hybrid character makes the voice highly useful in combination and helps it to blend admirably with other families and genera. The Gemshorn possesses the qualities of Flute and String tone, each clearly and separately discernible. The tone is agreeably full, yet speaks with an extraordinary clarity and fine definition, especially in the grave pitches. It seems that in low registers, the String quality, and in high registers, the Flute quality, comes to the fore with noteworthy effect.

As one of the most useful voices in the organ, the Gemshorn functions effectively as an inferior or interior member in plenum registrations, as a superior member in background registrations, and as a superior or interior unison or mutation voice in compound solo effects. The voice occurs at all unison and mutation pitches from 16' to 1'. It is particularly favored for those levels which require the ultimate in blend, such as 2 2/3' Nasat, 1 3/5' Terz, II Sesquialtera, II or III Rauschpfeife, II Terzian, and other mixed voices of similar character and function.[3]

The base values range between +4 HT and +7 HT above the Normprincipal, placing the register definitely into Group II with respect to its tonal function. Scales are often constant, in which case the static or decreasing types are favored. When segmental dispositions are employed, the ratios of diminution in the various segments are so arranged, that the scale decreases relatively as one or both extremes of the compass are reached; thus,

1. Decreasing toward the bass, static toward the treble (◁ ═══)

2. Decreasing toward the bass, decreasing toward the treble (◁ ▷)

The mouth widths must dwell in dimensions native to moderately narrow or narrow ratios (1/5 to 2/11). If the mouth is taken too wide, the true Gemshorn color cannot be achieved, and the voice will not function properly in registration. The cutup favors low and medium ratios. See Appendices L and O, 2. Plate LIV relates C 8' of the Gemshorn to the corresponding note of the Normprincipal.

From the fully covered family, the Gedacktfloete represents the wide-scaled genus. Inasmuch as in this family the pipes must be taken about five half-tones narrower than open pipes in order to achieve a parallel group classification, this voice, at about Normprincipal scale or slightly larger, belongs properly not to the moderate-scaled,

ut to the wide-scaled genus, and displays characteristics
f Group II.

The Gedacktfloete is perhaps the widest member of
the fully covered species that finds general application in
the organ, and that is able to function tonally with registers of the other families and genera. The tone is quite
round and full-bodied, somewhat thick, and impoverished in
its acoustic spectrum; it is not too clear in pitch definition, yet possesses considerable extensity. The voice is
particularly suited to large buildings where comprehensive
acoustical volumes must be satisfied. In registration, it
serves well to thicken or darken plenum combinations, especially when occupying fundamental or interior pitch levels.
For background, the voice is useful at 8' or at 4' pitch.
In solo effects its qualities make it suitable for interior
or possibly superior pitches.

The Gedacktfloete appears most often at 4', 2 2/3',
and 2' pitches, more seldom at 16' and 8'. In the Pedal its
value lies in the extreme pitches of 16', 2', and 1'.

Base values for the voice range between 0 HT and +3
HT above the Normprincipal. The scales are usually constant
and of the static (═══) or increasing (◁) variety.
When segmental, the scale tends to diminish relatively toward the bass (◁ ═══).

The mouth widths must be taken medium, at a ratio

of about 2/9. The cutup is usually normal. See Appendices
L and O, 2. Plate LV relates the C 8' of the Gedacktfloete
to the corresponding note of the Normprincipal.

The Rohrfloete, from the partly covered family, is
basically a covered pipe surmounted by a short and relatively narrow-scaled chimney, which, in turn, is open at both
ends. The pipe, therefore, functions primarily as a Gedackt
of wide scale in Group II, but to its primary set of odd
partials is added the rich and consecutive partial spectrum
of the diminutive and open chimney of about 1/4 to 1/3 the
diameter of the corpus. This open cylindrical member of the
compound corpus adds a bouquet of inharmonic overtones to
the fundamental tone, giving the voice an intriguing character, both full-bodied and singularly bright. Being partly
covered and partly open, the pipe seems to possess some of
the best qualities of both families.

The Rohrfloete is one of the very important organ
voices from the partly covered family. It finds frequent
application in dispositions of all kinds; quite often the
voice appears twice, even in moderate-sized instruments:
at 8' pitch in one division and at 4' in another. It may
appear at all pitches, including the mutations, from 16' to
1'. In the grave register of the compass, the chimney is
often discarded and the pipe simply constructed as fully
covered; in the very high areas, the pipes are supplanted

by open conical ones. The Rohrfloete is extremely versatile, serving at fundamental, interior, and superior pitches in all manner of registration. For a plenum, its best service lies at the fundamental and at interior pitches, both unison and mutation. In background and solo combinations, it serves equally well at the inferior, interior, or superior pitches.

Base values necessary for the development of an adequate Rohrfloete lie between +2 HT to +6 HT above the Normprincipal. Both constant and segmental scales are employed; the constant ones use static progressions (══), or such as diminish relatively toward the bass or toward the treble (◁) (▷); the segmental or variable ones combine both dispositions (◁ ▷). The mouth widths dwell in the moderately narrow and narrow categories, ranging from ratios of 1/5 to 5/27. See Appendix L. The cutup is kept medium or low, in order to encourage the development of a healthy overtone structure, so necessary to give the pipe a respectable degree of interesting tone color. See Appendix O, 2. Plate LVI relates C 8' of the Rohrfloete to the corresponding note of the Normprincipal.

Echo Forms: Wide Scale

The following echo voices represent the various families:

1. Schwegel from the open cylindrical family

2. Flûte douce from the open conical family

3. Gedackt-Zartfloete from the fully covered

family

Inasmuch as the Flûte douce and the Gedackt-Zartfloete were discussed previously under the moderate-scaled
genus, it will be necessary to discuss here only the Schwegel.

Technically, the Schwegel is looked upon as the echo
form of the Italian Principal which, in turn, is a wide form
of the true Principal. In effect, it can serve adequately
as an echo voice for all wide-scaled open cylindrical registers. The tone is delicate but very clear and light, having
an unmistakable, but very mild, Principal character. It is
usually voiced quite softly and winded gently, so that its
tonal effect is truly of echo dimensions. It appears most
often at 8' and more seldom at 4' pitch; rarely does it appear higher. As an echo voice, its function in the tonal
scheme of the organ is not one that contributes effectively
to the total sound; rather, its purpose is one to provide
relief or retirement, as it were, from the on-going effect
of the more full-throated parent voices. Accordingly, it is
used alone, or at best, in combination with other echo
voices, preferably of different pitch.

Diameters for the Schwegel use base values at or
near those of the Normprincipal, from -2 HT to +2 HT. The

scale is usually static and constant (=====). Mouth widths
are of moderately narrow or narrow ratios, ranging from 5/26
to 2/11. The cutup is normal or low. See Appendices L and
O, 2. Plate LVII relates C 8' of the Schwegel to the corresponding note of the Normprincipal.

Catalogs of Critical Dimensions

Following the physical, tonal, and functional descriptions of voices from each genus of the various families,
it would seem desirable to present more complete catalogs,
giving, in tabular form, the most necessary critical dimensions of all of the more commonly occurring voices in the
modern organ. Very few writers who deal with the subject of
modern organ voices have recorded sufficient information in
quantitative form, so that the dimensions can be effectively
developed, compared, and contrasted. Most noteworthy among
these are the German theorists, Mahrenholz and Jahnn, and
their Swiss counterpart, Ellerhorst. Table 43 presents
Mahrenholz's catalog in tabular form, Table 44 that of Jahnn,
and Table 45 that of Ellerhorst.[4]

TABLE 43

CATALOG OF CRITICAL DIMENSIONS--MAHRENHOLZ[a]

Species	Group	Base Values[b]	Scale Types	Mouth Widths[c]	Cutup[d]	Detail
Open Cylindrical Pipes: Overly Narrow Scale						
Bratsche	I/S	-10/-12	ǁ | ≡ <	5/19 1/4 3/13	low	. . . . .
Zartgeige	E	-13/-15	≡	5/21 3/13 2/9	low	. . . . .
Kontrabass	I/S	-6/-10	> ≡	2/9 5/23 4/19	low	. . . . .
Salizional	S	-5/-8	ǁ <	5/21 2/9 4/19	normal	. . . . .
Open Cylindrical Pipes: Narrow Scale						
Fugara	I	-3/-7	| <	5/19 5/21 2/9	normal-low	. . . . .
Geigend-principal	I	-2/-5	≡	3/11 5/19 1/4	low	. . . . .
Schweizer-pfeife	I	0/-4	ǁ <	1/4 4/17 2/9	low	Overblown

[a]Summarized from C. Mahrenholz, Die Orgelregister, ihre Geschichte und ihr Bau (2nd ed.; Kassel, 1942), pp. 37-121.

[b]Deviation in ± HT from the Normprincipal; maximum/minimum values.

[c]Ratios developed from tabular differences; maximum, mean, minimum values.

[d]For the present author's quantitative evaluations, see Appendix O, 2.

TABLE 43--Continued

[Maurenholz]

Species	Group	Base Values	Scale Types	Mouth Widths	Cutup	Detail
Open Cylindrical Pipes: Moderate Scale						
Principal	I	+1/-4	=|>|<	5/19 1/4 5/21	normal	. . . . .
Floeten-principal	E	-3/-6	||	5/22 2/9 5/23	normal-low	. . . . .
Harfen-principal	E	-4/-7	||	10/41 5/21 4/17	low	. . . . .
Open Cylindrical Pipes: Wide Scale						
Italian Principal	I/II	+8/+4	∧	4/19 5/24 1/5	low	. . . . .
Schwegel	E	+2/0	||	5/26 3/16 5/27	normal	. . . . .
Hohlfloete	I/II	+7/+4	>∧ ∧>	3/14 4/19 5/24	normal	. . . . .
Starkfloete	I/II	+7/+4	>∧ ||	5/19 1/4 5/21	normal	. . . . .
Querfloete	II	+8/+4	||	3/14 4/19 5/24	low	Overblown
Ueberblas. Dulzfloete	E	-2/-4	|=> || >∨	3/14 4/19 5/24	low	Overblown
Nachthorn	II	+14/+8	∧>	5/31 5/32 3/20	very low	. . . . .

TABLE 43--Continued [Mahrenholz]

Species	Group	Base Values	Scale Types	Mouth Widths	Cutup	Detail
			Open Conical Pipes: Narrow Scale			
Spitzgambe	I/S	-4/-6	= |= ∨	5/21 4/17 5/22	very low	T: 1/3-1/2[a]
Streich-floete	E	-6/-9	=	5/22 2/9 5/23	very low	T: 1/2
Konische Querfloete	I/S	0/-4	= | ∧	3/10 5/17 2/7	low	T: 2/3-5/6
			Open Conical Pipes: Moderate Scale			
Labial Dulzian I	I/S	+1/-4	= | ∧	2/9 5/23 3/14	low	T: 4/3
Labial Dulzian II	I/S	+1/-4	= | ∧	10/31 5/16 4/13	low	T: 4/3
Dulzian-floete	E	-5/-8	=	1/5 5/26 5/27	low	T: 11/10-7/5
Scharfgeige	E	-15/-18	=	3/11 4/15 5/19	low	T: 3/2
Spitzfloete	I	0/0	= |> | ∨	5/19 1/4 5/21	normal	T: 1/4
Flachfloete	I	+2/-2	=	5/16 3/10 2/7	very low	T: 5/8-2/3

[a] T = Taper (d/D), where $\underline{d}$ is the diameter at the top, and $\underline{D}$ is the diameter at the mouth. Read as follows: Taper equals 1/3 to 1/2.

Species	Group	Base Values	Scale Types	Mouth Widths	Cutup	Detail
Open Conical Pipes: Wide Scale						
Gemshorn	I/II	+6/+4	(symbols)	5/26 3/16 5/27	low	T: 1/3–3/8
Waldfloete	II	+7/+5	(symbol)	5/21 2/9 1/5	medium	T: 2/3
Blockfloete	II	+11/+8	(symbol)	3/19 5/32 2/13	medium–low	T: 2/5–1/2
Flûte douce	E	−5/−8	(symbol)	2/9 3/14 5/24	medium	T: 3/5–4/5
Fully Covered Pipes: Overly Narrow Scale						
Quintaden	I	−7/−14	(symbols)	3/11 4/15 5/19	low	• • •
Ueberblas. Gedackt I	I/S	−9/−14	(symbol)	1/4 3/13 2/9	low	Overblown
Fully Covered Pipes: Narrow Scale						
Gedackt-pommer	I/II	−4/−8	(symbols)	10/39 1/4 10/41	low	• • • •
Gedackt I	I	−5/−6	(symbol)	1/4 4/17 5/22	medium	• •
Ueberblas. Gedackt II	I	−3/−8	(symbol)	1/4 3/13 2/9	low	Overblown

TABLE 43--Continued

[Mahrenholz]

Species	Group	Base Values	Scale Types	Mouth Widths	Cutup	Detail
			Fully Covered Pipes: Moderate Scale			
Gedackt II	I/II	0/0	=	1/4 4/17 5/22	medium	• • • • •
Lieblich Gedackt	E	-8/-12	= |= V	1/4 10/41 5/21	medium-low	• • • • •
Spitzgedackt	I/II	+3/-3	=	10/51 5/26 4/21	medium-low	Conical
Ueberblas. Spitzged.	I	+3/0	> | = <= V	4/19 5/24 1/5	medium	Overblown
			Fully Covered Pipes: Wide Scale			
Gedackt-floete	II	0/0	= | <=	5/21 2/9 5/24	medium	• • • • •
Gedackt-Zartfloete	E	-4/-8	=	3/13 5/22	medium	• • • • •
			Partly Covered Pipes: Overly Narrow Scale			
Rohr-quintaden	I	-4/-12	= | V	10/39 1/4 10/41	low	D_c: 1/5-1/4C[a]

[a] D_c = diameter of chimney; C = diameter of corpus.

Species	Group	Base Values	Scale Types	Mouth Widths	Cutup	Detail
Partly Covered Pipes: Moderate Scale						
Spillpfeife	I	0/–4		5/23 4/19 1/5	medium	D_c: 1/3–2/3C
Rohrpfeife	I	0/–4		5/23 4/19 1/5	medium–low	D_c: 1/2–2/3C
Rohrgedackt	I/II	+2/–3		5/22 3/14 1/5	high–medium	D_c: 1/5–1/4C
Partly Covered Pipes: Wide Scale						
Rohrfloete	II	+6/+2		1/5 5/26 5/27	medium–low	D_c: 1/4–1/3C
Koppelfloete	II	+6/+2		1/5 5/26 5/27	medium	D_c: 1/4–1/3C

TABLE 44

CATALOG OF CRITICAL DIMENSIONS--JAHNN[a]

Species	Group	Base Values[b]	Scale Types	Mouth Widths	Cutup[c]	Detail
Open Cylindrical Pipes: Narrow Scale						
Aperta	. .	-1/-3	≡ | < | >	1/4	very low	. . . . .
Open Cylindrical Pipes: Moderate Scale						
Principal	. .	+3/-1	≡ | < | >	1/4	quite low	. . . . .
Querfloete I	. .	+3/+1	>	1/4	very low	Overblown
Open Cylindrical Pipes: Wide Scale						
Italian Principal	. .	+7/+5	> | ≡	1/5	very low	. . . . .
Starkfloete	. o	+7/+5	. . . . .	1/4	. . . . .	. . . . o
Quer-floete II	. .	+11/+5	>	1/5	very low	Overblown
Nachthorn	. .	+14/+10	> | ⟨=	1/6 2/13 1/7	very low	. . . . .

[a]Summarized from H. Jahnn, "Registernamen und ihr Inhalt," Beitraege zur Organistentagung Hamburg-Luebeck / 6. bis 8. Juli 1925 (Klecken, 1925), pp. 5-25.

[b]Deviation in ± HT from Normprincipal; maximum/minimum values.

[c]For the present author's quantitative evaluations, see Appendix O, 2.

Species	Group	Base Values	Scale Types	Mouth Widths	Cutup	Detail
Open Conical Pipes: Moderate Scale						
Dolzian	..	+2/-1	< | > | ==	1/5 2/11 1/6	very low	T: 4/3
Spitzfloete	..	+3/0	== | < | >	1/4	medium	T: 1/3
Open Conical Pipes: Wide Scale						
Flachfloete	..	+4/+3	== | < | >	1/4	low	T: 1/2
Gemshorn	..	+7/+5	== | > V ==	} 1/5 4/21 2/11	.....	T: 1/3
Waldfloete	..	+7/+5	== | =>	1/4	medium	T: 1/2–2/3[a]
Blockfloete	..	+11/+9	> | ==	1/5 3/16 2/11	..	T: 2/5
Fully Covered Pipes: Narrow Scale						
Quintadena	..	-6/-9	>	1/4	very low	......
Gedackt-pommer	..	-3/-5	>	1/4	very low	.....
Gedeckte Blockfloete	..	-2/-4	< | ==	1/4	low	.....

[a] T = Taper (d/D), where d is the diameter at the top, and D is the diameter at the mouth. Read as follows: Taper equals 1/2 to 2/3.

TABLE 44--Continued

[Jahnn]

Species	Group	Base Values	Scale Types	Mouth Widths	Cutup	Detail
			Fully Covered Pipes: Moderate Scale			
Gedackt	. .	0/0	= | ∨	1/4 2/9 1/5	normal	. . . . .
Kupfer-gedackt	. .	+2/+1	= | ∨	1/4 2/9 1/5	normal	Copper
Grossgedackt lieblich	. .	+3/+1	> | = | ∨	1/4 2/9 1/5	medium	Conical
			Partly Covered Pipes: Narrow Scale			
Schwiegel	. .	-1/-3	∨	1/5 2/11 1/6	low	Cyl.-Con.
			Partly Covered Pipes: Moderate Scale			
Spillfloete	. .	0/-2	∨ | =	1/5	. . . .	T: 1/3
			Partly Covered Pipes: Wide Scale			
Rohrfloete	. .	+5/+3	= | ∨ | >	1/5	. . . . . .	D_c: 1/4C[a]
Koppelfloete	. .	+5/+3	= | ∨ | >	1/5 2/11	. . . . . .	T: 1/2

[a]$\underline{D}_c$ = diameter of chimney; $\underline{C}$ = diameter of corpus.

TABLE 45

CATALOG OF CRITICAL DIMENSIONS--ELLERHORST[a]

Species	Group	Base Values[b]	Scale[c] Types	Mouth Widths	Cutup	Detail
			Open Cylindrical Pipes:	Overly Narrow Scale		
Viola	∴	-15 1/2	⟨	1/4	1/3 – 2/7	⋯
Salizional	∴	-11 1/2	⟨	9/40	9/40	⋯
Querfloete	∴	-8	⟨⟩	1/5 – 1/6	1/5<1/3>1/5	Arched[d]
			Open Cylindrical Pipes:	Narrow Scale		
Schweizer-floete	∴	-4/-8	⟩=⟩	1/4 – 9/40	1/4 – 9/40	Overblown
Geigend-principal	∴	-4/-8	⟩=⟩	1/4	19/80 – 9/40	⋯
Fugara	∴	-3	⟨	9/40	1/4	⋯

[a]Summarized from W. Ellerhorst, Handbuch der Orgelkunde (Einsiedeln, 1936), pp. 227-250.

[b]Deviation in ± HT from Normprincipal, reckoned at c' ; maximum/minimum values.

[c]The symbols for the scale types represent both constant and variable scales.

[d]An arched or vaulted upper lip.

TABLE 45--Continued   [Ellerhorst]

Species	Group	Base Values	Scale Types	Mouth Widths	Cutup	Detail
Open Cylindrical Pipes: Moderate Scale						
Prinzipal	•	-1/-2	⟩ ⟩ ＝ ⟩	1/4	1/4	• • • • •
Floete	•	-1/-2	⟨ ⟩	1/5	1/4 – 1/5	• • • • •
Italian Prinzipal	•	+2/+1	⟩	• • • • • •	1/4 – 9/40	• • • • •
Open Cylindrical Pipes: Wide Scale						
Nachthorn	•	+10	⟩	1/4 1/7	2/7 1/4	• • • • • •
Open Conical Pipes: Moderate Scale						
Spitzfloete	•	0	⟨ ⟩	1/4	1/4	T: 1/4
Flachfloete	•	0	⟩	1/3	1/5	T: 2/3
Open Conical Pipes: Wide Scale						
Gemshorn	•	+5/+3	⟩ ⟨ ⟩	1/5	1/4	T: 1/3-2/5[a]
Waldfloete	•	+5	＝ ⟩	2/7 – 1/5	1/4	T: 3/4

[a] $\underline{T}$ = Taper (d/D), where $\underline{d}$ is the diameter at the top, and $\underline{D}$ is the diameter at the mouth. Read as follows: Taper equals 1/3 to 2/5.

TABLE 45--Continued   [Ellerhorst]

Species	Group	Base Values	Scale Types	Mouth Widths	Cutup	Detail
Blockfloete	..	+6	=>	1/5	1/4	T: 1/2
Fully Covered Pipes: Overly Narrow Scale						
Quintadena A	..	-12	∨	1/4 – 9/40	1/4	.....
Quintadena B	.∘	-8/-13	∨ I ∧	9/40	1/4	.....
Gedackt A	..∘	-10	∨	1/5	1/3	.....
Fully Covered Pipes: Narrow Scale						
Nachthorn– Gedackt	..	-7	∨	1/5 – 1/6	2/7	.....
Gedackt B	..	-3 1/2	<>	1/5	1/3	.....
Fully Covered Pipes: Moderate Scale						
Spitzgedackt	.∘	-1 1/2	∧ =>	1/5	1/3 – 1/4	Conical
Gedackt– floete	..	+1	∨	1/5	1/4<1/3>1/4	Arched

TABLE 45--Continued

[Ellerhorst]

Species	Group	Baso Values	Scale Types	Mouth Widths	Cutup	Detail
Fully Covered Pipes: Wide Scale						
Grobgedackt	• °	+3	<	1/4 - 9/40	1/3 - 2/7	• • • • •
Partly Covered Pipes: Narrow Scale						
Rohrfloete A	• •	-6 1/2	>	1/5	1/3	• • •
Rohrgedackt	• •	-6 1/2	>	1/4 - 1/5	2/7	• ° •
Partly Covered Pipes: Moderate Scale						
Spillpfeife	• •	-2/-6	>	1/4 - 2/9	• • • • • •	T: 1/5-2/3
Partly Covered Pipes: Wide Scale						
Koppelfloete	• •	+2	>	1/5	1/4	T: 1/2
Rohrfloete B	• •	+4/+2	<>|<	1/5	1/3	• • • • •

CHAPTER VI

THE MODERN ORGAN: MUTATIONS

AND MIXED VOICES

Mutations

Beside its comprehensive array of individual voices,
the organ presents a unique marshaling of these resources to
develop the phenomenon of mutation voices. The practice
lies almost exclusively within the domain of the instrument
and has been consistently developed and practiced for many
centuries. Certainly, the history of the application of
this principle for the enrichment of the color palette of
the organ, exhibits crests and troughs, depending largely
upon the viewpoint with respect to the organ's artistic function and to the legitimacy of the concept from time to time.
With the recent renewed interest in the compelling principles underlying the concept of the organ, the interest in
the phenomenon of mutation voices is again reaching a peak
in the course of its checkered history.

In a general way, mutation voices are such as speak
at other than foundational pitches. Without a clear definition of what constitutes foundational pitches in the organ,
voices speaking at 2 2/3', 2', 1 3/5', 1 1/3', 1 1/7', 1'

177

pitch, etc. may be tentatively considered as mutation voices.
The term "mutation" is a fairly descriptive one because
voices, so named, have no compelling reason for independent
existence except in so far as they, through combination, influence, change, or mutate the tone color of other individual or collective foundational voices.

The French divide the entire fund of organ voices
into two main categories, as jeux de fond, i.e., foundation
stops, and jeux de combinaison or jeux de mutation, i.e.,
stops used in combination with the former, and which, in
turn, constitute the mutation voices here under discussion.[1]
The Germans, on the other hand, divide all organ voices into
Grundstimmen, i.e., foundational voices, and Aliquotstimmen
or Obertonstimmen, i.e., aliquot or overtone voices, because
these voices are developed out of integral parts of the Harmonic Series, which provides the basic ingredients for all
musical tone.[2] Mutation voices may, therefore, be generally
defined as voices whose fundamental pitch represents a partial tone of another foundational pitch in the organ. In
the theory of the organ, the definition has, through the
centuries, undergone certain refinements, as will presently
become evident.

The purpose of mutation voices in the organ is to
make available to the organist, certain tonal ingredients
which, by combination with other existing tone, present the

possibility of altering, readjusting, reinforcing, or recon-
stituting certain partial tones which are absent or incipi-
ently present in a given voice or combination of voices.
The addition of mutation voices to a registration materially changes the overall profile of the tonal spectrum which
the pipes exhibit in a natural way. They are, therefore,
influential color factors in the palette of organ voices.

Physical Bases

The development of mutation voices follows rather
strictly the physical laws of sound as they are reflected
in the Harmonic Series, which represents a fundamental tone
and the consecutive partial tones which, in sum, determine
the tone color of a given musical sound. Notationally, it
is often represented as shown in Appendix P, 1.

It must be understood that natural musical sounds
are far more complex than the usual notational representation of the Harmonic Series will indicate. For reasons of
space, only the first sixteen partials are shown, whereas,
in reality, an infinite number may constitute the full complement. In relation to the fundamental 1, partials 2, 4,
8, and 16 are octave-sounding ingredients; partials 3, 6,
and 12 are fifth-sounding; partials 5 and 10 are third-
sounding; partials 7 and 14 are seventh-sounding; partial 9
is second-sounding; partial 11 is fourth-sounding; and partial 13 is sixth-sounding.

The serial number of the partial is the quotient of the ratio of the frequency of that partial to the frequency of the fundamental in just intonation. Appendix P, 2 shows the frequencies of the various partial tones if 64 cycles per second are adopted as the frequency of the fundamental.

The various partials, if they are to be realized in independent voices as mutation stops, must be assigned an appropriate foot designation which can serve to identify the mutation voice and show its relation to any foundational voice. In practice, such a foundational voice may be either an 8', a 4', a 16', or a 32' voice; the one chosen and the one to which a given mutation stop is to be related is referred to as the "basis for reckoning," or more simply, the "basis." The formula which controls the foot designation is $D = B/P$ where $\underline{D}$ is the foot designation for the mutation stop, $\underline{B}$ the basis used for reckoning, and $\underline{P}$ the serial number of the partial which the mutation voice is to represent. Appendix P, 3 gives the foot designations of the mutation voices which find application in organ building, as reckoned from the various bases.

Mutation Pitches

There exists some difference of opinion among modern organ theorists as to what pitches or which partials of a given basis constitute the foundational pitches. When viewed from the panorama of implications which a definite

classification must satisfy, it would seem best to consider
the 8', 4', 16', and 32' pitches as foundational; the 64'
pitch is extremely rare, and the 2' pitch comes into question only if a 4' basis is used for reckoning the mutations.
Such a definition would, in the main, satisfy the proposal
of Klotz in this regard.[3] Smets, on the other hand, wishes
to include the 2' and 1' pitches into this classification,
but without adequate justification.[4] When reckoning mutations, the concept of the foundational voice as previously
developed would, in most cases, include the second partial
of any given basis as forming part of this classification.
The mutations themselves, then, would comprise all of those
voices whose pitch represents the third and consecutive partials beyond that point. These again are divided into harmonic and inharmonic mutations. The harmonic mutations are
those which do not exceed the sixth partial or limit of the
senario, while the inharmonic ones are considered to be such
as are developed from partials beyond this limit. Table 46
gives an overview of the pitches for mutation voices which
have or may find application in the concept of the organ of
today.

Suppression, Repetition, and Reduction

Two of the prime requisites for a mutation voice are
that it must definitely lie within the frequency range of
hearing and that it must lose its individual identity by

TABLE 46

PROPER FOOT DESIGNATION FOR VARIOUS SERIES OF MUTATIONS

| Foundational Registers | | Senario: Harmonic Mutations | | | | Super-Senario: Inharmonic Mutations | | | |
| Basis | Octave | Common | | | | Rare | Extremely Rare | | |
Fundamental	Second Partial, Octave-Sounding	Third Partial, Fifth-Sounding	Fourth Partial, Octave-Sounding	Fifth Partial, Third-Sounding	Sixth Partial, Fifth-Sounding	Seventh Partial, Seventh-Sounding	Ninth Partial, Second-Sounding	Eleventh Partial, Fourth-Sounding	Thirteenth Partial, Sixth-Sounding
8'	4'	2 2/3'	2'	1 3/5'	1 1/3'	1 1/7'	8/9'	8/11'	8/13'
4'	2'	1 1/3'	1'	4/5'	2/3'	4/7'	4/9'	4/11'	4/13'
16'	8'	5 1/3'	4'	3 1/5'	2 2/3'	2 2/7'	1 7/9'	1 5/11'	1 3/13'
32'	16'	10 2/3'	8'	6 2/5'	5 1/3'	4 4/7'	3 5/9'	2 10/11'	2 6/13'

blending completely with the foundational voice with which
it might be associated in registration. The practical realization of these prime conditions forces certain limitations upon the organ builder. One is the acute threshold of
pitch discrimination, which is generally accepted as about
8,000 to 8,500 cycles per second, being in the neighborhood
of c'''''' of an equal-tempered scale developed from a' =
440 cycles per second.[5] Within the compass of the standard
organ clavier (sixty-one notes ranging from C - c''''), any
voices predicated upon a pitch higher than 2' will exceed
the threshold of pitch discrimination, while those below
that pitch level will approach it at the upper limit of the
compass. Chart 26 gives the courses of two mutation voices
of which the 2 2/3' example approaches, while the 1 1/3'
example exceeds this limit.

Builders often accommodate themselves to this condition by merely discontinuing a voice when it reaches the a-
cute threshold of pitch discrimination; the voice is "suppressed." The example illustrated on Chart 26, should the
principle of suppression be exercised, would comprise fifty-
four pipes rather than the usual sixty-one; its course would
terminate at f'''.

A second limitation is imposed by the extreme difficulty of constructing and voicing diminutive pipes. In such
cases, resort is had to the practice of repetition, whereby

a voice, upon reaching the threshold, is broken and made to continue at its sub-octave; the last segment of the course, in effect, repeats the pitches of the corresponding preceding segment. The 1 1/3' example is often handled in this manner. Chart 27 shows the course for such a disposition.

A third limitation imposed by mutation voices is the incapacity of the pipes to blend adequately with foundational voices in grave pitch regions, or for the ear to discern such blend effectively. In such cases, resort is had to the principle of reduction, whereby a voice is made to begin its course at a higher pitch than the designation would indicate, falling to its rightful pitch at a convenient point in the course or at a point where blend can unmistakably be discerned. In this initial segment the pipes are "reduced" in their physical lengths. Chart 28 shows a 2 2/3' example which incorporates the principle of reduction. Notice that the voice still retains its intended foot designation which it pursues for the major segment of the course.

Inasmuch as the principles of suppression, repetition, and reduction interfere with the normal progress of the voice as it moves through the course of the compass, some justification other than physical convenience must support such a practice. Such justification is predicated upon three propositions which shore up the practice by considerations other than those of convenience.

1. The first proposition has already been presented; namely, that in the grave pitch regions certain low-pitched mutation voices fail to blend with the fundamental voice with which they may be associated. The ear does not perceive the composite sound as an entity, but as distinguishable pitches, each one operating in the foreground. The presence of a low-pitched mutation voice in that area constitutes a disturbing factor. On the other hand, the fact, that at the acute threshold of pitch discrimination certain high-pitched mutation voices are unable to convey a perceptibly discriminate pitch, justifies the suppression of the voice in that area

2. The second proposition maintains that mutation voices, when associated with a fundamental voice, serve chiefly the purpose of strongly characterizing the aural effect of the fundamental voice. For this reason, mutation voices find their prime application in the area of solo registrations. Since the literature for the organ, in most cases, limits its solo melodies to a range not exceeding that of $\underline{f}$ to $\underline{c}$''', the principles of suppression, repetition, and reduction do not interfere with the normal progress of the voice within such a melodic range. In fact it is a rigid principle in quality organ building

that adjustments at the grave and acute limits of the
compass remain outside the limits of the traditional
melodic range required by composers for the organ

3. The third proposition is a logical outgrowth
of the preceding. If the extreme segments of the
course are not urgently needed for solo registrations,
they may as well serve to strengthen weaknesses that
may be present in the overall disposition of the corpus of the division. For this purpose, the practice
of repetition and reduction may be applied to such
voices in order to marshal their resources in the interest of improving the fabric of the total compound
tonal structure of the division in which they occur.
The reduced segment in the grave area will contribute
clarity to this portion of the compass, while the repeated segment in the acute area will serve to contribute gravity and substance in that portion of the
compass. Chart 29 shows a small division containing
the voices, 8' Musiziergedackt, 4' Flachfloete, 2'
Scharfprincipal, and 1 1/3' Klein Nasat. The 1 1/3'
mutation voice has been reduced to 1' in the bass area
of the compass and repeats at 2 2/3' in the acute area
of the same

Tuning of Mutation Voices

In order for all mutation voices to blend perfectly

with the foundational voices, it is of the utmost importance that they be tuned to the foundational pitch in "just" ratios. The quotients of the ratios must be integers. Table 47 gives the ratios at which the frequencies of the individual notes of the various mutation voices must stand in relation to the corresponding notes of the foundational voices with which they may properly be associated.

If all of the frequencies of the individual notes of a mutation voice must stand in "just" ratios to the corresponding notes of a foundational voice, it becomes critically important that, if such voices are to function properly acoustically, they must be independent voices tuned "just" to the foundational pitch, and may not be derived from existing voices by borrowing. Tables 48 and 49 show the frequencies of a 2 2/3' and a 1 3/5' mutation voice when constructed independently and tuned "just," and when borrowed.

Scale and Mouth Treatment

The voicing of an effective mutation stop must be so controlled that its tone will reinforce or extend an overtone of a foundational voice without displaying aggressive characteristics of its own which might tend to make it individually noticeable. The listener should not be conscious of the fact that he hears, in reality, a bouquet of pitches rather than a single compound sound. The cohesion should be so firm as to assure perfect blend. Certain specifications

TABLE 47

RATIOS OF THE FREQUENCIES BETWEEN CORRESPONDING NOTES
OF MUTATION AND FOUNDATIONAL VOICES

Mutation Pitches	Ratio of Foundational Pitch / Mutation Pitch			
	8' Basis	4' Basis	16' Basis	32' Basis
10 2/3'	. . . . . .	. . . . . .	. . . . . .	3/1
5 1/3'	. . . . . .	. . . . . .	3/1	6/1
2 2/3'	3/1	. . . . . .	6/1	12/1
1 1/3'	6/1	3/1	12/1	24/1
2/3'	12/1	6/1	24/1	48/1
8'	. . . . . .	. . . . . .	. . . . . .	4/1
4'	. . . . . .	. . . . . .	4/1	8/1
2'	4/1	. . . . . .	8/1	16/1
1'	8/1	4/1	16/1	32/1
6 2/5'	. . . . . .	. . . . . .	. . . . . .	5/1
3 1/5'	. . . . . .	. . . . . .	5/1	10/1
1 3/5'	5/1	. . . . . .	10/1	20/1
4/5'	10/1	5/1	20/1	40/1
4 4/7'	. . . . . .	. . . . . .	. . . . . .	7/1
2 2/7'	. . . . . .	. . . . . .	7/1	14/1
1 1/7'	7/1	. . . . . .	14/1	28/1
3 5/9'	. . . . . .	. . . . . .	. . . . . .	9/1
1 7/9'	. . . . . .	. . . . . .	9/1	18/1
8/9'	9/1	. . . . . .	18/1	36/1
2 10/11'	. . . . . .	. . . . . .	. . . . . .	11/1
1 5/11'	. . . . . .	. . . . . .	11/1	22/1
8/11'	11/1	. . . . . .	22/1	44/1
2 6/13'	. . . . . .	. . . . . .	. . . . . .	13/1
1 3/13'	. . . . . .	. . . . . .	13/1	26/1
8/13'	13/1	. . . . . .	26/1	52/1

TABLE 48

VARIANT FREQUENCIES OF A BORROWED VERSUS AN INDEPENDENT
MUTATION VOICE AT 2 2/3' PITCH

Note	Frequency of 8' in Equal Temperament[a]	Frequency of 2 2/3' if Tuned "Just" to 8'	Frequency of 2 2/3' if Borrowed from 8'	Frequency Aberration in Cycles per Second
c'	261.63	784.89	783.99	.90
c♯'	277.18	831.54	830.61	.93
d'	293.66	880.98	880.00	.98
d♯'	311.13	933.39	932.33	1.06
e'	329.63	988.89	987.77	1.12
f'	349.23	1047.69	1046.50	1.19
f♯'	369.99	1109.97	1108.73	1.24
g'	392.00	1176.00	1174.66	1.34
g♯'	415.30	1245.90	1244.51	1.39
a'	440.00	1320.00	1318.51	1.49
a♯'	466.16	1398.48	1396.91	1.57
b'	493.88	1481.64	1479.98	1.66

[a]Based on American Standard Pitch, a' = 440 cycles
per second.

for the construction of mutation voices tend to assure the

achievement of such desirable qualities. Experience has

shown that species from any family of the labial order are

TABLE 49

VARIANT FREQUENCIES OF A BORROWED VERSUS AN INDEPENDENT
MUTATION VOICE AT 1 3/5' PITCH

Note	Frequency of 8' in Equal Temperament[a]	Frequency of 1 3/5' if Tuned "Just" to 8'	Frequency of 1 3/5' if Borrowed from 8'	Frequency Aberration in Cycles per Second
c'	261.63	1308.15	1318.51	10.36
c♯'	277.18	1385.90	1396.51	10.61
d'	293.66	1468.30	1479.98	11.68
d♯'	311.13	1555.65	1567.98	12.33
e'	329.63	1648.15	1661.22	13.07
f'	349.23	1746.15	1760.00	13.85
f♯'	369.99	1849.95	1864.66	14.71
g'	392.00	1960.00	1975.53	15.53
g♯'	415.30	2076.50	2093.00	16.50
a'	440.00	2200.00	2217.46	17.46
a♯'	466.16	2330.80	2349.32	18.52
b'	493.88	2469.40	2489.02	19.62

[a]Based on American Standard Pitch, a' = 440 cycles
per second.

suitable for mutation voices; open cylindrical, open conical, fully covered, and partly covered specimens can achieve
excellent results. The lower the actual pitch of the

utation, the more covered the pipes can be; the higher, the
more open. Fully covered pipes serve admirably at mutation
pitches like 10 2/3' and 5 1/3', partly covered ones at
3 1/3' and 2 2/3', open conical ones at 2 2/3' and 1 1/3',
and open cylindrical ones at the very high pitches of 1 1/3'
or 2/3' as well as at the lower pitches.

A second factor in the disposition of a mutation
voice that contributes materially toward good cohesion and
blend is the genus of the voice. Pipes from the moderate,
moderately-wide, and wide-scaled genera can be voiced to exhibit adequately recessive characteristics that will assure
good blend. Depending upon the foundational voice with
which they are intended to associate, the base values of the
mutation voices should, in every case, be several half-tones
larger than those of the foundational voice; the higher
pitched the mutation is, the greater can be the difference
between the two. Table 50 presents a sampling of a possible
dispersion of the families and genera of registers suitable
for mutation voices at various levels. It does not exhaust
the possibilities nor yet preclude considerably different
arrangements.

A final factor necessary to insure a successful mutation voice is the disposition of the mouth. Hardly ever
may the width of the mouth exceed 2/9 of the circumference;
it may be taken as narrow as 1/6 in the case of very wide-

TABLE 50

POSSIBLE DISPERSION OF FAMILIES AND GENERA AMONG MUTATION VOICES

Foundational Voice	Grave Mutations as 2 2/3' or 2'	Moderate Mutations as 1 3/5' or 1 1/3'	Acute Mutations as 1 1/7' or 1'
8' Holzfloete	Quint/Octave +2 HT Italian Principal +4 HT	Italian Principal +5 HT Gemshorn +6 HT	Waldfloete +7 HT Blockfloete +9 HT Nachthorn +11 HT
8' Gedackt	Flachfloete +2 HT Rohrfloete +4 HT	Spitzfloete +3 HT Italian Principal +5 HT	Hohlfloete +6 HT Blockfloete +8 HT
8' Rohrpfeife	Spitzfloete +2 HT Gemshorn +4 HT	Waldfloete +5 HT Italian Principal +6 HT	Blockfloete +8 HT Hohlfloete +7 HT
8' Spitzfloete	Italian Principal +4 HT Hohlfloete +5 HT	Gemshorn +6 HT Waldfloete +7 HT	Blockfloete +8 HT Nachthorn +10 HT . . . . . .

scaled pipes. In general, the mouth widths should be those normally required for the species of pipes which may be chosen for the mutation voice. By "rule of thumb," the wider the scale of the pipe, the narrower its mouth must be.

Classification

For purposes of ready reference, the mutation voices may conveniently be classified into types, depending upon the degree of coloration they add to foundational voices. Such a type-classification derives from the initial appearance of a given overtone in the Harmonic Series.

1. Type I exhibits all of the unison-sounding mutations, such as 4', 2', 1', and the like

2. Type II comprises all fifth-sounding mutations, such as 5 1/3', 2 2/3', 1 1/3', etc.

3. Type III embraces the third-sounding mutations, such as 3 1/5', 1 3/5', etc.

4. Type IV includes collectively all of the inharmonic overtones which, in order, are seventh-sounding (2 2/7', 1 1/7'), second-sounding (1 7/9', 8/9'), fourth-sounding (1 5/11', 8/11'), and sixth-sounding (1 3/13', 8/13')

Unison-Sounding Mutations

Unison-sounding mutations are such, which in relation to an 8' foundational voice, are at 2' and 1' pitch.

It must be remembered that at the 2' pitch, not all registers that might occur in a disposition are necessarily mutation voices. A tonal scheme may present a variety of voices
at this pitch from the narrow-scaled and moderate-scaled
genera of the various families, which serve other purposes
than that of coloring a foundational voice in the sense discussed previously. Among such are all the Principals, Pom-
mers, Rohrpfeifes, Geigendprincipals, Fugaras, Salicionals,
Rohrquintades, and the like. These voices, in the strict
sense of the concept, are not really mutation voices.

A résumé of suitable voices for mutation purposes as
recommended by Mahrenholz, Jahnn, and Smets appears in Table
51, where the families and genera of the same are differentiated.[6]

Fifth-Sounding Mutations

The fifth-sounding mutations (2 2/3' and 1 1/3' when
reckoning from an 8' basis) are perhaps the most important
and most common color factors in the organ. Even an economical tonal corpus is seldom developed without this mutation-
al ingredient. The tone must be yielding, comparatively
mild, and possess good carrying power or extensity.

The 2 2/3' pitch level often exhibits mutation voices
in a large variety of scales. Those voices which approach
Principal or moderate scale usually adopt the name Quint as
a root, suffix, or prefix, while those which are developed

TABLE 51

SPECIES SUITABLE FOR UNISON-SOUNDING MUTATIONS[a]

Family	2-Foot or 1-Foot Pitch		
	Moderate Scale	Moderately-Wide Scale	Wide Scale
Open Cylindrical	Schweizer-pfeife	Italian Principal	Hohlfloete Nachthorn Querfloete
Open Conical	Flachfloete	Spitzfloete	Gemshorn Waldfloete Blockfloete
Fully Covered	[Gedackt][b]	Gedacktfloete	. . . . .
Partly Covered	Spillpfeife Rohrpfeife	[Rohrgedackt][b]	Rohrfloete Koppelfloete

[a]Composite of Mahrenholz, Jahnn, and Smets. See Note 6.

[b]Interpolated by the present author.

from the wide-scaled genus are properly termed Nasat. Into the Quint classification belong such voices as Twelfth, Nineteenth, Scharfquint, Superquint, Spitzquint, Gedacktquint, Rohrquint, and the like. The term Nasat, on the other hand, identifies the wider-scaled members of the classification, such as Nasatquint, Hohlnasat, Larigot, Weitquint,

Gemsnasat, Gedacktnasat, Rohrnasat, etc. It will be noticed
that if the term "quint" appears among these also as a prefix or suffix, a qualifying adjective is added to denote the
fact that the voice is developed out of wide scales, and
therefore belongs properly into the Nasat classification.
Table 52 is a composite listing of registers recommended by
Mahrenholz, Jahnn, and Smets as useful for fifth-sounding
mutations.[7]

TABLE 52

SPECIES SUITABLE FOR FIFTH-SOUNDING MUTATIONS[a]

Family	2 2/3-Foot and 1 1/3-Foot Pitch		
	Moderate Scale	Moderately-Wide Scale	Wide Scale
Open Cylindrical	Principal	Italian Principal	Hohlfloete Nachthorn
Open Conical	....	Spitzfloete	Gemshorn Waldfloete
Fully Covered	Gedackt	Gedacktfloete	.....
Partly Covered	Rohrpfeife	....	Rohrfloete Koppelfloete

[a]Composite of Mahrenholz, Jahnn, and Smets. See
Note 6.

The fifth-sounding mutations sometimes appear an octave or two lower than at 2 2/3' pitch; in such cases, they are either Pedal mutations or are predicated upon a 16' foundation. Often the prefix Gross is then added to differentiate the item from other fifth-sounding mutations appearing in the same division or instrument.

Third-Sounding Mutations

The third-sounding mutations appear usually at 1 3/5' pitch and are normally associated with an 8' foundational voice. The sub-octave member at 3 1/5' identifies the voice as belonging properly to a 16' basis and appears occasionally in Pedal divisions. In such cases, the prefix Gross or Grob serves to differentiate the particular item from others of the same type. Mutations which reinforce the fifth partial bring an important and very strong color element into any tonal corpus in which they operate. If successfully executed, they tend to develop an aural illusion of reed color into otherwise purely labial combinations. To do this effectively, the voice must be kept near Principal scale; this is the reason why so frequently the Terz or Tierce is executed in pipes of the Italian Principal species. Pipes of narrower scale are hardly possible, but wider ones do appear. These, in turn, do not produce the reed effect nearly as well, but do provide interesting and eminently worthwhile color elements. Should two Tierces appear in the same

instrument, it is customary to provide one from the Italian
Principal species, and the other in wider-scaled pipes. The
terms used to identify the third-sounding mutations are <u>Terz</u>
or <u>Tierce</u>, <u>Gemsterz</u>, <u>Terzfloete</u>, or <u>Hohlterz</u>, the prefixes
serving to identify the species of pipe from which the Tierce
is constructed. Among these are chiefly Italian Principals,
Gemshorns, Rohrfloetes, and Hohlfloetes.

The Tierce almost always repeats in the top octave
of the compass and may very well be reduced in the lowest
segment of the compass, which often comprises an octave, and
occasionally an octave and one-half. At such a grave pitch,
the voice fails to blend and the ear is likely to be disturbed by the mutation voice functioning as a separately
discernible pitch rather than as a fully blended color element. Chart 30 shows a possible course for a Tierce.

Inharmonic Mutations

Independent voices which are intended to reinforce
the inharmonic partials (<u>i.e.</u>, those appearing outside the
traditional senario) are extraordinarily strong color elements and find application only in very large instruments.
Of these, the seventh-sounding <u>Septime</u> or <u>Septième</u> is rare,
while the remainder have occurred extremely rarely in actual practice.[8] All of them are made of wide and very wide-
scaled pipes unless extraordinarily compelling reasons dic-
tate the use of moderately-scaled pipes, such as the Italian

Principal. Generally the Blockfloete or Nachthorn species
serve as the ingredients for such voices. Most usually, the
extremes of the compass are suppressed rather than repeated
or reduced. See Chart 31.

Mixed Voices

Delineation

Mixed voices are fixed, pre-established combinations
of appropriate mutation voices, so arranged as not to be
playable separately. In effect, they are diminutive bouquets of selected mutation registers, particularly useful in
the more generously disposed tonal corpora of larger instruments. Mixed voices are often confused with mixtures; in
fact, the two concepts are seldom differentiated. In reality they exhibit such markedly opposing dispositions and
functions that the conditions which differentiate them need
to be carefully considered. There are at least ten factors
which serve to differentiate one concept from the other:

1. Mixed voices do not interrupt or break the
progress of their course within the limits of the melodic range, while mixtures employ the principle of
repetition or reduction throughout the compass

2. Mixed voices are compounded of few elements,
so that from two to five ranks serve as the practical
limit. Mixtures, on the other hand, generally exhibit

relatively more ingredients, so that from three to ten ranks comprise their most effective dispositions

3. Mixed voices operate at much lower pitches than do mixtures; in a division predicated upon an 8' basis, mixed voices may use pitches ranging from 8' to 1', while mixtures rarely go below 2' and may include pitches as high as 1/8'

4. Mixed voices are yielding in character rather than aggressive; they strive toward blend and absorption rather than toward eminence in registrational combinations, as do the mixtures

5. Mixed voices, for that reason, are compounded of species which exceed Principal scale, whereas mixtures are developed almost exclusively out of such scales, or narrower ones

6. Mixed voices must be equipped with mouths whose widths do not exceed 2/9 of the circumferences, whereas mixtures consistently display wider mouths

7. Mixed voices operate most effectively with foundational voices of non-Principal species, whereas mixtures associate well with either Principal or non-Principal foundations

8. Mixed voices are constructed of open cylindrical, open conical, fully covered, and partly covered families of pipes, whereas mixtures are developed

entirely out of open cylindrical pipes

9. Mixed voices are generally disposed, so that successively higher-pitched members are of increasingly larger scales, whereas in mixtures, an opposite disposition prevails

10. Mixed voices may be incorporated into a tonal corpus in dismembered form as individual mutation voices, whereas mixtures are not so dismembered

Basic Classification

In classifying mixed voices, the most remote overtone realized in the composition of such a voice determines the type into which a particular specimen falls. Five different types are distinguishable:

1. The Faberton type, which contains only unison or octave-sounding elements

2. The Rauschpfeife type, which contains fifth-sounding ranks as the most remote representatives of the overtone series

3. The Kornett type, among which third-sounding ranks will appear as the most remote elements

4. The Schreipfeife type, which exhibits a seventh-sounding member from the inharmonic group of overtones

5. The Hoelzern Gelaechter type, which may contain overtones as remote as second-sounding

Faberton

The Faberton type properly identifies mixed voices which contain only unison-sounding members. The most usual combination is the Faberton, or Tonus Fabri, or Gloeckleinton of two ranks at 2' and 1' pitches. In the Pedal, the type occurs as a Choralbass 4' and 2', or as a Zink 2' and 1', or, at times, as a Piffero 4' and 2' or 8', 4', and 2'. An acutely-pitched form of the Faberton type may appear in larger instruments as the Jauchzendpfeife 1' and 1/2'. All of these mixed voices are compounded of families and genera of pipes commonly used for mutation voices, such as Italian Principals, Flachfloetes, Spitzfloetes, Rohrfloetes, Waldfloetes, and Querfloetes. The lower the pitch level of the mixed voice, the more closely the pipes must approach Principal scale. Charts 32, 33, and 34 lay out the courses for various mixed voices of the Faberton type.

Rauschpfeife

The Rauschpfeife type of mixed voice exhibits representatives of partial tones which do not exceed fifth-sounding overtones. The basic composition from which the type derives its name is the II Rauschpfeife, Rauschquinte, or Rauschfloete 2 2/3' and 2'. At times, the term Quart or Quartan identifies the voice. When compounded of three ranks, the members appear at 4', 2 2/3', and 2' pitches; when of four, at 5 1/3', 4', 2 2/3', and 2' or at 4', 2 2/3',

2', and 1 1/3' pitches. In five ranks the voice contains
unisons and fifths from 5 1/3' through the 1 1/3' pitch.
Any Rauschpfeife type of mixed voice which contains members
lower than 2 2/3' is appropriate for Pedal divisions, or for
Manual divisions predicated upon a 16' foundation. In rare
instances, a Rauschpfeife may be compounded of 1 1/3' and 1'
pitches. Most generally, pipes of the Italian Principal species develop the finest specimens of the voice. Wider species find application when the pitch level is higher than
the basic disposition. Chart 35 presents a typical course
for a II Rauschpfeife.

Kornett

The inclusion of third-sounding mutations to represent the most remote species of overtone in the composition
of a mixed voice, places such an example into the Kornett
type. Any or all species of partials present in the Faberton or Rauschpfeife types may properly accompany the Tierce
element in one way or another. The full Kornett comprises
five ranks of pipes at 8', 4', 2 2/3', 2', and 1 3/5' pitches. The 8' member, being the foundational one, is tradi-
tionally a Rohrfloete, but may be represented instead by
similar species, such as the Gedacktpommer, Gedackt, Spillfloete, Koppelfloete, or Rohrpfeife. In every case, it
should be derived from moderately or generously-scaled fully covered or partly covered pipes. The unison-sounding

members of the Kornett may be Principals or other moderate-scaled open cylindrical or open conical pipes. The fifth and third-sounding members are usually of the Italian Principal species, if an effective horn quality is to be extracted from the Kornett.

The purpose of the Kornett is to serve as a noteworthy and strongly characteristic solo register and to assist in augmenting or strengthening the treble of reed voices in the same tonal corpus. For this reason many of the historical Kornetts commence at c' and proceed upward in the discant region of the compass.[9] Today the register is more often extended downward to the bass limit of the compass or appears in complete form no later than the lower limit of the melodic range (f). Quite often the register begins at C with three ranks, the missing members appearing during the second octave of the course. Charts 36 and 37 plot the courses for a full V Kornett and for a possible III-V Kornett example.

In most modern dispositions, the full Kornett seldom appears bound as one register; more often and quite commonly, the low-pitched members or the unison members of the combination are marshaled from existing registers of the respective division. In such cases, the remaining elements, when bound, are more properly termed Kornettino. This may be compounded of three ranks (then 2 2/3', 2', and 1 3/5' or

4', 2 2/3', and 1 3/5') or of four ranks (then 4', 2 2/3', 2', and 1 3/5'). When reduced to two ranks (as 2 2/3' and 1 3/5'), the mixed voice is renamed Sesquialtera and constructed chiefly of Italian Principal pipes. Should the two ranks be pitched at 2' and 1 3/5' the voice is more properly called a Hoernle. Occasionally the Sesquialtera appears in inverted form (as 1 3/5' and 1 1/3'); such a combination is known as a Terzian or Tertian. In three ranks, the Terzian is comprised of 1 3/5', 1 1/3', and 1' pitches. In some instances the Kornett, Sesquialtera, and Tertian are disposed at pitches an octave lower than customary, for use in Pedal divisions or in Manual divisions based upon a 16' foundation; in such cases, they are named Gross Kornett (5 1/3', 4', and 3 1/5'), Gross Sesquialtera (5 1/3' and 3 1/5'), or Gross Terzian (3 1/5' and 2 2/3'). The opposite practice, whereby the voices are shifted an octave upward, finds occasional use in large instruments and identifies the voices with the adjective Klein. At such high pitches, the voice can barely be carried unbroken through the melodic range of the compass. After c''' certain members are, therefore, either suppressed or repeated. Should elements of the Kornett appear on two separate divisions of an instrument, they will be differentiated by family, genus, and species or by degree of winding. The secondary voice is often called Echo Kornett. Chart 38 shows the course of a Sesquialtera, partly suppressed.

Schreipfeife, Hoelzern Gelaechter

Among mixed voices which incorporate elements representing the inharmonic overtones, the delineation and type-
classification is far from clear. Their extremely rare appearance in organ dispositions is insufficient to establish
consistent patterns. However, for the sake of completeness,
these types should at least be tentatively defined.

Schreipfeife may well serve as the type name for
mixed voices incorporating the Septime (1 1/7') while the
term Hoelzern Gelaechter (a term already appearing in Schlick
and Virdung) could suggest the presence of the None (8/9').[10]
According to Smets and others, Dr. Elis has recommended the
combination of 2 2/3', 1 3/5', and 1 1/7' for the Schreipfeife, while Rieger wants the Hoelzern Gelaechter to be
compounded of 1 1/7', 8/9', and 4/5' pitches.[11] In every
case, these very high-pitched mixed voices must be prepared
of wide-scaled pipes and are all subject to a certain amount
of suppression or repetition in the uppermost region of the
compass. Chart 39 exemplifies a Schreipfeife.

CHAPTER VII

THE MODERN ORGAN: TONAL CROWNS

The Concept of the Crown

As the mutations and mixed voices of the organ serve
to enrich and mature the foundational voices of Group II
(being a representation and gathering together into clusters
of the higher elements in the Harmonic Series of partials),
so the tonal crowns are similarly compounded of representative overtones to serve as the ultimate superstructure for
the Principal choirs present in the various tonal corpora of
the organ. They are a gathering together of relatively
high-pitched ranks of pipes which represent select overtones
properly associated with foundational voices.

In practice, such ranks represent almost exclusively
unison and fifth-sounding members (rarely, third-sounding),
and appear bound in clusters, presenting thus individual
bouquets of compound tone.

All tonal crowns are dependent registers, not useful
by themselves but requiring the support of one or more foundational voices; they belong to the fund of voices known as
jeux de combinaison by the French.

The purpose of the tonal crowns is to enlarge,

enrich, and cement together into a cohesive entity, the foundational Principal (or Principal-Ersatz) voices of a given tonal corpus. Crowns are indispensible in bringing the various Principal ensembles of the organ to brilliance and fullness. More particularly, their purpose is to add clarity to the bass portion of the compass, fullness to the middle, and gravity to the treble.

The exploitation of the phenomenon of tonal crowns in the full development of tonal corpora for the organ rests upon physical and psychological premises. Physically, the crowns combine the most simple elements of the senario and thus derive their justification from nature. Psychologically, the crowns are not essentially involved in the delineation of overall pitch; this is the compulsion of the foundational voices. For this reason, crowns appear in recurring and partly recurring segments, in order to operate beneath the threshold of acute pitch discrimination.[1] Their own overall compass equals only a portion of that of the foundational voices. The aural illusion of pitch, therefore, is established more effectively by the foundational voices than by the crowns.

Basic Ingredients

Inasmuch as tonal crowns are intended to culminate the Principal ensembles and bring them to richness, fullness, and brilliance, only Principal pipes in moderate and

narrow scales are employed as the ingredients from which
tonal crowns are developed. The higher pitched the crowns,
the narrower the base values for the scales of the pipes
must be. The overall range of scales that find effective
application in tonal crowns are those related to the narrow
Principal, Geigendprincipal, and Salicional species of
pipes, i.e., from about -2 HT to about -10 HT. The mouth
widths are generally 1/4 of the circumference with 2/9 ratios occurring at times among the fifth-sounding members.

The various segments of tonal crowns are normally
composed of unison and fifth-sounding ranks. Among these
will be found segmental courses on 8', 5 1/3', 4', 2 2/3',
2', 1 1/3', 1', 2/3', 1/2', 1/3', 1/4', 1/6', and 1/8'
pitches. Third-sounding ranks, when they do occur, will appear at 3 1/5', 1 3/5', 4/5', and 2/5' pitches. Any pitches
beyond these will appear extremely rarely and then only in
connection with very special dispositions.

Tonal crowns can be presented in tabular or in
graphic form. In tabular form, the method of presentation
should give an effective overview of the various segments
and the pitches of which each segment is comprised. Table
53 shows a Mixture composed of three segments, the first of
which begins at C with 1', 2/3', and 1/2' pitches; the second begins at f♯ with 2', 1 1/3', and 1' pitches; the third
begins at f♯'' with 4', 2 2/3', and 2' pitches. Chart 40

TABLE 53

HYPOTHETICAL DISPOSITION OF III MIXTURE 1'

Segment	Pitches of the Choirs					
C f♯ f♯''			4'	2 2/3' 2'	2' 1 1/3' 1 1/3'	1' 1' 1' 2/3' 1/2'

represents the identical Mixture in graphic form, which
helps to pictorialize the course of the choirs in each of
the segments.

It will be observed that the Mixture is of three
ranks throughout the course of the compass. Each of the
ranks is known as a <u>choir</u>. The lowest-pitched rank is the
<u>bass</u> <u>choir</u>, the highest-pitched one, the <u>treble</u> <u>choir</u>. The
course of the voice is interrupted twice; namely, at points
<u>A</u> and <u>B</u>. These points are referred to as <u>break</u> <u>points</u> and
occur in this example at <u>f-f♯</u> and at <u>f''-f♯''</u>, the two
breaks dividing the course into three <u>segments</u>. The foot
designations of the choirs in the first segment bespeak
their actual pitch at <u>C</u>, those of the second segment represent the foot designations as if the choirs were extended
downward to <u>C</u>, and those of the third segment, likewise.
Each segment occupies a certain range of the entire course.
The first segment has a range of eighteen notes or one and
one-half octaves, the second of twenty-four notes or two

octaves, and the third of nineteen notes or one and one-half octaves. At every break, each choir is interrupted to resume at the sub-octave; when so disposed, the device is known as _repetition_, or more particularly, as _wild_ _repetition_, since the entire configuration sinks by a large interval; in cases where the displacement is not so great, say only a fifth or a fourth, the device may be termed _quasi repetition_ or _mild_ _repetition_, as will be exemplified subsequently.

By inspection of the treble choir it will be noted that over the range of five octaves, the compound voice rises only three octaves in pitch, _i.e._, from 1/2' to 1/16'. In this case, the progress of the voice may be considered as _dynamic_, since the overall rise in pitch exceeds that of the range of any of its segments; in certain cases, where the overall pitch rise does _not_ exceed the range of the individual segments, the progress of the voice may be considered as _static_.

The complexity of the crown derives from the number of ranks it displays in its composition; those of two and three ranks are _meager_ crowns, those of four, five, or six ranks are _moderate_, while those of seven, eight, and more ranks are _rich_ crowns.

The designation of the entire Mixture is derived from the number of its ranks and from the pitch of the

lowest note of the bass choir. The voice under discussion
is, therefore, properly labelled as III Mixture 1'.

Hypothetical Applications

Table 53 and Chart 40 present a rather early method
of laying out a tonal crown; although the disposition exemplified there is rarely used today, it does provide an excellent example for developing the various terms and concepts which are associated with tonal crowns. A more modern
and more general application of the principles of crown disposition appears in Table 54 and Chart 41.

TABLE 54

HYPOTHETICAL DISPOSITION OF III MIXTURE 2'

Segment	Pitches of the Choirs
C̲	2' 1 1/3' 1'
f̲♯̲	2 2/3' 2' 1 1/3'
f̲♯̲''	4' 2 2/3' 2'

An analysis of the layout of the Mixture presented
in Table 54 and Chart 41 reveals the following conditions:

1. Its designation is III Mixture 2'

2. The components are unison and fifth-sounding
members

3. Its complexity is meager, since it is comprised of only three choirs

4. The type of repetition in this case is mild,
since the configuration drops only half an octave at
each break

5. The break points occur at $\underline{f}$-$\underline{f\sharp}$ and at $\underline{f}$''-$\underline{f\sharp}$''

6. The number of breaks throughout the course
equals two

7. The number of segments is three

8. The range of the segments varies between one-
and-one-half and two octaves

9. The overall progress of the crown displays
a dynamic character, traversing four octaves over a
range of five octaves of compass

Frequently the break points occur at other steps in
the compass, and the number of segments is increased in order to culminate the crown below the threshold of acute
pitch discrimination. Table 55 and Chart 42 present a
higher-pitched crown, which requires more and smaller segments, in order, by mild repetition, to stay within reasonable pitch limits.

The layout exhibits a three-rank Mixture of four
breaks and five segments, the break points occurring at $\underline{B}$-$\underline{c}$
and subsequent octaves. The bass choir at 1', defines the
crown. The progress of the voice, inasmuch as it rises
three octaves over a compass of five, is dynamic. The range
of the segments is consistently of one octave.

TABLE 55

HYPOTHETICAL DISPOSITION OF III MIXTURE 1'

Segment	Pitches of the Choirs					
C̲				1'	2/3'	1/2'
c̲				1 1/3'	1'	2/3'
c̲'			2'	1 1/3'	1'	
c̲''		2 2/3'	2'	1 1/3'		
c̲'''	4'	2 2/3'	2'			

Another example, this time of four ranks, will serve
to show a variety of break points and a variety in the
lengths of the segments; the fourth segment also shows an
adjustment of the bass choir to prevent the appearance of a
5 1/3' pitch in a crown intended for a division based upon
8' pitch. The wider spacing between the bass choir and its
next higher companion is called an octave gap above the bass
choir. Table 56 and Chart 43 reveal the disposition of the
crown.

TABLE 56

HYPOTHETICAL DISPOSITION OF IV MIXTURE 2'

Segment	Pitches of the Choirs					
C̲				2'	1 1/3'	1'	2/3'
f̲♯			2 2/3'	2'	1 1/3'	1'	
c̲''		4'	2 2/3'	2'	1 1/3'		
c̲'''	8'	4'	2 2/3'	2'			

The placement of the break points need not necessarily occur at c or f♯, nor need they necessarily be evenly spaced. Uneven spacing produces segments of different ranges. Table 57 and Chart 44 present a layout, where the break points occur after every ten notes.

TABLE 57

HYPOTHETICAL DISPOSITION OF IV MIXTURE 1'

Segment	Pitches of the Choirs								
c						1'	2/3'	1/2'	1/3'
A♯					1 1/3'	1'	2/3'	1/2'	
g♯				2'	1 1/3'	1'	2/3'		
f♯'			2 2/3'	2'	1 1/3'	1'			
e''		4'	2 2/3'	2'	1 1/3'				
d'''	8'	4'	2 2/3'	2'					

The Crown Area

Theoretically, a full crown is one that fills up, so to speak, by means of unison and fifth-sounding ranks, all of the pitch space between its bass choir and the acute threshold of pitch discrimination. To do this without duplication, the ranks are suppressed as they approach the threshold, and the complexity of the crown diminishes by one rank at each half octave of range. Chart 45 shows such a theoretical distribution.

It will be observed from the graph that the crown

diminishes in complexity in its successive segments. Table
58 summarizes this condition.

TABLE 58

COMPLEXITY OF FULL CROWN IN SUCCESSIVE SEGMENTS

Segment	Number of Ranks	Segment	Number of Ranks
C - F	. . . 10	f♯' - b'	. . . 5
F♯ - B	. . . 9	c'' - f''	. . . 4
c - f	. . . 8	f♯'' - b''	. . . 3
f♯ - b	. . . 7	c''' - f'''	. . . 2
c' - f'	. . . 6	f♯''' - c''''	. . . 1

Such a theoretical layout as just exemplified is
never executed in practice; on the contrary, the choirs,
once initiated, are carried through the full range of the
compass. To do this, repetition of some kind is resorted
to, which in turn, results in the appearance of double
choirs as the crown moves forward through the compass. To
show this phenomenon more clearly, the full crown of ten
ranks may be divided into two separate crowns each exhibiting five ranks. The lower crown is repeated every octave,
so that its bass choir assumes an 8' pitch in the last segment. Chart 46 presents such a theoretical layout. The
higher crown may be repeated every half octave, so that its
treble choir never exceeds the acute threshold of pitch discrimination. Chart 47 presents such a layout.

Should the two crowns be combined so as to fill out the entire pitch space between the bass choir and the acute threshold, the choirs will interlace and duplicate each other, so that each successive segment exhibits progressively more double choirs. Chart 48 pictorializes the combination of the two crowns.

Table 59 shows the increase in double choirs as the courses of the crowns move from segment to segment and begin to interlace and overlap more and more.

TABLE 59

RESULTANT DOUBLE CHOIRS BY COMBINATION
OF LOWER AND HIGHER CROWNS

Segment	Number of Ranks			Number of Double Choirs
	Lower Crown	Higher Crown	Total	
$\underline{C}$ — $\underline{F}$	5	5	10	0
$\underline{F\sharp}$ — $\underline{B}$	5	5	10	1
$\underline{c}$ — $\underline{f}$	5	5	10	1
$\underline{f\sharp}$ — $\underline{b}$	5	5	10	2
$\underline{c}'$ — $\underline{f}'$	5	5	10	2
$\underline{f\sharp}'$ — $\underline{b}'$	5	5	10	3
$\underline{c}''$ — $\underline{f}''$	5	5	10	3
$\underline{f\sharp}''$ — $\underline{b}''$	5	5	10	4
$\underline{c}'''$ — $\underline{f}'''$	5	5	10	4
$\underline{f\sharp}'''$ — $\underline{c}''''$	5	5	10	5

In actual practice, the entire possible pitch area

of the crown is not always fully developed; often the area
is divided among several crowns which may then occur in a
single tonal corpus or be distributed among several corpora.
When several crowns appear in an instrument, they are differentiated in various ways:

    1.   They may operate at different pitch levels

    2.   They may show different degrees of complexity

    3.   They may exhibit different segmental ranges

    4.   They may display a different number of seg-
ments in the course

    5.   They may present different break points

    6.   They may be compounded of differently scaled
pipes

    7.   They may be arranged to develop different de-
grees of dynamic progress

In fact, the permutations are so variegated, that it
is impossible to present all cases. The imagination of the
organ builder can be brought into full play in the artistic
disposition of the various tonal crowns within a given instrument.

Classification of Crowns

There has, however, developed historically, a classification of the crowns as derived from the pitch level of
their bass choirs, which seeks to differentiate them from
each other to some degree by appropriate appellations. The

full area of the crown is divisible, in theory, into at least three general areas; namely, low, medium, and high.[2] Depending upon the area in which a given example chiefly operates, the individual crowns are differentiated as Mixtures, Scharfs, and Zimbels. Crowns whose initial bass choirs are predicated upon a pitch of 2 2/3', 2', 1 1/3', or 1' may very well fall into the class of Mixtures, depending to some degree upon the manner in which they are subsequently developed. The Scharf needs to be predicated upon a somewhat higher pitch and requires a somewhat different overall profile than does the Mixture. Initial bass choirs of 1 1/3', 1', 2/3', 1/2', and even 1/3' may serve as the foundation from which Scharfs can be properly developed. The very high pitch region, dwelling near the threshold of acute pitch discrimination, is the characteristic area of the Zimbel. Its bass choirs are likely to be predicated upon 1/2', 1/3', 1/4', 1/6', and possibly 1/8' pitches. Since each classification exhibits a number of possible levels, it is desirable to qualify the various levels within each category as grave, normal, or acute. Table 60 gives a reasonably clear overview of the areas in which each classification of crown may operate, and qualifies the levels within each category. Further divisions of the plenary pitch area of the crown are possible, but serve more readily to confuse than to clarify the concept.

TABLE 60

THE VARIOUS CLASSES OF TONAL CROWNS AND
THEIR THEORETICAL DESIGNATIONS

Classi-fication	Pitch of Initial Bass Choir									
	2 2/3'	2'	1 1/3'	1'	2/3'	1/2'	1/3'	1/4'	1/6'	1/8'
Mixture	G[a]	N[b]	N	A[c]						
Scharf	. .	.	G	N	N	A	A			
Zimbel	. .	.	. .	.	. .	G	N	N	A	A

[a]G: grave. [b]N: normal [c]A: acute.

The Mixture

A few historical examples and modern prospectuses
may serve to show the general pitch level at which the true
Mixture operates, and the various permutations that appear
in the final disposition of the entire course. Chart 49
presents an early example of a Fourniture by Dom Bedos as
recorded by Mahrenholz.[3] The bass choir is predicated upon
2' pitch, the Mixture comprises five ranks, the repetition
is wild, the segments are of various ranges, and the progress of the voice is partly static and partly dynamic. The
upper limit of the compass is not defined, but likely lower
than c''''.

An example of a Mixture by Gottfried Silbermann
shows a very regular disposition. The bass choir is predicated upon a 2' pitch, the Mixture comprises four ranks, the

repetition is mild, the segments are of fairly equal range, and the progress of the voice is consistently dynamic. The upper limit of the compass is not defined by Mahrenholz, from whom the example is derived.[4] See Chart 50.

A modern layout for a III-V Mixture is proposed by Ellerhorst and presented in Chart 51, where it appears in graphic form.[5] The bass choir is predicated upon 2' pitch; the voice comprises three ranks in the first segment, four in the second, and five in the remainder; the repetition is generally mild except after the fourth segment, where the treble choir repeats wild; the segments are of equal ranges; the fourth segment exhibits an octave gap below the treble choir; and the progress is consistently dynamic.

A modern example exhibiting double choirs is proposed by Dr. Elis and quoted by Ellerhorst.[6] The bass choir is predicated upon 1 1/3' pitch, the Mixture comprises from four to six ranks, the repetition is consistently mild, the segments are of various ranges, one or two double choirs appear in the various segments, and the progress of the voice is dynamic. Chart 52 presents the layout as given by Ellerhorst.

A few additional observations may be helpful in refining the delineation of the Mixture class of crown. Smets points out that when double choirs are introduced into a Mixture, they must of necessity be developed from different scales, in order to forestall interference between pipes of the same pitch.[7] Mixtures of the Great division may be fairly bold, whereas those of secondary divisions must be so dimensioned and voiced as to be usable with only one or two foundational voices.[8] The disposition of a Mixture must be influenced by other crowns which a given division or an entire instrument may incorporate into its tonal plan.[9] Mixtures ought to be developed from moderate (Principal) or moderately-narrow scales (Geigendprincipal). Wider dimensions fail to produce adequate clarity and brilliance.[10] Ellerhorst indicates that the fifth-sounding ranks should be of somewhat wider scale (+1 to +2 HT) than the unison-sounding ranks, and should be equipped with slightly narrower mouths, about 9/40 of the circumference.[11] Supper derives the complexity of the crown from the Principalbasis of the division in which the Mixture is to appear.[12] He presupposes that the unison and quint pitches which lie between the foundational Principal and the bass choir of the Mixture are supplied in moderate-scaled Principal voices as independent registers. Should the 2' Octave not occur as an independent register, the crown must then contain it and so be increased by one choir. See Table 61.

The Scharf

The Scharf operates generally in the medium region of the crown area and normally exhibits less complexity than

TABLE 61

REQUISITE COMPLEXITY OF THE MIXTURE[a]

Principal-basis	Complexity of Crown (Number of Ranks)	Additional Ranks for Missing 2' Octave	Additional Ranks for Each Reed in Division
8'	4	1	1
4'	3	1	1
2'	2		1

[a]After W. Supper, *Fibel der Orgeldisposition* (Kassel, 1946), p. 14.

does the Mixture. Its name, which denotes "sharp" or "keen", derives from its pitch level and from its customary narrow scaling. The true Scharf, as Smets would have it, must be from two to three half-tones narrower than the Mixture.[13] For this reason, the name is sometimes, albeit unfortunately, applied to crowns which operate in the usual pitch level of the Mixture but are differentiated from it by narrower-scaled pipes.

When properly conceived and laid out, the Scharf is, so to say, the "Octave" of the Mixture, even though its bass choir may lie only a half octave above that of the Mixture. Such a condition usually prevails when the Scharf appears in another tonal corpus from that of the Mixture. Should the two crowns lie superposed in the same division, their bass choirs are likely to be at least an octave apart, so that

the lower one or two choirs of the Scharf overlap the upper
one or two choirs of the Mixture; when so disposed, double
choirs will appear throughout the course of the two crowns
when drawn together.

The definitive level of the Scharf in any given case
depends greatly upon which voices lie underneath it in the
same division, or which other species of crowns may be associated with it in other divisions of the same instrument.
Several types of Scharf have historically been delineated by
noteworthy organ builders and theorists.

The first example of the Scharf is one which is compounded of alternate unison and fifth-sounding ranks. Chart
53 presents the layout for such an example, the initial segment of which is recommended by Smets and the development of
the voice supplied by the present author.[14] The configuration exhibits a Scharf at a normal pitch of 1', of four
ranks, of five segments, of alternate unison and fifth-
sounding components, displaying an octave gap above the bass
choir in the last segment, and showing a partly dynamic and
partly static progression.

The second example is one which is dated 1619 and
quoted by Mahrenholz.[15] The upper limit of the compass is
not defined. The configuration exhibits a Scharf of four
ranks, of 2/3' pitch, of four segments, of an octave range
per segment, of wild repetition, and displaying a generally

static progression. See Chart 54.

The third example introduces a double choir into each segment. The Scharf is dated 1682 and quoted by Mahrenholz.[16] The configuration exhibits a Scharf of five ranks predicated upon a 1' bass choir with an internal double choir, of alternate unison and fifth-sounding ranks, of three segments, of wild repetition, and showing a partly static and partly dynamic progression. The upper limit is not defined. See Chart 55.

The fourth example shows a grave Scharf which also contains double choirs. The disposition is one by Arp Schnitger for the Rueckpositive of St. Jacobi, Hamburg, as quoted by Mahrenholz.[17] The configuration comprises from six to eight ranks predicated upon an initial bass choir of 1 1/3' pitch, alternate unison and fifth-sounding members, six segments, irregular repetition, double choirs, and combined dynamic and static progressions. The upper limit of the compass is not defined. See Chart 56.

The fifth example is a Baroque Scharf quoted by Mahrenholz.[18] Its pitch level places it into the class of acute Scharf. The configuration comprises three ranks predicated upon a 1/2' bass choir, alternate unison and fifth-sounding members, three segments of similar and dissimilar ranges, wild repetition, and combined static and dynamic progressions. The upper limit of the compass is given as c''', See Chart 57.

The sixth example presents a Scharf which shows an octave gap above its bass choir. The initial segment is suggested by Smets, while the remaining segments were developed by the present author.[19] The configuration comprises four ranks predicated upon a bass choir of 1' pitch, unison and fifth-sounding members displaying an octave gap above the bass choir, four segments of various ranges, wild repetition, and a combination of dynamic and static progressions. See Chart 58.

The seventh example shows, as it were, an inversion of the sixth, whereby the octave gap appears in certain segments underneath the treble choir. The layout is recommended by Ellerhorst and appears in Chart 59 in graphic form.[20]

The eighth example is a Scharf containing, beside unison and fifth-sounding ranks, also a third-sounding member. The example, quoted by Mahrenholz, is reputedly to have been the first Scharf equipped with a Tierce.[21] It is, according to Smets, by Joachim Wagner, an organ builder of the eighteenth century.[22] Note that although the unisons and quints break by mild repetition, the breaks of the Tierce are so staggered as to shift by one octave in every case; the Tierce rank is consistently retained as an inner member of the configuration. See Chart 60.

The Zimbel

The Zimbel operates in the very high region of the crown area, dwelling, throughout the range of its compass, near the acute threshold of pitch discrimination. For this reason, the voice exhibits many break points and a proportionately large number of segments, each of a very limited range. These conditions force the voice into a static progression, only occasionally modified to show a mild overall pitch rise over the entire compass.

Of all the classes of crowns, the Zimbel is least complex; in its best models it may contain as few as one rank and hardly ever more than three; in relation to the Mixture, which tends to be disposed richly, and the Scharf, which normally exhibits a moderate complexity, the Zimbel is likely to be meager.

For the Zimbel to be an effective voice, it must be constructed of very narrow scales. The scale of the Salicional represents its narrowest realization (-5 to -8 HT) and that of the Geigendprincipal, its widest (-2 to -5 HT).[23]

The question as to whether the Zimbel represents the upper region of the crown area (being considered as a detachment of the full crown), or whether it represents the ultimate culmination of the mutation and mixed voice fund of the organ, is perennially debated by the various organ theorists. Some feel that at the acute threshold of pitch discrimination, the two concepts (that of the Zimbel as the culmination of the Principal choir or as the peak of the feminine class of voices) merge and fuse, as it were, so that the Zimbel may be considered as the final peak of either group.

The level of the Zimbel is established by the pitch of the initial bass choir. Zimbels predicated upon a 1/2' bass choir may be considered as grave, those on 1/3' or 1/4' as normal, while those on 1/6' or 1/8' as acute.

The voice appears in three types. The first type contains only unison-sounding members, the second unison and fifth-sounding, while the third introduces also a third-sounding rank. To differentiate the different types, the terms Octavezimbel, Quintzimbel, and Terzzimbel are generally employed. A few historical examples and modern prospectuses will help to refine the delineation of the Zimbel.

The first example is a modern prospectus for a three-rank Octavezimbel presented by Mahrenholz.[24] The bass choir, at an initial pitch of 1/4', indicates a normal level for the voice. The configuration exhibits only unison-sounding ranks, and is partially double-choired. The repetition is wild, and its regularity establishes a static progression. Mahrenholz suggests the scale of the Salicional or even a narrower one as appropriate (-5 to -10 HT). See Chart 61.

The second example is a Quintzimbel of two ranks; it
is from the early period of German organbuilding and is
quoted by Mahrenholz.[25] The initial bass choir, at a pitch
of 1/6', indicates an acute level for the voice. The layout
is comprised of a unison and a fifth-sounding member, repeating by the interval of an octave at every octave of the
course. The progression is consistently static. The upper
limit of the compass is not defined. See Chart 62.

The third example is a Quintzimbel of three ranks;
it is from the early period of German organbuilding and is
quoted by Mahrenholz.[26] The bass choir, at an initial pitch
of 1/4', places the Zimbel at what may be considered a normal level for this voice. The repetition is wild, inasmuch
as the whole configuration drops an entire octave at the
break points. The range of the segments is unusually great
for a Zimbel, but bespeaks the earlier practice in this respect. The voice exhibits a static progression. Each segment is comprised of two unison and one fifth-sounding member. The upper limit of the compass is not defined. See
Chart 63.

The fourth example is a III Terzzimbel from the Arp
Schnitger organ at St. Jacobi in Hamburg, as presented by
Smets.[27] It is generally considered an unsurpassed model
from the classical era of organbuilding. It is an acute
form of the Zimbel, as indicated by the pitch of 1/6' for

its initial bass choir. In the successive segments of the
course, the third-sounding rank appears in the upper two
choirs but never in the bass choir. The scheme of repetition compounds both the mild and wild forms. The frequent
break points already prognosticate the modern practice of
continuous repetition. The progression is consistently
static. A unison, a fifth, and a third-sounding rank appear
in each segment. The upper limit of the compass is not defined. See Chart 64.

The fifth example is a Terzzimbel of three ranks as
proposed by Dr. Elis and presented by Ellerhorst.[28] Its
overall pitch level is slightly lower than that of the previous example, and approaches, for this reason, the normal
level of the Zimbel class. The Tierce rank is replaced by
a unison member in the last segment of the course. The repetition pattern is compounded of wild and mild forms, with
the Tierce appearing in the lower two choirs but never in
the treble choir. Break points occur twice per octave except in the last segment, producing thereby segments of
short range. The progression is largely static, but does
exhibit a dynamic character in the last segment. See Chart
65.

The sixth example is another Terzzimbel of three
ranks proposed by Dr. Elis and presented by Ellerhorst.[29]
It differs from the preceding example in that it begins at

grave pitch level for a Zimbel (2/5'). Inasmuch as a dy-
amic progression characterizes the voice throughout the
ourse of the compass, the entire pitch area of the Zimbel
s traversed. The Tierce rank appears in all three choirs--
ass, middle, and treble. The repetition pattern is con-
istently mild and shows frequent break points. See Chart
6.

The seventh example is a modern Terzzimbel of three
anks by Herman Schlicker, incorporated into the Positive of
he instrument at Grace Lutheran, River Forest, Illinois.[30]
redicated upon an initial bass choir of 1/5', and exhibi-
ing a dynamic progression, it still operates entirely with-
n the Zimbel area; in fact, it belongs to the class of a-
ute Zimbels. The Tierce rank appears as a bass, treble,
nd interior choir. The repetition pattern is compounded of
oth wild and mild forms and, inasmuch as the breaks occur
wice per octave, may be said to be continuous. See Chart
57.

NOTES AND REFERENCES

PART I

Chapter I: Notes and References

As expounded in M. Praetorius, Syntagmatis Musici Tomus
Secundus De Organographia . . . (Wolfenbuettel, 1619; fac-
simile ed. by W. Gurlitt, Kassel, 1929) and illustrated in
M. Praetorius, Syntagmatis Musici Theatrum Instrumentorum
seu Sciagraphia . . . (Wolfenbuettel, 1620; facs. ed. by
W. Gurlitt, Kassel, 1929).

See Plates I through VII of the Atlas for illustration of
the technical terms.

G. A. Audsley, The Art of Organ Building (New York, 1905),
II, 677.

Audsley, Art . . ., II, 677.

Audsley, Art . . ., II, 653.

Dom Bedos, L'Art du Facteur d'Orgues (1766; facs. by C.
Mahrenholz, Kassel, 1934), I, Planche XII, fig. 99 and 100.

J. G. Toepfer and M. Allihn, Die Theorie und Praxis des
Orgelbaues (2nd ed.; Weimar, 1888), Atlas Tafel I, fig. 42.

Chapter II: Notes and References

1 C. Mahrenholz, Die Orgelregister, ihre Geschichte und ihr
   Bau (2nd ed.; Kassel, 1942); Die Berechnung der Orgel-
   pfeifenmensuren (Kassel, 1938); Die neue Orgel in der St.
   Marienkirche zu Goettingen (Kassel, 1931).

2 H. H. Jahnn, "Registernamen und ihr Inhalt," Beitraege zur
   Organistentagung Hamburg-Luebeck / 6. bis 8. Juli, 1925
   (Klecken, 1925), pp. 5-25.

3 W. Supper, Die Orgeldisposition, eine Heranfuering
   (Kassel, 1950); Fibel der Orgeldisposition (Kassel, 1946).

4 W. Ellerhorst, Handbuch der Orgelkunde (Einsiedeln, 1936).

5 J. G. Toepfer and P. Smets, Lehrbuch der Orgelbaukunst
   (4 vols.; 4th and 5th ed.; Mainz, 1955). P. Smets, Die
   Orgelregister, ihr Klang und Gebrauch (Mainz, 1943).

6 Discrepancies between the frequencies given and those expected are caused by the temperament.

7 Such tables usually give the velocity of sound at 0° Centigrade or the equivalent 32° Fahrenheit.

8 After Grueneisen and Merkel, Annalen der Physik, Bd. 66,
   Jg. 1921. Quoted by Mahrenholz, Die Orgelregister . . .,
   p. 10.

9 C. D. Hodgman and others, Handbook of Chemistry and
   Physics (38th ed.; Cleveland, 1956), p. 2889.

10 Ellerhorst, Handbuch . . ., p. 212.

11 Ellerhorst, Handbuch . . ., p. 212.

12 Ellerhorst, Handbuch . . ., p. 212.

13 Ellerhorst, Handbuch . . ., p. 212.

14 R. Gerhardt, Nova Acta Academiae Naturae Curiosorum, Band
   47, and re-expressed by Mahrenholz, Orgelregister . . .,
   p. 112, footnote 1.

15 Mahrenholz, Orgelregister . . ., p. 111-12.

16 Mahrenholz, Orgelregister . . ., p. 167.

17 Mahrenholz, Orgelregister . . ., p. 163.

Chapter III: Notes and References

The cutup is the distance between the upper and lower lips, expressed as a ratio of the height of the mouth to its width; thus, C = H/W, where C is the ratio of the cutup, H the height of the mouth, and W the width of it.

A psychological expression used to refer to the capacity of a tone to fill a given acoustical volume (G. Trag-faehigkeit).

Thus: D/L = 10/100 or 1/10, where D is the diameter, and L the length of the corpus.

Thus: c/C = 1/2 or C/c = 2/1, where c is the shorter or higher pipe, and C the longer or lower pipe of the octave.

J. G. Toepfer and Max Allihn, Die Theorie und Praxis des Orgelbaues (2nd ed.; Weimar, 1888), pp. 122ff.

Toepfer, Theorie . . ., pp. 130-33.

Toepfer consistently developed his ratios from the cross-sectional areas (G. Flaechenverhaeltnisse). Today, diam-eter values (linear dimensions) are preferred, so the necessary conversions must be made.

Derivation thus: If a is the cross-sectional area of the smaller (higher octave) pipe, A that of the larger (lower octave) pipe, r and R the respective radiuses, and d and D the respective diameters, then

$$\frac{a}{A} = \frac{\pi r^2}{\pi R^2} \; ; \quad \text{by expressing } r \text{ and } R \text{ in terms of } d \text{ and } D:$$

$$\frac{a}{A} = \frac{\pi(d/2)^2}{\pi(D/2)^2} = \frac{\pi d^2/4}{\pi D^2/4} = \frac{\pi d^2 4}{\pi D^2 4} = \frac{d^2}{D^2} \circ \quad \text{If } \frac{a}{A} = \frac{d^2}{D^2}$$

$$\text{then } \frac{d}{D} = \sqrt{\frac{a}{A}} \circ \quad \text{Hence, if } \frac{a}{A} = \frac{1}{\sqrt{8}},$$

$$\text{then } \frac{d}{D} = \sqrt{\frac{1}{\sqrt{8}}} = \frac{1}{\sqrt[4]{8}} \circ$$

Derivation thus: If the octave ratio of the diameters is

Chapter III: Notes and References--Continued

$\dfrac{1}{\sqrt[4]{8}}$, then the step ratio will be equal to the twelfth

root of the same; thus, $\sqrt[12]{\dfrac{1}{\sqrt[4]{8}}} = \dfrac{1}{\sqrt[48]{8}} = \dfrac{1}{\sqrt[48]{2^3}} =$

$\dfrac{1}{\sqrt[16]{2}}$.

10 Observe the actual handling of the step ratio when calculating diameters:

Case 1: Suppose the diameter of the next larger
(lower) pipe is sought; B when c is given:

If $\dfrac{c}{B} = \dfrac{1}{\sqrt[16]{2}}$, then B $= c\sqrt[16]{2}$.

Case 2: Suppose the diameter of the next smaller
(higher) pipe is sought; c♯ when c is given:

If $\dfrac{c}{c\sharp} = \dfrac{\sqrt[16]{2}}{1}$, then c♯ $= \dfrac{c}{\sqrt[16]{2}}$.

11 Derivation thus: If x is the serial number of the step
which will double the original value, and since one step
is equal to $\sqrt[16]{2^1}$, then the double measure 2 $= \sqrt[16]{2^x}$.
By solving for the unknown quantity x:

$(\log 2) = \dfrac{x(\log 2)}{16}$ or $x = \dfrac{(\log 2)\,16}{(\log 2)} = 16.$

12 Toepfer, Theorie . . ., pp. 139-40.

13 C. Mahrenholz, Die Orgelregister, ihre Geschichte und
ihr Bau (2nd ed.; Kassel, 1942), pp. 13-14, footnote 2.

14 The value given (i.e., 154.17 mm. for C) is the equivalent of the one adopted by the Freiberger Orgelkommission
(i.e., 155.5 mm. for C). The apparent difference is the
result of the divergent standard pitches used in Europe
and America. The method of conversion must take into

Chapter III: Notes and References--Continued

consideration the operation of two ratios: one for the lengths and one for the diameters. See Appendix D, 2 for a full discussion of the requisite mathematical proposi- tions to effect the conversion; a full table of values over the entire compass is presented there as well, which exhibits a base value of 154.17 mm. for the diameter of $\underline{C}$ 8'.

15 By using $1/\sqrt[16]{2}$ as the step ratio:

$$\frac{C}{C\sharp} = \frac{\sqrt[16]{2}}{1} \text{ , hence } C\sharp = \frac{C}{\sqrt[16]{2}} = \frac{154.17}{\sqrt[16]{2}} = 147.63 \text{ mm.}$$

All the other notes for the prime segment of the compass may be computed from the base $\underline{C}$ as follows, by substitut- ing $\underline{1}$ for the value of $\underline{C}$:

$$C = 1 \text{ ; } C\sharp = \frac{1}{\sqrt[16]{2}} \text{ ; } D = \frac{1}{\sqrt[8]{2}} \text{ ; } D\sharp = \frac{1}{\sqrt[16]{2^3}} \text{ ;}$$

$$E = \frac{1}{\sqrt[4]{2}} \text{ ; } F = \frac{1}{\sqrt[16]{2^5}} \text{ ; } F\sharp = \frac{1}{\sqrt[8]{2^3}} \text{ ; } G = \frac{1}{\sqrt[16]{2^7}} \text{ ;}$$

$$G\sharp = \frac{1}{\sqrt[2]{2}} \text{ ; } A = \frac{1}{\sqrt[16]{2^9}} \text{ ; } A\sharp = \frac{1}{\sqrt[8]{2^5}} \text{ ; } B = \frac{1}{\sqrt[16]{2^{11}}} \text{ ;}$$

$$c = \frac{1}{\sqrt[4]{2^3}} \text{ ; } c\sharp = \frac{1}{\sqrt[16]{2^{13}}} \text{ ; } d = \frac{1}{\sqrt[8]{2^7}} \text{ ; } d\sharp = \frac{1}{\sqrt[16]{2^{15}}} \text{ ;}$$

$e = \frac{1}{2}$. Having thus arrived at the half-measure, one can

derive the values for the remaining segments of the com- pass by direct multiplication or division of the values of the prime segment. It is considerably easier to compute the values in a descending series, beginning with $\underline{e}$ as base, and using the value of 77.09 mm. in place of 154.17 mm. The equations would then be set up, using the recip- rocals of the previous ratios. By substituting $\underline{1}$ for the value of $\underline{e}$,

$$e = 1; \quad d\sharp = 1 \times \sqrt[16]{2} \text{ ; } d = 1 \times \sqrt[8]{2} \text{ ; } c\sharp = 1 \times \sqrt[16]{2^3} \text{ ;}$$

$$c = 1 \times \sqrt[4]{2} \text{ ; } B = 1 \times \sqrt[16]{2^5} \text{ ; } A\sharp = 1 \times \sqrt[8]{2^3} \text{ ;}$$

Chapter III: Notes and References--Continued

$$A = 1 \times \sqrt[16]{2^7} \;; \quad G\sharp\!\!\sharp = 1 \times \sqrt[2]{2} \;; \quad G = 1 \times \sqrt[16]{2^9} \;;$$

$$F\sharp\!\!\sharp = 1 \times \sqrt[8]{2^5} \;; \quad F = 1 \times \sqrt[16]{2^{11}} \;; \quad E = 1 \times \sqrt[4]{2^3} \;;$$

$$D\sharp\!\!\sharp = 1 \times \sqrt[16]{2^{13}} \;; \quad D = 1 \times \sqrt[8]{2^7} \;; \quad C\sharp\!\!\sharp = 1 \times \sqrt[16]{2^{15}} \;;$$

$$C = 2.$$

16 The fourth quadrant is understood as the grid of a Cartesian coordinate system comprising the negative Y-axis area of the positive X-axis area and circumscribed by angles ranging from 0° to -90° or from +270° to +360°.

17 For purposes of reference, this value (154.17 mm.) becomes O, and is often shown as 0 HT (zero half-tones). Should, in another case, the next greater tabular value (160.99 mm., see Appendix D, 2) be desired as the base, it would be referred to as +1 HT (plus one half-tone); should the next lesser tabular value (147.63 mm.) be desired, it would be referred to as -1 HT (minus one half-tone).

18 If the base O = 154.17 mm., then 1/2 = 77.09 mm., $(1/2)^2$ = 38.54 mm., $(1/2)^3$ = 19.27 mm., and $(1/2)^4$ = 9.64 mm. See Appendix D, 2. These values represent the origin (0 HT), sixteenth, thirty-second, forty-eighth, and sixty-fourth steps in the table. By interpolation, all other values are obtainable from the graph. On the ordinate (Y-axis), the tabular values for C$\sharp\!\!\sharp$, D, D$\sharp\!\!\sharp$, E, etc. lie on the successive downward calibrations from the origin O. Each calibration on the Y-axis represents a tabular diameter-dimension equal to one half-tone; downward, a half-tone smaller (-1 HT), upward, a half-tone larger (+1 HT).

19 Such values, taken from the table in Appendix D, 2, are as follows: 0 HT = 154.17 mm. for C; +1 HT = 160.99 mm. for C; +2 HT = 168.12 mm. for C; +3 HT = 175.57 mm. for C; +4 HT = 183.34 mm. for C; and +5 HT = 191.46 mm. for C.

20 Such values, taken from the table in Appendix D, 2, are as follows: 0 HT = 154.17 mm. for C; -1 HT = 147.63 mm. for C; -2 HT = 141.36 mm. for C; -3 HT = 135.38 mm. for C; -4 HT = 129.64 mm. for C; -5 HT = 124.14 mm. for C.

21 For a static constant scale, the octave ratio of diminution is exclusively $1/\sqrt[4]{8}$ for the diameters, or $1/\sqrt{8}$ for the cross-sectional areas.

22 For an increasing constant scale, the octave ratio of diminution may be $1/\sqrt[17]{2^{12}}$; $1/\sqrt[3]{4}$; $1/\sqrt[19]{2^{12}}$; $1/\sqrt[5]{8}$; $1/\sqrt[7]{16}$; $1/\sqrt[11]{64}$; etc. See Appendix H.

23 For a decreasing constant scale, the octave ratio of diminution may be $1/\sqrt[5]{16}$; $1/\sqrt[7]{64}$; $1/\sqrt[13]{2^{12}}$; $1/2$; etc. See Appendix H.

24 Inasmuch as the area of Principal tone permits a latitude of from -5 HT to +4 HT, neither of the two scales, 2a nor 2b, actually moves outside the general field of Principal tone; they move only in the direction of String or Flute tone.

25 Since the step ratio for the bridge is $\dfrac{1}{\sqrt[10]{\dfrac{t_1}{p_2}}}$, the various steps are computed as follows: 30th step = t_1 ;

$$31\text{st step} = \frac{t_1}{\sqrt[10]{(t_1/p_2)}} \; ; \quad 32\text{nd step} = \frac{t_1}{\sqrt[5]{(t_1/p_2)}} \; ;$$

$$33\text{rd step} = \frac{t_1}{\sqrt[10]{(t_1/p_2)^3}} \; ; \quad 34\text{th step} = \frac{t_1}{\sqrt[5]{(t_1/p_2)^2}} \; ;$$

$$35\text{th step} = \frac{t_1}{\sqrt[2]{(t_1/p_2)}} \; ; \quad 36\text{th step} = \frac{t_1}{\sqrt[5]{(t_1/p_2)^3}} \; ;$$

$$37\text{th step} = \frac{t_1}{\sqrt[10]{(t_1/p_2)^7}} \; ; \quad 38\text{th step} = \frac{t_1}{\sqrt[5]{(t_1/p_2)^4}} \; ;$$

$$39\text{th step} = \frac{t_1}{\sqrt[10]{(t_1/p_2)^9}} \; ; \quad 40\text{th step} = p_2 \; .$$

Chapter IV: Notes and References

1 The circumferences are often expressed as the width of
the plate, i.e., the width of the rectangular plate of
metal immediately after cutting from stock, and before
the corpus is shaped into a cylinder.

2 The ratio may be expressed in terms of the diameters as
well, because the circumferences and the diameters, being linear dimensions in the same progression, proceed
in the same ratio of diminution throughout the compass;
if R_m = W/C and C = Dπ , then R_m = W/Dπ , where $\underline{R}_m$ is the
ratio of the mouth, $\underline{W}$ the width of it, $\underline{C}$ the circumference of the corpus, and $\underline{D}$ its diameter.

3 The term unit ratios refers to all ratios which exhibit a
numerator of 1.

4 Thus, if $\underline{C}$ 8' is to have a diameter of 168.12 mm. (i.e.,
the diameter of $\underline{A}\sharp$ 16' of the Normprincipal), then, in
order for this pipe to have a 1/4 mouth, its dimension
must be 132.04 mm. (i.e., the mouth width of $\underline{A}\sharp$ 16' of
the Normprincipal).

5 H. Jahnn, "Registernamen und ihr Inhalt," Beitraege zur
Organistentagung Hamburg-Luebeck / 6. bis 8. Juli 1925
(Klecken, 1925), pp. 5-25. Mahrenholz, Orgelregister
. . ., pp. 37-125. W. Ellerhorst, Handbuch der Orgelkunde (Einsiedeln, 1936), pp. 227-50.

Chapter V: Notes and References

1 A plenum registration is necessary for all organ music in which the parts are to be treated as equal but not characteristic; such as hymns, chorales, fugues, many preludes, and the like. It is compounded of an aequal member and consecutive partial pitches, all of which may be Group I registers. If both groups of voices are to be marshaled for plenum purposes, then the inferior pitches may be represented by voices from Group II, while the superior pitches must be of Group I.

Background registrations are made up entirely of registers from Group II. An aequal member is required, upon which may be superposed one, two, or even three partial pitches. No interior foundational pitches (8', 4', 2') may be omitted from the combination. The purpose of the registration is to provide a clear, yet recessive tone color, suitable for background purposes.

Solo registrations are developed from registers of Group II. An aequal member serves as the basic ingredient, to which are then added one or several unison or mutation voices of higher pitch; the combination must exhibit the lack of an interior foundational pitch. In some instances a register from Group I may serve as the basic ingredient or as an interior unison member. The registration must develop a characteristic tone color, suitable for presenting a cantus in the foreground.

2 See chapter vi for delineation of the "Mutation" concept.

3 See chapter vi for delineation of the "Mixed Voice" concept.

4 C. Mahrenholz, Die Orgelregister, ihre Geschichte und ihr Bau (2nd ed.; Kassel, 1942), pp. 37-121. H. Jahnn, "Registernamen und ihr Inhalt," Beitraege zur Organistentagung Hamburg-Luebeck / 6. bis 8. Juli 1925 (Klecken, 1925), pp. 5-25. W. Ellerhorst, Handbuch der Orgelkunde (Einsiedeln, 1936), pp. 227-250.

Chapter VI: Notes and References

1 Dom Bedos, L'Art du Facteur d'Orgues (1766; facs. ed. by C. Mahrenholz, Kassel, 1934), I, 39.

2 Paul Smets, Die Orgelregister, ihr Klang und Gebrauch (Mainz, 1943), pp. 103, 170-71.

3 Hans Klotz, Das Buch von der Orgel (5th ed.; Kassel, 1955), p. 42.

4 Smets, Orgelregister . . ., p. 103.

5 The acute threshold of pitch discrimination is a conventionally accepted frequency level, beyond which the ear is supposedly unable to differentiate one pitch from another.

6 C. Mahrenholz, Die Orgelregister, ihre Geschichte und ihr Bau (2nd ed.; Kassel, 1942), pp. 37-125; 193-257. H. Jahnn, "Registernamen und ihr Inhalt," Beitraege zur Organistentagung Hamburg-Luebeck / 6. bis 8. Juli 1925 (Klecken, 1925), pp. 5-25. Smets, Orgelregister . . ., pp. 1-320.

7 Mahrenholz, Orgelregister . . . . Jahnn, "Registernamen . . . ." Smets, Orgelregister . . . .

8 Such as the None (8/9'), Undecime (8/11'), or Tredecime (8/13').

9 The discant region comprises the upper area of the Manual compass, usually beginning at c' or nearby.

10 A. Schlick, Spiegel der Orgelmacher und Organisten . . . (1511; newprint by Flade, Kassel, 1951), p. 28. S. Virdung, Musica getutscht . . . (1511; facs. ed. by L. Schrade, Kassel, 1931) p. Diij.

11 Smets, Orgelregister . . ., pp. 238 and 119.

Chapter VII: Notes and References

1 The acute threshold of pitch discrimination is a conventionally accepted frequency level, beyond which the ear is supposedly unable to differentiate one pitch from another. In organbuilding, a frequency level of from 8,000 to 8,500 cycles per second is usually taken as the practical limit.

2 The division of the crown area into three sections is not necessarily accepted by all theorists, nor has it always been manifest in the practice; some theorists and certain historical periods seem to recognize only a two-fold division of the plenary area.

3 C. Mahrenholz, Die Orgelregister, ihre Geschichte und ihr Bau (2nd ed.; Kassel, 1942), p. 217 and footnote 1 on same page.

4 Mahrenholz, Orgelregister . . ., p. 218.

5 W. Ellerhorst, Handbuch der Orgelkunde (Einsiedeln, 1936), p. 236.

6 Ellerhorst, Handbuch . . ., p. 239.

7 P. Smets, Die Orgelregister, Ihr Klang und Gebrauch (Mainz, 1943), p. 162.

8 Smets, Orgelregister . . ., p. 163.

9 Smets, Orgelregister . . ., p. 162.

10 Smets, Orgelregister . . ., p. 162.

11 Ellerhorst, Handbuch . . ., p. 235.

12 W. Supper, Fibel der Orgeldisposition (Kassel, 1946), p. 14.

13 Smets, Orgelregister . . ., pp. 236-37.

14 Smets, Orgelregister . . ., p. 236.

15 Mahrenholz, Orgelregister . . ., p. 216.

16 Mahrenholz, Orgelregister . . ., p. 216.

17 Mahrenholz, Orgelregister . . ., p. 223.

Chapter VII: Notes and References--Continued

18 Mahrenholz, Orgelregister . . ., p. 223.

19 Smets, Orgelregister . . ., p. 236.

20 Ellerhorst, Handbuch . . ., p. 244.

21 Mahrenholz, Orgelregister . . ., p. 229, footnote 2.

22 Smets, Orgelregister . . ., p. 236.

23 Mahrenholz, Orgelregister . . ., pp. 249, 250.

24 Mahrenholz, Orgelregister . . ., p. 250.

25 Mahrenholz, Orgelregister . . ., p. 251.

26 Mahrenholz, Orgelregister . . ., p. 251.

27 Smets, Orgelregister . . ., p. 32.

28 Ellerhorst, Handbuch . . ., p. 248.

29 Ellerhorst, Handbuch . . ., p. 248.

30 By interview with Mr. Herman Schlicker, president of
   Schlicker Organ Company, Buffalo, New York.

PART II

THE EARLY BAROQUE ORGAN:

MECHANICS AND PNEUMATICS

CHAPTER VIII

SINGLE CHEST MECHANISMS--
TRANSIENT COUPLING

Two basic forms of chest were in current use at the time of Praetorius and were definitely known by him. These were the spring chest and the slider chest. Essentially, these chests differed only in their stop actions, and it is for this reason that the device used for engaging or disengaging the stops became the appellation for the chest itself.

The Spring Chest

Mechanical Disposition

Both forms of chest, spring and slider, were developed side by side. They are identical in all respects except for the stop actions. In the spring chest, the stop is controlled by multiple pallet valves known as stop pallets, which are mounted inside the tone channel and seated against the under side of the table, whereas in the slider chest the stop is controlled by means of a slider mounted outside and above the tone channel, and seated against the upper side of the table.

247

A schematic drawing of the basic operational mechanism of the spring chest is presented on Plate LVIII. Whenever the bellows are operated, the pallet box $\underline{A}$ is supplied
with wind under pressure. The tracker $\underline{B}$ together with the
pull-down $\underline{C}$ is connected to the appropriate manual or pedal
key, as the case may be. When a key is depressed, the corresponding pallet valve $\underline{D}$ is pulled away from its seat and
the wind is admitted into the appropriate channel $\underline{E}$ which,
running latitudinally across the whole chest, is able to
communicate with any or every pipe of the corresponding note
on the chest. A stop pallet valve $\underline{F}$, is provided for each
pipe on the chest. A whole series of these, comprising the
valves for all of the pipes of one register, are harnessed
together and activated by a series of stickers $\underline{G}$ provided
with heads which, in turn, are engaged or disengaged by
means of a stop beam $\underline{H}$, which is raised by the tension of
the valve springs $\underline{I}$ when the stop is "off", and lowered (as
shown at $\underline{J}$), thus depressing the gang of stickers $\underline{G}$ and
opening the valves $\underline{K}$ for all the pipes of a given stop, when
the stop is "on". Accordingly, whenever wind is admitted to
the channel $\underline{E}$, by action of the key pallet valve $\underline{D}$, it will
immediately be admitted also to the appropriate note or pipe
whose stop pallet valve $\underline{K}$ is depressed or in the "on" position. The wind thus admitted excites the pipe $\underline{M}$. When the
stop-beam $\underline{H}$ is in the "off" position, its stop pallet valves
$\underline{F}$ will be closed and so no wind is admitted from the channel

E to the pipe M, even though a key may be depressed. Upon releasing the key, the key pallet D returns, by action of its spring L, to its position of rest, thus cutting off the wind to the channel E, and thereby also to the pipe M, causing the same to remain silent, no matter if the stop-beam H or J is in the "off" or "on" position.

The spring chest, during the time of the Early Baroque, appeared much more seldom than the slider chest, because of the greater expense and time involved in its construction and also, reputedly, because of its propensity toward malfunction. Klotz points out that among the organs built during the golden age of German organ building (ca. 1500-1775) and still in existence today, more than 99% are constructed of slider chests, and the balance (ca. 1%) of spring chests.[1]

Praetorius' Description

Praetorius has the following to say about the spring chest of his time:

Das XII. Capitel	Chapter XII
. . . .	. . . .
Welcher gestalt die Spring-laden / so wol auch die Schleiffladen anfangs her-fuer kommen.	In what form the spring chests, as well as the slider chests, originated.
EHe aber die Invention der Schleiffen / (darvon oben im 7. Cap. meldung geschehen) recht offenbahr worden / ist	Before the invention of the sliders (which was mentioned above in chapter vii) came into common use, the type of

diese Art der Laden / so noch bey vnser zeit Springladen genennet werden / mit grossem muehseligen nachsuchen erfunden / vnd in Niederlandt vnd Brabandt gemacht vnd gebraucht worden: Welche eigentlich (wie solches vorstendige Orgelmacher bekennen) aus der Invention, do man die vielheit der Pfeiffen voneinander hat absondern wollen / (davon im 14. Cap. meldung geschehen sol) jhren Vrsprung haben. Darumb dann auch diese Art oder erfindung der Springladen kein newes / wie etzliche sich beduncken lassen / sondern aus der eltesten Invention hergeflossen / vnd bey zweyhundert Jahren allbereit im gebrauch gewesen.

Wie dann im Bisthumb Wuertzburg in einem Muenche Closter / noch vor wenig Jahren eine solche Springladen von einem Orgelmacher Timotheus genandt / aus einem sehr alten Werck / so ein Muench gemacht / genommen / vnd an deren statt / hinwiderumb eine newe Lade mit Schleiffen / darinn gelegt worden ist.

Es hat aber in dieser Springladen eine jede Stimme jhre sonderliche Ventiel vnd viel Arbeit / doch wegen dessen / dasz es also nicht hat koennen zusammen lauffen vnd durchstechen / sehr gut: Welche Ventiel dann mit eim eintzigen Register zugleich vffgezogen / vnd doch darbeneben in der Laden zu einen jeden Clave sondere Ventiel, welche mit dem Cla-

chest which, even in our day, is called the spring chest, was developed by very painstaking research, and constructed and used in the Netherlands and in Brabant. This [development] really had its origin (as is generally admitted by eminent organ builders) in the desire to separate the [functions of the] multitude of pipes [in the older organs] from each other, (whereof note shall be made in chapter xiv). Therefore, this type or device of the spring chest is not new, as some seem to think, but springs from a most ancient invention and has already been in use for two hundred years.

In a monastery within the diocese of Wuerzburg, [for example,] such a spring chest, originally built by a monk, was taken out of a very old instrument by an organ builder named Timotheus, and in its place was laid a new chest with sliders.[2]

This spring chest, moreover, had separate pallets for each stop and much [constructional] detail; despite this [fact, the chest was] very good because it was impossible for the wind to escape and run into neighboring channels to cause ciphers. These pallet valves were opened simultaneously by a single draw knob. Beside these valves, there appeared within the chest also separate

vir nidergezogen werden /
verhanden.

Wie dann die Nieder- vnd
Hollaender von solchen
Springladen mehr als von den
Schleiffladen gehalten: Vnd
solches darumb / das der
Windt reiner / ohne vitia
vnd sonderbahre maengel /
vnter den Pfeiffen hat mue-
gen behalten werden; auch
in enderung desz Gewitters /
wegen des Schleiffwercks /
welches sonsten nicht ge-
ringe defecten seyn / be-
stendig blieben.

Als man sich aber auch in
diesen Landen die Schleiffladen Iust vnd perfect zumachen mit grosser muehe
beflissen / vnd die Nidder-
vnd Hollaender in Sachsen
kommen vnd gesehen / das
durch derselben vortheil
eben so wol auch die
Schleiffladen perfect zu-
fertigen mueglich; sind sie
nachgefolget / vnd sich der-
en anzumassen angefangen.
Wie denn M. Fabian Peters
von Schneeck / zu Rostock /
Strallsundt vnd andern or-
tern dergleichen gemacht
haben sol.

Vnd mus gewiszlich nicht
ein geringes Werck seyn /
die Springladen (als ich
von verstendigen Orgelmachern gehoert vnd selbst ver-
nuenfftig erachten kan) Iust
zumachen / wiewol auff den
Schleiffladen mehr wuender-
licher enderungen in Stimmwercken mit den abgesoender-
ten Baessen / holtz verleit-
ungen vnd sonsten zuerhalten

pallets for the keys, which
were pulled down by the manual
[trackers].

Accordingly, the natives of
the Netherlands and of Holland
rated the spring chests more
highly than the slider chests;
[largely] because it was possible to confine the wind more
perfectly underneath the pipes,
without [the usual] faults and
deficiencies which often caused
considerable problems in the
slider chests. The chests also remained static during cli-
matic changes.

After the organ builders in
our lands had, with great diligence, succeeded in perfecting
the slider chest, [the builders
of] the Netherlands and of
Holland, having come to Saxony
to observe that with [its in-
herent] advantages the slider
chest [provided an adequate
and] perfect mechanism, they
followed [our example] and began to develop them also. In
fact, it is claimed that Master
Fabian Peters of Schneeck built
such [slider chests] at Rostock,
Stralsund, and other places.

Certainly, it is not a simple
matter to fabricate a perfect
spring chest (as I have heard
from eminent organ builders and
also observed personally); however, with the slider chest it
is possible to elicit a greater and more wonderful variety
of voices from the instrument
by means of borrowed basses,
grooved channels, and the like,
than can be accomplished with

vnd zuwege zubringen seyn / als auff den Springladen dergestaldt nicht geschehen kan. Jedoch seynd alle beyde Inventiones / wie denn auch beyderley Art von Spaen vnd Ledder bezogenen Blaszbaelgen / auch gut vnd bestendig; wenn nur ein jeder Meister die hellen an Tag gebrachten Gaben recht vnd mit hoechsten fleisz in acht nehmen wolte: als leyder jtziger zeit der mangel mit grossem schaden der armen Leute (die in Staedten vnd Doerffern / Dem HErrn der Heerscharen zu ehren ein Orgelchen / nach jhrer Kirchen gelegenheit setzen vnd auffzurichten zum offtern nicht ein geringes kosten lassen) befunden wird.[4]

the spring chest. Nevertheless, both types [of chest], as also both kinds of bellows, the single and multiple fold, are good and durable, if only all masters would, with the utmost diligence, exercise their manifest talents [in the construction of the same]; unfortunately, the lack of [this exercise] works to the detriment of the poor people (who, in cities and in villages often expend not a little, in order to set up and erect in their churches, as occasion arises, a small organ in honor of the Lord of Hosts). [Translation by the present author]

Defects of the Spring Chest

Because of its rather complicated mechanism the spring chest seems often to have developed operational defects; Werckmeister enumerates ten common ailments:[5]

1. Occasionally the stickers fail to function properly

2. The upper boards have a tendency to warp

3. The stop-beams are likely to warp and twist out of shape

4. Frequently the springs become dislodged

5. The stickers have a tendency to bypass the pallet valves

6. The pallet valves fail to seat properly

7. The holes for the stickers are often not uniform, hence the stop-beam is likely to bend them out of shape

8. The stop-beam lifts up too high when disengaged, causing the stickers to spring up out of their bushings

9. The springs often are too weak and unable to return the stickers and stop-beam to a position of rest

10. Occasionally foreign particles become lodged under the pallet valves

The seemingly rather high regard in which these chests were held must have sprung from the fact that in the spring chests it was impossible to develop ciphers through wind leakage along a slider, a very common and annoying defect in the slider chest as Adlung points out.[6]

Illustrative Cases

In the fifth part of the De Organographia Praetorius presents an array of organ dispositions purporting to be eminent examples of the organ builder's art of his time, including also several model dispositions of his own devising and a few instruments obviously in the planning stage.[7] These dispositions were gathered by Praetorius through personal visits, by letter, or by hearsay. Unfortunately, his information was frequently incomplete or unreliable, and the effort of various writers since his day to present them intelligibly to the modern student of the organ have not always been successful; in fact, the results have quite often been overly speculative and misleading. The present writer proposes, as occasion may arise, to select applicable examples from Praetorius' catalog of dispositions to illustrate emerging concepts as they appear in this study, seizing the concomitant opportunity to present them in as accurate a form as previous and on-going research will permit. It is hoped that thereby, little by little and step by step, an intelligible theory of the Praetorius organ can be developed.

In presenting the organs of the city of Luebeck, Praetorius gives the disposition of the organ at St. Peters. Although he does not mention the case, it has been clearly established by subsequent research that this instrument, built in 1587-91, was equipped with spring chests.[8] The organ was, as far as can be determined, a straight three-manual-and-Pedal instrument of 45 voices.[9] Praetorius' presentation is incomplete and apparently erratic. For this reason, a composite presentation is made here; the first column gives Praetorius' listing exactly as it appears in the De Organographia; the second reconstitutes the disposition as supported by Praetorius and by other early and applicable sources:

V

In Luebeck.[10]

1.

Die Orgel zu S. Peters Kirchen / so M. Gottschaldt
Burckart ein Niederlaender[11]
gemacht / hat 45. Stimmen.
3. Manual Clavir von C bisz
ā Coppel zum Oberwerck vnnd
Rueckpositiff vnnd Coppel zum
Pedal vnd Rueckpositiff.[12]
Das Pedal aber gehet vom C
mit dem Gs vnd Fs bisz oben
ins d̄.

Im Ober Werck seynd
13. Stimmen

1. Principal von 16.Fuessen
2. Spilpipe   8.fi.
3. Klein Spillpipe   4
4. Superoctava[13]   4
5. Rauschquinta[14]   4
6. Kleinoctava   4
7. Grosz Octava[15]   4
8. Borduna[16]   24.fi.
9. Dulcian   16
10. Feld Trommeten   16
11. Scharff Zimbel[17]
12. Mixtura
13. Gedact   8.fi.

In der Brust 8
Stimmen.

1. Gedact vff   8.fi.
2. Offenfloeit   4.fi.
3. Scharff Regal[18]
4. Harffen Regal[19]
5. Geigen Regal[20]
6. Sifelitt[21]
7. klein Quintadehna[22]

V

In Luebeck

1

The organ at St. Peter's
church, built by Master Gottschalk Burchard [Borchert], a
Netherlander, has 45 voices.
[It has a] three-manual clavier
[with a compass] from C to a''.
A coupler for the Oberwerk and
Rueckpositive, and a coupler
for the Pedal and Rueckpositive. The Pedal reaches from
C with G♯ and F♯ up to d'.

In the Oberwerk,
13 voices

1. Principal of   16 feet
2. Spillpfeife   8 ft.
3. Klein Spillpfeife   4
4. Super Octave   [2']
5. Rauschquinte   [II]
6. Klein Octave   4
7. Gross Octave   [8']
8. Bourdon   [32']
9. Dulzian   16
10. Field Trumpet   16
11. Scharf Zimbel   [III]
12. Mixture
13. Gedackt   8 ft.

In the Brust,
8 voices

1. Gedackt of   8 ft.
2. Offenfloete   4 ft.
3. Scharf Regal   [8']
4. Harfen Regal   [4']
5. Geigend Regal   [4']
6. Siffloete   [1']
7. Klein Quintade   [4']

8. Sedecima[23]		8. Sedecima	[2']

Im Rueckpositiff 14. Stimmen.		In the Rueckpositive, 14 voices	
1. Principal von	8.Fusz	1. Principal of	8 foot
2. Octava	4	2. Octave	4
3. Quintadehna.[24]		3. Quintade	[16']
4. Gemszhorn[25]		4. Gemshorn	[8']
5. Krumbhoerner[26]		5. Krummhorn	[8']
6. Gedact vff	8.fi.	6. Gedackt of	8 ft.
7. Querpipe[27]		7. Querpfeife	[4']
8. Feldpipe[28]		8. Feldpfeife	[2']
9. Superoctava[29]		9. Super Octave	[2']
10. Trommeten	8.fi.	10. Trumpet	8 ft.
11. Baerpipen[30]		11. Baerpfeife	[4']
12. Blockfloeiten	4.fi.	12. Blockfloete	4 ft.
13. Zimbel[31]		13. Zimbel	[III]
14. Mixtur[32]		14. Mixture	[V]

Im Pedal 10 Stimmen.		In the Pedal, 10 voices	
1. Principal Basz	32.fi	1. Principal bass	32 ft.
2. Gedact Basz	16.fi.	2. Gedackt bass	16 ft.
3. Blockfloeiten B.	16	3. Blockfloete bass	16
4. Decem Basz[33]		4. Decem bass	[4']
5. Superoctaven B.[33]	8	5. Super Octave bass	8
6. Mixtur B.[34]	8	6. Mixture bass	8
7. Dusan B.[35]	16	7. Dulzian bass	16
8. Passunen Basz	16	8. Posaune bass	16
9. Schallmeyen B.[36]		9. Schalmei bass	[4']
10. Cornett Basz	8	10. Kornett bass	8

[Translation by the present author]

In order to provide a more intelligent overview of the instrument, the following disposition presents a modern equivalent:[37]

St. Peter, Luebeck

Built by Johannes Gottschalk and his son, Gottschalk Johannsen called Burchard (Borchert) from Husum, between 1587 and 1591. The younger man should be considered the real builder. [The disposition does not take into account nor delineate certain conditions that may have prevailed because of permanent coupling.]

Oberwerk

8. [32'] Bourdon (Great F)
1. 16' Principal
7. [8'] Gross Octave
13. 8' Gedackt
2. 8' Spillpfeife
6. 4' Klein Octave
3. 4' Klein Spillpfeife

4. [2'] Super Octave
5. [II] Rauschquinte
12. Mixture
11. [III] Scharf Zimbel
10. 16' Field Trumpet
9. 16' Dulzian

Brust

1. 8' Gedackt
7. [4'] Klein Quintade
2. 4' Offenfloete
8. [2'] Sedecima

6. [1'] Siffloete
3. [8'] Scharf Regal
4. [4'] Harfen Regal
5. [4'] Geigend Regal

Rueckpositive

3. [16'] Quintade
1. 8' Principal
6. 8' Gedackt
4. [8'] Gemshorn
2. 4' Octave
7. [4'] Querpfeife
12. 4' Blockfloete

9. [2'] Super Octave
8. [2'] Feldpfeife
14. [V] Mixture
13. [III] Zimbel
10. 8' Trumpet
5. [8'] Krummhorn
11. [4'] Baerpfeife

Pedal

1. 32' Principal
2. 16' Gedackt

6. Mixture
8. 16' Posaune

3. 16' Blockfloete

5. 8' [Octave]

4. [4' Super Octave]

7. 16' Dulzian

10. 8' Kornett

9. [4'] Schalmei

Accessories

Couplers: Rueckpositive to Oberwerk; Rueckpositive to
Pedal

A second, apparently straight, two-manual-and-Pedal
disposition using spring chests is presented by Praetorius
among his catalog of dispositions. It was located at the
St. Blasius Stift [cathedral] in Braunschweig.[38] In the
following presentation the first column quotes Praetorius
from the De Organographia, while the second column provides
a translation:

XIII.

Die Orgel zu Braunschweig
Im Stifft S. Blasij. Welche
M. Hennig aus Hildesheimb
gemacht / hat 35. Stimmen.[39]

Im Ober Werck seynd
13. Stimmen

1. Principal	16.fusz
2. Principal	8.fusz
3. Octava[40]	8.fusz
4. Quintadeena	16
5. Quinta[41]	3
6. Mixtur	2.fusz
oben im Discant 12. Pfeiffen. im Basz 7. starck.	
7. Zimbel 3 Pfeiffen starck	
8. Holfloeite	16

XIII

The organ at St. Blasius
Stift, which was built by Master Hennig of Hildesheim. It
has 35 [really 37] voices.

In the Oberwerk,
13 voices

1. Principal	16 foot
2. Principal	8 foot
3. Octave	[4] foot
4. Quintade	16
5. Quint	3
6. Mixture	2 foot
Twelve ranks in the tre-ble, seven in the bass [portion of the compass]	
7. Zimbel	III ranks
8. Hohlfloete	16

9. Holfloeite	8		9. Hohlfloete	8
10. Coppelfloeite	4		10. Koppelfloete	4
11. Gemszhorn	2		11. Gemshorn	2
12. Trommeten	8		12. Trumpet	8
13. Dulcian	8		13. Dulzian	8

Diese Stimmen / wie auch im Rueckpositiff gehen durchaus ins C sampt ds Fs gs vnd oben ins $\overline{\overline{c}}$ sampt $\overline{\overline{gs}}$ vnd $\overline{\overline{b}}$

These voices, as also those in the Rueckpositive, reach down to C including the d#, F#, and g#, and up to c''' including the g#''' [more likely g#''] and bb''.

Im Rueckpositiff
11. Stimmen.

1. Holfloeite	8.fusz
2. Quintadehna	8
3. Principal	4
4. Octava 42	4
5. Zimbel 2.Pfeiffen starck	
6. Querfloeiten	8
7. Schallmeyen	4
8. Krumbhoerner	8
9. Block Pfeiffe	4
10. Siffloeit	2
11. Zincken von h bis oben hinaus.43	

In the Rueckpositive,
11 voices

1. Hohlfloete	8 foot
2. Quintade	8
3. Principal	4
4. Octave	[2*]
5. Zimbel	II ranks
6. Querfloete	8
7. Schalmei	4
8. Krummhorn	8
9. Blockfloete	4
10. Siffloete	2
11. Zink, from b to the upper limit	[8*]

Im Pedal 14.
Stimmen

1. Gar grosser Untersatz Gedact	32.fusz
2. Principal	16
3. Octava	8
4. Gedact	16
5. Holfloeiten	8
6. Posaunen	16
7. Trommeten	8
8. Krumbhorn	16
9. Gemszhorn	4

In the Pedal,
14 voices

1. Gross Untersatz Gedackt, very large	32 foot
2. Principal	16
3. Octave	8
4. Gedackt	16
5. Hohlfloete	8
6. Posaune	16
7. Trumpet	8
8. Krummhorn	16
9. Gemshorn	4

Mixtur
{ 10. Zimbel 2.
       Pfeiffen starck
  11. Rauschpfeiffen[44]
  12. Super Octav 4.fi. }

13. Bawrfloeiten   2

14. Trummel 2 Pfeiffen
    starck[45]

Tremulant

Coppel zu beyden Clavirn

Fuenff Ventile,
   1. Zum Ober Werck
   2. Zun Baessen
   3. Zun Rueckpositiff
   4. Zur Sonnen
   5. Zun Sternen

Diese Baesse im Pedal sind
also gemacht / dasz man ein-
en jeglichen besonders gebrauchen kan: Vnd haben jhre
eigne Laden / gehen alle vnten ins grosse C sampt Ds.
Fs. gs. vnnd oben ins d̄
sampt c̄s.

Die Laden seynd nicht vff
die gemeine / sondern eine
andere Art gerichtet / vnd
werden Springladen genennet
/ davon im dritten Theil
dieses Tomi Secundi etwas
angedeutet werden.

Es sind auch die Span
Baelge / deren achte vorhanden / vff eine sondere Art
gemacht / also dasz ein jeglicher 9. guter Schuch lang
/ mit einer eintzigen Falten; Die Spuene sind 2.
starcke Eichene Bretter
gantz bestendig / vnd geh-
en dichte zusammen / dasz
keine Mausz darbey kommen
kan.

Mixture
{ 10. Zimbel   II ranks
  11. Rausch-
      pfeife [III ranks]
  12. Super Octave 4 ft. }

13. Bauerfloete   2

14. Tambura   2 pipes

Tremulant

Coupler for both manuals

Five ventils:
   1. For the Oberwerk
   2. For the Basses
   3. For the Rueckpositive
   4. For the Sun
   5. For the Stars

These bass voices in the
Pedal are so disposed that it
is possible to use each one
separately; they have their
own chests and all descend to
C including $D\sharp$, $F\sharp$, and $g\sharp$,
and ascend to d' including
$c\sharp'$.

The chests are not constructed in the common manner, but
are of a different type and
are called spring chests,
whereof certain things will be
pointed out in the third part
of this Tomus Secundus.

There are also single fold
bellows, of which eight occur,
which are constructed in a special manner: each one is nine
full feet long and has but a
single fold. The panels are
made of two strong oak boards,
very rigid; when folded they
clap firmly together, so that
no mouse can get at [the
folds].

Das oberste Werck hat fuenff Felder / in der mitten einen raum / die spitzen vnd ein flachfeld / auff beyden seiten die Baszthuermer.	The facade of the main organ has five [probably seven] fields: in the middle a round tower [of pipes, flanked by] flat planes and pointed towers [of pipes, concluding on] both sides with the pedal towers.
Das Rueckpositiff hat mitten eine spitzen / vnd den raum / flachfeld / vnd so vor dann hat 7. felder.	The Rueckpositive, located in the middle, has pointed towers, a round tower, and flat planes, and has, therefore, seven [probably five] fields. [Translation by the present author]

The following rearrangement of the registers presents the St. Blasius instrument in an equivalent modern form:[46]

St. Blasius, Braunschweig

Built by Henning Henke, ca. 1600-20.[47] [The disposition does not take into account nor delineate certain conditions that may have prevailed because of permanent coupling].

Oberwerk

1.	16' Principal	5.	2 2/3'	Quint
8.	16' Hohlfloete	11.	2'	Gemshorn
4.	16' Quintade	6.	VII-XII	Mixture (2')
2.	8' Principal	7.	III	Zimbel
9.	8' Hohlfloete	12.	8'	Trumpet
3.	[4'] Octave	13.	8'	Dulzian
10.	4' Koppelfloete			

Rueckpositive

6.	8' Querfloete	10.	2'	Siffloete
1.	8' Hohlfloete	5.	II	Zimbel
2.	8' Quintade	8.	8'	Krummhorn
3.	4' Principal	11.	[8']	Zink (from b on)

9. 4' Blockfloete

4. [2'] Octave

7. 4' Schalmei

Pedal

1. 32' Gross Gedackt
    Untersatz

2. 16' Principal

4. 16' Gedackt

3. 8' Octave

5. 8' Hohlfloete

12. 4' Super Octave

9. 4' Gemshorn

13. 2' Bauerfloete

11. [III] Rauschpfeife

10. II Zimbel

6. 16' Posaune

8. 16' Krummhorn

7. 8' Trumpet

14. Tamburo

Accessories

Tremulant

Coupler: Rueckpositive
            to Oberwerk

Sun

Stars

Five ventils:
  Oberwerk
  Pedal
  Rueckpositive
  Sun
  Stars

Although Praetorius, by inference, claims that in
the spring chest the borrowing of basses, duplexing of registers, and the like, was not possible, the fact remains
that he presents in his catalog of dispositions at least
two instruments which involved the use of the spring chest
and upon which borrowed basses definitely did occur.[48]
These instruments were:

1. St. Johannes in Lueneburg[49]

2. St. Gotthard in Hildesheim[50]

The method of handling such borrowing will be fully
discussed in chapter ix, after the slider chest of the time

has been more fully investigated and the necessary concepts

developed for an understanding of the same.

The Slider Chest

Mechanical Disposition

By far the most common method of controlling the

action of the organ of Praetorius was by means of the slider

chest. The chest derived its name from its stop action

which, in contrast to the spring chest, was effected by

means of movable sliders mounted between the table and the

upper boards and separated by bearers, rather than by means

of stop pallets for the individual pipes. The basic mecha-

nism of this type of chest and its operation is fully il-

lustrated and described in chapter i of this study, and ref-

erence should be made to that discussion while pursuing the

more pristine forms of the mechanism as exhibited in the

work of the organ builders of the late sixteenth and early

seventeenth centuries.

The various concepts relating to this chest were

known and practiced avidly during this time. The chest con-

tained the pallet box which was supplied with pressure wind

from the bellows; the box housed the pallet valves, one for

each key; each note had its corresponding latitudinal chan-

nel in the chest; the channels were covered by a table;

upon this lay the movable sliders and immovable bearers;

thereupon lay the upper boards on which the actual pipes

were planted. The chest, when constructed in its "straight"
form, operated precisely as explained in chapter i of this
study.

Generic Methods of Coupling

The first departure from the conventional form and
use of the slider chest as we know it from more recent practice, occurred in the various and more primitive methods of
coupling or combining the chests to make them playable also
on keyboards other than their own. Two generic methods of
coupling were used during the Early Baroque:

1. Transient coupling, i.e., the coupling of a
chest to a keyboard other than its native one by
means of a mechanism so disposed, that the player
could engage or disengage the coupling effect at
will[51]

2. Permanent coupling, i.e., the coupling of a
chest to a keyboard other than its native one by
means of a pre-arranged and fixed mechanism, not in
control of the player[52]

The principle of transient coupling was known and
practiced in the Early Baroque, but, from a modern point of
view, to a very limited extent. A perusal of the organs in
Praetorius' catalog of dispositions reveals hardly ever
more than one manual-to-manual coupler and one manual-to-
pedal coupler per instrument. Of the forty-seven instruments

delineated or proposed, manual-to-manual couplers are specifically mentioned in seventeen cases; of these two and
three-manual instruments, not more than one manual-to-
manual coupler appears in any one organ.[53] In the thirty
remaining instruments, manual-to-manual couplers may or, in
some cases, may not have occurred, since Praetorius' accounts of these instruments are often lacking in detail.
Manual-to-pedal couplers are clearly indicated in only fourteen examples and, in every case, no more than one such
coupler per instrument is specified.

     With few exceptions, the usual manual-to-manual cou-
pler mechanism was the one which coupled the Rueckpositive
to the Oberwerk. Since the Rueckpositive had by necessity
to occupy the lowest position in the console, the coupling
effect operated in an upward direction and coupled the lower
manual to the upper. Likewise, the only manual-to-pedal
coupler which can be found in the Praetorius dispositions
is the one which coupled the Rueckpositive to the Pedal.

     It appears that the requisite mechanisms for intro-
ducing transient couplers more generously into the instruments were lacking, or that the limitations of the keyboard
dispositions and the layout of the control harnesses prevented a more common use of transient coupling. It may also
be that the basic tonal concepts governing the incorporation
of the tonal resource made a greater employment of couplers
quite unnecessary, or were sufficiently satisfied with the

alternatives offered by the various methods of permanent
coupling to be defined below.[54]

Because of the great physical differences between
manual couplers and pedal couplers, it is necessary to take
up each species separately in an effort to discover the basic construction and operation.

Transient Manual Couplers

Inasmuch as only one early baroque instrument equipped
with a manual coupler mechanism is still in authentic existence today, an attempt to reconstitute the basic principles
employed for this purpose must rely upon several avenues of
research;[55] chief among these are:

1. The technical descriptions of ancient mechanisms by subsequent and reliable theorists who may
have had visual access to instruments of the Early
Baroque in their time

2. Photographs or detailed descriptions of vestigial remains of the old instruments as discovered
and verified by specialists who have or are investigating the work of specific builders of the period

3. Application and testing of hypotheses developed from the above sources against the qualitative
descriptions and apparent conditions evident in the
overall specifications provided by Praetorius

The earliest technically descriptive source for

reliable information on the early transient coupler mechanisms is Jakob Adlung who, in 1768, describes the manual couplers as follows:

Die Palmulae sind von einer Breite, und die verschiedenen Claviere muessen recht auf einander passen; denn es werden dieselben oft zusammen gekoppelt, dasz wenn das eine gedruckt wird, auch das andere, zuweilen auch wol das dritte mit niederfaellt. Die gemeinste Art sie zu koppeln ist, da unten an die Palmulas kleine Hoelzerchen mit Leime bevestiget werden, etwa einen Finger dick, auch so breit, und 1 Zoll lang; alsdann werden dergleichen auch an denen Palmulis des untern Claviers bevestiget, doch so, dasz sie oben zu stehen kommen.

Sie werden so abgerichtet, dasz diese zweyerley Koppelhoelzchen neben einander vorbeystreichen, und wenn das obere Clavier geruehret wird, es das untere nicht mit beruehre: wenn aber das obere Clavier hinterwaerts geschoben wird; so treten die obern Kloetzchen just ueber die Hoelzchen des andern Claviers, daher durch des obern Niederdrueckung auch das andere niederfallen musz. Und so wird es auch gehalten, wenn mehr, als 2 Claviere zu koppeln sind. Daraus folgt, dasz, wenn man das untere Clavier beruehret, das obere dadurch nicht

The [manual] keys are of uniform width, and the several claviers must be properly aligned [over each other] because they are often coupled together, so that when one [clavier] is played, [the keys of] a second and possibly a third [clavier] will fall correspondingly. The most common method of coupling the claviers requires small wooden cleats to be glued to the under side of the keys [of the upper clavier]. These cleats approximate in thickness and width the size of a finger and are made an inch long. A corresponding set of wooden cleats are mounted on the top side of the keys of the lower clavier, so that they stand erect.

The corresponding coupler cleats [of the two claviers] are so aligned, that they bypass each other; when the upper clavier is played, its keys will not depress those of the lower clavier. When, however, the upper clavier is pushed back [into coupling position], the upper cleats will line up precisely over the [corresponding] cleats of the other clavier, so that any depression of the upper keys will force the lower ones to fall as well. The same conditions prevail when more than two claviers are to be coupled. Accordingly, when [the keys of] the lower clavier are depressed, [the keys of] the

angeschlagen werde, weil das
Druecken unterwaerts ge-
schiehet. Ferner siehet ein
jeder, dasz man die Haende
nicht darf auf dem Ober-
werke haben, wenn man dasselbe schieben will, weil
die Hoelzchen gegen einander stoszen, und endlich
abbrechen wuerden: auf dem
untern Claviere aber koennen die Haende ohne Schad-
en bleiben, weil in dem
Schieben die Hoelzchen ueber-
einander wegpasziren.

Das Koppeln der Claviere
geschiehet auch wol so, dasz
das obere geschoben wird,
und doch von dem untern
niedergezogen wird durchs
Spielen; denn die obern Abstrakten haben besondere
Muetterchen oder Schlingen,
darein die untern sich
haengen. So ists in Naum-
burg zu St. Wenceslai und
St. Otmari. Da musz man
die Haende auf keinem Claviere haben.

Andere machen ihre Koppel
durch blinde Claviere, dabey die Tastatur unbeweglich
liegt; weil aber dieses
vielerley Ungelegenheit verursacht; so haelt man heut
zu Tage wenig oder nichts
davon.
. . . .

Es gibt aber noch andere
Arten zu koppeln. Man kop-
pelt auch wol drey Claviere
zusammen, und spielt auf
denen Mittelsten, wie z. Ex.

upper are not affected, since
the motion is in a downward
direction. It is further evident that when the Oberwerk,
[i.e., the upper clavier], is
to be moved into position [in
order to engage the coupling
action], the hands may not
depress any of its keys, since
the wooden cleats would col-
lide and finally cause break-
age; on the lower clavier,
however, the keys can be depressed [while engaging the
coupling action] without any
ill effects, since the cleats
will bypass each other.

The coupling of claviers is
also accomplished in such a
way that the upper clavier is
[similarly] pushed [to engage
the coupling action], but its
keys are drawn downward by
playing on the lower [clavier]
because the upper trackers are
equipped with special nuts and
loops into which those of the
lower clavier are engaged.
Thus it is at St. Wenceslas
and St. Otmar at Naumburg.
[In this case] the hands may
not depress any keys of either
clavier [when the coupler is
in the process of being en-
gaged].

Others construct their couplers by means of blind claviers, whereby the keyboards remain stationary. Since, however, this method presents
many inconveniences, it is
held in little or no regard
today.
. . . .

There are still other methods of coupling. Occasionally
three manuals are coupled together, and the playing is executed on the middle one as,

in Gera, it. zu Walters-	for example, in Gera, likewise
hausen.[56]	in Waltershausen. [Translation
	by the present author]

A summary outline of Adlung's descriptions will
serve to clarify at least three basic historic mechanisms
which he records as having been used in the past and, possibly, at his time:

A. The Cleat Coupler[57]

1. Coupling medium comprises a double set of
permanently mounted cleats, so aligned as to face each
other from adjacent keyboards. See Plate LIX, figs.
1-8

2. Represents a direct keyboard-to-keyboard
mechanism

3. Useful only for the coupling of adjacent keyboards

4. Generally couples upward, i.e., a lower manual to a higher one; never the reverse

5. Requires one of the respective keyboards to
be moved into alignment with the other one, in order
to achieve a coupling effect; the higher manual must
be inactive when the coupler is being engaged

6. Is particularly applicable to keyboards operating under a second class lever principle, where
the fulcrum is at the tail end of the key, the applied force at the front end, and the work is realized

between the extremes

B. The Fork Coupler[58]

    1. Coupling mechanism comprises tapped wires or equivalent extensions of the trackers attached to the active keyboard, a set of hardwood nuts positioned thereon and subject to refined adjustments, and wooden cleats in the form of forks mounted permanently on the top sides of the idle keys.[59] See Plate LX, figs. 1-6

    2. Represents a direct keyboard-to-keyboard mechanism

    3. Useful for coupling adjacent and non-adjacent keyboards

    4. Generally couples downward, i.e., a higher manual to a lower one

    5. Requires the idle keyboard to be moved in order to align and mesh the nuts and forks to achieve the coupling effect; in the case of a "down" coupler the lower keyboard must be inactive while the coupler is being engaged[60]

    6. Is particularly applicable to keyboards operating under a second class lever principle

C. The Lever Arm Coupler[61]

    1. Only mentioned by Adlung; appears, however, in a multitude of forms in the subsequent literature; assumes a variety of forms in its historic development

and gradually is metamorphosed into the backfall,
double backfall, and ram couplers; combines with other
species to create many permutations. See Plate LXI,
figs. 1-4

2. Represents an indirect keyboard-to-keyboard
mechanism, introducing a blind clavier as intermediary

3. Useful for coupling adjacent or non-adjacent
keyboards

4. Depending upon its disposition, it can be
used as a device to couple upward or downward

5. Keyboards remain in fixed position; coupling
is effected by adjusting the attitude of the blind
clavier

6. In its most primitive form it is especially
applicable to keyboards operating under a second
class lever principle

In reference to Plate LIX, figs. 1 and 2, the cleat
coupler, when applied to couple two manuals, operates as
follows:

The upper keyboard II and the lower keyboard I are
pivoted at A. The cleats B and C are securely attached to
their respective keys. When the keyboards are coupled
(fig. 1), a depression of key II influences key I in a similar (downward) direction; manual I is coupled to II and the
coupling effect is upward. To disengage (fig. 2), keyboard

I is moved to the left, so that cleats B and C bypass each other.

Plate LIX, fig. 3 shows the application of the device for coupling three manuals. A represents the fulcrums of all three keyboards. As shown, manual I is coupled to manual II, and manual II is coupled to manual III. When playing on II, I will respond; when playing on III, both I and II will respond. Fig. 4 shows manual III as disengaged because of its repositioning to the right. Fig. 5 shows manual I as disengaged because of its repositioning to the left. Fig. 6 shows both III and I disengaged by appropriate positioning. In every case the coupling effect is upward and involves only adjacent keyboards. I cannot be directly and independently coupled to III. Fig. 7 is a perspective sketch of a key having a surmounted cleat C, while fig. 8 shows a submounted cleat B. It will be noted that all keyboards are based upon the second class lever principle.

The fork coupler, illustrated on Plate LX, figs. 1-6, is shown when laid out to operate between two adjacent keyboards. It operates as follows:

The upper keyboard II and the lower keyboard I are pivoted at A. A perspective sketch in fig. 3 shows the mechanical accessories required to realize the coupler. The forked cleat B is securely attached to key II. The tapped wire C is imbedded into the shank of key I, projects upward

through an elongated slot in key II, and serves as a pull-
down for tracker F which communicates with a pallet in the
chest for keyboard I. The hardwood nut D is carefully adjusted to pass exactly over cleat B when keyboard II is
pushed into registration to achieve a coupling effect. Fig.
1 shows two keyboards in registration: manual II is coupled
to manual I. A depression of key I achieves a similar motion in key II. The coupling effect is downward: II-I.
Fig. 2 shows the coupler disengaged by repositioning keyboard
II to the left. Fig. 6 shows the mechanism in reverse attitude; the forked cleat B is mounted to the right of tapped
wire C. In fig. 4 the coupler is engaged; in fig. 5 it is
disengaged by moving the upper keyboard to the right. The
applications of the coupler here illustrated involve keyboards pivoted as second class levers.

Plate LXI presents two forms of the lever arm coupler
in relatively simple execution. In figs. 1 and 2 the attitude of the mechanism is disposed to achieve a downward coupling effect: II-I. The keys are pivoted at A. Fig. 1
shows the coupler engaged; B is a movable bearing stock into
which are mounted and pivoted as many lever arms C as the
keyboard exhibits keys.[62] A tapped wire D is imbedded into
the end of each lever arm C and projects upward through a
slightly oversize hole in key II. Leather button F is used
for fine adjustment. The tapped wire E is imbedded into key
I and projects upward through an oversize hole in lever arm

C, being surmounted by an adjustable leather button at G. By
depressing key I, the lever arm C moves downward and pulls
key II down with it. Fig. 2 illustrates the coupler as disengaged. Movable bearing stock B has been positioned downward, thus relaxing the effect of lever arm C on leather button G. In figs. 3 and 4 the attitude of the mechanism is
disposed to achieve an upward coupling effect: I-II. In
fig. 3 a depression of key II engages key I as well. Fig. 4
shows the coupler as disengaged; the movable bearing stock B
has been raised to free it from leather button F.

It is evident from the foregoing that up to the time
of Adlung (1699-1762) at least three, and possibly more,
basic species of transient manual couplers had developed to
a point to command the formal attention of organ theorists.
It is unlikely that all three were used by the early baroque
builders. Gottfried Silbermann (1683-1753) reputedly employed only the cleat coupler (for manual-to-manual coupling)
combined with keyboards based on a second class lever principle in his early instruments, introducing the fork coupler
only in his more mature instruments. Ernst Flade reports
the following observations:

> Further auxiliary registers of the Silbermann
> organs are the couplers. By examination of a Silber-
> mann keyboard, we find the following relationships
> between the point of applied force (finger position),
> the weight (connection point for the trackers) and the
> fulcrum (tail end of key): in the Hauptwerk 29 x 29
> cm., in the Oberwerk 22 x 25 cm. Silbermann followed,
> therefore, the method already urgently recommended by

Schlick and subsequently by Dom Bedos; namely, to
connect the trackers to the key at the mid-point
[or in its vicinity]. Thereby he gained the advantages of the lightest possible touch and a minimum key length. In his first organs, Silbermann
employed the cleat coupler. . . . Silbermann's
later instruments exhibited a more highly perfected
form of manual coupler in the fork coupler.[63]
[Translation by the present author]

Ulrich Daehnert presents very clear photographs of
two adjacent keyboards purportedly constructed by Zacharias
Hildebrandt (1688-1757) and found preserved in a church at
Langhennersdorf bei Freiberg.[64] The upper keyboard is constructed after the second class lever principle and shows
the tracker connections at the mid-points of the keys (top
side), while the lower keyboard is predicated upon the first
class lever principle and shows the appropriate wooden
cleats mounted on the top side of the key shanks directly
behind the sharps.[65] A cleat coupler system is, therefore,
indicated; this suggests an upward coupling effect between
the upper and lower keyboards. Inasmuch as the upper keyboard is equipped with handles on its key cheeks, and the
lower keyboard shows the cleats mounted with the inclined
edge toward the fronts of the keys, it would seem that the
coupler had to be engaged by pushing in the upper (active)
keyboard away from the player to achieve the coupling effect, while the lower (idle) keyboard remained stationary.

A final, unimpeachable source to help delimit the
concept of the transient manual coupler in the Early Baroque

is Dom Bedos (1709-1779). In his L'Art du Facteur d'Orgues
he presents carefully detailed plan, elevation, section,
and perspective drawings of manual keyboards on fourteen
different plates.[66] In every instance where specifically
shown, the keys are mounted as second class levers and the
tracker connections are always near the mid-points of the
key shanks. The coupler mechanisms are invariably those of
the cleat coupler species. The coupler is engaged by positioning one of the keyboards, appropriate handles being
provided on the key cheeks for this purpose. Schematically,
the mechanisms comprise the equipment and manner of mounting
as illustrated on Plate LIX, figs. 1-8.

On the basis, then, of Adlung's descriptions, of
Flade's research into the Gottfried Silbermann instruments,
of Daehnert's photographs of Hildebrandt keyboards, and of
Dom Bedos' drawings and perspectives, it would seem appropriate to surmise that for transient manual coupling the most
widespread and favored method was the cleat coupler. The
fork coupler seems to have developed somewhat later than the
Early Baroque, and the lever arm species still later. Through
a knowledge of the mechanical dispositions which the cleat
coupler requires, the physical effects which it can produce,
and the limitations it imposes, it remains necessary to apply the hypothesis against the qualitative descriptions contained in Praetorius' catalog of dispositions.

The conditions which the cleat coupler requires for

introduction into a system of keyboards are:

1. Keyboards generally mounted in second class lever fashion

2. Cleat mechanism mounted between keyboards

3. Key cheek handles or equivalent devices to registrate one of the involved keyboards

The symptoms and limitations which indicate the presence of a cleat coupler system are:

1. Specification of a manual coupler system

2. A minimum of one and a maximum of two manual couplers per instrument

3. Coupling of adjacent keyboards only

4. Active keyboard in a superior position to the idle one, so that the coupling effect is consistently upward

Praetorius specifically indicates transient manual couplers in seventeen of the forty-seven instruments presented in his catalog of dispositions. In six additional cases a transient coupler is mentioned, but it is not clear if a manual or a pedal coupler is intended.[67] His indications follow the usual form of expressing coupler systems in the Early Baroque, whereby the coupling effect is not reflected in the specification. They must, therefore, be restated in the modern sense if the coupling effect is to be properly understood. Today it is customary to list the idle keyboard first and the active keyboard last as, for example,

Swell-to-Great, where the coupling effect is downward. Following is a complete list of the designations used by Praetorius, together with a translation and commentary by the present author:

1. Coppel zum Oberwerck und Rueckpositiff[68]

1. Coupler for the Oberwerk and Rueckpositive

The designation means that a coupler mechanism occurs between the two keyboards; it may be understood to mean, in a modern sense, "Rueckpositive-to-Oberwerk"

2. Coppel zum (ins) Manual[69]

2. Coupler for the Manual

By Manual is to be understood the main keyboard in contrast to the Pedal and the Rueckpositive; the designation may be interpreted as "Rueckpositive-to-Hauptwerk (Oberwerk)"

3. Coppel in (zu) beyden Manualen (Clavieren)[70]

3. Coupler for both manuals (claviers)

The designations indicate one coupler mounted between two keyboards; in all probability, manual-to-manual couplers are meant

4. Coppel der beyden Manual Clavirn[71]

4. Coupler for both manual claviers

The designation indicates one coupler mechanism mounted between two keyboards

5. Coppel zum Oberwerck

5. Coupler for the Oberwerk

und Brust Clavir[72]   and Brust clavier

 The designation may be understood to mean <u>one</u> coupler

mechanism mounted between two keyboards; a modern

designation would read, "Brust-to-Oberwerk"

 It will be observed that the meager specifications

of Praetorius satisfy the necessary conditions for the in-

corporation of a cleat coupler system. The coupling effect

is consistently upward, the coupler engages two adjacent

keyboards, and the systems of the entire array of instru-

ments exhibit the limitations imposed by the cleat coupler

mechanism.

 An applicable example of an organ which contains

a clearly indicated manual coupler system is the Esaias

Compenius instrument built for Bueckeburg, which appears

among the entries in Praetorius' catalog of dispositions.[73]

Presented here in two-column form, the instrument is quoted

directly from the De Organographia in column one, while

column two translates Praetorius' commentaries and gives

reasonably modern equivalents for the registers. It should

be noted that the manual coupler, operating between the

Brust and Oberwerk, presupposes the manual arrangement to

be Oberwerk on top, Brust in the middle, and Rueckpositive

at the bottom, if the usual upward coupling effect is to oc-

cur. Such an arrangement is specifically indicated by Prae-

torius for the Rostock organ, and is applied here by

XVIII[75]

Das grosse Werck zu
Bueckeburgk So der Hochgeborne Graff vnd Herr / Herr
Ernst / Graff zu Holstein /
Schaumburgk vnd Sternberg /
Herren zu Gehmen / durch M.
Esaiam Compenium, Fuerstl.
Braunsch. Orgel- vnnd In-
strumentmacher / auch Organisten, An. 1615. verfertig-
en lassen. Hat 48. Stimmen.
3. Clavir im Manual. Coppel
zum Ober Werck vnd Brust
Clavir.[76] Drey Tremulanten
1. Im Ober Werck / 2. Rueckpositiff / vnd 3. im Pedal.
9. Spaenbaelge / oben vffn
Kirchgewelbe / gleich vber
der Orgel.

Ein Register / dasz die
Blaszbaelge allzuglich losz
lest / vnd zugleich ein-
schleust / dasz sie der Cal-
cant nicht mehr tretten kan.

Im Ober Werck seynd
12. Stimmen

1. Grosa Principal   16.fi.
2. Grosz Quintadehn   16
3. Grosz Octava   8
4. Gemszhorn   8
5. Gedacte Blockpfeiffe   8
6. Viol de Gamba   8
7. Querpfeiffe   4
8. Octava   4
9. Klein Gedact
   Blockpfeiff   4
10. Gemszhorn / Quinta   3
11. Klein Flachfloeit   2

XVIII

The large instrument at
Bueckeburg, which was fabricated [upon order of] the noble Count and Lord, Lord Ernst,
Count of Holstein, Schaumburg,
and Sternberg, Lord at Gehmen;
by Master Esaias Compenius, organist and princely organ and
instrument maker of Braunschweig, in 1615. It has 48
voices, 3 keyboards, a coupler
for the Oberwerk and Brust,
three tremulants for the (1)
Oberwerk, (2) Rueckpositive,
and (3) Pedal. Nine bellows
are mounted up in the ceiling
vaults of the church, directly above the organ.

[The organ contains] a control mechanism which immediately releases and locks the
bellows, so that the operator
cannot treadle them.

In the Oberwerk,
12 voices

1. Gross Principal   16 ft.
2. Gross Quintade   16
3. Gross Octave   8
4. Gemshorn   8
5. Gedackt Blockpfeife   8
6. Viola da Gamba   8
7. Querpfeife   4
8. Octave   4
9. Klein Gedackt
   Blockpfeife   4
10. Gemshorn Quint   3
11. Klein Flachfloete   2

| 12. Mixtur | | 12. Mixture | |
| 8.10.12.14.Chor.[77] | | 8, 10, 12, and 14 ranks | |

In der Brust 8. Stimmen		In the Brust, 8 voices	
1. Rohrfloeiten	8	1. Rohrfloete	8
2. Nachthorn	4	2. Nachthorn	4
3. Offenfloeit / sol fornen an zu steh-en kommen von Elffenbein	4.fi.	3. Offenfloete, to be mounted out in front; of ivory	4 ft.
4. Klein Gemszhorn	2	4. Klein Gemshorn	2
5. Holquintlein. anderthalb[78]		5. Hohlquint	1 1/2
6. Zimbeln kleine	2.Chor	6. Zimbel, small	II ranks
7. Regal	8	7. Regal	8
8. Geigend Regal von holtze	4	8. Geigend Regal of wood	4

Im Rueck Positiff 12. Stimmen		In the Rueckpositive, 12 voices	
1. Principal	8.fusz	1. Principal	8 foot
2. Grosz Nachthorn	8	2. Gross Nachthorn	8
3. Gedactfloeite von Holtz	8	3. Gedacktfloete of wood	8
4. Nasat Pfeiffe von Holtz[79]	4	4. Nasat Pfeife of wood	4
5. Spill Pfeiff	4	5. Spillpfeife	4
6. Klein Roehrfloeit	4	6. Klein Rohrfloete	4
7. Klein Octava	2	7. Klein Octave	2
8. Klein Gedact	2	8. Klein Gedackt	2
9. Suifloeit	1	9. Siffloete	1
10. Klingend Zimbel	3.Chor	10. Klingend Zimbel III ranks	
11. Rancket von Holtz	16	11. Rankett of wood	16
12. Krumbhorn.	8	12. Krummhorn	8

Im Pedal sind 13. Stimmen		In the Pedal, 13 [16] voices	
1. Sub Principal Basz	32	1. Sub Principal Bass	32
2. Grosz Rohrfloeit B.	16	2. Gross Rohrfloete Bass	16

		German				English	
3.	Grosz Gemszhorn B.	16		3.	Gross Gemshorn Bass	16
4.	Holpfeiffen B.	8		4.	Hohlpfeiffe Bass	8
5.	Grosz Nachthorn B.	8		5.	Gross Nachthorn Bass	8
6.	Querfloeiten Basz von Holtz	8		6.	Querfloete Bass of wood	8
7.	Octaven B.	4		7.	Octave Bass	4
8.	Klein Gemszhorn B.	4		8.	Klein Gemshorn Bass	4
9.	Trommeten B.	8		9.	Trumpet Bass	8
10.	Posaun oder Bombard B.	16		10.	Posaune or Bombarde Bass	16

Brust Pedalia   **Brust Pedal**

		German				English	
11.	Hornbaeszlein	2		11.	Horn Bass	2
12.	Bawrpfeifflein	1		12.	Bauerfloete Bass	1
13.	Zimbel Basz	3.Choericht		13.	Zimbel Bass	III ranks
14.	Sordunbasz von Holtz	16.fi.		14.	Sordun Bass of wood	16 ft.
15.	Dolcianbasz von Holtz	8.fi.		15.	Dulzian Bass of wood	8 ft.
16.	Cornett Basz	2.fi.		16.	Kornett Bass	2 ft.

Manual Clavirs Disposition.   Disposition of the manual claviers

```
              As                                      Ab
     Ds    Fs  Gs   B            D#    E#    F#  G#   Bb
 C D    E F   G    A   ♮      C D    E F   G    A    B

       es        as                  eb        ab
    cs  ds   fs  gs          c#   d#      f#   g#
 c    d    e f   g   a etc.  c   d    e f   g    a etc.

 bisz ins c̿ f̿              up to c''' f'''
```

Pedal Clavier.   Pedal clavier

Fs   Gs   F#   G#
  D   E   B   cs   D   E   Bb   c#
C F   G   A   ♮ c   d   C F   G   A   B c   d

es   as   eb   ab
ds   fs   gs   b   c̄s   d#   f#   g#   bb   c#'
  e f   g   a   h c̄   e f   g   a   b c'

d̄ ē.   d' e'

The following rearrangement of the registers pre-

sents the Bueckeburg instrument in an equivalent modern

form:[80]

Stadtkirche, Bueckeburg[81]

Built by Esaias Compenius in 1615. The planning
and execution of the instrument were undoubtedly carried out
under the direct supervision and cooperation of M. Praetorius. The disposition indicates a straight three-manual
instrument not encumbered with permanent coupling or with
borrowed basses.

Oberwerk

1. 16' Principal   8. 4' Octave

2. 16' Quintade   9. 4' Blockfloete
                                      (covered)
3. 8' Octave
                                  7. 4' Querfloete
5. 8' Blockfloete (covered)
                                  10. 2 2/3' Gemshorn
4. 8' Gemshorn
                                  11. 2' Flachfloete
6. 8' Viola da Gamba
                                  12. VIII-XIV Mixture

Brust

1. 8' Rohrfloete
3. 4' Offenfloete
2. 4' Nachthorn
4. 2' Gemshorn

5. 1 1/3' Hohlquint
6. II Zimbel
7. 8' Regal
8. 4' Geigend Regal

Rueckpositive

1. 8' Principal
3. 8' Gedacktfloete
2. 8' Nachthorn
4. 4' Nasat
6. 4' Rohrfloete
5. 4' Spillpfeife

7. 2' Octave
8. 2' Gedackt
9. 1' Siffloete
10. III Klingend Zimbel
11. 16' Rankett
12. 8' Krummhorn

Pedal

1. 32' Principal
2. 16' Rohrfloete
3. 16' Gemshorn
4. 8' Hohlfloete
5. 8' Nachthorn
6. 8' Querfloete
7. 4' Octave
8. 4' Gemshorn

11. 2' Horn
12. 1' Bauerfloete
13. III Zimbel
10. 16' Posaune (Bombarde)
14. 16' Sordun
9. 8' Trumpet
15. 8' Dulzian

Accessories

Coupler: Brust to Oberwerk
Tremulants: Oberwerk
            Rueckpositive
            Pedal
Bellows control

Short bass octave in manuals

Short bass octave in Pedal

Split keys for certain sub-semitones

Transient Pedal Couplers

To the present author's knowledge there is no pedal coupler from the Early Baroque still in existence today, and

the subsequent theoretical treatises either do not concern
themselves with the primitive forms of pedal couplers or
describe them only in a somewhat haphazardly qualitative
way. Practically all of them define the effects of the early
pedal couplers rather than delineate their construction or
precise operation within the system. The present author,
by extensive research into the classical theorists has been
unable to find any drawings or sketches that would provide
definitive information as to how the pedal couplers were
constructed or how they were incorporated into the actions
of the early instruments here under discussion. Photographs
of remnants relating to the subject appear to be non-existent.

It is necessary, therefore, to rely entirely upon
the descriptive accounts of subsequent theorists and to reconstruct in a hypothetical way, operating mechanisms which
reflect the engineering skill of the early builders as gathered from our previous discussion of the manual couplers,
take into account the prevailing methods of key disposition
and harness layout, and, thereupon, compare these possible
solutions with the qualitative descriptions that have come
down to us since that time, and which can be relied upon to
reflect a concern for detail and accuracy, and display an
acute historical sense.

Most noteworthy among these accounts are those of
Jakob Adlung (1699-1762), whose previous accounts served so
well in rediscovering the action of the manual couplers. His

account follows:

Wenn aber das Pedal an das
Manual gekoppelt werden soll,
so hat man ein absonderliches
manubrium und Registratur
dazu, welche auch Windkoppel
genennet wird. Manche sind
so gemacht, dasz die Fuesze
koennen auf dem Pedal stehen
bleiben, wenn das Koppel gezogen wird: aber zuweilen
ist das Gegentheil. Durch
das Koppel wird selten das
Manual an das Pedal verbunden: durch besondere Ab-
strakten, und andere Dinge,
wird es dahin gebracht,
dasz, wenn das Pedal getret-
en wird, auch die Register
des Manuals sich hoeren lassen.

• • • • • • • • • • • • •

When, however, the Pedal is
to be coupled to the Manual, a
special draw knob and registrational device is provided,
known also as a wind coupler.
Some [coupler mechanisms] are
so constructed that the feet
[of the player] may depress
the keys while the coupler is
being drawn [into registra-
tion]; occasionally, however,
the opposite is true. More
rarely, the Manual is connected to the Pedal by means of
the [mechanical] coupler, [in
contradistinction to the wind
coupler mentioned above].
Through special trackers and
other devices the mechanism is
so arranged that when the pedal keys are depressed, the
manual registers speak also.

• • • • • • • • • • • • •

Wo aber das Manual nicht
bestaendig mitgehet im
Pedal; so wird solches durch
einen Zug zuwege gebracht.
Und das geschiehet wieder
auf mancherley Weise. Denn
man macht entweder die Manuallade mit doppelten Ventilen, oder mit einem.
Macht man sie mit einem, so
werden zuweilen die Pedal-
palmuln durch besondere Abstrakten und Zuege mit den
Manualpalmuln so verbunden,
dasz sich diese mit nieder-
ziehen. Auf solche Art
wird in der Orgel zu St. An-
dreae in Erfurt das untere
Clavier an das Pedal verbunden.

Whenever the Manual is not
permanently coupled to the
Pedal, a draw knob is required
to engage [the coupling mecha-
nism]. This, in turn, is accomplished in several ways.
Either the manual chest is
constructed with single [pal-
lets] or with double pallets.
If the manual chests are provided with single [pallets],
then, in some cases, the pedal
keys are connected by special
trackers and draw knobs to the
manual keys in such a way,
that the latter are visibly
activated [when the pedal keys
are depressed while the coupler is "on"]. In the St. Andreas organ at Erfurt, the lowest Manual is connected to the
Pedal in this manner.

Oder, welches gemeiner ist, man verbindet durch besondere Zuege die Manualabstrakten an das Pedal, dasz die Manualpalmuln sich nicht bewegen. Und da koennen die Fuesze, wie auch im vorigen Falle, nicht auf dem Pedal stehen bleiben, wenn man das Koppel ziehet. Dieses Koppel ist zu Erfurt in der Kaufmannsorgel, auch an einigen andern Oertern, so, dasz man es mit den Fueszen schieben kann. Wie solches zugehe, ist besser zu sehen, als zu schreiben.

Or, more commonly, the manual trackers are connected to the Pedal by special draw knobs, so that the manual keys are not visibly activated [when the pedal keys are depressed while the coupler is "on"]. In this case, as also in the preceding, the feet may not depress the pedal [keys] when the knob [to engage the coupler] is being drawn. This coupler [mechanism] appears in the Kaufmann organ at Erfurt, and at several other places, and is so arranged, that [the mechanism] can be engaged by means of the feet. How this is accomplished is easier to see than to describe.

Die andere Hauptart der Koppel ist mit doppelten Ventilen auf der Manuallade. Diese Ventile liegen zuweilen hinten und vornen; da eine Reihe durch die Abstrakten, die an die Manualclaves verbunden sind, aufgezogen wird, die andere Reihe gegenueber durch besondere Abstrakten, so vom Pedal hinauf gefuehret werden: diese aber gehen nur durch soviel Cancellen, als das Pedal Claves hat. Folglich musz auch ein besonderer Windkasten auf der andern Seite gemacht seyn, und der Wind durch einen besonderen Kanal aus dem Manualkanale dahin gefuehret werden. Aber diese Art hat eine ganz besondere Incommoditaet bey sich, davon ich anderswo etwas gedenken will.[82]

The other chief method of coupling is by [means of] double pallets in the manual chest. These pallets are, at times, placed [both] under the front and rear [portions of the chest]; one row is opened by [a set of] trackers connected with the manual keys, the opposite row by a separate set of trackers connected with the pedal keys; these, however, involve only as many channels as are required by the number of pedal keys, [hence, only in the bass portion of the chest]. Accordingly, a special pallet box must be provided on the rear portion of the chest, and the wind must be conveyed to this additional [or, secondary] pallet box by means of a separate wind conductor leading from the manual wind trunk into it. This method [of coupling] brings with it certain inconveniences which I shall discuss elsewhere.

Daher andere die Ventile

For this reason, others place

des Manuals und Pedals auf eine Seite bringen, und neben einander legen, dasz z. E. die Cancelle C nur einmal da ist, aber im Windkasten hat sie zwo Oefnungen neben einander, deren jede mit einem besonderen Ventile bedeckt wird, und wird das eine durch die Pedalabstrakten, das andere durch das Manual aufgezogen.[83]

the pallets of the Manual and Pedal side by side along the [front portion of the] chest, so that, for example, only one channel is provided for [the note] C, but two openings are cut side by side between the [channel and] pallet box, each of which is covered with a separate pallet; one [pallet] is then opened by the pedal trackers, the other by the manual trackers. [Translation by the present author]

This somewhat garrulous exposition on the possible methods of pedal coupling prevalent in Adlung's day permits of several interpretations. The following outline summarizes the present author's interpretation of the various methods of coupling that were in use at Adlung's time and of which some were undoubtedly practiced by the early baroque builders at the time of Praetorius:

A. Mechanical Pedal Coupler

1. Transient, but direct mechanical connection between pedal key and manual key (the manual key is visibly activated by the pedal key). This form can be realized by the cleat coupler and the backfall coupler. See Plates LXII and LXIII

2. Transient mechanical connection between manual harness and pedal harness (the manual key is not visibly activated by the pedal key). This form can be realized by the square coupler. See Plate LXIV

3. Pedal transiently connected to pedal pallets of a dual set of pallets in the bass portion of a single pallet box attached to the manual chest (there is no direct connection to the corresponding manual key). This form can be realized by the square-pallet coupler. See Plate LXV

B. Pneumatic Pedal Coupler

1. Pedal permanently connected to pedal pallets of a dual set of pallets in a secondary pallet box attached to the bass portion of the manual chest; coupler effect is controlled by inflating or exhausting the secondary pallet box. This form is generally referred to by the theorists as the bass-ventil coupler. See Plate LXVI

A hypothetical reconstruction of the manual-to-pedal cleat coupler is given in one possible form on Plate LXII, figs. 1-3. In fig. 1, Rp designates the Rueckpositive or lowest manual clavier mounted typically as a second class lever. The sticker B passes downward through the roller system C and the movable register D (in the form of a bearing stock) and terminates in a notched form at its lower extremity. To it is permanently attached a bevelled cleat A which is positioned directly beneath the notched key nose of the pedal key P. When the pedal key P is depressed it will, by virtue of the cleat A move the sticker B downward, depressing

both the manual key Rp and the backfall E which, rising at
its opposite end, opens the pallet H of the Rueckpositive
chest G, thereby causing the appropriate manual note to sound.
Chest F is the regular pedal chest which is directly connected
to the pedal key without reference to the coupler mechanism.
Fig. 2 shows the position of the coupler when disengaged.
The bearing stock D, having been moved to the right an appropriate distance, has moved the gang of stickers B along with
it, and so disengaged all of the cleats A. The pedal key P
travels freely without engaging any notes of the Rueckpositive. As will be observed, the coupler cannot be drawn into
operating position while any pedal keys are depressed; the
Pedal must be idle during this operation. Fig. 3 gives a
perspective detail of the critical junctures of the device.

A possible realization of the backfall coupler is
presented on Plate LXIII, figs. 1-3. Although a more sophisticated form of a Rueckpositive-to-Pedal coupler than the
cleat coupler, its application or an equivalent one in the
Early Baroque is not entirely precluded, but is, in the present author's opinion, unlikely. It is presented here because
it illustrates one of the cases described by Adlung. In
fig. 1, Rp designates the Rueckpositive or lowest clavier
mounted in the usual fashion of the time as a second class
lever. The sticker A passes downward through the roller system B and terminates in the square G which transforms its
downward motion to a horizontal one, and by means of the

square $\underline{I}$ reconverts to a vertical motion upward, thus opening the pallet $\underline{J}$ in the Rueckpositive chest $\underline{N}$. To the sticker $\underline{A}$ are attached two cleats $\underline{E}$, one on each side of it. When
the pedal key $\underline{P}$ is depressed, its nose will depress backfall
$\underline{F}$, which, by means of the sticker $\underline{Q}$ and the backfall $\underline{C}$, will
exert a downward force on the cleats $\underline{E}$, thus moving the
sticker $\underline{A}$ downward and causing the appropriate note to sound
in the Rueckpositive chest $\underline{N}$. Fig. 2 shows the coupler in a
disengaged attitude. The bearing stock $\underline{D}$, having been raised
a certain distance, has removed the gang of backfalls $\underline{C}$ from
their juxtaposition to cleats $\underline{E}$, thereby permitting them to
run idle when the pedal keys $\underline{P}$ are depressed. Fig. 3 shows
one enlarged detail of the critical juncture in the coupler
mechanism. As shown, the coupler is disengaged. It will be
noted that the corresponding manual key will tend to fall
when the coupler is engaged and a pedal key is depressed.

The square coupler bespeaks the conditions set forth
by Adlung for a transient mechanical connection between the
manual harness and the pedal harness, whereby the manual key
is not visibly influenced by the depression of the pedal key
while the coupler is "on". Plate LXIV, figs. 1-3 is an adaptation of a square coupler as presented by Seidel.[84] Fig. 1
shows the mechanism in operating attitude. The motion of
the pedal key $\underline{P}$ is transmitted by means of sticker $\underline{A}$, square
$\underline{B}$, and tracker $\underline{C}$ to point $\underline{F}$ and beyond through bridge $\underline{G}$ to
the pedal pallet in the pedal chest $\underline{I}$. The cleat $\underline{F}$ influences

the square <u>E</u>, which, rotating in bearing stock <u>D</u>, transmits a downward motion to tracker <u>H</u> which rotates backfall <u>J</u> and opens the manual pallet in chest <u>K</u>. Fig. 2 shows the mechanism as disengaged. The bearing stock <u>D</u>, having been moved a certain distance to the left, has removed the gang of squares <u>E</u> from juxtaposition to the cleats <u>F</u>, allowing the tracker <u>C</u> to move freely without influencing the squares <u>E</u>, the trackers <u>H</u>, and the pallets in the manual chest <u>K</u>. Fig. 3 shows the critical juncture point of the coupler when engaged.

The <u>square-pallet coupler</u> illustrated in Plate LXV, meets Adlung's conditions for a pedal coupler communicating between the pedal key and separate pedal pallets mounted between the manual pallets in the bass portion of the manual chest.[85] The coupler operates in every respect as the square coupler discussed above, with this exception, that the tracker <u>A</u> (fig. 1) is not attached to the manual harness but to independent pallets introduced between the manual pallets. Accordingly, this is not a keyboard-to-keyboard coupler but an independent pedal harness communicating with the manual chest. Fig. 2 shows the coupler disengaged by appropriate positioning of bearing stock <u>B</u>. In fig. 3 a front view of the manual chest reveals the dual set of pallets. Pallets <u>A</u> are connected to the manual trackers, while pallets <u>B</u> are connected to the pedal harness. Both pallets <u>A</u> and <u>B</u> serve channel <u>C</u>, etc. and are mounted side by side.

The bass ventil coupler is really a permanent mechanical disposition in which the coupling effect can be nulli-
fied by deflating a pallet box, permitting the pallets therein to run idle. Plate LXVI, figs. 1-3, gives the necessary
accessories required to realize the coupling action. In fig.
1, the manual chest A is supplied with a primary pallet box
and pallets B which are harnessed directly to the Ow keyboard. The bass portion (or portions, if divided into C and
C♯ sides) of the chest exhibit a secondary pallet box and as
many pallets C as there are keys on the pedalboard P. The
manual keyboard operates pallets B while the pedalboard operates pallets C by a fixed harness G. Each pallet box is
provided with a wind-trunk ventil, the one at E serving to
admit or check the air flow from wind conductor D into the
primary (manual) pallet box, while the one at F serves the
same purpose for the secondary (pedal) pallet box. In fig.
1, air is admitted to both pallet boxes, but neither a manual nor a pedal key is depressed; hence, no notes are sounding. In fig. 2, wind is admitted to both boxes, and a pedal
pallet is open; hence the note controlled by the corresponding pedal key is responding to the depression of the key:
the coupler is "on". In fig. 3, although the pedal pallet
is open because of a depressed pedal key, the corresponding
note does not sound because the secondary pallet box is exhausted of wind; the pallet runs idle and the coupler is
"off".

The foregoing analysis and projection of Adlung's account reveals at least four, if not five, distinct methods of realizing the coupling effect between a manual and the Pedal. Of these, it would seem that the cleat coupler or some closely related variant of it, found general application in the early baroque instruments. The contention can be arrived at inductively by a careful examination of Praetorius' meager reports:

1. In almost every instance where a pedal coupler is specified, the coupling effect is between the lowest manual (Rueckpositive) and the Pedal

2. The Rueckpositive manual was, according to all available evidence, laid out as a second class lever mechanism

3. The earliest and best sources indicate a transmission of the manual key motion by means of a rigid sticker operating downward

4. Dom Bedos frequently shows an elongated backfall connection between the extremity of the sticker and the pallet box of the Rueckpositive chest[86]

5. The principle of the cleat coupler mechanism, having found wide application in the manual-to-manual systems, could, by analogy, easily and likely have been applied to a manual-to-pedal situation, even though its application required the additional feature of a blind clavier in the form of a gang of stickers

6. Its application to the manual-to-pedal situation exhibited the same inconveniences which occurred in its manual-to-manual application[87]

In the present author's judgment, it is unlikely that the backfall coupler, the square coupler, or the square-pallet coupler mechanisms constituted routine mechanical appliances for the early baroque builders. It cannot be definitely proved that these were later inventions, but the greatest evidence for their absence are:

1. They show a degree of sophistication in mechanical engineering for which no real analogy can be found in the work of the early masters

2. They are all Oberwerk (upper clavier)-to-Pedal couplers, and none of the specifications in Praetorius' catalog ever mention such a coupling effect by mechanical means. The one case (Luebeck, Liebfrauen) which does indicate some such connection specifies the presence of a ventil system which could indicate the presence of a pneumatic pedal coupler

3. Any connections between manuals (other than the Rueckpositive) and the Pedal seem to have been of a permanent nature, not subject to engagement or disengagement by the player

The pneumatic coupler, requiring a double set of pallets in twin pallet boxes in the bass portions of the manual chest, is alluded to in several instances by Praetorius. We

know that Gottfried Silbermann (1683-1753) returned to the
device in his mature instruments; there is, therefore, much
reason to believe that its invention and application took
place among the early baroque builders. It found an appropriate use whenever it was desired to establish a transient
coupling effect between the Manual (not Rueckpositive) chest
and the Pedal.

The various statements used by Praetorius to indicate
a transient manual-to-pedal coupler are here presented in
full together with the present author's interpretation in a
modern sense:

1. Coppel zum Pedal vnd   1. Coupler for the Pedal
Rueckpositiff[88]   and Rueckpositive

   In a modern sense one would say, "Rueckpositive-to-
   Pedal"; no doubt this is intended to designate a
   transient mechanical coupler analagous to the cleat
   coupler

2. Coppel des Pedals im   2. Coupler of the Pedal in
(zum) Rueckpositiff (Posi-   the Rueckpositive (Positive)
tiff)[89]

   These are archaic expressions for "Rueckpositive-to-
   Pedal"; a transient mechanical coupler is indicated;
   most likely some form of cleat coupler

3. Coppel zum Rueckposi-   3. Coupler for the Rueck-
tiff / vnd Pedal[90]   positive and Pedal

The expression indicates a mechanical but transient
"Rueckpositive-to-Pedal" coupler

4. Coppel zum Pedal[91]   4. Coupler for the Pedal

The precise meaning is not apparent, but likely a
"Rueckpositive-to-Pedal" coupler. The actual effect
can only be surmised from the context

5. Coppel[92]   5. Coupler

The appellation is indeterminate; it can indicate
either a manual-to-manual or a manual-to-pedal
coupler

6. Coppel zum Pedal vnnd   6. Coupler for the Pedal
Manual[93]   and Manual

The designation is not clear whether one or two couplers are meant. However, internal specifications in
the Praetorius account of this instrument would indicate a bass-ventil coupler between the Oberwerk
manual chest and the Pedal[94]

Conclusions

On the basis of the foregoing detailed discussion of
transient coupling, a few conclusions can be drawn and summarized here, which seem to bespeak the extent to which the
concept was applied to the instruments of the early baroque
organ builders:

1. Transient manual-to-manual couplers were employed to a limited extent in the instruments of the

time

2. The coupling was achieved by simple mechanical means; it appears that the cleat coupler was generally used; the act of engaging the coupler required the displacement of one clavier; while drawing the coupler, the lower manual had to remain in a state of rest

3. The coupling effect was generally upward; a lower manual could be coupled to an upper one, not the reverse; the usual coupling was Rueckpositive-to-Oberwerk (or equivalent manual); coupling always involved two adjacent keyboards

4. Transient manual-to-pedal coupling found a limited application

5. The coupling was achieved by simple mechanical means; it can be surmised that some form of cleat coupler was employed; the act of engaging the coupler required the displacement of a blind clavier; while drawing the coupler, the Pedal had to remain in a state of rest

6. The mechanical coupler was used to couple the Rueckpositive to the Pedal; no other combinations are anywhere in evidence

7. Occasionally but rarely, coupling of another manual (other than the Rueckpositive) and the Pedal was achieved by means of the bass-ventil coupler; this

comprised a fixed harness between the Pedal and the main manual chest, and the coupling effect was engaged or disengaged by controlling the access of wind to a secondary pallet box containing the pedal ventils

The apparent lack or omission of other coupling effects beyond those enumerated suggests that some other method besides transient coupling found application in these instruments. The following chapter (ix) will seek to explore the concept of permanent coupling and delineate its function as it may have found application in the Early Baroque.

CHAPTER IX

CHEST LAYOUT AND CONTROL

In order to arrive at a knowledgeable understanding
of the theory of the Praetorius organ, it is of the utmost
importance to reconstruct, as far as possible, the schematic
layouts of the various chests of the instruments of his time
and to develop the methods used in harnessing the same to
the several keyboards. These methods were various and often
compound and, as the ramifications of the harness systems
had a considerable influence upon the tonal dispositions of
the instruments, a careful perusal of the layout and harness
dispositions must be undertaken. Many, if not most, of the
dispositions presented by Praetorius in his catalog of dispositions[1] are unintelligible to the modern student of the
organ unless a clear understanding of layout and harness together with their possibilities and limitations are brought
to bear upon any analyses of the instruments he discusses.
By such an approach, the tonal resources and their incorporation in these instruments come back to life, as it were,
and reasonably clear understandings can be gained and critical appraisals made. Truly enough, not every single instance permits of a total solution, but the gain in

understanding is of such considerable dimensions, that a detailed study is warranted.

Subsequent theorists[2] of the organ are remarkably meager in substantial information on the subject. A few allusions or references to historical practice do appear, but these are barely sufficient to serve as points of departure. The bulk of the information must be painstakingly gleaned from Praetorius' own allusions and references as they are scattered throughout the De Organographia. By a careful selection, appraisal, and synthesis of these morsels, a fairly acceptable theory can be built up and reinforced by diligent application to the various examples of instruments appearing in the catalog of dispositions. The most obvious avenue of research, that of inspecting existing remaining monuments of the time, lies closed to our study. All of the instruments of the time, save one, have largely disappeared, and those which do present vestigial mechanisms have been subject to repeated revisions and modifications, so that no authentic information can be gathered from them, particularly in the area of mechanical disposition.[3] Remnants that do still exist are largely individual sets of pipes and, in some cases, the facades and consoles of the instruments. The Frederiksborg instrument in Denmark happens to exhibit a very normal type of harness, already commonly known from more recent examples of the organ builder's art.

<u>Terminology</u> <u>and</u> <u>Codification</u>

Any study of the layout and control mechanism of the early baroque instruments must assort the various terms used by Praetorius in describing these portions of the mechanism. All literature pertaining to instruments of the time describes the layout of the organ from the vantage point of the main chest, relating all other chests to this central member by appropriate designations which serve to indicate their physical location in reference to the main chest. This point of view is in direct contrast to the modern practice of describing the instrument from the vantage point of the console and of the keyboards. Accordingly, great care must be exercised, both in the presentation and interpretation of information gleaned from the <u>De Organographia</u>, to differentiate the various terms. The following terms, together with an appropriate and useful code letter provided by the present author, are used by Praetorius to describe the various chests of the instrument:[4]

W :	Werk	Up :	Unterpositive
OW :	Oberwerk	Vp :	Vorpositive
GW :	Grosswerk	Rp :	Rueckpositive
M :	Manual	Sp :	Seitenpositive
B :	Brust	P :	Pedal
Bo :	Brust, above[5]	Pw :	Pedal-in-the-Werk
Bu :	Brust, below[6]	Po :	Pedal-in-the-Oberwerk

Bp : Brustpositive   Pm : Pedal-in-the-Manual

Op : Oberpositive   BP : Brust Pedalia

The main chest is generally designated by the terms Werk, Oberwerk, Grosswerk, or Manual, as the case may be. The second major and consistently independent division is usually identified by the terms Rueckpositive or Seitenpositive. The occasionally independent division but, more usually, a subdivision of the main chest is identified by such terms as Brust, Brust oben, Brust unten, Brustpositive, Oberpositive, Unterpositive, or Vorpositive. The independent pedal division is designated simply as Pedal, Pedal-Baesse, Pedal auf beyden Seiten, or Pedal in den Tuermen.[7] A subdivision of the pedal chest when mounted in the proximity of the Brust is variously called Brust Pedalia, Pedal in der Brust, Brust Pedal, etc. Individual segments (one or two stops) of the Pedal when mounted with the main chest and supported by the cradle (G. Stuhl) are occasionally referred to as Pedal im Werk, Pedal im Oberwerk, or Pedal im Manual, as the case may be.

The Single Harness

The single harness was frequently used in the Early Baroque and identifies a single control mechanism for each individual full chest of the instrument. It was, in its engineering aspects, equivalent to the tracker harnesses that are known to us from more recent examples of mechanical organs in our own time. By means of squares, backfalls, trackers, stickers, and roller board systems the motion of the key was transmitted from the individual keyboards to the pertinent chests to be controlled by the respective keyboards.

The Straight Two-Manual

A straight[8] two-manual and Pedal organ normally required three independent harnesses; one served the Oberwerk, a second, the Rueckpositive, and a third, the Pedal.

A typical layout for such an instrument is schematically illustrated in Plate LXVII, fig. 1, which shows the physical orientation of the component chests. The Oberwerk chest OW was centrally positioned and generally mounted off the floor (in fact, a considerable distance, sufficient to clear the console, the music rack, and the necessary internal machinery, such as roller boards and the like) and supported by a structural framework known as a cradle. The Pedal chest P was usually (though not always) divided into two separate parts, one exhibiting the pipes C, D, E, F$\sharp$, G$\sharp$, A$\sharp$, etc., and the other, the alternate pipes C$\sharp$, D$\sharp$, F, G, A, B, etc.[9] These chests were most often placed much nearer to the floor and were arranged to flank the Oberwerk chest OW on both sides. The Rueckpositive chest Rp was in almost all cases mounted by the gallery rail and behind the player, the chest being very nearly at floor level. The console was positioned centrally between the Oberwerk OW and the Rueck-

positive Rp, the player facing the Oberwerk OW.

The harness for such a two-manual and Pedal layout
is schematically presented in Plate LXVII, figs. 2 and 3.
To the Oberwerk key OW is attached a tracker leading upward
through a roller board B (necessary to respace the planes of
the trackers) to the pallet C in the Oberwerk chest OW. A
depression of the Oberwerk key will open pallet C. A sticker
D leads downward from the Rueckpositive key Rp and is loosely
attached to backfall E. Another sticker F leads upward from
the opposite end of backfall E to the pallet G in the Rueckpositive chest Rp. The gang of backfalls E are arranged in
the form of a fan frame, so as to respace the planes of
stickers D in stickers F. A depression of the Rueckpositive
key will open pallet G. A short sticker H leads from the
nose of pedal key P to square I. From here the tracker J
leads to roller K whose projecting arms are at right angles
to each other. A tracker L leads from roller K to square M,
from which another tracker N leads upward to pallet O in
pedal chest P. A depression of the pedal key will open
pallet O. The three harnesses described are all single harnesses, i.e., each harness communicates only between one keyboard and one chest.

The single harness found application in nearly every
instrument found described in Praetorius' catalog of dispositions. Its main application is found in the control mechanism

of the Rueckpositive. The writer has been unable, by careful examination of all the examples presented by Praetorius,
to find a single instance where other than a single harness
control was introduced into the Rueckpositive manual and
chest. From this apparent fact it can be deduced that the
Rueckpositive was always handled mechanically as an independent division and, therefore, any attempt to discover the concept of a tonal corpus as practiced in the Early Baroque must
look to the Rueckpositive dispositions as exemplary. In most
cases, all other divisions of the instruments involved the
use of compound harnesses; they present, therefore, only
fractional corpora.

The Straight Three-Manual

Occasionally a straight three-manual and Pedal plan
appears among the dispositions of Praetorius. Such a layout
is certainly not general or common, but it does occur and
must be presented here in its logical place among the single
harness controls. In such cases single harnesses are applicable and adequate, and the layout presents four complete
divisions or equivalents: Oberwerk, Brust, Rueckpositive,
and Pedal.

Plate LXVIII, fig. 1 shows a typical arrangement for
this condition. The Oberwerk OW again occupies the central
position. Underneath and in front of it is positioned the
Brustwerk B. The Pedal P, divided into two sections, flanks

the Oberwerk OW on both sides. The Rueckpositive Rp lies behind the console and in front of the Oberwerk. The chest levels are similar to those described for the two-manual situation, except for the additional member of the Brust, which generally appears beneath the Oberwerk chest.

The harness for a straight three-manual and Pedal layout is schematically presented in Plate LXVIII, fig. 2. The Rueckpositive and Pedal are controlled similarly as in the two-manual layout. The Brust chest B is directly attached to the topmost keyboard by tracker A. A depression of the Brust key will open the corresponding pallet C. A roller board may or may not be necessary, depending upon the spacing of the pallets C. To the Oberwerk key is attached a tracker D which passes through an oversize hole in the corresponding key of the Brust key B. Tracker D is attached to square E, from which another tracker F leads to square G; here the motion is reconverted to a vertical direction and leads by means of tracker H through the roller board I to pallet J. A depression of the Oberwerk key will open pallet J in the Oberwerk chest. Fig. 3 shows a possible harness where the Oberwerk keyboard occupies the topmost position while the Brust keyboard occupies a middle position in the console.

Basic Situations

All single harness situations can be visualized more

easily by stating them in code form. The code is in the form of a fraction, where the numerator (a letter) represents the chest while the denominator (also a letter) represents the keyboard. Accordingly, the three harnesses described in connection with the two-manual and Pedal situation may be concisely represented and interpreted as:

1. OW / OW : The Oberwerk chest is controlled by the Oberwerk keyboard

2. Rp / Rp : The Rueckpositive chest is controlled by the Rueckpositive keyboard

3. P / P : The Pedal chest is controlled by the Pedal keyboard

The four harnesses of the three-manual and Pedal layout described above may be represented and interpreted as:

1. B / B : The Brust chest is controlled by the Brust keyboard

2. OW / OW : The Oberwerk chest is controlled by the Oberwerk keyboard

3. Rp / Rp : The Rueckpositive chest is controlled by the Rueckpositive keyboard

4. P / P : The Pedal chest is controlled by the Pedal keyboard

Survey of Examples

A perusal of the instruments presented in Praetorius' catalog of dispositions reveals very few straight layouts employing single harnesses; more usually, double and compound harnesses were necessary to realize the control of the instruments. The following cases show what appear to have been straight organs which could have been adequately controlled by sets of single harnesses:

1. Braunschweig, St. Blasius.[10] A two-manual and Pedal instrument exhibiting the model layout form described above. Probably single harnesses throughout: OW / OW; Rp / Rp; P / P. It will be observed that the three tonal corpora are numerically well balanced: Oberwerk, 13 voices; Rueckpositive, 11 voices; Pedal, 14 voices. Each tonal corpus exhibits a full complement containing a core of Principal and non-Principal voices, an appropriate crown structure, and a representation of mutation pitches. Praetorius draws especial attention to the unique character of the Pedal, pointing out that all of the bass voices are independent and placed on a full pedal chest.[11]

2. Hessen, Schlosz.[12] A straight two-manual and Pedal instrument compactly laid out into a single case. Single harnesses only are indicated: OM / OM (Ober Manual chest controlled by Ober Manual keyboard); UM / UM (Unter Manual chest controlled by Unter Manual keyboard); P / P. The tonal corpora are perfectly balanced: Ober Manual, 9 voices; Unter Manual, 9 voices; Pedal, 9 voices. A full

presentation of the instrument appears below

3. _Monk's Organ_.[13] A straight two-manual and
Pedal instrument laid out compactly into one case.
Single harnesses are suggested: OC / OC (Ober Clavier chest controlled by Ober Clavier keyboard);
UC / UC (Unter Clavier chest controlled by Unter Clavier keyboard); P / P. Again, the instrument exhibits a good balance between the several corpora: Ober
Clavier, 5 voices; Unter Clavier, 4 voices; Pedal, 5
voices

There is, of course, no real guarantee that all three
instruments were straight layouts, or that in every case only
single harnesses were used; these conditions are, at present,
impossible to prove. However, the balanced corpora, their
internal complements, and the occasional bits of information
provided by Praetorius would lead the present author to believe very strongly, that the layouts and harnesses could
have been, and very likely were, as suggested.

A famous example of a straight two-manual and Pedal
instrument, worthy of closer examination, is the _Hessen_,
Schlosz instrument.[14] This organ was built by Esaias Com-
penius in close cooperation with Michael Praetorius. Both
men were simultaneously in the official employ of Bishop and
Prince Heinrich Julius of the Braunschweig-Lueneburg court.[15]
The instrument was erected at the Hessen _Schlosz_ in 1612.[16]
Upon the death of Heinrich Julius it was presented to the

King of Denmark by the widow, who was a sister of Christian IV, the Danish monarch.[17] Compenius personally re-erected the instrument in the Frederiksborg <u>Schloszkirche</u> in 1616-1617. Compenius died and was buried there. The instrument is still in working order today, having been painstakingly reconditioned without significant change in 1895 by Felix Reinburg of the French firm of Cavaillé-Coll.[18] It is the only remaining complete instrument of the Early Baroque whose authenticity is beyond question.

XXI.

Zu Hessen vffm Schlosse.[19]

Das hoeltzern / Aber doch sehr herrliche Orgelwerck so von M. Esaia Compenio An. 1612. gemacht. Jetzo aber dem Koenig in Dennemarck verehret / vnd Anno 1616. doselbsten zu Friedrichsburg in der Kirchen gesetzet worden / ist starck von 27. Stimmen / Coppel zu beyden Manualn. Tremulant. Grosser Bock. Sackpfeife. Kleinhuemlichen.

Im obern Manual
9. Stimmen

1. Principal	8.fusz
2. Klein Principal von Elffenbein vnd Ebenholtz	4
3. Gedactfloeite	8
4. Gemszhorn oder klein Violn	4
5. Nachthorn	4
6. Blockpfeiffen	4

XXI

At Hessen in the Castle.

The wooden, but very magnificent instrument built by Master Esaias Compenius in the year 1612, and since presented to the King of Denmark; it was erected in the church at Frederiksborg in 1616. It comprises 27 voices, a coupler for the two manuals, a tremulant, a Bock tremulant, a bagpipe drone, and a musette.

For the Upper Manual,
9 voices

1. Principal	8 foot
2. Klein Principal of ivory and ebony	4
3. Gedacktfloete	8
4. Gemshorn or Klein Viola	4
5. Nachthorn	4
6. Blockpfeife	4

7. Gedact Quint	3	7. Gedackt Quint	3
8. Supergedactfloeitlin	2	8. Super Gedacktfloete	2
9. Rancket	16	9. Rankett	16

Im Unter Manual /
vnten an statt des
Positiffs
9. Stimmen

For the Lower Manual,
below and in place of the
Positive,
9 voices

1. Quintadehna	8.fi.	1. Quintade	8 ft.
2. Klein Gedactfloeite	4	2. Klein Gedacktfloete	4
3. Super Gemsz-hoernlein	2	3. Super Gemshorn	2
4. Nasatt	anderthalb	4. Nasat	1 1/2
5. Klein repetirt Zimbel	einfach	5. Klein Repetierend Zimbel	I rank
6. Principal Discant	4	6. Principal (discant)	4
7. Blockpfeiffen Discant	4	7. Blockpfeife (discant)	4
8. Krumbhorn	8	8. Krummhorn	8
9. Geigend Regal	4	9. Geigend Regal	4

Im Pedal
9. Stimmen

In the Pedal,
9 voices

1. Grosser Gedact-floeiten Basz	16.fusz	1. Gross Gedacktfloete Bass	16 foot
2. Gemszhorn B.	8	2. Gemshorn Bass	8
3. Quintadeen B.	8	3. Quintade Bass	8
4. Querfloeiten B.	4	4. Querfloete Bass	4
5. Nachthorn B.	2	5. Nachthorn Bass	2
6. Bawrfloeiten Baeszlein	1	6. Bauerfloete Bass	1
7. Sordunen B.	16	7. Sordun Bass	16
8. Doltzian B.	8	8. Dulzian Bass	8
9. Jungfrawen Regal Basz	4	9. Jungfrau Regal Bass	4

[Translation by the present author]

The following rearrangement of the registers presents the <u>Frederiksborg</u> instrument in equivalent modern form:[20]

Frederiksborg (Hessen, Schlosz)

Built and completed by Esaias Compenius and Michael Praetorius in 1612; moved to <u>Frederiksborg</u> Schlosz, Hillerød, Denmark in 1617. All pipes are of wood. Ornate Late Renaissance case. Under protection of the Danish government at the present time. The instrument survives in an extraordinarily authentic form.

Upper Manual

1. 8' Principal
3. 8' Gedacktfloete
2. 4' Klein Principal
4. 4' Gemshorn (Viola)
5. 4' Nachthorn
6. 4' Blockfloete
7. 2 2/3' Gedackt Quint
8. 2' Gedacktfloete
9. 16' Rankett

Lower Manual

1. 8' Quintade
6. 4' Principal (discant)
2. 4' Klein Gedacktfloete
7. 4' Blockfloete (discant)
3. 2' Gemshorn
4. 1 1/3' Nasat
5. I Repetierend Zimbel
8. 8' Krummhorn
9. 4' Geigend Regal

Pedal

1. 16' Gross Gedacktfloete
2. 8' Gemshorn
3. 8' Quintade
4. 4' Querfloete
5. 2' Nachthorn
6. 1' Bauerfloete
7. 16' Sordun
8. 8' Dulzian
9. 4' Jungfrau Regal

Accessories

Coupler: Lower Manual to Upper Manual

Tremulant

Bock Tremulant

Bagpipe Drone

Musette

Among the three-manual and Pedal instruments listed
by Praetorius, only two seem to have clearly been straight
instruments controlled by single harnesses throughout:

1. <u>Stralsund</u>.[21] Very probably, a three-manual
and Pedal instrument, laid out, likely as not, in
the model form given above. A set of single harnesses
are indicated: OW / OW; B / B; Rp / Rp; and P / P.
The tonal corpora are closely balanced: Oberwerk,
10 voices; Brust, 11 voices; Rueckpositive, 11 voices;
and Pedal, 11 voices. Each corpus exhibits a full
complement of voices culminating in the usual crown
structure of Mixture and Zimbel, or Zimbel alone

2. <u>Lueneburg</u>, <u>St</u>. <u>Lambrecht</u>.[22] A three-manual
and Pedal instrument, laid out somewhat differently
from the model form given above. In this instance,
the Grosswerk replaces the usual Oberwerk, and the
Oberwerk replaces the usual Brust. A set of single
harnesses are indicated: GW / GW (Grosswerk chest
controlled by Grosswerk keyboard); OW / OW; Rp / Rp;
P / P. The tonal corpora are well balanced: Grosswerk, 13 voices, Oberwerk, 14 voices; Rueckpositive,
15 voices; Pedal, 17 voices. Each corpus exhibits a
full complement of voices culminating in full or in
part in the crown structure of Mixture, Scharf, and
Zimbel

As an example of a straight three-manual and Pedal instrument, a detailed presentation of the St. Lambrecht organ follows:[23]

Orgel zu S. Lambrecht in Lueneburg / hat 60. Stimmen vnd drey Manual Clavier.	The organ at St. Lambrecht in Lueneburg has 60 voices and three manual keyboards.

Mittel oder Grosz Werk: zum Mitlern Clavier: Hat 13. Stimmen.		Middle or Grosswerk, for the middle keyboard, has 13 voices	
1. Principal.	16 Fuesz.	1. Principal	16 foot
2. Gedact.	16 Fuesz.	2. Gedackt	16 foot
3. Octava.	8 Fuesz.	3. Octave	8 foot
4. Iula oder Spitzfloeit.[24]	8.	4. Jula or Spitzfloete	8
5. Querpfeiff.	8.	5. Querpfeife	8
6. Octava.	4.	6. Octave	4
7. Spillpfeiff.	4.	7. Spillpfeife	4
8. Floeite.	4.	8. Floete	4
9. Spitz Quinta[25]	3.	9. Spitzquinte	3
10. Octava.	2.	10. Octave	2
11. Ruszpfeiff.		11. Rauschpfeife	
12. Zimbel.		12. Zimbel	
13. Mixtur.		13. Mixture	

Ober Werck: zum Obern Clavier. Hat 14. Stimmen.		Oberwerk, for the upper keyboard, has 14 voices	
14. Principal.	8 Fuesz.	14. Principal	8 foot
15. Hellpfeiff.	8.	15. Hellpfeife	8
16. Querpfeiff.8.Halbirt.[26]		16. Querpfeife (halved)	8
17. Quintfloeit.[27]	3.	17. Quintfloete	3
18. Nasat.	3.	18. Nasat	3
19. Gedact.	2.	19. Gedackt	2
20. Gemszhorn.	1.	20. Gemshorn	1

21. Waldfloetlin[28]	1.	21. Waldfloetlein	1
22. Feldpfeiff	1/2.	22. Feldpfeife	1/2
23. Zimbel.		23. Zimbel	
24. Trummet.	8.	24. Trompete	8
25. Regal.	8.	25. Regal	8
26. Krumbhorn.	8.	26. Krummhorn	8
27. Zinck halbirt.	8.	27. Zink (halved)	8

Rueckpositieff.
Hat 15. Stimmen.

Rueckpositive,
has 15 voices

28. Principal.	8.	28. Principal	8
29. Quintadehna.	8.	29. Quintade	8
30. Gedact.	8.	30. Gedackt	8
31. Blockfloeit.	4.	31. Blockfloete	4
32. Holfloeit.	4.	32. Hohlfloete	4
33. Quintfloeit.	3.	33. Quintfloete	3
34. Octava.	2.	34. Octave	2
35. Sedetzen Quint.[29]	1 1/2	35. Sedecima quint	1 1/2
36. Seifloeit.	1.	36. Siffloete	1
37. Repetirend Zimbel.		37. Repetierend Zimbel	
38. Scharp.		38. Scharf	
39. Mixtur.		39. Mixture	
40. Regal.		40. Regal	
41. Schalmey.		41. Schalmei	
42. Baarpfeiff.		42. Baerpfeife	

Pedal-Baesse:
17. Stimmen.

Pedal Basses,
17 voices

43. Principal-Basz 16.Fuesz		43. Principal Bass	16 foot
44. Vntersatz.	16.	44. Untersatz	16
45. Octava.	8.	45. Octave	8
46. Gedact.	8.	46. Gedackt	8
47. Super-Octava.	4.	47. Super Octave	4
48. Nachthorn.	4.	48. Nachthorn	4
49. Spitz-Quint.	3.	49. Spitzquinte	3
50. Gemszhorn.	2.	50. Gemshorn	2

51. Bawr Floeit.	1.	51. Bauerfloete	
52. Rauschpfeiff.		52. Rauschpfeife	
53. Zimbel.		53. Zimbel	
54. Mixtur.		54. Mixture	
55. Posaunen.	16.	55. Posaune	16
56. Krumhorn.	16.	56. Krummhorn	16
57. Trommetten	8.	57. Trompete	8
58. Schalmey.	4.	58. Schalmei	4
59. Cornet.	2.	59. Kornett	2

Tremulant.

1.
2. Ventiel zum Oberwerck.
3. Mittelwerck.
Pedael.

1. Coppel zu beyden Manualen.[30]
2. Coppel / Pedal zum Rueckpositiff.[31]

Tremulant

Ventils for the
1. Oberwerk
2. Mittelwerk
3. Pedal

1. Coupler for both manuals
2. Coupler: Rueckpositive to Pedal

[Translation by the present author]

The following rearrangement of the registers presents the St. Lambrecht organ in an equivalent modern form:[32]

St. Lambrecht, Lueneburg

The instrument, often attributed to Hans Scherer, d. A., is in reality the work of Christian Bockelmann, 1604-1610. The instrument was officially accepted by Hieronymus Praetorius.[33]

Grosswerk

1. 16' Principal
2. 16' Gedackt
3. 8' Octave
4. 8' Jula or Spitzfloete
5. 8' Querfloete

8. 4' Floete
9. 2 2/3' Spitzquinte
10. 2' Octave
11. Rauschpfeife
13. Mixture

6. 4' Octave   12.   Zimbel
7. 4' Spillpfeife

Oberwerk

14. 8' Principal   21. [2/3'] Waldfloete
15. 8' Hellpfeife   22. 1/2' Feldpfeife
16. 8' Querpfeife [discant]   23.   Zimbel
17. [4'] Quintfloete   24. 8' Trumpet
18. 2 2/3' Nasat   25. 8' Regal
19. 2' Gedackt   26. 8' Krummhorn
20. 1' Gemshorn   27. 8' Zink [discant]

Rueckpositive

28. 8' Principal   36. 1' Siffloete
30. 8' Gedackt   39.   Mixture
29. 8' Quintade   38.   Scharf
31. 4' Blockfloete   37.   Repetierend Zimbel
32. 4' Hohlfloete   40.   Regal
33. 2 2/3' Quintfloete   41.   Schalmei
34. 2' Octave   42.   Baerpfeife
35. 1 1/3' Sedecima quint

Pedal

43. 16' Principal   52.   Rauschpfeife
44. 16' Untersatz   54.   Mixture
45. 8' Octave   53.   Zimbel
46. 8' Gedackt   55. 16' Posaune
47. 4' Super Octave   56. 16' Krummhorn
48. 4' Nachthorn   57. 8' Trompete
49. 2 2/3' Spitzquinte   58. 4' Schalmei
50. 2' Gemshorn   59. 2' Kornett
51. 1' Bauerfloete

Accessories

Ventils for: Couplers:
  Oberwerk   Rueckpositive to Grosswerk

Grosswerk   Rueckpositive to Pedal
Pedal   Tremulant

In addition to complete sets of single harnesses,
practically all of the instruments exhibit a single harness
control for one or another of the chests. In nearly every
instance, the Rueckpositive is thus controlled and can be
presumed to present, therefore, a full complement of voices
and an independent tonal corpus. It is difficult to say
what constitutes cause and effect in this situation: Was
the Rueckpositive set up as an independent corpus because
mechanical limitations prevented its being harnessed otherwise than by a single harness, or was the double and triple
harness carefully avoided in order to preserve the individual
tonal identity of the division?

Summary

From the conditions established in the foregoing
analyses and interpretations, a few general hypotheses may
be drawn and contributed toward the theory of the Praetorius
organ:

1. A full set of single harnesses for the entire
instrument is extremely rare; it is suggested in instruments that exhibit a straight disposition

2. A single harness for one or another chest of
an instrument seems to be a frequent occurrence; most
often and consistently, the Rueckpositive is controlled

in this manner

3. A single harness control can be deduced from the disposition of the tonal corpus presented by a given chest

4. A straight instrument is suggested if the tonal corpora exhibit a balanced (i.e., a numerically equivalent) complement for each division of the instrument

5. The self-sufficiency of a tonal corpus is suggested by a culminating crown structure, a full set of Principal or Principal-ersatz voices at the foundation pitches, a respectable representation of non-Principal voices at the foundation and mutation pitches, and a reasonably full spectrum of pitches from the respective bases to the threshold of pitch discrimination and represented by unison and fifth-sounding members

The Double Harness

The double harness finds reasonably frequent application in the instruments of the Early Baroque. It was usually executed as a type of permanent coupling system not subject to engagement or disengagement by the player, and permitted the consistent control of two chests from one keyboard. Its most elemental application is found in layout situations where it became necessary to mount the full complement of one tonal corpus on two chests. A number of different situations required a double harness for adequate control, and our investigation will be best served by analyzing a number of individual instances, arranging our pursuit in such a way as to show, if possible, a developmental growth of the concept as manifested in the dispositions presented by Praetorius.

Division of the Manual Corpus

The first and most rudimentary case is that presented by the Hamburg, St. Peter instrument.[34] This organ contained five divisions playable from a three-manual and Pedal console.[35] The divisions and their contents present the following picture: an Oberwerk of 9 voices playable from the middle keyboard; a Brustpositive of 10 voices playable from the uppermost keyboard; a submounted Brustpositive of 1 voice attached to the larger Brustpositive; a Rueckpositive of 11 voices playable from the lowest keyboard; and a Pedal of 11 voices.[36]

A possible schematic layout for such an instrument is shown on Plate LXIX, fig. 1, where the larger Brustpositive is identified as Bp_1, and the smaller one as Bp_2. The Oberwerk OW can be surmised to have been centrally positioned, the pedal chests P probably flanked the same on both sides, and the Rueckpositive Rp, true to its name, probably found its place behind the player. A double harness is

suggested by the division of the Brustpositive into two
chests and by Praetorius' notation that the smaller Brustpositive was attached (G. angehaengt) to the larger one. In
code form, the situation may be represented as $Bp_1 + Bp_2$ / B
(Brustpositive 1 and Brustpositive 2 are controlled by the
Brust keyboard).

Plate LXIX, fig. 2 shows a possible method of controlling the two chests from one keyboard, where the harness
for one chest is simply hung on to the harness for the other.
A tracker D leads from the Brust keyboard upward through
square F to pallet N. A second tracker G connects squares
F and L. A third tracker I leads from square L upward through
roller board R to pallet Q. A depression of the Brust key
opens pallets N and Q simultaneously. A permanent coupling
of the two chests Bp_1 and Bp_2 is thereby effected. The two
chests, in sum, present one tonal corpus, while each of the
other chests, namely, the Oberwerk, the Rueckpositive, and
the Pedal present separate tonal corpora.

A full presentation of the St. Peter instrument follows herewith:[37]

VII.	VII
In Hamburg	In Hamburg
. . . .	. . . .
II.	II
Die bey S. Peter helt in sich gleicher gestalt 3. Clavir 42. Stimmen / 9. Baelge vnd Tremulanten.	[The organ] at St. Peter comprises similarly 3 claviers and 42 voices.[38] [There are] 9 bellows and tremulants.

Das Ober Werck im mittelsten Clavier hat 9. Stimmen.			The Oberwerk (for the middle keyboard) has 9 voices	
1. Principal 12. Fusz angehende im F.[39]			1. Principal, beginning at F	12 foot
2. Quintadehna	12.fusz F		2. Quintade	12 foot, F
3. Octava	6.fusz F		3. Octave	6 foot, F
4. Gedact[40]	8.fusz C		4. Gedackt	8 foot, C
5. Holfloeite	3.fusz F		5. Hohlfloete	3 foot, F
6. Ruszpipe[41]			6. Rauschpfeife	[4']
7. Scharp			7. Scharf	[III]
8. Mixtur			8. Mixture	[VI]
9. Zimbel			9. Zimbel	[II]

Das Brustpositiff oben in der Orgel / gehoert zum obersten Clavir, vnd hat 10. Stimmen.		The Brustpositive up in the organ belongs to the upper keyboard and has 10 voices	
1. Principal	8.fusz C	1. Principal	8 foot, C
2. Holpipe	8.fusz	2. Hohlpfeife	8 foot
3. Holfloeite	4.fusz	3. Hohlfloete	4 foot
4. Nasatt auff die Quinta	3.fusz	4. Nasat at the quint	3 foot
5. Gemszhorn[42]	2.fusz	5. Gemshorn	[4] foot
6. Kleinfloeit	2.fusz	6. Klein Floete	2 foot
7. Zimbel 3. Pfeiffen starck		7. Zimbel	III ranks
8. Trompette	8.fusz	8. Trompete	8 foot
9. Regal	8.fusz	9. Regal	8 foot
10. Zincke[43]	8.fusz	10. Zink	[4] foot

Das vnterste Brust Positiff ist an das Ober Brust Positiff angehenget: Vnnd hat nur.		The lower Brustpositive is attached to the upper Brustpositive, and has only:	
1. Krumbhorn	8.fusz	1. Krummhorn	8 foot

Das Rueck Positiff gehoeret zum vntersten Clavir Und hat 11. Stimmen.		The Rueckpositive belongs to the lowest keyboard and has 11 voices	
1. Principal.[44]	8.fusz E.	1. Principal	8 foot, E

2. Quintadehna.	8.fusz	2. Quintade	8 foot
3. Gedact.	8.fusz	3. Gedackt	8 foot
4. Hollfloeite.	4.fusz	4. Hohlfloete	4 foot
5. Octava.	4.fusz	5. Octave	4 foot
6. Sifloeit.[45]		6. Siffloete	[1']
7. Scharp.		7. Scharf	[III]
8. Mixtur.		8. Mixture	[IV]
9. Baarpfeife.	8.fusz	9. Baerpfeife	8 foot
10. Regall.[46]	8.fusz	10. Regal	[4] foot
11. Krumbhorn	8.fusz	11. Krummhorn	8 foot

Im Pedal
seynd 11 Stimmen.

In the Pedal,
11 voices

1. Principal[47] 24.fi. ex F		1. Principal 24 ft., from F	
2. Grosz Basz oder Vnter-satz von 16.fusz ins C		2. Gross Bass, or Untersatz of 16 foot, C	
3. Octava	8.fi.	3. Octave	8 ft.
4. Gedact	8.fi.	4. Gedackt	8 ft.
5. Gemszhorn Basz[48]		5. Gemshorn Bass	[16']
6. Zimbel		6. Zimbel	[III]
7. Mixtur		7. Mixture	[VI]
8. Bassaune	16.fusz	8. Posaune	16 foot
9. Trompette	8.fusz	9. Trompete	8 foot
10. Krumbhorn	16.fusz	10. Krummhorn	16 foot
11. Cornett.	2.fusz	11. Kornett	2 foot

[Translation by the present author]

From a modern point of view, the order of the registers and their pitch designations would present the following equivalent picture:[49]

St. Peter, Hamburg

The instrument purportedly was built in 1548 by Hinrich Niehoff and rebuilt in 1603-04 by Hans Scherer, d. A.[50]

The disposition exhibits a great similarity to the <u>Hamburg</u>, <u>St</u>. <u>Jacob</u> instrument.[51]

Oberwerk

1. 16' Principal (to Great <u>F</u>)
2. 16' Quintade (to Great <u>F</u>)
3. 8' Octave (to Great <u>F</u>)
4. 8' Gedackt
5. 4' Hohlfloete (to Great <u>F</u>)
6. [4'] Rauschpfeife
8. [VI] Mixture
7. [III] Scharf
9. [II] Zimbel

Brustpositive

1. 8' Principal
2. 8' Hohlpfeife
3. 4' Hohlfloete
5. [4'] Gemshorn
4. 2 2/3' Nasat
6. 2' Klein Floete
7. III Zimbel
8. 8' Trompete
9. 8' Regal
1. 8' Krummhorn
10. [4'] Zink

Rueckpositive

1. 8' Principal
3. 8' Gedackt
2. 8' Quintade
5. 4' Octave
4. 4' Hohlfloete
6. [1'] Siffloete
8. [IV] Mixture
7. [III] Scharf
9. 8' Baerpfeife
11. 8' Krummhorn
10. [4'] Regal

Pedal

1. 32' Principal (to Great <u>F</u>)
2. 16' Gross Bass, or Untersatz
5. [16'] Gemshorn
3. 8' Octave
4. 8' Gedackt
7. [VI] Mixture
6. [III] Zimbel
8. 16' Posaune
10. 16' Krummhorn
9. 8' Trompete
11. 2' Kornett

Accessories

Nine bellows

Tremulants

Division of the Pedal Corpus

At times the pedal forces of the organ were divided
into two chests, which required a double harness in order to
control them. This second instance of a double harness became necessary when the tonal corpus of the Pedal was divided
between the customary side pedal towers and the Brust Pedalia. It should be remembered that the apparent division of
the Pedal voices on two flanking sides of the Oberwerk required really only one single harness since only alternate
notes normally appeared on each side. The addition of a Brust
Pedalia, however, required an additional harness, regardless
if the Brust Pedalia appeared as one chest or as two chests
of alternate notes. In code form the situation may be represented as P + BP / P (Pedal and Brustpedalia are controlled
by the pedal keyboard). The Bueckeburg instrument presents
an instance where the pedal forces seem to have been divided
in this fashion and controlled by the pedal keyboard.[52]

Plate LXIX, fig. 3 shows a schematic layout, possible
for an organ whose pedal forces were divided between flanking
side towers and a divided Brust Pedalia. The Oberwerk OW, as
customary, probably occupied the central position and was
flanked on both sides by the main pedal chests P. The Brust
B, lying underneath and near the front of the Oberwerk, was
similarly flanked on both sides by a pair of secondary pedal
chests, often referred to as a Brust Pedalia BP. The Rueckpositive Rp, as its name implies, was, in all likelihood,

stationed behind the player in a central position.

Plate LXIX, fig. 4, 5, and 6 show a possible double harness for the Pedal and Brust Pedalia in schematic form. The first harness begins at the nose of pedal key P and leads downward through sticker A to square C. A tracker D passes from square C to roller E which turns the motion alternately left and right for the successive notes of the compass. A second tracker O leads from roller E to square F which turns the motion upward. A third tracker G leads from square F up to pallet H in the main pedal chest P. A depression of the pedal key opens pallet H. The second harness (fig. 4) begins also at the nose of pedal key P. A tracker I leads from the nose of pedal key P up to roller J whose projecting arms are placed perpendicular to each other, in order to effect a change of direction in the transmitted motion. A second tracker K leads from the secondary arm of roller J to square L, from which a third tracker M leads upward to pallet N in the Brust Pedalia chest BP. A depression of the pedal key opens pallet N as well as H. Fig. 6 shows a segment of the Pedal and Brust Pedalia harnesses in perspective. A double harness is, therefore, attached to the pedal keyboard in order to be able to open two corresponding pallets simultaneously. The double harness functions like a permanent coupling action not subject to engagement or disengagement by the player. In a case like Bueckeburg, the voices of both the Pedal and Brust Pedalia constitute one tonal corpus.[53]

The Pedal-in-the-Oberwerk

A third double harness situation which arises in the organs presented by Praetorius is the one where the pedal forces are so divided that a major portion is mounted in the customary side towers flanking the Oberwerk, while a selected few voices are mounted either on the cradle of the Oberwerk chest or in its vicinity. The designations for these separate voices vary as, Im Pedal zum Ober Wercke (in the Pedal by the Oberwerk), Untersatz im Oberwerk (Untersatz in the Oberwerk), Pedal auff der Oberlade (Pedal on the Oberwerk chest), Hinderm Werck auff einer sonderlichen Lade (behind the Werk on a special chest)', Untersatz von Holtz (Untersatz of wood), Zum Pedal alleine im Oberwerck (for the Pedal alone in the Oberwerk), and similar expressions.[54] It is not possible today to make certain claims for the precise meanings of these designations; they do, however, suggest a disposition of the resources in some fashion similar to that suggested above. In code form the situation may be represented as P + Po / P (Pedal and Pedal-in-the-Oberwerk are controlled by the pedal keyboard. The organ at Danzig, St. Maricn is a case in point.[55] Beside the Oberwerk, Brust, and Rueck-positive, the Pedal appears in two separate compartments specified as Im Pedal zum Ober Wercke (in the Pedal by the Oberwerk) and Im Pedal auff beyden Seitten (in the Pedal on both sides).

It would appear that a schematic layout for the

instrument could be similar to that shown on Plate LXX, fig. 1. The Oberwerk OW occupies, as usual, the central position; the Brust B lies centrally underneath it; the Rueck-positive Rp lies centrally at some distance in front of it. The main pedal chest P is in two segments of alternate notes flanking the Oberwerk on both sides; the secondary pedal chest Po lies divided into two segments of alternate notes behind the Oberwerk and on the cradle. In this manner the traditional layout of the various chests is fully realized.

A possible disposition of the double harness for the Pedal is shown in section in fig. 2, in plan in fig. 3, and in perspective in fig. 4. Sticker A leads from the nose of the pedal key P to square O. A tracker C leads to roller E which is one of a gang of rollers mounted in a diagonal-horizontal roller board D, which is arranged to turn the motion alternately right and left in order to distribute the alternate notes of the compass to the divided main pedal chests P. A second tracker M leads from roller E to square N. Here the motion is turned upward and directed to pallet G in pedal chest P by means of tracker F. The second harness begins at roller E and leads by means of tracker H to square I. Tracker J leads from square I through the roller board K to pallet L. A depression of the pedal key opens both pallets G and L. Designation Po identifies the fractional pedal chest mounted in the cradle of the Oberwerk OW. Fig. 3 shows a portion of the double pedal harness in plan, while fig. 4

represents a perspective sketch of the junction of the two
harnesses at roller E and the subsequent progress of each
harness to pallets G and L respectively. A double harness
is, therefore, attached to the pedal keyboard in order to open
two corresponding pallets at the same time. It functions like
a permanent coupling action not subject to engagement or disengagement by the player.

The full disposition of the Danzig organ follows
according to the record of Praetorius and others:[56]

III.	III
Die grosse Orgel zu Dantzig	The great organ at Danzig

In S. Marienkirche / So Anno 1585. von Iulio Anton-io[57] erbawet worden / helt 55. Stimmen.	In the St. Maria Church, which was built by Julio Antonio in the year 1585. It contains 55 voices

Im Ober Werck seynd 13. Stimmen	In the Oberwerk, 13 voices[58]

Dieser
ser
Stim-
men
ein
jede
hat
48.
Pfeif-
fen.

1.Principal	16.fusz
2.Holfloeite	16.fusz
3.Quintadehna	16.fusz
4.Spillpfeiffe	8.fusz
5.Octava	8.fusz
6.Quintadehna	8.fusz
7.Offenfloeite oder Viol[59]	8.fusz
8.Spillpfeiffe 9.Viol[60]	4.fusz
10.Sedecima	
11.Rauschquint	

Each
of
these
voic-
es
con-
tains
48
pipes

1.Principal	16 foot
2.Hohlfloete	16 foot
3.Quintade	16 foot
4.Spillpfeife	8 foot
5.Octave	8 foot
6.Quintade	8 foot
7.Offenfloete or Viola	8 foot
8.Spillpfeife	4 foot
9.Viola	4 foot
10.Sedecima	[2']
11.Rauschquint	[II]

12. Zimbel hat 144. Pfeiffen. Ist derwegen drey Choericht.	12. Zimbel comprises 144 pipes, hence of III ranks
13. Mixtur hat in alles 1152. vnd auff jeder Clavem 24. Pfeiffen.	13. Mixture has altogether 1152, hence 24 pipes per key

<table>
<tr><td colspan="2" align="center">In der Brust—
oder Vor Positiff
8. Stimmen.</td><td colspan="2" align="center">In the Brust
or Vorpositive,
8 voices</td></tr>
<tr><td>1. Gedacte Stimm</td><td>8.fusz</td><td>1. Gedackt Stimme</td><td>8 foot</td></tr>
<tr><td>2. Gedact</td><td>4.fusz</td><td>2. Gedackt</td><td>4 foot</td></tr>
<tr><td>3. Principal</td><td>4.fusz</td><td>3. Principal</td><td>4 foot</td></tr>
<tr><td>4. Quintadehna</td><td>4.fusz</td><td>4. Quintade</td><td>4 foot</td></tr>
<tr><td>5. Zimbel</td><td></td><td>5. Zimbel</td><td>[III]</td></tr>
<tr><td>6. Dunecken[61]</td><td>2.fusz</td><td>6. [Decima]</td><td>2 foot</td></tr>
<tr><td>7. Regal singend</td><td>8.</td><td>7. Singend Regal</td><td>8</td></tr>
<tr><td>8. Zincken</td><td>4</td><td>8. Zink</td><td>4</td></tr>
</table>

<table>
<tr><td colspan="2" align="center">Im Rueckpositiff.
18. Stimmen.</td><td colspan="2" align="center">In the Rueckpositive,
18 voices</td></tr>
<tr><td>1. Principal</td><td></td><td>1. Principal</td><td>8 foot</td></tr>
<tr><td>2. Holfloeit oder Holpfeiff[62]</td><td rowspan="2">8.fusz</td><td>2. Hohlfloete or Hohlpfeife</td><td>8 foot</td></tr>
<tr><td>3. Spillpfeiff oder Blockfl.[63]</td><td>3. Spillpfeife or Blockfloete</td><td>8 foot</td></tr>
<tr><td>4. Octav</td><td rowspan="3">4.fusz</td><td>4. Octave</td><td>4 foot</td></tr>
<tr><td>5. Offenfloeit oder Viol[64]</td><td>5. Offenfloete or Viola</td><td>4 foot</td></tr>
<tr><td>6. Kleine Blockfloeit</td><td>6. Klein Blockfloete</td><td>4 foot</td></tr>
<tr><td>7. Gemszhorn</td><td></td><td>7. Gemshorn</td><td>[2']</td></tr>
<tr><td>8. Sedecima[65]</td><td></td><td>8. Sedecima</td><td>[2']</td></tr>
<tr><td>9. Floeit</td><td></td><td>9. Floete</td><td>[2 2/3']</td></tr>
<tr><td>10. Waldfloeit</td><td></td><td>10. Waldfloete</td><td>[1']</td></tr>
<tr><td>11. Rauschquint</td><td></td><td>11. Rauschquinte</td><td>[II]</td></tr>
<tr><td>12. Nasatt</td><td></td><td>12. Nasat</td><td>[1 1/3']</td></tr>
<tr><td>13. Zimbel von 144. Pfeiffen</td><td></td><td>13. Zimbel 144 pipes</td><td>[III]</td></tr>
</table>

14. Mixtur von 220 Pfeiffen		14. Mixture 220 pipes	[V]
15. Trommet	} 8.fusz	15. Trompete	8 foot
16. Krumbhorn		16. Krummhorn	8 foot
17. Zincken	} 4.fusz	17. Zink	4 foot
18. Schallmeyen		18. Schalmei	4 foot

Im Pedal zum Ober Wercke 4. Stimmen / ein jede von 43. Pfeiffen.66		For the Pedal-in-the-Oberwerk, 4 voices, each of 43 [23?] pipes	
1. Grosz Vnter Basz von	32.fusz	1. Gross Unterbass of	32 foot
2. Vnter Basz	16	2. Unterbass	16
3. Posaunen Basz	16	3. Posaune Bass	16
4. Trommete	8.fusz	4. Trompete	8 foot

Im Pedal auff beyden Seitten. 12. Stimmen.		In the Pedal on both sides, 12 voices	
1. Floeiten oder Octava67	8.fusz	1. Floete or Octave	8 foot
2. Gedact	8.fusz	2. Gedackt	8 foot
3. Quintadehna	4.fusz	3. Quintade	4 foot
4. Superoctav	2.	4. Super Octave	[4']
5. Nachthorn		5. Nachthorn	[2']
6. Rauschquint		6. Rauschquinte	[II]
7. Bawerpfeiff		7. Bauerpfeife	[1']
8. Zimbel von 144. Pfeiffen		8. Zimbel of 144 pipes	[III]
9. Mixtur von 220. Pfeiffen		9. Mixture of 220 pipes	[V]
10. Spitz oder Cornett		10. Spitz or Kornett	[2']
11. Trommeten oder Schallmeyen		11. Trompete or Schalmei	[4']
12. Krumbhoerner		12. Krummhorn	[8']

Vber das seynd noch in der gantzen Orgel 3. Tremulanten, vnd 1. Trummel im Basz.

Beyond this the instrument exhibits 3 tremulants and a Tympanum in the bass.

[Translation by the present author]

By taking into account not only Praetorius' record, but also the information supplied by Frotscher, a more complete and possibly more accurate disposition of the organ can here be reproduced in the customary modern manner.[68]

St. Maria, Danzig

The instrument was built by Julius Antonius Friese during the years 1583-85. Various deviations in the specifications occur in the historic literature pertaining to this instrument.[69]

Oberwerk

1.	16' Principal	9.	4'	Octave
2.	16' Hohlfloete	8.	4'	Spillpfeife
3.	16' Quintade	10.	[2']	Sedecima
5.	8' Octave	11.	[II]	Rauschquinte
7.	8' Offenfloete	13.	XXIV	Mixture
4.	8' Spillpfeife	12.	III	Zimbel
6.	8' Quintade			

Brustpositive

1.	8' Gedackt	6.	2'	[Decima]
3.	4' Principal	5.	[III]	Zimbel
2.	4' Gedackt	7.	8'	Singend Regal
4.	4' Quintade	8.	4'	Zink

Rueckpositive

1.	8' Principal	12.	[1 1/3']	Nasat
2.	8' Hohlfloete	10.	[1']	Waldfloete
3.	8' Spillpfeife	11.	[II]	Rauschquinte
4.	4' Octave	14.	[V]	Mixture
5.	4' Offenfloete	13.	[III]	Zimbel
6.	4' Blockfloete	15.	8'	Trompete
9.	[2 2/3'] Floete	16.	8'	Krummhorn

8. [2'] Sedecima   18. 4' Schalmei
7. [2'] Gemshorn   17. 4' Zink

Pedal

1. 32' Gross Unterbass (Po)   6. [II] Rauschquinte
2. 16' Unterbass (Po)   9. [V] Mixture
1. 8' Octave   8. III Zimbel
2. 8' Gedackt   3. 16' Posaune (Po)
4. [4'] Octave   4. 8' Trompete (Po)
3. 4' Quintade   12. [8'] Krummhorn
5. [2'] Nachthorn   11. [4'] Schalmei
7. [1'] Bauerpfeife   10. [2'] Kornett

Accessories

Three tremulants   Tympanum

The Oberwerk-and-Brust

A fourth double harness situation which prevailed
among the early baroque instruments involved the combination
of the Brust chest and the Oberwerk chest in such a manner
that both were playable from one keyboard. The condition
can be represented in code form as OW + B / OW (Oberwerk-and-
Brust are controlled by the Oberwerk keyboard) or, occasionally, as W + B / W (Werk-and-Brust are controlled by the Werk
keyboard). Both situations are identical since Oberwerk and
Werk may be considered as interchangeable terms.

The physical layout of the chests is shown in simple
schematic form on Plate LXXI, fig. 1. The Oberwerk OW is
centrally positioned; flanking it on both sides are the divided chests of the Pedal P; underneath it lies the Brust B;

in front of it and in the center lies the Rueckpositive Rp.
The layout is classical for the period.

The control harnesses for this layout are extremely
simple. Plate LXXI, fig. 2 shows a possible way of harnessing the two chests to one keyboard. A tracker A leads upward
from the Oberwerk key OW through square Z to pallet I in the
Brust chest B. A second tracker C leads from square Z to
square E. A third tracker J leads from square E through
roller board K to pallet L in the Oberwerk chest OW. A depression of the manual key opens both pallets I and L simultaneously. Again, a permanent coupling action is thereby
effected, which is not subject to engagement or disengagement
by the player.

A double harness, such as the one described above,
could find pertinent application in the Halberstadt, St. Martini organ.[70] The instrument exhibits four chests, in all
likelihood controlled by two manuals and a pedal keyboard.
The Oberwerk had 8 voices; the Brust, 6 voices; the Rueckpositive, 12 voices; and the Pedal, 12 voices. The relatively meager complement of voices in the Oberwerk and Brust
strongly indicates a combination of Oberwerk-and-Brust as
one tonal corpus representing the real Werk of the instrument. Under this concept, the Werk is able to exhibit 14
voices as against 12 in the Rueckpositive and Pedal. An examination of the internal tonal structure of the Oberwerk-
and-Brust does, however, not provide an adequate compulsion

for considering the two chests as one division; each chest does possess a fairly complete tonal structure, culminating in both instances in the usual crown structure of Mixture and Zimbel. The question, therefore, remains open. If the two chests were independent of each other, a three-manual and Pedal console must be surmised.

Following is a full presentation of the St. Martini instrument:[71]

XVI.

Verzeichnuesz derer Register vnd Stimmen / so in den Orgeln zu

Halberstadt
zu finden.

Das 1. Werck in S. Martini Kirchen hat M. David Becke mit 39. Stimmen vnd einem Tremulant gesetzet. Der Tremulant, ob er wol keinen laut von sich gibt / so wird er doch von etlichen / Auch vor eine Stimme (weil man viel verenderung damit haben kan) gerechnet.

Im Ober Wercke
8. Stimmen.

1. Quintadehna   16.fusz
2. Principal
3. Grobgedact.
4. Grob Gemszhorn
5. Octava
6. Quinta
7. Mixtur
8. Zimbel.

XVI

Inventory of the registers and voices which are to be found in the organs of

Halberstadt

The first instrument, comprising 39 voices and a tremulant, was erected in St. Martini Church by Master David Beck. The tremulant, even though it is unable to produce a tone, is sometimes reckoned as a voice (because of the many variations one can derive from it).

In the Oberwerk,
8 voices[72]

1. Quintade   16 foot
2. Principal   [8']
3. Grob Gedackt   [16']
4. Grob Gemshorn   [8']
5. Octave   [4']
6. Quinte   [3']
7. Mixture   [VI]
8. Zimbel   [III]

In der Brust 6. Stimmen.		In the Brust 6 voices	
1.	Principal	1. Principal	[4']
2.	Gedact	2. Gedackt	[8']
3.	Nachthorn[73]	3. Nachthorn	[2'?]
4.	Zimbel	4. Zimbel	[1']
5.	Mixtur	5. Mixture	[III]
6.	Regal.	6. Regal	[8']

Im Pedal 12. Stimmen.		In the Pedal 12 voices	
1.	Vntersatz	1. Untersatz	[16']
2.	Principal	2. Principal	[16']
3.	Gedact Basz	3. Gedackt Bass	[16']
4.	Octaven Basz	4. Octave Bass	[8']
5.	Zimbel Basz	5. Zimbel Bass	[II]
6.	Floeiten B.	6. Floete Bass	[4']
7.	Hol Quinten B.	7. Hohlquinte Bass	[6']
8.	Quintfloeiten B.	8. Quintfloete Bass	[3']
9.	Posaunen B.	9. Posaune Bass	[16']
10.	Trommeten B.	10. Trompete Bass	[8']
11.	Schallmeyen B.	11. Schalmei Bass	[4']
12.	Cornetten B.	12. Kornett Bass	[2']

Im Rueck Positiff 12. Stimmen.		In the Rueckpositive, 12 voices	
1.	Principal	1. Principal	[8']
2.	Quinta	2. Quinte	[3']
3.	Octava	3. Octave	[4']
4.	Quintadeena	4. Quintade	[8']
5.	Mixtur	5. Mixture	[IV]
6.	Zimbel	6. Zimbel	[II]
7.	Spitzfloeite	7. Spitzfloete	[4']
8.	Gemszhorn	8. Gemshorn	[2']
9.	Gedact	9. Gedackt	[8']
10.	Suiffloeit	10. Siffloete	[1']

11. Krumbhorn.   11. Krummhorn   [8']

12. Geigend Regal.   12. Geigend Regal   [4']

By combining the record of Praetorius with the more detailed specifications of the <u>Dresdener Handschrift</u>, the Halberstadt instrument presents the following, more familiar, appearance in equivalent modern form:[74]

St. Martini, Halberstadt

Built by David Beck before 1619. The instrument was in the church in which Andreas Werckmeister served as organist around the end of the seventeenth century.[75] In 1769-70 the <u>St. Martini</u> Church inherited the old <u>Grueningen</u>, <u>Schlosz</u> organ, which had also been built by David Beck in 1596 and renovated in 1705 under the supervision of Werckmeister.[76]

Oberwerk and Brust

3. [16'] Grob Gedackt   6. [2 2/3'] Quinte
1. 16' Quintade   3. [2'?] Nachthorn (B)
2. [8'] Principal   7. [VI] Mixture
4. [8'] Grob Gemshorn   5. [III] Mixture (B)
2. [8'] Gedackt (B)   8. [III] Zimbel
5. [4'] Octave   4. [1'] Rep. Zimbel (B)
1. [4'] Principal (B)   6. [8'] Regal (B)

Rueckpositive

1. [8'] Principal   8. [2'] Gemshorn
9. [8'] Gedackt   10. [1'] Siffloete
4. [8'] Quintade   5. [IV] Mixture
3. [4'] Octave   6. [II] Zimbel
7. [4'] Spitzfloete   11. [8'] Krummhorn
2. [2 2/3'] Quinte   12. [4'] Geigend Regal

Pedal

2. [16'] Principal   8. [2 2/3'] Quintfloete

1.	[16'] Untersatz	5.	[II] Zimbel
3.	[16'] Gedackt	9.	[16'] Posaune
4.	[8'] Octave	10.	[8'] Trompete
7.	[5 1/3'] Hohlquinte	11.	[4'] Schalmei
6.	[4'] Floete	12.	[2'] Kornett

Accessories

Tremulant

Symptoms of the Double Harness

The symptoms for the presence of a double harness to control both the Oberwerk and the Brust from one keyboard can be detected most easily from the internal disposition of the voices on each chest. A double harness and, concomitantly, a divided corpus, is suggested:

1. If the Oberwerk exhibits materially fewer voices than do the Rueckpositive or the Pedal

2. If the Brust, likewise, exhibits a considerable numerical inferiority to the Rueckpositive or the Pedal

3. If either the Oberwerk or the Brust omit a crown structure in whole or in part

4. If the higher-pitched (hence, physically diminutive) voices are missing in the Oberwerk and appear in the Brust instead

5. If the Brust does not over-duplicate species of voices found in the Oberwerk

6. If the Brust exhibits isolated voices not

sufficient to give a respectable semblance of a tonal corpus

7. If the tonal complements of both chests constitute a single respectable tonal corpus reaching from the base through the normal unison and fifth-sounding voices up to the crown structure

Survey of Examples

By diligent application of the above-mentioned principles to the organs presented in Praetorius' catalog of dispositions, it would seem that a double harness for the control of Oberwerk-and-Brust or of Werk-and-Brust from one keyboard is suggested in the following instances:

1. Danzig, St. Marien.[77] Oberwerk of 13 voices, Brust of 8 voices, Rueckpositive of 18 voices, Pedal of 16 voices. The Brust disposition is relatively meager and somewhat fragmentary

2. Hamburg, St. Jacob.[78] Oberwerk of 9 voices, Brust oben of 11 voices, Brust unten of 4 voices, Rueckpositive of 15 voices, and Pedal of 14 voices. An examination of the internal disposition of the Oberwerk and the Brust unten would suggest these two chests as probably having been combined by a double harness for control from the Oberwerk keyboard. The Brust oben is relatively complete and already contains similar species of voices at corresponding pitches.

On the other hand, the Brust unten supplies the very
voices which are lacking in the Oberwerk to complete
its tonal corpus

3. Magdeburg, St. Ulrich.[79] Oberwerk of actually 11 voices,[80] Brust of 4 or 5 voices,[81] and Pedal
of apparently 5 voices.[82] The Brust contains the
higher-pitched voices lacking in the Oberwerk. A
double harness for Oberwerk-and-Brust is suggested

4. Torgau.[83] Oberwerk of 11 voices, Brust of
2 voices, Rueckpositive of 10 voices, and Pedal of 3
voices. Obviously, the highly fragmentary Brust belongs in the tonal corpus of the Oberwerk. A double
harness for Oberwerk-and-Brust is suggested

5. Halberstadt, St. Martini.[84] This instrument
is discussed above as the initial example for the
double harness control for Oberwerk-and-Brust

6. Halberstadt, Barfuesser.[85] Werk of 9 voices,
Brust of 5 voices, Rueckpositive of 13 voices, and
Pedal of 11 voices.[86] The combination of Brust-and-
Werk is specified by Praetorius as In der Brust zum
Manual (in the Brust for the Manual)

7. Grueningen, Schlosz.[87] Oberwerk of 12
voices, Brust of 7 voices, Rueckpositive of 14 voices,
and Pedal of 26 voices. The combination of Brust and
Oberwerk is specified by Praetorius as Fornen in der
Brust zum Manual (forward in the Brust for the Manual)

8. <u>Model Disposition 1</u>.[88] Oberwerk of 9 voices, Brustpositive of 4 voices, Rueckpositive of 9 voices, and Pedal of 5 voices. The Brust contains only higher-pitched labial voices and a reed with fractional resonators, none of which duplicate voices on the Oberwerk but rather supply missing tonal elements. A double harness controlling Oberwerk-and-Brust from one keyboard is suggested

9. <u>Model Disposition 2</u>.[89] Oberwerk of 7 voices, Brust of 3 voices, Rueckpositive of 6 voices, and Pedal of 3 voices. The Brust contains a higher-pitched labial voice and a pair of reeds with fractional resonators. These tonal elements supplement the resources of the Oberwerk. A double harness for Oberwerk-and-Brust is suggested

10. <u>Model Disposition 3</u>.[90] Werk of 6 voices, Brust of 2 voices, Seitenpositive of 5 voices, and Pedal of 2 voices. The Brust contains two reeds with fractional resonators which supplement the tonal resources of the Werk. A double harness for Werk-and-Brust is suggested

11. <u>Sondershausen</u>.[91] Oberwerk of 10 voices,[92] Brust of 6 voices, Rueckpositive of 8 voices,[93] and Pedal of 9 voices.[94] The Brust contains only higher-pitched labial voices and a reed with fractional resonators. The tonal elements of the Brust complement

the tonal corpus of the Oberwerk. A double harness
is suggested for Oberwerk-and-Brust

From this survey it becomes evident that the combination of Brust-and-Oberwerk by means of a double harness to make them playable on one keyboard seems to have been a very common practice among the early baroque builders. The machinery for achieving this effect was a very simple engineering problem. It is concomitantly evident also, that in many instances, the Brust was conceived as a tonal supplement of the Oberwerk and was introduced quite frequently as a space-saving device to relieve the Oberwerk of too many voices. The fractional resonators found a convenient home here as well, since the location of the Brust provided ready access for the frequent tunings which these reeds required.

The Oberwerk-and-Pedal

A fifth application of the double harness to control two chests found wide use in the Early Baroque in an effort to enrich the frequently meager resources of the Pedal by attaching the entire Oberwerk permanently to the pedal harness. The condition can be represented in code form as OW + P / P (Oberwerk-and-Pedal are controlled by the pedal keyboard), and the equivalent W + P / P (Werk-and-Pedal are controlled by the pedal keyboard).

The layout conducive to such application of the double harness is the rather classical one represented on

Plate LXXI, fig. 1. It seems to have been applied also in
the more concise form of instrument illustrated on Plate
LXVII, fig. 1, where a Brust component is absent. Deviations
from these two basic layouts will be illustrated as the cases
may subsequently arise.

The control harness for engaging the Oberwerk chest
permanently into the Pedal is fairly simple. Plate LXXI,
fig. 3 shows a possible way of realizing the situation. A
sticker M leads from pedal key P to square N. A tracker Q
leads from square N through square S (which is notched in
order to engage the cleats R which are fastened to both sides
of tracker Q) to roller T which turns the motion sideways
toward square U. A third tracker V leads from square U up
to pallet W. The second harness attaches at square S, from
which tracker X leads upward through square E and roller
board K to pallet L. A depression of the pedal key will open
both pallets W and L; the Oberwerk is thereby permanently
coupled to the Pedal and is not subject to engagement or disengagement by the player.

A double harness, such as the one described could
find application in Praetorius' Model Disposition VI.[95] The
instrument exhibits three chests controlled by two manuals
and the pedal keyboard. The Oberwerk has 5 voices, the
Unterpositive has 6 voices, and the Pedal has 2 voices. The
impoverished disposition of the Pedal, comprising only two
voices at 16' pitch, suggests a permanent coupling of the

Oberwerk to the Pedal, likely as not, by means of a double harness in the manner described. A closer and more comprehensive inspection of Praetorius' Model Disposition VI will serve to show the necessity for effecting a permanent alliance between the Oberwerk and the Pedal.

VI.	VI
Noch ein Disposition Zu eim kleinen Wercklein vff gar liebliche Art gerichtet / Von 13. Stimmen.	Another disposition for a small instrument of 13 voices set out in a delightful manner.

Oberwerck.		Oberwerk	
1. Liebliche Rohr-floit	8.fusz	1. Lieblich Rohr-floete	8 foot
2. Nachthorn	4	2. Nachthorn	4
3. Gemshorn Spitzfloit	4	3. Gemshorn [or] Spitzfloete	4
4. Octaevlin scharff	2	4. Octave, keen	2
5. Krumbhorn	8	5. Krummhorn	8

Vnter Positiff.		Unterpositive	
6. Quintadehna	8	6. Quintade	8
7. Blockfloit	4	7. Blockfloete	4
8. Zimbel scharff gar klein	2.3 fach	8. Scharf Zimbel, very small	II-III ranks
9. Nasat-quint	anderthalb fusz	9. Nasat Quint	1 1/2 foot
10. Ranckett: 16. oder Baer Pfeiff	8.fusz.	10. Rankett 16, or Baerpfeife	8 foot
11. Klein Regal		11. Klein Regal[96]	[4']

Pedal.		Pedal	
12. Vntersatz	16	12. Untersatz	16
13. Sorduen / oder gar stille liebliche Posaunen	16.fusz	13. Sordun, or very mild Lieblich Posaune	16 foot

Coppel zu beydon Manualn /
Vnd was sonsten mehr bey andern Orgeln erinnert werden.

Coupler for both manuals,
and whatever else is normally
[expected] in other organs.

Wolte man es etwas schaerf-
fer haben / so kan man ein
lieblich principal von 4.
Fuessen darzu setzen.

Should one wish a somewhat
keener [ensemble], a Lieblich
Principal of 4 foot could be
added.

Es muessen aber alle Stimmen / auff die enge Mensuren
gerichtet / vnnd gar lieblich intoniret werden.

All voices must, however, be
developed out of narrow scales,
and be mildly voiced.

The following rearrangement of the registers presents
the instrument in an equivalent modern form:[97]

Model Disposition VI

Proposed by Praetorius. The disposition takes into
account the probability of a permanent coupling effect between the Oberwerk and the Pedal.

Oberwerk

1. 8' Lieblich Rohrfloete
2. 4' Nachthorn
3. 4' Gemshorn or
       Spitzfloete

4. 2' Octave
5. 8' Krummhorn

Unterpositive

6. 8' Quintade
7. 4' Blockfloete
9. 1 1/3' Nasat
8. II-III Zimbel

10. 16' Rankett, or
        8' Baerpfeife
11. [4'] Klein Regal

Pedal

12. 16' Untersatz
1. 8' Lieblich Rohrfloete (OW)
2. 4' Nachthorn (OW)
3. 4' Gemshorn or
       Spitzfloete (OW)

4. 2' Octave (OW)
13. 16' Sordun or
        Lieblich Posaune
5. 8' Krummhorn (OW)

Accessories

Coupler: Unterpositive to   Other customary
Oberwerk   accessories

Among certain recent theorists of the organ, a more
sophisticated combination of Oberwerk-and-Pedal is occasionally indicated for the period. This combination suggests
that at times only a portion of the Oberwerk was permanently
attached to the Pedal, the remainder being playable on the
Oberwerk keyboard only. In specific cases it seems that the
resources of the Oberwerk were divided right on the chest,
so that the grave and moderately-pitched voices were concentrated, for example, on the front portion of the chest, while
the acutely-pitched voices, and particularly the crowns, were
concentrated on the back portion. To accomplish such a separation, the channels of the chest needed to be latitudinally
partitioned and a pallet box provided for each portion of the
chest. The front portion was then, supposedly, attached to
the Oberwerk and Pedal, while the back portion was attached
to the Oberwerk manual only. The Pedal would then exhibit
its own, independent crown structure on its native chests.

The present writer has found no compelling reasons
for suggesting this possible organization of the Oberwerk
chest because, among the dispositions presented in Praetorius'
catalog, the case does not seem to apply. It is, of course,
possible that situations outside of Praetorius' catalog and
within the historical period may compel such an analysis,

but the problem lies, in reality, outside the burden of the
present study.

However, for the sake of completeness, it may prove
helpful to exhibit a hypothetical control for the supposedly
prevailing condition. The engineering problems, in the present writer's opinion, lay well within the scope of the early
baroque builders, since it required no additional mechanical
insights not already exhibited by the craftsmen in more pristine situations.

Plate LXXI, fig. 4 shows a possible double harness
for both the Oberwerk manual and the pedal keyboard, in order
to realize the condition described. Tracker A leads from the
Oberwerk key OW to square Z; a second tracker C, equipped with
a pair of cleats D fastened securely on both sides of it,
passes through notched square E and continues to square F.
Here tracker G leads upward through roller board H to pallet
I. The second harness for the Oberwerk begins with tracker J
which leads from square E through roller board K to pallet L.
A depression of the Oberwerk key opens both pallets L and I
simultaneously. A sticker M leads from the nose of pedal
key P to square N. From here a tracker Q, equipped with a
pair of cleats R securely attached to it on both sides, passes through notched square S and continues to roller T where
the motion is turned at a right angle to communicate with
square U. A tracker V leads upward to pallet W. The second
pedal harness begins with tracker X which leads from square S

through roller board $\underline{Y}$ and attaches to square $\underline{E}$. From here, by means of the second Oberwerk harness the motion is transmitted to pallet $\underline{L}$. A depression of the pedal key opens pallets $\underline{W}$ and $\underline{L}$ at the same time.

The Oberwerk chest, section 1 carries the grave and moderately-pitched foundation and mutation voices, while section 2 carries the elements of the crown structure. The pedal chest $\underline{P}$, in turn, contains the bass voices and an independent crown structure. By means of such a disposition of layout and control the Pedal achieves a greater differentiation from the Oberwerk than in the more common layout and harness as described above and found exemplified among the dispositions of Praetorius.

Conditions and Implications

Among the dispositions of the various instruments contained in Praetorius' catalog, certain symptoms suggest the permanent alliance of Oberwerk-and-Pedal:

1. The lack of a transient coupler accessory operating between the Oberwerk and the Pedal

2. An impoverished pedal disposition; the Pedal exhibits merely supplemental bass voices or an otherwise incomplete corpus; quite frequently the pedal resources are restricted to 16' bass voices and to acutely-pitched solo voices at 2' and 1' pitch; occasionally, the Pedal possesses an independent crown.

Usually the moderate pitches at 8', 4', and 2 2/3'
are likely to be absent from the pedal corpus or appear there in random fashion

The permanent control of the Oberwerk chest by the
Pedal and the Oberwerk keyboard set up certain conditions
that affected the artistic manipulation of the instrument:

1. One set of draw knobs was provided for the
voices of the Oberwerk chest; their engagement was
immediately reflected in the registration of both
the Oberwerk manual and the pedal keyboard

2. Whatever registers were "drawn" would play
whenever the keys of either the Oberwerk or the Pedal
were depressed

3. The independent pedal voices mounted on the
pedal chests (should the instrument have been able to
exhibit such) could be added to or subtracted from the
pedal registration at the will of the player

4. Registrationwise, the Pedal could be differentiated from the tonal texture of the Oberwerk manual in two ways: (a) additional independent grave or
acute voices could be engaged; (b) if an additional
division and manual (such as a Rueckpositive) were
present, the hands could play upon it, while the resources of the Oberwerk could be reserved for the
Pedal

The advantages for combining the resources of the

Oberwerk and Pedal were dubious:

1. It was possible to restrict the pedal resources to the most essential voices

2. It was a convenience to effect (a) economy
of cost, (b) economy of space, and (c) economy of
wind

The disadvantages were serious and led to the eventual abandonment of a permanent alliance between the Oberwerk and the Pedal:

1. The Pedal, relying upon the voices of the
Oberwerk chest to supplement its own impoverished resources, failed to present a tonal corpus with any
claim to completeness

2. The permanent entanglement of the Pedal with
the Oberwerk made it impossible to registrate the
Pedal with any degree of independence

3. The Oberwerk voices, built to suit manual
functions, were unable to provide the Pedal with the
requisite extensity of tone

Survey of Examples

Following is a list of instruments from Praetorius'
catalog of dispositions in which the application of the
double harness for purposes of combining the resources of
the Oberwerk and the Pedal is strongly suggested:

1. Rostock.[98] A three-manual and Pedal

instrument exhibiting 6 voices in the Oberwerk, 12 in the Brustwerk, 12 in the Rueckpositive, and 9 in the Pedal. The Pedal lacks a crown structure of any kind, a labial voice at 16' pitch, and an Octave at 8' pitch; all of these basic elements are exhibited in the Oberwerk; hence, an alliance between Oberwerk and Pedal seems to have been likely

2. Luebeck, St. Peter.[99] A three-manual and Pedal instrument exhibiting 13 voices in the Oberwerk, 8 in the Brust, 14 in the Rueckpositive, and 10 in the Pedal. The Pedal lacks a transient coupler between it and the Oberwerk, the acute element (Zimbel) of the crown structure, and any voices higher than 4' pitch; all of these elements are exhibited in the Oberwerk,[100] so a double harness for Oberwerk-and-Pedal can be surmised

3. Luebeck, Cathedral.[101] A two-manual and Pedal instrument which had 7 voices in the Oberwerk, 14 in the Rueckpositive, and 9 in the Pedal. The Pedal lacks entirely any kind of crown structure and an 8' Principal voice; these are available in the Oberwerk. It is possible that both the Oberwerk and the Pedal were tied in to the pedal keyboard

4. Lueneburg, St. Johannes.[102] A three-manual and Pedal instrument. The Werk had 4 voices; the Oberpositive, 8 voices; the Rueckpositive, 11 voices;

and the Pedal, 4 voices.[103] Of the pedal voices,
one was an Untersatz which was added later, and the
other three were apparently mounted with the Werk
chest and constituted, therefore, what was known as
Pedal im Werk (Pedal-in-the-Werk). Praetorius points
out with some care that the Werk chest contained an
extra octave of bass pipes for each of its voices,
which was attached to the Pedal.[104] It appears, then,
that this combination of the Werk-and-Pedal by a
double harness represents an attachment of the secondary pedal harness to the Oberwerk chest at the sub-
octave. This instrument has, in its course through
the subsequent literature, suffered highly speculative
interpretations, most of which indicate a lack of
understanding as to the method of engineering required
to realize the effect which Praetorius describes; in
most instances, Praetorius' meager description has
been misinterpreted, so that the successive hypothetical reconstructions of the instrument differ from
each other in case after case. It is hoped that the
present author's interpretation may help to clarify
the issue rather than confuse it still further. It
is impossible to guarantee the validity of the present
contention in this regard, but the conclusions drawn
are an outgrowth of a fairly comprehensive and penetrating perusal of the subject of permanent coupling.

5. <u>Magdeburg, St. Catharina</u>.[105] A three-manual and Pedal instrument which contained 10 voices in the Oberwerk, 6 in the Brustpositive, 10 in the Rueckpositive, and 10 in the Pedal. The layout of this instrument departs slightly from the classical form in that the pedal towers were mounted on both sides of the Rueckpositive rather than in the more usual location as flanks of the Oberwerk. Although the Pedal exhibits a numerical strength equal to the Oberwerk and the Rueckpositive, its internal disposition suggests a significant lack of 8' and 4' voices. Its complement comprises four 16' voices, one 8' voice, no 4' voice, two 2' voices, two 1' voices, and one Mixture. This noticeable poverty in the moderately-pitched voices suggests an alliance of the Pedal with the Oberwerk. The case cannot be proven, but is very likely

6. <u>Torgau</u>.[106] In all probability this was a two-manual and Pedal instrument. The Oberwerk exhibits 11 voices, the Brust, 2 voices, the Rueckpositive 10 voices, and the Pedal 3 voices. The Pedal comprises two 16' voices and one 4' voice. The lack of a transient coupler accessory between the Oberwerk and Pedal, the numerical inferiority of the Pedal, the lack of moderately-pitched and acutely-pitched voices, and the total lack of a crown structure suggest a

permanent alliance between the Oberwerk and Pedal

7. <u>Cassel</u>, <u>Freiheit</u>.[107] The disposition of the various tonal corpora strongly suggest a three-manual and Pedal instrument.[108] The components of the various divisions comprise 8 voices for the Oberwerk, 8 for the Oberpositive, 9 for the Rueckpositive, and 8 for the Pedal. It is possible that the Pedal may have been independent, but the lack of a significant crown structure and the total absence of labial voices any higher than 8' pitch suggest that the Oberwerk was made playable in the Pedal as well.[109]

8. <u>Cassel</u>, <u>Brueder</u>.[110] Undoubtedly a two-manual and Pedal instrument. The Werk comprised 10 voices, the Rueckpositive 8 voices, and the Pedal 7 voices. The Pedal exhibits the following complement: four voices at 16' pitch, two at 8' pitch, and one at 2' pitch.[111] The obvious lack of 4' and 2' labial voices plus the lack of a crown structure of any sort strongly suggest the attachment of the Oberwerk to the Pedal in permanent fashion

9. <u>Cassel</u>, <u>Schlosz</u>.[112] A two-manual and Pedal instrument. The disposition assigns 8 voices to the Werk, 6 to the Oberpositive, and 6 to the Pedal. The Pedal comprises two voices of 16' pitch, two of 8' pitch, and two of 4' pitch.[113] Noteworthy omissions are the higher-pitched voices and a crown. A

combination of Oberwerk-and-Pedal is strongly suggested

10. Model Disposition 1.[114] Very likely a two-
manual and Pedal instrument. It shows 9 voices for
the Oberwerk, 4 for the Brustpositive, 9 for the
Rueckpositive, and 5 for the Pedal. The Pedal itself
exhibits two voices at 16' pitch, one at 8' pitch, one
at 2' pitch, and one at 1' pitch. The lack of a transient Oberwerk-to-Pedal coupler, the paucity of
moderately-pitched voices at 8' and 4' pitch, plus the
lack of a crown suggest a harness to combine the resources of the Oberwerk permanently with those of the
Pedal

11. Model Disposition 2.[115] Clearly a two-
manual and Pedal instrument. The Oberwerk has 7
voices; the Rueckpositive, 6; the Brust, 3; and the
Pedal, 3. The Pedal forces comprise two voices at 16'
pitch and one voice at 2' pitch. The lack of a transient Oberwerk-to-Pedal coupler plus the impoverished
tonal corpus of the Pedal point to a permanent attachment of the Oberwerk to the Pedal

12. Model Disposition 3.[116] Again, a two-manual
and Pedal instrument. The resources are divided so as
to give 6 voices to the Oberwerk, 2 to the Brust, 5 to
the Seitenpositive, and 2 to the Pedal. The Pedal,
with two 16' voices (or one 16' voice and one 8' voice

as an alternate suggestion by Praetorius), suggests a

permanent alliance between the Oberwerk and Pedal

13. <u>Model</u> <u>Disposition</u> <u>VI</u>.[117] The instrument

was laid out in detail above

With such an extensive array of examples from Prae-

torius' catalog of dispositions, among which the use of a

double harness in order to control the resources of the Ober-

werk-and-Pedal from the pedal keyboard is strongly suggested,

it would seem very likely that the permanent alliance of

Oberwerk-and-Pedal bespeaks a fairly standard practice for

the Early Baroque. In analyzing any dispositions from this

period, it would seem advisable to suspect such a harness

system and to seek for appropriate internal symptoms to help

fortify such a suspicion. The fully independent pedal divi-

sion is, in reality, an uncommon phenomenon for the period;

it is to be found only in the most comprehensive instruments.

It should, however, be reiterated, that no authentic monu-

ments remain that reveal these conditions and that subsequent

theorists, who may have enjoyed personal access to some of

these instruments, leave us no definitive information that

could establish the condition without doubt in every indi-

vidual case. All of the evidence must be deduced from the

internal dispositions of the instruments, and the hypotheses

submitted must be carefully applied and tested to see if such

mechanical layouts were within the apparent scope of the en-

gineering skills of the period.

The Oberwerk-and-Pedal-in-the-Oberwerk

A sixth and final application of the double harness to control two chests is exemplified in one instance among Praetorius' dispositions. It involves the combination of the Oberwerk and a few pedal voices mounted with the Oberwerk, most likely in the cradle. Such occasional mounting has previously already been alluded to as Pedal im Oberwerk (Pedal-in-the-Oberwerk). The situation can be expressed in code form as OW + Po / P (Oberwerk and Pedal in the Oberwerk are controlled by the pedal keyboard).

A likely layout for this situation is shown on Plate LXXII, fig. 1, where the Oberwerk OW occupies, as usual, the central position; in front of it lies the Rueckpositive Rp; in back of it and probably mounted in the same cradle as the Oberwerk are the few pedal voices Po.

The double control harness for this condition could be achieved very simply in the form shown on Plate LXXII, fig. 2. A sticker A leads from the nose of pedal key P to square B. A tracker C, attached to square B leads through a notched square D to square E. A second tracker F leads onward through roller board G to pallet H. The tracker C must be equipped with a pair of cleats I securely mounted on both sides of it which can engage square D when tracker C is moved. The second harness attaches at square D in the form of tracker J, which leads upward through roller board K, square L, and roller board M to pallet N in the Oberwerk chest OW. A depression of pedal key P opens both pallets H and N.

A double harness such as the one described could find application in Praetorius' Model Disposition 6.[118] This two-manual and Pedal instrument commanded 7 or 8 voices in the Oberwerk, 9 in the Rueckpositive, and 1 or 2 in the Pedal.[119] The poverty exhibited for the resources of the Pedal strongly suggest a double harness in order to make the Oberwerk resources available to the Pedal in permanent form.

A full presentation of this instrument is herewith subjoined:[120]

6.	6
Disposition einer Orgel von 18. Stimmen.	Disposition of an instrument of 18 voices
Im Ober Wercke 9. Stimmen.	In the Oberwerk, 9 voices
1. Principal von 8.fusz	1. Principal of 8 foot
2. Koppel oder Block-floeite / oder lieb-lich Gedact von 8.fi.	2. Koppelfloete or Block-floete or Lieblich Gedackt, of 8 ft.
3. Nachthorn 4.fi.	3. Nachthorn 4 ft.
4. Octava von 4.fi.	4. Octave of 4 ft.
5. Gemszhorn lieb-lich von 2.fusz	5. Lieblich Gems-horn of 2 ft.
6. Quinta von drittehalb fusz	6. Quinte of 2 1/2 foot
7. Mixtur von 2.fi. Pfeiffen starck.[121]	7. Mixture of 2 ft. [?] ranks
8. Vntersatz von Holtz[122] vff 16.fusz	8. Untersatz of wood at 16 foot
9. Trommeten vff 8.fusz Thon / vnnd 8.fusz lang	9. Trompete of 8 foot tone, and 8 foot length

Im Rueck Positiff 9. Stimmen.		In the Rueckpositive, 9 voices	
1. Principal von	4.fusz	1. Principal of	4 foot
2. Koppelfloeiten von	4.fusz	2. Koppelfloete of	4 foot
3. Quintadeen	8.fusz	3. Quintade	8 foot
4. Assat vff die Quinten anderthalb fi.		4. Nasat at the fifths	1 1/2 ft.
5. Querpfeiffe lieb- lich[123] von	4.fusz	5. Lieblich Quer- pfeife of	[2] foot
6. Cymballen lieblich /		6. Lieblich Zimbel	
7. Ziflitt von	1.fusz	7. Siffloete of	1 foot
8. Schallmeyen von	4.fusz	8. Schalmei of	4 foot
9. Krumbhorn von	8.fusz	9. Krummhorn of	8 foot

Tremulant.
2. Coppeln / etc.[124]

Tremulant
2. Couplers, etc.

[Translation by the present author]

In order to gain a clear overview of the disposition, particularly with respect to the Pedal which, at first glance, seems to be non-existent, a reconstruction of the specification in more familiar modern form may prove helpful. It should be remembered that if the Oberwerk was attached to the Pedal, as seems highly likely, its voices could not be disengaged from the Pedal; whatever was drawn in the Oberwerk would automatically play in the Pedal as well.[125]

Model Disposition 6

Oberwerk

1. 8' Principal   3. 4' Nachthorn

2. 8' Koppelfloete or
   Blockfloete or
   Lieblich Gedackt

4. 4' Octave

6. 2 2/3' Quinte

5. 2' Lieblich Gemshorn

7. 2' Mixture

9. 8' Trompete

Rueckpositive

3. 8' Quintade

1. 4' Principal

2. 4' Koppelfloete

5. [2'] Lieblich Querpfeife

4. 1 1/3' Nasat

7. 1' Siffloete

6.   Lieblich Zimbel

9. 8' Krummhorn

8. 4' Schalmei

Pedal

8. 16' Untersatz

1. 8' Principal (OW)

2. 8' Koppelfloete or
   Blockfloete or
   Lieblich Gedackt (OW)

4. 4' Octave (OW)

3. 4' Nachthorn (OW)

6. 2 2/3' Quinte (OW)

5. 2' Lieblich Gems-
   horn (OW)

7. 2' Mixture (OW)

9. 8' Trompete (OW)

Accessories

Tremulant

Couplers: [Rueckpositive to
Pedal]
[Rueckpositive to
Oberwerk]

The Compound Harness

In a few instances found in Praetorius' catalog of
dispositions, the layout and disposition of the resources of
one or two divisions necessitated the introduction of a compound harness in order to control the various portions effectively. There is really no conclusive proof that such harnesses found application in the instruments of the time; however, at least four instances remain where such a control

mechanism or one to achieve an equivalent effect seems to have been required. The multiple harness, in every one of the instances, could easily have been realized as a combination of two double harnesses, so arranged as to engage the various components.

Various Dispositions

The first instance is illustrated by the Grueningen, Schlosz instrument,[126] where the voices in the pedal towers, plus the ones on the Oberwerk cradle, plus the Brust Pedalia had to be made playable from the pedal keyboard. The situation may be expressed in code form as P + BP + Po / P (the Pedal, the Brust Pedalia, and the Pedal-in-the-Oberwerk are controlled by the pedal keyboard). The actual mechanism could have been a compound double harness; it represents an application of the two double harness situations described above; namely, P + BP / P and P + Po / P. No additional engineering problems needed to be solved in order to effect such a compound harness.

The second instance which suggests a multiple harness control is the instrument at Sondershausen.[127] Here the voices of the Oberwerk, of the Pedal-in-the-towers, and of the Pedal-in-the-Oberwerk needed to be controlled by the pedal keyboard. In code form the situation may be represented as OW + P + Po / P (the Oberwerk, the Pedal, and the Pedal-in-the-Oberwerk are controlled by the pedal keyboard). Again a compound double harness would have been sufficient to control these scattered members. Of the double harness systems developed above, two would have sufficed; namely, OW + P / P and P + Po / P.

The third instance of a probable multiple harness control is the organ at <u>Halberstadt</u>, <u>Barfuesser</u>.[128] It is debatable if the Werk was attached to the Pedal. If it was, then it became necessary to harness the Werk, the Pedal, and the Brust Pedal to the pedal keyboard. In code, the situation presents the following picture: W + P + BP / P (the Werk, the Pedal, and the Brust Pedal are controlled by the pedal keyboard). A combination of two double harnesses previously described would have sufficed to solve the problem: W + P / P and P + BP / P.

The fourth instance requires the combination of Oberwerk, Brust Pedal, and Pedal-in-the-Oberwerk to achieve full control by one keyboard. The case is illustrated by the <u>Magdeburg</u>, <u>St. Ulrich</u>[129] instrument. The organ does not exhibit an independent pedal division in the side towers as was generally customary. On the contrary, a single pedal voice appears in the cradle, while three or four pedal voices appear mounted in the Brust. The attachment of the Oberwerk to the Pedal was mandatory if the Pedal was expected to cope at all adequately with the tonal corpora of the other divisions. In code form the situation may be represented as OW + Po + BP / P (the Oberwerk, the Pedal-in-the-Oberwerk,

and the Brust Pedal are controlled by the pedal keyboard).
Again a combination of two double harnesses seems to be the
logical solution of the problem: OW + Po / P and Po + BP / P.

Conclusions

On the basis of the preceding analyses with respect
to the existence and application of double and compound harness mechanisms in the instruments of the Early Baroque, it
would seem appropriate to summarize the conditions and implications of this practice as it may have affected the layout,
control, and concept of the organ of Praetorius.

1. The employment of a double harness system
executed in a mechanical way was, according to all
indications, a common practice for the time

2. Most popular were the double harnesses which
combined the Oberwerk-and-Brust to be playable upon
the Oberwerk keyboard, and the combination of the
Oberwerk-and-Pedal to be playable upon the pedal keyboard

3. The double harness mechanism seems to have
found occasional application in a number of different
situations as well; among these were the combination
of a divided Brust corpus (as Brust 1 and Brust 2)
and the combination of a divided Pedal corpus (as Pedal and Brust Pedalia or as Pedal and Pedal-in-the-
Oberwerk)

4. The double harness systems were fixed and immutable alliances not subject to engagement or disengagement by the player

5. The double harness principle permitted and abetted the membering of occasional divisions of the organ into fractional corpora

6. Its frequent application to engage the Brust with the Oberwerk and the Oberwerk with the Pedal gave the Oberwerk a dominant position in the instrument. In fact, the term Werk took on a connotation that collectively comprised the Brust, the Oberwerk, and the Pedal as the central organic unity in the instrument

7. Such a permanent intercommunication between the Brust, the Oberwerk, and the Pedal served to isolate the Rueckpositive as a contrasting element in the concept of the organ. It consistently maintained an independent and unalloyed existence

8. The permanent fusion of Brust, Oberwerk, and Pedal obviated the necessity for developing and applying transient couplers between these divisions; it also explains the consistent omission of these devices

9. The inviolate entity of the Rueckpositive required the provision of transient coupler systems to operate between it and the Pedal, and between it and the Oberwerk; it also explains the rather consistent presence of these devices in the specifications

for the instruments

10. The common introduction of a double harness
system had implications for the tonal disposition of
the pedal corpus. It generally reveals an hourglass
structure insofar as the Pedal often exhibited a number of grave bass voices, an impoverished central core
structure, and a bouquet of acute voices. At times
and in several cases the Pedal was restricted to
gravely-pitched bass voices only

11. The Oberwerk, should its division be suggested by the presence of a double harness between it
and a Brust, comprised the grave and moderately-
pitched voices, while the high-pitched and physically
diminutive voices (such as reeds with fractional resonators) were dismembered from it and placed into a
separate compartment, such as the Brust

12. The dismembering of the Oberwerk into Oberwerk and Brust permitted a registrational application
of the wind-trunk ventil. Should this be brought into play in connection with the Brust, for example,
its engagement or disengagement permitted a collective change in registration by pneumatic means

13. The whole concept of multiple harnessing
and its application had a determining influence upon
the methods of laying out the tonal corpora during
this period. Without a knowledgeable understanding

of the principle, the dispositions presented by Praetorius in his catalog are hardly intelligible to the
modern student of the organ

CHAPTER X

THE PRINCIPLE AND PRACTICE

OF TRANSMISSION

Delineation of the Concept

Having discovered, developed, and refined the various methods of multiple and compound harnessing as discussed
in chapter ix, the early baroque builders had accumulated the
total technical skill required to introduce into their instruments the principle and practice of transmission. Under
this concept is understood the operational condition whereby
a voice native to one chest and playable from a certain keyboard can be made selectively playable upon another keyboard;
each keyboard can then engage the same voice independently of
the other. The principle seemed to provide the eagerly
sought-for escape from the entangling alliances engendered
by the various methods of permanent coupling or attachment
whereby a voice so disposed would invariably respond to the
action of both keyboards whenever it was engaged by the draw
knob. By way of illustration, certain methods of harnessing
could set up a condition where, for example, a 16' Principal
could be made to play from the Oberwerk and from the pedal
keyboard; however, in every case, when the draw knob engaged

the voice it would respond to both keyboards and could not be used separately from either one. By transmission, on the other hand, the voice could be played from either keyboard separately or from both simultaneously at the wish of the player. The advantages to be gained from such a disentanglement were compelling enough for the early baroque builders to cause them to pursue the problem with a view toward developing the requisite mechanism to achieve such an operational condition.

Historic Evidence

Neither in his text nor in his comments on existing instruments does Praetorius fully describe the methods or mechanisms whereby transmission could be achieved, but there do occur many references to the principle in the dispositions of various contemporary instruments which he presents. In order to understand these tonal dispositions fully and intelligently, it becomes necessary to explore the principle and its application in the instruments of the time.

The procedure most likely to give a full and detailed picture of the principle of transmission and its implementation entails a minute examination of references found in the important historical treatises of the organ, beginning with the most recent and ending with the most ancient. The fullest and most accurate description is given by Elis (1949) in his dictionary under the entry:

Transmissions: Attempts to make a voice playable from two keyboards reach back to very early times.
In the final analysis, many of the partially independent pedals of the sixteenth century were nothing more
than transmissions of manual registers into the Pedal.
The mechanism to set up transmissions within the slider chest requires double channels (one for clavier A,
the other for clavier B); likewise, double sliders and
grooves in the upper boards which are fed from both
sliders. Each of the intake-bores for the grooves is
covered with a small checkvalve (G. Rueckschlagven-
til).[1]

A further recent source of information on transmission

in the slider chest is Mahrenholz (1942) who, in discussing

the application of the principle in the old organs, indicates

the apparent motivation for the practice but gives an incom-

plete account of the technical requirements for it in the

slider chest. He says:

At some yet undetermined time the desire became
evident to be able to play on the Pedal, voices from
the chest other than those already drawn for the Manual. Technically, this was solved in the manner that
the single chest in the organ was equipped with double
sliders and double pallets of which one set was attached to the manual keyboard, the other to the pedal
keyboard. Thereby the Pedal was released from its
dependence upon the manual keyboard and achieved an
apparently independent status.[2]

Adlung (1768), under the entry "Coppel", throws fur-

ther light on the principle, its practical application, ef-

fect, advantages, and disadvantages:

Coppel (Koppel) has another interpretation.
Where the space [for an organ] is restricted, or when
the church has inadequate means, several of the organ
registers are occasionally constructed in such a way
that they may, by means of individual draw knobs, be

used separately in the Manual and Pedal. However, the
draw knobs are not labelled Koppel, but the actual
name of the register [is inscribed] on each. For example, in a village near Erfurt, called Hohenfelden,
there are two draw knobs for the Quintaton 8'; both
are inscribed as Quintaton 8', but there is only one
register [i.e., set of pipes]. When one knob is
drawn, the register speaks only in the Manual; when
the other one is drawn, it speaks only in the Pedal.
When both are drawn [the voice] speaks both above
[in the Manual] and below [in the Pedal]. In the
Kreuzkirche in Dresden, the Mixture is thus disposed
in the Manual and Pedal. This is an abridgment for
churches of moderate means; if there is any oversight
in the construction of the mechanism or in the wind
conductors, considerable difficulties arise; such
divided registers often speak improperly, especially
the reeds if the wind supply is not equal, or if a
condition of turbulence develops, or if the wind is
conducted to the pipe from unequal distances . . . .[3]

Adlung further points up the compelling motivation

for resort to the principle of transmission:

What was mentioned in paragraph 124 concerning
the duplication of register draw knobs, serves also
to reduce the costs and to increase the variety [of
registration].[4]

Werckmeister (1698) criticizes transmissions gener-

ally, allowing incorporation of the principle only in organs

for churches of impoverished means. Important is his almost

casual reference to the checkvalves, a critical device for

realizing a transmission in an effective manner:

That some show an inclination toward such register dispositions where one voice [is arranged] to be
used individually and separately in the Pedal and Manual, is not always advisable; experience proves that
it does not always succeed and often sounds false, especially in reeds. The cause lies in the unequal

distribution of the wind, or in its turbulence, or in
the variable distances over which the wind is conducted to the pipe, causing it to lose its equality.
Therefore, it is better that every voice be supplied
with its own pipes, or careful consideration is made
to see if [transmission] is feasible, so that the work
is not undertaken in vain. Beyond that, it is a fine
abridgment for poor churches which are unable to pay
for many large voices. [Transmission] occurs ordinarily among the large voices. Often the so-called
checkvalves in the chests cause inconveniences.[5]

Finally, two references to transmission from Prae-

torius (1619) himself will serve to indicate that the prin-

ciple was known and applied in organs of his time. Follow-

ing the title of his Universal Tabel there appears a paren-

thetic clause seeking to explain certain of his designations

that follow in the table. He says:

N.B. Where [the letters] M. and P. are found
designated in the margin, it must be understood that
such a voice can be used alone in the Manual as well
as alone in the Pedal (in which case it will be labelled Principalbass, Gedacktbass, etc.) Furthermore, such a voice can be used simultaneously in the
Manual and Pedal by means of one or two separate
registers [i.e., stop actions].[6]

In comparing the slider chest with the spring chest,

Praetorius points up the advantages of the slider chest for

purposes of transmission:

. . . in the slider chests more wonderful variations in the voices are possible of achievement by
means of borrowed basses, wood groovings, and the
like, than can be developed with the spring chest.[7]

The historic evidence, here presented in reverse

chronological order, firmly establishes the existence of the concept of transmission in the early baroque period and collectively reveals the necessary conditions and mechanical appointments needed to put it into practice in connection with the slider chest.

Internal Evidence

Several terms will need to be considered which occur in the various dispositions presented by Praetorius to indicate the presence of some form of transmission in the organs of the time. The ones occurring most frequently are the terms absonderlich, abgesondert, abgesonderter Basz, and the like. The terms mean separated, isolated, segregated bass, etc. In modern parlance, such a voice or bass would be termed borrowed, borrowed bass, etc. For example, in discussing a Positive comprised of one set of pipes, Praetorius says:

> . . . and every register can be drawn and used by itself alone and segregated; then also two, and finally all three . . . .[8]

Again, in discussing the relative merits of the slider chest over against the spring chest, he points out:

> . . . although in the slider chests more wonderful variations in the voices [are possible of achievement] by means of segregated basses . . . .[9]

From Praetorius' catalog of dispositions a number of references can be quoted to show various terms used to indicate transmissions:

Magdeburg, Cathedral.[10] In the Oberwerk are
listed: "1. Principal 16', 2. Principalbass, segregated, 16'." Also items 6 and 7: "Quintade Untersatz
with a segregated bass, 16'."

Occasionally transmissions are indicated by the
phrase, mit zwei Registern (with two registers [sliders]) as,
for example, in the organ by Fritzsche:

Schoeningen, Schlosz.[11] In the Oberwerk are
listed: "4. Gedackt Subbass at 16', throughout the
clavier, but with two registers, so that each can be
used segregated, one for the Manual, the other for
the Pedal. 5. and for this reason there are two
voices."

At times the terms manualiter, pedaliter, im Manual,
durchs Manual (in the Manual, in the Pedal, throughout the
Manual) are used to show transmissions:

    1. Leipzig, St. Nicholas.[12] In the Oberwerk
are listed: "11. Grobgedackt at 16' in the Manual.
12. and in the Pedal as a segregated bass"

    2. Leipzig, St. Thomas.[13] In the Oberwerk are
listed: "1. Principal 16' in the Pedal and in the
Manual"

    3. Model Disposition 7.[14] In the Oberwerk are
listed: "2. Gross Quintade 16' in the Manual and in
the Pedal, segregated"

4. <u>Bayreuth</u>.[15] In the Oberwerk are listed:

"6. Lieblich Gedackt Subbass 16' throughout the entire

Manual, with a segregated bass for the Pedal alone.

7. which comprises two voices"

Other terms that occur occasionally are <u>in 2 Registern</u>
<u>zerteilt</u> (divided into two registers), <u>doppelt</u> (double), and
the like. These terms are, however, sometimes used to mean
sliders divided into discant and bass portions; hence, the
full context must be taken into consideration when interpreting these terms.

<u>Mechanism and Control</u>

The historic evidence, gleaned from the treatises of
representative organ theorists and found in the dispositions
of the instruments of the time, not only forces us to accept
the principle of transmission as having been known and practiced by Praetorius and his contemporaries, but also supplies
us with the motivation for it, its operational effects, its
technical aspects, its advantages, and its disadvantages. It
is now possible and desirable to develop the requisite mechanism by description and illustration in order to gain a clear
understanding of its operation and the effect its application
may have had in the tonal dispositions of the instruments.
In many cases the tonal layouts of the organs are unintelligible unless a fairly accurate understanding of the principle
and application of permanent coupling and transmission can be

brought to bear upon the problem.

Inasmuch as transmissions from the Manual into the Pedal were exclusively restricted to voices from the Werk or Oberwerk and to registers of large physical dimensions, such voices may be presumed to have been mounted on the front or rear (more likely, the latter) portion of the Werk or Oberwerk chest, so as to make the additional chest appointments accessible for maintenance.[16] Furthermore, since the Pedal needed to engage only the bass pipes of the voice in transmission, double appointments needed to be provided only in the bass portions of the Oberwerk chest; more than likely, one-half of these were on the left side of the chest, the remainder, on the right. Since the average pedal keyboard of the time had only about 23 keys, each side of the chest needed to be equipped with double mechanism for about 12 bass notes. Praetorius' catalog of dispositions lists single-stop transmissions most often, with multiple-stop transmissions occurring in occasional examples only; accordingly, the mechanism needed for transmission purposes had to be provided for one, two, or three stops at the most. In only one example is an entire Werk division of 16 voices fully equipped for transmission of all of its voices to a second keyboard.

For purposes of future reference, the Oberwerk chest which contains an element of transmission may be conveniently designated in code form as OW + t (Oberwerk chest with transmission) to distinguish it from the unencumbered Oberwerk, which has already been designated in code form as OW. Should

it be desirable to refer to the transmission section alone

the code letter t (transmission portion) will serve.

Transmission Chest Disposition

In order to effect a transmission in an Oberwerk

slider chest, additional modifications and appointments had

to be provided beyond those described in chapter i of this

study. Such modifications were reflected in three areas of

the mechanism:

1. There needed to be the following conditions

available in the console: (a) Two keyboards, con-

nected to the Oberwerk-transmission chest; in every

case, one of these was the Oberwerk keyboard, the oth-

er, the pedal keyboard, since almost all of the trans-

missions occurred between the Oberwerk and the Pedal.

(b) Two draw knobs for the single voice, one to en-

gage the manual slider, the other, the pedal slider

2. A compound harness system had to be provided:

(a) One was needed to control the Oberwerk-transmission

chest so as to be playable from the Oberwerk keyboard.

(b) Another one was required to combine the pedal

chest, the transmission portion of the Oberwerk chest,

and, quite often, the regular portion of the Oberwerk

chest so as to be playable from the pedal keyboard

3. The transmission portion of the Oberwerk

chest needed double equipment from the pallet boxes
up to the pipe bores in the bass portions of the
chest, as follows: (a) An Oberwerk pallet box e-
quipped with sufficient pallets to satisfy the requirements of the Oberwerk keyboard; a pedal pallet
box equipped with sufficient pallets to satisfy the
requirements of the pedal keyboard. (b) A double set
of pallets; those in the Oberwerk pallet box communicated with the Oberwerk channels, while those in the
pedal pallet box communicated with the pedal channels.
(c) Double channels in the chest for each borrowed
note; one channel was fed by the Oberwerk pallet, the
other, by the pedal pallet. (d) Double bores in the
table and primary upper board for each borrowed note;
one set communicated with the Oberwerk channels, the
other, with the pedal channels.[17] (e) Double sliders
for the borrowed voice; one was controlled by the
Oberwerk draw knob, the other, by the pedal draw knob;
the bores of the Oberwerk slider corresponded with
those bores of the table and upper board which communicated with the Oberwerk channels, while those of the
pedal slider corresponded with those bores of the
table and upper board which communicated with the pedal channels. (f) An auxiliary upper board over the
bass portions of the Oberwerk-transmission chest and
overlying the primary upper board; the board was

grooved to connect the double intake-bores in the primary upper board with the requisite pipe bores which
the double channels had to feed; depending upon the
attitude of the sliders, the pipe bores could be fed
from the Oberwerk and pedal channels, either separately or simultaneously. (g) A set of hinged checkvalves, imbedded into the auxiliary upper board and
overlying the intake-bores, so as to prevent dissipation of the pressure from one channel into the other,
should the companion slider be in registration and
the neighboring channel at atmospheric pressure

The chest mechanism necessary for the realization
of transmission in an Oberwerk slider chest is shown in a
series of drawings in the Atlas. Plate LXXII, fig. 3 shows
the basic method of partitioning the left bass portion of a
normal chest (unaffected by transmission) into a series of
separated channel compartments, each serving one note. The
chest frame is identified by A; it is divided into compartments H by partitions F and G. There remain dead spaces J
between the channel compartments H.[18] The floor of each compartment reveals an oblong opening I on the underside of
which is seated the Oberwerk pallet in order to control the
access of pressure into the compartment from the pallet box.
Underneath the chest and in front is attached the Oberwerk
pallet box (not shown) which extends longitudinally along the
entire chest and latitudinally from the front edge back to

point K.

Plate LXXIII, fig. 1 shows how the previously dead spaces between the Oberwerk channel compartments have been pressed into service as pedal channels. The chest frame is identified by A. The formerly dead spaces J have been latitudinally partitioned by members M to provide pedal channels reaching half-way across the chest and in the rear portion of it. They actually need to be long enough to span the space occupied by the transmission voices to be mounted on the chest. Pedal channels J reveal oblong openings through the floor of the chest under which are seated the pedal pallets in order to control the access of pressure into the pedal channels. The pedal pallets (not shown) are enclosed by an appropriate pallet box, similar to the one provided for the Oberwerk pallets. Fig. 2 is a latitudinal section of fig. 1 and shows the disposition of the pallets and pallet boxes. The chest frame is shown at A. Oberwerk channel H extends entirely across the chest from front to rear. Pedal channel J extends half-way across the chest from latitudinal partition M to the rear. Opening I in the Oberwerk channel provides the seat for pallet N, while opening L in the pedal channel provides the same for pallet O. The Oberwerk pallet box is identified by P, while the pedal box is identified by Q.

Plate LXXIV, fig. 1 exhibits the requisite chest overlays in a single, compound drawing. Area A of the drawing (in plan) shows the Oberwerk and pedal channel compartments

and partitions as well as the pallet openings in the front
and rear portions of the chest. Area B shows the intake-bores
in the table; those at F communicate with the Oberwerk channels, while those at G communicate with the pedal channels.
Area C shows the sliders. Sliders H and I comprise a double
set required for purposes of transmission. Those at J are
individual Oberwerk sliders. The bores in slider H are in
registration with bores F of the table and communicate with
the Oberwerk channels, while those in slider I correspond with
bores G of the table and communicate with the pedal channels.
Area D shows the countersunk bores K of the primary upper
boards upon which the pipes are set. Area E shows the auxiliary upper board which is necessary for the transmission
voices. The board is bored partly through from the under side
with a somewhat enlarged bore at L and at M. A further bore
is made from the top side at M and countersunk to provide a
ᵤat for the pipe. A groove N is tunneled from bore L to bore
M to provide the necessary communication for the intake-bore
of the pedal channel and pipe bore M.

Plate LXXIV, fig. 2 presents a longitudinal section
of fig. 1 at Z-Z. Groove N connects bores L and M. Hinged
checkvalve O operates in bore L which is connected with the
pedal channel, while hinged checkvalve P operates in bore M
which is connected with the Oberwerk channel.

On Plate LXXV, fig. 1, the pedal slider T is shown
in "on" position, thus opening intake-bores N to grooves R.

Tracker V is shown as engaging pedal pallet L, thereby inflating channel H with pressure wind from the pedal pallet
box. The pressure from channel H passes through intake-bore
N and the corresponding hole in slider T, and opens hinged
checkvalve P. From here the pressure inflates groove R, and
exhausts through pipe bore S, causing the note C to sound in
response to the depression of pedal key, note C. Should the
Oberwerk key, note C draw down tracker W and thus engage
Oberwerk pallet M, the pressure from the Oberwerk pallet box
would, likewise, inflate channel I. Since, however, slider
U (not effectively shown in fig. 1) would be out of registration, the key action would be effectively checked at this
point and the note would not respond. Should, however, the
Oberwerk slider U be "on" and the pedal slider T be "off",
the situation would be reversed: the note C would respond to
the stimulus of the corresponding Oberwerk key, but would not
react to that of the corresponding pedal key.

Control Harness for Transmissions

The harness for the incorporation of an Oberwerk-
transmission chest into the control system of two keyboards
such as the Oberwerk and Pedal, is dependent upon the total
disposition of chest layout and the overall control of the
same. The most common situation, which may be looked upon
as classical for the period, requires the Oberwerk harness
to engage the Oberwerk pallets; it also requires the pedal

harness to engage the pallets of the pedal chest, the pedal pallets of the transmission chest, and generally also the Oberwerk pallets of the Oberwerk-transmission chest in the form of a triple harness. In code form the condition may be expressed as OW + t / OW (Oberwerk-transmission chest is controlled by the Oberwerk keyboard) and OW + t + P / P (Oberwerk, transmission, and pedal chest are controlled by the pedal keyboard).

A possible harness for the compound situation is shown on Plate LXXV, fig. 2, which is adequate to handle the condition described above. The manual harness begins at the Oberwerk key OW. Tracker A leads upward to square B; a second tracker C, equipped with cleats D securely fastened to it, passes through notched square E and leads to pendant arm F, necessary to hold tracker C in properly suspended position; a third tracker G leads from square E through roller board H to Oberwerk pallet I in the Oberwerk chest OW. A depression of the Oberwerk key opens pallet I. The pedal harness begins at pedal key P. A sticker J engages square K, from which a tracker L, equipped with cleats M, passes through notched square N and through roller O and leads to square Q; a second tracker R leads through roller board S to pedal pallet T in the transmission chest. The second pedal harness attaches at square N, from which tracker U leads through roller board V and is attached to an appropriate projecting arm in roller board H. The third pedal harness is the usual one which

attaches at roller O, leads by means of a tracker (not shown)
to square W, and thence by tracker X to pallet Y in the pedal
chest P. A depression of the pedal key opens pallets T, I,
and Y simultaneously.

Registrational Effects

There remain to be investigated the various registrational effects which could be produced by a transmission
chest, depending upon the attitudes of the stop action and
the key action. It must also be proven that the voice could
be made separately and independently playable from the Oberwerk keyboard and from the pedal keyboard.

The following basic attitudes of the two actions will
serve to show the independent control of the voice from either
keyboard; all other situations can easily be extrapolated.

1. If both draw knobs for the voice are engaged
and corresponding keys are depressed on both keyboards,
the chest mechanism will assume the attitudes shown
on Plate LXXVI, fig. 1: Sliders T and U will be in
registration, pallets L and M will be open, checkvalves P and Q will be opened and the pipe fed by
pressure from channels H and I

2. If the pedal draw knob is engaged, the manual one disengaged, and corresponding keys depressed
on both keyboards, the chest mechanism will react as
shown on Plate LXXVI, fig. 2: Slider T will be in

registration while slider U will be out of registration, pallets L and M will be open; checkvalve P will
be opened and the pipe fed by pressure from channel
H, while checkvalve Q will remain closed by gravity

3. If the manual draw knob is engaged, the pedal one disengaged, and corresponding keys are depressed on both keyboards, the chest mechanism will
exhibit the attitudes shown on Plate LXXVI, fig. 3:
Slider U will be in registration, while slider T will
be out of registration, pallets L and M will be open,
checkvalve Q will be opened and the pipe fed by pressure from channel I, while checkvalve P will remain
closed by gravity

4. If both draw knobs are disengaged and corresponding keys are depressed on both keyboards, the
chest mechanism will assume the attitudes shown on
Plate LXXVI, fig. 4: Sliders T and U will be out of
registration, pallets L and M will be open, checkvalves P and Q will remain closed by gravity, and the
pipe will not respond

5. If both draw knobs are engaged and the pedal key is depressed, while the manual key remains
idle, the chest mechanism will respond as shown on
Plate LXXVI, fig. 5: Sliders T and U will be in registration, pallet L will be open, while pallet M will
be closed, checkvalve P will be opened and the pipe

fed by pressure from channel $\underline{H}$ while checkvalve $\underline{Q}$ will remain closed because of gravity and pressure within the groove

6. If both draw knobs are engaged and the manual key is depressed, while the pedal key remains idle, the chest mechanism will assume the attitudes shown on Plate LXXVI, fig. 6: Sliders $\underline{T}$ and $\underline{U}$ will be in registration, pallet $\underline{L}$ will be closed, while pallet $\underline{M}$ will be open, checkvalve $\underline{Q}$ will be opened by pressure from channel $\underline{I}$, while checkvalve $\underline{P}$ will remain closed because of gravity and the pressure in the groove, and the pipe will respond to pressure from channel $\underline{I}$

Types of Transmissions

With the principle of transmission established as a practice of the Early Baroque, the requisite mechanism and harness control developed, and the registrational effects examined, it becomes possible to approach Praetorius' catalog of dispositions with a view toward analyzing the application of the concept in the instruments of the time. The entire catalog seemingly differentiates between various types of transmissions, of which three are clearly identifiable; these are:

1. Single-stop, unison transmissions

2. Multiple-stop, unison transmissions

3. Single and multiple-stop, octave transmissions

Single-stop, Unison Transmissions

To set up the mechanism for transmission in a tracker organ of slider chests involved the incorporation of considerable mechanical equipment into the instrument. Accordingly, most of the instruments which give evidence of transmission present the case of a single transmission from the Oberwerk into the Pedal at the unison. Thus applied, the principle became economically feasible and worthy of implementation. Usually such transmissions were applied to large manual or pedal voices of grave pitch, whose double use seemed to warrant the time, effort, and expense to effect it.

For single-stop, unison transmissions the requisite mechanism consisted of duplicate draw knobs in the console, compound harnesses from the keyboards to the chest, and a fairly complex chest mechanism as described above.

The control harness for the unison transmission is schematically exemplified on Plate LXXV, fig. 2 and discussed above; it was necessary, however, that the Oberwerk and pedal harnesses were attached to pallets of adjacent channels, in order to communicate with corresponding notes of the same pitch.

Illustrative Cases

A number of instances can now be marshaled from Praetorius' catalog of dispositions to show how the principle of transmission was incorporated into the tonal dispositions of

the instruments of the time. The first example is Praetorius'
Model Disposition 4, which illustrates a single-stop, unison
transmission from the Werk into the Pedal.[19] The Pedal also
exhibits an independent voice listed among the Werk voices in
the form of a Pedal im Werk (Pedal-in-the-Werk); the attachment of the entire Werk to the Pedal in permanent form appears
to have been mandatory.

	4.			4	
Disposition einer gar kleinen Orgel: von 10. oder 11. Stimmen.[20]			Disposition of a very small organ of 10 or 11 voices		
1. Principal	4.fusz		1. Principal	4 foot	
2. Rohrfloeit oder Gedact mit einem abgesondertem Basz	8.fusz		2. Rohrfloete or Gedackt, with a segregated bass	8 foot	
3. Octava	2.fusz		3. Octave	2 foot	
4. Scifloeit	1.fusz		4. Siffloete	1 foot	
5. Nasatt Quinta anderthalb fusz			5. Nasatquinte	1 1/2 foot	
6. Zimbel gar klein, 2. oder 3. Choer- icht / an statt der Mixtur.			6. Zimbel, very small; 2 or 3-choired, in place of the Mixture		
7. Blockfloeit	4.fusz		7. Blockfloete	4 foot	
8. Nachthorn	4.fusz		8. Nachthorn	4 foot	
9. Krumbhorn	8.fusz		9. Krummhorn	8 foot	
10. Pedal Vntersatz von Holtz[21]	16.fusz		10. Pedal, Untersatz of wood	16 foot	

Koendte er aber durchs
gantze Manual durchgehen /
vnd hernacher zum Pedal abgesondert werden: were es
desto besser.

If it [i.e., Untersatz,]
could be carried throughout
[the compass of] the Manual
and then be segregated for the
Pedal, it would be better.

Ein Clavier / doch dasz vff beyden seiten die Register halbirt / bisz ins c etc. darmit man den Choral druff fuehren kan / mit vnterschiedlichen Stimmen.[22]

One clavier, but so that the registers can be [used] divided on both sides at c', etc., so that the Chorale [cantus] can be presented with differentiated voices [for its accompaniment].

Tremulant

Tremulant

Vom C bisz ins c̄ oder d̄ / welches besser. Pedal vom C bisz ins d̄.

[The manual compass is] from C up to c''' or d''', which is preferred. Pedal [compass] from C up to d'.

Der organist sol hinter dem Wercke sitzen / dasz das Werck fornen heraus koempt.

The organist should sit behind the organ, so that the instrument projects out forward.

Weil man eine Quintadeen von 8.fuessen darzu setzen / vnd den Basz auch absondern / so kan mans in acht nemen.

If one should wish to add an 8' Quintade and segregate the bass, it may well be considered.

[Translation by the present author]

The following organization of the disposition presents the instrument in familiar and equivalent modern form:[23]

Model Disposition 4

[Werk]

2.	8' Rohrfloete or Gedackt	5.	1 1/3' Nasat
1.	4' Principal	4.	1' Siffloete
7.	4' Blockfloete	6.	II or III Zimbel
8.	4' Nachthorn	9.	8' Krummhorn
3.	2' Octave		

[Pedal][24]

10.	16' Untersatz (Po)	3.	2' Octave (W)
2.	8' Rohrfloete (t)	5.	1 1/3' Nasat (W)

1. 4' Principal (W)   4. 1' Siffloete (W)
7. 4' Blockfloete (W)   6. II or III Zimbel (W)
8. 4' Nachthorn (W)   9. 8' Krummhorn (W)

Accessories

Tremulant   Divided sliders
Manual: C̲ - c̲''' or d̲'''   Pedal: C̲ - d̲'
Optional voices: 8' Quintade in the Manual and Pedal
                   16' Untersatz in the Manual also

A possible schematic harness for Model Disposition 4
is presented on Plate LXXVII, fig. 1. The motion of the Werk
key W̲ is transmitted by tracker A̲, square B̲, tracker C̲, square
D̲, tracker E̲ and roller board F̲ to pallet G̲ within the Werk
chest W̲. The motion of pedal key P̲ is carried by sticker H̲,
square I̲, tracker J̲, square K̲, square L̲, tracker M̲, and roller
board N̲ to pallet O̲ in the combined transmission chest t̲ and
Pedal-in-the-Werk chest P̲w̲; in addition, the motion of tracker
J̲ is conveyed by square K̲, tracker Q̲, and roller board R̲ to
appropriate projecting arms in roller board F̲, from where it
is led to pallet G̲ in the Werk chest W̲. In code form the
harness system may be rendered as W + t / W and W + t + Pw
/ P.

In this instance the transmission chest and the Pedal-in-the-Werk chest could very easily and most economically
have been combined as a single operational unit as shown on
Plate LXXVII, fig. 2. Channels H̲ are fed through pallet openings L̲ while channels I̲ are fed by Werk pallets in the front
of the chest. The separation of the independent pedal voice

from the transmission voice is accomplished by proper disposition of the sliders. The transmission voice is controlled by sliders T and U, the former being associated with pedal channels and the latter with Werk channels. The independent pedal voice is then equipped with a single slider Pw which communicates only with the pedal channels H and is sealed off from Werk channels I.

A second example is Praetorius' Model Disposition 7, which requires, however, a somewhat more complex harness system. It also shows a single-stop, unison transmission from the Oberwerk into the Pedal. The Oberwerk and Brust are permanently coupled, while the Pedal presents an independent set of voices, a transmission from the Oberwerk into the Pedal, and is probably permanently coupled to the Oberwerk.

7.		7	
Disposition einer Orgel von 22. Stimmen.[25]		Disposition for an organ of 22 voices	
Ober Werck zum Manual.		Oberwerk for the Manual	
1. Principal	8.fusz	1. Principal	8 foot
2.) Grosz Quinta-deena (Im Man.) 3.) (Im Ped. abg)	16 fi.	2.) Gross Quintade (In the Manual) 3.) (Segregated Pedal)	16 ft.
4. Gedacte Floeit: Oder Rohrfloeit lieblich	8.fusz	4. Gedacktfloete or Lieblich Rohrfloete	8 foot
5. Octava enger Mensur	4.fusz	5. Octave of narrow scale	4 foot
6. Nachthorn oder Quintadeena	4.fusz	6. Nachthorn or Quintade	4 foot
7. Nasatt Quinta	3.fusz	7. Nasatquinte	3 foot

8. Mixtur, 4.5.6.7. Choericht / do man denn auch ein abgesondert Register zur 2.Choerichten Zimbel machen koendte.[26]

Zum Pedal alleine im Oberwerck.

9. Gedacter starcker Vntersatz   16.fusz

10. Posaunen Basz   16

Brust.

11. Klein Blockfloeit   2.fusz

12. Sifloeit oder Schwiegelpfeiff   1.fusz

13. Geigend Regal.   4.fusz

NB.

Wo nicht fleissige Organisten verhanden / do sind viel Regal- vnd Schnarwercke nichts nuetze / sonderlich von 4. fuessen / denn dieselbe wollen einen vnverdrossenen fleissigen Organisten haben / der sich nicht verdriessen lest / alle acht tage alle Schnarrwercke durch vnd durch zustimmen / vnd in jhrem Stande zu erhalten: Jnmassen ich dann in der Gruningischen Orgel bey den viertzehen Schnarrwercken solches ohne Ruhm mir nicht wenig angelegen seyn lassen.

Wolte man nun auch die Brust gantz aussen lassen; So kan man das kleine Blockfloeitlin von 2.fuessen ins Oberwercke / vnd das Sifloeitlein von 1.Fusz ins Rueckpositiff bringen.

Rueck Positiff.		Rueckpositive	
1. Schweitzer Pfeiff zum Principal fornen an	4.fusz	1. Schweizerpfeife as display in the front	4 foot
2. Quintadeena	8	2. Quintade	8
3. Gemszhorn oder Spitzfloeit	4	3. Gemshorn or Spitzfloete	4
4. Holfloeit oder Querfloeit	4	4. Hohlfloete or Querfloete	4
5. Klein Octava	2	5. Klein Octave	2
6. Holquinten oder Scharffquinten anderthalb		6. Hohlquinte or Scharfquinte	1 1/2
7. Zimbeln	2.Choerich	7. Zimbel	II ranks
8. Trommeten	8	8. Trompete	8
9. Krumbhorn	8.fusz	9. Krummhorn	8 foot

Wiewol man eins vnter diesen beyden Schnarrwercken auch aussen lassen koendte.

For that matter, one of these two reed voices could be omitted.

Coppeln vnd Tremulanten, wie in den vorigen Dispositionibus.

Couplers and tremulants, as in the preceding dispositions.

[Translation by the present author]

In order to give a clearer overview of the resources of each division, the following organization of the disposition presents the instrument in more familiar, yet equivalent modern form:[27]

Model Disposition 7
Oberwerk-and-Brust[28]

2. 16' Gross Quintade

1. 8' Principal

4. 8' Gedacktfloete or Rohrfloete

7. 2 2/3' Nasat

11. 2' Blockfloete (B)

12. 1' Siffloete or Schwegel (B)

5. 4' Octave

6. 4' Nachthorn or Quintade

8. IV-VII Mixture

9. 4' Geigend Regal (B)

Rueckpositive

2. 8' Quintade

1. 4' Schweizerpfeife

4. 4' Hohlfloete or Querfloete

3. 4' Gemshorn or Spitzfloete

5. 2' Klein Octave

6. 1 1/3' Hohlquinte or Scharfquinte

7. II Zimbel

8. 8' Trompete

9. 8' Krummhorn

Pedal

9. 16' Gedackt Untersatz (Po)

3. 16' Quintade (t)

1. 8' Principal (OW)

4. 8' Gedacktfloete (OW)

5. 4' Octave (OW)

6. 4' Nachthorn (OW)

7. 2 2/3' Nasat (OW)

8. IV-VII Mixture (OW)

10. 16' Posaune (Po)

Options and Accessories

Options: Eliminate Brust entirely, but move the 2' Block-floete into the Oberwerk and the 1' Siffloete into the Rueckpositive; borrow a II rank Zimbel from the IV-VII Mixture of the Oberwerk

Couplers: As in the preceding dispositions

Tremulants: As in the preceding dispositions

A possible schematic harness for Model Disposition 7 is diagrammed on Plate LXXVIII, fig. 1. The motion of Ober-werk key OW is transmitted by tracker A, square U, tracker C, square D, tracker E, and roller board F to pallet G in the Oberwerk-transmission chest Ow + t. An additional tracker H leads from square U to pallet I in the Brust chest B. A depression of the Oberwerk key opens both pallets G and I. The motion of pedal key P is transmitted by sticker J, square K,

tracker L, square M, tracker N, and roller board O to pedal
pallet Q in the transmission chest. An additional harness
leads from square R, through tracker S, and roller board T
to a properly-positioned projecting arm in roller board F,
which engages pallet G in the Oberwerk chest OW. A depression
of the pedal key opens pallets Q and G. In code form the harnesses may be represented as OW + t + B / OW and OW + t + Po
/ P.

A third example shows an actual instrument, the specifications of which are rather completely recorded by Praetorius and appear to be quite reliable. It is the disposition
for the Stadtkirche at Bayreuth, completed in the year of the
publication of the De Organographia.[29] It shows a single-
stop, unison transmission from the Oberwerk into the Pedal.
The Oberwerk and Brust are permanently coupled, while the Pedal presents a chest of independent voices, a transmission from
the Oberwerk into the Pedal, and is probably permanently coupled to the Oberwerk.

V.	V
Eine andere.[30]	Another

Ohngefehrliche Disposition eines Orgelwercks von 34. oder 35. Stimmen nach Art der Dreszdnischen vnnd Schoeningischen: Der-gleichen vielleicht zu Ba-rait im Voigtlande von mehr gedachtem Churf. Saechs. Or-

Approximate disposition for an instrument of 34 or 35 voic-es after the manner of the Dresden and Schoeningen [or-gans], which will possibly be completed this summer at Bay-reuth in Voigtland, by the previously-mentioned Gottfried

gelmacher Gottfried Frit-
schen / diesen Sommer wird
gefertiget werden.

Fritzsche, organ builder to
the Elector of Saxony.

Oberwercke.
13. Stimmen.

Oberwerk,
13 voices

Drey
prin-
ci-
pal-
Pfeif-
fen
so
im
Au-
gen-
schein
kom-
men.

1. Posaunen von
holtz gantz vber-
gueldet. Am laut
Trommeten art / vff
8.fusz Thon.
Vnnd ist das erste
principal.

2. Das ander prin-
cipal Zinnern Oc-
tav offen von 4.
fusz Thon.

3. Das dritte prin-
cipal Zinnern Prin-
cipal von 8. fusz
Thon.

Three
reg-
is-
ters
of
dis-
play
pipes,
visi-
ble
to
the
eye

1. Posaune of wood,
completely gilded;
tonally of the Trom-
pete species and of
8' pitch.
This is the first
display item.

2. The second display
item [is an] open
Octave of tin at 4'
pitch.

3. The third display
item [is a] Principal
of tin at 8' pitch

4. Zimbel 2.fach.

4. Zimbel   II ranks

5. Mixtur 6.fach.

5. Mixture   VI ranks

6. Gedacter Sub Bass lieblich durchs gantze
Manual, mit einem
abgesonderten Basz
zum Pedal allein.

6. Lieblich Gedackt Sub-
bass, throughout the
[compass of the] Manual,
with a segregated bass
for the Pedal alone,

7. Vnd gibt zwo
Stimmen   16.fusz

7. Which comprises
two voices   16 foot

8. Hoeltzern Prin-
cipal enger Men-
sur vff rechte
Blockfloeten art 8.fusz

8. Holzprincipal of
narrow scale and
of the Block-
floete species   8 foot

9. Quintadehna vff 8.fusz

9. Quintade at   8 foot

10. Spitzfloeyt
lieblich   4.fusz

10. Lieblich
Spitzfloete   4 foot

11. Nachthorn / offen
weiter Mensur
gar lieblich   4.fusz

11. Nachthorn, open
and wide scale,
gently voiced   4 foot

12. Quinta scharff   3.fusz

12. Scharfquinte   3 foot

13. Rancket oder
Sorduen vff 16.f.thon.

13. Rankett or
Sordun   16 foot pitch

Brust Positifflin.
   6. Stimmen

Brustpositive,
   6 voices

Auch 3. principalia.

14. Geigend Regal
von holtz gantz
vergueldet
vff   4.fusz

15. Schoen Zin-
nern Schwiegel
oder Hollfloet-
en vff   1.f.

16. Gembszhorn
still oder klein
Gedact / auch
von schoenem
Zinn   4.fusz

Also three display items

14. Geigend Regal of
wood, completely
gilded,
at   4 foot

15. A Schwegel or
Hohlfloete of fine
tin
at   1 ft.

16. Still Gemshorn
or Klein Gedackt,
also of fine
tin   4 foot

17. Superoctavlin
scharff vff   2.f.th.

17. Super Octave,
keen   2 ft. pitch

18. Blockfloettlin 2.fusz

18. Blockfloete   2 foot

19. Klein Quintadetz /
an stadt der
Zimbeln31

19. Klein Quinta decima,
in place of the
Zimbel   [2/3']

Rueck Positiff.
   11. Stimmen.

Rueckpositive,
   11 voices

Auch drey principalia.

20. Kleine Trom-
meten / von Holtz
ganz vergueldet
muessen aber blind
seyn / dieweil
man von fornen
zum stimmen nit
kommen kan: es
were denn dasz ein
Chor oder Poer Kir-
che vnter die Orgel
von deren man zu den
foerder Pfeiffen des
Rueck-Positiffs kom-
men koente.32

Also three display items

20. Small trumpets of
wood, completely gilded;
[they] must, however,
be mute, since it is
impossible to approach
them from the front for
tuning, unless there
would be a choir gallery
under the organ from
which the front pipes
of the Rueckpositive
could be approached.

21. Schoen Zinnern
Superoctava Querp-
feiffen Art 2.fusz.

21. A Super Octave of
fine tin, of the Querp-
feife species 2 foot

22. Schoen Zinnern
Principal   4.fusz

22. A Principal of
fine tin   4 foot

23. Grosse Coppel: oder liebliche floeten vff	8.fusz	23. Gross Koppel or Lieblich Floete — 8 foot
24. Klein Quintadehn	4.fusz	24. Klein Quintade — 4 foot
25. Querfloeten	4.fusz	25. Querfloete — 4 foot
26. Gembshoernlein oder gedact floetlein	2.fusz	26. Gemshorn or Gedackt-floete — 2 foot
27. Nasat Quinta lieblich	anderthalb fusz.	27. Nasatquinte, delicate — 1 1/2 foot
28. Zimbeln klein	einfach	28. Klein Zimbel — I rank
29. Ranckett oder Baer Pfeiffen	8.fusz	29. Rankett or Baerpfeife — 8 foot
30. Krumbhoerner	8.fusz	30. Krummhorn — 8 foot

Baesse im Pedal 5. Stimmen. — **Basses in the Pedal, 5 voices**

3. Principalia
- 31. Grosz Posaunen Basz   16.fusz.
- 32. Starcker Sub Bass gedact Zinnern   16.fusz
- 33. Grob principal Bass Zinnern von   16.fusz

Three display items
- 31. Gross Posaune-bass   16 foot
- 32. Gedackt Sub-bass of tin; bold   16 foot
- 33. Grob Principal-bass of tin at   16 foot

34. Cornet Baeszlin.[33]   34. Kornettbass [2 foot]

35. Vogelgesang / durchs gantze Pedal.   35. Vogelgesang, throughout the entire Pedal

Extraordinarii Stimmen. — **Auxiliary Voices**

36. Vmblauffender Stern mit Zimbel gloecklin.   35. Rotating Star with Zimbel bells

37. Kuckuck: Nachtigal.   36. Cuckoo; Nightingale

1. Coppel zu beyden Manualen.   1. Coupler for both manuals

2. Coppel zum Pedal vnnd Rueck Positiff.   2. Coupler for the Pedal and Rueckpositive

Wolte man drey manual Clavir haben / so koente man noch eins zum Brust Positiff machen.

Should one desire three manual claviers, an additional one could be provided for the Brustpositive.

1. Tremulant zum gantzen Wercke durch vnd durch.

2. Tremulant zum Rueck Positiff absonderlich[34] / wird sonsten der Bock genant.

9. oder 11. Blasbaelge.

Clavier zum Manual.

```
      Fs   Gs                es
      D    E    B            ds
C F   G    A    H C d        e
```

f etc. bis in $\overline{\overline{d}}$ oder $\overline{\overline{f}}$

Zum Pedal.

```
      Ds        Fs   Gs   B
C D   E F       G    A    H C
```

```
      ds        fs
d     e  f         etc. bis ins
```

```
      ‾c‾s
c̄     d̄ ē
```

Es gefelt mir auch gar wol / dasz man zu einer jeden Laden / ein absonderlich Ventil macht / damit 1. nicht ein jeder / so vff die Orgel gelauffen koempt wisse / sich drein finden koenne / ob er gleich die Register ziehet. 2. Dasz der Wind nicht so bald alle Laden erfuellet / wenn man nicht vff allen Claviren schlagen wil.

---

1. Tremulant for the entire instrument, through and through

2. Separate tremulant for the Rueckpositive, ordinarily known as the Bock [tremulant]

From 9 to 11 bellows

Clavier for the Manual

```
      F♯   G♯                e♭
      D    E    B♭           d♯
C F   G    A    B c d        e
```

f, etc. up to d''' or f'''

For the Pedal

```
      D♯        F♯   G♯   B♭
C D   E F       G    A    B c
```

```
      d♯        f♯
d     e  f         etc. up to c'
```

```
      c♯'
      d' e'
```

It pleases me greatly, that for each chest a separate ventil is provided, so that 1. not everyone who happens to come upon the organ can find his way around [i.e., play it] even though he may draw the registers 2. The wind does not always fill all the chests, when one does not wish to play on all of the Manuals

[Translation by the present author]

From the almost bewildering array of specifications presented by Praetorius, the following organization in more familiar modern form will serve to give a clearer, yet equivalent, overview:[35]

Stadtkirche, Bayreuth

The instrument was built by Gottfried Fritzsche during 1618-19 and was supposedly dedicated by Samuel Scheidt in the presence of Michael Praetorius, Johannes Staden, and Heinrich Schuetz.[36]

Oberwerk-and-Brust[37]

6.	16' Gedackt Subbass	17.	2' Super Octave (B)
3.	8' Principal	18.	2' Blockfloete (B)
8.	8' Holzprincipal	15.	1' Schwegel (B)
9.	8' Quintade	19.	[2/3'] Quinta decima (B)
2.	4' Octave	5.	VI Mixture
10.	4' Spitzfloete	4.	II Zimbel
16.	4' Still Gemshorn (B)	13.	16' Rankett or Sordun
11.	4' Nachthorn	1.	8' Posaune
12.	2 2/3' Scharfquinte	14.	4' Geigend Regal (B)

Rueckpositive

23.	8' Gross Koppel	27.	1 1/3' Nasatquinte
22.	4' Principal	28.	I Klein Zimbel
25.	4' Querfloete	29.	8' Rankett or Baerpfeife
24.	4' Klein Quintade	30.	8' Krummhorn
21.	2' Super Octave	20.	Klein Trompete (mute)
26.	2' Gemshorn		

Pedal

33.	16' Grob Principalbass	11.	4' Nachthorn (OW)
32.	16' Gedackt Subbass	12.	2 2/3' Scharfquinte (OW)
7.	16' Lieblich Subbass (t)		

3.	8' Principal (OW)		5.	VI Mixture (OW)
8.	8' Holzprincipal (OW)		4.	II Zimbel (OW)
9.	8' Quintade (OW)		31.	16' Gross Posaune
2.	4' Octave (OW)		13.	16' Rankett or Sordun (OW)
10.	4' Spitzfloete (OW)		1.	8' Posaune (OW)
			34.	[2'] Kornett

Accessories

Vogelgesang

Rotating Star with bells

Cuckoo and Nightingale

Couplers: [Rueckpositive to Oberwerk] Rueckpositive to Pedal

From nine to eleven bellows

Tremulant for the Werk

Bock tremulant for the Rueck-positive

[Wind-trunk ventils for
    Oberwerk
    Brustpositive
    Rueckpositive
    Pedal]

An appropriate harness for this instrument would be similar to the diagram shown for Model Disposition 7, except that an independent pedal chest needs to be engaged by the pedal harness, and the Oberwerk chest would exhibit only a transmission section without any independent pedal stops in the cradle. Plate LXXVIII, fig. 2 shows an appropriate harness for the Bayreuth instrument. It operates in similar fashion to previous examples and represents a combination of the classical form of harness as diagrammed on Plate LXXV, fig. 2, plus the addition of the Brust component as shown on Plate LXXVIII, fig. 1. In code form, the harness would be designated as OW + t + B / OW and OW + t + P / P, and represents a second classical form for the period.

Survey of Examples

A survey of the remaining dispositions in Praetorius'
catalog will serve to show the fairly common occurrence of
single-stop, unison transmissions in the instruments of the
Early Baroque:

Bernau.[38] The Untersatz 16' operates both in
the Werk and in the Pedal; it is probably a transmission voice. In addition, the Pedal exhibits a
Posaunebass and a Bauerpfeifebass as a Pedal im Werk.
A Regal is specified as a Brust item. Accordingly,
the harnesses may be designated as W + B + t / W and
W + Pw + t / P, and could have been similarly disposed
as Model Disposition 7 and diagrammed on Plate
LXXVIII, fig. 1

2. Leipzig, St. Nicholas.[39] The 16' Grobgedackt
occurs as a unison transmission from the Werk into the
Pedal. The Brust, which exhibits only Regal stops,
may be considered as having been attached to the Werk.
The Pedal of three independent stops engaged a transmission voice from the Oberwerk, and was probably permanently coupled to the Werk. In code form, the harness system seems to have been W + B + t / W and
W + P + t / P, may be diagrammed as shown on Plate
LXXVIII, fig. 2, and represents one of the classical
methods of combining chests in the period

3. Leipzig, St. Thomas.[40] The 16' Principal of

the Oberwerk is a transmission voice at the unison, selectively playable from both the Oberwerk and pedal keyboards. The Brust, comprising only two Regal voices was, no doubt, permanently coupled to the Oberwerk. The Pedal of two independent voices engaged the transmission voice and may be presumed to have been permanently coupled to the Oberwerk. In code, the situation is strictly classical: OW + B + t / OW and OW + P + t / P. It may be diagrammed as shown on Plate LXXVIII, fig. 2

4. _Dresden, Schlosz._[41] This organ, by Gottfried Fritzsche, is an example of the typical _deluxe_ layouts of the builder. The principle of transmission was avidly practiced by Fritzsche and almost all of his instruments exhibit the typical compound harness systems as developed above. The present author suspects a unison transmission between item 4 of the Oberwerk and item 3 of the Pedal. The transmission is not clearly defined, but both of these voices are listed as 16' Gross Quintade. The Brust, comprising higher-pitched labial voices and a 4' Regal seems to have been permanently coupled to the Oberwerk. The Pedal, of six independent voices, probably engaged the suspected transmission voice and was, very likely, permanently coupled to the Oberwerk. Accordingly, the control of the chestwork seems to exhibit the

following disposition in code form: OW + B + t / OW
and OW + P + t / P. It is a classical harness disposition for the time and may be diagrammed as shown on
Plate LXXVIII, fig. 2

    5. Model Disposition 4.[42] A detailed analysis
of this instrument appears above

    6. Model Disposition 7.[43] A full presentation
of the instrument appears above

    7. Hildesheim, St. Gotthard.[44] A single-stop,
unison transmission occurs between the Oberwerk and
Pedal as items 6 and 7: 16' Untersatz Gedackt in the
Pedal and 16' Gedacktfloete in the Manual. Perhaps
items 11 and 12, since they are specifically designated as im Manual, may have been transmissions into
the Pedal as well, the precise definition of the condition having been an oversight of Praetorius. The
harness system is relatively simpler than in the preceding examples and may be surmised to have been similar to the following (in code form): OW + t / OW
and OW + t / P, which represents, in effect, the harness for Model Disposition 4 described above and diagrammed on Plate LXXVII, fig. 1

    8. Riddagshausen, Cloister.[45] A single-stop,
unison transmission is indicated between the Oberwerk
and Pedal as items 2 and 3 of the disposition. It is
a 16' Gross Rohrfloete. The Brust contains four

stops, of which two are lingual stops and the other
two, higher-pitched labial voices; it was probably a
supplemental division of the Oberwerk and permanently
coupled to it. The Pedal commanded six independent
voices, engaged the transmission voice from the Oberwerk, and was, likely, permanently coupled to the
Oberwerk. The condition may be represented in code
form as: OW + B + t / OW and OW + P + t / P, the typical harness layout for instruments containing a
transmission. The diagram on Plate LXXVIII, fig. 2
may serve as the basic harness system for this instrument

9. Bayreuth, Stadtkirche.[46] A full presentation of this instrument appears above

Multiple-stop, Unison Transmissions

Occasionally, the early baroque builders extended the
principle of unison transmission to involve more than a single
stop. The maximum number of voices disposed in such a manner
among the actual instruments listed in Praetorius' catalog
were three; one instance reveals only two voices.[47] The
transmissions, as formerly, were always between the Oberwerk
and Pedal, were applied to voices of grave pitch, and were
generally executed at the unison. Since the voices spoke at
the same pitch in the Oberwerk and Pedal, corresponding harness elements from both keyboards needed to be attached to

adjacent channels.

The equipment needed in the chest to effect multiple-stop transmission was the same as for single-stop transmission. The only obvious difference lay in the extent of the equipment:

    1. The pedal channels had to be long enough to span the transverse space on the chest to be occupied by the transmission voices or be carried across the entire chest

    2. Each stop involved in transmission had to be equipped with double sets of sliders and the requisite draw knobs to operate them

Illustrative Cases

The organ at the Schloszkapelle, Schoeningen, built by Gottfried Fritzsche ca. 1619, presents a disposition using multiple-stop, unison transmission. Praetorius' account of it is very complete, even descriptive, and appears, by comparison with other early sources, to be very reliable. It shows unison transmission of two voices from the Oberwerk into the Pedal. The Oberwerk and Brust are permanently coupled; the Pedal presents no independent voices beyond the transmissions, and is, probably, permanently coupled to the Oberwerk.

XXIII.[48]	XXII
Die Fuerstliche Widwe[49] zu Braunschweig vnnd Lueneburg	The princely widow at Braunschweig and Lueneburg is having

lest jetzo in ihrer F. G. Schlosz Capell zu Schoening-en[50] durch den Churf. Saechsischen Orgelmacher M. Gottfried Fritzschen eine Orgel von schwartzgebeistem[51] formirtem[52] Holtz mit Golde gestaffiret / fertigen:

an organ built of black-stained and varnished wood decorated with gold, by the organ builder to the Elector of Saxony, Master Gottfried Fritzsche, for the Court chapel of Her Princely Grace at Schoeningen.

Welche nachfolgende 20. Stimmen in sich begreifft.[53]

[The instrument] embraces the following 21 voices:

Im Ober Wercke
10. Stimmen.

In the Oberwerk,
10 voices

1. Gantz vergueldete Posaunen dem eusserlichem ansehen nach / sonsten sol es Krumbhoerner Art seyn / vnd also das erste vnd foerderste Principal vff   8.fusz

1. Completely gilded Posaune according to its external appearance; otherwise of the Krummhorn species; this comprises the first and foremost display item at   8 foot

2. Schoen zinnern Super Octav von   2.fi. vnd ist das ander Principal.

2. Super Octave of fine tin at   2 foot which is the second display item

3. Schoen zinnern Octav von   4.fusz vnd ist das dritte Principal.

3. Octave of fine tin at   4 foot which is the third display item

4. Gedacter Subbasz vff   16.fusz Durchs gantze Clavir / aber doch mit zwey Registern / also / das ein jedes absonderlich / eins zum Manual / das ander zum Pedal zu gebrauchen.

4. Gedackt Subbass at   16 foot Throughout the entire keyboard, but [controlled] by two draw knobs, so that each can be used to [control] the voice separately, the one for the Manual, the other for the Pedal

5. Vnd dahero seynd es zwo Stimmen.

5. And, therefore, it is [counted as] two voices

6. Hoeltzern Principal gar enger Mensur, lieblich / vnd rechter Floeiten Art von 8.fusz

6. A wooden Principal of narrow scale, gently [voiced] and really of the Flute species 8 foot

7. Quintadeena von 8.fusz

7. Quintade at   8 foot

8. Spitzfloeit / ist
   fast wie ein Gemsz-
   horn / doch
   lieblicher.   4.fusz

9. Mixtur   3.fach

10. Posaunen / doch nicht
    so gar starck / son-
    dern vff Dolcianen
    art vff   16.fusz
    Welche auch mit zwey
    Registern / gleich wie
    der Subbasz sol ge-
    macht werden / Wofern
    es wegen des engen
    vnd kleinen raums die
    Lade ertragen vnnd
    leyden wil.

   In der Brust
   5. Stimmen.

11. Blockfloeitlin   2.fusz

12. Nasatt Quinta
              anderthalb fusz

13. Sieffloeitlin oder
    Schwiegelpfeiff   1.fi.

14. Zimbeln   2.Choericht

15. Geigend Regal.   4.fusz

   Im Rueckpositiff
   5. Stimmen.

16. Kleine Trommeten / oder
    Posaunen zum foedder-
    sten Principal, allein
    zum Augenschein / vnnd
    dasz es mit dem Ober-
    wercklin dem ansehen
    nach correspondiret;
    Seind aber blind: vnd
    an deren statt eine
    Baerpfeiffe von 8.fusz

17. Octaevlin das ander
    Principal Querpfeif-
    fen Art.   2.fusz

18. Querfloeiten / das

8. Spitzfloete, [which]
   is almost like a Gems-
   horn, but more
   gently [voiced]   4 foot

9. Mixture   III ranks

10. Posaune, but not over-
    ly bold; rather of
    the Dulzian
    species   16 foot
    Which also shall be
    made with two registers,
    like the Subbass, pro-
    vided that the chest,
    because of the narrow
    and limited space, will
    suffer and permit
    it

   In the Brust,
   5 voices

11. Blockfloete   2 foot

12. Nasatquinte   1 1/2 foot

13. Siffloete or
    Schwegelpfeife   1 ft.

14. Zimbel   II ranks

15. Geigend Regal   4 foot

   In the Rueckpositive,
   5 voices

16. Small Trompete or Posaune
    as the foremost display
    item, but only for the
    [sake of] appearance, so
    that it will correspond
    with the [display of the]
    Oberwerk. [The pipes] must,
    however, be mute, and in
    their place [shall be in-
    serted] a Baerpfeife
    at   8 foot

17. Octave, the second dis-
    play item, of the Quer-
    pfeife species   2 foot

18. Querfloete, the third

dritte vnnd rechte Principal von		4.fusz	and true display item at		2 foot
19. Nachthorn von		4.fusz	19. Nachthorn at		4 foot
20. Quintlein scharff offen		anderhalb fi.	20. Scharfquinte, open		1 1/2 ft.

1. Coppel zu beyden Claviren.

1. Coupler for both manuals

2. Tremulant zum gantzen Werck durch vnd durch.

2. Tremulant for the Werk, through and through

3. Bock zum Rueckpositiff absonderlich.

3. Separate Bock [tremulant] for the Rueckpositive

4. Zimbelgloecklin.

4. Zimbel bells

5. Vogelgesang.

5. Vogelgesang

Die Clav. im Manual.

The Manual Clavier

$$\text{C F} \quad \overset{D}{G} \quad \overset{E}{A} \text{ bis ins } \overline{\overline{cs}} \ \overline{\overline{d}} \qquad \underline{C} \ \underline{F} \quad \overset{D}{\underline{G}} \quad \overset{E}{\underline{A}} \text{ up to } \underline{c\sharp}''' \ \underline{d}'''$$

vnd die dis gedoppelt.

with split d♯ [keys]

Claves im Pedal.

The Pedal Keys

$$\text{C F} \quad \overset{D}{G} \quad \overset{E}{A} \text{ bisz ins } \overline{cs} \ \overline{d} \qquad \underline{C} \ \underline{F} \quad \overset{D}{\underline{G}} \quad \overset{E}{\underline{A}} \text{ up to } \underline{c\sharp}' \ \underline{d}'$$

[Translation by the present author]

By sorting out the voices, dropping the descriptions, and arranging the registers in the customary modern manner, a much better overview of the instrument can be gained:[54]

Schlosskapelle, Schoeningen

Built in 1617 by Gottfried Fritzsche.[55] It is typical of the rich appointments with which Fritzsche outfitted his instruments that were intended for palace courts and chapels. It is quite possible that the instrument, although erected elsewhere, filled the void occasioned by the removal of the <u>Hessen, Schlosz</u> instrument to Denmark at about this time.

Oberwerk-and-Brust[56]

4.	16' Gedackt Subbass		12.	1 1/3' Nasatquinte (B)
6.	8' Holzprincipal		13.	1' Siffloete (B)
7.	8' Quintade		9.	III Mixture
3.	4' Octave		14.	II Zimbel (B)
8.	4' Spitzfloete		10.	16' Posaune (Dulzian)
2.	2' Super Octave		1.	8' Posaune (Krummhorn)
11.	2' Blockfloete (B)		15.	4' Geigend Regal (B)

Rueckpositive

18.	4' Querfloete		20.	1 1/3' Scharfquinte
19.	4' Nachthorn		16.	8' Baerpfeife
17.	2' Octave			

Pedal

5.	16' Gedackt Subbass (t)		2.	2' Super Octave (OW)
6.	8' Holzprincipal (OW)		9.	III Mixture (OW)
7.	8' Quintade (OW)		10.	16' Posaune (Dulzian) (t)
3.	4' Octave (OW)		1.	8' Posaune (Krummhorn) (OW)
8.	4' Spitzfloete (OW)			

Accessories

Dark-stained and varnished case, decorated with gold

Coupler: [Rueckpositive to Oberwerk]

Tremulant for the Werk
Bocktremulant for the Rueckpositive

Zimbel bells

Vogelgesang

Short bass octave in the manual and pedal claviers

Sub-semitones for the manual claviers

An adequate harness for the instrument would be the

one diagrammed for <u>Model Disposition 7</u> and shown on Plate LXXVIII, fig. 1. In code form the situation at Schoeningen can be expressed as: OW + B + t / OW and OW + t / P.

A second example of multiple-stop, unison transmission occurs in the disposition of the organ at the <u>Cathedral</u>, <u>Magdeburg</u>. The Oberwerk and Brust may be presumed to have been permanently coupled together, while the Pedal presents seven independent voices mounted in the side towers plus two voices mounted on a special chest behind the Oberwerk (Po), engages three transmission voices from the Oberwerk, and was, probably, permanently coupled to the Oberwerk.

X.	X
Verzeichnisz der Stimmen vnd Registern in den Orgeln zu Magdeburg.	Inventory of the voices and registers in the organs at Magdeburg
Die 1. im Thumb[57]	The first, in the Cathedral
Von M. Heinrico Compenio vffgerichtet / vermag 42. Stimmen. 2. Tremulant. Vogelgesang / Trummel. 2. Clavir com C bisz $\overline{\overline{c}}$.[58] Pedal von g bisz ins $\overline{d}$.[59] 12. Lederne Blasbaelge.	Erected by Master Heinrich Compenius, it comprises 42 voices, two tremulants, Vogelgesang, and Tympanum. Two claviers from C to c'' [c''']. Pedal from g [C] up to d'. Twelve bellows of leather.
Im Ober Werck	In the Oberwerk

Im Ober Werck		In the Oberwerk	
1. Principal	16.fusz	1. Principal	16 foot
2. Principal Basz abgesondert[60]	16.fusz	2. Principalbass, segregated	16 foot
3. Principal grosser Vntersatz bisz ins F.[61] von	24.fusz	3. Gross Principal Untersatz extending to F at	24 foot
4. Zimbel mit 3. Pfeiffen		4. Zimbel of	III ranks

5.	Mixtur mit 12. vnd 15. Pfeiffen[62]		5.	Mixture of XII-XV ranks
6.⎫ 7.⎭	Quintadehn Vntersatz mit ein abgesonderten Basz[63]	16.fusz	6.⎫ 7.⎭	Quintade Untersatz with a segregated bass 16 foot
8.⎫ 9.⎭	Grosse Octava mit eim abgesondertem Basz[64]	8.fusz	8.⎫ 9.⎭	Gross Octave 8 foot with a segregated bass
10.	Grosse Quinta[65]	6.fi.	10.	Gross Quinte 6 ft.
11.	Klein Octava	4.fi.	11.	Klein Octave 4 ft.
12.	Grob Gedact	8.fi.	12.	Grob Gedackt 8 ft.
13.	Klein Gedact	4.fi.	13.	Klein Gedackt 4 ft.
14.	Klein Quint	3.fi.	14.	Klein Quinte 3 ft.
15.	Nasatt[66]	1.oder 3.fi.	15.	Nasat 1 or 3 ft.
16.	Nachthorn	4.fi.	16.	Nachthorn 4 ft.

In der Brust
6. Stimmen.

In the Brust,
6 voices

1.	Principal	2.fi.	1.	Principal 2 ft.
2.	Zimbel doppelt		2.	Zimbel II ranks
3.	Mixtur	6.fach	3.	Mixture VI ranks
4.	Flachfloete	4.fi.	4.	Flachfloete 4 ft.
5.	Grob Messing Regal	8.fi.	5.	Grob Regal of brass 8 ft.
6.	Messing Regal singend	4.fusz	6.	Singend Regal of brass 4 foot

Zum Pedal
auff beyden Seitten
9. Stimmen.

For the Pedal,
[mounted] on both sides,
9 voices

1.	Posaun Basz	16.fusz	1.	Posaunebass 16 foot
2.	Klein Posaun Basz	8.fusz	2.	Klein Posaunebass 8 foot
3.	Schalmey oder Cornet	4.fusz	3.	Schalmei or Kornett 4 foot
4.	Singend Cornett von Messing	2.fusz	4.	Singend Kornett of brass 2 foot
5.	Bawrfloeit Basz	1.fusz	5.	Bauerfloete bass 1 foot
6.	Nachthorn Basz	4.fusz	6.	Nachthorn bass 4 foot
7.	Zimbel Basz 3. Pfeiffen starck		7.	Zimbel bass of III ranks

Hinderm Wercke stehet auff einer sonderlichen Lade.		Behind the instrument, and mounted on an individual chest	
8. Gedacter Vnter Basz	16.fusz	8. Gedackt Unterbass	16 foot
9. Grosz Gemszhorn Basz	8.fusz	9. Gross Gemshornbass	8 foot

Im Rueckpositiff.		In the Rueckpositive	
1. Principal	8.fusz	1. Principal	8 foot
2. Zimbel doppelt		2. Zimbel	II ranks
3. Mixtur	3.fach	3. Mixture	III ranks
4. Rohrfloeite	4.fusz	4. Rohrfloete	4 foot
5. Quintadehn	8.fusz	5. Quintade	8 foot
6. Schwiegel	4.fusz	6. Schwegel	4 foot
7. Octava	4.fusz	7. Octave	4 foot
8. Gemszhorn	4.fusz	8. Gemshorn	4 foot
9. Quinta	3.fusz	9. Quinte	3 foot
10. Suifloeit	2.fusz	10. Siffloete	2 foot
11. Gedact Quinta	3.fusz	11. Gedacktquinte	3 foot
12. Kleine Gedact	2.fusz	12. Klein Gedackt	2 foot
13. Trommeten	8.fusz	13. Trompete	8 foot
14. Dulcian von Holtz	16.fusz	14. Dulzian of wood	16 foot

[Translation by the present author]

The apparent disorder of the registers presents a more intelligible picture to the student of the organ when arranged in an equivalent modern fashion:[67]

Cathedral, Magdeburg

Built in 1604 by Heinrich Compenius, der Juengere.[68] Heinrich (ca. 1565-1631) was a younger brother of Praetorius' co-worker, Esaias Compenius I, at the Braunschweig-Lueneburg court.

Oberwerk-and-Brust[69]

1. 16' Principal
6. 16' Quintade
8. 8' Gross Octave
12. 8' Grob Gedackt
10. 5 1/3' Gross Quinte
11. 4' Klein Octave
16. 4' Nachthorn
4. 4' Flachfloete (B)
13. 4' Klein Gedackt

14. 2 2/3' Klein Quinte
1. 2' Principal (B)
15. 1 1/3' or 2 2/3' Nasat
5. XII-XV Mixture
3. VI Mixture (B)
4. III Zimbel
2. II Zimbel (B)
5. 8' Grob Regal (B)
6. 4' Singend Regal (B)

Rueckpositive

1. 8' Principal
5. 8' Quintade
7. 4' Octave
6. 4' Schwegel
8. 4' Gemshorn
4. 4' Rohrfloete
9. 2 2/3' Quinte

11. 2 2/3' Gedacktquinte
10. 2' Siffloete
12. 2' Klein Gedackt
3. III Mixture
2. II Zimbel
14. 16' Dulzian
13. 8' Trompete

Pedal

3. 32' Gross Principal Untersatz (Po)
2. 16' Principal (t)
8. 16' Gedackt Unterbass (Po)
7. 16' Quintade (t)
9. 8' Gross Octave (t)
9. 8' Gross Gemshorn (Po)
12. 8' Grob Gedackt (OW)
10. 5 1/3' Gross Quinte (OW)
11. 4' Klein Octave (OW)
16. 4' Nachthorn (OW)
6. 4' Nachthorn

13. 4' Klein Gedackt (OW)
14. 2 2/3' Klein Quinte (OW)
15. 1 1/3' or 2 2/3' Nasat (OW)
5. 1' Bauerfloete
5. XII-XV Mixture (OW)
4. III Zimbel (OW)
7. III Zimbel
1. 16' Posaune
2. 8' Klein Posaune
3. 4' Schalmei or Kornett
4. 2' Singend Kornett

Accessories

Two tremulants   Vogelgesang

Tympanum

The harness system for the Magdeburg, Cathedral instrument is somewhat more extensive than usual. It is, in
effect, the classical form shown for the Bayreuth instrument,
but incorporates also a special pedal chest mounted behind
the Oberwerk. A possible realization in scheme is presented
on Plate LXXIX, fig. 1. Its operation is similar to that of
previous examples and needs no further description here. In
code form the harnesses may be represented as: OW + B + t
/ OW and OW + P + Po + t / P.

Besides the two instruments presented, there occurs
one additional instance of a multiple-stop, unison transmission among the dispositions in Praetorius' catalog. This is
the Magdeburg, St. Johannes instrument.[70] In the Oberwerk,
item 3 is a transmission into the Pedal of item 2: 16' Quintade. It seems also that item 13 (Quint bass) is a transmission of item 10 (Quinte), and that item 14 (Zimbel bass) is
a transmission of item 12 (Zimbel). If so, then the instrument exhibits three transmissions from the Oberwerk into the
Pedal. It should be further noticed that the voices enumerated under the Brust comprise, in reality, a Brust of three
voices and a Brust Pedalia of three voices. Item 4 of the
Oberwerk appears to be an independent pedal voice. In code

form the situation may be represented as: OW + B + t / OW
and OW + Po + BP + t / P.

Suboctave Transmissions

Having achieved both single and multiple-stop, unison
transmissions, the early baroque builders found the case for
suboctave transmissions close at hand. Among the dispositions presented by Praetorius, two clear instances of sub-
octave transmissions are incorporated among the actual instruments. The equipment needed to achieve this condition
in the slider chest was the same as for unison transmissions.
The only difference lay in the attachment of the harness to
the transmission chest.

In the case of unison transmissions, it will be remembered, corresponding trackers from the Manual and Pedal
were attached to pallets which fed adjacent channels which,
in turn, by means of the grooving in the auxiliary upper
board, communicated with the corresponding pipes or notes.
In the case of suboctave transmissions, on the other hand,
the harness from one keyboard was attached as before (i.e.,
a given key to its corresponding pallet on the chest), whereas the harness from the pedal keyboard was attached to the
alternate pallets lying an octave lower. Accordingly, sub-
octave transmission was achieved without altering the chest
mechanism, but by adjusting the attachment of the pedal harness to the pedal pallets.

<u>Illustrative</u> <u>Cases</u>

A case in point, showing a single-stop, suboctave transmission from the Oberwerk into the Pedal, is the instrument at <u>Halle</u>, <u>Liebfrauen</u>, which is presented by Praetorius in a fairly complete form. The suboctave transmission is clearly indicated and involves a single stop; namely, item 1 of the Oberwerk: <u>Principal</u> <u>im</u> <u>Pedal</u> <u>16</u>. <u>Im</u> <u>Manual</u> <u>8.fusz</u> <u>Thon</u>. As usual, the Oberwerk and Brust appear to have been permanently coupled,[71] while the Pedal presents an array of independent voices, engages the transmission voice at the suboctave, and was, probably, permanently coupled to the Oberwerk.

XII.	XII
Das Werck zu Hall[72]	The instrument at Halle
Bey vnser lieben Frauen Kirchen. Hat 31. Stimmen.	At <u>Unser</u> <u>lieben</u> <u>Frauen</u>, has 31 voices
Im Ober Werck 6. Stimmen	In the Oberwerk, 6 voices
1. Principal im Pedal 16. Im Manual 8.fusz Thon[73]	1. Principal, in the Pedal 16, in the Manual 8 foot pitch
2. Octava, 4.fi. Thon im Manual allein.	2. Octave, 4 ft. pitch in the Manual alone
3. Mixtur	3. Mixture[74] [VI ranks]
4. Zimbel	4. Zimbel [III ranks]

5. Nachthorn   } im
   4.fusz thon   } Man-
               } ual
6. Querpfeiff   } al-
   8.fusz thon   } lein
	5. Nachthorn } in
	   4 foot pitch } the
	               } Man-
	6. Querpfeife } ual
	   8 foot pitch } alone

In der Brust 6. Stimmen	In the Brust 6 voices
1. Principal 2.fusz Thon	1. Principal 2 foot pitch

2.	Mixtur		2.	Mixture	[IV ranks]
3.	Zimbel		3.	Zimbel	[II ranks]
4.	Regal	8.fusz	4.	Regal	8 foot
5.	Waltfloetgen	1.fusz	5.	Waldfloete	1 foot
6.	Flachfloetgen	4.fusz	6.	Flachfloete	4 foot

Neben der Brust
4. Stimmen.

Beside the Brust
4 voices

1.	Trommeten Basz	8.fusz	1.	Trompete bass	8 foot
2.	Schallmeyen Basz	4.fusz	2.	Schalmei bass	4 foot
3.	Zimbel Basz		3.	Zimbel bass	
4.	Quintfloete Basz	3.fusz	4.	Quintfloete bass	3 foot

Auff der Seitten
sind newlich hinan gesetzet
3. Stimmen

Three voices have
recently been set at the side

1.	Grober Posaunen Vntersatz	16.fusz	1.	Grob Posaune Untersatz	16 foot
2.	Quintadehn Basz	8.fusz	2.	Quintade bass	8 foot
3.	Nachthorn	4.fusz	3.	Nachthorn	4 foot

Im Rueck Positiff.

In the Rueckpositive

1.	Principal	4.fusz Thon	1.	Principal	4 foot pitch
2.	Mixtur		2.	Mixture	
3.	Zimbel		3.	Zimbel	
4.	Octava	2.fusz	4.	Octave	2 foot
5.	Quinta[75]	9.fusz	5.	Quinte	[3] foot
6.	Quintadeen	8.fusz	6.	Quintade	8 foot
7.	Gedactes	4.fusz	7.	Gedackt	4 foot
8.	Kleingedactes	2.fusz	8.	Klein Gedackt	2 foot
9.	Spiszfloeit[76]	2.fusz	9.	Spitzfloete	[4] foot
10.	Siffloeit	2.fusz	10.	Siffloete	2 foot
11.	Trommeten	8.fusz	11.	Trompete	8 foot
12.	Singend Regal	4.fusz	12.	Singend Regal	4 foot

[Translation by the present author]

By combining the fractional corpora and rearranging the order of the registers, the <u>Halle</u> instrument presents the following, more familiar, picture in equivalent modern form:[77]

Liebfrauen, Halle

Very little information concerning this instrument has come down through the literature.

Oberwerk-and-Brust[78]

1.	8' Principal	5.	1' Waldfloete (B)
6.	8' Querpfeiffe	3.	[VI] Mixture
2.	4' Octave	2.	[IV] Mixture (B)
5.	4' Nachthorn	4.	[III] Zimbel
6.	4' Flachfloete (B)	3.	[II] Zimbel (B)
1.	2' Principal (B)	4.	8' Regal (B)

Rueckpositive

6.	8' Quintade	10.	2' Siffloete
1.	4' Principal	8.	2' Klein Gedackt
9.	[4'] Spitzfloete	2.	Mixture
7.	4' Gedackt	3.	Zimbel
5.	[2 2/3'] Quinte	11.	8' Trompete
4.	2' Octave	12.	4' Singend Regal

Pedal

1.	16' Principal (t)	3.	[VI] Mixture (OW)
6.	8' Querpfeife (OW)	4.	[III] Zimbel (OW)
2.	8' Quintade	3.	Zimbel (BP)
2.	4' Octave (OW)	1.	16' Posaune
5.	4' Nachthorn (OW)	1.	8' Trompete (BP)
3.	4' Nachthorn	2.	4' Schalmei (BP)
4.	2 2/3' Quintfloete (BP)		

A harness scheme designed to engage the component chests of the various corpora and to effect a suboctave transmission from the Oberwerk presents a complex problem. Obviously, it is impossible at this late date to specify exactly how the harness was disposed. It is, however, worthwhile to propose a possible realization of the control of the instrument in some schematic form. Plate LXXIX, fig. 2 presents a possible network by means of which the chests could have been controlled in order to realize the probable combination of the components. If the transmission voice was mounted on the Oberwerk chest, as seems most practical, the Great octave (C̲, D̲, E̲, F̲, G̲, A̲, B̲♭, and B̲, the usual notes of the short bass octave) would have had to be set off on a separate bass chest and the pedal harness divided, so that its suboctave trackers would have led to the off-set chest and the remainder to the transmission portion of the Oberwerk chest. For example, the C̲ tracker would have been attached to the 16' C̲ pallet of the off-set chest, and the c̲ tracker to the 8' C̲ pallet of the transmission chest. The bass pipes of the transmission voice could, of course, have been mounted on the regular pedal chests. In such a case, only the upper portion (beyond the bass octave) of the transmission harness would need to have been provided.

The manual harness on Plate LXXIX, fig. 2 presents no features which have not already been described above, but the pedal harness needs to be traced to understand its complex alliances. The motion of pedal key P is transmitted:

1. By sticker H, square I, tracker J, square K, tracker L, and roller boards M (and for the off-set chest, square N and tracker O) to pallets Q in the transmission chest and its suboctave off-set t

2. By sticker H, square I, tracker J, roller R, square S, and tracker T to pallet U in pedal chest P

3. By sticker H, square I, tracker J, square V, tracker W, and roller board X to appropriate projecting arms in, roller board Y, and thence to pallet Z in the Oberwerk chest OW

4. By tracker a, roller b, tracker c (not shown), square d, and tracker e to pallet f in the Brust Pedalia chest BP. A depression of pedal key P opens pallets Q, U, Z, and f. See Plate LXIX, fig. 6 for a perspective sketch of the harness leading to the Brust Pedalia. In code form, the harness system for this instrument can be expressed as: OW + B + t / OW and OW + P + BP + t / P

A second example shows multiple-stop, suboctave transmission. The disposition is the one for Magdeburg, St. Peter. Praetorius' presentation is incomplete, lacking a number of pitch designations, but the multiple-stop, suboctave transmission is clearly indicated, and we are constrained to press this example into service, relying upon the Dresdener Handschrift to provide the necessary information to reconstruct the disposition somewhat more adequately.

In this example the Manual and Brust appear to have
been permanently coupled, while the Pedal presents an array
of independent voices, engages the transmission voice at the
suboctave, and was, probably, permanently coupled to the Manual.

The suboctave transmission is not indicated in the
usual way by Praetorius, but may be presumed to have been:

1. Item 7 of the Manual, Grobgedact Manualiter
8.fusz, which reappears as item 2 in the Pedal, Gedacter Vntersatz 16.fusz

2. Item 9 of the Manual, Grosz Quintadeen /
manualiter 8.fusz, which reappears as item 1 in the
Pedal, Grosz Quintadeen Basz 16.fusz

Specified in this manner, it would seem that the sub-
octave notes of the two voices which were to be playable in
the Pedal alone would, likely, have been mounted on the regular pedal chests and included under the heading, Baesse im
Pedal (Basses in the Pedal). The draw knobs intended to control the voices for the Pedal would need to have been arranged
so as to engage segmented sliders. The bass octave segment
of the pedal slider would need to have been placed into the
pedal chest, while the segment intended to control the remainder of the voice, would need to have been placed into the
transmission chest.

X.

Verzeichnisz der Stimmen vnd Registern in den Orgeln zu Magdeburg.

. . . .

IV.

In der Orgel zu S. Peter / sind alles in allen 33. Stimmen.[79]

1.	Principal	8.fuessen
2.	Zimbeln	
3.	Quint	3.fusz
4.	Mixtur	
5.	Octav	4.fusz
6.	Querfloeiten	4.fusz
7.	Grobgedact Manualiter[81]	8.fusz
8.	Grob Gemszhorn	8.fusz
9.	Grosz Quintadeen / manualiter[82]	8.fusz

Baesse im Pedal.

1.	Grosz Quintedeen Basz.	16.fusz
2.	Gedacter Vntersatz	16.fusz
3.	Zimbeln Basz	
4.	Bawrfloeiten Basz	1.fusz
5.	Holfloeiten Basz	2.fusz
6.	Quintfloeiten Basz.	

In der Brust zum Manual 4. Stimmen.[83]

1.	Nachthorn	4.fusz
2.	Quintfloeit oder klein Gedact	2.fusz
3.	Zimbeln zweyfach	
4.	Regal.	

X

Inventory of the voices and registers in the organs at Magdeburg

. . . .

IV

In the organ at St. Peter, there are altogether 34 voices

1.	Principal	8 foot
2.	Zimbel[80]	[II ranks]
3.	Quinte	3 foot
4.	Mixture	[IV ranks]
5.	Octave	4 foot
6.	Querfloete	4 foot
7.	Grobgedackt, in the Manual	8 foot
8.	Grob Gemshorn	8 foot
9.	Gross Quintade, in the Manual	8 foot

Basses in the Pedal

1.	Gross Quintade bass	16 foot
2.	Gedackt Untersatz	16 foot
3.	Zimbel bass	[III ranks]
4.	Bauerfloete bass	1 foot
5.	Hohlfloete bass	2 foot
6.	Quintfloete bass	[8 foot]

In the Brust for the Manual, 4 voices

1.	Nachthorn	4 foot
2.	Quintfloete or Klein Gedackt	2 foot
3.	Zimbel	II ranks
4.	Regal	[8 foot]

In der Brust auff beyden seiten zum Pedal. 3. Stimmen.		On both sides of the Brust, for the Pedal 3 voices	
1. Posaunen Basz		1. Posaune bass	[16 foot]
2. Trommeten Basz		2. Trompete bass	[8 foot]
3. Schallmeyen Basz.		3. Schalmei bass	[4 foot]

Im Rueckpositiff 12. Stimmen.		In the Rueckpositive 12 voices	
1. Principal	4.fusz	1. Principal	4 foot
2. Trommeten	8.fusz	2. Trompete	8 foot
3. Quintadehna	8.fusz	3. Quintade	8 foot
4. Gemszhorn	4.fusz	4. Gemshorn	4 foot
5. Mittelgedact	4.fusz	5. Mittel Gedackt	4 foot
6. Klein Regal		6. Klein Regal	[4 foot]
7. Octava		7. Octave	[2 foot]
8. Quinta		8. Quinte	[1 1/2 foot]
9. Kleingedact		9. Klein Gedackt	[2 foot]
10. Sifflit		10. Siffloete	[1 foot]
11. Mixtur		11. Mixture	[III ranks]
12. Zimbeln.		12. Zimbel	[II ranks]

[Translation by the present author]

By rearranging the registers into an equivalent modern form, a better picture of the resources and their disposition can be gained:[84]

St. Peter, Magdeburg

The history of this instrument is largely lost in oblivion; very few, and no significant, references are to be found in the historic literature of the organ.

Oberwerk-and-Brust[85]

1. 8' Principal	3. 2 2/3' Quinte

8. 8' Grob Gemshorn

7. 8' Grob Gedackt

9. 8' Gross Quintade

5. 4' Octave

6. 4' Querfloete

1. 4' Nachthorn (B)

2. 2' Quintfloete (B)

4. [IV] Mixture

2. [II] Zimbel

3. [II] Zimbel (B)

4. [8'] Regal (B)

Rueckpositive

3. 8' Quintade

1. 4' Principal

4. 4' Gemshorn

5. 4' Mittel Gedackt

7. [2'] Octave

9. [2'] Klein Gedackt

8. [1 1/3'] Quinte

10. [1'] Siffloete

11. [III] Mixture

12. [II] Zimbel

2. 8' Trompete

6. [4'] Klein Regal

Pedal

2. 16' Gedackt Untersatz [t]

1. 16' Gross Quintade [t]

1. 8' Principal (M)

8. 8' Grob Gemshorn (M)

6. [8'] Quintfloete

5. 4' Octave (M)

6. 4' Querfloete (M)

3. 2 2/3' Quinte (M)

5. 2' Hohlfloete

4. 1' Bauerfloete

4. [IV] Mixture (M)

2. [II] Zimbel (M)

3. [III] Zimbel

1. [16'] Posaune (BP)

2. [8'] Trompete (BP)

3. [4'] Schalmei (BP)

A possible control harness for the St. Peter instrument could in almost every respect have been similar to the scheme developed for Halle, Liebfrauen and diagrammed on Plate LXXIX, fig. 2. The only difference lay in the probable mounting of the suboctave of the transmission voice on the regular pedal chests. Accordingly, the lowest octave of the transmission harness could have been omitted, since the regular pedal harness would have been sufficient to engage the suboctave notes through the pallets of the pedal chest. In code form, the harness system for this instrument may be expressed as: M + B + t / M and M + P + BP + t / P.

Miscellanea

Model Disposition 5

Among Praetorius' model dispositions there appears a specification, purportedly drawn up by him, which carries the principle of transmission to its ultimate extreme. It presents an entire chest of sixteen voices equipped with a full transmission mechanism, in order to make all of the voices playable an octave higher on another manual keyboard. Accordingly, we have here a case of multiple-stop, superoctave transmission. Inasmuch as no pedal extensions are provided, it must be assumed that the Pedal was to be permanently coupled to the transmission chest, being connected to the manual pallets, but not to the Oberpositive pallets, since these fed channels associated only with itself. The equipment needed to realize this instrument was the total mechanism required for multiple-stop, suboctave transmission previously described, plus a permanent coupling arrangement between the Pedal and the Manual. The only difference lay in the attachment of the Oberpositive harness which, instead of being attached to pallets lying an octave lower, was attached to pallets lying an octave higher. The bass octave, accordingly, required only single mechanism.

5.

Disposition einer Orgel von 16. vnd 48. Stimmen.[86]

Haupt		Ober Positiff.	
1. Vnter Basz von dickem Dannenholtz	16.fi.	Vntersatz	8.fusz
2. Gedactfloeite	16.fusz	Gedactfloeit	8
3. Sordun oder Posaun	16	Sorduen	8
4. Krumbhorn	8	Krumbhorn	4
5. Trommet oder starck Regal	8	Regal	4
6. Principal	8	Principal	4
7. Gemszhorn	8	Gemszhorn	4
8. Quintadeen	8	Quintadeena	4
9. Octava offen	4	Superoctava	2
10. Klein Blockfloeit	4	Super Blockfloeitlein	2
11. Gemszhorn	4	S. Gemszhoernlein	2
12. Nachthorn	4	S. Nachthoernlein	2
13. Quinta	3	Nassat	anderthalb
14. Superoctava	2	Sieffloit	1
15. Klein Zimbel		Klein Zimbel.	
16. Mixtur 4.5.6.Pfeiffen oder mehr.		Mixtur.	

(vertical note between the two lists) Gibt im Ober Positiff eben so viel Stimmen / doch alle in der Octava hoeher.[87]

Summa 48. Stimmen
vnd noch darueber.

1. Tremulant
2. Stern Zimbelgloecklin
3. Kuckuck
4. Vogelgesang
5. Huemmelchen
6. Bock
7. Trummel.

The instrument may be considered a novelty in the form of a prospectus which was never actually realized. It sought to extend the principle of transmission beyond the practice of the time. In more customary modern form, the disposition would present the following appearance:[88]

Model Disposition 5

[Werk]

1.	16' Unterbass	12.	4' Nachthorn
2.	16' Gedacktfloete	13.	2 2/3' Quinte
6.	8' Principal	14.	2' Super Octave
7.	8' Gemshorn	16.	IV-VI Mixture
8.	8' Quintade	15.	Zimbel
9.	4' Octave	3.	16' Sordun or Posaune
10.	4' Blockfloete	5.	8' Trompete or Regal
11.	4' Gemshorn	4.	8' Krummhorn

Oberpositive

1.	8' Untersatz (t)	12.	2' Nachthorn (t)
2.	8' Gedacktfloete (t)	13.	1 1/3' Nasat (t)
6.	4' Principal (t)	14.	1' Siffloete (t)
7.	4' Gemshorn (t)	16.	IV-VI Mixture (t)
8.	4' Quintade (t)	15.	Klein Zimbel (t)
9.	2' Super Octave (t)	3.	8' Sordun (t)
10.	2' Blockfloete (t)	5.	4' Regal (t)
11.	2' Gemshorn (t)	4.	4' Krummhorn (t)

[Pedal]

1.	16' Unterbass (W)	12.	4' Nachthorn (W)
2.	16' Gedacktfloete (W)	13.	2 2/3' Quinte (W)
6.	8' Principal (W)	14.	2' Super Octave (W)
7.	8' Gemshorn (W)	16.	IV-VI Mixture (W)
8.	8' Quintade (W)	15.	Zimbel (W)
9.	4' Octave (W)	3.	16' Sordun or Po- saune (W)
10.	4' Blockfloete (W)	5.	8' Trompete or Regal (W)
11.	4' Gemshorn (W)	4.	8' Krummhorn (W)

Accessories

Tremulant   Vogelgesang

Zimbelstern   Huemmelchen

Cuckoo   Bock [tremulant]

Tympanum

A possible harness scheme for Model Disposition 5 is shown on Plate LXXX. Its operation is quite obvious and needs no further explanation here. In code form, the situation can best be expressed as: t / W + Op + P (the transmission chest is controlled by the Werk, Oberpositive, and Pedal keyboards).

The Old Positive

A final case needs to be discussed and brought under critical inspection. This has to do with the Old Positive which Praetorius describes in the De Organographia[90] and presents in perspective on Plate I of the Theatrum Instrumentorum.[91] Often quoted as a classical instance of intra-manual quint and octave transmission, the instrument, in reality, can be realized by a somewhat different mechanical disposition than that described above for super and suboctave transmission. Basically, the difference lies in this, that the pipes of one chest are to be variously controlled by one keyboard rather than by two, as formerly. Praetorius' description and a translation of the same follow:

Das XLVIII. Capitel   Chapter XLVIII

Von dem Positiff (Col.   Concerning the Positive
XXXVII.) so zu einerley   (Plate XXXVII)[92] which has
Pfeiffen drey absonderliche   three separate registers[93] for

Register hat.

ALlhier musz ich auch dieses gedencken / dasz ein alt Positiff / doch von gar sauberer / reiner vnd subtiler Arbeit / so von einem Muench sol gemacht worden seyn / mir zu handen kommen; Welches dem Koenige zu Dennemarck / Christiano IV. zubracht (dessen Form vnd structur im Theatrum Instrumentorum Col. .94 zu finden.

Jn demselben sind nur einerley Pfeiffen / nemlich ein Offen Principaelgen von 2.Fusz Thon / vnd wiewol nur 38. Claves oder Clavir vom F bisz ins ā / so sind doch der Pfeiffen noch eine Octav drueber / oben in der mitten des corporis in die runde herumber gewunden gesetzet.

Zu solchen eintzigen Pfeiffen sind drey Register / 1. zum rechten Thon der vntersten Pfeiffen / das 2. zur Quint; das 3. zur Octav drueber, vnd kan ein jedes Register vor sich selbsten alleine vnd absonderlich; hernacher auch zwo / vnd dann alle drey Register zugleich gezogen vnd gebraucht werden / dasz also in einerley Pfeiffen vff einem Clave zween vnd auch drey discreti soni, vnd vnterschiedene Laut / als nemblich neben dem rechten Tono, die Quint vnd Octav resoniret vnd sich hoeren lest. Wie nu solches zugehe / lasz ich einen verstaendigen Orgelmacher darvon judiciren, vnd wolte wuendschen / dasz ein Kuenst-

one [set of] pipes

Here I should also like to make mention of this, that an old Positive of very clean, fine, and delicate workmanship, which is supposed to have been constructed by a monk, came to my attention; it had been presented to the King of Denmark, Christian IV. (Its form and structure may be found in the Theatrum Instrumentorum, Plate [I].)

In the same is [contained] only one [set of] pipes; namely, an open Principal of 2 foot pitch. Even though there are only 38 keys in the keyboard, from F to a'', there are pipes for an additional octave beyond [this range], which are mounted up in the center of the instrument and wound around in a circle.

For this single [set of] pipes there are three registers: one, for the true pitch of the lowest pipes; the second, for the fifth above; and the third, for the octave above. Each register can be used alone; thereupon, also two, and finally all three can be drawn and used together, so that from this one [set of] pipes, two or three distinct tones of different pitch can be sounded by one key; namely, that beside the true pitch, also the fifth and the octave will sound and be heard. How this is brought about, I leave to the judgment of a knowledgeable organ builder. I wish that some craftsman would undertake to construct such an instrument.

ler solch Werck nachzumachen
sich vnternemen wolte.

Vber das so ist auch dieses noch ein Kunststuecke an
diesem Wercklin / dasz es /
wenn die eine helffte der
Bley oder Gewichten / so
dieserwegen von einander zer-
theilet vnd halbieret seyn /
von den Blaszbaelgen abge-
nommen werden / gar ein
sanfften stillen Resonantz /
gleich den Querfloetten von
sich gibt / vnd sich nicht
anders hoeren lest / als
wenn ein Stimmwerck Quer-
floetten zusammen accordirt
vnd geblasen wuerden.95

Beyond this, there is another
clever device associated with
this instrument, whereby, when
half of the lead or weights
(which, for this reason are
dismembered and divided) are
removed from the bellows, the
pipes produce a very soft and
quiet tone, much like the Quer-
floeten. [The effect resem-
bles] that of a chorus of Quer-
floeten, playing together in
parts. [Translation by the
present author]

The legend on Plate I of the Theatrum Instrumentorum

gives additional information concerning this instrument. It

reads as follows:

Alt Positiff mit einerley
Pfeiffen / vnd dreyen unter-
schiedenen Registern: Also
das es dreyerley absonderliche Stimmen gibt / vff
zween Fuesz / auch ander-
halb / vnd 1. Fuesz-Thon.96

An old Positive with one [set
of] pipes and three separate
registers, so that three separate voices are available: at
2 foot, at 1 1/2 [i.e., 1 1/3]
foot, and at 1 foot pitch.
[Translation by the present
author]

What Praetorius describes here is, in effect, a uni-

fication of one set of pipes into three pitches, all playable

upon the same keyboard. The pitches are 2', 1 1/3', and 1'.

There are different ways of accomplishing this effect in a

mechanical instrument, and since the Old Positive has long

since disappeared, no one will be able to claim any authen-

ticity for his solution. Inasmuch, however, as this Positive

is occasionally referred to in the literature of the organ
as a classical example of transmission at other than unison
pitch,[97] it would seem worthwhile to examine the condition
and see in what respects the transmission mechanism and control described above is applicable, or whether the Old Positive lies outside the concept.

Plate LXXXI, figs. 1, 2, 3, 4, and 5 show a possible
method of realizing the conditions Praetorius prescribes. It
will be observed that only a single set of pallets H and single channels I are necessary, since only one keyboard is involved. The multiple mechanism begins at bores J, K, and L
in the table. These feed into corresponding bores in the
sliders: bore J, into the 1 1/3' slider; bore K, into the
2' slider; and bore L into the 1' slider. The sliders, in
turn, feed into the bores of the primary upper board: the
1 1/3' slider, into bore M; the 2' slider, into bore N; and
the 1' slider, into bore O. At some agreeable distance from
the primary upper board is placed a double auxiliary upper
board comprised of lower panel P and upper panel Q. Panel P
exhibits three bores (R, S, and T) per note. By means of
tube X, bore M is connected to bore R at the interval of a
fifth higher; by tube W, bore N is joined to bore S at the
unison; by tube a, bore O communicates with bore T at the interval of an octave higher. The upper panel Q of the auxiliary upper board has only a pipe bore S which is connected to
bores R, S, and T of the lower panel by groove U. Each bore

in panel P̲ is covered with a hinged checkvalve Y̲ which pre-
vents dissipation of pressure into idle companion tubes and
channels should the pertinent sliders be also in registration.

The mechanism operates, so that by depression of key
C̲ and the opening of pallet H̲:

1. Should only the 2' slider be in registration,
the pressure from channel I̲ will pass through bores K̲
and N̲, tube W̲, bore S̲, checkvalve Y̲, and pipe bore S̲
into pipe C̲, exciting the same

2. Should only the 1' slider be in registration,
the pressure from channel I̲ will pass through bores L̲
and O̲, tube a̲, bore T̲, checkvalve Y̲, and pipe bore S̲
into pipe c̲, exciting the same

3. Should only the 1 1/3' slider be in registration, the pressure from channel I̲ will pass through
bores J̲ and H̲, tube X̲, bore R̲, checkvalve Y̲, and pipe
bore S̲ into pipe G̲, exciting the same

4. Should any combination of sliders be in registration, all of the effects described by Praetorius
could be fully realized

Accordingly, three bores are required in the table,
the primary upper board, and the lower panel of the auxiliary
upper board for each channel in the chest. Three sliders are
necessary, one for each pitch desired. A series of tubes
leads from the sliders to the desired pipes. Grooves tunneled into the upper panel of the auxiliary upper board convey

the pressure from the tubes to the requisite pipes, while checkvalves prevent unwanted dissipation of the pressure.

The drawings, of course, do not take into account the concentric display of the pipework as shown in the Theatrum Instrumentorum. It would be highly confusing to present the mechanism in such a fashion. The drawings also exhibit complete octaves rather than the short bass octave which may have found application in the Old Positive.

From this discussion it can be suggested that the purported "transmission" mechanism and control necessary for the Old Positive are altogether different matters than the principle and practice of transmission as generally pursued by the early baroque builders, exemplified in Praetorius' catalog of dispositions, and developed within the present chapter.

Conclusions

From the preceding investigation certain conclusions can be drawn which bespeak the principle and practice of transmission and its effect upon the concept of the organ and its tonal composition in the Early Baroque:

1. The practice of transmission was of fairly common occurrence among the early baroque builders

2. The concept envisioned the isolation of certain tonal elements from a single chest to be separately and independently controllable from two

keyboards

3. Application of the principle was almost always restricted to voices of the Werk or Oberwerk to be independently playable on their native keyboard and the Pedal; it was never applied to the Rueckpositive or to the Brust

4. In practice, only selected voices (one, two, or three) of large physical size and grave pitch were used for transmission purposes

5. The effect seems to have been realized by means of double mechanism in that segment of the chest containing the pertinent voices

6. A special extension of the pedal harness was required to engage the duplicate chest mechanism

7. Three basic types of transmission seem to have been developed and used: (a) single-stop, unison transmission (common), (b) multiple-stop, unison transmission (occasional), and (c) octave transmission (rare).

8. The application of the principle did not by any means replace the entangling alliances of permanent coupling; it merely served to ameliorate the condition for individual voices; in fact, in almost all instances, permanent coupling and transmission were applied side by side

9. Transmission did not serve to enrich the usually impoverished resources of the Pedal in instruments where it was applied; it only offered a minimal increase in the registrational flexibility of the division

10. The combination of permanent coupling and transmission served to reinforce the dominant character of the Oberwerk as the central tonal corpus of the instrument; divisions associated with it, such as the Brust and Pedal, became increasingly dependent upon it to help establish their own identities

11. The tonal isolation of the Rueckpositive was thereby sharpened still further; it assumed the position of a secondary tonal corpus, entirely independent of the central Werk

12. Transmission in conjunction with permanent coupling served to impoverish the independent resources of the Pedal still further; in most cases, the Pedal disappears as a tonal corpus and becomes merely a bare addendum to the Werk

CHAPTER XI

PROVISION, APPLICATION, AND MEASUREMENT
OF THE WIND SUPPLY

In developing the theory of the Praetorius organ, it
is important to inspect as minutely as possible all aspects
of the mechanical and pneumatic disposition of the instruments of the time. The arrangement and disposition of the
"lungs" had a limiting effect upon the tonal resources of
the organ, circumscribing the horizon, as it were, by permitting some features to be explored and realized and others
to be denied. Certain appointments which appear in the old
instruments are a direct outcome of the manner of securing
and delivering the wind; certain other features, more recently invented and applied, were lacking, and by their very
absence placed a strong limitation upon the full realization
of the instrument.

The more recent theorists of the mechanical organ,
such as Dom Bedos, Toepfer, and others (who, in effect, are
really the first ones whose treatises on the instrument move
from the qualitative character of the earlier writers into a
more definitive, quantitative discussion) do not always concern themselves with the full history of the development of

the basic principles (especially with regard to the generation of the wind), so that in this area a certain amount of
investigation, aimed at ferreting out the practical implementation of the principle in the organ of Praetorius, may prove
helpful and rewarding. Thereby, the study becomes contributory to the whole art of the organ of the Early Baroque and
will serve to delineate and enlighten related aspects in the
conceptual theory of the same.

Capture, Storage, and Compression
of the Wind

A discussion of the various appliances dealing with
the generation of the wind, and their effective organization,
appears in chapter i of this study and will serve as a point
of departure for more critical and penetrating research into
the manner in which the basic principles were applied in the
Early Baroque. The previous discussion is based largely upon
Toepfer[1] who, in turn, had ample recourse to, and relied
heavily upon the definitive writings of Dom Bedos.[2] Both
theorists dealt with contemporary problems and theory, the
former for the nineteenth, the latter for the eighteenth century. Their treatises are encyclopedic repositories of the
theory and practical applications of it in their time; their
works were chiefly pedagogic and only casually historic. Accordingly, a certain amount of error and apparent misconcep-
tion dogged their writings with respect to the principle and

practice of wind generation in the older organs, with which they were not particularly concerned. The first problem of the present study must, then, concern itself with the removal of a certain aura of confusion with respect to the basic appliance of wind generation, the bellows.

The Non-ribbed Species of Bellows

From the writings of Praetorius and his contemporary, Compenius[3] (whose writings must be admitted here as equally worthy primary sources), it becomes evident that three distinct types of bellows, covering two species, were known by them and appear in their writings. The two species are:

1. The non-ribbed species

2. The ribbed species

Of these, the first one is the more ancient; Praetorius describes it in the De Organographia and sketches a gang of them in the Theatrum Instrumentorum. In discussing the dispositions of several organs which he cites as historic monuments of his day, he says:

MAn mus aber zur selbigen obberuehrten zeit / vor drithalb oder dreyhundert Jahren (als solche grosse Werck / wie das zu Halberstadt / davon jetzo gehandelt wird / gebawet worden) noch geringe Inventiones vnd nachdencken auff Blaszbaelge gehabt haben; Sintemahl an diesem Domwercke zu Halberstadt / 20. vnd an deme zu Magdeburg / 24. gar kleine

During the afore-mentioned time, about 250 to 300 years ago [i.e., 1320-1370], when such large organs as the one at Halberstadt (of which we shall treat presently) were built, very meager reflection and skill must have been spent upon the bellows. The organ at the cathedral of Halberstadt was provided with twenty, the one at Magdeburg, with twenty-four very small bellows (in

Baelge / (nach Ordnung vnd gestalt / wie in der Sciograph. Col. XXVI. zubefinden) vorgeleget worden. Welche vnsern jtzigen Schmiedebaelgen an groesse vnd Proportz nicht sehr vngleich gewesen: Sintemahl sie nicht durch bleyern oder steinern gewichte / sondern eben durch solch ein Mittel regiert worden / das man allzeit zu zweyen Baelgen eine Person zum tretten gebraucht / vnd wann mit einem Fuesz der eine Balck durch die schwere desz Calcanten nieder getretten ist / der ander mit dem andern Fuesz wider in die hoehe gezogen worden; das also zu 20. Baelgen / zehen Personen / vnd zu 24. jhrer zwoelffe nothwendig haben verhanden sein muessen.[4]

their appearance and arrangement as pictured on Plate XXVI of the Sciagraphia [i.e., the Theatrum Instrumentorum]). With respect to their size and proportions, they were not unlike present-day forge bellows. They were not regulated by lead or stone weights, but in this manner, that at all times one person was required to operate two bellows. Whenever the operator, by one foot, brought his weight down upon one bellows, the other foot would raise the second one, so that for twenty bellows, ten persons, and for every twenty-four, twelve persons had of necessity to be available. [Translation by the present author]

From Praetorius' perspective sketch of the Halberstadt bellows' chamber, a pair of non-ribbed bellows may be extracted to help illustrate his description.[5] Plate LXXXII, fig. 1 identifies the various exterior parts of the bellows. The bottom panel A rests on a horizontal plane and is securely mounted to rigid supports. The top panel B is hinged to panel A at the front end E and is movable, circumscribing an arc segment at each movement. The flexible leather apron C encloses a compartment for capturing and compressing the air, while stirrup D is securely mounted upon the top panel at the rear of the bellows and provides a convenient support for the foot of the treadler. Fig. 2 illustrates the attitude of the bellows during the first phase of the pumping cycle when the bellows is being opened (by lifting the top panel), in order to charge the compartment with air from the atmosphere; the leather apron or gusset assumes a concave appearance because of the partial vacuum within the compartment. Fig. 3 illustrates the attitude during the second phase of the pumping cycle when the bellows is being closed (by depressing the top panel), in order to compress and expend the air from the compartment into the throat and canal; the leather apron or gusset assumes a convex appearance because of the developing pressure inside the compartment. Fig. 4 illustrates the bellows in a state of rest after having exhausted itself.

A further, more detailed, description of the old wind system is provided by Praetorius:

Vnd ist in den Eltesten Wercken ebener massen zubefinden / das dieselben auch / wie die vnsrigen / durch den Windt vnd Blaeszbaelge regiret / vnd zum klang gebracht worden seyn: Item / das die Baelge eben dieselben mittel / nemlich die Windtklappen oder Ventiel, dadurch der Windt in aus dem Balg gefuehrt wird / gehabt haben; vnd mit ledder vberzogen vnd beschlagen worden seyn.[6]

And in the most ancient instruments there is, likewise, this to be found, that they, like ours, were driven by wind and bellows, and thus made to sound. Also, the bellows were provided with the same appliances; namely, intake and exhaust valves, whereby the wind was brought into and out of of them; they were overlaid and outfitted with leather. [Translation by the present author]

A confirming statement by Werckmeister reinforces Praetorius' descriptions and supplies the all-important dimensions used for this type of bellows. He says:

So ist demnach insonder-
heit aus dem Syntagmati Prae-
torii bekant / . . . . Noch
wunderlicher koemmt mir vor /
dasz man zu solchen Orgeln in
die 20. bisz 24. kleine bla-
se-Baelge etwa 3. bisz 4.
Schuhe lang nach Arth der le-
dern Schmiede-Baelge ge-
brauchet . . . . ich koente
es selber nicht glauben /
wenn ich die . . . Baelge
nicht selber gesehen haette.[7]

It is, therefore, known,
particularly from the Syntagma
of Praetorius . . . . and appears even more strange to me,
that for such organs from
twenty to twenty-four bellows,
about three to four feet long
and similar to leather forge
bellows, were used . . . .
this would be incredible to me,
had I not seen . . . the bellows personally. [Translation
by the present author]

From these descriptions and sketches a fairly complete system for generating the wind can be extracted and reconstructed:

1. Externally, the bellows were comprised of a
bottom panel of about three to four-foot length and
securely mounted in a horizontal plane; to this was
attached, by means of a hinge at the front, a corresponding top panel, overlying it, but movable in a
vertical plane so as to inscribe an arc. The two
plates were combined and sealed by means of a leather
gusset (non-rigid) which encompassed the sides and
the rear. On the top panel was provided a stirrup to
receive the shoe of the treadler

2. Internally, the bellows exhibited an intake
and an exhaust system, so arranged as to work in opposite phase: while one (intake) opened, the other
(exhaust) closed; the opposite effect occurred during
the second phase of the cycle

With the mechanism thus basically established, it is possible to suggest its operation:

1. Every two pairs of bellows required one operator, who mounted the bellows by placing one shoe into each stirrup. A rigid bar was provided overhead to serve as a convenient handrail for support

2. In treadling the bellows, the operator would simultaneously inflate one while deflating the other, the cycle being realized in opposite phases. While one bellows would capture the wind, the other would compress and expend it. The internal valves operated automatically, opening and shutting properly to achieve the desired results

3. Accordingly, the bellows were operated directly; the wind was pumped. The dynamic weight of the human body served to compress the wind within the bellows. The density of the wind thus compressed was continuously subject to the motions of the operator in the second phase. By this method of wind generation, the pressure varied greatly, tending to be irregular, uneven, and fluctuating; all of these conditions were faithfully reflected in the live wind as it approached, entered, and excited the pipes

4. For direct operation of the non-ribbed bellows, either two pairs of bellows or multiples of the same had to be provided, and arranged so as to pulsate

in opposite directions. Since no provisions were made
for the intermediate storing, recompression, and re-
distribution of the wind in order to divorce it from
the vagrant motions of the operators, it became a matter of critical importance for the maintenance of a
nominally consistent wind pressure, that the operators
were of reasonably equal bodily weight, that they exercised a similar style of treadling, and that a carefully worked out sequence of cycles was firmly established and rigidly adhered to

5. Inasmuch as only a limited amount of vertical
motion could be achieved by the operator, the non-
ribbed bellows when operated directly, had to be of
fairly small size; what the bellows lacked in volume
was overcome by a comparatively large number of items.
Accordingly, three conditions provide symptoms for the
presence of this type of wind system: (a) a comparatively large number of individual bellows, (b) an even
total number of items, and (c) each item of relatively
small size

The operation of the non-ribbed bellows changed, in
time, from the _direct_ to the _indirect_ method. Praetorius
relates:

Wie denn gleichsfalls or-
dentliche Baelge mit recht-
messigem Windt vnnd Gewicht /
vorhundert vnd neuntzen Ja-

About one-hundred-nineteen
years ago [_i.e._, _ca._ 1500]
more respectable bellows
were developed for use, which

ren ohngefehr auch zum Gebrauch erfunden worden seyn:
Welche aber gleichwol / noch
wie vor etlichen hundert
Jahren mit Lohegaren Rosz-
vnd Ochsenhaeutten vberzogen gewesen / vnnd alle
fuenff Jahr haben einge-
schmieret werden muessen.[8]

had a properly measured wind
and weight. However, these
were [still] overlaid with
tanned horse and ox-hides,
just like [the ones] of several hundred years ago; they
had to be greased every five
years. [Translation by the
present author]

The significant advance indicated here is the change
from direct to indirect operation. The dynamic, uneven motions of the operator were replaced by the more even compression exerted by inert weights mounted on the movable top panel and passing through the segment of an arc; thereby, gravity had been harnessed as the driving force. The operator
needed only to set up a potential energy, which could be
achieved in two ways:

    1. He could raise the top panel from the rear
of the bellows by hand

    2. He could raise the top panel from the front
of the bellows by means of a string and pully or by
means of a first class lever

The various possibilities are illustrated schematically on Plate LXXXIII, figs. 1-4. Fig. 1 shows the bellows
at rest; the bottom panel A lies on a horizontal plane and is
appropriately secured; the movable top panel B is equipped
with a handle C and an inert weight D. The front of the bellows is at E, the rear, at F. Fig. 2 shows the bellows as
being cocked from the rear by means of a hand raising the top

panel. This method found frequent application in small table organs and portatives.[9] Fig. 3 shows a string and pulley assembly for cocking the bellows from in front. This method is used in the Compenius organ at Frederiksborg, Schloss.[10] Fig. 4 shows a common method of cocking from the front of the bellows by means of a first class lever assembly. This method seems to have found frequent application in most of the instruments of the time, especially in the larger ones.[11]

Because of the basic change from direct to indirect operation, certain conditions began to prevail:

1. The bellows were no longer pumped, they were merely cocked

2. The dynamic motions of the body were replaced by the inert masses of the weights; the bellows were less subjected to wear and tear

3. The wind compression became more static and the distribution more even

4. An odd or even number of bellows (beyond the theoretical minimum of two) could now be employed

5. The size of the individual bellows had to remain largely the same, in order to facilitate the effective operation of the non-ribbed leather gusset

6. One operator could handle more than two bellows, since he was only active in the comparatively easy first phase of the cycle

7. The operation of the bellows could be

performed more safely and effectively by hand rather

than by foot

The Ribbed Species of Bellows

The next advance was realized when the non-rigid

leather apron or gusset was replaced by a system of collaps-

ible and expansible ribs, causing the bellows to present the

appearance of multiple folds. When this happened, the era

of the ribbed species of bellows had arrived. Praetorius re-

cords this event in the De Organographia. He says:

Vor neuntzig Jahren ist man den Sachen aber naeher kommen . . . . Vnd seynd auch Spaenbaelge gearbeitet worden.[12]	Ninety years ago [i.e., ca. 1530] significant advances were made . . . . Ribbed bellows began to be fabricated. [Translation by the present author]

The generic German term for this type of bellows dur-

ing Praetorius' time was Spaenbaelge, i.e., bellows con-

structed with "chips" of wood. These chips were the trian-

gular and trapezoidal members which were fitted together,

hinged, and gusseted to provide the expansible enclosure be-

tween the top and bottom panels of the wedge-shaped bellows.

Toepfer uses the term Spannbalg only for the much later ap-

pearing single-fold bellows, reserving the term Faltenbalg

for the multiple-fold member of the species.[13] Literally

translated, the term Faltenbalg means fold-bellows and is

quite appropriate for this species, although the name is

equally applicable to the multiple-fold and the single-fold

type; the same is true of the term _Spaenbalg_; literally translated, the term means _chip bellows_ and refers to the chips or pieces of wood which were used to enclose the panels. There is nothing in the names to restrict their meanings to either multiple or single folds. Accordingly, where in Toepfer and subsequent theorists the term _Faltenbalg_ is reserved for the multiple-fold bellows, and the term _Spaenbalg_, for the single-fold bellows, the latter term, at the time of Praetorius, served to identify either the multiple-fold or single-fold forms of the ribbed bellows. It is only by this interpretation that the confusion existing with respect to these terms can be lifted and an intelligent approach to the wind system of the Praetorius organ realized.

The <u>Multiple-fold</u> <u>Type</u>
<u>of</u> <u>Bellows</u>

Our investigation of the first member of the ribbed species of bellows concerns itself, then, with the multiple-fold type, which seems to have been in full flowering at the time of Praetorius and may be considered as taken for granted when no further qualifying specification was added to the term.

Werckmeister, in his treatise concerning the renovation of the _Grueningen_, _Schloss_ organ in 1704, describes the instrument as it was before the renovation began.[14] Among other things, he says:

Hinter diesem Wercke lie-
gen Acht Starcke Baelge /
zwar nach der alten Arth /
mit vielen Falten gemachet /
jedoch gehen sie fast 2. Ellen hoch auff und geben
ihren guten bestaendigen
Wind / sonderlich da sie nun
auszgebessert / und wo es
noethig gewesen / mit neuen
Leder ueberlegt worden. Sie
sind 8. Schuhe lang und 4.
breit und von lautern Eichen
Holtze.[15]

Behind the instrument lie
eight substantial bellows,
constructed in the old manner
with many folds, to be sure,
but they open almost two Ellen
[i.e., ca. four feet] and deliver a good, steady wind, especially now that they have
been reconditioned and, where
necessary, overlaid with new
leather. They are eight feet
long and four feet wide and
are made of solid oak. [Trans-
lation by the present author]

A second, reliable source of information for the
wind system in use at the time is Esaias Compenius I, whose
manuscript on the inspection of organs discusses the bellows
of the time as follows:[16]

Zur Besichtigung gehoeret
neher:

The following bears closer
inspection:

1. Dasz Balghausz wegen
des Geblaeses, oder der Baelgen dabey man gerne Licht
der finstern oerter halben,
haben musz. Vnd ist in acht
zu nehmen, dasz die Belgen
ohne Beruehrung des Clavirs
getretten werden, und zuse-
hen ob sie auch einen feinen
satsamen gang haben.

1. [In] the bellows-chamber,
which houses the blowplant or
bellows, one will need a light
because of the prevailing dark-
ness. It should be observed
that the bellows must be treadled without touching the keys
of the Manual, in order to see
if they operate with a fine,
full movement.

2. Ob Sie auch mit zu gar
schweren Gewichte beleget
seyn.

2. If they are perhaps laden
with overly heavy weights.

3. Ob Sie auch sonderlich
die auf eine Wiege liegen
an der Zahl Steine gleich
viel haben.

3. If they are supplied with
an equal number of stones, especially those which are mounted in a cradle.

4. Ob Sie auch schottern
wen getreten wird, den solches ist der mangel dasz die

4. If they chatter when being cocked; the defect here
will be caused by a weak

Wagebalcken, oder Calcatur-claves zu schwach sein, welcher defect zu tadeln stehet. / lever, which [condition] should be criticized.

5. Ob der Windt iust stille vnd wol verwahret sey. / 5. If the wind remains static and is well sealed.

6. Ob Sie auch wol zu treten. / 6. If they are comfortable to treadle.

7. Sonderlich gebe der Iudex mit groszen Fleisze hiervff achtung ob sie schwer von Gewichte sein, oder ob sie davon so faul und schwerlich unter sich weichen wollen, dasz der Balcke nicht den wind im Huj vnd schnell in sich bekommen kan. Welches hiermit zu probiren, wen man den Balg haestig niedertritt, folget er nun fein artig, so ist es Kein mangel, Helt er aber gegen das geschwinde gewaltsahme hastige niedertreten, gahr faul oder ie zeher wiederumb, so ist es ein fundament mangell vnd stehet darinne dasz die Ventiel so den wind in den Baelgen lassen sollen, zu klein sey vnd damit nun solches noch gewisser zu erkundigen vnd davon zu iudiciren so giebt sich die Probe noch einmahl in denen, wen der Balg hastig, darin den alle Maengel, was etwan wird, und die Ventil unten im Balge sein zu klein, wie oben gemeldet so zeugt der Wind die Ledderfalten mit Gewalt in sich hinein, vnd wen der Balg sich wieder vff den Wind sezzet so springen die falten wieder herausz, welches ein gros geprasseln vnd Poltern vervrsachet auch nicht Lange gehen Koennen, sondern von tage zu tage zum ende eyle.

7. Especially should the examiner diligently observe if the bellows rise heavily or if they, for this reason, yield with too great a resistance, so that the bellows cannot capture the wind with efficiency and dispatch. Such a condition may be tested as follows: When the bellows are treadled forcefully and respond immediately, there exists no deficiency; should, however, the bellows resist the swift and forceful motion, or react sluggishly, a major defect exists in so far, that the intake valves which give access to the wind are too small. This condition should then be more thoroughly examined and a judgment given. This same test will produce another symptom: When the bellows are abruptly treadled, all inherent defects, including that of inadequate intake valves, as mentioned above [will be revealed in this wise] that the wind will forcefully suck in the leather folds; when the bellows, thereupon, reverse their motion to compress the wind, the folds will snap outward and cause a great din and clatter which the bellows cannot suffer for any length of time but which will lead to their eventual destruction.

8. Auch musz man in diesen defect darauff acht haben wen schon die Ventill Loecher unten am Balge, davon iezt gesagt grosz genug sein, kan demnach dieser mangel daher entstehen, wen die Ventill all zu hart gefast und zu keinen rechten Vffgange kommen koennen, solches stehet nach etzlichermaszen durch den Meister balde zu helffen, aber sonst wie oben angezeigt ist.

8. The symptoms of this defect may have another cause: Even though the openings for the intake valves in the bottom panel are of adequate size, the defect may be caused by the intake valves being too closely and tightly fitted, so that they cannot open properly. This condition can often be directly corrected by the organ builder; if not, it must be judged inadequate as before. [Translation by the present author]

A third source of information for the system of wind supply is the De Organographia itself or, more accurately, the Theatrum Instrumentorum, which is its accompanying atlas. Three bellows systems are pictured herein in perspective:

1. The first is the one attached to the Old Positive.[18] A double pair of bellows is shown in a state of rest; the folds are clearly recognizable as multiple folds, but the ribs cannot be clearly seen. Weights are shown on the top panel, and handles appear as extensions of the same to indicate indirect operation by hand from the rear of the bellows

2. The second system is attached to a Positieff.[19] Here one pair of bellows is at rest, the other, cocked. The open one reveals five folds and exhibits a weighted top panel including a handle for cocking. The folded pair of bellows is pictured exactly as the one for the Old Positive

3. The third system is attached to a <u>Regahll</u>.[20]

It is in all respects similar to the wind system of

the <u>Positieff</u>

The fourth source of information is extracted from

the catalog of dispositions where, in some instances, Prae-

torius makes reference to the wind system of the instrument

he presents. Of the forty-seven dispositions, only fifteen

give some information in this respect. Table 62 lists the

pertinent cases together with related information.

For the organ at <u>Braunschweig</u>, <u>St</u>. <u>Blasius</u>, Prae-

torius devotes a special paragraph toward describing the un-

usual bellows provided for this instrument. He says:

Es sind auch die Span Baelge / deren achte vorhanden /
vff eine sondere Art gemacht
/ also dasz ein jeglicher 9.
guter Schuch lang / mit einer eintzigen Falten;[21] Die
Spuene sind 2. starcke Eichene Bretter gantz bestendig /
vnd gehen dichte zusammen /
dasz keine Mausz darbey kommen kan.[22]

There are also ribbed bel-
lows [<u>i.e.</u>, <u>Spaenbaelge</u>], of
which eight occur, which are
constructed in a special manner; each one is nine full
feet long and has but a single fold. The tongued-and-
grooved panels are made of two
strong oak boards, very durable; when folded, they clap
together, so that no mouse can
get at the [folds]. [<u>Trans-
lation</u> <u>by</u> <u>the</u> <u>present</u> <u>author</u>]

Another special paragraph is attached to the speci-

fication of the <u>Hildesheim</u>, <u>St</u>. <u>Gotthard</u> organ, in order to

describe more fully the unusual features of the bellows.

Praetorius says:

Es hat aber dieser Meister
Henning eine gar sonderliche

This Master Henning uses a
special type of bellows, which

TABLE 62

BELLOWS SPECIFICATIONS FOR
SPECIFIC INSTRUMENTS

Instrument and Reference to the De Organographia	Number of Voices	Number of Bellows	Description
Constanz, pp. 161-62	70	22	Blaszbaelge
Rostock, pp. 163-64	39	14	Blaszbaelge
Hamburg, St. Jacob, pp. 168-69	53	18	Small Blaszbaelge
Hamburg, St. Peter, pp. 169-70	42	9	Baelge
Magdeburg, Cathedral, pp. 172-73	42 [45]	12	Leather Blaszbaelge
Magdeburg, St. Catharina, pp. 175-76	33 [36]	8	Spaenbaelge
Braunschweig, St. Blasius, pp. 178-79	35 [37]	8	Special type[a] of Spaenbaelge
Leipzig, St. Nicholas, pp. 179-80	29	10	Spaenbaelge
Halberstadt, Barfuesser, pp. 182-83	27 [38]	8	Blaszbaelge
Bueckeburg, pp. 185-86	48	9	Spaenbaelge
Model Disposition 1, p. 191	27	8	Good, durable Blaszbaelge
Sondershausen, p. 197	36 [33]	12	Blaszbaelge
Hildesheim, St. Gotthard, pp. 198-99	23	5	Special type[a] of Blaszbaelge
Riddagshausen, Cloister, pp. 199-200	31		Spaenbaelge
Bayreuth, pp. 200-02	34	9-11	Blasbaelge

[a]See below for detailed specifications of the special type of bellows here indicated.

Art von Blasbaelgen im
brauch / die den andern
Spaenbaelgen / viel mehr
aber den Laeddern baelgen
weit vorgehen / vnnd haben
nur ein einige falten so
eines Schuchs[23]/ das ist einer halben Ellen hoch in die
hoeh / auffgehet: Vnd sich
gleich als 2. dicke (drey
finger breit) Eichene Bretter zusammen schleust /
dasz man also nichts mehr
davon siehet; vnd also weder von der Lufft noch von
Meusen schaden nemen kan.
Die Leng ist gemeiniglich
8. oder neuntehalb schuch
lang / vnnd fuenfftehalb
schuch breit[24] / zu den
grossen Orgeln aber 9. schuch
lang / vnnd 5. oder sechstehalb schuch[25] breit.[26]

far excel the other ribbed bellows [i.e., Spaenbaelge] and,
in particular, the leather bellows. These have only a single
fold which opens to one foot,
that is, one-half Ell. When
closed, they appear like two
thick oak boards (about three
fingers wide), so that nothing
more can be seen of the folds;
they cannot be damaged by either the atmosphere or mice.
Their length is generally 8 or
8 1/2 feet, and their width,
4 1/2 feet. For large organs,
however, they are 9 feet long
and 5 or 5 1/2 feet wide.
[Translation by the present
author]

From these quotations, sketches, and abstracts a very
complete wind generation system, as generally employed at the
time of Praetorius, can be reconstructed:

1. The term Blaszbaelge is used as an overall
term, applying to all types and species of bellows

2. The term Spaenbaelge identifies the ribbed
species, either of the multiple-fold or of the single-
fold type

3. It appears that the multiple-fold type of
ribbed bellows, introduced ca. 1530, was the one in
common use at the time of Praetorius. Since their
inner ribs were not directly attached to the panels,
they must be considered as having been floating ribs,

inclined to chatter

4. The single-fold type of ribbed bellows were just being introduced in a few instances at about this time [ca. 1620], and were welcomed not only as a novelty, but also as a great improvement

5. The general method of operation was indirect, the bellows being cocked rather than pumped, and stones or lead weights serving as the inert mass intended to compress the air by gravity

6. The bellows were mounted in some form of cradle, and the bellows lever seems to have operated from underneath the bellows, so that it could be treadled by foot from a position in front of the bellows. Plate LXXXIII, figs. 5 and 6 presents a schematic mounting of a multiple-fold bellows set into a cradle. The bottom panel A is securely imbedded upon supports B and C. The top-panel D moves through an arc segment, being hinged at E and connected to the bottom panel A by means of triangular and trapezoidal ribs F which provide the enclosure for the compartment of the bellows. Lever G rotates on fulcrum H and is attached to the top panel D by means of rod I and projecting arm J. Lever G is equipped with a treadling plate K for the convenience of the operator. Fig. 6 shows the bellows in an attitude of rest

7. Intake and exhaust openings and valves for

the same were provided to operate automatically[27]

8. For indirect operation, a minimum of two pairs or any number (odd or even) beyond the minimum needed to be supplied. The determining factor was the number of voices in the organ, the sizes of the channels and pallet boxes, the sizes and volumes of the wind trunks and conductors, and the number and character of all auxiliary devices requiring a pressure wind

9. In certain cases, some locking or anchoring device was provided to prevent promiscuous operation of the bellows and use of the instrument

10. In certain instances, a separate and enclosed bellows chamber housed the entire blowplant

The <u>Single-fold</u> <u>Type</u>
of <u>Bellows</u>

The single-fold, ribbed bellows are mentioned only twice by Praetorius: once with the disposition of the <u>Braunschweig</u>, <u>St</u>. <u>Blasius</u> organ, and again at <u>Hildesheim</u>, <u>St</u>. <u>Gotthard</u>.[28] Both of these instruments were built by Henning Henke of Hildesheim around the second decade of the seventeenth century. In both cases, Praetorius describes the construction of the bellows and points out the advantages. They were, in their mechanical disposition, much the same as described in chapter i of this study and need no further discussion here beyond the fact that at this time they were constructed of about the same size as the multiple-fold type.

Both types of ribbed bellows (the multiple-fold and the single-fold), if they were arranged to be operated indirectly, required that certain refined conditions be met in their construction and operation which are not directly apparent:

1. By the indirect method, the operator did not pump the bellows, but would cock one after the other at leisure, relying upon the weights to compress and deliver the wind. It was always necessary that a second bellows would be cocked before the first one had completed its cycle and exhausted itself. For such indirect operation, any number of bellows, odd or even, needed to be provided, the theoretical minimum being two. While one folded, the remaining ones were either idle or remained cocked until the pressure on the remote side of the exhaust valves became lower than that within the bellows. Thereupon, another bellows would take over and exhaust itself

2. In such a compound mechanism, it became critically important that each bellows of the series be constructed of exactly the same size and weight as any of its fellows. All of the bellows appointments, such as intake valves, exhaust valves, etc., needed to be of precisely the same size and had to be

adjusted in perfect balance with all others; equal
resistance had, likewise, to be maintained in all
hinges and bearings

3. It will be evident that in a bellows system
of this nature, without the additional convenience
of a magazine or reservoir for storing the wind under
regulated pressure, each bellows had to supply the
total requisite wind for the entire organ when passing through the second phase of its cycle. In short,
the system operated the bellows in series, one after
the other, not in parallel

It is clear, then, that the principle of the generation and conservation of wind became an obsession with the
organ builders of the Early Baroque.

Distribution and Disturbance
of the Wind

Having generated an adequate supply of pressure wind
for the organ by means of the bellows system provided for
this purpose, the organ builders of the period needed to
transport it into the instrument and lead it eventually into
the pallet boxes, at which point the chest mechanism harnessed
the wind anew for purposes of exciting the pipes. Here the
necessary devices were set up to control the wind in such a
way as to reflect every attainable wish of the player.

It is to be noted, that one of the chief and most

effective devices of today for controlling the pressure wind
and propelling it forward was lacking in the early baroque
organs. This pneumatic device is the reservoir (variously
called receiver, magazine, etc.), wherein the wind is stored,
recompressed, made static, and delivered into the wind trunks.
The reservoir divorces the wind in the bellows from that in
the wind trunks, eliminating from it all disturbances and
fluctuations which the compound motions, structural conditions, and operational imbalances of the bellows may have imposed upon it. It is hardly conceivable, how even in an intermediary stage of wind generation which the early baroque
builders of this period had painstakingly achieved, a steady,
adequate, and reliable wind system could be satisfactorily
achieved.

No mention, indication, or hint as to the presence of
some intermediate storage device appears anywhere in the primary sources concerned with this period. The conclusion is
self-evident: no such stage had as yet been developed. Accordingly, the organ of Praetorius accepted its wind from the
bellows directly into the canals, wind trunks, and conductors.
Their restless preoccupation with the bellows system, seeking
constantly therein to secure an adequate, regular, even, and
reliable pressure wind, attest to the critical importance the
early baroque builders attached to it in the initial stage of
generation.

The Basic Wind Conducting System

The transportation and distribution of the pressure wind begins, therefore, at the exhaust valves of the bellows. From here the wind, by means of a throat (which could be either a direct opening into the canal, or a conductor leading from the bellows' exhaust valves to the canal) was forced into the canal. The canal was, in effect, a gathering device for the wind exhausted by the various bellows. At times, and under certain conditions, the canal could serve as the wind trunk itself, moving directly into the instrument; at other times it led into a separately identifiable wind trunk. The wind trunk, thereupon, served to store the wind in the precise condition it received it; it could not alter it, divorce it from the bellows, nor recompress it; the wind retained all the characteristics with which the bellows had endowed it. At convenient places along the line traversed by the wind trunk, smaller, subsidiary trunks (known as conductors) were cut into it, in order to distribute the wind fractionally to the various pallet boxes. The overall disposition is clearly presented in chapter i and illustrated on Plate XXIV, fig. 1. It should be noted that in the pertinent sources, the fine distinction between throat, canal, wind trunk, and conductor does not usually appear; the terms most often used are Canal, Kanal, and Windfuehrungen. The accompanying descriptions, however, clearly show that several or all of the members were present.

The division of the bellows into two groups, each with its own wind conducting system (as, for example, one system for the Pedal and another for the manuals), does not seem to have as yet been developed and used by 1620.

The earliest extant technical description of wind conducting in the early organs appears in Adlung (1768):

Es folgen die Windkanaele, die den Wind von den Baelgen nach der Orgel fuehren. Wenn die Baelge mit Winde versehen, so gehen unter der Oeffnung derselben, davon § 62. gesagt ist, Kanaele weg, und fangen den Wind aus den Balgen auf; und diese haben die § 62. beschriebenen Kanalventile in sich. Hernach aber laufen diese Kanaele zusammen in einen groszen Kanal, der zuweilen 2 Schuh, auch wol mehr, auch weniger, dick und hoch ist.

Oder die Pedalbaelge schicken ihren Wind in einen besonderen Kanal, die Manualbaelge auch. In oder nicht weit vor der Orgel theilen sich diese Kanaele in kleinere Arme, deren einer nach dieser, der andere nach jener Windlade zu gehet. Zuweilen gehen etliche Arme nach einer Lade; doch alle in den Windkasten. Die Kanaele sind viereckigt, von Brettern oder Bohlen gemacht, und wohl verbunden, auch mit Leder ueberlegt, wo die Fugen sind, und durchaus mit der Masse bestrichen, wovon § 38. zu lesen, damit ja der Wind sich nicht verschleiche.29

There follow the wind trunks which conduct the wind from the bellows into the organ. When the bellows are filled with wind, the canals described in paragraph 62 and attached to the openings provided for them, gather the wind from the bellows; within the former are contained the exhaust valves described in paragraph 62. Thereupon, the various canals run together into a wind trunk which is two feet, more or less, and square, in cross section.

Occasionally, the pedal bellows deliver their wind into a canal separate from that provided for the manual bellows. Within or near the organ, the wind trunks divide into smaller conductors, which go to various wind chests. Occasionally, several conductors lead to one chest, but are always attached to the pallet box. The canals, wind trunks, and conductors are square in cross section, constructed of boards or planks, well joined, overlaid with leather at the seams, and impregnated with glue-size, so that no wind can escape. [Translation by the present author]

Devices to Check the Wind

In the instruments of the Early Baroque, certain appliances were often incorporated into the wind trunk or one
of its conductors whose purpose was to check the flow of the
pressure wind in its course from the bellows to the pallet
boxes. Practically all manner of valves that appeared in the
organs of this time were called ventils. Those that served
a specific purpose were often qualified by an appropriate
adjective, the ones in question being often termed Sperr-
ventile or check ventils.

Depending upon where they were located, the check
ventils could affect either the entire instrument or a portion of it. Those occurring in the general or primary wind
trunk before any branch conductors had been tapped off would
affect the whole instrument; when engaged, they would shut
off the wind from all subsequent conductors and pallet boxes.
This type of general check ventil does not appear to have
been used to any extent in these organs; it was easier simply to cease treadling the bellows, should no wind be desired,
or to close off all divisional ventils collectively.

The divisional check ventils were, however, much in
vogue at the time. These were introduced into the various
branch conductors and affected whatever pallet box a given
conductor would normally supply with wind. Of the forty-
seven instruments appearing in Praetorius' catalog, eight are
reported as having such divisional check ventils; in the

parallel instances presented by the Dresdener Handschrift,
twenty-four of the instruments are reported as having been
so equipped. A few instances will show how they were disposed:

1. Lueneburg, St. Johan-
nes. 2. Ventil, vnter welchem eines zum obersten Clavier / das andere zum Rueckpositiff gehoeret.[30]

1. Lueneburg, St. Johannes.
Two ventils, among which one
belongs to the upper clavier,
the other, to the Rueckpositive

2. Magdeburg, St. Ulrich.
Ventil zum Werck, Brust, vnd
Positiff.[31]

2. Magdeburg, St. Ulrich.
Ventil for the Werk, Brust,
and Positive

3. Braunschweig, St. Bla-
sius. Fuenff Ventile, 1.
Zum Ober Werck. 2. Zun
Baessen. 3. Zun Rueck Posi-
tiff. 4. Zur Sonnen. 5.
Zun Sternen.[32]

3. Braunschweig, St. Bla-
sius. Five ventils: (1) for
the Oberwerk, (2) for the
Basses, (3) for the Rueckpositive, (4) for the Sun, and
(5) for the Stars

4. Torgau. Ventiel zum
Rueckpositiff.[33]

4. Torgau. Ventil for the
Rueckpositive

5. Riddagshausen, Klo-
ster. Vier ventile: 1. Zum
Ober Werck. 2. Brust. 3.
Rueckpositiff. 4. Pedal.[34]

5. Riddagshausen, Clois-
ter. Four ventils: (1) for
the Oberwerk, (2) Brust, (3)
Rueckpositive, and (4) Pedal
[Translations by the present
author]

The Dresdener Handschrift, in parallel cases, gives
much more detailed information concerning the check ventils,
and establishes their use for divisional wind checks as
common practice.

The purpose and value of these ventils are extolled
by Praetorius. In discussing the accessories of the organ
at the Bayreuth, [Stadtkirche], he says:

Es gefelt mir auch gar wol / dasz man zu einer jeden Laden / ein absonderlich Ventil macht / damit 1. nicht ein jeder / so vff die Orgel gelauffen koempt wisse / sich drein finden koenne / ob er gleich die Register ziehet. 2. Dasz der Wind nicht so bald alle Laden erfuellet / wenn man nicht vff allen Claviren schlagen wil.35	It pleases me greatly, that for each chest a separate ventil is provided, so that (1) not every one who happens to come upon the organ can find his way around even though he may draw all the registers, and (2) the wind does not always fill all the chests when one does not wish to play on all manuals. [Translation by the present author]

In sum, the divisional check ventils provided the
following conditions and conveniences for the player:

    1. They discouraged tampering with the instru-
ment by the uninitiated

    2. They conserved the wind for active chests

    3. They made it possible to disengage a mal-
functioning chest from the wind system

    4. They permitted a limited amount of fore-
registration and served as a registrational cut-out

    The last condition needs some application to show its
value to the player. In a case where the Oberwerk and Brust
were controlled by one keyboard, for example, it was possible
to set up a registration on each chest. By a skillful use of
the pertinent check ventil, either chest could be cut in
(engaged) or cut out (disengaged) of the registration at will,
making possible a collective change in registration. One
manual could, to some extent, provide the flexibility of two.

    A schematic form of check ventil is illustrated on

Plate XXV, fig. 2.

Basic Forms of the Tremulant

The wind trunks and conductors of the early organs were frequently equipped with devices to disturb the flow of the wind, so as to achieve certain effects in the speech of the pipes. Noteworthy among these devices were the tremulants. Built in various forms, they were much-beloved appointments in the instruments of the time and were held in such high regard that Praetorius and others often considered them as important and as useful as actual voices in the organ:

Der Tremulant, ob er wol keinen laut von sich gibt / so wird er doch von etlichen Auch vor eine Stimme (weil man viel verenderung damit haben kan) gerechnet.[36]	The tremulant, even though it is unable to produce a sound, is considered by some as an [actual] voice in the organ, because so many modifications can be effected by it. [Translation by the present author]

In the primary sources underlying the present study, the devices for disturbing the wind are differentiated only by the terms Tremulant and Bocktremulant. Fortunately, the Compenius organ at the Frederiksborg palace in Denmark contains an example of each type, so that a clear differentiation can yet be firmly established. Praetorius differentiates the two by name as Tremulant and Grosser Bock.[37] Thekla Schneider describes the two as follows:

The register, Grosser Bock, is the older design of the tremulant. It consists of a ventil which is opened and shut by a spring with the help of the wind in the trunk. The second, a mildly-beating type of tremulant is connected with the Manual. The two differ from each other in that the <u>Bocktremulant</u> beats more quickly than the second one.[38] [<u>Translation by the present author</u>]

Woersching differentiates the tremulants of the <u>Frederiksborg</u>, <u>Schloss</u> organ as follows:

In the Manual we find the milder, adjustable tremulant, while a heavier tremulant, the <u>Grosser Bock</u>, affects the Pedal.[39] [<u>Translation by the present author</u>]

Accordingly, the two types of tremulants are differentiated from each other by their effect upon the speech of the pipes:

1. The <u>tremulant per se</u> produced mild beats at a moderate pace and appears to have been equivalent to the <u>tremblant doux</u> described and illustrated in chapter i of the present study

2. The <u>Bock tremulant</u> produced heavier beats at a faster pace and appears to have been equivalent to the <u>tremblant fort</u> as described and illustrated in chapter i

Introduction and Differentiation

The tremulant mechanism seems to have been introduced into the wind systems in various ways, in order to affect the entire instrument, a major portion of it, or individual divisional chests. Dom Bedos consistently shows the <u>tremblant</u>

doux mounted into the general or main wind trunk near the canal and before any branch conductors are tapped off.[40] This would indicate a condition whereby such a tremulant should affect the entire instrument, including all chests, such as the Oberwerk, the Brust, the Rueckpositive, and the Pedal. Such a disposition can be surmised in those cases where a tremulant is included among the specifications without additional delimiting descriptions. In Praetorius' catalog of dispositions, each of the following instruments has a tremulant specified in this manner:[41] Bernau; Braunschweig, St. Blasius; Torgau; Halberstadt, St. Martini; Cassel, Brueder; Cassel, Schlosz; Grueningen, Schlosz; and Model Dispositions 4, 5, and 6. Of course, the specifications of the instruments may be incomplete and it should be remembered that Praetorius does not specifically say that these tremulants affected the entire instrument. On the other hand, he usually makes special mention of the fact when two tremulants did occur in an instrument. In such cases the tremulant was introduced to affect the Werk (zum gantzen Werck), while the Bock tremulant was arranged to affect the Rueckpositive only and separately from the Werk. It is, however, debatable just what the term zum gantzen Wercke implied. It may have meant either:

1. The entire instrument, through and through including the elements comprising the Werk, and the Rueckpositive as well; in such a case, the tremulant

would have had to occur in the main wind trunk before the Rueckpositive conductor was tapped off. This is the method consistently exemplified by Dom Bedos, and represents a _series_ disposition[42]

2. Only those chests which normally were understood to comprise the _Werk_; namely, the Oberwerk, the Brust, and the Pedal, plus any fractional chests associated with these corpora; in such a case, the tremulant would have had to occur in the wind trunk beyond the branch conductor for the Rueckpositive. In this case the Bock tremulant for the Rueckpositive would, in effect, be truly segregated from the other tremulant and operate entirely independently as Praetorius seems to want to indicate in several of his descriptions. Such a layout represents a _parallel_ disposition

The present author is inclined toward the latter interpretation but is unable to prove the case. The following descriptions from Praetorius' catalog will serve to exemplify the condition:

1. Schoeningen, Schlosz-kirche. Tremulant zum gantzen Werck durch vnd durch. Bock zum Rueckpositiff absonderlich.[43]

1. Schoeningen, Schloss-kirche. Tremulant for the entire Werk through and through; Bock for the Rueckpositive, separately

2. Riddagshausen, Kloster. Tremulant zum gantzen Werck. Bocktremulant zum

2. Riddagshausen, Cloister. Tremulant for the entire Werk; Bock tremulant for the

Rueckpositiff allein / vnd dasz die Regal vnnd Schnarwercke / auch zum Tremulanten gebraucht werden koennen.[44]

Rueckpositive alone, so that the regals and reeds can also be used with it.

3. Barait. Tremulant zum gantzen Wercke durch vnd durch. Tremulant zum Rueck Positiff absonderlich / wird sonsten der Bock genant.[45]

3. Bayreuth, [Stadtkirche]. Tremulant for the entire Werk, through and through; tremulant for the Rueckpositive, separately, usually called the Bock

4. [Model Disposition] 1. Tremulanten im Ober Wercke vnnd Rueck Positiff ein jeden sonderlichen zu gebrauchen.[46]

4. Model Disposition 1. Tremulants for the Oberwerk and the Rueckpositive, each one to be usable separately

5. [Model Disposition] 3. Tremulant zum gantzen Werck. Bock zum Rueckpositiff.[47]

5. Model Disposition 3. Tremulant for the entire Werk; Bock for the Rueckpositive [Translations by the present author]

Occasionally, a separate tremulant was provided for each major chest in the instrument. In such instances, the mechanism would need to have been introduced into the pertinent branch conductors which supplied the respective chests. Noteworthy is the application of the device to the pedal division. Examples from Praetorius' catalog follow:

1. Bueckeburg. Drey Tremulanten 1. Im Ober Werck / 2. Rueckpositiff / vnd 3. im Pedal.[48]

1. Bueckeburg, [Stadtkirche]. Three tremulants: (1) in the Oberwerk, (2) in the Rueckpositive, and (3) in the Pedal

2. Dreszden, Schloszkirche. Ober Werck: Tremulant; Brust Positiff: Tremulant; Positiff vff beyden seiten: Tremulant.[49]

2. Dresden, Schlosskirche. Separate tremulants for the Oberwerk, Brustpositive, and Seitenpositive [Translations by the present author]

Characteristic Effects

Compenius, Praetorius' co-worker at the Braunschweig court, sheds some light on what were considered desirable characteristics for the tremulant in his time. He says:

1. Man findet aber mancherley art schlaege Tremulanten aber das sind die Lieblichsten, die 8 schlaege vff einen Tact oder Mensur schlagen . . . .

1. One finds many types of tremulants, but those are the most desirable which beat eight times per Takt or measure . . . .

2. Auch werden ihr viel gefunden, die dieser art sein, dasz wan man oben in der Hoehe . . . greifft so schlagen sie geschwinde, sobald man aber unter sich im Basz . . . etwas vollstimmig greiffet . . . so fallen sie vnd schlagen Langsam, . . . welche dan billich getadelt . . . .

2. Many can be found which react on this wise that, when one plays . . . in the upper range, they beat rapidly; as soon as one plays in the lower range, . . . they weaken and beat more slowly . . . . Such a condition should be criticized . . . .

3. Darumb ist das die Beste art, wen sie 8 schlaege vff einen rechtmaeszigen Tact schlagen vnd fein sanffte beben, auch bestendig denselben schlag vnd Mensur behalten. Sonderlich aber wen Sie sollen zu Schnarrwerkken gebraucht werden, wie dan wol geschehen mag, auch darzu eine sondrer art Tremulanten, Boecke genandt sich zum Besten vnd Lieblichsten darzu arten.

3. The best type is, therefore, the one which delivers eight beats for each properly executed Takt, undulates mildly, and maintains the same steady beat and measure, especially when it is to be used with reeds, which [generally] are sympathetic to this effect. For this purpose, special types of tremulants, known as Bocks, are best suited and most desirable

4. Man findet ihr auch die sich gar bequem auff zweyerley art alsz Langsam, vnd dan geschwinde hoeren lassen, welches nur durch einen Registerzug oder enderung des Windes geschiehet.50

4. There are also those which are able to undulate in two speeds, slow and fast; this [variation] is accomplished by means of a register control, or by a change in the wind. [Translation by the present author]

It seems that the effect of the tremulant was particularly cultivated in connection with the regal and reed pipes of the organ. Compenius alludes to this in the above quotation. Praetorius occasionally points it out as well:

1. Leipzig, S. Niclas. Tremulant zum Schnarr Wercke gut.51

1. Leipzig, St. Nicholas. Tremulant, good for reeds

2. Riddagshausen, Kloster. Bocktremulant zum Rueckpositiff allein / vnd dasz die Regal vnnd Schnarwercke / auch zum Tremulanten gebraucht werden koennen.52

2. Riddagshausen, Cloister. Bock tremulant for the Rueckpositive alone, so that the regals and reeds can be used with it. [Translations by the present author]

Constructional Features

By tracing the mechanical realization of the tremulant through the subsequent theoretical treatises of the eighteenth and nineteenth centuries, it is possible to differentiate the construction of the two types of tremulants, but it must be realized that the manner in which they eventually emerge into drawings or descriptions reflects the probable improvements that had from time to time been incorporated into them. The two types which appear again and again in the literature are:

1. The closed tremulant

2. The open tremulant

The closed tremulant lay entirely within the wind trunk and reveals no communication with the outer atmosphere. It amounted to a device which in some manner disturbed the

normal and even flow of the pressure wind without releasing
any of it to the outside. The effect achieved by it seems
to have been one of mild and gentle undulation. It seems to
have been used for the entire Werk and can be suspected when
no special specification as Bock, stark schlagend, and the
like would indicate the other type of tremulant. Adlung describes an external mounting for it,[53] while Dom Bedos pictures a fairly simple form of it mounted entirely within the
main wind trunk.[54]

The open tremulant differed from the closed type in
that it periodically released a segment of the pressure wind
to the outer atmosphere; it thereby created alternate compressions and rarefactions in the air column of the conductor
to which it was usually attached. To achieve this effect,
an opening had to be provided in the conductor upon which the
tremulant mechanism was mounted and could act. A sophisticated form of the open tremulant is developed from Dom Bedos
in chapter i of the present study, fully described, and illustrated on Plate XXVI, fig. 2.

Pneumatic Appliances

The early baroque organ presents a number of pneumatic devices which are referred to by Praetorius as Extraordinarii Stimmen. All of them produced sounds which imitated instruments from the orchestra, or intriguing sounds
from nature. There occur the Zimbelstern, the Vogelgesang or

Nachtigall, the Trommel or Tympanum, the Kuckuck, and various forms of the Sackpfeife. These were freely introduced into salon or church organs, and are often enthusiastically described in the various pamphlets issued by the respective churches from time to time. There is hardly an instrument listed in Praetorius' catalog, which does not list at least one, several, or all of these pneumatic devices.

One of the purposes of the present study is to rediscover, as far as possible, the device itself, how it operated, and what tonal effect was achieved thereby. The only ones that can be faithfully described are those which occur in the Frederiksborg, Schloss organ, since this is the only authentic, surviving monument of the time. For the others, reliance must be placed upon descriptions handed down by others who saw them and recorded illuminating descriptions of them.

The Zimbelstern

The Zimbelstern occurs frequently among the early instruments; Praetorius mentions it as appearing in eight of the forty-seven organs of his catalog, while the Dresdener Handschrift, among the same instruments, lists twenty-nine occurrences of it. In the De Organographia the following references appear:[55]

1. Braunschweig, St. Blasius. Ventil for the sun and for the stars

2. Dresden, Schloss. Zimbel bells at the star

3. Schoeningen, Schloss. Zimbel bells

4. Model Disposition 2. Star for the Zimbel
bells

5. Model Disposition 5. Star Zimbel bells

6. Sondershausen. Rotating star

7. Riddagshausen, Cloister. Zimbel bells with
a star

8. Bayreuth, [Stadtkirche]. Rotating star with
Zimbel bells

From the descriptions given, the following points can
be extracted:

1. The sounding medium was a cluster of high-
pitched cymbal bells

2. The visible form of the device was either a
star or a sun which rotated

3. Occasionally, the device occurred several
times in one instrument

For all of these forms, the term today is Zimbelstern, a number of examples having been introduced, in modern
adaptation, into recent American instruments; they all are,
however, executed in a different manner than is indicated in
the present study.

One such rotating Zimbelstern is carefully described
by Mattheson. Speaking of the St. Gertrude organ in Hamburg,
he says:

By this organ there is a remarkable Zimbelstern
over the framework and underneath the pedestal, upon
which appears a likeness of St. Gertrude with the
chapel on her arm. The star is heavily gilded. In
the middle of the star is a rose of polished steel in
diamond form, which sparkles when the sun shines upon
it while rotating. To the points of the star are attached similar, but smaller, polished rosettes, between which projecting flames are painted to simulate
the effect of a rainbow when in motion. Eight Zimbel
bells are mounted on the star, so that when it rotates, the bells produce an exquisite sound. The instrument was renovated in 1700 by Arp Schnitger.[56]
[Translation by the present author]

In describing the Zimbelstern in more technical de-

tail, Adlung adds the following information:

The Zimbelstern used little bells of a very
bright and silvery tone and of a very high pitch.
Most often, different-sized bells were introduced.
The star, projecting out through the case of the organ, was driven by an axle which, in turn, was set
in motion at its opposite end within the case, by a
turbine fed with wind from the bellows. A register
control to engage or disengage the turbine was provided in the console. The bells, containing miniature
clappers within them, were securely attached to the
axle, so that when it rotated, a lively and confused
ringing of high-pitched bells was induced. Occasionally, somewhat larger and tuned bells were employed,
but these could only be used when playing in corresponding keys.[57] [Translated abstract by the present
author]

The Vogelgesang or Nachtigall

The Vogelgesang or Nachtigall seems to have enjoyed

especial favor among the builders of the time. Of the forty-

seven instruments in Praetorius' catalog, no less than fif-

teen are recorded as having been equipped with the device in

one form or another. The entries in the De Organographia are various, but it seems that all of them are synonymous with the term, Vogelgesang:

1. Vogelgesang.[58] (Magdeburg, Cathedral; Magdeburg, St. Ulrich; Leipzig, St. Nicholas; Torgau; Schoeningen, Schlosz; Model Dispositions 2 and 5; Sondershausen, Monk's Organ; Riddagshausen, Cloister)

2. Vogelgeschrey.[59] (Magdeburg, St. Catharina; Model Disposition 3; Hildesheim, St. Gotthard)

3. Allerley Vogelgesang.[60] (Sondershausen)

4. Vogelgesang durchs gantze Pedal.[61] (Dresden, Schloss; Bayreuth, [Stadtkirche])

5. Nachtigall.[62] (Magdeburg, St. Ulrich; Bayreuth, [Stadtkirche])

Some additional light is shed upon certain parallel instances recorded in the Dresdener Handschrift:

1. Sondershausen.[63] All kinds of Vogelgesang on every pedal key (Organ builder Fritzsche)

2. Bayreuth, Stadtkirche.[64] Vogelgesang, throughout the entire Pedal, as a small repeating mixture (Organ builder Fritzsche)

Adlung gives a detailed account of the technical execution of one form of the Vogelgesang. He says:

Vogelgesang is also called Nachtigall. The former name is very common . . . . It is also called Vogelgeschrey . . . . It is comprised of a canister made of metal, of an agreeable size, about four inches wide, high, and long. Underneath is a short tube through which the wind blows into the canister when attached to the wind trunk. Above it, three, four, or

more small pipes are mounted; they are several inches
long, covered, etc. All are blown at once. Should it
be desired to engage the register, the canister is
filled with water, for which purpose a funnel is provided. The pipes, thereupon, produce a fluttering
tone similar to that of the owls, or whatever they
are called, which the youngsters purchase from the
potter at the annual fairs for a few cents, in order
to amuse themselves.[65] [Translation by the present
author]

Gustav Fock, in a monograph dealing with the old or-

gans in and about Hamburg, throws further light upon the

Vogelgesang, especially in the novel form occasionally em-

ployed by Gottfried Fritzsche:

Beside the true organ voices, Fritzsche brings
a whole series of extraordinary registers which are
either entirely unknown in the North, or are known in
other forms: Kuckuck, Nachtigall, Vogelgesang. The
latter name denotes two realizations: The register
is either the above-mentioned Zimbel-like mixed voice
("throughout the entire Pedal," "an entire chorus of
Vogelgesang") as in Dresden, Braunschweig-Martini,
Bayreuth, or Sondershausen; or it is executed after
the manner of the Nachtigall, hence, with small pipes
which blow into a canister filled with water as in
Schoeningen, where it is listed among the accessories.[66] [Translation by the present author]

In sum, the Vogelgesang (Vogelgeschrei, Nachtigall)

appears in the early baroque instruments in two forms:

1. A tonally static device

2. A tonally progressive voice

In the first instance, several high-pitched open pipes were

excited by a wind which had been or would be disturbed by

passing through a mass of water. The device was engaged by

draw knob but was otherwise not connected with the key

action. Once excited, it would sound continuously until the
draw knob disengaged the wind. Subsequent writers on the subject want to differentiate the Nachtigall from the Vogelgesang
by pointing out that the former effect was realized by one
pipe or by two to four pipes tuned as a major chord, while
the latter was realized by very high pipes of indeterminate
pitch.[67]

The second form of the Vogelgesang (as, "throughout
the entire Pedal", etc.) seems to have been a progressive
voice subject to the stop and key action, hence, a kind of
high-pitched mixed voice, dwelling on the acute threshold of
pitch discrimination after the manner of the Zimbel or Terzzimbel.

The Trommel or Tympanum

The effort to simulate or actually reproduce the effect of drums or tympani in the organs of the Early Baroque
followed, in general, two directions. One was to simulate
the effect acoustically by means of wind-blown pipes; the
other, by introducing actual drums or tympani, and having
them struck by some pneumatic contrivance, often in the form
of sculptured figures handling appropriate drum sticks. Praetorius cites the device in thirteen of the forty-seven dispositions of his catalog under the following entries:

1. Trummel.[68] (Magdeburg, Cathedral; Magdeburg,
St. Ulrich; Torgau; Model Dispositions 2, 3, and 5;

Sondershausen, Monk's Organ; Hildesheim, St. Gotthard;

Riddagshausen, Cloister)

2. Trummel im Basz.[69] (Danzig, St. Maria)

3. Trummel, 2. Pfeiffen starck.[70] (Braun-

schweig, St. Blasius)

4. Heer Trummeln E vnd F.[71] (Dresden, Schloss)

5. Rechte Heerpaucken.[72] (Sondershausen)

From these entries at least two species of the device

can be differentiated:

1. The acoustically simulated effect derived

from at least two pipes as at Braunschweig, St. Bla-

sius

2. Genuine tympani operated pneumatically, as

strongly suggested by Dresden, Schloss and Sonders-

hausen

The acoustically derived effect of the drum is some-

what further elucidated by the parallel references in the

Dresdener Handschrift, where the device is almost exclusively

referred to as Tamburo, and in a number of instances as Tam-

buro out of 16', indicating a generally grave pitch level.

Adlung is largely disinterested in the device, and dispatches

it with a noteworthily brief description. He says:

> Tympanum, . . . Pauke, . . . Tamburo, and Tam-
> bour . . . . In the organ it has been attempted to
> simulate the effect by means of two pipes in the range
> of the Subbass.[73] [Translation by the present author]

The use of genuine tympani finds some elaboration in the Dresdener Handschrift:

Dresden, Friedrichs-Stadt.[74] Tympani are two very large copper kettle drums which are mounted high on the right and left sides of the organ; they are struck by two angels. The controls appear as four keys mounted over the Pedal, of which two strike the pitch C, and two, the pitch G. [Translation by the present author]

It is to be wondered whether Praetorius' designation of E and F for the Heer Trummeln of the Dresden, Schloss organ might not be typographical errors for the notes C and F or G. The writer has been unable to find clarification of this problem in any of the subsequent literature pertaining to this instrument, nor yet in a reprint of the original proposal of Fritzsche, the organ builder, to which he had access.[75]

The Kuckuck

The Kuckuck device occurs much more seldom than do the ones previously discussed. The De Organographia reports it as an accessory in only four of the instruments listed. The designation is invariably entered into the specifications as Kuckuck[76] (Magdeburg, St. Catharina; Model Disposition 5; Hildesheim, St. Gotthard; Bayreuth, [Stadtkirche]). The Dresdener Handschrift reports the device in three of the instruments mentioned, but provides no additional information. Adlung describes it only briefly:

The Kuckuck . . . consists of the pipes which produce two tones at the interval of a third, similar to the bird from which it derives its name.[77] [Translation by the present author]

Mahrenholz defines it a little more clearly. He describes it as follows:

The call of the cuckoo was imitated by two pipes tuned to each other at the interval of a major third, and planted on a little chest. The pallet valves were alternately opened by means of a cam driven by the wind. The cuckoo appears in the Early Baroque and disappears again toward the end of the eighteenth century.[78] [Translation by the present author]

The popular present-day cuckoo clock imitates the call of the cuckoo by means of two covered wooden pipes, each fed by a single miniature bellows. The interval of the tones is usually a perfect fourth, often slightly out of tune.

The Huemmelchen and Sackpfeife

The Huemmelchen and Sackpfeife are somewhat related devices which occur but very rarely in the organs of the time. Fortunately, both are featured in the surviving Frederiksborg, Schloss organ. In Praetorius' catalog, the devices appear as follows:[79]

1. Huemmelchen. (Model Disposition 5)

2. Kleinhuemlichen. (Hessen, Schloss)

3. Sackpfeife. (Hessen, Schlosz)

The best description of these pneumatic accessories is given by Woersching in his monograph on the Compenius organ at Frederiksborg:

> "Sackpfeife" und "Huemmelchen" are bagpipe reg-
> isters. The Sackpfeife, which is engaged by a draw
> knob in the form of an owl, produces a gentle, hum-
> ming effect which functions like an organ point and
> lies somewhere between B and C. The Kleinhuemlichen,
> which is engaged by a draw knob in the form of a
> fool's head, consists of six reed pipes of the tone
> series F - c - f - c' - f' - c'', and produces a mu-
> sette effect. Each of the six pipes can be engaged
> separately, so that the player can exercise a con-
> siderable option in choosing tonal combinations. Be-
> yond that, the F pipes can be mutated to G.[80] [Trans-
> lation by the present author]

To differentiate the two appliances a little more
clearly, it may be helpful to describe them by contrast:

	Huemmelchen	Sackpfeife
1.	One pipe	1. Six pipes, usable separately or in various combinations
2.	Pitch: C	2. Pitch: F - c - f - c' - f' - c''
3.	Covered labial pipe	3. Reed pipes (probably regals)
4.	Soft, humming effect	4. Reedy bagpipe tone
5.	Note and pitch: fixed	5. Note and pitch: semi-variable
6.	Type of effect: Organ point	6. Type of effect: Musette
7.	Used as one note	7. Used, most usually, in pairs

Miscellanea

One additional accessory is found among the early

baroque instruments in Praetorius' catalog which, so far, has proven to be inexplicable. A multitude of conjectures prevails in the literature, and the problem appears impossible of solution. The device is the Alteration mentioned by Praetorius as an accessory in the Magdeburg, St. Ulrich instrument.[81] It cannot even be established if the device is pneumatic or mechanical. No attempt will be made here to offer any explanation beyond recording the appearance of it.

Measurement of the Wind Pressure

No wind pressures were recorded by Praetorius for any of the instruments which he presents in his catalog, nor yet is any specific wind pressure mentioned anywhere in the De Organographia as suitable for use in organs. Obviously, no direct method for measuring the pressure of the wind had as yet been devised. It seems that the pressure was arrived at indirectly; the number, size, and volumetric contents of the collective bellows determined the quantity of wind that could be supplied; the pressure was determined entirely by the total moving weight of each bellows. This weight included the inert mass of stone or lead placed upon the top panel, plus the dead weight of the panel and its appointments, and the weight of the moving ribs. Any operational device attached to the bellows could increase or decrease the effective pressure of the wind, depending upon how it was balanced into the system. By a careful adjustment of all contributing

factors, a theoretically equal wind pressure could be established and maintained; there was, however, no way to measure
the pressure or to record it intelligibly for posterity.

It is, nevertheless, of extraordinary importance for
this study to know with some degree of accuracy what pressure
was generally employed by the builders of these early instruments.

Surviving Records

Fortunately, two instances of record are yet available:

1. The Frederiksborg, Schloss (formerly Hessen,
Schloss) organ, now in Denmark, has been most carefully preserved in its original condition including
the entire wind system. It is at present a completely
functional instrument. Its pressure is most reliably
given as 55 to 65 millimeters of water[82]

2. The wind pressure of the Grueningen, Schloss
organ, Praetorius' own performing instrument, was
measured in 1704-05 by Andreas Werckmeister, who was
officially in charge of the renovation which took
place at that time. Werckmeister measured the pressure just before the renovation and recorded it in his
official report as having been 28 degrees[83]

The pressure of the Grueningen, Schloss organ as
handed down by Werckmeister is meaningless, unless it is

possible to establish the instrument he used for measurement,

its calibration, and the method used for reading the pressure

from the scale. Werckmeister says:

Der Wind aber / war nach
der allgemeinen Wind-Probe
(da 6. Zoll in 60. Grad getheilet werden) vorher 28.
Grad: Jetzo aber steiget er
36. Grad, welches der ge-
woehnliche Wind anderer guten Wercke zu seyn pfleget.
Jedoch hat der seel. Foerner
seinen Orgel-Wercken mehrentheils 45. bisz 46. Grad gegeben / welchen Wind denn
auch mein unterhandenes
Werck zu St. Martini auch
hat / weszwegen es auch
sehr scharff klinget.84

The wind, however, according to the common windgauge
(where 6 inches are divided
into 60 degrees), was, formerly, 28 degrees. Now it rises
to 36 degrees, which is the
usual pressure of other worthwhile instruments. However,
the sainted Foerner most often used to give his instruments [a pressure of] 45 to
46 degrees; this is, likewise,
the pressure of my instrument
at St. Martini, for which reason it sounds very aggressive.
[Translation by the present
author]

Three facts from this report set up a situation which

will make it possible, by careful research, to interpret the

recorded wind pressure in modern terms. These facts are:

1. The inventor of the windgauge was Christian

Foerner

2. The recorded pressure was 28 degrees

3. The gauge was calibrated, so that 6 inches

were equal to 60 degrees (or, 1 degree was equal to

1/10 inch)

The Foerner Windprobe

A very careful study of the Foerner windgauge must be

undertaken if, by means of it, an intelligible value for the actual wind pressure of the Grueningen, Schloss organ is to be realized. J. G. Walther gives the basic facts concerning Foerner and his activity in connection with the windgauge. He says:

> Foerner (Christian), the son of a burgomaster and carpenter, was born in Wettin, learned the art of organ building . . . from his brother-in-law Johann Wilhelm Stegmann, an organ builder . . . . He understood very thoroughly the physical properties of fire and water. Among other things he invented the useful instrument known as the Windprobe or windgauge . . . . In 1677 he was still alive, 67 years of age, and unmarried.[85]

Werckmeister, who used the windgauge in measuring the pressure of the Grueningen organ, describes the instrument quite carefully:

Nach dem auch von der Wind-Probe . . . etlichemahl ist erwehnt worden / und viele nicht wissen / was es vor ein Instrument sey / so habe ich eine kurtze Beschreibung davon abstatten wollen:

Erstlich wird ein Kaestlein von Metalle gemachet / etwa 2. oder 3. Zoll lang / und halb so breit und tieff / hier werde ein Canal auffgesetzet / etwa in dem diameter eines halben Zolles / jedoch gekroepffet / dasz man es anstecken kann / hierneben werde ein ander kurtz Canaelchen gesetzet / worauff man eine glaeserne Roehre / so auch in dem Diametro einen halben Zoll haelt / stecken kann: Darnach wird ein Maaszstaebichen 6. Zoll

Inasmuch as the Windprobe . . . has been mentioned several times, and many do not know what kind of instrument it is, I have decided to render a brief description of it.

First, a small canister of metal is constructed about two or three inches long and half of that in width and depth. On it is mounted a mitered tube about one-half inch in diameter, so that a connection can be made [with the wind conductor]. Thereupon, another little tube is mounted, into which a glass tube, likewise, one-half inch in diameter, can be set. Then a rule, six inches or a quarter of an Ell long, is divided into sixty parts or degrees; this

oder 1/4 Ellen lang in 60.
Theile oder Grad getheilet /
selbiges kann nun an das
Glaeserne Canal gesetztet
werden / wenn nun der Wind
hinein gelassen wird / so
kann man sehen / wie hoch
der Wind treibet.[86]

can be set up against the glass
tube. Now, when the wind is
admitted [into the canister],
it can be observed how high
the wind will drive [the wa-
ter]. [Translation by the
present author]

Werckmeister's description establishes certain facts
about the Foerner Windprobe. One of the most significant is
that it was in reality a single-column open manometer in contrast to the double-column open manometer generally, if not
exclusively, used today. The calibration was in degrees, each
degree representing one-tenth of an inch. The unit of measure
(kind of inch) is not yet revealed. The pressure was undoubtedly read from the scale-rule as the displacement of the meniscus from the zero-point. The recession of the water surface in the opposite column occurred inside the canister and
could not be seen nor taken into consideration without complicated volumetric calculations.

Adlung delivers a very fine and detailed description
of the gauge in quantitative terms which is sufficient in all
respects to serve as the basis for the construction of a model of the Foerner Windprobe. He supplies also the all-
important unit of measure for the calibration of the scale-
rule and reveals the method of determining the pressure directly from it:

Wir haben eine Windwage,
welche § 240 ihrer Einrich-

We have a windgauge whose
arrangement will become more

tung nach besser bekannt werden soll; dieselbige wird mit Wasser gefuellet, und an den Canal gehaenget, wo eben hierzu eine gebohrete Oeffnung zu finden ist. Eine glaeserne Roehre, welche auf der Windwage befestiget ist, wird das Steigen und Fallen des Windes, dessen Gleichheit oder Ungleichheit, kurz, alle Veraenderungen uns sehen lassen. Wenn man ein Staebgen etwa 6 Zoll lang abtheilt, erst in seine 6 rheinlaendische Zolle, hernach jeden Zoll in 10 gleiche Theile; so nennen die Orgelmacher solche Theile Grade, da denn bey einigen Orgeln kaum 25 Grade des Windes zu finden, wenn man das Staebchen neben die Roehre haelt, und acht hat, wie hoch das Wasser steigt.[87]

evident in paragraph 240. The same is filled with water and attached to the canal where, for this purpose, a perforation is to be found. A glass tube, which is mounted on the windgauge, will permit us to observe the rise and fall, the steadiness and unsteadiness, in short, all the variations of the wind. If a rule, about six inches long is divided into its six Rhenish inches and, thereupon, each inch into ten equal parts, each such part will be designated as one degree by the organ builders. In some instruments hardly twenty-five degrees are reached when the rule is placed next to the glass tube and the rise of the water is observed. [Translation by the present author]

The foregoing account establishes the unit of measure as the Rhenish inch, a critical fact if the windgauge described represents the Foerner Windprobe. The pressure was read directly from the water level in the glass tube as surmised, and represented the displacement of the meniscus from the zero-point and ignored the concomitant recession in the opposite column. Every degree of displacement represented one-tenth of a Rhenish inch.

Adlung's reference to paragraph 240 finally reveals that his discussion concerns itself with the Foerner Windprobe and gives the necessary quantitative measurements required to reproduce a model of it:

Von der Windwage . . . .
Ihr Erfinder ist Christian
Foerner aus Wettin, ein Orgelmacher . . . . Ihre aeus-
serliche Einrichtung ist
hier zu Lande diese, wie die
23te Figur einigermassen vor-
stellt, dasz ein rund Kaestgen von Metall, etwa 4 bis 5
Zoll im Durchschnitte, und
etwa anderthalb Zoll hoch,
auf der Oberflaeche 3 Oeff-
nungen habe.

Die eine zeigt sich mit
einem aufgesetzten cylind-
rischen offenen Roehrgen,
einen halben oder ganzen
Zoll hoch, nahe am Rande,
darein wird das Glasroehrgen
(f, k) gesetzt, so, dasz weder Luft noch Wasser zwi-
schen solchem durchkommen
koenne, wenn der Wind das
Wasser in solches hebt, und
welches zu verwahren ist mit
Wachs, Linnen, oder weichem
Papiere . . . .

Durch die zwote Oeffnung
(g) wird durch Aufsetzung
eines kleinen Trichters das
Wasser in das Kaestgen gebracht, bis es ganz voll,
welche nachdem mit einem
Stoepsel wohl zu verwahren,
dasz bei der Probe nichts
verschuettet werde.

Ueber der 3ten Oeffnung
sitzt eine senkrechte Roehre
(h, 1), mit welcher eine ho-
rizontale Roehre (i, h) einen geraden Winkel macht;
wir wollen sie beyde zusammen den Hahn nennen. An
meiner Windwage ist die erste 1 Zoll hoch, und haelt
im Durchmesser 3 viertel
Zoll; die andere ist eben so
weit, wo sie mit der ersten

Concerning the windgauge
. . . . its inventor is Christian Foerner of Wettin, an organ builder . . . . In our part
of the country its external
disposition is similar to that
shown in Figure 23. [See Plate
LXXXIV, figs. 1, 2, and 3]. A
round canister of metal, a-
bout four or five inches in diameter and about one and one-
half inches high, has three
openings on top.

The first opening, near the
edge, is fitted with an open
cylindrical tube which extends
an inch or one-half inch upward; into this is fitted a
glass tube ($\underline{f}$, $\underline{k}$), so that neither air nor water can escape
when the wind pushes the water
up in the tube; this joint
should be packed with wax, lin-
en, or soft paper . . . .

By mounting a small funnel
over the second opening ($\underline{g}$),
water can be poured into the
canister until it is filled;
thereupon, it must be sealed
with a stopper, so that nothing will be spilled during the
test.

Into the third opening is
fitted a vertical tube ($\underline{h}$, $\underline{1}$),
to which is attached a hori-
zontal tube ($\underline{i}$, $\underline{h}$), in order
to make a right angle; the two
pieces together could be called
a cock. In my own gauge, the
first member is one inch high
and three-fourths inch in diameter; the other member is of
the same cross section where
it is joined to the first one,

zusammen gekroepft ist; aber das Ende musz etwas enger seyn, dasz das Instrument besser in der Oeffnung des Canals sich befestigen lasse, und keine Luft zwischen demselben durchkommen koenne . . . . Solche Beschreibung steht in Werkmeisters Orgelprobe, wenigstens betrifft der Unterschied das Wesen des Instruments nicht.[88]

but the opposite end must be somewhat narrower, so that the instrument can be more securely fitted into the canal, and any escape of the wind avoided . . . . Such a description appears in Werckmeister's Orgelprobe; any differences will not materially affect the function of the instrument. [Translation by the present author]

From these quantitative descriptions, the present author had a model of the Foerner Windprobe constructed in brass, in order to investigate what effect the single-column manometer would have on the reading of the pressure in comparison to the common double-column manometer used today. Adlung's dimensions were converted to metric equivalents according to the table of Rhenish measure presented in Appendix Q, 1, and the windgauge was constructed according to plan and elevation drawings given on Plate LXXXV, figs. 1 and 2.

Interpretation of Recorded Pressures

The rather detailed discussion and development of the Foerner Windprobe, its construction, disposition, calibration, and method of reading the wind pressure, plus the actual reproduction of a model was undertaken because it soon became obvious to the writer while pursuing a study of wind pressures in an academic way, that pressure should register different values on the modern, double-column, open, and S-tube form of windgauge than on the single-column Foerner Windprobe.

Invented by Foerner[89] in 1667, the gauge seems to have enjoyed an increasingly widespread use until some time between
Dom Bedos (ca. 1766) and Toepfer (ca. 1833). Toepfer was
concerned about the general disregard of the recession of the
water table from the zero-point and proposed modifications
which resulted in a double-column manometer exhibiting equal
cross-sectional areas and visible zero-points in both primary
and secondary columns. See Plate XVII, fig. 2. The registered value was to be read off as the linear distance between
the depressed water table in the primary tube and the elevated water table in the secondary tube, in precisely the
manner that wind pressures in organs are evaluated and recorded today.

Accordingly, all recorded pressures between the time
of Foerner's invention and Toepfer's modification of the same
may not be considered equivalent to pressures registered by
modern windgauges as is so often, if not generally, assumed
today. The values registered by single-column and double-
column manometers are related to each other by rule of thumb
in the ratio of 1 to 2, thus: $S / D = 1 / 2$, where $\underline{S}$ represents the registered value of a single-column, and $\underline{D}$, that
of a double-column manometer. Actually, the Foerner Windprobe registers the pressure at slightly less than half the
value registered by a double-column manometer because the
initial zero-point is disturbed by the proportionately larger
area of the water table in the primary portion of the system.

This phenomenon was observed by the writer when measuring a given pressure with both types of gauges simultaneously.

Pending further and more exhaustive investigations, the writer proposes that organ wind pressures recorded between 1667 and, say, about 1800, in degree units derived from single-column manometers be re-evaluated by at least doubling the value in order to arrive at a reasonably, faithful modern equivalent registered on a double-column manometer.

Accordingly, the pressure of the Grueningen, Schloss organ as measured by Werckmeister at the time of the renovation in 1704 registered 73 mm. on the Foerner Windprobe.[90] This value is equivalent to 2.88 inches British measure. On a double-column manometer this pressure would register at 146 mm. or 5.76 British inches.

Conclusions

From the discussion of the entire pneumatic disposition of the early baroque organ, including the capture, compression, distribution, disturbance, and application of the wind, a few summarizing statements can be extracted to contribute to the theory of the Praetorius organ. These are:

1. The non-ribbed species of bellows were known by the early baroque builders in surviving examples of the time, but do not seem to have been constructed by them for new instruments

2. Of the ribbed species, the multiple-fold type

was in very common use and represents the norm for the time

3. The single-fold type began to appear in a few instances and was hailed as a novelty and as an improvement over the multiple-fold type

4. The bellows were equipped with automatic internal valves to control intake and exhaust

5. The operation of the bellows was indirect, being effected by inert weights which were set into potential force by cocking the bellows

6. In such a system, each bellows had to be capable of delivering the full pressure and quantity of wind required by the instrument while the bellows passed through the second phase of its cycle

7. The system could operate with any number of bellows save one, provided they supplied a sufficient volume of wind to allow the operator ample time to cock the units one after another

8. An arrangement of levers made it possible to cock the bellows by foot. Hand cocking was used for small table organs and Portatives

9. Generally, the compressed air was delivered by the bellows through appropriate throats into a common canal which, in turn, fed it into the general wind trunk; conductors, attached to the wind trunk at convenient points, distributed the wind to the various

pallet boxes

10. There seems to have been no intermediate compartment for storing, equalizing, or redistributing the compressed wind; the bellows communicated quite directly with the pallet boxes

11. Check ventils were introduced, at times, into the wind trunk, but more generally into the divisional conductors

12. They helped to conserve the wind, provided a method for cancelling a malfunction, and offered some opportunity for making collective changes in registration by pneumatic means

13. The tremulant was a much-beloved pneumatic appliance, and appeared often in two forms as (a) tremulant and (b) Bocktremulant

14. The effect of the open tremulant was particularly cultivated in connection with reed pipes and regals, and occurred generally in the Rueckpositive where reeds were often disposed

15. Certain pneumatic appliances were generously introduced into the instruments of the time; among these the Zimbelstern and Vogelgesang were often used, while the Trommel, the Kuckuck, the Huemmelchen, and the Sackpfeife occur more rarely

16. The wind pressures for some of the organs of the time were measured by organists and technicians

after 1667, the date of the appearance of the Foerner
Windprobe

17. Reliably recorded pressures are available
for two pertinent instruments, and show a range of
from about 60 to 75 mm. of water as registered on a
single-column manometer

18. It is probable, but not yet firmly established, that these pressures ought be evaluated at
twice their face value in order to arrive at an equivalent value as registered by a modern double-column
manometer

19. The difficulty of capturing air, compressing
it, and supplying it to the instrument placed strong
limitations upon the early baroque builders. It helps
to explain the frequently meager tonal resources provided for the Pedal, and probably encouraged the practice of trying to achieve a respectable pedal corpus
through permanent coupling and transmission, where
much could be gained without impoverishing the wind
supply too greatly

NOTES AND REFERENCES

PART II

Chapter VIII: Notes and References

1 H. Klotz, Das Buch von der Orgel (5th ed.; Kassel, 1955), p. 17.

2 T. Schneider, "Die Orgelbauerfamilie Compenius," Archiv fuer Musikforschung, II (1937), 9 points out that this organ builder was Timotheus Compenius from Oberfranken.

3 W. Haacke, Die Entwicklungsgeschichte des Orgelbaus im Lande Mecklenburg-Schwerin (Wolfenbuettel-Berlin, 1935), pp. 24-25 established this organ builder as Fabian Petersen from the town of Sneek in the Netherlands province of Ostfriesland.

4 M. Praetorius, Syntagmatis Musici Tomus Secundus De Organographia . . . (Wolfenbuettel, 1619; facs. ed. by W. Gurlitt, Kassel, 1929), pp. 107-09.

5 A. Werckmeister, Erweiterte und verbesserte Orgelprobe (Quedlinburg, 1698; facs. ed. Kassel, 1927), pp. 39-40.

6 J. Adlung, Musica mechanica organoedi (edited and published posthumously by J. L. Albrecht, Berlin, 1768; facs. ed. by C. Mahrenholz, Kassel, 1931), I, 34.

7 Praetorius, De Organographia . . ., pp. 161-195, 197-203, 233-234. For the sake of convenient reference, the complete set of dispositions presented on these pages will hereinafter be referred to as "catalog of dispositions."

8 W. Stahl, Musikgeschichte Luebecks (Kassel, 1952), II, 35-36.

9 Stahl, Musikgeschichte . . ., II, 36.

10 Praetorius, De Organographia . . ., pp. 164-65.

11 Master Johannes Gottschalk and his son, Gottschalk Johannsen called Burchard (Borchert) from Husum. The younger man should be considered the real builder. See Stahl, Musikgeschichte . . ., II, 35.

12 Coppel zum Oberwerck vnnd Rueckpositiff may be read as "Coupler between Oberwerk and Rueckpositive," and interpreted as "Rueckpositive-to-Oberwerk." Likewise, Coppel zum Pedal vnd Rueckpositiff may be interpreted as a coupler between the respective divisions, and interpreted as "Rueckpositive to Pedal."

Chapter VIII: Notes and References--Continued

13 P. Smets, Die Dresdener Handschrift Orgeldispositionen
   (Kassel, 1931), p. 47 has Superoctava 2', while Stahl,
   Musikgeschichte . . ., p. 36 has Superoktav 4' (2?).

14 Smets, Dresdener . . ., p. 47 has Rausch Quinta 3'; Stahl,
   Musikgeschichte . . ., p. 36 has Rauschpfeife (2 fach);
   Adlung, Musica . . ., I, 133 surmises that Praetorius
   means Rauschquinta over 4', hence 2 2/3' and 2'; J. Adlung,
   Anleitung zu der musikalischen Gelahrtheit (Erfurt, 1758;
   facs. ed. by Moser, Kassel, 1953), p. 453 surmises it might
   be of three ranks, the largest being 4'.

15 Stahl, Musikgeschichte . . ., p. 36 has Groszoktav 4'
   (8'?); Smets, Dresdener . . ., p. 47 has Grosz Octava 8'.

16 Beginning at F, this register was approximately of 24'
   length at this note. Stahl, Musikgeschichte . . ., p. 36
   has Bordun 24' (von F an); Smets, Dresdener . . ., p. 47
   has Bordun 16'; Adlung, Musica . . ., I, 77 considers the
   foot designation (24') a typographical error. In modern
   practice it would be labelled as 32'.

17 Smets, Dresdener . . ., p. 47 has Cymbel scharff 3 fach.

18 Smets, Dresdener . . ., p. 47 has Scharff Regal 8'.

19 Smets, Dresdener . . ., p. 47 has Harffen Regal 4'.

20 Stahl, Musikgeschichte . . ., p. 36 has Geigen Regal (4');
   Smets, Dresdener . . ., p. 47 has Viola Regal 4'.

21 Smets, Dresdener . . ., p. 47 has Sifflet 1'; Stahl, Musikgeschichte . . ., p. 36 has Siffloete (2').

22 Stahl, Musikgeschichte . . ., p. 36 has Klein Quintadena
   (4'); Smets, Dresdener . . ., has Quintadena 4'.

23 Smets, Dresdener . . ., p. 47 has Sedecima 2'; Stahl,
   Musikgeschichte . . ., p. 36 has Sedecima (1'); Mahrenholz,
   Orgelregister . . ., points out that the term Sedecima was
   generally used for the Octave 2', very seldom for Octave
   4', occasionally for Octave 1'. The term sedecima (16th)
   is, likely, a confusion for the more accurate term quinta
   decima (15th).

24 Smets, Dresdener . . ., has Quintadena 16'.

25 Stahl, Musikgeschichte . . ., p. 36 has Gemshorn (8'); Smets, Dresdener . . ., p. 47 has Gemszhorn 8'.

26 Smets, Dresdener . . ., p. 47 has Krumbhorn 4'; Stahl, Musikgeschichte . . ., p. 36 has Krummhorn (8').

27 Stahl, Musikgeschichte . . ., p. 36 has Querpipe 8' or 4'; Smets, Dresdener . . ., p. 47 has Traversa 4'.

28 Smets, Dresdener . . ., p. 47 has Queer Floethe 2'; Stahl, Musikgeschichte . . ., p. 36 has Feldpipe (2').

29 Smets, Dresdener . . ., p. 47 has Superoctava 2'; Stahl, Musikgeschichte . . ., p. 36 has Superoktav (2').

30 Stahl, Musikgeschichte . . ., p. 36 has Baerpipe (4'); Smets, Dresdener . . ., p. 47 has Clarinen 4'.

31 Smets, Dresdener . . ., p. 47 has Cymbeln 3.fach.

32 Smets, Dresdener . . ., p. 47 has Mixtur 5.fach.

33 Smets, Dresdener . . ., p. 47 has Octava 8, Superoctava 4'. The term Decem is very likely a corruption of decima quinta, i.e., the 15th or the 4' when reckoning from a 16' basis, or the 8' when reckoning from a 32' basis. It is highly improbable that a 10th or third-sounding voice is meant, since the Tierce, during this time and according to accumulated evidence, seems to occur only in the extremely acute pitches of the Klingend Zimbel. Mahrenholz, Orgelregister . . ., p. 45 points out that the name Decima was very generally used to designate the Octave 4', seldom 8' or 2'. Accordingly, the two voices may be rendered as Octave 8', and Super Octave 4'.

34 Smets, Dresdener . . ., p. 47 has Grosz Mixtur aus 8'; this designation would indicate that the lowest choir of the Mixture began at 8' pitch, or possibly at 5 1/3'; it has thus far been impossible to establish the number of choirs in this voice.

35 Smets, Dresdener . . ., p. 47 has Dulcian 16'.

36 Smets, Dresdener . . ., p. 47 has Schallmey 4'.

37 The arrangement of the voices adheres to modern practice; the numbering follows Praetorius for the sake of accurate cross reference.

38 Praetorius, De Organographia . . ., p. 178-79.

39 H. Klotz in personal interview at Cologne, May 9, 1956
gave the builder's name as Henning Henke. E. Palandt in
J. Biermann, Organographia Hildesiensis Specialis (Hildesheim, 1738; facs. by E. Palandt, Kassel, 1930), p. 19 of
the "Nachwort", establishes Henning Henke as the builder.

40 Smets, Dresdener . . ., p. 48 has Octava 4'; inasmuch as
the Principal 16' is accompanied by a Principal 8', it is
strongly suggested that Praetorius may be in error here,
and that an Octave 4' is meant.

41 In the early organs the 3' designation served to identify
the quint over the Octave 4', hence, more accurately,
2 2/3'.

42 Smets, Dresdener . . ., has Octava 4'. Inasmuch as both
Praetorius and Smets indicate a 4' pitch level for this
voice, it possibly was 4', and the 2' designation must be
taken as a strong surmise of the present author. H. Klotz
in personal interview at Cologne, May 9, 1956, considers
this voice to have been at 2' pitch.

43 Smets, Dresdener . . ., p. 48 has "Zinck, durchs halbe
Clavier." Adlung, Anleitung . . ., p. 481 footnote x
gives convincing evidence for the voice to have been at
8' pitch. H. Klotz in personal interview at Cologne,
May 9, 1956, surmises that h (i.e., b-natural directly below middle-c) is meant here rather than h' (i.e., b♮ ').

44 Smets, Dresdener . . ., p. 48 has Rausch Pfeiffen 3.fach.

45 Adlung, Musica . . ., I, 152 says, "Trummel . . . is also
called Tamburo or Tambour . . . . In the organ, builders
have tried to represent it by two pipes in the range of
the Subbass. I don't think much of it. These two pipes
sound the tones C and G . . . . That the term 'Trommel'
is identical to 'Tympanum' I have observed from Praetorius'
disposition of the organ at Braunschweig, where the 'Trommel' is of '2 Pfeifen stark'."

46 The arrangement of the voices adheres to modern practice;
the numbering follows Praetorius for the sake of accurate
cross reference.

47 Inasmuch as the St. Gotthard organ in Hildesheim was built by the same builder between 1612-17, the Braunschweig organ may be reckoned as having been built in the same decade or, possibly, the preceding.

48 Praetorius, De Organographia . . ., p. 108: ". . . however, with the slider chest it is possible to elicit a greater and more wonderful variety of voices by means of borrowed basses, grooved channels, and the like, than can be accomplished with the spring chest."

49 Praetorius, De Organographia . . ., p. 170-71.

50 Praetorius, De Organographia . . ., p. 198-99.

51 Practically all modern methods of coupling in the organ use transient couplers.

52 The concept and application of permanent coupling is almost totally non-existent today.

53 The specific instruments as listed in Praetorius, De Organographia . . . are: Luebeck, St. Peter (pp. 164-65); Bernau (pp. 176-77); Braunschweig, St. Blasius (pp. 178-79); Leipzig, St. Nicholas (pp. 179-80); Leipzig, St. Thomas (p. 180); Torgau (pp. 180-81); Bueckeburg (pp. 185-86); Dresden, Schlosz (pp. 186-88); Grueningen, Schlosz (pp. 188-89); Hessen, Schlosz (p. 189); Schoeningen, Schlosz (pp. 189-90); Model Disposition 1 (p. 191); Model Disposition 2 (pp. 191-92); Model Disposition 3 (p. 192); Barait (pp. 200-02); Model Disposition VI (p. 202); Lueneburg, St. Lambrecht (pp. 233-34).

54 See chapter ix.

55 This is the original Hessen, Schlosz instrument of Esaias Compenius built between 1605-1610, erected in the Hessen Schlosz in 1612, and moved to Denmark and re-erected in 1617. Presently it stands in the Frederiksborg Castle near Hillerød, Denmark. M. Praetorius was personally deeply involved in the design and preparation of this instrument according to the best sources. See T. Schneider, "Die Orgelbauerfamilie . . .," pp. 22-25.

56 Adlung, Musica . . ., I, 21-22.

57 G.: Kloetzchenkoppel.

Chapter VIII: Notes and References--Continued

58 G.: Gabelkoppel.

59 By the "active keyboard" is understood that keyboard which
   is to be played after the coupling is in effect.

60 By the "idle keyboard" is understood that keyboard upon
   which the playing does not take place after the coupling
   is in effect.

61 G.: Wippenkoppel.

62 This assemblage constitutes a form of "blind clavier."

63 E. Flade, Gottfried Silbermann (Leipzig, 1953), pp. 169-
   70.

64 U. Daehnert, Der Orgel und Instrumentenbauer Zacharias
   Hildebrandt (Leipzig, 1960), Plates 24-25.

65 The first class lever is a basic mechanical disposition of
   levers where the applied force and the work or weight are
   positioned at the extremes of the lever, while the fulcrum
   occurs between the extremes.

66 Dom Bedos, L'Art du Facteur d'Orgues (1766-1778; facs. ed.
   by C. Mahrenholz, Kassel, 1934), Plates XXXIII, XXXIX, XL,
   XLI, XLII, XLIII, LII, LVIII, LIX, LXXX, LXXXI, LXXXII,
   LXXXIV, LXXXV.

67 The specific cases as listed in Praetorius, De Organographia . . . are: Luebeck, Liebfrauen (pp. 165-66);
   Cassel, Freiheit (pp. 183-84); Cassel, Brueder (p. 184);
   Cassel, Schlosz (pp. 184-85); Model Disposition 6 (pp. 193-
   94); Model Disposition 7 (pp. 194-95).

68 Praetorius, De Organographia . . ., p. 164.

69 Praetorius, De Organographia . . ., p. 181.

70 Praetorius, De Organographia . . ., pp. 176, 179, 186,
   188, 189, 190, 191, 192, 201, 202, and 234.

71 Praetorius, De Organographia . . ., p. 180.

72 Praetorius, De Organographia . . ., p. 185.

73 Praetorius, De Organographia . . ., pp. 185-86.

74 Praetorius, De Organographia . . ., pp. 163-64.

75 Praetorius, De Organographia . . ., pp. 185-86.

76 In view of the previous discussion, the coupling effect
   may be understood as "Brust-to-Oberwerk."

77 The disposition of the Mixture indicates, most likely, 8
   ranks in the bass, 10 in the tenor, 12 in the alto, and
   14 in the soprano or discant portion of the compass.

78 The archaic expression, "anderthalb" (literally, "the second half-designation"), may be understood as 1 1/2.

79 Since the term, "Nasat", never appears elsewhere as an appellation for a unison-sounding rank, the present author
   suspects a typographical error for 3' (2 2/3'). Smets,
   Dresdener . . ., p. 46 indicates "Nasat Octava 4 Fusz."

80 The arrangement of the voices adheres to modern practice;
   the numbering follows Praetorius for the sake of accurate
   cross reference.

81 See Schneider, "Die Orgelbauerfamilie . . .," p. 34 for
   exact definition of the locale.

82 One can surmise that the inconvenience here alluded to is
   a necessary by-product of the condition set up by two
   pneumatically independent pallet boxes communicating with
   a common key channel. Should, for example, the secondary
   (pedal) pallet box be exhausted and a pedal pallet opened
   by a given pedal key while the corresponding note is also
   played upon the manual keyboard, the inflation of the
   channel from the primary pallet box would be dissipated
   through the open pedal pallet into the exhausted secondary
   pallet box and the note would be unable to speak at all
   or, at best, only partially.

83 Adlung, Musica . . ., pp. 79-80.

84 J. J. Seidel, Die Orgel und ihr Bau (Breslau 1843; reprint
   by F. Knuf, Amsterdam, 1962), Table 4, fig. 11.

85 Since the manual chests were usually divided between C and
   C# sides, a chest so equipped would exhibit two bass portions.

86 See, for example, Dom Bedos, L'Art . . ., Plate XLVI, fig. 6, or Plate LII.

87 More particularly, the necessity of keeping the pedal keys at rest while drawing the coupler.

88 Praetorius, De Organographia . . ., pp. 164, 186, and 201.

89 Praetorius, De Organographia . . ., pp. 176, 180, 191, 192, and 234.

90 Praetorius, De Organographia . . ., pp. 179 and 200.

91 Praetorius, De Organographia . . ., pp. 165 and 181.

92 Praetorius, De Organographia . . ., pp. 183, 184, 194, and 195.

93 Praetorius, De Organographia . . ., p. 165.

94 Praetorius, De Organographia . . ., p. 165-66. The account of the Liebfrauen organ at Luebeck is perhaps the most confused one of Praetorius. However, he does record the following statements among the pedal registers: "Ventile zu allen Roehren Baessen oben in der Orgel; Ventile zu allen Pfeiffen vnd Baessen im Stuel; Ventile zum Bassunen- vnd Trommeten B. im Stuele."

Chapter IX: Notes and References

1 Praetorius' catalog of dispositions comprises the following pages of M. Praetorius, Syntagmatis Musici Tomus Secundus De Organographia . . . (Wolfenbuettel, 1619; facs.
ed. by W. Gurlitt, Kassel, 1929), pp. 161-95; 197-203;
233-34. Hereinafter the term Praetorius' catalog or Praetorius' catalog of dispositions refers to these pages collectively.

2 Such as Werkmeister, Adlung, Dom Bedos, Toepfer, Hopkins,
Audsley, et al.

3 The only existing, almost entirely unchanged, and authentic instrument of the Early Baroque stands under govern-
mental protection in Frederiksborg Schlosz in Hillerød,
Denmark. It was planned and built by Compenius and Praetorius in 1612 for the Hessen Schlosz, and removed to
Denmark in 1617.

4 The terms are customarily not translated but are generally taken over into English in original form.

5 Bo: Brust oben; literally: Brust, above.

6 Bu: Brust unten; literally: Brust, below.

7 Literally: Pedal, Pedal basses, Pedal on both sides, or
Pedal in the towers.

8 The term straight is here used in its modern sense to designate an instrument in which each chest and its complement of voices is controlled by a separate keyboard, native
to that chest; there is no communication between the voices
of one chest and an "alien" keyboard except through the
transient couplers; there are no "borrows" or "duplexes"
of any kind.

9 Thus in modern keyboard dispositions; in the Early Baroque
the short octave appeared frequently in the Pedal as, C,
F, D, G, E, A, B♭, B, etc.; in such cases the one side
would, most likely, exhibit C, D, E, and B♭ and the other
side F, G, A, and B in the Great Octave.

10 Praetorius, De Organographia . . ., pp. 178-79. See also
chapter viii of the present study for a full presentation
of the instrument.

11 Praetorius, De Organographia . . ., p. 179.

Chapter IX: Notes and References--Continued

12 Praetorius, De Organographia . . ., p. 189.

13 Praetorius, De Organographia . . ., p. 198.

14 For detailed information concerning this historic and famous instrument, see T. Schneider, "Die Orgelbauerfamilie
Compenius," Archiv fuer Musikforschung, II (1937), 22-34;
J. Woersching, Die Compenius-Orgel auf Schlosz Frederiksborg (Kopenhagen) (Mainz, 1946); A. Hammerich, "Eine historische Orgel auf Frederiksborg Schlosz bei Kopenhagen,"
Bulletin de la Société Union Musicologique II (1922),
65-78.

15 Esaias Compenius I was born ca. 1560, was appointed as
Princely Organ and Instrument Maker in Braunschweig in
1605, and died while in Denmark in 1617. Michael Praetorius (Latin for Schulteis) was born ca. 1571, was appointed Princely Kapellmeister in Braunschweig in 1603
(having been a member of the musical entourage of Heinrich
Julius since 1589), and died in 1621. Cf. W. Gurlitt,
Michael Praetorius Creuzburgensis, sein Leben und seine
Werke (Leipzig, 1915) for a detailed account of Praetorius'
ancestry and formative years of his life.

16 According to Schneider, "Orgelbauerfamilie" . . ., p. 24,
the Hessen Schlosz should not be confused with a castle
in Kassel, but lay in Braunschweig and served for a time
as the princely seat of the Braunschweiger dukes; she further maintains that, according to an inscription within
the instrument, the organ was built in 1610, not 1612 as
Praetorius indicates. The present author is inclined to
the view that the organ was in the process of construction
when the inscription was attached, and that Praetorius'
date probably indicates the date of completion or erection
in the castle.

17 According to Schneider, "Orgelbauerfamilie" . . ., p. 25,
the widow's name was Elizabeth, who passed away in 1623;
she was a daughter of Friedrich II of Denmark. Woersching,
Compenius-Orgel . . ., p. 6, points out that Heinrich
Julius died in 1613 and that his widow was also a sister-
in-law of James I of England.

18 Woersching, Compenius-Orgel . . ., pp. 6-7 provides the
following additional information concerning the instrument
while in Denmark: From 1617-1693 the organ stood in
Schlosz Frederiksborg; in 1693 King Christian V had the
organ moved into the Rittersaal of the Schlosz by Hans and

Chapter IX: Notes and References--Continued

Peter Pertersen-Botzen; in 1704 the bellows were repaired;
shortly before 1859 the instrument was again removed and
set up in the vicinity of Copenhagen; in 1859 the Frederiksborg Schlosz burned; in 1864 the organ was returned
to the Schloszkapelle of Frederiksborg and erected over
the altar in the Chapel of the Danebrog-Ritter; several
decades later a certain Meldahl drew renewed attention to
the instrument; in 1891 C. M. Philbert (French consul in
Helsingor) wrote a report in Le Monde musical (1891); in
1895 the instrument was restored and placed into working
order by the firm of Aristide Cavaillé-Coll of Paris under the supervision of a staff of experts.

19 Praetorius, De Organographia . . ., p. 189. The left column presents the disposition exactly as recorded by Praetorius; the right column provides a translation and a more
modern spelling of the terms.

20 The arrangement of the voices adheres to modern practice;
the numbering of the individual items follows Praetorius'
account for the sake of accurate reference.

21 Praetorius, De Organographia . . ., pp. 167-68.

22 Praetorius, De Organographia . . ., pp. 233-34.

23 Praetorius, De Organographia . . ., pp. 233-34. The left
column presents the disposition exactly as recorded by
Praetorius; the right column provides a translation and
a more modern spelling of the terms.

24 C. Mahrenholz, Die Orgelregister ihre Geschichte und ihr
Bau (2nd ed.; Kassel, 1942), p. 73, footnote 1, quotes the
Dresdener Manuscript as describing the Iula as "an open,
narrow-scaled, and keenly voiced register which, because
of its narrow scale is very delicate, but not penetrating
in character." He considers the voices Iula and Spitzfloete as neither identical nor similar.

25 The pitch designation 3' must be understood as 2 2/3' in
modern organ parlance.

26 The term halbiert is not entirely clear; it probably means
that only a portion of the compass was supplied with pipes
as, for example, the upper or discant half.

27 The pitch designation of 3' seems spurious; the present
writer is inclined to suspect an error here, and that the

designation probably was intended to be 4'. The term
Quintfloete may be understood to describe the "quinting"
character of the tone rather than the actual pitch level
of the voice. Please note that the division lacks a 4'
voice, while exhibiting two at 3' pitch.

28 H. Klotz in personal interview at Cologne on May 9, 1956
indicated that he suspects the designation of 1' to be an
error for 2/3'.

29 The term Sedetzen Quint signifies a pitch level lying a
fifth over the fifteenth, the term sedecima being a corruption of quinta decima.

30 The present author surmises the designation to indicate
one transient coupler for two adjacent keyboards; likely
as not, "Rueckpositive-to-Grosswerk."

31 In modern expression, "Rueckpositive-to-Pedal."

32 The arrangement of the voices exhibits customary modern
practice; the numbering of the individual items follows
Praetorius' account for the sake of accurate reference.
The pitch designations enclosed in brackets are beyond
proof; they represent either personal surmises, suggestions
adopted from concordances, or the considered opinions of
colleagues.

33 Cf. G. Fock, "Hamburgs Anteil am Orgelbau im niederdeutschen Kulturgebiet," Zeitschrift des Vereins fuer
Hamburgische Geschichte (1939), 325, footnote 96.

34 Praetorius, De Organographia . . ., pp. 169-70.

35 Specified thus by Praetorius.

36 The assignment of the keyboards to the specific chests is
by Praetorius.

37 Praetorius, De Organographia . . ., pp. 169-70. The left
column presents the organ exactly as recorded by Praetorius; the right column provides appropriate translations
of the text and a more modern spelling of the registers.

38 The instrument is in many respects similar to the preceding St. Jacob organ as recorded in Praetorius, De Organographia . . ., pp. 168-69.

Chapter IX: Notes and References--Continued

39 The Oberwerk for this instrument had a limited compass
downward; it seems to have been Great F; hence, a designation of 12' would, from a modern point of view, be considered as a 16' pitch; one of 6', as 8' pitch; one of
3', as 4' pitch, etc.

40 For some, as yet, inexplicable reason the Gedackt seems
to have had a compass that extended downward to Great C;
hence, the designation 8', must be left inviolate.

41 P. Smets, Die Dresdener Handschrift Orgeldispositionen
(Kassel, 1931), p. 59 has Rusz Pfeiffe 4', Scharff 3.fach,
Mixtur 6.fach, and Cymbeln 2.fach.

42 Smets, Dresdener . . ., p. 59 has Gemshorn 4'.

43 Smets, Dresdener . . ., p. 59 has Zinck 4'.

44 The indicated compass limit of E is either an error for
C or the limit is not reflected in the pitch designation
as previously.

45 Smets, Dresdener . . ., p. 59 has Sifflet 1', Scharff
3.fach, Mixtur 4.fach.

46 Smets, Dresdener . . ., p. 59 has Regal 4'.

47 A 24' length at a compass limit of F would presume a pitch
level of 32' for the voice according to a modern designation.

48 Smets, Dresdener . . ., p. 59 has Grosz Gemshorn 16',
Cymbel 3.fach, Mixtur 6.fach aus 4 Fusz.

49 The order of the registers has been rearranged to agree
with modern practice; the individual items follow the
numbering of Praetorius in order to facilitate accurate
reference.

50 See Fock, "Hamburgs Anteil" . . ., pp. 330-31.

51 See Praetorius, De Organographia . . ., pp. 168-69.

52 Praetorius, De Organographia . . ., pp. 185-86.

53 See chapter viii of the present study for a full presentation of the Bueckeburg instrument.

54 See Praetorius, De Organographia . . ., pp. 163, 174, 188, 173, and 194.

55 Praetorius, De Organographia . . ., pp. 162-63.

56 Praetorius, De Organographia . . ., pp. 162-63.

57 More accurately, Julius Antonius Friese. See G. Frotscher, Deutsche Orgeldispositionen aus fuenf Jahrhunderten (Wolfenbuettel, 1939), p. 14.

58 Frotscher, Orgeldispositionen . . ., p. 14 serves as the source for all pitch designations of the right column which are enclosed in brackets.

59 Frotscher, Orgeldispositionen . . ., p. 14 establishes the voice as Offenfloete 8'.

60 Frotscher, Orgeldispositionen . . ., p. 14 has Oktave 4'.

61 The designation Dunecken is unclear. Frotscher, Orgeldispositionen . . ., p. 14 substitutes the term Decima, which may be interpreted as Decima quinta.

62 Frotscher, Orgeldispositionen . . ., p. 14 has Gedackt 8'.

63 Frotscher, Orgeldispositionen . . ., p. 14 has Spillfloete 8'.

64 Frotscher, Orgeldispositionen . . ., p. 14 establishes the voice as Offenfloete 4'.

65 Incorrect archaic expression for Quinta decima.

66 The number of pipes given for the pedal voices seems inordinately great; an error for 23 pipes can be suspected.

67 Frotscher, Orgeldispositionen . . ., p. 14 establishes the voice as Oktave 8'.

68 The voices are arranged in the more familiar order used in the present day; the individual items follow Praetorius' numbering for the sake of accurate reference.

69 The most reliable source available for this instrument is Frotscher, Orgeldispositionen . . ., p. 14, who gathered his information from the Aufzeichnung vom Jahre 1611 im Staatsarchiv Danzig.

70 Praetorius, De Organographia . . ., pp. 181-82.

71 Praetorius, De Organographia . . ., pp. 181-82.

72 All of the missing designations have been derived from Smets, Dresdener . . ., p. 53, and entered in the right column in brackets.

73 Smets, Dresdener . . ., p. 53 has Nachthorn 4'. The present author strongly suspects a 2' pitch and has so indicated his suspicion.

74 The registers are arranged in typical modern form; the numbering of the items follows Praetorius for the sake of accurate reference.

75 A. Werckmeister, Organum Gruningense redivivum (Quedlinburg und Aschersleben, 1705; newprint by P. Smets, Mainz, 1932), p. 9.

76 Smets, Dresdener . . ., p. 133 and Werckmeister, Organum . . ., p. 7.

77 Praetorius, De Organographia . . ., pp. 162-63.

78 Praetorius, De Organographia . . ., pp. 168-69.

79 Praetorius, De Organographia . . ., pp. 174-75.

80 Item 11, Untersatz Basz may be considered as a pedal voice mounted in the cradle of the Oberwerk, or set down on the floor and tubed from the Oberwerk channels.

81 It is questionable if item 5, Coppel, was an actual voice or merely a coupler mechanism.

82 The five voices for the Pedal could very likely have been the Untersatz Basz of the Oberwerk, and the Posaun Basz, Regal Basz, Floeiten Basz, and Kleinen Schreyer of the Brustpositive.

83 Praetorius, De Organographia . . ., pp. 180-81.

84 Praetorius, De Organographia . . ., pp. 181-82.

85 Praetorius, De Organographia . . ., pp. 182-83.

86 Divided by Praetorius as In Pedal oben (8 voices) and In der Brust zum Pedal (3 voices).

87 Praetorius, De Organographia . . ., pp. 188-89. Praetorius was organist at this palace for a time.

88 Praetorius, De Organographia . . ., p. 191.

89 Praetorius, De Organographia . . ., pp. 191-92.

90 Praetorius, De Organographia . . ., p. 192.

91 Praetorius, De Organographia . . ., p. 197.

92 Item 10 Quintadehn Sub Bass may be considered as belonging exclusively to the Pedal but mounted in the Oberwerk cradle.

93 Praetorius specifies 7 voices for the Rueckpositive but records 8 voices.

94 The Quintadehn Sub Bass, listed in the Oberwerk, may be considered an additional pedal voice beside those listed under Pedal Baesse in den Thormen (Pedal basses in the towers).

95 Praetorius, De Organographia . . ., pp. 202-03.

96 The 4' designation for this voice is a surmise of the present author.

97 The order of the registers follows typical modern practice; the numbering agrees with Praetorius for the sake of accurate reference.

98 Praetorius, De Organographia . . ., pp. 163-64.

99 Praetorius, De Organographia . . ., pp. 164-65.

100 The pitch designations of Praetorius for the voices of the Oberwerk are obviously erratic. Smets, Dresdener . . ., p. 47 records the following pitches for the Oberwerk voices: Principal 16'; Bordun 16'; Spill-Floethen 8'; kleine Spill-Floethen 4'; Grosz Octava 8'; Octava 4'; Superoctava 2'; Gedackt 8'; Rausch Quinta 3'; Dulcian 16'; Trompone 16'; Cymbel scharff 3.fach; Mixtura.

Chapter IX: Notes and References--Continued

101 Praetorius, De Organographia . . ., pp. 166-67. The cathedral is referred to as the Thumbkirche.

102 Praetorius, De Organographia . . ., pp. 170-71.

103 Items 4, 6, 7, and 8 of the resources listed for the mittelste Clavir may be considered as independent pedal voices of which the Nachthorn Basz, Trommeten Basz, and Bauerfloeiten Basz were mounted in the cradle of the Werk.

104 He says in his introductory remarks that "the middle [clavier] which controls the main chest has a complete octave more than usual; namely, an additional octave below Great C, which is attached to the Pedal and used for this purpose."

105 Praetorius, De Organographia . . ., pp. 175-76.

106 Praetorius, De Organographia . . ., pp. 180-81.

107 Praetorius, De Organographia . . ., pp. 183-84.

108 Designated as a three-manual instrument in H. Klotz, Ueber die Orgelkunst der Gotik, der Renaissance, und des Barock (Kassel, 1934), p. 78.

109 The pitches of the pedal voices can be derived from Smets, Dresdener . . ., p. 54, where they are recorded as follows: Principal 32'; Octav Principal 16'; Untersatz 16'; Gedackt 8'; Rausch-Pfeiffe 3.fach; Posaunen 16'; Trompeta 8'; Cornet 2'.

110 Praetorius, De Organographia . . ., p. 184.

111 Praetorius' designation of a 3' pitch is probably an error for 2' pitch.

112 Praetorius, De Organographia . . ., pp. 184-85.

113 The pitches of the pedal voices can be derived from Smets, Dresdener . . ., p. 54, where they are recorded as follows: Untersatz 16'; Gedackt 8'; Gemszhorn 4'; Posaunen 16'; Trompeta 8'; Cornet 4'.

114 Praetorius, De Organographia . . ., p. 191.

115 Praetorius, De Organographia . . ., pp. 191-92. This disposition has more than passing interest. It served as the

model for the construction of a Praetorius organ for the
Musikwissenschaftliche Institut der Universitaet Freiburg
in Breisgau. Instigated by Prof. Dr. W. Gurlitt, the
project was undertaken by the Walcker firm of Ludwigsburg
under the leadership of Dr. h. c. Oskar Walcker and completed in 1921. On Dec. 4 of the same year, Dr. Karl
Straube dedicated the instrument. One additional voice
(a Dolcianbasz 8') was added to the Pedal, bringing the
resources up to 20 voices. The project created international interest and served as a strong motivation for
the organ movement in Germany.

116 Praetorius, De Organographia . . ., p. 192.

117 Praetorius, De Organographia . . ., pp. 202-03.

118 Praetorius, De Organographia . . ., pp. 193-94.

119 The present author suggests that the Untersatz von Holtz
should be considered a pedal voice. The Trommeten vff
8.fusz Thon could also have been a pedal voice mounted in
the Oberwerk, but the case cannot be proven.

120 Praetorius, De Organographia . . ., pp. 193-94.

121 An unusual Mixture designation by Praetorius; he is either
specifying the pitch of the bass choir of the Mixture as
2' or he intended to write von 2 Pfeiffen starck (II
ranks).

122 The Untersatz should be considered as a pedal voice mounted in the Oberwerk cradle or set on the floor and tubed
from the channels of the Oberwerk.

123 The present author suspects an error in pitch designation;
the general disposition of the corpus would suggest a 2'
pitch for this voice.

124 The index figure 2 may suggest either item 2, then one
coupler, or it may indicate two couplers.

125 As customary for this study, the registers are arranged
in conformity with modern practice, while the numbering
adheres to Praetorius in order to facilitate accurate
reference.

126 Praetorius, De Organographia . . ., pp. 188-89.

127 Praetorius, De Organographia . . ., p. 197.

128 Praetorius, De Organographia . . ., pp. 182-83.

129 Praetorius, De Organographia . . ., pp. 174-75.

Chapter X: Notes and References

1 C. Elis, Orgelwoerterbuch (3rd ed.; Mainz, 1949), p. 97.
Original in German, translation by the present author.

2 C. Mahrenholz, Die Orgelregister, ihre Geschichte und ihr
Bau (2nd ed.; Kassel, 1942), p. 275. Noteworthy omissions
in this account are the double channels and checkvalves.
Translation by the present author.

3 J. Adlung, Musica mechanica organoedi (edited and published
posthumously by J. L. Albrecht, Berlin, 1768; facs. ed. by
C. Mahrenholz, Kassel, 1931), I, 81-82. Translation by
the present author.

4 J. Adlung, Anleitung zu der musikalischen Gelahrtheit
(Erfurt, 1758; facs. ed. by H. Moser, Kassel, 1953),
p. 529. Translation by the present author.

5 A. Werckmeister, Erweiterte und verbesserte Orgelprobe
(Quedlinburg, 1698; facs. ed. Kassel, 1927), pp. 42-43.
Translation by the present author.

6 M. Praetorius, Syntagmatis Musici Tomus Secundus De Organographia . . . (Wolfenbuettel, 1619; facs. ed. by W. Gurlitt, Kassel, 1929), opposite p. 126. Translation by the
present author.

7 Praetorius, De Organographia . . ., p. 108.   Translation
by the present author.

8 Praetorius, De Organographia . . ., p. 80.

9 Praetorius, De Organographia . . ., p. 108.

10 Praetorius, De Organographia . . ., pp. 172-73.

11 Praetorius, De Organographia . . ., pp. 189-90.

12 Praetorius, De Organographia . . ., pp. 179-80.

13 Praetorius, De Organographia . . ., p. 180.

14 Praetorius, De Organographia . . ., pp. 194-95.

15 Praetorius, De Organographia . . ., pp. 200-02.

16 Since the terms Werk and Oberwerk are often used interchangeably in the older instruments, the subsequent

discussion will restrict itself to the term Oberwerk to identify these divisions in general.

17 Inasmuch as a second, or false, or auxiliary upper board will be required in the double mechanism, the term primary will serve to differentiate the regular or normal upper board from the auxiliary one.

18 It should be borne in mind that a normal chest will exhibit dead spaces only at the lowest extremes of the compass where the pipes require a greater chest space than do the channels; gradually the dead spaces diminish as the pipes become smaller and eventually disappear when the physical space needed for the pipes is equal to and less than the space required for the channel. Should the chest be e-quipped for transmission purposes, the pipes will need to be spaced farther apart than normally, so as to provide adequate room for the introduction of alternate pedal channels.

19 Praetorius, De Organographia . . ., pp. 192-93.

20 Praetorius, De Organographia . . ., pp. 192-93; the left column reproduces Praetorius' account, while the right column provides a direct translation and modern spellings for the registers by the present author.

21 The Untersatz was probably benched, i.e., set off the main chest on the floor and fed by tubes from appropriate pedal channels in the Werk chest, only a pedal slider being provided for it.

22 The intent of the specification is to provide divided sliders, so that the bass and discant portions of the voice can be separately registrated.

23 The arrangement of the voices follows modern practice; the numbering of the items follows Praetorius' account for the sake of accurate reference.

24 The code letters in parentheses identify the chests upon which the various voices are mounted.

25 Praetorius, De Organographia . . ., pp. 194-95; the left column quotes Praetorius, while the right column provides a direct translation and modern spellings for the registers by the present author.

Chapter X: Notes and References--Continued

26 The term abgesondert may be interpreted in another sense
   as heretofore. What is probably intended is that the manual slider be provided in two segments; the first segment
   could then engage the lower choirs for the entire length
   of the chest, the second, the upper two choirs. By drawing the second slider, a two-rank Zimbel could then be
   registrated, while the registration of both sliders would
   engage the full Mixture. In the present author's opinion,
   the segmentation of the Mixture is probably not related to
   the principle of transmission; on the other hand, Praetorius may have had a transmission into the Pedal in mind.
   In such a case, the layout would have to be engineered in
   conformity with the requirements for transmission.

27 The arrangement of the voices conforms to modern practice;
   the numbering adheres to Praetorius for the sake of accurate reference.

28 The code letters in parentheses identify the chests upon
   which the voices are mounted.

29 The church is identified as the Stadtkirche in H. Klotz,
   Das Buch von der Orgel (5th ed.; Kassel, 1955), p. 117.

30 Praetorius, De Organographia . . ., pp. 200-02. The left
   column gives Praetorius' exact account, while the right
   column provides a direct translation and a modern spelling for the registers by the present author.

31 Mahrenholz, Orgelregister . . ., p. 45 suggests a 2/3'
   pitch level for this voice, with apparently good reasons.

32 P. Smets, Die Dresdener Handschrift Orgeldispositionen
   (Kassel, 1931), p. 112 identifies a Borkirche (Poerkirche)
   as an Empore (gallery).

33 Klotz, Buch . . ., p. 117 specifies Kornettbaeszlein 2'.

34 Corrected thus in the Errata; cf. Praetorius, De Organographia . . ., p. 236.

35 The voices are arranged according to modern practice; the
   numbering follows Praetorius for the sake of accurate reference.

36 W. Gurlitt, "Der Kursaechsische Hoforgelmacher Gottfried
   Fritzsche," Festschrift Arnold Schering (Berlin, 1937),
   p. 116.

Chapter X: Notes and References--Continued

37 The code letters in parentheses identify the chests upon which the voices were mounted.

38 Praetorius, De Organographia . . ., pp. 176-77.

39 Praetorius, De Organographia . . ., pp. 179-80.

40 Praetorius, De Organographia . . ., p. 180.

41 Praetorius, De Organographia . . ., pp. 186-88.

42 Praetorius, De Organographia . . ., pp. 192-93.

43 Praetorius, De Organographia . . ., pp. 194-95.

44 Praetorius, De Organographia . . ., pp. 198-99.

45 Praetorius, De Organographia . . ., pp. 199-200.

46 Praetorius, De Organographia . . ., pp. 200-02.

47 Praetorius does present a prospectus, however, which envisioned multiple-stop, octave transmission for 16 voices from one manual chest to another Manual rather than to the Pedal.

48 Praetorius, De Organographia . . ., pp. 189-190. The example is misnumbered by Praetorius; it should be disposition XXII. According to Christhard Mahrenholz (personal interview at Hanover, May 13, 1956) this instrument was the successor to the Hessen, Schlosz organ when the latter was moved to Frederiksborg, Schlosz in Denmark in 1616-17.

49 Probably the widow of Prince Heinrich Julius of Braunschweig, Praetorius' employer, who died in 1613.

50 Corrected thus in the Errata; cf. Praetorius, De Organographia . . ., p. 236.

51 Corruption of schwarzgebeiztem, i.e., black-stained. Cf. Gurlitt, "Kursaechsische . . .," p. 115.

52 Formirtem: probably a corruption of firnisztem (Dativ case), i.e., varnished or lacquered.

53 Actually 21 voices according to Praetorius' usual custom of reckoning transmissions as two voices.

Chapter X: Notes and References--Continued

54 The numbering of the items, however, follows Praetorius'
   account for the sake of accurate reference.

55 The date is given thus in Gurlitt, "Kursaechsische . . .,"
   p. 115.

56 The code letters in parentheses identify the chests on
   which the voices were mounted.

57 Praetorius, De Organographia . . ., pp. 172-73. As customary in this study, the left column gives Praetorius'
   record, while the right column provides a translation and
   a modern spelling for the registers by the present author.

58 A typographical error for the upper limit of the manual
   compass can be suspected; it probably was intended to be
   c''' rather than c''. H. Klotz, in personal interview on
   May 9, 1956, drew attention to the suspected error.

59 The writer suspects an error for the lower limit of the
   pedal compass as well; probably C was intended, rather
   than g.

60 Indicates transmission into the Pedal.

61 Extends downward only to F, hence of 24' physical length
   but actually of 32' pitch.

62 The designation indicates variable complexity in different
   areas of the compass.

63 Indicates transmission into the Pedal.

64 Indicates transmission into the Pedal.

65 Actually 5 1/3'.

66 More likely of 1' (i.e., 1 1/3') pitch.

67 The numbering of the items follows Praetorius for the sake
   of accurate reference.

68 So dated by T. Schneider, "Die Orgelbauerfamilie Compenius," Archiv fuer Musikforschung II (1937), p. 14.

69 The code letters in parentheses identify the chests upon
   which the voices were mounted.

Chapter X: Notes and References--Continued

70 Praetorius, De Organographia . . ., pp. 173-74.

71 Smets, Dresdener . . ., p. 48 specifies the attachment of the Brust to the Oberwerk.

72 Praetorius, De Organographia . . ., pp. 177-78.

73 The specification, 16' in the Pedal and 8' in the Manual, designates a suboctave transmission into the Pedal.

74 The designations in brackets are from Smets, Dresdener . . ., p. 48.

75 Praetorius' designation of 9.fusz is undoubtedly a typographical error. Smets, Dresdener . . ., p. 48 specifies 3 foot.

76 Smets, Dresdener . . ., p. 48 specifies 4 foot.

77 The numbering adheres to Praetorius' account for the sake of accurate reference.

78 The code letters in parentheses identify the chests upon which the voices were mounted.

79 In reality, 34 voices.

80 The designations enclosed in brackets are from Smets, Dresdener . . ., p. 51.

81 The designation Manualiter suggests a transmission into the Pedal.

82 A transmission into the Pedal may be suspected.

83 The designation indicates that the Brust is permanently coupled to the Manual.

84 The items follow Praetorius' numbering in order to facilitate accurate reference.

85 The code letters in parentheses identify the chests upon which the voices were mounted.

86 Praetorius, De Organographia . . ., p. 193. Inasmuch as the original presentation by Praetorius is reasonably self-explanatory and a full translation would tend to

Chapter X: Notes and References--Continued

confuse the page, the usual two-column presentation is omitted this time.

87 Translation: "[Transmission] will give an equal number of voices in the Oberpositive, but all an octave higher."

88 The items are numbered to agree with the original of Praetorius to facilitate accurate reference.

89 The code letters in parentheses identify the chest upon which the voices are mounted.

90 Praetorius, De Organographia . . ., pp. 79-80.

91 M. Praetorius, Theatrum Instrumentorum seu Sciagraphia . . . (Wolfenbuettel, 1620; facs. ed. by W. Gurlitt, Kassel, 1929), Plate I.

92 A false reference; the instrument is actually pictured in perspective on Plate I.

93 The term Register may as well be translated as sliders, since these are the ones that actually effect a registration.

94 The plate number is omitted in the original text.

95 Praetorius, De Organographia . . ., pp. 79-80.

96 Praetorius, Theatrum . . ., Plate I.

97 Thus in Mahrenholz, Orgelregister . . ., p. 276, where he says:

> "After unison and even octave transmission had once been tested out for the Pedal, it was imminent that similar mechanisms should be constructed for the manual chests. To be sure, experiments along this line did not move in the direction of making voices from one keyboard playable upon another as one might easily conjecture. The tonal entity of each chest, as well as the different vertical placement of the chests, consciously arrived at, prevented this. However, attempts were made by means of double and triple ventils to make a register playable within the same keyboard, also at the fifth and octave. On Plate I, Praetorius

Chapter <u>X</u>:   <u>Notes</u> <u>and</u> <u>References</u>--Continued

gives us the picture of an old Positive, which borrows two registers, the Quint 1 1/3', and the Octave 1', from a 2' Principal rank."

Chapter XI: Notes and References

1 More specifically upon J. Toepfer and M. Allihn, Die Theorie und Praxis des Orgelbaues (2nd ed.; Weimar, 1888).

2 Dom Bedos, L'Art du Facteur d'Orgues (1766-78; facs. ed. by C. Mahrenholz, Kassel, 1934).

3 M. Praetorius and E. Compenius, Orgeln Verdingnis . . . (Ms., edited and published by F. Blume in Kieler Beitraege zur Musikwissenschaft, IV; Wolfenbuettel-Berlin, 1936).

4 M. Praetorius, Syntagmatis Musici Tomus Secundus De Organographia . . . (Wolfenbuettel, 1619; facs. ed. by W. Gurlitt, Kassel, 1929), p. 103.

5 M. Praetorius, Theatrum Instrumentorum seu Sciagraphia . . . (Wolfenbuettel, 1620; facs. ed. by W. Gurlitt, Kassel, 1929), Plate XXVI.

6 Praetorius, De Organographia . . ., p. 106.

7 A. Werckmeister, Musicalische Paradoxal-discourse . . . (Quedlinburg, 1707), pp. 83-84.

8 Praetorius, De Organographia . . ., p. 115.

9 Praetorius, Theatrum . . ., Plates I and IV. Only the method is illustrated, the bellows being of another species.

10 F. Viderø, "Compenius Organ Album," Gramophone Shop Celebrities (New York, [n. d.]), p. [2]: "The wind pressure is about 55-60 mm. and the air is supplied by four fan-shaped bellows with a stringpull." The bellows are, probably, of another species, however.

11 Also, probably, with another species of bellows. Dom Bedos, L'Art . . . illustrates all of his bellows as using this method of cocking.

12 Praetorius, De Organographia . . ., pp. 115-16.

13 Toepfer, Theorie . . ., p. 506.

14 The Grueningen, Schloss organ was located in the castle church of Heinrich Julius, Duke of Braunschweig-Lueneburg and Bishop of Halberstadt. He was Praetorius' employer for the greater portion of the latter's life, at least up to 1613, when the prince passed away and Praetorius removed

to Dresden. The organ was originally built by David Beck between 1592 and 1596, was completed and installed in the castle church in 1596 with great pomp and circumstance, and was renovated in 1704 by Christoph Contius under the supervision of Andreas Werckmeister. Praetorius was thoroughly and intimately acquainted with this instrument and it is reasonable to suppose that Esaias Compenius, the official organ and instrument maker at the same court, had much to do with its maintenance.

15 A. Werckmeister, Organum Gruningense redivivum (Quedlinburg, 1705; newprint ed. by P. Smets, Mainz, 1932), p. 10. The dimensions given by Werckmeister, namely, 8 feet long and 4 feet wide, are probably in Brunswick measure, and would be equivalent to 7' - 5 7/8" x 3' - 9" in British measure. See Appendix Q, 2.

16 The apparently co-authored manuscript of Praetorius and Compenius on the inspection of organs was announced several times by Praetorius in the De Organographia under various titles. Since it never seems to have appeared in published form until just a few years ago, a firm title had never been provided for it. The manuscript begins somewhat curiously with a preamble apparently added by another hand: Kurtzer Bericht, Wasz bey uberliefferung einer Klein und grosverfertigten Orgell zu observiren, wie die fundamentaliter durchgelauffen, mit Fleisz besichtiget, und nach dem Gehoer examiniret werden musz. Von Fuerstl. Br. Orgeln und Instrumentmachers Esaio Compenio hinterlaszen vnd von Michael Praetorio in vorgehenden Tractat Fol. 160 versprochen. Praetorius does, in fact, announce the preparation of such a treatise on page 160 of the De Organographia. A second announcement on page 203 suggests a title for it as Tractaetlein vom Verdingnis, Bawen, vnd Liefferung einer Orgel, from which a title has finally been contrived for the manuscript and has come to be adopted in the literature as M. Praetorius and E. Compenius, Orgeln Verdingnis. This is the title used by F. Blume in his publication of the manuscript as the fourth volume of the Kieler Beitraege zur Musikwissenschaft (Wolfenbuettel-Berlin, 1936).

17 Compenius, Verdingnis, pp. 18-19.

18 Praetorius, Theatrum . . ., Plate I.

19 Praetorius, Theatrum . . ., Plate IV, 1.

20 Praetorius, Theatrum . . ., Plate IV, 2.

Chapter XI: Notes and References--Continued

21 Assuming the length to be given in Brunswick measure, a
British equivalent for 9. guter Schuch would be approximately 8' - 6". See Appendix Q, 2.

22 Praetorius, De Organographia . . ., p. 179.

23 The Brunswick measure of ein Schuch is equal to 11 1/4
British inches. See Appendix Q, 2.

24 The Brunswick measure of 8. oder neuntehalb [8 1/2] schuch
lang / vnnd fuenfftehalb [4 1/2] schuch breit is equal to
7' - 5 7/8" x 4' - 2 1/2" or 8' - 0" x 4' - 2 1/2" in
British measure. See Appendix Q, 2.

25 The Brunswick measure of 9. schuch lang / vnnd 5. oder
sechstehalb schuch breit is equal to 8' - 5 1/8" x
4' - 8 1/6" or 8' - 5 1/8" x 5' - 1 4/5" in British measure. See Appendix Q, 2.

26 Praetorius, De Organographia . . ., p. 199.

27 See chapter i of the present study for detailed information concerning the construction and operation of the internal valves and openings in the bellows.

28 Praetorius, De Organographia . . ., pp. 178-79 and 198-99.

29 J. Adlung, Musica mechanica organoedi (edited and published
posthumously by J. L. Albrecht, Berlin, 1768; facs. ed. by
C. Mahrenholz, Kassel, 1931), I, 49.

30 Praetorius, De Organographia . . ., p. 170.

31 Praetorius, De Organographia . . ., p. 174.

32 Praetorius, De Organographia . . ., p. 179.

33 Praetorius, De Organographia . . ., p. 181.

34 Praetorius, De Organographia . . ., p. 200.

35 Praetorius, De Organographia . . ., p. 202.

36 Praetorius, De Organographia . . ., p. 181.

37 Praetorius, De Organographia . . ., p. 189. The Frederiksborg, Schloss instrument is the one originally built for
and erected in the Hessen, Schloss.

38 T. Schneider, "Die Orgelbauerfamilie Compenius," Archiv fuer Musikforschung, II (1937), 30.

39 J. Woersching, Die Compenius-Orgel auf Schlosz Frederiksborg (Kopenhagen) (Mainz, 1946), p. 12.

40 Dom Bedos, L'Art . . ., Plates XLVIII, fig. 2 and LII.

41 Praetorius, De Organographia . . ., pp. 176, 179, 181, 181, 184, 184, 188, and 192-94 respectively.

42 Dom Bedos, L'Art . . ., Plate LII.

43 Praetorius, De Organographia . . ., p. 190.

44 Praetorius, De Organographia . . ., p. 200.

45 Praetorius, De Organographia . . ., pp. 201-02.

46 Praetorius, De Organographia . . ., p. 191.

47 Praetorius, De Organographia . . ., p. 192.

48 Praetorius, De Organographia . . ., p. 185.

49 Praetorius, De Organographia . . ., p. 187.

50 Compenius, Verdingnis, p. 23.

51 Praetorius, De Organographia . . ., p. 179.

52 Praetorius, De Organographia . . ., p. 200.

53 Adlung, Musica . . ., I, 149.

54 See chapter i of the present study for a description of the same and Plate XXVI, fig. 1 for an illustration.

55 Praetorius, De Organographia . . ., pp. 179, 187, 190, 191, 193, 197, 200, and 201 respectively.

56 J. Mattheson, Friedrich Erhard Niedtens Musicalischer Handleitung Anderer Theil von der Variation des General-Basses . . . (Hamburg, 1721), p. 181.

57 Adlung, Musica . . ., I, 84-85. The text presents an abbreviated paraphrase of a long and wordy description.

Chapter XI: Notes and References—Continued

58 Praetorius, De Organographia . . ., pp. 172, 174, 179, 181, 190, 191, 193, 198, and 200 respectively.

59 Praetorius, De Organographia . . ., pp. 175, 192, and 199 respectively.

60 Praetorius, De Organographia . . ., p. 197.

61 Praetorius, De Organographia . . ., pp. 188 and 201 respectively.

62 Praetorius, De Organographia . . ., pp. 174 and 201 respectively.

63 P. Smets, Die Dresdener Handschrift Orgeldispositionen (Kassel, 1931), p. 49.

64 Smets, Dresdener . . ., p. 61.

65 Adlung, Musica . . ., I, 154-55.

66 G. Fock, "Hamburgs Anteil am Orgelbau im niederdeutschen Kulturgebiet," Zeitschrift des Vereins fuer Hamburgische Geschichte (1939), 346.

67 Thus C. Mahrenholz, Die Orgelregister, ihre Geschichte und ihr Bau (2nd ed.; Kassel, 1942), pp. 262-63.

68 Praetorius, De Organographia . . ., pp. 172, 174, 181, 191, 192, 193, 198, 199, and 200 respectively.

69 Praetorius, De Organographia . . ., p. 163.

70 Praetorius, De Organographia . . ., p. 179.

71 Praetorius, De Organographia . . ., p. 187. It is likely that the pitch designation of E is a misprint for C.

72 Praetorius, De Organographia . . ., p. 197.

73 Adlung, Musica . . ., I, 152.

74 Smets, Dresdener . . ., p. 69. This instrument stood formerly in the Evangelische Schloss-Kirche at Dresden and was removed to Dresden, Friedrichs-Stadt in 1738 and rebuilt by Haehnel. It is, therefore, the original instrument of Gottfried Fritzsche as presented in Praetorius,

Chapter XI: Notes and References--Continued

De Organographia . . ., pp. 186-88, and revised by Haehnel.

75 O. Kade, "Gottfried Fritzsche. Bericht ueber die neue
Orgel in der Schlosskirche zu Dresden: anno 1612. den 3ten
Juli," Monatshefte fuer Musikgeschichte III (1871), 90-94.

76 Praetorius, De Organographia . . ., pp. 175, 193, 199, and
201 respectively.

77 Adlung, Musica . . ., I, 104.

78 Mahrenholz, Orgelregister . . ., p. 264.

79 Praetorius, De Organographia . . ., pp. 193, 189, and 189
respectively.

80 Woersching, Compenius-Orgel . . ., p. 12.

81 Praetorius, De Organographia . . ., p. 174.

82 P. Andersen, Orgelbogen Klangteknik, Arkitektur og Historie
(København, 1955), p. 207.

83 Werckmeister, Organum . . ., p. 20.

84 Werckmeister, Organum . . ., p. 20.

85 J. G. Walther, Musikalisches Lexikon (Leipzig, 1732; facs.
ed. by R. Schaal, Kassel, 1953), p. 251.

86 A. Werckmeister, Erweiterte und verbesserte Orgel-Probe
(Quedlinburg, 1698; facs. ed. by Baerenreiter Verlag,
Kassel, 1927), p. 63.

87 J. Adlung, Anleitung zu der musikalischen Gelahrtheit
(Erfurt, 1758; facs. ed. by H. Moser, Kassel, 1953), p. 363.

88 Adlung, Anleitung . . ., pp. 542-43.

89 K. Fellerer, Orgel und Orgelmusik, ihre Geschichte (Augsburg, 1929), p. 17.

90 See Appendix Q, 1 for a table of Rhenish and British equivalents of linear measure.

PART III

THE EARLY BAROQUE ORGAN:

THE TONAL RESOURCE

CHAPTER XII

THE ORGAN VOICES OF PRAETORIUS:

PRINCIPALS AND CROWNS

Method of designation

The fourth part of the Syntagmatis Musici Tomus Secundus De Organographia contains several chapters in which
Praetorius carefully describes the voices of the organ as
he knows them or conceives of them. He also sets up a classification for the voices of the organ which follows, in the
main, the usual modern classifications, but departs from
these in several respects.

His discussion is introduced by an explanation of
designations and how he applies them in his subsequent discussions. It will be necessary to inspect his method of
designation since certain provincial expressions are here
carefully explained.

Designation of Pitch

For the aequal pitch, i.e., the normal, non-trans-
posing pitch (8'), whereby the sound reflects the notation
at par value, he uses the term Chormasz.[1] Super or sub-
octave pitch designations are either duplications or

divisions of the Chormasz. Hence, 16' pitch sounds an octave lower; 32' pitch, two octaves lower than Chormasz.
Conversely, 4' pitch sounds an octave higher; 2' pitch, two
octaves higher; and 1' pitch, three octaves higher than
Chormasz. See Plate LXXXVI, 1.

Having carefully related the various unison designations, Praetorius makes only casual reference to the quint
designations. From his dictionary of organ voices[2] and catalog of dispositions[3] it becomes evident that the quints
were simply designated as of 6', 3', and 1 1/2' pitches, in
place of the more familiar modern designations of 5 1/3',
2 2/3', and 1 1/3', respectively.[4] The Tierce designation
does not occur in the De Organographia because mutations of
this type had not yet been isolated as independent ingredients of what was considered a proper tonal corpus; they appeared only in the very acute pitch regions of certain Zimbels and, as such, did not require specific pitch designation.

Certain registers from Praetorius' catalog of dispositions exhibit what appear to be erroneous pitch designations, but which are, in reality, influenced by the lower
limit of the compass for the voice; thus, in Luebeck,
St. Peter,[5] the Oberwerk Borduna, 24. fi. must be interpreted as of 32' pitch since the voice extended downward,
in all likelihood, only to F. In fact, such lower limits
are specifically delineated in Hamburg, St. Jacob,[6] where

the first pedal voice is given as <u>Principal</u> <u>aus</u> <u>dem</u> F <u>24.</u>
<u>fusz</u>, <u>i.e.</u>, "Principal from <u>F</u>, 24 foot [pitch]." Likewise,
in <u>Hamburg</u>, <u>St. Peter</u>,[7] the first pedal voice is listed as
<u>Principal</u> <u>24.</u> <u>fi.</u> <u>ex</u> <u>F</u>, <u>i.e.</u>, "Principal 24 foot [pitch],
from <u>F</u>." Also, at <u>Magdeburg</u>, <u>Thumb</u>,[8] the Oberwerk exhibits
a <u>Principal</u> <u>grosser</u> <u>Vntersatz</u> <u>bisz</u> <u>ins</u> <u>F.</u> <u>von</u> <u>24.</u> <u>fusz</u>, <u>i.e.</u>,
"Gross Principal Untersatz to <u>F</u> of 24 foot [pitch]." All of
these designations indicate, in reality, a true 32' pitch,
since the designation as given reflects the lower limit of
the compass of each of the voices.

At times, an entire division reveals unusual pitch
designations, as in the case of <u>Hamburg</u>, <u>St. Jacob</u>,[9] where
the Oberwerk designations must be carefully interpreted, in
order to arrive at the true pitch of the voices. The following presentation of this division gives Praetorius' original
record in the first column and an appropriate modern corollary in the second:

VII.

In Hamburg

I.

Die zu S. Jacob hat 53.
Stimmen neben den Trebulan-
ten, vnd 18. kleinen Blaszbaelgen / auch 3. Clavir.

Im Ober Werck
9 Stimmen.

1. Principal   12. Fusz Thon
   im F angehende

VII

In Hamburg

I

The [organ] at <u>St. Jacob</u>
has 53 voices besides the
Tremulant, and 18 small bellows; also 3 manual claviers.

In the Oberwerk
9 voices

1.   16' Principal,
      starting at <u>F</u>

2. Octava	6. Fusz	3.	16' Quintade		
3. Quintadeen	12. Fusz	2.	8' Octave		
4. Holpipe	6. Fusz	4.	8' Hohlpfeife		
5. Holfloeit	3. Fusz	6.	8' Querpfeife; 12' long, and open		
6. Querpipe 6. fusz Thon 12. Schue lang / vnd ist offen.		5.	4' Hohlfloete		
		7.	[?] Rauschpfeife		
7. Ruszpipe		9.	[VIII] Mixture[10]		
8. Scharp		8.	[III] Scharf[11]		
9. Mixtur					

[Translation by the present author]

It is clear that the lower limit of the compass, namely F, dictated the seemingly erroneous pitch designations.

A similar situation obtains in the specifications for the Oberwerk of the Hamburg, St. Peter instrument.[12]

Some clarification is necessary in resolving the apparent confusion of the Latin terms quinta decima and sedecima. Quinta decima is the Latin ordinal for the fifteenth, which, reckoned from an aequal or 8' basis, represents a 2' pitch. Sedecima, however, appears frequently in the dispositions of the Early Baroque as an alternate term for the same pitch. It is the Latin ordinal for the sixteenth and came into use, most probably, as the result of considering the 2' as the double octave (2 x 8) over aequal pitch.[13]

Designation of Divisions

The individual divisions of the instrument are often designated in foot-terms, the basic Principal voice serving

as the point of reference. Praetorius delineates three identifiable situations:[14]

1. <u>Klein</u> <u>Werk</u>, of 4' pitch, is a division whose
basic Principal voice sounds the note <u>c</u> on the <u>C</u> key,
either in the Manual or Pedal;[15] hence, the basis of
such a division is a 4' Principal register. See
Plate LXXXVI, 2

2. <u>Mittel</u> or <u>Chormaessig</u> <u>Werk</u>, of 8' pitch, is
a division whose basic Principal voice sounds the note
<u>C</u> on the <u>C</u> key, either in the Manual or Pedal; hence,
the basis of such a division is an 8' Principal register. See Plate LXXXVI, 3

3. <u>Gross</u> <u>Werk</u>, of 16' pitch, is a division whose
basic Principal voice sounds the note <u>CC</u> on the <u>C</u> key,
and is therefore an octave lower than the preceding;
hence, the basis of such a division is a 16' Principal register. See Plate LXXXVI, 4

Praetorius' own <u>Model</u> <u>Disposition</u> <u>1</u> may serve to show
an appropriate application of the terms as used with individual divisions of an instrument.[16] The Rueckpositive,
since it exhibits a 4' <u>Schoen</u> <u>Zinnern</u> <u>Principal</u> as the basic
Principal voice of the division, may be called a <u>Klein</u> <u>Werk</u>;
the Oberwerk, predicated upon an 8' <u>Zinnern</u> <u>Principal</u>, is
properly designated as a <u>Mittel</u> or <u>Chor</u> <u>Werk</u>; the Pedal,
with a 16' <u>Offener</u> <u>Vntersatz</u> as its basic Principal voice,
exemplifies a <u>Gross</u> <u>Werk</u>.

Designation of Instruments

Having established the premise that a _division_ is designated by the pitch-level of the lowest Principal contained therein, Praetorius proceeds to develop the manner in which an _entire instrument_, _i.e._, a whole organ, might and should be designated.

The designation of the instrument derives from the pitch-level of the lowest Principal in the Manual, Oberwerk, or Werk (whichever represents the central organic core of the instrument), regardless of the basic Principal voices contained in other divisions, such as the Rueckpositive, Brust, Pedal, etc. Quite generally, but not always, this voice is exhibited in the case or facade. The following abstracts of Praetorius' account delineate the designations:[17]

1. _Gross Principal Instrument_. Such an instrument derives its name from the fact that it will display in the facade, a 16' Principal from the Manual. It may also possess a Gross Octave 8', an Octave 4', and, possibly, also a Principal 32' in the Pedal; however, the designation of the instrument does not derive from these latter items

2. _Aequal Principal Instrument_. Such an instrument may also be called a _Mittel Principal Instrument_ or a _Chor Principal Instrument_. It may also possess an Octave 4', a Klein Octave 2', or a pedal Principal 16', indeed, even appearing in the side towers; however, the designation of the instrument does not derive from these latter items, but from the 8' Principal in the Manual which appears in the facade

3. _Klein Principal Instrument_. Such an instrument may also be called an _Octave Principal Instrument_. It may also possess an Octave 2' and a Super Octave 1', but the designation of the instrument is derived from the pitch-level of the 4' Principal in the Manual .

Having established his fundamental terminology, Praetorius goes on to reinforce it by denying all apparent exceptions. He says, in effect:[18]

> For any of the three types of instruments just enumerated, the casework of the organ may, at times, not be adequate to contain the lowest (i.e., largest) pipes of the manual Principal register; such overlong pipes may, therefore, be placed elsewhere. At other times, the framework of the case may require larger (i.e. longer) pipes to fill out the facade than the register is able to supply; in such situations, overlength or dumb pipes may be used to complete the design. In every instance, however, the designation of the instrument is not affected thereby, but derives strictly from the basic Principal upon which the tonal corpus of the Manual (or Oberwerk, or Werk) is predicated, even if a larger voice occurs in the Pedal and is mounted in the facade.
>
> Any instruments which display smaller (i.e., higher-pitched) basic Principals than the ones listed, do not belong into the class of organs, but into the class of instruments known as Positives. In these, the Manual is predicated upon a Principalbasis of 2' pitch and they are more properly designated as Gross Positive, Kirchen Positive or Klein-Octave-Principal Instrument. Such instruments derive their aequal pitch-level from species of pipes other than Principals, such as Gedackts or Quintades of 8' and 4' pitch, and the like.

Praetorius' Classification of

the Tonal Resource

Praetorius opens his chapter[19] on the organ voices by making certain observations concerning the physical characteristics of pipes and the general effect these have on the pitch and tone. He defines the corpus, shows the influential effect of scale (i.e., diameter or cross-sectional area) on the length of the corpus, differentiates open and covered pipes, and establishes the policy that all of his

designations are to be interpreted as describing the pitch
of the tone rather than the physical lengths of the pipes.
He says, in effect:[20]

> The length of the corpus of a labial pipe is reckoned
> from the mouth of the pipe to the opposite end, excluding the
> foot.

> Principals and all other open pipes are usually of
> about the same physical length as the pitch designation would
> indicate. The diameter of the pipe does, however, influence
> the requisite length of the corpus: a wide pipe needs to be
> a little shorter, and a narrow pipe a little longer than a
> moderate-scaled pipe in order to produce the same pitch.

> The Gedackts are not quite half as long as the pitch
> designation would indicate, even if their diameter is as
> great or even greater than that of correspondingly-pitched
> open pipes. For example, if a Principal of 8' pitch has an
> 8' corpus, the Gedackt of 8' pitch, even if of the same di-
> ameter, has a corpus of 4' length or, possibly, a little
> shorter. The reason for this is that as soon as an open pipe
> is covered, the pitch sinks an octave, a fifth, or a sixth
> as the situation may require. This can be illustrated by
> the Quintade, which is much longer than a corresponding Ge-
> dackt, because its diameter approaches that of a 4' Princi-
> pal while that of the Gedackt agrees with the 8' Principal.
> A result of this condition, that these two forms of covered
> pipes exhibit such an unequal diameter and yet produce the
> same pitch, is that the Quintade develops a perceptible quint
> because of its narrow scale; this effect is strengthened by
> its box-beard and the rather low cutup of the mouth. With-
> out these factors, the pipe will not produce the quint ef-
> fect, but will sound just like a Gedackt.

> In order that the difference in the physical lengths
> of open and covered pipes will not confuse the pitch desig-
> nation it is proper, when referring to open pipes, to say,
> Principal of 8' tone, Octave of 4' tone, etc. When speaking
> of covered pipes, where the physical length does not agree
> with the pitch designation, one should say, Gedackt of 8'
> tone, Quintade of 8' tone, Nachthorn of 4' tone, Blockfloete
> of 2' tone, etc.

Classification by Order and Family

Before presenting the various species of registers,

Praetorius classifies the entire tonal resource of the organ into large categories comprising the orders and families. This discussion serves as a brief introduction to his rather comprehensive table of organ voices, which he calls, Universal Tabel (i.e., a universal table). In order to project his approach clearly and without bias, a parallel presentation is subjoined, giving the original text and a direct translation of it.

Disz ist aber anfaenglich / wol und mit fleisz in acht zu nehmen / dasz nur zweyerley Art / Nemblich offene und zugedaeckte Pfeiffen seyn / daraus alle andere Arten unnd Lautsenderungen erfolgen: Und ob schon mancher zum dritten die Schnarr Wercke allhier nicht mit eingerechnet haben wolte / so befindet sich doch unwidersprechlich / dasz die enderung des Klanges in demselben eben so wol aus der enderung derer Corporum, (Inmassen mit andern offnen- und gedacten Pfeiffen geschicht) erfolget; darum sie billich / weil in ihnen noch viel wunderliche und mehr Variationes, als in anderen Pfeiffwercken erwiesen und erfunden werden / koennen und muessen mit eingeschlossen werden.

From the very beginning it must be clearly and diligently observed, that there are only two types of pipes, namely, open and covered, from which all [other] species [of pipes] and variations of tone are derived. Although some do not care to reckon the reeds as falling under this classification, it is undeniably evident that among them the contrast of sound is caused by the variant dispositions of the corpora (as happens with other open and covered pipes). It is, therefore, reasonable that they can and must be included, since more and even greater variations of tone can be discovered and demonstrated among them.

Und werden nu also 1. die Pfeiffen in Orgeln abgetheilet in Floeit- und Schnarrwerck.

1. Accordingly, organ pipes are divided into labial [flue] and lingual [reed] pipes.

2. Das Floeitwerck ist oben an seinem Corpore entweder

2. The labial voices are either open or covered at the

offen / oder zugedaeckt.

3. Der offenen Floeitwerck etliche sind gleich aus Proportioniret und haben gleichweite Corpora; Etliche aber sind nicht gleich aus weit proportioniret.

4. Die gleichaus proportioniret seyn / haben einstheils lange / enge und schmale Corpora; Anders theils aber kurtze und weite Corpora, als die Holfloeitten allerley Art.

5. Die nicht gleichaus proportioniret, deren sind auch zweyerley: Etliche unten weit / und oben enge / als die Gemszhoerner / Spitzfloeitten / und Flachfloeitten: Etliche aber oben weit und unten enge / als der Dulzaen.

6. Die zugedaeckte Floeitwercke / seynd entweder gantz zugedeckt / als die Quintadehnen und Gedacten allerley Art: Aber seynd oben uffm deckel in etwas wiederumb eroeffnet / als die Rohrfloeitten.

7. Der schnarrwercken seynd auch zweyerley: Etliche offen / als die Posaunen / Trummeten / Schalmeyen / Krumbhorn / Regall / Zincken / Cornett: Etliche zugedaeckt / als die Sordunen / Rancket / Baerpipen / Bombart / Fagott / Apffel und Koeplinregal / etc. Wie in nachfolgender Tabell mit mehrerm zu ersehen.[21]

top of the corpus.

3. Several of the labial [voices] are equally proportioned and have cylindrical bodies; others, however, are not equally proportioned.

4. Among the equally proportioned ones, some have long and narrow bodies; others, short and wide, as the Hohlfloetes of various kinds.

5. There are also two types of unequally proportioned [pipes]: some are wide at the bottom and narrow at the top, as Gemshorns, Spitzfloetes, and Flachfloetes; others are wide at the top and narrow at the bottom, as the Dulzian.

6. The covered labial voices are either fully covered, as the Quintades and the various kinds of Gedackts; or they are pierced in the cap surmounting the body, as the Rohrfloetes.

7. The lingual voices are also of two kinds: some are open, as the Posaune, Trompete, Schalmei, Krummhorn, Regal, Zink, and Kornett; others are covered as the Sordun, Rankett, Baerpfeife, Bombardon, Fagott, Apfelregal, Kopfregal, etc. A more comprehensive presentation appears in the following table. [Translation by the present author]

From this introductory classification preceding the

Universal Table, a brief, tentative outline of Praetorius'
assortment of the organ voices into orders and families can
be set up:

    I. Labial Voices

        A. Open

            1. Cylindrical

                a. Long and Narrow

                b. Short and Wide

            2. Non-cylindrical

                a. Upright Conical

                b. Invert Conical

        B. Covered

            1. Fully

            2. Partly

    II. Lingual Voices

        A. Open

        B. Covered

The classifications of organ voices as presented in
most of the recent modern works on the organ agree to a large
extent with this early outline of Praetorius; the departures
from it are largely ones of detail, except in the case of
reeds where the classification shows another concept. Note,
particularly, that Praetorius' classification is not predicated upon a concept of organ voices as it prevailed in the
nineteenth and early twentieth centuries, where the pipes

were classified as bodies of tone reminiscent of the orchestra, somewhat as follows:

I. Flue Pipes

    A. Diapasons

    B. Flutes

    C. Strings

II. Reed Pipes

    A. Chorus Reeds

    B. Solo Reeds

The two classifications reveal opposite concepts with respect to the organ as a legitimate musical instrument. Praetorius' classification (as well as the modern) differentiates the voices by means of the disposition and properties of the vibrating air columns that generate the tone (a physical concept), whereas in the other classification, the voices are differentiated largely by the perceptible effect of the tone upon the ear as related to another medium of musical expression (a psychological concept).

The first classification seeks to differentiate those factors in the organ voices which _cause_ a difference in the tone color, while the second seeks to differentiate the tonal _symptoms_, no matter in what manner they might have been achieved. From the former classification, the social behavior of organ voices can be effectively analyzed to serve as a legitimate and useful foundation for registration;

from the latter no such principles have ever been established
or promulgated with any degree of conviction.

Classification by Species

Although his classification of orders and families
is somewhat sparse, and one could wish that it were somewhat
more detailed in certain areas, Praetorius' outline does establish his basic concepts of organ tone; he uses this broad
outline as the framework for his table of species which is
inserted as a broadsheet into the De Organographia and entitled, Universal Tabel.[22] For the sake of completeness and
as an aid in pursuing Praetorius' concepts concerning the
individual organ voices, the table will be subjoined in outline, rather than in tabular form. It lists practically all
of the registers he later describes in his dictionary of organ voices, and is arranged to show the classification of
voices according to Praetorius' concepts. The foot-designations indicate pitches, not physical lengths of the pipe
bodies; Praetorius is precise about this, heading the respective columns with the legend, am Thon / Fusz. The reconstruction of the table as given in the present study varies from the original as follows:

1. The names of the registers have been re-
spelled to conform with the list given in Appendix R,
to which reference may be had in case of doubt

2. The Pedal registers which are indicated in

the original with the letter P in the margins, have
here been written out; (Praetorius does not do so,
but specifies these voices in his NB. preceding the
table). To have them written out greatly facilitates
an accurate and quick overview of the rich supply of
voices available to the Pedal, and not so evident in
the original table. In every case, when such a pedal
voice has been inserted by the present author but in
conformity with Praetorius' directions, the designation has been enclosed in brackets

3. With respect to the pitch designations, obsolete entries as 6', 3', 1 1/2' have been corrected to
5 1/3', 2 2/3', 1 1/3' in conformity with modern practice

4. Typographical imperfections or apparent errors have been "corrected" by reference to the descriptions of the registers as they appear in Praetorius' dictionary of organ voices

Praetorius' Universal Tabel is presented in Table 63
in equivalent outline form.

From the full array of voices presented in the table,
a brief, giving a summary of the tabular contents, will prove
helpful in overviewing Praetorius' organization and his assignment of the individual voices to various categories. It
will be noted that certain names appear under different classifications than usual, hence, suggest different construction

TABLE 63

UNIVERSAL TABLE

Wherein are differentiated not all, but most of the voices
and designations found in contemporary organs

(N.B. Where M and P are found designated in the margin, it
should be understood that such a voice can be used both in
the Manual alone, as well as in the Pedal alone, in which
case it is called Principalbass, Gedacktbass, etc., and then
also in the Manual and Pedal simultaneously, by means of one
or two separate register controls.)

Organ Pipes

[Manual]   [Pedal]

Labials: Open and Equally-proportioned
I. Long, Narrow, and Slender: Principal Scale

Principals

P.		32' Gross Subprincipalbass
M.	16' Gross Principal	
P.		16' Gross Principal, or
		Principaluntersatz
M. P.	8' Principal or	[8' Principalbass, or
	Praestant	Praestantbass]
M. P.	4' Klein Principal	[4' Klein Principalbass]
M.	4' Klein	
	Principaldiscant	

Octaves

M. P.	8' Gross Octave	[8' Gross Octavebass]
M. P.	4' Octave	[4' Octavebass]
M. P.	2' Klein Octave	[2' Klein Octavebass]
M.	1' Super Octave	

Quintes

M. P.5 1/3' Gross Quinte		[5 1/3' Gross Quintebass]
M. P.2 2/3' Quinte		[2 2/3' Quintebass]
M. 1 1/3' Klein Quinte		

Rauschpfeife or Rauschquinte 2 2/3' and 2'

TABLE 63--<u>Continued</u>

<u>Schweizerpfeifes</u>
M. P.	8'	Gross Schweizer- pfeife	[8' Gross Schweizer- pfeifebass]
M.	4'	Klein Schweizer- pfeife	
M.	4'	Klein Schweizer- pfeifediscant	
P.			1' Klein Schweizer- pfeifebass

<u>Mixtures</u>
M. P.	4'	Gross Mixture	[4' Gross Mixturebass]
M. P. 2'/1'		Mixture	[2'/1' Mixturebass]
M. P.		Klein Mixture, or Scharf	(Klein Mixturebass, or Scharfbass]

<u>Zimbels</u>
M. P.	Grob Zimbel	[Grob Zimbelbass]
M. P.	Klingend Zimbel	[Klingend Zimbelbass]
M. P.	Zimbel	[Zimbelbass]
M.	Klein Zimbel	
M.	Repetierend Zimbel	
P.		Zimbelbass

[Labials: Open and Equally-proportioned]
II. Short and Wide

<u>Hohlfloetes</u> of <u>Various</u> <u>Kinds</u>
M. P.	8'	Gross Hohlfloete	[8' Gross Hohlfloetebass]
M. P.	4'	Hohlfloete	[4' Hohlfloetebass]
M.	4'	Hohlpfeifediscant	
M. P. 2 2/3'		Hohlquinte	[2 2/3' Hohlquintebass]
M. P.	2'	Klein Hohlfloete	[2' Kleinfloetebass]
M.	1 1/3'	Klein Hohlquinte, or Quintfloete	
M.	1'	Siffloete	
M.	[2/3']	Waldfloete	
P.			1' Klein Floetebass
M. P.	8'	Gross Schwegel	[8' Gross Schwegelbass]
M. P.	4'	Klein Schwegel	[4' Klein Schwegelbass]

TABLE 63--Continued

III. [Labials:] Open and Unequally-proportioned
Wide below and Narrow above [upright conical]

Gemshorns or Spillfloetes
M. P.   16' Gross Gemshorn   [16' Gross Gemshornbass]
M. P.   8' Gemshorn   [8' Gemshornbass]
M. P.   4' Octave Gemshorn   [4' Octave Gemshornbass]
M. P.2 2/3' Gemsquinte   [2 2/3' Gemsquintebass]
M. P.   2' Klein Gemshorn, or   [2' Klein Gemshornbass, or
               Super Gemshorn   Super Gemshornbass]
M.   1 1/3' Klein Gemsquinte,
               or Nasat
            4' Spillfloete

Spitzfloetes
M.   4' Spitzfloete
M. P.   2' Klein Spitzfloete   [2' Klein Spitzfloetebass]
M.   1 1/3' Spitzquinte
            4' Blockfloete, or
               Blockpfeife

Flachfloetes
M. P.   8' Gross Flachfloete   [8' Gross Flachfloetebass]
M. P.   4' Flachfloete   [4' Flachfloetebass]
M. P.   2' Klein Flachfloete   [2' Klein Flachfloetebass]
M.   2' Klein Flachfloete-
               discant

[III. Labials: Open and Unequally-proportioned]
Wide above and Narrow below [invert conical]

[Dulzians]
            8' Dulzian

[Labials:] Fully Covered
IV. Quintade Scales

Quintades
M. P.   16' Gross Quintade   [16' Gross Quintadebass]
M. P.   8' Quintade   [8' Quintadebass]
M. P.   4' Klein Quintade   [4' Klein Quintadebass]

TABLE 63--<u>Continued</u>

<u>Nachthorns</u>
M. P.   4' Nachthorn   [4' Nachthornbass]
     P.   2' Klein Nachthornbass

<u>Querfloetes</u>
M. P.   8' Gross Querfloete   [8' Gross Querfloetebass]
M. P.   4' Querfloete   [4' Querfloetebass]

[Labials: Fully Covered]
V. Gedackts of Various Kinds

[<u>Gedackts</u>]
     P.   32' Gross Gedacktsubbass
M.   16' Gross Gedackt
     P.   16' Gross Gedacktbass, or
                                          Gedacktuntersatz
M. P.   8' Gedackt   [8' Gedacktbass]
M. P.   4' Klein Gedackt   [4' Klein Gedacktbass]
M.   2 2/3' Gedacktquint
M.   2' Super Gedackt
     P.   1' Bauerfloetebass

[Labials:] Partly Covered
VI. Rohrfloetes of Various Kinds

[<u>Rohrfloetes</u>]
M. P.   16' Gross Rohrfloete   [16' Gross Rohrfloetebass]
M. P.   8' Rohrfloete   [8' Rohrfloetebass]
M. P.   4' Klein Rohrfloete   [4' Klein Rohrfloetebass]
M.   2' Super Rohrfloete
     P.   1' Bauer Rohrfloetebass,
                                          or Rohrschelle

Linguals
VII. Open

[<u>Open</u> <u>reeds</u>]
     P.   16' Posaunebass
M.   8' Trumpet
     P.   8' Trumpetbass

TABLE 63--Continued

M. P.	8' Schalmei	[8' Schalmeibass]
P.		4' Klein Schalmei
P.		16' Gross Krummhornbass
M. P.	8' Krummhorn	[8' Krummhornbass]
P.		4' Klein Krummhornbass
M.	8' Gross Regal	
M. P.	4' Klein Geigendregal, or Jungfrauregal	[4' Klein Geigendregalbass, or Jungfrauregalbass]
M.	1' Zimbel Regal	
M.	8' Zinkdiscant	
P.		4' Kornettbass
P.		2' Kornettbass

[Linguals]
VIII. Covered

[Covered reeds]

M. P.	16' Sordun	[16' Sordunbass]
M. P.	16' Gross Rankett	[16' Gross Rankettbass]
M. P.	8' Rankett	[8' Rankettbass]
P.		16' Gross Baerpfeife[bass]
M. P.	8' Baerpfeife	[8' Baerpfeifebass]
M. P.	16' Gross Bombardon	[16' Gross Bombardonbass]
M. P.	8' Bombardon	[8' Bombardonbass]
M.	8' Fagott	
P.		8' Dulzianbass
M.	8' Apfelregal, or Knopfregal	
M.	4' Kopfregal	

[Translation by the present author]

and tonal properties than commonly associated with them today. The brief reflects to a remarkable degree, a close
kinship to the modern taxonomy of organ voices which separates the tonal resource of the organ into labial and lingual orders; into open cylindrical, open conical, fully covered, partly covered, cylindrical resonator, conical

resonator, and fractional resonator families; and into overly narrow, narrow, moderate, wide, and very wide genera.

Brief of the Universal Table

I. Labials

   A. Open Pipes

      1. Cylindrical

         a. Long and Narrow

            Principal--Octave--Quinte--Rausch-pfeife--Schweizerpfeife--Mixture--Scharf--Zimbel

         b. Short and Wide

            Hohlfloete--Quintfloete--Siffloete--Waldfloete--Schwegel

      2. Non-cylindrical

         a. Upright Conical

            Gemshorn--Nasat--Spillfloete--Spitz-floete--Blockfloete--Flachfloete

         b. Invert Conical

            Dulzian

   B. Covered Pipes

      1. Fully Covered

         a. Of Quintade Scale

            Quintade--Nachthorn--Querfloete

         b. Of Gedackt Scale

            Gedackt--Subbass--Untersatz--Bauerfloete

    2. Partly Covered

        Rohrfloete--Bauerrohrfloete--Rohrschelle

II. Lingual Pipes

    A. Open Resonators

        Posaune--Trumpet--Schalmei--Krummhorn--Regal--

        Zink--Kornett

    B. Covered Resonators

        Sordun--Rankett--Baerpfeife--Bombardon--Fagott--

        Dulzian--Regal

Comparison to Modern Classifications

In most modern organizations of organ voices, the following registers are classified another way, because they exhibit a different construction and possess other tonal qualities than the corresponding items in Praetorius' classification.

The modern classifications consider:

1. The Principal, Octave, and Quinte as of open cylindrical construction in moderate scale

2. The Waldfloete as of open conical construction in wide scale

3. The Spillfloete as of partly covered construction in moderate scale

4. The Nachthorn as of open cylindrical construction in wide scale

5. The Querfloete of open cylindrical construction in wide scale

The lingual voices are classified according to an altogether different organization in modern theory. Instead of open and covered, the major divisions are cylindrical, conical, and fractional; accordingly, all items will disperse differently and no direct comparisons can be made.

Open Cylindrical Pipes: Principal Scale

Having classified the organ voices both in outline and tabular forms, Praetorius sets about earnestly to describe and discuss each family and member of the various species of pipes in detail in his dictionary of organ voices. Inasmuch as his own discussion is of critical importance in any effort to explore and understand his concept of organ voices and tone, the writer will present Praetorius' own account, provide a parallel translation in English, and subjoin a commentary after each classification which will seek to organize and delineate the concepts.

Praetorius opens his dictionary of organ voices by coordinating family, genus, and species of the Principal and enumerating the varieties which properly fall into this classification.

Von offenen Stimmwercken / so gleichaus proportioniret vnd an jhrer weite Principal Mensur seyn. Als nemblich: Principal, Octaven,

Concerning open pipes which are equally proportioned[23] [i.e., cylindrical] and in their width [i.e., diameter] of Principal scale;[24] such

Quinten, Rauschpfeiffen /
Schweitzerpfeiffen / Mixturen, Zimbeln vnd derglei-
chen.[25]

as Principals, Octaves,
Quintes, Rauschpfeifes,
Schweizerpfeifes, Mixtures,
Zimbels, and the like.
[Translation by the present
author]

The Principals

Praetorius presents first and foremost the Princi-

pals at 32', 16', 8', and 4' pitches. He considers each one

individually as a Principalbasis and as a primary element in

the development of Principal choirs. A tonal corpus, he im-

plies, may possess no more than one of these, and its pres-

ence serves to identify the particular corpus in the scheme

of the whole. He says:

Principal.

DIeser Name PRINCIPAL (welches die Alten / vnsere lie-
be Vorfahren / Praestanten
genennet haben) ist nicht
ohngefehr / oder nach ge-
duncken solchem Pfeiffwerk-
ke zugeeignet worden.
Dann dieweil dieselbigen
nicht allein des Wercks Zier-
de vnnd Ornament seyn / sondern auch das jenige / was
vor erwehnet / vnd geliebter
kuertz halber allhier noch-
mals zu gedencken vnnoetig /
praestiren koennen / werden
sie recht / wol vnd billich
mit dem Namen Principaln intituliret. Wiewol es von etlichen mit dem Namen Doeff
genennit wird.

Es seynd aber derselben
viererley Art:

Principal

This name, Principal (for
which our beloved forefathers
used the term, Prestant), did
not come to be associated
with this species of pipes by
chance or caprice; [on the
contrary], the name, Principal, became attached to them
justly and simply because
they not only serve as deco-
ration and ornament for the
instrument,[26] but also because
of the reasons set forth before, and for the sake of
brevity unnecessary to repeat
here.[27] Even so, some call
these pipes by the name,
Doeff.

There are four varieties
[of Principals] in this [spe-
cies]:

1. Grosz Sub Principal Basz von 32. Fusz.

Diese Stimme kan nicht / wie vorhergedacht / zum Manual Clavier, sondern allein zum Pedal gebraucht werden; Darumb / weil deroselben so gar tieffer Thon vnnatuerlich ist / dasz wenn auch nur ein Clavis alleine / als ein Basz respondiren sol / es mehr ein Windsausen vnd schnauben / als ein rechter vernehmlicher reiner Thon zu hoeren ist; Was wolte denn / wenn es Concordantenweise Manualiter geschlagen wuerde / fuer eine grewliche vndeutlich vnd abschewliche Harmony erfolgen / also / dasz es Organisten vnd Zuhoerer bald satt werden / vnd mit verdrusz anhoeren wuerden: Darumb solche nur allein Pedaliter neben einer dazugezogenen Stimme von 16. Fusz sol vnd musz gebraucht werden.

2. Grosz Principal von 16. Fusz.

Diese Stimme ist nun gebraeuchlich / vnd kan von derselben / wenn sie aus rechter fundamentalischer Theilung an dem Corpore vnd Labien fleissig / vnd just gemacht vnd Intonirt wird / ein rechter vornemlicher Klang vnd Sonus erhoeret auch Manualiter (wenn nur in der tieffen nicht zu grobe Concordanten mit Tertien und Quinten gegriffen) wol alleine geschlagen / vnd lieblich vff einen langsamen Tact gebraucht werden; Aber noch besser / wenn sie eine andere Stimme / wie folgen sol / ne-

1. Gross Subprincipalbass of 32' [pitch].

This voice, as pointed out previously, cannot be used in the Manual, but only in the Pedal. Since its pitch is so unnaturally low, even a single bass note resembles more a panting and rushing of wind than a true, recognizable tone. If it were played in chords, what a gruesome, unclear, and abominable harmony would result! Both organists and audience would soon tire of it and tolerate it only with disgust. Therefore, this voice should and must be used only in the Pedal, and then only in combination with another voice of 16' pitch.

2. Gross Principal of 16' [pitch].

This voice is useful and, when carefully and properly made and proportioned with respect to its body and mouth, and skillfully voiced, can deliver a true and noble tone and resonance. It can, in a slow tempo, be used alone on the Manual (if chords containing thirds and fifths are avoided in its low register). It is, however, better for the propogation and expansion of its tone if a voice of higher pitch from among those which follow, is drawn with it.

ben sich zur auszbreitung
des Klanges haben mag.

3. Aequal Principal von 8. Fusz Thon.

Dieser Corpus groesse oder
8. fuessiger Thon / ist der
allerlieblichste / auch der
Menschen Stimme / vnd aller
vornembsten Instrumenten
ehnlichster Aequal Thon /
inmassen denn alle Stimmen
die 8. Fusz Thon seyn / zu
Motetten vnd Choralconcor-
danten gantz bequeme / ohne bedencken vnd Vitiis im
Gehoer / nach rechter ge-
setzter Composition vnd
praeceptis gebraucht wer-
den koennen vnd moegen.
Darinnen auch eine sonder-
bare Geheimnisz verborgen /
solcher 8. Fusz Thon / aller
anderer kleinen Stimmen /
ihre heimlich in sich haben-
de vnreinigkeit auff vnd an
sich nimpt / zu seiner ei-
genen Reinigkeit vnd Eh-
ren bringet / vnd derselben
sich theilhafftig machet:
Davon auff eine andere Zeit
/ geliebts Gott / ausz-
fuehrlicher geschrieben werden kan.

3. Aequal Principal of 8' pitch.

The [Principal tone] of 8'
pitch is the loveliest [of
the species]. Its pitch is
equal to that of the human
voice and of the most important instruments; for all
registers of 8' pitch are
quite convenient for motets
and chorale harmonizations
and can be used with all com-
positions set according to
the [usual] precepts. There
is an unusual secret connected with this voice: such an
8' voice will integrate the
impurities which smaller
voices may tend to display,
and absorb them into its own
purity and nobility.[28] Of
this [phenomenon] we can, God
willing, write more fully
another time.

4. Klein Principal oder Octaven Principal 4. Fusz.

Jst zwar auch eine lieb-
liche Stimme alleine zu gebrauchen / aber dieweil sie
fuer sich / sonderlich in der
hoehe / keine sonderlich
Suavitet oder Lieblichkeit hat
/ wird in solchen Octav- oder
kleinen Principalwercken
als anfaenglich gedacht / gemeiniglich ein Fundament-
stimme / Quintadehn oder Ge-

4. Klein Principal or Octave Principal of 4' [pitch]

[This], to be sure, is also
a lovely voice and can be used
by itself. However, because
it does not possess any particular smoothness in its upper
register, it is customary
among the Octave or Klein
Principal instruments mentioned before, to introduce
and develop a foundational
voice to go with it, such as

dact von 8. Fuszthon dazu disponiret vnd gearbeitet.

In etlichen Aequal Wercken/ wird auch wol ein klein Principal Discant von 4. f. gearbeitet / welches sich im vngestrichenem f von 1 1/2. fi. Thon anhebet vnnd ascendiret, so weit das Clavier oben wendet: Wiewol sie sonsten nur im mittel c̄ oder c̄s angefangen werden.[31]

a Quintade or Gedackt of 8' pitch.

In some Aequal instruments a small Principaldiscant of 4' [pitch][29] is often introduced, which begins with small f at 1 1/3' [actual pitch][30] and ascends to the limit of the manual compass; ordinarily such [discant voices] begin at c' or c#'. [Translation by the present author]

Organization of the Principal Concept

Praetorius discusses the family of Principals as fundamental voices which are intended to serve as Principalbases for the various divisions of the organ or, in certain cases, for the entire instrument.[32] His concept may be conveniently organized as follows:

1. The 32' Gross Subprincipalbass may serve as a fundamental Principal voice (i.e., Principalbasis) in the Pedal only, not in the Manual

2. The 16' Gross Principal may serve similarly in the Pedal, or in the Manual of Gross Principal instruments

3. The 8' Aequal Principal may serve as a Principalbasis in the Manual of Aequal Principal instruments

4. The 4' Klein or Octave Principal may serve, in like manner, in the Manual of Klein Principal instruments

In the Universal Table, the names of the Principals

are a little more closely defined and differentiated for
Manual and Pedal use. For Manual use, Praetorius lists:

  16' Gross Principal

  8' Principal or Praestant

  4' Klein Principal or Klein Principaldiscant

For Pedal use, he lists:

  32' Gross Subprincipalbass

  16' Gross Principal or Principaluntersatz

  8' Principal

  4' Klein Principal

From the Theatrum Instrumentorum[33] the scale of C
for an 8' Principal can be quantitatively defined and related to the modern Normprincipal and to a theoretical Praetorius Norm.[34] See Table 64. A copy of the pipe is reproduced on Plate LXXXVII, 2.

The Schweizerpfeifes

Before moving on to the other varieties of the Principal, such as the Octave, the Quinte, the Mixture, etc.,
Praetorius takes up the narrow-scaled genus of the open cylindrical family and delineates the species known as Schweizerpfeife. Even though the modern Schweizerpfeife is generally an overblown pipe, his discussion fails to indicate
this condition. He does, however, point out that this species is slow of speech and resembles String tone.

TABLE 64

RELATIVE SCALE OF THE 8' PRINCIPAL

Item	Reference	Diameter in mm.	Deviation from Modern Normprincipal	Deviation from Praetorius Norm[d]
8' Principal	37-1[a]	142.6[b]	-1.5 HT[c]	-1.0 HT

[a]Reference to M. Praetorius, _Theatrum Instrumentorum seu Sciagraphia_ . . . (Wolfenbuettel, 1620; facs. ed. by W. Gurlitt, Kassel, 1929), Plates XXXVII and XXXVIII. The first number identifies the Plate, the second, the specific item on the Plate.

[b]Actual diameter as interpreted from Praetorius' scale drawings in the _Theatrum Instrumentorum_ . . . . See chapter xiv of the present study for the development of the actual dimensions.

[c]Deviation from the _Normprincipal_ in ± half-tones (HT). See Appendix D, 3 for derivation and values of the _Normprincipal_ as adjusted to Praetorius' _Chorton_.

[d]See Appendix S for derivation and values of the _Praetorius Norm_.

Schweitzerpfeiff.

ES ist aber noch eine Art Stimmwerck dieser Principalen art / aber gar enger Mensur, welche von den Nieder vnd Hollaendern Schweitzerpfeiffen genennet worden seyn; Vnd solches vielleicht darumb / weil sie so lang / vnd gegen der enge des Corporis im ansehen gleich der Proportion einer Schweitzerpfeiffen erscheinen: Haben gleichwol einen gar besondern / lieblichen / scharffen / vnd bald ei-

Schweizerpfeife

There exists, furthermore, another variety of pipes in the Principal species[35] but of very narrow scale. These were designated as _Schweizerpfeifes_ by the Netherlanders, probably because they appear as long and as slender in their [physical] proportions as the [mouth-blown] Schweizerpfeifes.[36] They possess a singular, lovely, and intense tone color which resembles that of Violins and is the result of their very narrow scale. The

ner Violn Resonantz / welcher durch jhre Engigkeit
entstehet; Seynd mit kleinen Saeitbaertlein vnd
Vnterleistlin / Als es die
Orgelmacher nennen / ge-
macht / sonst wolten sie
schwehrlich wegen der gar
zu engen Mensur zur guten
Intonation kommen. Wie man
sie denn auch dieserwegen
im Discant vnd kleinen
Pfeiffen etwas weiter machen
musz.

pipes are fitted with what organ builders call ears and
beards.[37] Without these it
would be difficult for the
pipes, since they are of such
narrow scale, to develop their
speech. For this reason they
must be scaled relatively wider in the small pipes of the
treble.[38]

Es seynd aber derselben
nur zweyerley:
1. Grosse Schweitzerpfeiff
von 8. Fusz Thon.
2. Kleine Schweitzerpfeiff
4. Fusz Thon.

There exist only two types
of the same:
1. Gross Schweizerpfeife
of 8' pitch
2. Klein Schweizerpfeife
of 4' pitch

Aus dieser kleinen Schweitzerpfeiff wird von etlichen
nur der Discant gearbeitet /
vnd Schweitzerpfeiffen Discant genennet: Deszgleichen
auch im Pedal allein von 1.
Fusz Thon / vnd wird (3.)
Schweitzerpfeiffen Basz /
oder Schweitzer Basz genant.

Out of these small Schweizerpfeifes some develop only
the treble and call [the reg-
ister] Schweizerpfeife discant. Likewise, in the Pedal
[some develop this voice] in
1' pitch, and call it 3)
Schweizerpfeifebass or Schwei-
zerbass.

Diese Stimmen aber sind
nicht gemein / werden auch
nicht leichtlich gearbeitet
/ denn sie mit jhrer schweren Intonation halber einen
rechtschaffenen vnnd geuebe-
ten Meister suchen vnd haben
wollen.

Since these voices require
an experienced and skillful
master to bring them to proper
speech, they are not easily
constructed nor very common.

Die grosse Schweitzer-
pfeiff gibt im Pedal auch
einen schoenen lieblichen
Basz / vnd gar einer Basz-
geigen ehnlich / wenn sie zu
stillen Stimmen gebraucht
wird. Es ist aber zu merk-
ken / dasz diese Stimme im
Manual mit einem langsamen
Tact vnnd reinen Griffen /

The Gross Schweizerpfeife
[8'] provides a lovely bass
voice in the Pedal and, when
used in conjunction with other
soft voices, resembles the
tone color of a Bass Viol. It
should be noted that in the
Manual, this voice, because
of the slow attack of its
speech, needs to be played in

ohne sonderbahre Collora-
turen wegen jhres langsamen
anfallens geschlagen seyn
wil / sonsten sie zu jhrer
Liebligkeit vnnd Reinigkeit
nicht kommen kan.

a slow tempo and without unusual colorations. Otherwise
the tone can never develop
into its [natural] beauty and
purity.

Es findet sich auch noch
eine andere Art von Schweitzerpfeiffen / welche recht
vff praestanten oder Principal Mensur gerichtet /
oben aber gedaeckt seyn;
Vnd vngeachtet sie sich dahero nothwendig vberblasen
muessen / so fallen sie doch
in rechtem Thon / gleich /
als wenn sie offen / vnd
gar nicht gedaeckt weren.[41]

There exists also another
type of Schweizerpfeife which
leans more toward the true
Praestant or Principal scale,[39]
but is covered at the top.
Despite the fact that [the
pipes] must then be overblown,
they fall into the proper
pitch, just as if they were
open and not covered.[40]
[Translation by the present
author]

The record fails to establish whether the open

Schweizerpfeife is of simple length or overblown; Praetorius'

description would strongly suggest an overblown pipe. If

so, the corpus would need to be of double length, thereby

presenting an inordinately slim appearance. The covered form

of the Schweizerpfeife was definitely overblown into the

third partial, hence of three times the simple physical

length or 1 1/2 times the pitch length. The Schweizerpfeifes

represent very early attempts to approach String tone in the

organ. Three members of the family are recognized by Prae-

torius:

8' Gross Schweizerpfeife

4' Klein Schweizerpfeife

1' Schweizerpfeifebass

In the Universal Table, the items are clearly

differentiated between the Manual and Pedal. For Manual use
he suggests:

    8' Gross Schweizerpfeife

    4' Klein Schweizerpfeife, or Discant of the same

For Pedal use he suggests:

    8' Gross Schweizerpfeife

    1' Klein Schweizerpfeifebass or Schweizerbass

In a subsequent discussion relating to covered cylindrical pipes Praetorius delineates a special form of open and
overblown pipes from the Querfloete species, which must be
considered here under the open cylindrical pipes and related
to the Schweizerpfeife.[42] It is constructed of open cylindrical pipes in double length; hence, overblown at the octave. He much prefers this species to the covered one,
claiming for it greater fidelity to the tone of the mouth-
blown Querfloetes. Its relative scale can be extracted from
the model of it which appears in the Theatrum Instrumentorum[43]
and is reproduced on Plate XC, 4. See Table 65.

TABLE 65

RELATIVE SCALE OF THE 4' OPEN QUERFLOETE

Item	Refer-ence	Diameter in mm.	Deviation from Modern Normprincipal	Deviation from Prae-torius Norm
4' Octave	37-2	92.3	+0.5 HT	+1.0 HT
4' Querfloete (open)	37-13	99.3	+2.0 HT	+3.0 HT

The overblown open Querfloete falls, then, very nearly into the Principal scales; more accurately it may be considered as a member of the Italian Principals which Praetorius, however, does not discuss; its scale lies between the modern Schweizerpfeife at 0 HT and the modern open Querfloete at +4.0 HT.

The Octaves and Quintes

In presenting the Octaves and Quintes, Praetorius is careful to relate them to the Principalbases of the instruments or tonal corpora in which they are properly to find a place. He develops a very precise nomenclature for these sub-species as is evident in his account, which follows verbatim.

Octava.

GLeich wie nun von viererley Principalen Art jetzt gesetzt ist; Also folgen auch viererley Octaven aus derselben Principal Mensur, als Octava / Groszoctava / Octava / klein Octava / vnd Superoctaevlin.

1. Groszoctava ist von 8. Fusz Thon.

Diese Octava gehoeret allein ins grosz Principal Werck / vnd ist an der Mensur vnd Klange nicht anders / als ein AEqualPrincipal, Wie es denn von etlichen gegen das grosse Principal, klein Principal genennet wird. Weil aber im Rueck

Octave

Just as we have presented four varieties of Principals, there follow also four [varieties of] Octaves, constructed of the same [basic] Principal scale. These are Gross Octave, Octave, Klein Octave, and Super Octave.

1. Gross Octave is of 8' pitch

This Octave belongs properly into a Gross Principal instrument, and is in its scale and tone color nothing else than an Aequal Principal. Some call this voice a Klein Principal in contrast to the Gross Principal, just as in the Rueckpositive the

Positiff dasselbige kleine Principal von 4. Fuessen / zum vnterscheyd das von 8. Fusz Thon stehet: Uber disz auch die Principal mehrerstheils von Zien / die Octaven aber aus Bley oder halbwerck (das ist halb Zien vnd halb Bley gearbeitet / vnd in die Orgelwercke hinein / die Principal aber forn an gesetzt werden / wird diese Stimme billich grosse Octava genennet.

2. Octava ist von
4. Fusz Thon.

Vnd gehoeret in die AEqual Wercke / vnd heisset darumb also / weil sie im Mittel mit jhrem Thon eine Octava hoeher / als das AEqualPrincipal, vnd dergleichen 8. Fusz Thon Stimmwercke ist; Auch ausser dem allein gebraucht werden kan / vnd sich zu hoehern vnd niedern Stimmen ziehen lesset.

3. Kleinoctava ist von
2. Fusz Thon.

Vnd wird sonsten Superoctava genennet: Weil aber noch kleiner Octaven / wie folget / verhanden / kan diese Stimme nicht recht Super- oder Supremaoctava heissen: Vnd gibts auch die Obergesetzte Ordnung / Groszoctava 8. Fusz Thon / Octava 4. Fusz Thon sey / darumb musz diese ja billich klein Octava 2. Fusz Thon / vnd die folgende Superoctaevlein 1. Fusz Thon

4. Superoctaevlein ist von 1. Fusz Thon.

4' voice is labelled Klein Principal in contrast to the one at 8' pitch. Furthermore, the Principals are usually of tin, while the Octaves are cast in lead or in metal compounded of equal parts of tin and lead. [The Octaves] are mounted within the organ proper, while the Principals are set out in the front.[44] For these reasons this voice is simply called Gross Octave.

2. Octave is of
4' pitch

[. . .] and belongs into the Aequal instruments. It is so designated because it is a voice in the middle,[45] [as it were,] with a pitch an octave higher than that of the Aequal Principal or similar voices of 8' pitch. Besides, it can be used alone or together with voices of higher and lower pitches.

3. Klein Octave is of
2' pitch

[. . .] and is otherwise [often] called, Super Octave. Since, as will be shown, still smaller Octaves are available, this voice cannot properly be designated Super or Supreme Octave. According to the afore-mentioned order, the Gross Octave must be of 8' pitch, the Octave of 4' pitch; therefore, this one must be designated as Klein Octave 2', and the following one as Super Octave of 1' pitch.[46]

4. Super Octave is of
1' pitch

Heisset sonst Sedetze /
weil es zwo Octaven vber der
Octaven 4. Fusz Thon stehet:
Aber weil die Octava 4.
Fusz / keine Fundament oder
AEqual Stimme ist / kan diese nicht wol von derselben
anzurechnen / Sedetz genennet werden: Sondern behelt
billich den Namen Superoctava, vnd gehoeret vornehmlich in die grossen Posi-
tiff / darinnen Principal
von 2. Fusz disponiret
seyn.

[. . .] and otherwise called
Sedecima because it is pitched
two octaves higher than 4'
pitch. However, since the 4'
Octave is not a foundational
or aequal voice, this register
cannot very well be reckoned
from it and called Sedecima,
but retains simply the name,
Super Octave. It belongs
chiefly into the large Positives where the Principal-
[basis] is of 2' pitch.[47]

[5. Quintes of 5 1/3',
2 2/3', and 1 1/3' pitch]

5. Hieher gehoeren auch
die Quinten von 6. 3. vnd
1 1/2. Fusz Thon / vnnd
diese letzte Art wird von
etlichen Quindetz genennet /
aber vnrecht.

Here belong also the Quintes
of 5 1/3', 2 2/3', and 1 1/3'
pitch. The latter voice is
often and incorrectly labelled
as Quinta decima by some
[builders].[48]

[6. Rauschpfeife of
II ranks]

6. Item / die Rausch
Pfeiffen / welches ein Alter Name / von den Alten
erfunden. Do dann etliche
diese zwo Stimmen vnd Re-
gister / Als Quint 3. Fusz
vnd Superoctava 2. fi. zusammen gezogen: Etliche
aber auff ein Register zusammen gesetzet / vnd eine
absonderliche Stimme daraus
gemacht / welche sie mit
dem Namen Rauschpfeiff intituliret, gleich wie die
Mixtur vnd Zimbeln einen
Namen vnd Register / doch
mehr als eine Pfeiffen haben: Etliche haben es auch
Rauschquinten genennet /
dieweil die Quinta groeber
ist / als die Superoctava.
Also haben sie auch eine
Rauschpfeiffen Basz gehabt /

Rauschpfeife is an old name,
which was discovered by our
forefathers. [To produce the
effect of the Rauschpfeife,]
some draw the Quinte 2 2/3'
and the Super Octave 2' together; others have made a
separate mixed voice [out of
the combination] and entitled
it as Rauschpfeife.[49] In
this [latter] case the Rauschpfeife resembles the Mixture
and Zimbel, which also have
more than one pipe [per key].
Because the Quinte is more
grave in pitch than the Super
Octave, some have designated
this voice as a Rauschquinte.
They also had a Rauschpfeife-
bass, examples of which can
still be found in use today.
[Translation by the present
author]

welcher jetzt noch im Ge-
brauch gefunden wird.[50]

<u>Organization</u> <u>of</u> <u>the</u> <u>Octave</u> <u>and</u> <u>Quinte</u> <u>Concept</u>

Praetorius relates the Octaves to the various fundamental Principals he discussed earlier, but does not quite
complete the correlation. His use of the qualifying terms
<u>Gross</u> and <u>Klein</u> relate these voices to the Principalbases
established in the preceding paragraphs:

1. The <u>8</u>' <u>Gross</u> <u>Octave</u> may serve as an <u>octave</u>
<u>voice</u> in <u>Gross</u> <u>Principal</u> <u>instruments</u> or in divisions
based on a 16' Principal

2. The <u>4</u>' <u>Octave</u> may serve similarly in <u>Aequal</u>
<u>Principal</u> <u>instruments</u> or in divisions based on an 8'
Principal

3. The <u>2</u>' <u>Klein</u> <u>Octave</u> may serve as an <u>octave</u>
<u>voice</u> [in <u>Klein</u> <u>Principal</u> <u>instruments</u> or in divisions
based on a 4' Principal]

4. The <u>1</u>' <u>Super</u> <u>Octave</u> may serve, in like
manner, in <u>Positives</u> based on a 2' Principal

The Octaves are further differentiated from the Principals in three ways:

1. They do not serve as fundamental members of
a tonal corpus, but are supported by a Principal an
octave lower in pitch

2. The Octaves do not appear in the case

3. They are constructed of baser metal than the

Principals

His discussion of the 8' Gross Octave would seem to indicate that he considered the Octaves as exhibiting the same basic scales as their supporting Principals; namely, a base value equal to that of the Principalbasis, and a similar if not identical tone quality. However, in the sketches for the Principal and Octave voices found in the Theatrum Instrumentorum[51] and reproduced on Plate LXXXVII, 2; LXXXIX, 2; and XCI, 4 the basic scales are not equal but disperse as shown in Table 66.

TABLE 66

RELATIVE SCALES AMONG PRINCIPAL VARIETIES

Item	Refer-ence	Diameter in mm.	Deviation from Modern Normprincipal	Deviation from Prae-torius Norm
8' Principal	37-1	142.6	-1.5 HT	-1.0 HT
4' Octave	37-2	92.3	+0.5 HT	+1.0 HT
2' Klein Octave	37-4	46.7	-3.5 HT	-3.0 HT

In the Universal Table Praetorius distributes the varieties of Octaves between Manual and Pedal. For Manual use he recommends:

8' Gross Octave   2' Klein Octave

4' Octave   1' Super Octave

For Pedal use he proposes:

8' Gross Octave   2' Klein Octave

4' Octave

Although Praetorius does not actually specify it, his arrangement of the Principals and Octaves as properly belonging to certain-sized instruments, can logically be extended to the group of Quinte voices which he enumerates:

1. The 5 1/3' Quinte may serve as a twelfth voice in Gross Principal instruments or in divisions based on a 16' Principal

2. The 2 2/3' Quinte may serve the same function in Aequal instruments or in divisions based on an 8' Principal

3. The 1 1/3' Quinte may serve, in like manner, in Klein Principal instruments or in divisions based on a 4' Principal

The example of the 2 2/3' Quinte pictured in the Theatrum Instrumentorum[52] and reproduced on Plate XCI, 2 is related to the 8' Principal as shown in Table 67.

TABLE 67

RELATIVE SCALE OF THE 2 2/3' QUINTE

Item	Reference	Diameter in mm.	Deviation from Modern Normprincipal	Deviation from Praetorius Norm
8' Principal	37-1	142.6	-1.5 HT	-1.0 HT
2 2/3' Quinte	37-3	70.1	+1.0 HT	+2.0 HT

Praetorius presents the Rauschpfeife in two different

forms. He lists it as a single mixed voice of two ranks, one at 2 2/3', the other at 2' pitch; or as two independent voices, one at each of the forenamed pitches which, when drawn together, comprise the effect of the Rauschpfeife. The former case is, in effect, a register, while the latter is a registration.

The Universal Table distributes the Quintes between the Manual and the Pedal. For Manual use, Praetorius recommends:

5 1/3' Gross Quinte   1 1/3' Klein Quinte

2 2/3' Quinte

For Pedal use, he suggests:

5 1/3' Gross Quinte   2 2/3' Quinte

The Mixtures and Scharfs

Although Praetorius entitles his section on crowns as Mixtures and Zimbels, he actually separates the concepts by discussing, first of all, Mixtures and Scharfs, and subsequently the Zimbel under its own heading. He again carefully relates the varieties of crowns to the instruments or corpora in which they are intended to operate. His discussion is comparatively brief, and one could wish that he had delineated the concept more fully and precisely; it seems, however, that he chose to prepare his account for the interested layman rather than for the technician, and so tends to avoid overly technical presentations. His paragraphs on the

Mixtures and Scharfs follows:

Mixtur Zimbeln.

UNter oder aus dieser Mensur werden nu die Mixturen
vnd Zimbeln grosz vnd kleiner disposition genommen
vnd gearbeitet / vnd gehoeren dieselbige billich zu
den Principal vnnd Octav
Stimmwercken / dieweil sie
eben derselben Mensur seynd
/ vnd die Octaven vnd Quinten ohne das zur Mixtur vnd
Zimbeln des vollen Wercks
halben gezogen werden. Vnd
weil derselben dispositiones
vnd Variationes von den Orgelmachern mancherley / nach
Art vnd Gelegenheit der
Wercke vnd Kirchen / gemacht
werden / ist hiervon in spe-
cie nit zuschreiben: Nur
allein das / ob sie wol allezeit eine einige Octaven
hinauff steigen / vnd denn
also bald wieder repetiret
werden / doch dieser vnterscheyd hierinn verhanden:
Dasz einerley Art 1. grosse
Mixtur genennet wird / welch
die Alten in jhren Wercken /
(weil sie domaln noch nicht
von mancherley Art Stimmen /
wie jetzo gewust) gesetzet
haben: Vnd wiebevor ange-
zeigt worden / offte von
30. 40. vnd mehr Pfeiffen
starck / darunter die
groeszte von 8. Fuessen gewesen: Jetziger zeit aber
seynd die grossen Mixturen
allein von 10. 12. biszweilen doch gar selten 20.
Pfeiffen starck auff einem
Chor / vnd die eine grosse
Pfeiffe im vntersten Clave
von 4. fi. Thon.

Mixtures [and] Zimbels

Mixtures and Zimbels in
large and small layouts are
taken and developed out of
the same general scales; they
belong simply to the species
of Principal and Octave voices
because they are of the same
basic measure, except that the
Octaves[53] and Quintes are drawn
together with the Mixtures
and Zimbels, in order to realize the full sound [of the
organ].[54] Since the natures
and circumstances of the instruments and the churches
cause the different builders
to dispose and lay out these
[compound] voices so variously, we [do not intend] to
write specifically about them
here. Only this [should be
noted] that, although they all
rise in pitch for a single
octave and then repeat, this
difference obtains: Formerly,
among our forefathers, who
were unaware of the various
differentiated families of
pipes [now in use], the
1) Gross Mixture often comprised 30, 40, or more pipes
per key, the largest being of
8' pitch.[55] Nowadays, [on
the other hand,] the Gross
Mixture comprises only 10,
12, and rarely [as high as]
20 pipes per key, the largest being of 4' pitch.

2. Die andere Art heisset Mixtur, weil dieselbige im mittel / vnd nicht zu grosz noch zu klein mit Pfeiffen besetzet: Vnd ist eben die / welche jetzund in die AequalPrincipal, auch wol in die grosse Principalwercke von 4. 5. 6. 7. 8. vnd 9. Pfeiffen oder Choren gemacht wird: Darinnen die groeste Pfeiffe gemeiniglich von 2. oder 1. fi. Thon ist.

3. Die dritte Art wird genennet kleine Mixtur, oder wie sie die Niederlaender vor Jahren genennet haben / Scharp: vnd nicht vnrecht / denn es ist eine recht scharffe Stimme / vnd doch nur von drey Pfeiffen / als f c̄ f̄ / etc. disponiret, vnd wird offt repetiret: Wol in grossen Wercken in die Brust / oder im kleinen vor seine rechte Mixtur gesetzet vnd geordnet. Etliche nemen gar kleine / subtile vnnd junge Pfeifflin darzu / die groeste 3 Zoll lang / als f̄ f̄ c̄ f̄ :[57] oder drey oder vier Pfeifflin in unisono, vnd ein Octaevlein / aber keine Quint, vnd gehen von einer Octav zur andern: Dasselb heissen sie Scharp. (Repetirt heist / zu etlichen malen in einem Clavir durch octaven wiederholen / als von einem c oder f zum andern / vnd ist einerley / derowegen dann die Mixturen vnd Zimbeln zum schlagen vor sich selbst alleine nicht koennen gebraucht werden.)[59]

2. The second type is simply called _Mixture_ because it is moderately laid out without too many or too few [ranks of] pipes. It is the one which nowadays is composed of 4, 5, 6, 7, 8, or 9 ranks and [placed into] Aequal Principal or Gross Principal instruments. The largest pipe [in this Mixture] is usually of 2' or 1' pitch.[56]

3. The third type is called _Klein Mixture_ or _Scharf_, as the Netherlanders, not incorrectly, have called it for years. It is a rather aggressive voice, even though laid out in only three ranks, such as _f_, _c'_, _f'_, etc., with frequent repetition. This [Klein Mixture] is properly arranged and placed into the Brust of large instruments, or [takes the place of] the true Mixture in small instruments. Some compound it of very small and delicate pipes, the largest only 3 inches long, as _f'_, _f'_, _c''_, _f''_. Others take three or four pipes in unison plus an octave and no fifth, and proceed thus from one octave to the next. This is the reason for the name Scharf.[58] (_Repetition_ means to duplicate by octaves several times throughout [the compass of] the Manual: as, when one proceeds from one _c_ or _f_ to the next, the [original pitch] repeats itself. This condition is immaterial, but for this reason Mixtures and Zimbels cannot be used alone. [_Translation by the present author_]

Delineation of the Mixture and

Scharf Concepts

From the preceding record and commentary by Praetorius, certain basic concepts and principles can be extracted:

1. The tonal elements from which Mixtures were
compounded were unison and quint voices

2. The number of choirs or ranks (i.e., the
complexity) in Mixtures varied, depending upon the
type in question; the Gross Mixture exhibited generally from ten to twelve, and rarely twenty ranks; the
Mixture was generally comprised of from four to nine
ranks; and the Klein Mixture, of from three to four
ranks

3. The bass choir provided the pitch designation
for the Mixture by reference to its pitch at C. The
Gross Mixture was properly of 4' pitch; the Mixture,
of 2' and 1' pitch; and the Klein Mixture, of [1/2']
and 1/4' pitch

4. The Principalbasis of the instrument (or,
possibly, of the division) dictated the initial pitch-
level of the bass choir

5. The base values for the diameters of the
Mixture pipes, were to correspond to those of the
supporting Principals and Octaves

6. The breaks occurred at various points in the

compass, and each rank resumed its course at the sub-octave pitch-level. The repetition, accordingly, was wild[60]

By extension of item 4 above, a clearer overview of the relation of the Mixture variety to the Principalbasis can be gained:

1. The Gross Mixture 4' may serve as the true Mixture in Gross Principal instruments or in divisions based on a 16' Principal

2. The Mixture 2' or 1' may serve the same function in Gross Principal instruments, in Aequal Principal instruments, or in divisions based on an 8' Principal

3. The Klein Mixture or Scharf 1/2' or 1/4' may serve as the true Mixture in Klein Principal instruments, in divisions based on a 4' Principal, or in secondary divisions (such as a Brust) of larger instruments

The view that the base values of the pipes of the Mixture should correspond to those of the supporting Principals and Octaves still prevailed some 80 years later, and is reinforced more emphatically by Werckmeister:

So ist auch viel daran gelegen / dasz man die Stimmen / so da muessen zugleich gezogen werden / aus einem Principio mensuriret und disponiret; Als zum

Much devolves upon this, that the voices which must be drawn together be developed and scaled out of a single basic principle [i.e., base value]; for example, the c'

Exempel: das c in 8 Fus
Principal musz mit dem c
in der Octava 4. Fus / aus
einer Mensur fliessen /
diesem musz das F in der 2.
Fus quinte gleich seyn /
wie auch das C in der 2.
Fus-octava, und also muessen alle Pfeiffen in der
Mensur bleiben / auch die
Mixturen, sonsten wird man
kein Werck rein stimmen
koennen / und wenn es schon
einmal rein ist / so ver-
aendert sich es doch mit
dem Wetter.[61]

of the 8' Principal must exhibit the same base value as
the c of the 4' Octave; so also the F of the 2 2/3' Quinte
as well as the C of the 2' Octave. All of these voices
must have the same scale, also
the Mixtures; otherwise it
would be impossible to tune
any instrument true; or, if it
had been true, it would change
with the weather. [Transla-
tion by the present author]

Mahrenholz presents the layout of a IV [Klein] Mixture 2/3' from an organ of 1619, which may serve as a case
in point to exemplify the various characteristics of Mixtures
as Praetorius would have them. See Table 68 and Chart 68.

TABLE 68

ACTUAL DISPOSITION OF IV MIXTURE 2/3' (1619)[a]

Segment	Pitches of the Choirs							
C					2/3'	1/2'	1/3'	1/4'
c				1 1/3'	1'	2/3'	1/2'	
c'		2 2/3'	2'	1 1/3'	1'			
c''	5 1/3'	4'	2 2/3'	2'				

[a]C. Mahrenholz, Die Orgelregister, ihre Geschichte
und ihr Bau (2nd ed., Kassel, 1942), p. 216.

The upper limit of the compass is not defined; the
configuration exhibits a [Klein] Mixture of four ranks, of
2/3' pitch, of four segments, of an octave range per segment,

of wild repetition, of three breaks, and displaying, in general, a static progression.

It would be fortunate for this study if actual surviving examples of early baroque Mixtures were available, or if layouts of the same were reliably recorded. Since this is not the case, hypothetical dispositions are all that can be developed. Inasmuch as such may prove provocative and help to throw some light on the layout of Mixtures, a few cases may be undertaken here.

Using the 1619 example just cited as a point of departure, a IV Mixture 1' as recommended by Praetorius for use in Aequal and Gross Principal instruments might be attempted. Praetorius specifies three limitations:

1. Unisons and quints are to comprise the ingredients for Mixtures generally

2. An octave drop is to occur at each break and bespeaks the normal method of repetition for the time

3. The initial pitch of the bass choir is to be 1'

Table 69 and Chart 69 realize these conditions in the main, except that a break at c'' must be suppressed, in order to allow the tonal configuration to proceed upward in pitch to the limit of the compass.

The upper limit of the compass cannot be firmly established but seems to be in the vicinity of c''' since most keyboards of the time reveal a compass of about 48 notes.

TABLE 69

POSSIBLE DISPOSITION OF IV MIXTURE 1'

Segment	Pitches of the Choirs
c	1' 2/3' 1/2' 1/3'
c	2' 1 1/3' 1' 2/3'
c'	4' 2 2/3' 2' 1 1/3'
c''	4' 2 2/3' 2' 1 1/3'

The configuration exhibits a Mixture of four ranks, of 1'
pitch, of three segments of an octave and two octaves in
range, of wild repetition, of two breaks, and displaying
both static and dynamic progressions.

Similarly, a IV Mixture 2' may be attempted. Here,
two breaks have to be suppressed in order to allow the tonal
configuration to remain generally above the aequal voice.
The breaks are suppressed at c and at c'', so that only one
occurs at c', dropping the configuration by one octave. See
Table 70 and Chart 70.

TABLE 70

POSSIBLE DISPOSITION OF IV MIXTURE 2'

Segment	Pitches of the Choirs
c	2' 1 1/3' 1' 2/3'
c	2' 1 1/3' 1' 2/3'
c'	4' 2 2/3' 2' 1 1/3'
c''	4' 2 2/3' 2' 1 1/3'

Praetorius' reference to the Gross Mixture and his delineation of it at 4' pitch for probable use in Gross Principal instruments serves as the basis for a possible layout for one of X ranks.

His specifications for Mixtures generally set certain limitations:

1. Unison and quint pitch-levels serve as the ingredients from which Mixtures are compounded

2. An octave drop at each break bespeaks the normal practice of the time for repetition

3. An initial pitch of 4' for the bass choir

There is, of course, no indication in the De Organographia whether the acute ranks of the Mixture were merely discontinued when they reached the acute threshold of pitch discrimination, or if they were repeated an octave lower and thus introduced double choirs into the subsequent segments. The latter seems more likely and is suggested also by Mahrenholz, who says:

Eine Eigentuemlichkeit der aelteren Mixturen musz noch erwaehnt werden, naemlich das Vorhandensein von mehreren gleich hohen Choeren in der Mixtur (sog. Doppelchoeren), die heute ganz unbekannt geworden und erst in allerjuengster Zeit wieder praktisch erprobt sind. Diese Doppelreihen, die sich in fast jeder alten Mixtur vorfinden, sind zumeist verschieden mensu-

A characteristic of the older Mixtures must yet be mentioned; namely, the presence in the Mixture of several choirs of identical pitch (so-called double choirs) which, largely extinct today, have only in the most recent time been practically re-examined. These double choirs, which are found in nearly every old Mixture, were most often different in scale and mouth treatment, in so far that the

riert und oft auch verschieden labiert in der Weise,
dasz die weitere Pfeife das
schmalere Labium besitzt.
Dies Nebeneinander zweier
gleichgestimmter aber un-
gleich mensurierter Pfei-
fenreihen erzeugt ein ge-
wisses Schweben, das den
alten Orgeln den strahlen-
den Glanz verleiht.[62]

wider pipe received the narrower mouth. This juxtaposition of identically-pitched
but differently-scaled pipes
produces a certain undulation
which lends a radiant luster
to the tone of the old organs.
[Translation by the present
author]

Table 71 and Chart 71 represent a restrained attempt
to realize the X Gross Mixture 4' of Praetorius. The upper
limit of the compass is uncertain, but seems to have been
in the vicinity of c''' among the instruments of the time.
The configuration exhibits a very comprehensive structure of
ten ranks, of 4' pitch, of two segments of two octaves in
range in the lower choirs and four segments of one octave in
range in the higher ones, of one break in the lower choirs
and three breaks in the higher ones, of wild repetition, and
of a dynamic progression in the lower choirs and a static
one in the higher ones.

An alternate disposition for the X Gross Mixture 4'
avoids the accumulation of triple choirs in the uppermost
octave of the compass. A possible solution is shown in Table
72 and Chart 72.

Some contributory information, although meager, can
be gleaned from Praetorius' catalog of dispositions, among
which thirty-one entries give specific information about the
Mixture. These entries will serve to show how the theoretical

TABLE 71

POSSIBLE DISPOSITION OF X GROSS MIXTURE 4'

Segment	Pitches of the Choirs											
	8'	5 1/3'	4'	2 2/3'	2'	1 1/3'	1'	2/3'	1/2'	1/3'	1/4'	1/6'
C			4'	2 2/3'	2'	1 1/3'	1'	2/3'	1/2'	1/3'	1/4'	1/6'
c			4'	2 2/3'	2'	1 1/3'	1'	2/3'	1/2'	1/3'		
									1/2'	1/3'		
c'	8'	5 1/3'	4'	2 2/3'	2'	1 1/3'	1'	2/3'				
							1'	2/3'				
c''	8'	5 1/3'	4'	2 2/3'	2'	1 1/3'						
					2'	1 1/3'						
					2'	1 1/3'						

TABLE 72

ALTERNATE POSSIBLE DISPOSITION OF X GROSS MIXTURE 4'

Segment	Pitches of the Choirs											
	8'	5 1/3'	4'	2 2/3'	2'	1 1/3'	1'	2/3'	1/2'	1/3'	1/4'	1/6'
C			4'	2 2/3'	2'	1 1/3'	1'	2/3'	1/2'	1/3'	1/4'	1/6'
c			4'	2 2/3'	2'	1 1/3'	1'	2/3'	1/2'	1/3'		
c'	8'	5 1/3'	4'	2 2/3'	2'	1 1/3'	1'	2/3'	1/2'	1/3'		
							1'	2/3'	1/2'	1/3'		
c''	8'	5 1/3'	4'	2 2/3'	2'	1 1/3'	1'	2/3'				
			4'	2 2/3'	2'	1 1/3'	1'	2/3'				

concept of the Mixture was actually incorporated into the instruments by the early baroque builders. Table 73 lists the instruments and the complexity of the Mixtures contained therein, as specified by Praetorius.

Of the thirty-one Mixtures exhibited in Table 73, nineteen are simple Mixtures, i.e., they contain the same number of ranks throughout the course of the compass. The number of choirs range from a minimum of three to a maximum of twenty-four. The median number of choirs is five. The remaining twelve Mixtures are compound, i.e., the discant exhibits more choirs than does the bass portion of the compass. Among these, the complexity of the bass portion of the compass varies from four to twelve choirs, while that of the discant portion varies from five to fifteen. The median complexity is from five-and-one-half choirs in the bass portion to eight in the discant portion of the compass.

In six instances from the thirty-one defined Mixtures of the catalog of dispositions, the relationship between the initial pitch of the bass choir of the Mixture and the Principalbasis can be determined. Table 74 exhibits this relationship.

The table serves exhibit purposes only, since no real trend or compelling principle governing the relationship sought, can actually be drawn from it.

Beside the Gross Mixture and Mixture, Praetorius delineates the Scharf, which he also calls a Klein Mixture.

TABLE 73

COMPLEXITY OF MIXTURES IN PRAETORIUS' CATALOG OF DISPOSITIONS

Instrument and Reference to De Organographia	Division	Number of Choirs														
		1	2	3	4	5	6	7	8	9	10	11	12	13	14	15	More
Danzig, St. Marien, pp. 162-63	Ow Rp P																
Stralsund, pp. 167-68	Ow																
Magdeburg, Cathedral, pp. 172-73	Ow Rp																
Magdeburg, St. Ulrich, pp. 174-75	Ow Ow																
Bernau, pp. 176-77	Ow																
Braunschweig, St. Blasius, pp. 178-79	Ow																
Leipzig, St. Nicholas, pp. 179-80	[Ow]																
Leipzig, St. Thomas, p. 180	Ow																
Torgau, pp. 180-81	Ow																

TABLE 73--Continued

Number of Choirs

Instrument and Reference to De Organographia	Di-vi-sion	1	2	3	4	5	6	7	8	9	10	11	12	13	14	15	More
Halberstadt, Barfuesser, pp. 182-83	W B Rp																
Bueckeburg, pp. 185-86	Ow																
Dresden, Schloss, pp. 186-88	Ow																
Grueningen,[a] Schloss, pp. 188-89	Ow P B Rp																
Schoeningen, Schloss, pp. 189-90	Ow																
Model Disp. 1, p. 191	Ow																
Model Disp. 2, pp. 191-92	Ow																
Model Disp. 5, p. 193	W																

[a]A. Werckmeister, Organum Gruningense redivivum (Quedlinburg and Aschersleben, 1705; newprint ed. by P. Smets, Mainz, 1932), pp. 9-10.

TABLE 73--Continued

Instrument and Reference to De _Organographia_	Di-vi-sion	Number of Choirs														
		1	2	3	4	5	6	7	8	9	10	11	12	13	14	15	More
Model Disp. 7, pp. 194-95	Ow																
Sondershausen, p. 197	Ow																
Hildesheim,[a] St. Gotthard, pp. 198-99	Ow																
Riddagshausen, Kloster, pp. 199-200	Ow																
Bayreuth, pp. 200-02	Ow																

[a] J. Biermann, _Organographia Hildesiensis specialis_ (Hildesheim, 1728; facs. ed. by E. Palandt, Kassel, 1930), p. 3.

TABLE 74

RELATION OF BASS CHOIR TO PRINCIPALBASIS

Instrument and Reference to De Organographia	Division of Instrument	Lowest Voice on Division	Principal-basis of Division	Pitch of Bass Choir at C
Luebeck, St. Peter, p. 165	P	32'	32'	8'[a]
Hamburg, St. Jacob, p. 169	P	32'	32'	10 2/3'
Braunschweig, St. Blasius, pp. 178-79	Ow / P	16' / 32'	16' / 16'	2' / 4'
Model Disposition 2, p. 191	Ow	16'	8'	2'
Model Disposition 6, p. 194	Ow	8'	8'	2'
Riddagshausen, Kloster, p. 199	Ow	16'	8'	4'

[a]The pitch of the bass choir is from P. Smets, Die Dresdener Handschrift Orgeldispositionen (Kassel, 1931), p. 47.

He describes it as being very bright and aggressive and of a fairly sparse number of ranks, usually three or four.

The first case is of three choirs, related to each other as f, c', and f'; it is impossible to reproduce this example exactly or authentically, because Praetorius' delineation is too meager, but the writer will propose a disposition which is possible and agreeable to Praetorius' description and general concept of the Mixture, but beyond proof. See Table 75 and Chart 73.

TABLE 75

POSSIBLE DISPOSITION OF KLEIN MIXTURE OR SCHARF
(Case 1)

Segment	Pitches of the Choirs
F	1/2' 1/3' 1/4'
f	1' 2/3' 1/2'
f'	2' 1 1/3' 1'
f''	4' 2 2/3' 2'

For purposes of analyzing and laying out this Scharf, a compass ranging from F to f''' is the only logical possibility; the configuration (Table 75 and Chart 73) exhibits a Scharf of three ranks, of 1/2' pitch, of four segments each an octave in range, of three breaks, and of a generally static progression.

The second case is equally vague since the type in the De Organographia reproduced very imperfectly at this

point. In an interview with Dr. Mahrenholz[63] it was established that the bass choir was probably intended to be represented by two ranks of pipes, with the remaining ranks a
fifth and an octave above it; thus, f' - f' - c'' - f''.
Praetorius specifies the bass choir as 3" or 1/4'. A hypothetical realization of this second case of the Klein Mixture or Scharf is presented in Table 76 and Chart 74.

TABLE 76

POSSIBLE DISPOSITION OF KLEIN MIXTURE OR SCHARF
(Case 2)

Segment	Pitches of the Choirs		
F			1/4' 1/6' 1/8' 1/4'
f		1/2' 1/3' 1/4' 1/2'	
f'	1' 2/3' 1/2' 1'		
f''	2' 1 1/3' 1' 2'		

The range of the compass must again be taken as
from F to f''' as, in fact, it did occur among certain instruments of the time.[64] Without this basic premise it is
impossible to work out even a hypothetical solution. The
configuration represents a Scharf of four ranks, of 1/4'
pitch, of four segments each an octave in range, of three
breaks, of a double bass choir throughout the compass, and

of a static progression.

Praetorius briefly delineates a third example of the Klein Mixture or Scharf, describing it as of "three or four pipes in unison plus an octave, but no quint, which proceed from one octave to the next."[65]

By using a bass choir with an initial pitch of 1/2' as proposed in the first case above, a possible layout can be developed. See Table 77 and Chart 75.

TABLE 77

POSSIBLE DISPOSITION OF
KLEIN MIXTURE OR SCHARF
(Case 3)

Segment	Pitches of the Choirs			
F			1/2' 1/2' 1/2'	1/4'
f		1' 1' 1'	1/2'	
f'	2' 2' 2'	1'		
f''	4' 4' 4'	2'		

The range of the compass must again be taken as from F to f'''. The configuration displays a Scharf of four ranks, of 1/2' pitch, of four segments each an octave in

range, of three breaks, of a triple bass choir, of an octave
gap between the bass and treble choirs, and of a generally
static progression.

The fourth and final case is, in reality, an alternate realization of the third case, whereby the bass choirs
are taken at 1/4' rather than at 1/2', after the manner of
the second case. Table 78 and Chart 76 give a possible
realization of the Klein Mixture or Scharf at this rather
acute pitch.

TABLE 78

POSSIBLE DISPOSITION OF
KLEIN MIXTURE OR SCHARF
(Case 4)

Segment	Pitches of the Choirs			
F			1/4'	1/8'
			1/4'	
			1/4'	
f		1/2'	1/4'	
		1/2'		
		1/2'		
f'	1'	1/2'		
	1'			
	1'			
f''	2'	1'		
	2'			
	2'			

The range of the compass must again be taken as
from F to f'''. The configuration is in all respects similar

to the third case, except for the initial pitch of the bass
choirs, which, in this example, is 1/4'.

The Zimbels

Praetorius' discussion of the Zimbel is inordinately
brief and terse, but he actually identifies at least seven,
if not eight, varieties of the species. By a careful assortment of the collective information a fairly clear concept of
the Zimbel can be developed. His account follows:

Zimbeln.

1. Grober Zimbel ist von
3. Pfeiffen besetzet.

2. Klingende Zimbel / 3.
Pfeiffen starck repetiret
durch gantze Clavir in f
vnd in c̄ / vnd wird also
gesetzt f a c̄: welches die
kunstreichste seyn sol.

3. Zimbel ist von 2.
Pfeiffen / vnd wird etlich-
mal mehrentheils per Octa-
vas repetiret.

4. Kleiner Zimbel ist von
einer Pfeiffen vnd offt repetiret.

5. Repetirende Zimbel ist
von 2. vnd 1. Pfeiffen besetzet / vnd repetiret sich
fort vnd fort.

6. Zimbel Baesse seynd
zwey- oder zum hoechsten
dreyerley Arten: Die groesten etwan ein halben Fusz
Thon; vnd werden einmal repetiret: Die andern seynd

Zimbels

1. The Grob Zimbel is composed of 3 [ranks of] pipes.

2. The Klingend Zimbel is
composed of 3 [ranks of] pipes
and repeats throughout the
compass on f and c'; it is
laid out as f, a, c', and is
considered the most artistic
[of the species].

3. The Zimbel is of 2 ranks
and sometimes repeats several times per octave.

4. The Klein Zimbel is of
one rank and repeats often.

5. The Repetierend Zimbel
is of two ranks and one rank,
and repeats constantly.

6. Zimbelbasses are of two
and, at most, three types.
The largest type is of 1/2'
pitch and is repeated once;
the others are somewhat
smaller and are repeated

etwas geringer / werden	twice; all are composed of
zweymal repetiret, vnd doch	fourths and fifths.[66] [Trans-
alle durch Quarten ynnd	lation by the present author]
Quinten disponiret.[67]	

Delineation of the Zimbel Concept

Praetorius differentiates the seven or eight varieties of Zimbels by their individual characteristics, which may be assorted as follows:

1. Certain ones are most applicable in the Manual, others in the Pedal

2. They vary in their complexity from one to three ranks

3. The ingredients comprise a) unisons and fifths, or b) unisons, fifths, and thirds

4. The initial pitches of the bass choirs vary from 1/2' to 1/6'

Praetorius lists five varieties of Zimbels which are useful in the Manual. These are:

1. The Grob Zimbel of III ranks

2. The Zimbel of II ranks

3. The Klein Zimbel of I rank

4. The Repetierend Zimbel of II ranks and I rank

5. The Klingend Zimbel of III ranks

For Pedal use, he mentions three types, but defines only two:

1. The Zimbelbass 1/2'

2. The Zimbelbass [1/3'] or [1/4']

With respect to their complexity, Praetorius divides
the varieties of Zimbels as follows:

    1. Zimbels of III ranks are a) the Grob Zimbel,
b) the Klingend Zimbel, c) the Repetierend Zimbel,
and d) the [Zimbel bass][68]

    2. Zimbels of II ranks are a) the Zimbel, and
b) the [Zimbel bass][69]

    3. Zimbels of I rank are limited to one variety,
the Klein Zimbel

    It seems that all varieties of the Zimbel were com-
prised of unison and quint ranks; the Klingend Zimbel seems
to have been the only one to contain a tierce rank. In fact,
by examination of all the dispositions in Praetorius' catalog
and the accounts in his dictionary of organ voices, the tierce
occurs only in the high pitch region of the Zimbel, near the
acute threshold of pitch discrimination. None of the instruments exhibit any tierce ranks as independent mutation stops
or as components of Mixtures except in the case of the Klingend Zimbel. Werckmeister, who inherited all of Praetorius'
manuscripts upon the latter's demise,[70] records the incident
when Praetorius heard a Tierce in the form of a Sesquialtera
for the first time. He says:

    . . . this voice, the Sesquialtera, which the
afore-mentioned Praetorius met for the first time in
the Cathedral at Hildesheim in 1620 . . . .[71]

    This date, then, represents one of the early

occurrences of a tierce rank at a pitch lower than the usual
1/5' or 1/10' of the Klingend Zimbel.

As to the initial pitch of the bass choir, Praetorius
suggests only one and that in connection with the largest
Zimbelbass; for this voice he recommends 1/2' pitch. For
the other Zimbelbass voice he proposes a bass choir "somewhat smaller"; accordingly, 1/4' or, possibly, 1/3' can be
considered as his intent. To be in proper relation, the manual Zimbels can be surmised to have been predicated upon bass
choirs not larger than 1/4' and, possibly, as small as 1/6'
or even 1/8'.

A summary of partially defined entries of the Zimbel
among the instruments in Praetorius' catalog of dispositions
reveals certain preferences in connection with the actual
implementation of the theoretical concept of the Zimbel in
the instruments of the time. Forty-five entries yield some
information concerning the voice. Table 79 shows the distribution of the Zimbel between Manual and Pedal.

TABLE 79

DISTRIBUTION OF ZIMBEL VARIETIES
IN MANUAL AND PEDAL DIVISIONS

Division	Varieties of Zimbel			
	I rank	II ranks	III ranks	Klingend Zimbel
Manual	3	21	12	4
Pedal	. . . .	1	4	. . . . . .

Table 80 delineates the dispersion a little more closely by identifying the precise divisions into which the varieties of Zimbels were placed.

TABLE 80

DISTRIBUTION OF ZIMBEL VARIETIES
AMONG INDIVIDUAL DIVISIONS

Specific Division	Varieties of Zimbel			
	I rank	II ranks	III ranks	Klingend Zimbel
Oberwerk } Werk	. . . .	6	7	. . . .
Rueckpositive Seitenpositive Unter Manual	3	8	4	3
Brust	. . . .	7	1	. . . .
Pedal	. . . .	1	4	. . . .

The frequency dispersion for each division of the organ exhibits the preferences shown in Table 81.

Although Praetorius alludes to the pitches of bass choirs and to repetition of the ranks in his account of the Zimbel, he never gives a full picture of the layout of the compound voice in either tabular or graphic form. Inasmuch as it is eminently worthwhile to be able to see the full layouts of the Zimbels, other sources beside the De Organographia must be marshaled, in order to provide a little deeper insight into the composition of the Zimbel as developed and

TABLE 81

FREQUENCY DISPERSION OF ZIMBELS

Division	Frequently	Occasionally
Oberwerk or Werk	III ranks	II ranks
Rueckpositive, Seiten-positive, or Unter Manual	II ranks	I rank, III ranks, or Klingend Zimbel
Brust	II ranks	III ranks or Klingend Zimbel
Pedal	III ranks	II ranks

used at this time. The first and fully reliable source is the surviving example of the I Zimbel 1/6' of the Frederiksborg organ (Hessen, Schloss), built by Compenius and Praetorius,[72] both of whose signatures appear inside the instrument. From Praetorius' specification, Andersen's realization,[73] and from the official record of the technical disposition of the instrument and its pipes in the Danish Royal Library,[74] a very accurate layout of the I Zimbel 1/6' can be reconstructed. Table 82 and Chart 77 reproduce the disposition in tabular and graphic form.

From this technical information, the following characteristics can be mustered:

1. The Zimbel lies in the octave nearest the acute threshold of pitch discrimination, i.e., in the pitch area of 1/8' to 1/16'. This condition would suggest that the Zimbels generally lay very high, in

TABLE 82

ACTUAL DISPOSITION OF I ZIMBEL 1/6'
(FREDERIKSBORG)

Segment	Pitches of the Choirs
c	1/6'
A♯	1/4'
f	1/3'
a♯	1/2'
e'	2/3'
a♯'	1'
e''	1 1/3'

the approximate region of the Frederiksborg example

2. Unison and quint ranks serve as tonal ingredients in the Zimbel, as such

3. The repetition occurs twice per octave, each
one dropping the pitch about one-half octave to the
next lower unison or quint rank. The repetition,
therefore, is mild. Whereas in the Mixtures the break
involves a drop (by wild repetition) from 1' to 2', or
1/2' to 1', or 1/4' to 1/2', in the Zimbels the break
drops the pitch (by mild repetition) from 1' to
1 1/3', or 1/2' to 2/3', or 1/3' to 1/2', or 1/6' to
1/4', etc. Because of this incessant repetition, the
effect of the voice is quite neutral as far as the
rise and fall of pitch is concerned

4. The bass choir begins at 1/6' and alternates

between a unison and quint level, lending thereby a
materially different ingredient and tonal character
to each segment of the course

It is apparent that the segments of the course are
of unequal lengths. One of the segments of the octave, in
those cases where two breaks occur within the octave, comprises five or six notes, while the other segment embraces
six or seven notes. This general practice of dividing the
octave unequally seems to have been a consistent one for
the early baroque builders. It will have been observed that
in most modern layouts where two breaks per octave are involved, the division of the same usually tends toward the
presentation of more equal segments, generally of six notes.
The more frequent breaks were, most likely, forced upon the
early designers in their efforts to avoid exceeding the limits of the acute threshold of pitch discrimination.

The more frequent breaks of the compound voice bring
with them a new principle of repetition which is, for the
early baroque instruments, a feature not to be found in the
Mixtures and Scharfs. Inasmuch as the repetition occurs
twice per octave, mild repetition appears as an accepted
principle among the early baroque builders in the high pitch
region of the Zimbel. There is no concrete evidence in
Praetorius' discussions that such repetition occurred among
the lower-pitched Mixtures. The conclusion is that the eventual application of mild repetition among Mixtures of all

types in the subsequent era found its first application in
the disposition of the Zimbel of this time. Having discovered and explored the acoustical propriety and usefulness of
mild repetition in the disposition of the Zimbel, the builders required only time before applying and exploring the
principle in connection with lower-lying Mixtures.

Another fairly reliable source for delineation of
the Zimbel concept is the surviving example of a III Klingend Zimbel by Hans Scherer found in the St. Jacobi organ of
Hamburg.[75] In citing the example, Mahrenholz states:

> The famous Zimbel built by Hans Scherer for the
> St. Jacobi organ of Hamburg is probably the only Terz-
> zimbel which has survived untouched.[76]

A tabular and graphic representation of the disposition of this voice is found in Table 83 and in Chart 78.

From this noteworthy example of the Early Baroque
certain principles underlying the Klingend Zimbel become evident:

1. The voice operates near the acute threshold
of pitch discrimination. It occupies an area slightly
exceeding the range from 1/6' to 1/12'

2. It is composed of unison, quint, and tierce
ranks. In every segment of the course the tierce is
supported underneath by a unison rank

3. The breaks occur twice per octave, which dis-
places the tonal configuration by an interval drop of

TABLE 83

ACTUAL DISPOSITION OF III KLINGEND ZIMBEL 1/6'
(SCHERER, ST. JACOBI-HAMBURG)

Segment	Pitches of the Choirs		
C	1/6'	1/8'	1/10'
F	1/4'	1/5'	1/6'
c	1/3'	1/4'	1/5'
f	1/2'	2/5'	1/3'
c'	2/3'	1/2'	2/5'
f'	1'	4/5'	2/3'
c''	1 1/3'	1'	4/5'
f''	2'	1 3/5'	1 1/3'

a sixth and a third alternately. Actually, the individual ranks drop a whole octave at each break, but the breaks are staggered. Thus, at _F_, the 1/8' and 1/10' ranks resume at 1/4' and 1/5', while the 1/6' rank continues unbroken; at _c_, the 1/6' rank resumes at 1/3', while the 1/4' and 1/5' ranks continue. The breaking method assumes, therefore, a compound character. At one point two ranks break, at another, one. By this method, the basic principle of an octave break is held inviolate, although the aural effect at each break-point is perceived as an interval drop of a sixth or a third, as the case may be

4. The bass choir begins at 1/6' and alternates between a unison and a quint level. The tonal character of the configuration remains largely static because it exhibits the same ingredients in each segment, although variously superposed

With the experience gained from realizing the Frederiksborg I Zimbel and the Hamburg, St. Jacobi III Klingend Zimbel, an effort can be made to delineate the Zimbelbasses along similar lines, using Praetorius' meager specifications as a premise and the preceding essays as guidelines. The realizations will be conjectures, to be sure, but, inasmuch as they are shored up by earlier surviving examples, a tentative solution may have some value.

For the first example of the Zimbelbass Praetorius

specifies the following conditions:

1. A bass choir of 1/2' pitch

2. A layout exhibiting fourths and fifths,
hence, of three ranks and one repetition

A possible layout for the Zimbelbass, which answers
Praetorius' specifications and reflects the characteristics
of the Frederiksborg and Hamburg models is shown in Table 84
and Chart 79.

TABLE 84

POSSIBLE DISPOSITION OF
III ZIMBELBASS 1/2'

Segment	Pitches of the Choirs		
C		1/2'	1/3' 1/4'
c	1' 2/3'	1/2'	

For the second example of the Zimbelbass, Praetorius
specifies the following conditions:

1. A Zimbel somewhat smaller than the first example; this would suggest a bass choir having an initial pitch slightly higher than the first example. A
1/3' pitch can quite properly be surmised

2. A layout exhibiting fourths and fifths, hence
of three ranks

3. Two repetitions [per octave ?]

Table 85 and Chart 80 reflect these specifications

as nearly as possible.

TABLE 85

POSSIBLE DISPOSITION OF III ZIMBELBASS 1/3'

Segment	Pitches of the Choirs					
C				1/3'	1/4'	1/6'
F			1/2'	1/3'	1/4'	
c		2/3'	1/2'	1/3'		
f	1'	2/3'	1/2'			

If, then, the Zimbelbass is predicated upon a bass choir of 1/2' or 1/3', and the Klein Zimbel, on one of 1/8', it would seem reasonable to interpolate the Grob Zimbel at 1/4' and the Zimbel at 1/6'. For the last two no specification relating to the bass choir is given by Praetorius. The interpolations are suggested by the present author in an attempt to round out a full presentation. Two specifications of Praetorius may serve as a premise for the Grob Zimbel:

1. It is of three ranks

2. It is Grob, a qualifying term used to relate a voice to others in the same class; in this case it would indicate a Zimbel of a pitch more grave than its fellows. If a 1/4' pitch is adopted for this voice and higher pitches for the remaining manual Zimbels, the term Grob becomes meaningful

The repetition scheme probably calls for two

repetitions per octave, as exemplified by the previous instances of manual Zimbels lying in a fairly acute pitch
range. Table 86 and Chart 81 seek to realize the Grob Zimbel
in tabular and graphic forms.

TABLE 86

POSSIBLE DISPOSITION OF III GROB ZIMBEL 1/4'

Segment	Pitches of the Choirs					
<u>C</u>				1/4'	1/6'	1/8'
<u>F</u>				1/3'	1/4'	1/6'
<u>c</u>			1/2'	1/3'	1/4'	
<u>f</u>		2/3'	1/2'	1/3'		
<u>c</u>'		1'	2/3'	1/2'		
<u>f</u>'	1 1/3'	1'	2/3'			
<u>c</u>''	2'	1 1/3'	1'			
<u>f</u>''	2 2/3'	2'	1 1/3'			

With the Grob Zimbel 1/4' thus fairly well delineated,
it is possible to move to the <u>Zimbel</u> <u>per</u> <u>se</u>. The initial
pitch-level of its bass choir may be taken as 1/6', so that
it lies squarely between the Grob Zimbel at 1/4' and the
Klein Zimbel at 1/8'. Praetorius specifies:

1. A complexity of two ranks

2. Several repetitions per octave

Table 87 and Chart 82 realize these conditions in the
main.

There remains the <u>Repetierend</u> <u>Zimbel</u>, which can only

TABLE 87

POSSIBLE DISPOSITION OF II ZIMBEL 1/6'

Segment	Pitches of the Choirs								
c̲								1/6'	1/8'
F̲							1/4'	1/6'	
c̲						1/3'	1/4'		
f̲					1/2'	1/3'			
c̲'				2/3'	1/2'				
f̲'			1'	2/3'					
c̲''		1 1/3'	1'						
f̲''	2'	1 1/3'							

be realized by a subjective interpretation of Praetorius'
description and by relating it to the other varieties of
Zimbel previously explored and developed. Praetorius specifies:

1. Two and one ranks

2. Continuous repetition

A possible realization of the Repetierend Zimbel is
presented in Table 88 and Chart 83. The double-choired
course cannot be proven, but it is not excluded, since such
double choirs are known to have existed in instruments of an
even earlier vintage.

From the considerable array of Zimbels which Praetorius presents in his dictionary of organ voices and the
consistent appearance of the same in the dispositions of

TABLE 88

POSSIBLE DISPOSITION OF II-I REPETIEREND ZIMBEL 1/6'

Segment	Pitches of the Choirs								
C								1/6'	1/8'
									1/8'
F							1/4'	1/6'	
							1/4'		
c						1/3'	1/4'		
							1/4'		
f					1/2'	1/3'			
					1/2'				
c'				2/3'	1/2'				
					1/2'				
f'			1'	2/3'					
			1'						
c''		1 1/3'	1'						
			1'						
f''	2'	1 1/3'							
	2'								

contemporary instruments which he presents in his catalog of dispositions, it becomes apparent that the Early Baroque not only favored the voice but considered it an indispensible ingredient for the full realization of the tonal concept of the organ of the time.

Conclusions

Praetorius' dissertation on the organs and organ voices of his time shows a fine organizational mind at work. His concepts concerning the Principals and crowns are, in the main, so well postulated that they prognosticate the

modern theory concerning the same. In fact, in many respects, modern theorists plumb the depths of the Baroque and
the Early Baroque in an effort to formulate an acceptable and
practical theory of the organ for the present time. A few
succinct statements, gleaned from the discussions of the
present chapter, will serve to set into sharper relief the
basic concepts of organ voices in the Early Baroque and contribute much toward a knowledgeable understanding of the total theory of the organ of Praetorius:

1. All pitch designations were related to the
Chormasz which represented the aequal or 8' pitch.
Super and sub-octave designations were derived by progressive duplications or divisions of the same. Off-
unison pitches were designated only approximately

2. Praetorius' pitch designations derive consistently from the aural effect of the pitch of a
voice; they do not describe the physical lengths of
the pipe bodies, except by chance

3. Individual divisions of instruments were differentiated by their Principalbases, so that a 16'
Principal established a Gross Werk; an 8' Principal,
a Mittel or Chor Werk; and a 4' Principal, a Klein
Werk

4. Entire instruments were differentiated by the
Principalbasis of the central Werk in the organ,

variously designated as the Werk, the Oberwerk, or the Manual, so that a <u>Gross Principal instrument</u> was required to exhibit a 16' Principal; an <u>Aequal Principal instrument</u>, an 8' Principal; and a <u>Klein Principal instrument</u>, a 4' Principal, in the Werk. <u>Positives</u> were generally based upon a 2' Principal

5. Praetorius set up a method of assorting and classifying the tonal resources of the organ, which was predicated upon the physical characteristics of the pipes or, more properly, of the air columns which they enclosed. His classification is, in the main, very much in vogue in modern times

6. Praetorius recognized two orders of pipes, the labial and the lingual. These he subdivided into six families as open cylindrical, open conical, fully covered, and partly covered labial pipes, and open and covered lingual pipes

7. Praetorius often expresses scale (<u>i.e.</u>, diameter or cross-sectional area of a pipe) as a function of the length of the corpus because it has an influential effect upon the same, while the actual length is generally easily recognizable as a symptom of the diameter or cross-sectional area. Accordingly, a <u>long</u> scale may be interpreted as the symptom of a <u>narrow</u> corpus, and a <u>short</u> scale, as the symptom of a <u>wide</u> corpus

8. In any attempt to compare actual diameters of Praetorius' pipes with the modern Normprincipal, account must be taken of the fact that modern tables of mensuration are generally based upon International pitch, while Praetorius' diameters are predicated upon his <u>Chorton</u>. Accordingly, a table of mensuration must be prepared which reflects this difference

9. Modern classifications of labial pipes follow Praetorius very closely; those of lingual pipes, however, derive from an altogether different concept

10. Except for isolated instances, Praetorius' nomenclature of the species of voices and the pertinent modern appellations are in general agreement

11. Praetorius considered the Principal as the most eminent voice in the organ. He classified entire instruments by it and used it as well to identify component corpora. The Principalbasis became a consistent organizing factor in the incorporation of the tonal resource, serving as a reference point to which nearly all tonal ingredients were related

12. The Praetorius Norm is a theoretical rule of measure which, by means of diameter dimensions, bespeaks an average practice with regard to the mensuration of Principals; it is closely related to the modern Normprincipal in that it deviates from it by only one-half half-tone

13. The Early Baroque recognized String tone in the organ, but derived it from open cylindrical and moderately narrow-scaled pipes identified as Schweizerpfeifes

14. The disposition of the Octaves in the various corpora was related to the Principalbases in such a way that they were expected to be supported by Principals an octave lower in pitch

15. It seems, by implication, that the Quintes were, likewise, related to the Principalbases, and in such a way that they were expected to be supported by Principals an octave-and-a-half lower in pitch

16. Praetorius indicates and Werckmeister reinforces the viewpoint that the diameters of members of the Principal choir should be developed out of identical base values, but his drawings of the same belie this contention

17. According to Praetorius, the plenary area of the crown was served by two species of compound voices; namely (a) the Mixture and (b) the Zimbel. However, he identifies also a sub-variety of the Mixture as a Scharf

18. The Mixtures and Zimbels exhibited, generally, unison and quint elements; the tierce element appeared only in the very high pitch-region of the Klingend Zimbel

19. The members of the several varieties and sub-varieties of crowns derived their pitch designation from the pitch level of the bass choir in the initial segment of the course

20. Repetition in Mixtures and Scharfs was largely of the wild form whereby the choirs were displaced an octave downward at each break. Breaks occurred almost always at octave intervals

21. The breaks in Mixtures and Scharfs occurred once per octave, while in Zimbels, two breaks per octave seem to have been the rule

22. Praetorius relates the Mixtures and Scharfs to the Principalbases of the corpora in which they operated. The relationship was, however, less rigid than with Octaves and Quintes, and permitted, therefore, a somewhat greater latitude in their disposition

23. It appears that Praetorius' concept of the crown structures envisioned the Mixture to be predicated upon initial bass choirs of 4', 2', or 1' pitches; the Scharf, upon 1/2' or 1/4' pitches; and the Zimbel, upon 1/2', 1/3', 1/4', and 1/6' pitches

24. A résumé of Mixture dispositions in Praetorius' catalog of dispositions reveals a median complexity of five ranks in simple Mixtures, and one of five-and-one-half to eight ranks in compound Mixtures,

the greater number of ranks appearing in the discant
portions of the courses

25. To Praetorius, the Scharf concept identified
a sub-variety of the Mixture, more particularly, acute
realizations of the same; the term is synonymous with
Klein Mixture, which was predicated upon initial bass
choirs of 1/2' and 1/4' pitches

26. In the Scharf, unison ranks seem often to
have preponderated; at times, double or triple bass
choirs in unison appeared throughout the course,
while at other times, the quint ingredient was entirely suppressed. In such cases the configuration exhibited a continuous octave gap in all segments of
the course

27. The Zimbel was conceived as a voice which
dwelled consistently near the acute threshold of pitch
discrimination; its breaks and method of repetition
gave it a purely static and neutral character, which
did not influence the delineation of pitch within the
corpus in which it operated

28. The pitch ingredients of Zimbels comprised
unisons and fifths; or unisons, fifths, and thirds

29. Initial bass choirs of this species were
predicated upon pitch levels ranging from 1/2' to 1/6'

30. The complexity of Zimbels exhibited a sparse
disposition; from one to three ranks were the general,

if not exclusive, rule

31. Repetition occurred more frequently in Zimbels than in Mixtures or Scharfs, and generally revealed a mild form. The norm was two repetitions per octave, each break displacing the voice by the fractional part of an octave. The segments of the course were of unequal range, so that the primary segment of each octave comprised usually five to six notes, while the secondary segment comprised six to seven notes as a rule

CHAPTER XIII

THE ORGAN VOICES OF PRAETORIUS:

FLUTES, GEDACKTS, AND REEDS

Open Cylindrical Pipes: Wide Scale

Having assorted, classified, and organized the entire
fund of Principal voices and closely related varieties of the
same, Praetorius turns his attention to the non-Principal
voices of the open cylindrical family and particularly to
those of the wide-scaled genus. Under this concept he includes the Hohlfloete together with its attendant sub-species, such as the Waldfloete, Floete, Quintfloete, and the
Siffloete. He says:

II.

Holfloeit.

ISt ein offenes Stimm-
werck / welches viel weite-
rer / doch etwas kuertzerer
Mensur, als die Principaln,
vnd gleichaus weitere Corpora hat: Vnd an jhrer weitten
bald Gedacter Mensur seynd /
ohne dasz sie engere Labia
haben. Vnd dieweil sie offen / vnd so weit sind /
klingen sie auch so hol /
daher jhnen dann der Name
Holfloeit gegeben worden.[3]

II

Hohlfloete

[. . .] is an open register
of much wider and [proportion-
ately] shorter scale than the
Principals;[1] the pipe body is
cylindrical and in its width
approaches the scale of Gedackts[2] except that the mouths
are narrower. Because they
are open and of wide [scale]
they produce a hollow tone;
for this reason they were
given the name Hohlfloete.
[Translation by the present
author]

His brief description relates the species to the

Principals by differentiating their physical characteristics

from the same:

    1. They are of open and cylindrical construction

    2. They exhibit wider scales (i.e., greater di-

ameters) than do corresponding Principal pipes

    3. They have, for this reason, somewhat shorter

corpora than do corresponding Principal pipes

    4. Their mouth widths are consistently narrower

    5. Because they are open and wide in scale their

tone is somewhat hollow in its aural effect

The Hohlfloetes

Praetorius presents an array of Hohlfloete varieties

and sub-species, discussing each one briefly and showing the

qualifying nomenclature that seems to have been in use at

his time to differentiate the higher and lower-pitched mem-

bers of the species.[4]

1. Grosz Holfloeiten 8. Fusz Thon.	1. Gross Hohlfloete of 8' pitch
Es haben aber die alten Orgelmacher vor 60. vnd mehr Jahren in die Choral- oder Thumbkirchen Wercke solche Stimme ins Pedal, vnd so grosz am Thon / als das Principal gemacht; Sintemal man domals von den vnterschiedenen Baessen oder Vntersaetzen noch nichts gewust / vnd solchen Basz / Subbasz vnd Thunbasz / auch	Sixty and more years ago the old organ builders used to place such a voice into the pedal [division] of instruments destined for cathedral churches, and set it at the same pitch as the Principal. At that time nothing was known of the various bass voices or Untersatzes. Such a bass [voice] was called Subbass, Thunbass, or Coppel

Coppel geheissen / darumb dasz er weit vnd Tohnend geklungen / vnd den Werk-ken / weil sie eine Quinta tieffer / als Chor Thon ge-wesen / eine besondere brau-sende Art / in solcher tief-fe gegeben hat. Wie derer noch in vielen alten Thumb Wercken gefunden werden / dasz ein vnwissender meynen solte / es were wegen seines Thonens vnd erfuellens ein Vntersatz / weil es an des-sen Stadt zum vollen Wercke gebraucht worden / dabey verhanden.

because of its broad and ex-tensive resonance; it gave the instruments, since they were pitched a fifth below the [present] <u>Chorton</u>, a strange, blustering character in such a low register. In-asmuch as this [voice] is still to be found in the old cathedral instruments, it often happens that a layman, because of the fullness and extensity of its tone, con-fuses this voice with the [modern] Untersatz, especial-ly when it is used in the full plenum in place of it.

2. Holfloeiten
   4. Fusz Thon.
3. Holquinten
   3. Fusz Thon

2. Hohlfloete
   of 4' pitch
3. Hohlquinte
   of 2 2/3' pitch

Werden durchs Manual vnd Pedal, wie man wil / ge-braucht; Vnd haben die Al-ten den Holquinten Basz gern in den Choral Wercken / den Sang Meister vnd die Chora-les, biszweilen zur Schalck-heit / auszm rechten Thon vnd anfang des Chorals zu verfuehren gehabt.

These voices may be used throughout the Manual and Ped-al as one may wish. The old [organ builders], occasionally out of roguishness, used to enjoy placing a Hohlquintebass [into the Pedal] of choir in-struments, in order to deceive the choirmaster and the sing-ers by giving them thus a false pitch for the opening of the chorale.

4. Kleine Holfloeit
   2. Fusz Thon.

4. Klein Hohlfloete
   of 2' pitch

Diese ist von etlichen auch Nachthorn genennet / darumb dasz es hol / vnd fast als ein Hornklang sich im Resonantz Artet: Jst aber nicht gar recht nach jhrem klang genennet / Sin-temal sich die Quintadehnen Art viel besser darzu schik-ket.

Some call this [voice] a Nachthorn because it sounds hollow and almost assumes the tone color of a horn. Its tone, however, does not jus-tify such an appellation, since pipes of the Quintade species are much more suita-ble [for this purpose].[5]

5. Kleinfloeitten Basz /
2. fi.

ist auch gar gut zum Cho-
ral zu gebrauchen.

    6. Quintfloeitten
    anderthalb Fusz Thon.
    7. Suifloeit
    1. Fusz Thon.

Das Suifloeit ofer Sieff-
litt rechnen etliche vnter
die Principal Stimmen.

    8. Waldfloeitlin
    anderthalb Fusz Thon.

Welche Stimm in Seestaed-
ten an jetzo noch gebraeuchlich / vnd wird 2. oder 3.
mal / weil es so kleine
ist / repetiret.

    9. Klein Floeiten Basz
    ist 1. Fusz Thon.

Wird an statt / vnd wie
die Bawrfloeitlein disponiret, ist aber etwas heller
vnd lautterer am Klange.
Vnd sind nun diese kleine
Stimmen / wenn dieselbe zu
Aequal Stimm Wercken mit
vnd ohne den Tremulant gezogen werden / gar gut vnd
frembd am Klange zu hoe-
ren.[9]

5. Klein Floetebass
of 2' [pitch]

[. . .] is also a good voice
for use with the chorale.[6]

    6. Quintfloete
    of 1 1/3' pitch
    7. Siffloete
    of 1' pitch

Some reckon the Siffloete
among the Principal voices.

    8. Waldfloete
    of 1 1/3' pitch[7]

[. . .] is a voice still
used today in [certain]
coastal cities; it is repeated
two or three times because
[the pipes] are so small.[8]

    9. Klein Floetebass
    of 1' pitch

[. . .] is introduced [in-
to the Pedal] like the Bauerfloete and [at times] in
place of it; its tone, however, is louder and brighter.
These small voices, when used
in combination with aequal
voices either with or without
the Tremulant, are unusual in
their tone color and delight-
ful to hear. [Translation by
the present author]

Organization of the Hohlfloete Concept

Praetorius classifies the species of Hohlfloetes as
open cylindrical pipes of wide scale, thereby separating the
species from the Rohrfloete, for which the term Hohlfloete
had served as a customary appellation in the Early Baroque.

In fact, in the Theatrum Instrumentorum Praetorius uses both terms synonymously to serve as the name of a partly covered pipe.[10] Mahrenholz expresses the same view:

> In the North and West and partly also in Central Germany, the term Hohlfloete was so rigidly attached to the Rohrfloete, that an open Hohlfloete was specifically delineated as "Hohlfloete 8', not covered."[11]

Despite this prevailing concept at the time, Praetorius apparently wants the term Hohlfloete to be reserved for open cylindrical pipes, and proceeds to lay out a whole set of voices for this species. His basic scale for the Hohlfloete requires a diameter which is considerably wider than that of the Principal; in fact, the different varieties cover a span which ranges between that of the Offenfloete and the Nachthorn Offen as illustrated in the Theatrum Instrumentorum[12] and reproduced on Plate LXXXIX, 3 and 4. Table 89 compares the two extremes to the base value of Praetorius' 4' Octave.

The Hohlfloetes of Praetorius together with their related sub-species comprise, therefore, a group of wide-scaled registers ranging in scale from +5.0 HT to +11.5 HT. The modern concept differentiates three identifiable species from the same family within this range span:

1. The Italian Principal: +4.0 HT to +8.0 HT
2. The Hohlfloete: +4.0 HT to +7.0 HT
3. The Nachthorn: +8.0 HT to +14.0 HT

TABLE 89

RELATIVE SCALES OF THE 4' OFFENFLOETE AND
4' NACHTHORN OFFEN

Item	Reference	Diameter in mm.	Deviation from Modern Normprincipal	Deviation from Praetorius Norm[d]
4' Octave	37-2[a]	92.3[b]	+0.5 HT[c]	+1.0 HT
4' Offenfloete	38-5	109.9	+4.5 HT	+5.0 HT
4' Nachthorn offen	37-5	146.1	+11.0 HT	+11.5 HT

[a]Reference to M. Praetorius, Theatrum Instrumentorum
seu Sciagraphia . . . (Wolfenbuettel, 1620; facs. ed. by W.
Gurlitt, Kassel, 1929), Plates XXXVII and XXXVIII. The first
number identifies the Plate, the second, the specific item
on the Plate.

[b]Actual diameters as interpreted from Praetorius'
scale drawings in the Theatrum . . . . See chapter xiv of
the present study for the development of the actual dimensions.

[c]Deviation from the Normprincipal in ± half-tones
(HT). See Appendix D, 3 for derivation and values of the
Normprincipal adjusted to Praetorius' Chorton.

[d]See Appendix S for derivation and values of the
Praetorius Norm.

The mouth widths for the Hohlfloetes, even though
difficult to establish from Praetorius' scale drawings, seem
to dwell between 1/5 and 1/6 of the circumference of the corpus; these are comparatively narrow mouths, and contribute
much, when associated with a wide scale, toward developing
the hollow effect which Praetorius claims as characteristic
for this species.

By virtue of his constantly recurring qualifying
designations of Gross and Klein, the unison and octave pitches of the Hohlfloete may very well be related to the Principalbases which Praetorius established in his dictionary of
organ voices.[13] Thus considered, the various members of the
species and sub-species disperse as follows:

   1. The 8' Gross Hohlfloete may serve as an octave voice in Gross Principal instruments or in divisions based on a 16' Principal

   2. The 4' Hohlfloete may serve similarly in Aequal Principal instruments or in divisions based on
an 8' Principal

   3. The 2' Klein Hohlfloete[14] may serve a similar
function in Klein Principal instruments or in divisions based on a 4' Principal

   4. The 1' Siffloete may appear as an octave
voice in Positives based on a 2' Principal

   A whole set of mutation or aliquot voices, developed
out of Hohlfloete scales, is presented by Praetorius. In
his dictionary of organ voices, these are grouped together
with the corresponding unison and octave voices and thus reveal their intended relationship to the Principalbases:

   1. The 2 2/3' Hohlquinte may serve as a mutation
voice over a Principalbasis no higher than 8'

   2. The 1 1/3' Quintfloete may serve as a mutation
voice over a Principalbasis no higher than 4'

3. The [2/3'] <u>Waldfloete</u>[15] may serve as a mutation voice over a Principalbasis no higher than 2'

Praetorius proposes two pedal voices from the Hohlfloete species:

1. 2' Klein Floetebass

2. 1' Klein Floetebass

The former was considered useful in Choralbass registrations,[16] while the latter was brighter and louder than the usual 1' Bauerfloete of partly-covered pipes, and could be used in its place.[17]

A perusal of the Universal Table[18] establishes the preferred locations for the separate varieties of the Hohlfloete species. For Manual use Praetorius recommends:

8' Gross Hohlfloete	1 1/3' Klein Hohlquinte or Quintfloete
4' Hohlfloete, or only the discant of the same	1' Siffloete
2 2/3' Hohlquinte	[2/3'] Waldfloete
2' Klein Hohlfloete	

For Pedal use, he proposes:

8' Gross Hohlfloete	2' Klein Hohlfloete
4' Hohlfloete	1' Klein Floetebass
2 2/3' Hohlquinte	

The Schwegels

Out of the wide-scaled genus of the open cylindrical family, Praetorius identifies a separate species which,

although related to the Hohlfloetes, produces a somewhat
more refined and quiet aural effect. He labels this species
as the Schwegel.

Schwiegell	Schwegel

ALlhier ist noch eine be-
sondere Art von Laut oder
Resonantz vnd Namen / die
nicht so gar weiter Mensur,
als diese Holfloeiten / verhanden / welche von den Nie-
derlaendern auch fast vor
hundert Jahren / wie aus des
Sebastiani Virdungs Musica
zuersehen / Schwiegel (weil
sie gegen ander enge Mensur
Pfeiff Werck zurechnen auch
hol / vnnd doch sanffte /
vnd am Resonantz den Querfloeiten gar ehnlich klingen) genennet worden. Sie
sind biszweilen vff Gemszhoerner form gerichtet /
doch vnten vnd oben etwas
weiter / gleichwol oben
wiederumb zugeschmiegt / das
Labium ist schmahl / vnd
sind stiller als Spilfloeit-
ten. Es seynd aber derselben nur zweyerley Art: Als

1. Grosse Schwiegel
   8. Fusz Thon
2. Kleine Schwiegel
   4. Fusz Thon.

Woher aber solch sanffter
Klang komme / lasz ich andere dessen verstendige bericht geben. Vnd disz sey
also von dieser Mensur vom
Groesten bisz zum kleinesten
genug gesagt.[21]

Here is still another unique
type of sound, tone color, and
name; [the pipes] are not of
so wide a scale as the Hohlfloetes. According to Sebastian Virdung's Musica,[19] the
Netherlanders, for over a hundred years, have called them
Schwegel (because in contrast
to other pipes of narrow
scale, they possess a hollow,
yet delicate sound, and a tone
color which resembles that of
Querfloetes). Sometimes they
are made of a shape which is
similar to Gemshorns, except
that the scale is made somewhat wider both above and below, and the top bevelled inward.[20] The mouth is narrow
and the speech somewhat more
quiet than that of the Spillfloetes. There are only two
varieties:

1. Gross Schwegel
   of 8' pitch
2. Klein Schwegel
   of 4' pitch

On the causes for the delicate tone, I must let others
report who understand this.
And so, from the largest to
the smallest, let this be
enough regarding [pipes] of
this scale. [Translation by
the present author]

Organization of the Schwegel Concept

Praetorius' description indicates an echo form of the Hohlfloete species. The conditions which he enumerates bespeak an echo character. He requests:

1. An open cylindrical disposition

2. A somewhat narrower scale than that of the Hohlfloete

3. A narrow mouth, probably even narrower than that of the Hohlfloete

4. A hollow tone color similar to that of the Hohlfloete

5. A soft dynamic level

Praetorius defers to others for an explanation of the soft effect of the voice; it is obviously the result of a parallel recession in scale and mouth width, and light winding. He also points out that an alternate form for the voice is derived by some through the use of open conical rather than open cylindrical pipes. Two varieties of the species are proposed:

8' Gross Schwegel   4' Klein Schwegel

The Universal Table[22] recommends both pitch levels of the Schwegel as suitable for Manual and Pedal use.

Open Conical Pipes

In opening the discussion on open conical pipes, Praetorius lays down certain general specifications which are characteristic for the family:

1. They are not equally proportioned, i.e., their corpora exhibit unequal or graduated diameters

2. They are of a fairly generous scale at the level of the mouth

3. They are tapered, so that their conicity produces the effect of covering the pipe more than one-half

4. Five identifiable species can be recognized within the family: Gemshorn, Blockfloete, Spitz-floete, Flachfloete, and Dulzian

The Gemshorns and Related Species

Praetorius, first of all, delineates a comprehensive variety of Gemshorns in both unison, octave, and mutation pitches, including in his discussion certain related species of the same, as the Spillfloete, the Blockfloete, and the Spitzgedackt:

III.	III
Offene Stimmwerck / welche nicht gleichaus weite Corpora haben.	Open pipes which do not have equally proportioned bodies[23]
DIsz ist nun die andere Art der offnen Pfeiffen / welche / weil sie vnten ziemlich weit / vnd oben zu-gespitzet / vnd also mehr / als halb zugedaecket seyn / viel ein andern Resonantz / als vorbeschriebener Princi-	This is the other family of open pipes which, because they are rather wide below, pointed above, and more than half covered, have a considerably different tone color than the pipes of Principal scale described above. Because their

palmensuren Art an vnd in sich haben. Vnd werden dieselben darumb / dasz sie an der Proportz vnnd Resonantz als ein Horn klingen / billich Gemszhorn genennet: Vnd sind deroselben Art vnterschiedlich / als Gemszhorn / Plockfloeit / Spitzfloeit / Flachfloeit; Dultzian vnd dergleichen.

tone color and sonority resemble that of horns, they are simply called Gemshorn. The following registers of this group can be distinguished: Gemshorn, Blockfloete, Spitzfloete, Flachfloete, [Labial] Dulzian, and others.

Gemszhorn

1. Grosz Gemszhorn ist am Thon 16. Fusz.

Dieses ist eine liebliche Stimme / aber besser im Pedal als Manual Clavir zu gebrauchen / es sey dann / dasz eine andere Stimme von 8. oder 4. fi. Thon darzu genommen werde.

2. Aequal Gemszhorn ist am Thon 8. Fusz.

Vnd ist eine sonderbahre liebliche vnd suesse Stimme / wenn sie aus rechter fundamentalischer Theilung nach allen jhren Vmbstaenden gemacht vnnd Intoniret wird / zu hoeren; Gibt wunderliche enderungen mit andern Stimmen zu verwechseln: Moechte auch wol Viol de Gamba, weil sie solchem Instrument am Resonantz sehr nachartet / wenn sie recht gemacht wird / intituliret werden. Die Niederlaender nennen es auch Coppelfloeiten; vnd sind laenger als ein Gedackt / aber kuertzer als ein Principal.

3. Octaven Gemszhorn ist am Thon 4. Fusz

Gemshorn

1. Gross Gemshorn of 16' pitch

This is a lovely voice, but more useful in the Pedal than in the Manual, unless another voice of 8' or 4' pitch be drawn with it.

2. Aequal Gemshorn of 8' pitch

This voice is a singularly lovely and sweet one to hear, when it is properly and justly proportioned in all particulars, and [carefully] voiced. It provides wonderful registrations when [combined] or contrasted with other voices. It might quite well be entitled Viola da Gamba since, if properly made, its tone color resembles such an instrument very closely. The Netherlanders also call it Koppelfloete. [The Gemshorns] are longer than a Gedackt but shorter than a Principal.

3. Octave Gemshorn of 4' pitch

Diese Stimme ist der nechstobgesetzten von 8. Fusz zu vielen lieblichen enderungen nicht vngleich zu gebrauchen: Vnd koennen beyde so wol in groszals in klein Principalwerkken gesetzt vnd gebraucht werden.

Like the preceding one, this voice can be used for many lovely registrations. Both can be placed and used in Gross Principal as well as in Klein Principal divisions.

4. Klein Octaven Gemszhorn ist am Thon 2. Fusz.

4. Klein Octave Gemshorn of 2' pitch

Gehoeret mehr ins Rueckpositiff vnd klein Octaven Principal Wercklein / als im grossen: Jedoch kan sie von andern vnd grossen dispositionen auch nicht auszgeschlossen seyn; Denn sie doselbst eben so wol eine liebliche Art im Manual, vnd auch ein schoenen Basz im Pedal zum Choral zu gebrauchen gibt / vnd sich gar vernemblich vnd eigentlich hoeren lesset.

[. . .] belongs more in Rueckpositives and Klein Octave Principal instruments than in larger ones. However, it cannot be excluded from other and [even] large dispositions, since it will provide these equally well with a lovely effect in the Manual and a fine bass in the Pedal, where its tone remains distinct and unique when used with the chorale.

Es werden auch aus dieser Gemszhoernern Art Quinten disponiret: Als

Quint voices constructed out of Gemshorn pipes are often introduced:

5. Die grosse Gemszhorn Quinta 6. Fusz Thon.
6. Die Gemszhorn Quinta 3. Fusz Thon: Vnd denn
7. Die klein Gemszhorn Quinta anderthalb Fusz Thon:

5. Gross Gemshornquinte of 5 1/3' pitch
6. Gemshornquinte of 2 2/3' pitch
7. Klein Gemshornquinte of 1 1/3' pitch

Ist oben halb so weit als vnten: Das labium wird in fuenff Theil getheilet / ein Theil ist des Mundes breitte / alsdann wird die helffte vffgeschnitten.

[. . .] is half as wide above as below. The [circumference at the] mouth is divided into five parts, of which one is taken for the width of the mouth. The cutup equals one-half of the width.

Vnd wird diese letzte Stimme sonsten nicht vnrecht NASATH genennet / dieweil

Otherwise, the latter voice is, not unjustly, called Nasat, since because of its

sie wegen jhrer kleine zu
andern Stimmen gleichsam
noesselt / sonderlich wenn
sie recht / vnd nicht so
scharff intoniret ist;
Gibt auch einen schoenen
Discant in der rechten
Hand / mit andern darzuge-
zogenen Stimmen zu gebrauchen. Etliche arbeiten das
Nasath vff weit Pfeiffwerck
Mensur, vnd enge labiret

Etliche heissen dasz
Gemszhorn auch Spillfloei-
ten / vnd dasselbige allein
wegen der Gestalt vnd Proportion, dasz solche Pfeiffen einer Hand Spillen gar
gleich vnd ehnlich anzuse-
hen seyn.

Etliche nennen die Gemsz-
hoerner noch an jetzo Plockpfeiffen: Jst aber nicht
rech getaeufft. Denn Plockpfeiffen eine andere Gestalt
vnd Klang haben / vnd koennen die Spitzfloeitten von
4. fi. Thon (darvan jetzt
alsbald sol gesagt werden)
wenn jhnen oben die rechte
weite / etwas weiter / als
den Gemszhoernern / gegeben
wird / des Klanges halben
billicher Plockpfeiffen oder
Plockfloeiten geheissen werden: Weil sie alsdann einen
Resonantz / natuerlich als
die andere blasende Instrumenta, welche Plockpfeiffen
genennet werden / von sich
geben. Kleiner aber als
von 2. Fuessen / werden
dieser Art Stimmen von verstendigen Meistern nicht gearbeitet.

Etliche arbeiten die
Plockfloeiten fast vff Querfloeiten Art / also / dasz

diminutive size, the tone is
somewhat nasal in effect when
compared to other voices, especially when it is properly
voiced and not too intense.
It provides also a fine discant in the right hand when
used in combination with other
voices. Some [builders] develop the Nasat out of wide
scales [in open cylindrical
pipes] and narrow mouths.

Some call the Gemshorn a
Spillfloete, and that only
because of its shape and proportion which give these pipes
an appearance similar to that
of a hand funnel.

Some still call the Gems-
horns, Blockfloetes. This is
not a proper designation because Blockfloetes have a different shape and tone color.
The Spitzfloetes of 4' pitch
(of which we shall speak presently), if they are given the
proper scale, (i.e., somewhat wider than [the scale] of
Gemshorns) can, because of
their tone color, more justly
be called Blockpfeifes or
Blockfloetes. When so constructed they produce a tone
color which resembles, in a
natural way, the tone of the
[mouth]-blown instruments
known as Blockpfeifes. Intelligent masters do not develop this type of voice in
any higher than 2' pitch.

Some develop Blockfloetes
after the fashion of Querfloetes, in that the pipe

das Corpus noch eins so lang
wird / als sonsten die rechte Mensur mit sich bringt /
oben zugedaeckt / vnd daher
sich in der Octav vbersetzen
vnd vberblasen musz.[24]

body is made twice as long as
ordinarily, and covered at
the top. Consequently, [the
pipe] must transpose [and
overblow] into the octave.
[Translation by the present
author]

Organization of the Gemshorn Concept

Praetorius presents the Gemshorn as a unison, an
octave, and a super octave voice and develops also a set of
mutation voices from this scale and disposition. In conformity with his usual method, the varieties of Gemshorns
can be clearly related to the Principalbases of instruments
or of divisions with which they may properly be associated:

1. The 16' Gross Gemshorn may serve as a unison
voice in Gross Principal instruments or in divisions
based on a 16' Principal; it may also be used as such
in the Pedal

2. The 8' Aequal Gemshorn may serve similarly
in Aequal Principal instruments or in divisions based
on an 8' Principal

3. The 4' Octave Gemshorn may serve in like manner in Klein Principal instruments or in divisions
based on a 4' Principal

4. The 2' Klein Octave Gemshorn may serve likewise in Positives or in divisions based on a 2' Principal

The correlation between the Gemshorn varieties and

the Principalbasis can be subjectively extended to show how
it may function as an octave voice:

    1. The 8' Aequal Gemshorn may serve as an octave
voice in Gross Principal instruments or in divisions
based on a 16' Principal

    2. The 4' Octave Gemshorn may serve similarly
in Aequal Principal instruments or in divisions based
on an 8' Principal

    3. The 2' Klein Octave Gemshorn may serve simi-
larly in Klein Principal instruments or in divisions
based on a 4' Principal

    A final correlation may be subjectively proposed be-
tween certain Gemshorn varieties and the Principalbasis,
whereby the Gemshorn may function as a super octave voice:

    1. The 4' Octave Gemshorn may serve as a super
octave voice in Gross Principal instruments or in divisions based on a 16' Principal

    2. The 2' Klein Octave Gemshorn may serve simi-
larly in Aequal Principal instruments or in divisions
based on an 8' Principal

    Such a rich array of functions demonstrates the ver-
satile character of the Gemshorn and justifies the considerable amount of time and space which Praetorius expends upon
it.

    Praetorius comments sparsely upon the registrational
values of certain of the unison and octave varieties of the

Gemshorn. He points out that the 16' Gross Gemshorn is more effective in registration when combined with another voice of 8' or 4' pitch. The 2' Klein Octave Gemshorn, he notes, can serve well as a pedal voice, particularly in canto-solo registrations.

Praetorius develops a set of mutation voices out of the Gemshorn species. He specifies a taper of 1/2, a mouth width of 1/5; and a cutup equal to 1/2 of the width.[25] His qualifying nomenclature assorts the voices as follows:

1. The 5 1/3' Gross Gemshornquinte may serve as a mutation voice over a Principalbasis no higher than 16' pitch

2. The 2 2/3' Gemshornquinte may serve similarly over a Principalbasis no higher than 8' pitch

3. The 1 1/3' Klein Gemshornquinte may serve similarly over a Principalbasis no higher than 4' pitch

The 1 1/3' Klein Gemshornquinte is often called Nasat. The voice is particularly useful in canto-solo registrations when combined with appropriate foundational voices. Praetorius indicates further that some builders develop the Nasat out of wide-scaled, open cylindrical pipes.

His allusion to the Viola da Gamba as the instrument whose tone the 8' Aequal Gemshorn resembles, points to a moderate or narrow scale as Praetorius' intention for this voice, but his actual sketch of the pipe in the Theatrum

Instrumentorum[26] and as reproduced on Plate LXXXVII, 3 belies this contention. By reference to this sketch, a comparison of the diameters of the 8' Principal and the 8' Gemshorn establishes the latter voice as one of fairly wide scale at the mouth.[27] See Table 90.

TABLE 90

RELATIVE SCALE OF 8' GEMSHORN

Item	Reference	Diameter in mm.	Deviation from Modern Normprincipal	Deviation from Praetorius Norm
8' Principal	37-1	142.6	-1.5 HT	-1.0 HT
8' Gemshorn	37-10	191.7	+5.0 HT	+6.0 HT

The Universal Table[28] distributes the varieties of Gemshorns. For Manual use Praetorius recommends:

16' Gross Gemshorn

8' Gemshorn

4' Octave Gemshorn

2 2/3' Gemshornquinte

2' Klein Gemshorn

1 1/3' Klein Gemshorn-
                    quinte or Nasat

For Pedal use he proposes:

16' Gross Gemshorn

8' Gemshorn

4' Octave Gemshorn

2 2/3' Gemshornquinte

2' Klein Gemshorn

Species Related to the Gemshorn

Praetorius adds certain observations to each of the

unison and octave voices in the Gemshorn species from which certain related species can be isolated and developed. He observes that the 8' Aequal Gemshorn approaches the tone quality of a Viola da Gamba[29] and asserts that among the Netherlanders, the term Koppelfloete seems frequently to have been used for this voice; occasionally also the term Spillfloete was used to designate a Gemshorn.

Inasmuch as practically all modern classifications of organ voices incorporate the Koppelfloete and the Spillfloete into the partly-covered family, it would seem desirable to differentiate them a little more closely. The Theatrum Instrumentorum[30] presents one example of each species as reproduced on Plate LXXXIX, 7 and 8. The dimensions and relationship of these voices to the 4' Octave are shown in Table 91.

TABLE 91

RELATIVE SCALE OF 4' KOPPELFLOETE
AND 4' SPILLFLOETE

Item	Reference	Diameter in mm.	Deviation from Modern Normprincipal	Deviation from Praetorius Norm
4' Octave	37-2	92.3	+0.5 HT	+1.0 HT
4' Koppelfloete	38-2	115.7	+5.5 HT	+6.0 HT
4' Spillfloete	37-11	93.5	+0.5 HT	+1.0 HT

These dimensions come very close to the usual

diameters adopted for these pipes today. Mahrenholz[31] recommends measurements for these voices as shown in Table 92.

TABLE 92

MAHRENHOLZ SCALES FOR THE KOPPELFLOETE
AND SPILLPFEIFE

Item	Deviation from Normprincipal
Koppelfloete	+2.0 HT to +6.0 HT
Spillpfeife	0.0 HT to -4.0 HT

Praetorius' sketch of the Koppelfloete exhibits a much longer conical chimney than do most modern examples.[32] The Universal Table[33] enters the Spillfloete among the Gemshorns and lists it only at 4' pitch. The Koppelfloete does not appear there.

Although Praetorius does not treat the Blockfloete separately, but rather under the general heading of Gemshorn, he does delineate it carefully enough to warrant its separation from the Gemshorn as a related but differentiated species; the Theatrum Instrumentorum[34] also presents a sketch of the Blockfloete which differs materially from the other open conical registers. He describes the Blockfloete as of a wider diameter than the Gemshorn; hence, more akin to the Spitzfloete in this respect. Its conicity, however, is less strong than that of the Gemshorn, and considerably less than that of the Spitzfloete. Praetorius' sketch of this voice

as found in the <u>Theatrum Instrumentorum</u> and reproduced on
Plate XCI, 5 establishes the voice as one of very wide scale.
See Table 93.

TABLE 93

RELATIVE SCALE OF 2' BLOCKFLOETE

Item	Refer- ence	Diameter in mm.	Deviation from Modern Normprincipal	Deviation from Prae- torius Norm
2' Octave	37-4	46.7	-3.5 HT	-3.0 HT
2' Blockfloete	37-12	87.7	+11.0 HT	+12.0 HT

Praetorius limits the use of the Blockfloete to two
varieties at the following pitches:

4' Blockfloete

2' [Klein] Blockfloete

The Universal Table[35] enters the Blockfloete among the Spitzfloetes and lists only one example of it; namely, at 4' pitch.

A second type of conical pipe, briefly described by
Praetorius, is the covered conical and overblown <u>Spitzgedackt</u>.
According to his account, and in fact, this corpus needs to
be of twice its normal length and will, therefore, overblow
into its octave since this species exhibits a full set of
partials in its acoustic spectrum. Since the simple length
for the covered conical family equals 3/4 of the pitch designation, the pipe, when overblown, needs to be 12' long for

8' pitch. An example of the Spitzgedackt in simple length occurs in the <u>Theatrum Instrumentorum</u>[36] as <u>8'</u> <u>Grossgedackt Lieblich</u>; a reproduction of the same appears on Plate LXXXVII, 4. Its dimensions and relation to the Principal are shown in Table 94.

TABLE 94

RELATIVE SCALE OF 8' GROSSGEDACKT
LIEBLICH [SPITZGEDACKT]

Item	Reference	Diameter in mm.	Deviation from Modern Normprincipal	Deviation from Praetorius Norm
8' Principal	37-1	142.6	-1.5 HT	-1.0 HT
8' Grossgedackt Lieblich	37-9	149.6	-0.5 HT	0.0 HT

This dimension lies well within Mahrenholz' recommendations for this voice; he lists it at from -3.0 HT to +3.0 HT.[37] Jahnn also conceives of this voice as moderate-scaled; he recommends a base value of +1.0 HT to +3.0 HT.[38] The voice does not appear as an item in Praetorius' Universal Table.

The Spitzfloetes

Praetorius considers the <u>Spitzfloete</u> species of sufficiently different character from the Gemshorn that he discusses its varieties separately and under their own title. At his time, the Spitzfloete seems to have been a recent development according to his account:

Spitzfloeit.	Spitzfloete
ES sind noch andere vnd fast dieser Art Stimmen / welche auch also zugespitzet seyn / vnd Spitzfloeiten genennet werden. Vnd dieser Art Mensur ist auch nicht gar lange vblich vnd im Gebrauch gewesen.	There is another species of voice similar [to Gemshorns], which also come to a point at the top and are called <u>Spitzfloetes</u>. Pipes of this species have not long been customary or in use.
Es ist aber ein ziemlicher vnterscheid zwischen den Gemszhoernern / vnd dieser Spitzfloeiten; Weil dieselbe vnten im labio weiter / vnd oben mehr zugespitzet wird / als gedackte[39] Gemszhoerner: Darumb sie recht Spitzfloeit geheissen. Vnd sind derselben nicht mehr / als zweyerley an Groesse vnd Thon.	There is, however, a considerable difference between Gemshorns and these Spitzfloetes. The latter are of a wider [scale] at the mouth and more pointed at the top than the above-mentioned Gemshorns. Therefore, they have justly been called Spitzfloetes, and are available in no more than two sizes and pitches.

1. Spitzfloeit
   4. Fusz am Thon.
2. Klein Spitzfloeit
   2. Fusz Thon.
	1. Spitzfloete
	   of 4' pitch
	2. Klein Spitzfloete
	   of 2' pitch

Auch habe ich Spitzfloeiten Art funden / welche oben gar wenig offen / vnd vnten gar enge labiret seyn; Dahero einen aus dermassen lieblichen Resonantz von sich geben: Aber mit grosser Muehe zur reinen vnd rechten Intonation zu bringen seynd.[40]	I have also found a subspecies of Spitzfloete which is only slightly open at the top and has a narrow mouth. Accordingly, it produces a lovely tone color. It requires much effort to develop a pure and proper speech [in these pipes]. [<u>Translation by the present author</u>]

Organization of the <u>Spitzfloete</u> Concept

Praetorius differentiates the Spitzfloete from the Gemshorn by the physical characteristics of its construction. He points out that:

1. The Spitzfloete is of greater diameter at the mouth than is the Gemshorn

2. It has a greater degree of conicity, <u>i.e.</u>, it is more nearly closed at the top of the corpus than is the Gemshorn

By virtue of his qualifying terms, it seems that Praetorius looks upon the Spitzfloete as an <u>octave</u> voice; if his usual classification is carried through, the Spitzfloete relates to the various Principalbases as follows:

1. The <u>4'</u> <u>Spitzfloete</u> may serve as an octave voice in <u>Aequal</u> <u>Principal</u> <u>instruments</u> or in divisions based upon an 8' Principal

2. The <u>2'</u> <u>Klein</u> <u>Spitzfloete</u> may serve similarly in <u>Klein</u> <u>Principal</u> <u>instruments</u> or in divisions based upon a 4' Principal

The Universal Table[41] includes also a mutation voice of the Spitzfloete species and distributes the varieties, so that for Manual use the following are recommended:

4' Spitzfloete   1 1/3' Spitzquinte

2' Klein Spitzfloete

For Pedal use, only one is proposed:

2' Klein Spitzfloete

The <u>Theatrum</u> <u>Instrumentorum</u> does not exemplify the Spitzfloete.[42]

From the Spitzfloete species, a sub-species in the form of an echo voice in open conical pipes is delineated by

Praetorius. It presents a very narrow mouth and exhibits a high degree of conicity, so much so that the pipe is nearly closed at the top of the corpus. Although Praetorius provides no name for this species, it is quite possible that he knew it as a <u>Conical Schwegel</u> to which he made reference under his presentation of the open cylindrical species of Schwegel, and both of which he considered as echo voices. No direct modern corollary can be found for this voice but it seems to have some relationship to the <u>Flûte douce</u>.

The <u>Flachfloetes</u>

Within the framework of open conical pipes, Praetorius isolates a species which differs materially from the Gemshorn and the Spitzfloete in its scale, mouth width, and degree of conicity. He identifies the species as the <u>Flachfloete</u>:

Flachfloeit.

NUn ist noch eine Art Stimme fast von dieser Mensur, vnd werden Flachfloeiten geheissen; Die seynd vnten im labio nicht gar weit / mit einem engen niedrigen vffschnidt / doch gar breit labiret, daher es auch so flach vnd nicht pompich klinget / vnd seynd oben nur ein wenig zugespitzet / wollen aber jhrer Intonation halben ein erfahrnen Meister haben; Klingen sonsten gar wol / vnd etwas flacher / als Gemszhoerner / drumb

Flachfloete

There is another species of voice, of almost the same scale, called <u>Flachfloete</u>. The diameter at the mouth is only moderately wide, the cutup low, and the mouth wide; for [these reasons] the tone is somewhat shallow and not so pompous. The pipes are only slightly tapered and require an experienced master to bring them into speech. Otherwise their tone color is quite agreeable and they sound somewhat more shallow than the Gemshorns; hence, the name,

sie recht mit dem Namen /
Flachfloeit getaufft seyn.
Es ist aber dieselbe dreyerley Art am Thon vnd Fusz
lenge. Als

   1. Grosz Flachfloeit
     8. Fusz Thon.
   2. Flachfloeit
     4. Fusz Thon.
   3. Klein Flachfloeit
     2. Fusz Thon.

Seynd alle drey gar gut
vnd nuetze / wenn viele
Stimmen in einem Werck disponiret seyn / zu lieblichen
enderungen zu gebrauchen:
Geben auch im Pedal schoene
Baesse zu vornehmen / denn
sie etwas lauter / jedoch
frembder / als die Gemsz-
hoerner am Klange seyn.

Moegen auch sonderlich die
kleine Flachfloeit / wenn
sie nach der Quinten Art
disponiret ist / im Rueck
Positiff mit einer Zimbel
vnd Quintadehn zu einem
geigenden Discant gebraucht
werden; denn es dem gar ehnlichen sich hoeren lest.
Vnd so viel sey von dieser
Art berichtet.[43]

Flachfloete, is a justifiable
designation. There are three
varieties [of Flachfloetes]
with respect to pitch and
length:

   1. Gross Flachfloete
     of 8' pitch
   2. Flachfloete
     of 4' pitch
   3. Klein Flachfloete
     of 2' pitch

All three are quite good and
useful for lovely registrations when a large number of
voices are specified for an
instrument. They provide also fine bass voices for the
Pedal because they sound somewhat louder and more unusual
than the Gemshorns.

The Klein Flachfloete, especially when introduced as a
quinting voice [i.e., likely
at 1 1/3' pitch] may be used
together with a Zimbel and a
Quintade of the Rueckpositive,
to produce a String-toned discant, since [the combination]
will resemble such a tone col-
or. Let this report be enough
concerning this species.
[Translation by the present
author]

The specifications for the Flachfloete reveal a moderate scale, a comparatively wide mouth, a very low cutup,
and a slight degree of conicity. The tone is described as
somewhat shallow and not nearly so pompous as that of the
wide-scaled open conical pipes, such as the Gemshorn or
Spitzfloete.

In conformity with his usual classification by qualifying terms, the Flachfloete seems to have been considered
an <u>octave</u> voice by Praetorius. Accordingly, it would relate
to the Principalbasis somewhat as follows:

    1. The <u>8</u>' <u>Gross</u> <u>Flachfloete</u> may serve as an oc-
tave voice in <u>Gross</u> <u>Principal</u> <u>instruments</u> or in divisions based on a 16' Principal

    2. The <u>4</u>' <u>Flachfloete</u> may serve a similar func-
tion in <u>Aequal</u> <u>Principal</u> <u>instruments</u> or in divisions
based on an 8' Principal

    3. The <u>2</u>' <u>Klein</u> <u>Flachfloete</u> may serve likewise
in <u>Klein</u> <u>Principal</u> <u>instruments</u> or in divisions based
on a 4' Principal

    A 4' example of the voice appears in the <u>Theatrum</u>
<u>Instrumentorum</u>,[44] and is reproduced on Plate LXXXIX, 6, where
its diameter reveals a moderate to moderately-wide scale.
See Table 95.

TABLE 95

RELATIVE SCALE OF 4' FLACHFLOETE

Item	Refer-ence	Diameter in mm.	Deviation from Modern Normprincipal	Deviation from Prae-torius Norm
4' Octave	37-2	92.3	+0.5 HT	+1.0 HT
4' Flachfloete	38-3	104.1	+3.0 HT	+4.0 HT

It will be noted that Praetorius' dimension approaches that of Jahnn, who recommends a base value of +3.0 HT to +4.0 HT for this voice.[45]

Praetorius recommends the use of voices from this species as registers in the Pedal; he points out that they are admirably suited to this function in that their tone is somewhat louder than that of Gemshorns and their tone color more unique.

He adds, further, a quinting Flachfloete (probably intended at 1 1/3' pitch), useful for canto-solo registration when combined with a Quintade and a Zimbel; the effect, he says, resembles that of a solo violin. Under his discussion of Gedackts, Praetorius alludes again to the Flachfloete, and says, "In my opinion, no species is better suited for a 32' pedal voice, than a Flachfloete."[46]

In the Universal Table[47] Praetorius distributes the varieties of Flachfloetes, so that for Manual use he recommends:

8' Gross Flachfloete	2' Klein Flachfloete or discant of the same
4' Flachfloete	

For Pedal use, he proposes:

8' Gross Flachfloete	2' Klein Flachfloete
4' Flachfloete	

The Labial Dulzian

From the family of open conical pipes Praetorius

isolates an invert-conical form which he labels <u>Dulzian</u>, <u>Dul-</u>
<u>zaen</u>, or <u>Dolcan</u>.[48] Most modern catalogs render the name as
<u>Dulzian</u> or, more particularly, as <u>Labial Dulzian</u>, in order to
distinguish it from a lingual species which uses the same
name. His account follows:

Dulzain.

ES ist noch eine Stimme /
die vngleicher weitten ist /
uebrig / oben weit / vnten
aber im labio vmb ein ziemliches enger: Solche stimme wird Dulzain genennet /
stehet zum Stralsond im
newen Wercke / vnd ist 8.
Fusz Thon / kan auch wegen
der gar schwehren Intonation
kleiner nicht gemacht werden: Klinget darumb dem
Dulzian etwas ehnlich / weil
sich das Corpus oben aus /
gleich wie das Instrument
Dulzain erweittert / vnd im
labio enger ist. Weil aber
der Dulzian an jhm selbsten
ein Rohr oder schnarrent Instrument bleiben musz / vnd
jetztbeschriebene Stimme
vnter das Floeit oder Pfeiffwerck gehoeret / kan dieselbige dem Rohr Instrument
nicht gar gleich Stimmen.
Man lest es aber also bey
des Meisters gegebenen Namen bleiben.[49]

[Labial] Dulzian

There is another voice of
non-cylindrical shape, which
is wide at the top and considerably narrower at the mouth.
Such a voice is known as a
[Labial] <u>Dulzian</u> and appears
in the new instrument at
Stralsund at 8' pitch. Because of [inherent] voicing
difficulties, it cannot [very
well] be constructed at higher
pitches. Its tone color resembles that of the [mouth-
blown] Dulzian because the
pipe body expands toward the
top but remains narrow near
the mouth, just as in the
case of the [mouth-blown] instrument. Since the [mouth-
blown] Dulzian must be considered a reed instrument, and
the present voice falls into
the labial order of organ
pipes, the [Labial] Dulzian
may not be voiced too similar
to the reed instrument. It
is, however, [advisable] to
retain the name given to it
by the masters. [<u>Translation</u>
<u>by the present author</u>]

<u>Organization of the Labial Dulzian Concept</u>

Praetorius' specifications delineate the voice as of
invert-conical shape; he requires:

1. An unequally proportioned corpus, i.e., a
corpus which does not exhibit a consistent diameter
throughout its length, but rather graduated diameters

2. A wide diameter at the top of the corpus

3. A moderate diameter at the mouth

The voice is recommended for use at 8ᵗ pitch only,
since Praetorius claims that it is difficult to voice at
higher pitches. However, a 4ᵗ example of the voice which ap‑
pears in the Theatrum Instrumentorum,[50] and is reproduced on
Plate XC, 2, exhibits a moderate scale at the mouth. See
Table 96.

TABLE 96

RELATIVE SCALE OF 4ᵗ LABIAL DULZIAN

Item	Refer‑ence	Diameter in mm.	Deviation from Modern Normprincipal	Deviation from Prae‑torius Norm
4ᵗ Octave	37‑2	92.3	+0.5 HT	+1.0 HT
4ᵗ Labial Dulzian	38‑1	98.3	+2.0 HT	+2.5 HT

The Universal Table[51] lists the Dulzian at 8ᵗ pitch
only and does not specify the divisions for which it might
be suitable.

Fully Covered Pipes

Praetorius divides his assortment of fully covered
pipes into two groups. The first group includes those species

which are related to the <u>Quintade</u>, the second group, those related to the <u>Gedackt</u>.

The Quintades

The first part of the account on covered pipes deals with registers of narrow scale; of these, Praetorius isolates three distinct species; namely, the <u>Quintade</u>, the <u>Nachthorn-Gedackt</u>, and the <u>Querfloete-Gedackt</u>:

<table>
<tr><td align="center">IV.</td><td align="center">IV</td></tr>
<tr>
<td align="center">Von Gedacten Pfeiffen / Vnd
erstlich von der Quinta-
dehna / Nachthorn vnd
Querfloeit.</td>
<td align="center">Of Covered Pipes, and First of
the Quintade, Nachthorn,
and Querfloete</td>
</tr>
<tr>
<td align="center">Quintadehna.</td>
<td align="center">Quintade</td>
</tr>
</table>

ES ist diese Stimme nicht lange / sondern etwa 40. o- der 50. Jahr im Gebrauch ge- wesen / wie sie denn in al- ten Orgeln nicht gefunden wird; Vnd ist eine liebliche Stimme (von etlichen Hol- schelle genennet) darinnen zweene vnterschiedliche Laut / als die Quinta, <u>ut</u>, <u>sol</u>, im Gehoer zu vernehmen seyn; Daher sie anfaenglich Quinta <u>ad</u> <u>una</u> genennet wor- den; Sie ist fast / jedoch ein ziemliches weiter / an Proportz jhres Corporis / als die Principal an der Mensur seyn; Vnd weil sie gedaeckt / ein Octava tief- fer als offene Pfeiffwerck gegen jhrer lenge zurech- nen. Es seyn aber dersel- ben / die aus einer Mensur vnterschiedlichen nach dem Thon oder Fuessen gearbei-

This voice has been in use for only about 40 or 50 years, and is not to be found in the old organs. It is a lovely voice (called <u>Hohlschelle</u> by some) wherein two distinguish- able sounds are discernible by the ear; namely, the funda- mental and twelfth, <u>do</u> and <u>sol</u>. It was, for this reason, originally designated Quinta ad una. It has almost the same proportions [<u>i.e.</u>, width and length] as the Principal, although its diameter is greater. Because it is cov- ered, its pitch must be reck- oned an octave lower than that of open pipes of the same length. There are three vari- eties [of Quintades] developed out of identical scales, but differentiated by pitch or length.

tet werden / nur dreyerley
Art verhanden: Als /

1. Grosse Quintadeen
16. Fusz Thon.

Diese Stimme ist Manuali-
ter vnd Pedaliter, wenn eine andere Stimme von 8. fi.
dazu genommen wird / gantz
lieblich zu gebrauchen vnd
zuhoeren.

2. Quintadeen
8. Fusz Thon.

Dieses ist beydes im
Rueck Positiff / oder im
kleinen Octaven Principal
Werck zum Fundament. Wie
denn auch im Pedal zum Choral Basz gar bequem zu gebrauchen.

3. Quintadeen
4. Fusz Thon.

Jst eine liebliche Stim-
me / sonderlich bey vnd zu
groessern Stimmen in der
Variation anzuhoeren; Kleiner aber wird sie nicht gefunden / wie sie denn auch
nicht geringer gearbeitet
[werden] kan.52

1. Gross Quintade
of 16' pitch

This voice is lovely to play
and to hear, both in the Manual and Pedal when another
voice of 8' pitch is added to
it.

2. Quintade
of 8' pitch

This is the fundamental
[voice] in the Rueckpositive
or in the Klein Octave Principal instrument. It can also be conveniently used in
the Pedal as a bass voice to
the Choralbass.

3. Quintade
of 4' pitch

[. . .] is also a lovely
voice to hear especially when
associated with larger voices
in registration. It is not,
however, to be found in higher pitches, since it cannot
be constructed [in diminutive
sizes]. [Translation by the
present author]

Organization of the Quintade Concept

The Quintade apparently was a newly developed voice
in Praetorius' day; he describes its tone as compound, presenting both a fundamental and a clearly perceptible twelfth.
Although it appears that Praetorius is specifying a large
scale for the Quintade when he says that it is wider than a
Principal, he is, in all probability, comparing an 8' Quintade

with a 4' Principal which exhibits a similar length of corpus. Hence, the scale is actually considerably narrower than
that of a Principal of equal pitch length. The dimensions
of the 8' Quintade as given in the Theatrum Instrumentorum,[53]
and reproduced on Plate LXXXVIII, 2, reveal the relationship
of its diameter to that of the Principal. See Table 97.

TABLE 97

RELATIVE SCALE OF 8' QUINTADE

Item	Refer-ence	Diameter in mm.	Deviation from Modern Normprincipal	Deviation from Prae-torius Norm
8' Principal	37-1	142.6	-1.5 HT	-1.0 HT
8' Quintade	37-7	105.2	-8.5 HT	-8.0 HT

The relationship of the Quintade to the Principalbasis is not clearly defined; however, Praetorius' suggestion
that the 8' member could serve as a fundamental voice in
Klein Principal instruments or even in Positives would point
to a sub-octave or possibly a double sub-octave function for
the Quintade group, as such. In the following presentation,
the 16' and 4' functions are subjective extensions of the
principle stated for the 8' member:

1. The 16' Gross Quintade may serve as a sub-
octave voice in Aequal Principal instruments or in divisions based on an 8' Principal

2. The 8' Quintade may serve similarly in Klein Principal instruments or in divisions based on a 4' Principal

3. The 4' [Klein] Quintade may serve similarly in Positives based on a 2' Principal

The double sub-octave function of the Quintade as defined for the 8' member may be subjectively extended to include the 16' member as well:

1. The 16' Gross Quintade may serve as a double sub-octave voice in Klein Principal instruments or in divisions based on a 4' Principal

2. The 8' Quintade may serve similarly in Positives based on a 2' Principal

In addition, Praetorius recommends other incidental uses for the Quintade. He suggests the 16' member as useful in the Pedal; the 8' member in the Pedal, he suggests as a useful, mild, sub-octave voice for canto-solo registrations, particularly those which involve the use of the Choralbass. In the Universal Table,[54] Praetorius recommends for Manual use:

16' Gross Quintade   4' Klein Quintade

8' Quintade

For Pedal use, he suggests:

16' Gross Quintade   4' Klein Quintade

8' Quintade

The Nachthorn-Gedackts

From the narrow-scaled genus of the fully covered family, Praetorius isolates and defines another species which he terms a Nachthorn, but which should more accurately be identified as Nachthorn-Gedackt, in order to differentiate it from the Nachthorn Offen which he describes under the very wide-scaled genus of the open cylindrical family. His account follows:

Nachthorn.

ES wird aber diese kleine Quintadeena von etlichen Orgelmachern an der Mensur, Jedoch vff gewisse masse erweitert / vnd daher / (weil sie aus solcher erweiterung einen Hornklang bekoempt / vnd die Quinta etwas stiller darinnen wird) Nachthorn geheissen. Welcher Name auch recht ist. Es mag aber diese Art ebenmessig zu vielen andern Stimmen gar lieblich vnd mannigfaltig verendert werden.

Aus dieser Mensur oder Art koemmet auch der Nachthorn Basz / beydes von 4. Fusz / so denn auch von 2. Fusz Thon her / vnd ist eine zierliche Stimme / bevorab im Basz anzuhoeren.

Die Niederlaender arbeiten das Nachthorn offen / wie eine Holfloeite / doch oben vmb etwas enger / vnd brechen allmehlich jmmer etwas ab / ist auch im Labio nicht so hoch vffgeschnitten / als die Hol-

Nachthorn

Some organ builders enlarge, to a certain degree, the scale [i.e., the diameter] of the Klein Quintade and (since by such enlargement the pipe assumes a horn tone and the twelfth becomes less audible) call it Nachthorn[-Gedackt], which is a proper designation. This species of voice may very well be used with many other voices for lovely and manifold registrations.

From this scale or variety is also derived the Nachthorn-bass, both in 4' and 2' pitch, which provides a decorative voice, especially in the Pedal.

The Netherlanders build the Nachthorn of open pipes like a Hohlfloete, although somewhat narrower at the top, and with a gradual but constant diminution. Since the mouth is not cut up as high as in the Hohlfloete, the [pipes]

floeit / daher es einen sonderlichen Klang bekoempt /
gleichsam / als wie einer
zuchete oder schluggete.[55]

develop a unique tone, reminiscent of someone trembling
or sobbing. [Translation by
the present author]

Organization of the Nachthorn-Gedackt Concept

Praetorius isolates the Nachthorn-Gedackt as a species distinct from the Quintade. He specifies it as of a
somewhat larger scale which, besides suppressing the twelfth
and reinforcing the fundamental, gives the voice a definite
horn character. The example of a Nachthorn-Gedackt from the
Theatrum Instrumentorum,[56] as reproduced on Plate XC, 3, relates to the 4' Octave as shown in Table 98.

TABLE 98

RELATIVE SCALE OF 4' NACHTHORN-GEDACKT

Item	Refer-ence	Diameter in mm.	Deviation from Modern Normprincipal	Deviation from Prae-torius Norm
4' Octave	37-2	92.3	+0.5 HT	+1.0 HT
4' Nachthorn-Gedackt	37-8	76.0	-4.0 HT	-3.5 HT

The dimension for the diameter of the Nachthorn-
Gedackt is very nearly that adopted by Mahrenholz for the
Gedacktpommer, which he lists at from -4.0 HT to -8.0 HT.[57]
Inasmuch as the Quintade was found to be about -8.0 HT in
its base value, the Nachthorn-Gedackt at -3.5 HT is about
4.5 HT larger than the Quintade. It resembles in its scale

and tonal characteristics the modern Gedacktpommer or possibly
the Musiziergedackt, and may be considered the early baroque
corollary for this voice.

Praetorius recommends the Nachthorn-Gedackt for use
at 4' pitch, since he considers it an adaptation of the 4'
Klein Quintade. He finds the voice useful in the Pedal as:

4' Nachthorn-Gedacktbass   2' Nachthorn-Gedacktbass

He acknowledges the fact that the term Nachthorn is
also used for an entirely different voice from another family and genus. This is the Nachthorn of the open cylindrical
family, of very wide scale, narrow mouth, and very low cutup.
He classifies it among the Hohlfloetes but states his personal preference for the Nachthorn-Gedackt of the fully covered
family, here under discussion.

The Querfloete-Gedackts

Praetorius' concept of the Querfloete permits the
voice to be executed in two different species; one is covered,
the other, open. In order to differentiate between them, it
should be observed that his present discussion concerns itself chiefly with the Querfloete-Gedackt:

Querfloeit.	Querfloete
NOch ist aus dieser Inven- tion der Quintadeen / eine newe Art erfunden worden / welche sich mit den Quer- floeiten / wie sie denn auch Querfloeit genennet wird / gar ehnlich im Klange ver-	Out of the discovery of the Quintade, still another spe- cies has been developed whose tone color compares closely and relates intimately to that of the [mouth-blown] Querfloe- te from which it derives its

gleichet vnd vereinbaret.

Es koempt aber derselbe
Klang nicht aus freywilliger
natuerlicher Intonation,
sondern auszm vbersetzen
oder vbergallen; Das vbergallen oder vbersetzen aber
daher / weil das Corpus gegen seiner enge mehr als
noch eines / vnd fast noch
anderthalb mal so lang ist.

Als zum Bericht; Wenn das
c / 4. Fusz Thon seinen
Klang hoeren lest / so ist
desselben Corpus an der lenge so lang / dasz / ob es
zwar wegen seiner lenge auff
12. Fusz respondiren solte
vnd koendte / so intoniret
doch in denselben nur al-
lein die Quinta, die vom
vbersetzen oder vbergallen
herruehret; Wie denn auch
solch Corpus wegen der vn-
natuerlichen lenge gegen
der enge / anders nicht als
Quinten kan.

Diese art der Querfloei-
ten ist zwar gut / vnd auch
newer Invention; Aber die
offener Mensur vnd an der
Corpus lenge noch eins so
lang seyn / welcher Art
denn auch in dem Fuerstli-
chen newen hoeltzernen Orgelwerck / (welches der
Hochwuerdige / Durchleuch-
tige hochgeborne Fuerst vnd
Herr / Herr Heinrich Julius / Postulirter Bischoff
zu Halberstadt / Hertzog zu
Braunschweig vnd Lueneburg /
Mein gnaediger Fuerst vnd
Herr hochloeblicher gedecht-
nisz / S. Fuerstl. G. hertzl.

name.

The tone, however, is not
the outcome of a free and natural speech, but the result of
transposition by overblowing.
The transposition, [in turn,]
is caused by the fact that
the length of the corpus, in
relation to [the normal length
which] its scale [would ordinarily require,] is more than
2 times and almost 2 1/2 times
its simple length.[58]

For example: if a c of 4'
pitch is made to sound, then
the body of the pipe will
[need to] be of such a length
as should and could ordinarily
produce approximately a 12'
pitch [i.e., a pitch equal to
FF]; yet the [phenomenon] of
transposition will permit the
pipe to overblow only at the
twelfth. This is reasonable,
since a pipe of such an un-
natural length [i.e., a 6'
length] in relation to [the
length which] its scale [would
ordinarily require] cannot do
otherwise than sound a
twelfth.

This species of Querfloete,
to be sure, is a good [voice]
and of recent invention. But
another species, [constructed
of] open [pipes] and in double length, pleases me more.
This is the one placed into
the princely new wooden organ
of 27 voices and 3 claviers
enclosed in a decorative case
and described in section V,
which the Right Reverend, Il-
lustrious, and Honourable Sovereign and Lord, Lord Heinrich Julius, Postulated Bishop
of Halberstadt, Duke of Braunschweig and Lueneburg, my gra-
cious Sovereign and Lord of

Gemahl. vff deroselben
Schlosz zu Hessen durch den
vornemen Orgel- vnd Instru-
mentmacher / Meister Esaiam
Compenium von 27. Stimmen /
mit dreyen Claviren in einem zierlichen Schappe /
dessen Disposition hinten
im V. Theil zu finden / setzen lassen) an jetzo von
Holtz / sonsten aber von
andern hiebevor auch in Metall gearbeittet worden
seyn / gefallen mir besser;
Denn es ist natuerlicher /
dasz es sich in der Octava
vbersetzet / als dasz es
noch weiter sich vberset-
zen / vnd ferner in die
Quint fallen solte. Vnd
sind dem natuerlichen Quer-
floeitenklang am Resonantz
noch gleicher / als die Gedacte / derer Art auch in
vor hochgedachter S. F. G.
herrlichen grossen Orgel zu
Grueningen / von 8. vnd 4.
Fusz Thon im Manual vnd Pedal verhanden seyn.⁶⁰

most blessed memory, had constructed by Master Esaias Compenius, distinguished organ
and instrument builder, for
His Sovereign Grace's beloved
spouse, and erected in her
palace at Hessen.⁵⁹ Here
[the Querfloetes] are made of
wood, although other builders
had previously constructed
them also of metal. For it is
more natural that [the pipes]
should transpose into the octave than go beyond and fall
into the twelfth. These [open
ones] resemble the tone color
of the [mouth-blown] Querfloete more closely than do
the covered ones, of which [a
pair] at 8' and 4' pitch appear both in the Manual and
Pedal of the large and magnificent organ of H[is]
P[rincely] G[race] at Grueningen. [Translation by the
present author]

Organization of the Querfloete-Gedackt Concept

The Querfloete-Gedackt is classified as a form of
overblown Quintade, although it is more closely related in
its scale to the Nachthorn-Gedackt. In fact, its deviation
in half-tones from both of these species compels Praetorius
to identify it as a separate species. His explanation of
the phenomenon of overblowing bespeaks the facts in the case;
the pipe overblows into the twelfth because the corpus is a
covered cylindrical one and, for this reason, presents only
the odd-numbered partials in its acoustic spectrum. Hence,

the corpus must be 3 times its simple physical length and 1 1/2 times its pitch length; as for example, 6' length for 4' pitch.

The Querfloete-Gedackt seems to be considered as an octave voice by virtue of the qualifying terms associated with the name of the register. Accordingly, its relation to the Principalbasis can be subjectively postulated as follows:

1. The 8' Gross Querfloete-Gedackt may serve as an octave voice in Gross Principal instruments or in divisions based upon a 16' Principal

2. The 4' Querfloete-Gedackt may serve similarly in Aequal Principal instruments or in divisions based on an 8' Principal

Praetorius' sketch of the 4' Querfloete-Gedackt as it appears in the Theatrum Instrumentorum,[61] and is reproduced on Plate XC, 5, relates the voice to the 4' Octave as shown in Table 99.

TABLE 99

RELATIVE SCALE OF 4' QUERFLOETE-GEDACKT

Item	Reference	Diameter in mm.	Deviation from Modern Normprincipal	Deviation from Praetorius Norm
4' Octave	37-2	92.3	+0.5 HT	+1.0 HT
4' Querfloete-Gedackt	37-14	87.7	-1.0 HT	0.0 HT

The Querfloete-Gedackt occurs in the Universal Table[62]
among the fully covered pipes of narrow scale. For Manual
use Praetorius recommends:

8' Gross Querfloete-Gedackt   4' Querfloete-Gedackt

For Pedal use he proposes:

8' Gross Querfloete-Gedackt   4' Querfloete-Gedackt

Praetorius also delineates and sketches an open cylindrical and overblown form of the Querfloete. The same is
discussed in chapter xii of the present study in connection
with the Schweizerpfeifes.

The Gedackts

From the general and overall concept of the Gedackt,
Praetorius detaches and isolates a separate species in the
form of the more narrow-scaled Bordun or Klein Barduen, and
an echo form for the entire family which he labels, Barem.
By far the major portion of his discussion, however, deals
with the several varieties of the Gedackt proper:

V.	V
Gedacten allerley Art.	Varieties of the Gedackt

DIese Stimme ist von den Alten in jhren Wercken nur allein schlecht mit dem Namen Floeitten genennet worden. Die Niederlaender vnd etliche andere nennen sie Bordun / sonderlich wenn sie enger Mensur sind: Etliche nennen sie auch Ba-rem / wenn sie gar still vnd linde intonirt wird.	Among the instruments of our forefathers, this voice [i.e., the Gedackt] was simply desig-nated as Floete. The Nether-landers and a few others call it Bordun, especially when constructed of a narrow scale. When voiced rather softly and gently, some call it Barem. Of the Gedackts or fully cov-ered voices there are six

Es seynd aber der Gedacten oder gantz zugedaeckten Stimmen nach jhrem Thon vnd Fusz gerechnet / sechserley Arten.

1. Grosz Gedact vff 16. Fusz Thon.

Diese Stimme wird mehrern theils ins Pedal gesetzt / vnd grosz Gedackter Vntersatz geheissen: Sie wird auch wol ins Manual herdurch gefuehret. Aber wegen jres thunen vnd stillen Klanges vnd jhrer Tieffe nicht so gar anmutig vnd vorstendtlich zuhoeren / wie die Erfahrung vnd Natur bezeuget. Vnd ob zwar diese gedackte Mensur, auch wol zu zeiten von 32. Fusz Thon im Pedal gesetzet / vnd grosz Gedacter Sub Basz genennet wird / so ist doch / wie vorher vom grossen Sub Principal berichtet worden / daraus viel weniger / als in offenen Pfeiffen ein rechter verstaendlicher Thon zu vernemen. Meines erachtens were vff 32. Fusz Thon keine bessere Art anzubringen / als die Flachfloeiten: Doch wil ich solches einem verstaendigen Orgelmacher zu probieren anheim gestellet haben.

2. Gedact am Thon 8. Fusz.

Dieses ist nu eine gemeine Stimme im Gebrauch / wird, auch wol in kleine Octav Principalwerck zum Fundament / wie denn auch in grosse Rueckpositiff gesetzt vnd disponiret.

varieties which are differentiated by pitch.

1. Gross Gedackt of 16' pitch

This voice, for the most part, is placed into the Pedal and called <u>Gross Gedackt Untersatz</u>. It is also carried through on the Manual. However, because of its extensive yet quiet tone and low pitch it is not very charming or distinct. This is clear from experience and from the very nature of the voice. Even though, from time to time, [a variety of this] species is placed into the Pedal at 32' pitch and called <u>Gross Gedackt Subbass</u>, it produces a much less distinct tone than do open pipes, as described earlier in connection with the Gross Subprincipal. In my opinion no better species of voice could be adopted for the 32' pitch than the Flachfloete. However, I shall leave such an experiment to the discretion of a skillful organ builder.

2. Gedackt of 8' pitch

This is a voice now in common use, and is placed into Klein Octave Principal instruments and into large Positives as a fundamental register.

3. Klein Gedackt
am Thon 4. Fusz.

Wird auch in gemein in allerhand dispositionen der Wercken vnd Positiffen gesetzet: Jst aber gut / vnd gibt feine vnd mannigfaltige / sonderlich mit Quintadehnen vnd Gemszhoernern vorenderungen.

Es ist ohngefehr vor 28. Jahren von einem domals jungen Meister E. C. eine seltzam Art erfunden / nach dem derselbe ein gedackt 4. Fusz Thon / mit zweyen labiis, die just einander gleich respondiren, gemacht / also / dasz man die Pfeiffen durchsehen kan / welche er Duifloet genennet hat. Dieselbe verendert jhren Klang gar vor anderer Gedacten Arten. Jst aber noch zur zeit nicht gemein worden.

4. Supergedaectlein
ist 2. Fusz am Thon.

Ob dieses schon gleich ist / so gibt es doch auch liebliche Variationes mit grossen Stimmwercken / Wie von dem Suifloeit vnd andern mehr erwehnet worden; sonderlich aber / wo ein guter Tremulant verhanden ist. Jnmassen es dann / wofern es juster Mensur, vnd reine gleichlautend intoniret, einen auszbuendigen guten Discant in der rechten Hand zu gebrauchen / vnd einem kleinen Plockfloeitlein gantz gleich vnd ehnlichen; Wie es denn auch zum grossen Rancket oder Sorduen von 16. Fuessen einen frembden Klang

3. Klein Gedackt
of 4' pitch

[. . .] is commonly specified for all kinds of instruments and Positives. It is a worthwhile [voice] and provides many and fine registrations, especially with the Quintade and the Gemshorn.

About 28 years ago a young master [builder], E[saias] C[ompenius], developed an unusual species [of voice] in the form of a 4' Gedackt with two identical mouths, [laid out] so that it was possible to look [transversely] through the pipe; he called [this voice] Duifloete.[63] Its tone varies considerably from other varieties of Gedackts. As yet, it has not become popular.

4. Super Gedackt
of 2' pitch

Even though this [voice] is identical [to the others of this species], it provides many lovely registrations with larger [i.e., more grave] voices, as was mentioned [above] in connection with the Siffloete and others, especially when a good Tremulant is available. When of the proper scale and uniformly voiced, it is useful as an excellent discant in the right hand, resembling very closely a small Blockfloete. It is a pleasure to hear it [played] together with a Gross Rankett or Sordun of 16' pitch with which it provides an unusual

vnd enderung gibt / vnd mit Lust anzuhoeren ist.

registration resulting in a strange tone color.

> 5. Gedacte Quinta
> 3. Fusz Thon.

> 5. Gedacktquinte
> of 2 2/3' pitch

Diese Stimme ist von et-lichen / als Gregorio Vo-gel / Pfeifferfloeit / wel-ches eine Quinta vom Chor Thon gestanden / genennet worden.

Some, as for example, Grego-rius Vogel, have called this voice Pfeiferfloete, [an in-strument] which was pitched at [the interval of] a fifth from the Chorton.

> 6. Bawerfloeit Basz /
> oder Paeurlin
> 1. Fusz Thon.

> 6. Bauerfloetebass
> of 1' pitch

Von dieser Stimme wird bey vns in Deutschland / sonderlich / wenn man den Choral im Pedal fuehren wil / gar viel gehalten: Die Italiaener aber verach-ten alle solche kleine Baszstimmen von 2. oder 1. Fusz Thon / dieweil sie / als eitel Octaven lautten / vnd im Resonantz mit sich bringen.[64]

Here in Germany we lay great store by this voice, especial-ly when one wishes to lead the chorale in the Pedal. The Italians, however, despise all such small bass voices of 2' or 1' pitch, because to them they sound like empty octaves. [Translation by the present author]

Organization of the Gedackt Concept

By assorting the several varieties of the Gedackt, it will be noted that Praetorius lists four of them at uni-son and octave pitches:

1. The 16' Gross Gedackt   3. The 4' Klein Gedackt

2. The 8' Gedackt   4. The 2' Super Gedackt

He proposes a single variety as a mutation voice:

1. The 2 2/3' Gedacktquinte

For the Pedal exclusively, he adds:

1. The 1' Bauerfloete

The Universal Table[65] lists the varieties similarly, but defines the pedal members more comprehensively. For Manual use, the table proposes:

1. The 16' Gross Gedackt   4. The 2 2/3' Gedacktquinte

2. The 8' Gedackt   5. The 2' Super Gedackt

3. The 4' Klein Gedackt

For Pedal use, the table lists:

1. The 32' Gross Gedacktsubbass

2. The 16' Gross Gedacktbass or Gedackt Untersatz

3. The 8' Gedackt

4. The 4' Klein Gedackt

5. The 1' Bauerfloetebass

The relative scales of the Gedackt and the Klein Barduen or Bordun can be observed in Table 100, which gives the diameters of the pertinent examples as illustrated in the Theatrum Instrumentorum,[66] and reproduced on Plate LXXXVIII, 3 and 4, and relates them to the 8' Principal.

TABLE 100

RELATIVE SCALE OF 8' GEDACKT AND 8' KLEIN BARDUEN

Item	Reference	Diameter in mm.	Deviation from Modern Normprincipal	Deviation from Praetorius Norm
8' Principal	37-1	142.6	-1.5 HT	-1.0 HT
8' Gedackt	38-6	133.0	-3.0 HT	-2.5 HT
8' Klein Barduen	38-4	123.8	-5.0 HT	-4.5 HT

In line with Praetorius' usual classification by
qualifying terms as Gross, Klein, etc., the Gedackt species
may be considered as chiefly a unison voice, taking its place
beside the Principalbases at corresponding pitch levels.
From such a viewpoint, subjectively arrived at, the following relationships may be proposed:

1. The 16' Gross Gedackt may serve as a unison
voice in Gross Principal instruments or in divisions
based on a 16' Principal

2. The 8' Gedackt may serve similarly in Aequal
Principal instruments or in divisions based on an 8'
Principal

3. The 4' Klein Gedackt may serve in like manner
in Klein Principal instruments or in divisions based
on a 4' Principal

4. The 2' Super Gedackt may serve likewise in
Positives based on a 2' Principal

In his account it soon becomes evident that Praetorius envisions a far greater versatility for the Gedackts than
the preceding outline would indicate. A sub-octave and occasional double sub-octave function for this species can
easily be surmised from certain specific indications he gives
in his account; but his recommendations are selective:

1. The 16' Gross Gedackt may serve as a sub-
octave voice in the Pedal, being superior in function
here than in the Manual. It is of common occurrence

2. The 8' Gedackt may serve as a sub-octave voice in Klein Principal instruments or in divisions based on a 4' Principal; it may serve as a double sub-octave voice in Positives based on a 2' Principal

In addition, Praetorius discusses certain other functions for specific varieties which do not bear rigid organization. Thus, he finds the 4' Klein Gedackt very gratifying in various divisions of instruments and in Positives. The 2' Super Gedackt he finds admirable in canto-solo registrations with the 16' Rankett or the 16' Sordun. The present author suspects that Praetorius might have intended the 2' Super Gedackt for the Pedal also, even though he fails to mention this possibility. The voice can more easily be carried through the range of the Pedal than that of the Manual. Nevertheless, the Universal Table[67] lists the voice for Manual use but not for Pedal, thus reinforcing Praetorius' written account.

The 1' Bauerfloete represents this popular pedal voice as executed in covered cylindrical pipes, taking its place alongside the 1' Bauerfloete of open cylindrical and wide-scaled Hohlfloete pipes recommended in the first part of the present chapter. Praetorius conceives of the Bauerfloete in either form as a noteworthy voice for all manner of canto-solo registrations in the Pedal.

In connection with the 4' Klein Gedackt, Praetorius reports Esaias Compenius' execution of this voice with double

mouths introduced into opposite sides of covered wooden pipes.
Designated as <u>Duifloete</u> (<u>i</u>.<u>e</u>., <u>Doppelfloete</u> in modern nomenclature), the voice had not yet gained general acceptance in
his day.

<u>Partly Covered Pipes</u>

Praetorius limits his discussion of the partly covered family to the varieties of the <u>Rohrfloete</u> species, having already treated the Spillfloete and Koppelfloete (which
most modern writers associate with partly covered pipes)
under the open conical family.

<u>The Rohrfloetes</u>

Considering the fact that the <u>Rohrfloete</u> has achieved
a considerable importance in the organ of today, it is somewhat remarkable that Praetorius discusses it rather briefly
in comparison to some of the other significant voices in the
organ. His account follows:

VI.	VI
Die zwar gedaect / aber wiederumb oben in etwas eroeffnet seyn: Als	Pipes Which are Covered but have been Somewhat Reopened at the Top, As, for Example,
Roehrfloeiten.	Rohrfloetes
AVs dieser Gedacten Mensur vnd Art ist nun eine andere erfunden / welche durch ge- wisse mensurirte Roehrlein / wiederumb in etwas eroeffnet wird: dahero sie denn recht Rohrfloeit heisset.	Out of the family and genera of the Gedackts another spe- cies has been developed, of which [the covered pipes] have been somewhat reopened at the top by means of carefully- scaled cylinders [<u>i</u>.<u>e</u>.,

Dieser Art Stimmen aber werden vnterschiedlich gearbeitet. Etliche lassen die Roehren halb herausser / vnd halb hinein gehen: Etliche gar hinein / dasz man nichts sihet / als oben das Loch / vnnd diese seynd zum bestaendigsten / denn die Roehren koennen alsdenn nicht verbeuget werden: Dieselbige aber musz man alsdenn mit Deckhuetten stimmen.

   1. Grosse Roehrfloeit
     16. Fusz Thon.

Wann nun ja von solchen grossen Gedacten Stimmwerken eine durchs gantze Manual gehen solte / so were diese grosse Rohrfloeit wegen dessen / dasz sie lautter vnd reiner klingt / weit besser / denn die gantze Gedacte Art / weil sie noch eine feine wolklingende Quintam darneben mit hoeren lesset.

   2. Rohrfloeit
     ist 8. Fusz Thon.
   3. Kleine Roehrfloeit
     ist 4. Fusz Thon.
   4. Super Roehrfloeitlein
     2. Fusz Thon.

Diese sind alle gar fueglich vnd lieblich zu aller Art Stimmen / sonderlich aber zur Quintadehnen zu gebrauchen.

5. Es gibt auch keine Art

chimneys]; the species is appropriately labelled Rohrfloete.

This species of voice is fabricated in different ways. Some allow the chimneys to extend partly into and partly out of the pipe; others sink them entirely, so that only an opening remains at the top. The latter are the more desirable because the chimneys are not [so likely to be] bent [out of shape]. [In any case] all must be tuned by [means of] fitted covers [i.e., calottes or canisters].

   1. Gross Rohrfloete
     of 16' pitch

If it should be desired to carry one of the large covered voices clear through [the compass of] the Manual, it would be better to choose this Gross Rohrfloete than a fully covered species, since it presents a fine, distinct, and pleasant fifth[-sounding] tone beside [the fundamental].

   2. Rohrfloete
     of 8' pitch
   3. Klein Rohrfloete
     of 4' pitch
   4. Super Rohrfloete
     of 2' pitch

These are all suitable and lovely to use with all kinds of registers, especially with Quintades.

   [5. Rohrschellebass
     of 1' pitch]

There is no better species

Stimmwerck ein besser Bawr-
floeit Baeszlin von 1. Fusz
Thon / als diese; Denn sie
gar eigendlich solchen
Klang / als wenn einer mit
dem Munde pfiffe / in der
hoehe in sich hat / vnd dasselbige wegen des vffgesetz-
ten Roehrleins. Disz Stimm-
lein ist von etlichen /
weils eine helle Quint in
sich hat / vnnd hoeren
lest / Rohrschell / Aber
wenn seine Eigenschafft wol
betrachtet wird / nicht
recht genennet worden.[68]

of register to produce the
Bauerfloetebass of 1' pitch
than this [very] one because
at such a high pitch it possesses a tone color much as
if one were to whistle with
the mouth. This [effect] is
caused by the surmounted
chimney. This little voice,
because it contains a bright
fifth[-sound] in its tone,
is called Rohrschelle by some;
this is, however, an inappropriate designation when one
considers its properties
carefully. [Translation by
the present author]

Organization of the Rohrfloete Concept

Praetorius points out that the Rohrfloete requires
carefully-scaled chimneys which are mounted either half in
and half out, or are entirely hidden within the pipe; he prefers the latter method of mounting, since thereby the diminutive chimneys are not so readily subject to abuse.

The variety of Rohrfloetes enumerated by Praetorius
are all of unison and octave pitches and seem to be intended
as unison voices, i.e., agreeing in pitch level with the
Principalbases of the divisions in which they are mounted.
His qualifying terms give the clue for this relationship,
which may subjectively be stated as follows:

1. The 16' Gross Rohrfloete may serve as a unison voice in Gross Principal instruments or in divisions based on a 16' Principal

2. The 8' Rohrfloete may serve similarly in

Aequal Principal instruments or in divisions based on
an 8' Principal

3. The 4' Klein Rohrfloete may serve in like
manner in Klein Principal instruments or in divisions
based on a 4' Principal

4. The 2' Super Rohrfloete may serve likewise in
Positives based on a 2' Principal

Praetorius' sketch of the Rohrfloete as found in the
Theatrum Instrumentorum,[69] and reproduced on Plate LXXXVIII,
5, relates its scale to the 8' Principal. See Table 101.

TABLE 101

RELATIVE SCALE OF 8' ROHRFLOETE

Item	Refer- ence	Diameter in mm.	Deviation from Modern Normprincipal	Deviation from Prae- torius Norm
8' Principal	37-1	142.6	-1.5 HT	-1.0 HT
8' Rohrfloete	38-7	156.2	+0.5 HT	+1.0 HT

Praetorius points out that the 16' Gross Rohrfloete
is better suited for the Manual than a Gedackt of the same
pitch, since it produces a louder and more distinct tone
which has a clearly perceptible overtone in it. The voice
combines particularly well with the Quintade. In the Pedal,
Praetorius points out, the Rohrfloete makes a noteworthy 1'
Bauerrohrfloete, often called a Rohrschelle, because of the

bright overtone present in its tone. This is the third species of Bauerfloete which Praetorius recommends, taking its place alongside the Bauerfloete of wide-scaled open cylindrical pipes, and the one of covered cylindrical pipes. Of the three distinct species, Praetorius prefers the Bauerfloete constructed of partly covered pipes.

The Universal Table[70] distributes the varieties of Rohrfloetes, so that for the Manual are recommended:

16' Gross Rohrfloete	4' Klein Rohrfloete
8' Rohrfloete	2' Super Rohrfloete

For the Pedal are recommended:

16' Gross Rohrfloete	4' Klein Rohrfloete
8' Rohrfloete	1' Bauerrohrfloete

Mahrenholz develops the contention that the Rohrfloete experienced a much longer history than did its designation. He says:

> The name, Rohrfloete, seems to be of a more recent vintage. Praetorius, because of his close association with Compenius does not necessarily bespeak a North German viewpoint; in his dispositions he designates nearly twenty Hohlfloetes, which are quite certainly of a covered construction, and almost the same number of Bauerfloetes of similar disposition. He uses the term, Rohrfloete, as a designation only for the instruments of the Compenius family at Magdeburg, Dom; Magdeburg, St. Katharinen; Bueckeburg; and Riddagshausen. Outside of these, the name is met only one additional time in the Fritzsche organ at Sondershausen; (the use of the term in his own prospectuses is obviously the result of Compenius' influence). It is quite likely, therefore, that the term, Rohrfloete, originated with the Compenius school.[71]

Pipes in Wood

Having presented his full array of labial pipes and given the critical dimensions for many of them in his Thea-trum Instrumentorum[72] as executed in metal, Praetorius appends a few cursory paragraphs to his account in which he very briefly draws attention to the possibility and practice of constructing many of the species in wood. He relates:

Allhier solte auch wol das hoeltzern Pfeiffwercks ge-dacht werden; Dieweil aber dasselbige / wegen allerhand Fundament Theilung / wie ichs selbst gar fleissig mit angesehen / so wol auch im Klange / gantz eine andere Meynung davon zuschreiben hat / vnd mit andern Orgel-wercken an Laut vnd arbeit fast wenig zu vergleichen: Welches dann mit vorgedach-tem Musicalischem vff dem Schlosz Hessen stehenden Or-gel Werck zu beweisen.

The wooden form of organ pipes ought be discussed here; since, however, the layout of their [various] proportions (which I personally have ob-served with great diligence) as well as their [resultant] tone color require an alto-gether different description [from that given here], they are hardly to be compared in tone and construction to [the examples found in] other in-struments. These facts are [adequately] proven by the aforementioned instrument in the palace at Hesse.[73]

Dessen frembder / sanff-ter / subtiler Klang vnd Liebligkeit aber im Schrei-ben so eigentlich nicht ver-meldet werden kan: Als habe ich weitlaeufftigkeit zu vermeyden / von solchen Pfeiffwerck vor diszmal all-hie etwas mehr zu erinnern vnnd anzudeuten vor unnoetig erachtet. Es kan aber hier-nechst vnd vielleicht bald von gedachtem Compenio selb-sten von diesen vnd andern Sachen mehr fundamentaliter nach Geometrischem Bericht etwas auszfuehrlichers an

This strange, mild, deli-cate, and lovely tone cannot really be described in writ-ing; so, for the sake of brev-ity, I have considered it un-necessary to go into further detail concerning these [wood-en] stops. Perhaps Compenius himself will in due time issue a report concerning these and other matters in a more com-prehensive and thoroughly mathematical manner, since this is really not my profes-sion.[74] Nevertheless, I prom-ise not to neglect my part in diligently furthering this art

Tag gegeben werden; Sintemal solches eigendlich meiner Profession nicht ist. Gleichwol wil ich meines Theils dieser Kunst Liebhabern zum besten solches mit fleisz zu befoerdern nicht vnterlassen; Jnmassen denn auch billich von dem Monochordo, daraus alle Instrumenta Musicalia vnd Pfeifwerck jhren Vrsprung / rechten Thon / vnd fundamentalische Theilung haben muessen / vnd billich eine Mutter aller Instrumenten vnd der gantzen Music moechte genennet werden / auch dasselbige eintzig vnd allein aus dem Zirckel herfleust / vnd mit demselbigen bewiesen vnd demonstriret seyn wil / daran jhrer viel mit grosser muehe / aber doch vergeblich gearbeitet haben / etwas erwehnung vnd Bericht ob Gott wil / erfolgen sol. Vnd so viel von offen vnd zugedaeckten Pfeiff- vnd Stimmwercken.

Folget von den Schnarrwercken.[75]

for the benefit of those interested in it. Accordingly, some reference and discussion concerning the monochord shall, God willing, follow soon, because out of it all musical instruments and pipes, their tone, and their basic proportions have their origin. It must, therefore, be considered the progenitor of all instruments and of music itself; its behavior is subject to the laws and functions of a circle, and can be demonstrated and proven thereby, even though many have unsuccessfully tried to realize such relationships. Let this suffice regarding open and covered voices; what follows concerns the reeds. [Translation by the present author]

Praetorius' reference to the instrument at Hesse calls to mind the very de luxe instrument which was built by Esaias Compenius in association with Michael Praetorius and erected at the Hessen Schlosz in 1612. In this unusual instrument, all pipes of all registers were fabricated in wood. The instrument survives to the present day in the Frederiksborg Schlosz, Hillerød, Denmark. A full presentation of this exciting musical monument appears in chapter ix of the present study.

Summary of Praetorius' Labial Registers

Aside from the Universal Table, Praetorius does not provide a summarizing résumé of the labial registers which he discusses throughout the course of the De Organographia. In order, however, to be able to present a fairly comprehensive and compelling theory concerning the registers of the organ, it may be rewarding to gather together all of the information which he presents, assort it, and organize it into brief form, so that his concepts and those of the Early Baroque may emerge more clearly and forcefully.

Contributory Resources

Praetorius' fund of information is scattered over three identifiable areas, each of which not only contributes significant information, but also serves to enlarge and refine the concepts developed in each of the others. These three areas are found in the following sections of the De Organographia:

1. The Universal Table[76]

2. The cursive account in his dictionary of organ voices[77]

3. The pertinent scale drawings of the Theatrum Instrumentorum[78]

Of these, the Universal Table has already been analyzed, discussed, and outlined in chapter xii of the present

study to which recourse may be had for purposes of comparison.
A brief of the cursive account and a summary of the scale
drawings will be subjoined.

The Dictionary of Organ Voices

From Praetorius' cursive account of the organ voices
included in his dictionary together with occasional comple-
mentary references to the scale drawings from the Theatrum
Instrumentorum, it is possible to prepare a brief which will
help to relate these voices to the usual modern classification grid generally used today to differentiate the species
by their physical specifications. Such a grid coordinates
the families and genera and thereby identifies the several
species:

A Brief of Praetorius' Cursive Account from his Dictionary of Organ Voices

I. Labial Pipes

    A. Open Cylindrical

        1. Narrow Scale

            a. Various Crowns

            b. Schweizerpfeife

        2. Moderate Scale

            a. Principal, Quinte, Octave, Rauschpfeife

        3. Wide Scale

            a. Hohlfloete, Waldfloete, Floete, Quint-
               floete, Siffloete, [Bauerfloete]

      b.   Schwegel

      c.   Open Querfloete

   4. Very Wide Scale

      a.   Open Nachthorn

B. Open Conical

   1. Narrow Scale

      a. [Conical Schwegel or Flûte douce]

   2. Moderate Scale

      a.   Flachfloete

      b.   Spillfloete

      c.   Labial Dulzian

   3. Wide Scale

      a.   Gemshorn, Nasat

      b.   Spitzfloete, Spitzquinte

      c.   Koppelfloete

   4. Very Wide Scale

      a.   Blockfloete

C. Fully Covered

   1. Narrow Scale

      a.   Quintade, Nachthorn–Gedackt

      b.   Barduen

      c.   Barem

   2. Moderate Scale

      a.   Gedackt Schweizerpfeife, Querfloete–Gedackt[79]

      b.   Gedackt, Gedacktquinte, Bauerfloete

      c. Duifloete

      d. Spitzgedackt

  3. Wide Scale

      a. None

  4. Very Wide Scale

      a. None

D. Partly Covered

  1. Narrow Scale

      a. None

  2. Moderate Scale

      a. Rohrfloete, Bauerrohrfloete or Rohr-
          schelle

  3. Wide Scale

      a. None

  4. Very Wide Scale

      a. None

It will be observed, that with but a very few additions and omissions, the brief resembles the Brief of the Universal Table[80] to a very large extent, except that here, the genera have been more clearly delineated by the present author.

In analysing the overview presented by the brief, it will be noted that a few of the species find a different or partly different classification with Praetorius than they do with modern theorists or organ builders:

1. Praetorius classifies the <u>Waldfloete</u> as of
the wide-scaled genus of the <u>open</u> <u>cylindrical</u> family,
while most modern theorists consider it of the wide-
scaled genus of the <u>open</u> <u>conical</u> family

2. Praetorius identifies two distinct and markedly different classifications for the <u>Nachthorn</u>--the
<u>very</u> <u>wide-scaled</u>, <u>open</u> <u>cylindrical</u> and the <u>narrow-</u>
<u>scaled</u> <u>covered</u> <u>cylindrical</u> form--while in present-day
practice the voice is generally considered, and the
term used for, a <u>very</u> <u>wide-scaled</u>, <u>open</u> <u>cylindrical</u>
species

3. Praetorius includes the <u>Spillfloete</u> with
moderate-scaled, <u>open</u> <u>conical</u> pipes, while most theorists today conceive of it as of moderate-scaled,
<u>partly-covered</u> pipes. The difference is one of point
of view only, and largely academic

4. Praetorius classifies the <u>Spitzfloete</u> as
larger in scale than the Gemshorn, including it with
<u>wide-scaled</u>, open conical pipes, whereas today it is
generally accepted as of <u>moderate-scaled</u>, open conical
pipes

5. Praetorius' <u>Koppelfloete</u> agrees with modern
theory with respect to its genus, but while he includes it in the <u>open</u> <u>conical</u> family, it is today generally considered as a member of the <u>partly-covered</u>
family. Again the difference is largely academic and

of no real consequence

6. Praetorius' <u>Barduen</u> represents a refined and useful concept, since it vividly isolates a <u>narrow-scaled</u> and fully covered species. Modern organ builders have not clearly identified the species, relying simply upon an overly comprehensive span in their concept of the <u>Gedackt</u> to command too great a variety in the genera of the same. The present author's experience in organ design strongly suggests isolation and delineation of the species and adoption of the name <u>Barduen</u> for the same

7. Praetorius' <u>Querfloete</u>-<u>Gedackt</u> is not reflected in modern practice; most overblown Gedackts appear today in considerably narrower scale than suggested by Praetorius

8. Praetorius classifies the <u>Rohrfloete</u> as a <u>moderate-scaled</u> genus in partly-covered pipes, whereas modern practice again accepts too wide a span for the concept, but uses it chiefly for <u>wide-scaled</u> pipes. The term <u>Rohrgedackt</u> seems useful to isolate the moderate-scaled form of the species from the Rohrfloete

Résumé of Scale Dimensions

The third available contributory resource, helpful for the refined delineation of Praetorius' concepts concerning the tonal resources of the organ is the _Theatrum Instrumen-torum_, wherein Praetorius includes two plates[81] which exhib-it scale drawings of 21 labial pipes and the resonators for 16 lingual pipes. Of these, the labial examples are repro-duced in equivalent scale, using metric measure, on Plates LXXXVII through XCI inclusive, of the atlas included with this study. These were fabricated by the Schlicker Organ Company of Buffalo, New York under the present author's per-sonal supervision and become a part of this study by refer-ence.[82] From these models, exact diameter dimensions can be extracted, which will help to define the voices in a quanti-tative way, and so contribute to a more precise understanding regarding the concepts of the Early Baroque with respect to the voices of the organ. Table 102 and Appendix T give the diameter dimensions for all of the labial voices which Prae-torius exemplifies, and relates them to the Praetorius Norm[83] by noting their deviation from the same in half-tones.

Equivalent Voices in the Modern Repertoire

A final step needs to be taken, in order to round out more fully the present discussion of Praetorius' labial organ voices. This step seeks to show how Praetorius' con-cepts of the voices are reflected in the modern repertoire, noting similar and alternate appellations for the same. Table 103 presents a comparative listing of Praetorius' voices together with their deviations from the Praetorius

TABLE 102

SUMMARY OF RELATIVE SCALES
OF LABIAL PIPES

Item	Reference to Theatrum ...: Plate-No.	Reference to Present Atlas: Plate-No.	Diameter at Mouth in Mm.	Deviation from Praetorius Norm[a]
[8' Praetorius Norm	. . .	LXXXVII-1	148.77	. . . .]
16' Quintade	37-6	LXXXVII-5	153.1	-11.5 HT
8' Principal	37-1	LXXXVII-2	142.6	-1.0 HT
8' Gemshorn	37-10	LXXXVII-3	191.7	+6.0 HT
8' Grossgedackt	37-9	LXXXVII-4	149.6	0.0 HT
8' Quintade	37-7	LXXXVIII-2	105.2	-8.0 HT
8' Klein Barduen	38-4	LXXXVIII-3	123.8	-4.5 HT
8' Gedackt	38-6	LXXXVIII-4	133.0	-2.5 HT
8' Rohrfloete	38-7	LXXXVIII-5	156.2	+1.0 HT
[4' Praetorius Norm	. . .	LXXXIX-1	88.46	. . . .]
4' Octave	37-2	LXXXIX-2	92.3	+1.0 HT
4' Offenfloete	38-5	LXXXIX-3	109.9	+5.0 HT
4' Nachthorn, open	37-5	LXXXIX-4	146.1	+11.5 HT
4' Flachfloete	38-3	LXXXIX-6	104.1	+4.0 HT
4' Spillfloete	37-11	LXXXIX-7	93.5	+1.0 HT
4' Koppelfloete	38-2	LXXXIX-8	115.7	+6.0 HT
4' Labial Dulzian	38-1	XC-2	98.3	+2.5 HT
4' Nachthorn-Gedackt	37-8	XC-3	76.0	-3.5 HT
4' Querfloete, open	37-13	XC-4	99.3	+3.0 HT
4' Querfloete-Gedackt	37-14	XC-5	87.7	0.0 HT
[2 2/3' Praetor. Norm	. . .	XCI-1	65.32	. . . .]
2 2/3' Quinte	37-3	XCI-2	70.1	+2.0 HT
[2' Praetorius Norm	. . .	XCI-3	52.6	. . . .]
2' Klein Octave	37-4	XCI-4	46.7	-3.0 HT
2' Blockfloete	37-12	XCI-5	87.7	+12.0 HT

[a]For an explanation and derivation of the Praetorius
Norm, see Appendix S.

TABLE 103 674

MODERN EQUIVALENTS OF PRAETORIUS' REGISTERS

Praetorius' Registers	Deviation from Praetorius Norm in HT	Equivalent Modern Registers	Deviation from Modern Normprincipal in HT
16' Quintade	-11.5	Quintaden[a]	-7/-14[c]
8' Principal	-1.0	Principal[a]	+1/-4
8' Gemshorn	+6.0	Gemshorn[a]	+6/+4
8' Grossgedackt	0.0	Spitzgedackt[a]	+3/-3
8' Quintade	-8.0	Quintaden[a]	-7/-14
8' Klein Barduen	-4.5	Gedackt I[a]	-5/-6
8' Gedackt	-2.5	Nachthorn-Gedackt[b]	-2/-4
8' Rohrfloete	+1.0	Rohrgedackt[a]	+2/-3
4' Octave	+1.0	Principal[a]	+1/-4
4' Offenfloete	+5.0	Italian Principal[a]	+8/+4
4' Nachthorn, Offen	+11.5	Nachthorn[a]	+14/+8
4' Flachfloete	+4.0	Flachfloete[b]	+4/+3
4' Spillfloete	+1.0	Spillpfeife[a]	0/-4
4' Koppelfloete	+6.0	Koppelfloete[a]	+6/+2
4' Labial Dulzian	+2.5	Labial Dulzian[b]	+2/0
4' Nachthorn-Gedackt	-3.5	Nachthorn-Gedackt[b]	-2/-4
4' Querfloete, Offen	+3.0	Querfloete I[b]	+3/+1
4' Querfloete-Gedackt	0.0	. . . .	. . .
2 2/3' Quinte	+2.0	Principal[b]	+3/-1
2' Klein Octave	-3.0	Principal[a]	+1/-4
2' Blockfloete	+12.0	Blockfloete[a]	+11/+8

[a] C. Mahrenholz, Die Orgelregister, ihre Geschichte und ihr Bau (2nd ed.; Kassel, 1942).

[b] H. Jahnn, "Registernamen und ihr Inhalt," Beitraege zur Organistentagung Hamburg-Luebeck / 6. bis 8. Juli 1925 (Klecken, 1925).

[c] The two deviations shown limit the extremes permissible for the voice.

Norm,[84] and gives the modern equivalents together with their
generally accepted deviations from the modern Normprincipal.[85]

Lingual Pipes with Open Resonators

Praetorius' discussion of lingual pipes is less firmly organized than his treatise on the labial registers; it
suffers also from a certain amount of garrulousness and gives
the general impression of uncertainty. He divides the entire
fund of lingual voices into two families; namely, open resonators and shaded resonators. He does not consider the basic
shape of the resonator as a determinant factor in the classification of families, as does the modern theory with respect
to the same.

Praetorius' Account

He opens his account by setting up basic laws controlling the lengths of resonators, makes proposals concerning
the width of reed tongues, and discusses at great length the
influence of temperature upon the tuning of reed pipes and
the causes for the symptomatic effects of the same:

VII.	VII
Von offenen Schnarrwercken.	Concerning Open Reeds

WEil die Schnarrwercke
fast gemein vnd einem jeden
bekant / ist vnnoetig darvon allhier viel zu erin-
nern / nur allein / dasz allezeit in der lenge vnd
structur dieser offenen Corporum zu disponiren, der ei-

Since reed voices are so
common and known to everyone,
it is unnecessary that much be
recalled here, with the exception that in the disposition
of the length and structure
of the open resonators, practically every master proceeds

ne Meister ein andere Art hat / als der ander; Jn dem etliche die Posaunen / gleich wie sie am Resonantz 16. Fusz Thon halten / also auch am Corpore, doch gar selten / von 16. Fuessen lang arbeiten: Etliche aber von 12. fi. dasz es also von dem rechten Thon in die Quint abweiche / vnd das ist die beste art: Die gemeinste art ist von 8. fi. Mensur. Etliche arbeiten die Posaunen nur von 6. fuessen. Etliche von 5. fuessen lang / oben etwas zugedaeckt / vnd ein loch / als ein Spund vierecket drinn geschnitten / etc. Dieselbige aber / weil die Corpora so klein / haben gar ein flachen vnd plattwegfallenden Klang vnd Resonantz. Wenn es aber pralen / prangen / vnd gravitetisch klingen sol / musz es von 12. fuessen seyn. Vnd solche Variation wird auch in den andern succedirenten offenen Schnarrwercken gehalten: Also/

Wenn die Mensur der Posaunen von $\left.\begin{array}{l}16.\ \text{Fusz}\\ 12\\ 8\\ 6\end{array}\right\}$

So sind die Trommeten von $\left.\begin{array}{l}8\ \text{Fusz}\\ 6\\ 4\\ 3\end{array}\right\}$

Schalmeyen von $\left.\begin{array}{l}4\\ 3\\ 2\\ 1\ 1/2\end{array}\right\}\text{Fusz}$

Dasz aber so gar viel an der Mensur vnd lenge der Corporum in Schnarrwercken nicht gelegen / koempt da-

differently from every other. In the case of the Posaunes, which sound a 16' pitch, some (although seldom) construct a resonator of 16' length, while others make it 12' long; in this case the [voice] transposes from the fundamental into the fifth. This [three-quarter] length provides the best type [of resonator]. The most common type is of 8' length. Some develop the Posaune in 6' length, others in 5' length--partly shaded at the top and provided with a rectangular hole similar to a bung. The reed voices, however, which are equipped with such small resonators have a shallow and dull tone color and sonority. If the tone is expected to sound resilient, opulent, and extensive, [the resonators] must be of 12' length. A [proportionate] relationship [between the pitch length and the physical length] should also be maintained in the succeeding [higher-pitched] open reed voices. Thus:

When the length of the Posaunes is [taken as] $\left.\begin{array}{l}16\ \text{feet}\\ 12\ \text{feet}\\ 8\ \text{feet}\\ 6\ \text{feet}\end{array}\right\}$

then that of the Trumpet should be $\left.\begin{array}{l}8\ \text{feet}\\ 6\ \text{feet}\\ 4\ \text{feet}\\ 3\ \text{feet}\end{array}\right\}$

and that of the Schalmei should be $\left.\begin{array}{l}4\ \text{feet}\\ 3\ \text{feet}\\ 2\ \text{feet}\\ 1\ 1/2\ \text{feet}\end{array}\right.$

The scale and length of the resonators in reed pipes is not of primary importance, since the pitch of the tone

her / dieweil die tieffe
oder hoehe des Resonantzes
nicht vom Corpore oder
structur (welche aber
gleichwol auch jhre rich-
tigkeit vnnd rechte masz haben musz) sondern von den
Mundstuecken herruehret:
Vnd ist disz dabey / wenn
die Mundstuecke lenglicht
vnd schmal seyn / so geben
sie viel ein lieblichern
Resonantz / als wenn sie
kurtz vnd breit seyn: Welches denn auch in den andern
Pfeiff vnd Floeitwercken
sich gleicher gestalt also
befindet / dasz die weiter
Mensur nimmer so lieblich
am Resonantz seyn / als die
enge.

Darumb sich billich ein
jeder Orgelmacher der gar
engen Mensuren befleissigen
solte; denn je enger / je
lieblicher vnd anmutiger.
Aber weil solche enge Mensuren zur rechten intonation
zubringen / nicht eines jeden Orgelmachers thun ist /
sintemal es guten verstand /
grossen fleisz / vnd tref-
liche muehe erfodert: So
bleiben die meisten / welche faule Patres vnd etwas
mehrers zu lernen verdros-
sen sind / gemeiniglich bey
den gewoehnlichen weiten
Mensuren, so duerffen sie
den Kopff nicht allzusehr
trueber zerbrechen / desto
geschwinder der arbeit ab-
kommen / vnd den Beutel besser fuellen.

Jm Land zu Hessen ist in
einem Kloster eine sonderliche Art von Posaunen funden worden / do vff das
Mundstueck ein Messing boe-

does not derive from the resonator or its structure (which,
in any case, must have its own
correct proportions), but
rather from the shallots.
Note that when the shallots
are long and narrow [the pipe]
delivers a much lovelier sonority than when they are
short and wide; this condition
obtains similarly in the labial pipes of the organ: the
wide scales will never produce
as lovely a tone as the narrow.

Therefore, every organbuilder ought to take pains [to
develop] the narrow scales;
for, the narrower [the shal-
lots], the more lovely and
charming [the tone will be].
However, since it requires
a thorough understanding,
great diligence, and considerable effort, it is not within every organbuilder's skill
to develop a true tone out of
such narrow scales. Accordingly, most [builders], being
lazy friars and loath to increase their knowledge [and
skill], hold generally with
the wide scales [for the shal-
lots]. In this way they need
not rack their brains, can
dispatch the work more hasti-
ly, and thus fill the purse
more readily.

An unusual type of Posaune
has been discovered in a
cloister [in the province] of
Hessen, where a brass plate
soldered to the shallot has a

demchen vffgeloetet / vnd
in der mitten ein ziemlich
lenglicht loechlein drinn /
darueber dann allererst das
rechte zuenglein oder blaetlein gelegt / vnd mit geglue-
eten Messings oder Staelenen
Saeiten druff gebunden wird /
dasz es nicht also sehr
schnarren vnd plarren kan.
Vnd weil es dergestalt etwas mehr als sonsten ge-
dempffet wird / gibt es
gleich einer Posaunen / wenn
die von einem guten Meister
recht intonirt vnd geblasen
wird / einen pompenden /
dumpichten / vnd nicht
schnarrenden Resonantz.

rather elongated opening cut
into the center of it, upon
which the actual tongue or
reed is fitted by means of
heated brass or steel wires,
in order to minimize the buzz-
ing and rattling. Since this
causes [the pipe] to be more
than usually muted, it produces a sonority that is
stately and muffled, and with
less rattle [than normally].
The tone is similar to that
of a [mouth-blown] trombone
when properly intoned and
blown by a skillful performer.

Doch muessen sie gleichwol
mit vff vnd niederziehung
des obersten Corporis gestimmet werden / vnd war bleiben / Regalia mobilia: Sintemal das falsch werden
nicht / wie etliche meynen /
vom vff- vnd niederweichen
der kroeckel oder droetlin /
daran die Regal sonsten eingestimmet werden muessen /
herruehret; Sintemal vnmoeglich / dasz die kroeckel von
sich selbsten hin vnd herwider / auff vnd nieder steigen koennen: Sondern von
wegen der subtilen Messings-
blaetlin / welche sich im
warmen Wetter von der hitze /
(dasz denn auch am Papier
oder duennem holtze kan pro-
biert werden) auszwerts
kruemmen; Vnd weil dadurch
das Loch am Mundstuecke erweitert wird / der Resonantz
etwas tieffer vnter sich
steiget. Jm kalten Wetter
aber das blaetlein sich in-
werts vnnd naeher zu dem
Mundstuecke wendet / da-
durch das Loch kleiner /

[The Posaune] must be tuned
and kept true by lengthening
and shortening the resonator.
Regalia mobilia.[86] Contrary
to the prevalent opinion, reed
voices are not thrown out of
tune by the rising and falling
of the tuning wires by means
of which the Regals are normally tuned; it is impossible for
the tuning wires to move up
and down by themselves. Rather, the cause lies in the delicate reed tongues, which, in
the heat of warm weather (as
can be demonstrated by a piece
of paper or a thin slice of
wood) curl outward, enlarge
the opening [at the shallot],
and thus lower the pitch. In
cold weather, the tongue curls
inward toward the shallot, diminishes the opening, and thus
raises the pitch. This is a
daily experience among those
who have to deal with organs
and Regals. In winter, as
soon as the cold weather turns
milder, the Regals become lower in pitch; conversely, as
soon as the weather returns to

vnd der Resonantz hoeher
vber sich steiget: Wie dieselbige verenderung ein jeder so mit Orgeln vnd Regaln
vmbgehet / taeglich erfaeh-
ret: Dasz / so bald im Vin-
ter das kalte Wetter sich
endert / vnnd zum Dawwetter
anlesset / die Regal vnter
sich steigen / vnnd tief-
fer werden: So bald es a-
ber hinwiederumb zu frieren
beginnet / werden sie also
bald hoeher: Darumb denn
auch das vffbinden der
Kroeckel nicht viel helffen
kan.

freezing, they rise in pitch.
Consequently, [the device] of
tying up the tuning wires is
of little help.

Vnnd disz befindet sich
auch gleicher gestalt nicht
allein vff den Clavicymbeln
vnd Symphonien an den Staelenen vnnd Messingssaeitten /
sondern auch vff den Lauten
vnd Geigen an den Saeiten /
so von Schaffsdaermen ge-
macht seynd. Dasz sie von
der hitze nachlassen / sich
ausdehnen vnd erweitern /
vnd derowegen der Resonantz
descendiret; von der kaelte
aber contrahiret, vnd sich
mehr in einander ziehen /
davon denn der Resonantz
auch ascendiret, also / dasz
im Winter die Instrumenta,
wenn sie continue etliche
Wochen im kalten gestanden /
fast vmb einen halben Thon
vnd mehr ascendiret vnd ge-
stiegen seyn. Daher dann /
wann von einem verstaendigen Meister die Mensur vff
Clavicymbeln vnnd Symphoni-
en also / dasz ein jede
Saeite vmb ein halben Thon
zur noth sich hoeher ziehen
lassen kan / nicht abgetheilet worden / fast alle Saeiten abgesprungen seyn. Wel-

The same condition prevails
not only with the steel and
brass strings of the Clavi-
cymbel and Symphonium, but also with the gut strings of
Lutes and Violins. As the
temperature rises they will
expand and relax their tension, causing a drop in pitch;
as the temperature falls they
will contract and increase
their tension, causing a rise
in pitch. In the winter, if
such instruments repose in
the cold continuously for
several weeks they rise in
pitch by nearly a half tone
or more. For this reason, if
the strings of Clavicymbels
and Symphonia are not properly graduated by a skillful
master, so that each one will
tolerate an increase in tension amounting to at least a
half tone, they will have a
tendency to snap. This I
have often experienced with
great annoyance and not without damage [to the instru-
ments].

ches ich nicht sonder schaden vnnd grossen Vnmuth zum
offtern selbst erfahren.

Vnd aus diesem Fundamento,
dasz die Verenderung im Regall vnd Schnarrwercken von
Messingsblaetlein herrueh-
re / entstehet eine Proba,
dadurch man erfahren kan /
Ob ein Regall mit den Zuenglein oder blaetlein durch
vnd durch just vnd fleissig
abgerichtet sey. Dann wann
ein Schnarrwerck von einem
guten Meister fleissig ver-
fertiget ist / so weichet es
in wandelung des Wetters
durchs gantze Clavier zu-
gleich mit einander / vnd
tretten entweder in der
waerm vnd hitz zugleich mit
einander weiter ab: Oder
begeben sich in der Kaelt
vnd Frost naeher zu dem
Mundstuecke / also / dasz
man vff einer Orgel / oder
sonsten / dasselbige ohne
mitzuziehung des Floeit-
wercks vnd anderer Pfeif-
fen gar wol / als wenn es
noch gar just eingestimmet /
bestaendig blieben waere /
gebrauchen kan.

Wann aber ein Floeitwerck
darzu gezogen wird / so befindet sich der mangel /
dasz sich entweder das
Schnarrwerck vnter / oder
vber sich vom Floeitwerck
durch vnnd durch abgewendet
habe: Vnd alsdenn ist dasselbe Schnarrwerck fleissig
vnd just bereitet. Befindet
sich aber / dasz das Schnarrwerck nicht zugleich mit
einander durchs gantze Clavier abgetretten ist / sondern der eine Clavis ist gegen dem Floeitwerck zu

Out of this fundamental concept, [namely,] that the
[pitch] variations in Regals
and reeds derive from the
brass tongues, there emerges
a test, whereby one can de-
tect if a Regal with its diminutive tongues is accurately adjusted throughout [the
range of its compass]. For,
if a reed [voice] is carefully finished by a skillful
master, it will, during a
change of weather, go uniformly out of tune; in warm
[weather, the pipes] will drop
in pitch together, whereas in
cold weather [the reed tongues]
will approach the shallots
[uniformly], so that on an organ or other instrument it is
possible, without adding a
labial voice or other register,
to use the [stop] as if it
were still in tune and had
remained constant.

If, however, a labial voice
is added [to the reed], the
discrepancy [in pitch] becomes
[immediately] apparent in that
the reed voice will prove to
be too high or too low [in a
constant ratio] throughout.
When this condition prevails,
then the reed voice can be
adjudged to have been diligently and accurately constructed. Should it happen
that the reed voice is not
uniformly out of tune throughout [the compass of] the Manual, but that one note is too

tieff / der andere zu hoch / der dritte rein / so ists ein gewisz Zeichen / dasz die Mundstuecke nicht gleich beblettert / sondern ein blaetlein starck / das ander schwach sey / denn sich das starcke dicke nicht so bald von der hitze oder kaelte zwingen lest / als das duenne vnnd schwache.[87]

high, a second too low, and a third in tune with the labial voice, it is a sure sign that the shallots have not been equipped with [relatively] uniform reed tongues, but that one tongue is too heavy, the other too light. The heavy [tongue] will not allow itself to be so readily affected by heat or cold as the light and weak one. [Translation by the present author]

Basic Concepts Concerning Reed Voices

Praetorius lays down three important concepts concerning the lingual voices in the organ. These need to be extracted from his account and brought into sharp relief. The concepts concern themselves with:

1. The proportional lengths of the resonators

2. The size of the shallots together with their surmounted tongues

3. The influence of temperature on the tuning

With respect to the first concern Praetorius has specific proposals to make. He mentions, first of all, the various conditions which are effectively realizable. He proposes resonators of:

1. Full length, i.e., resonators whose physical length equals the pitch

2. Three-quarter length, i.e., resonators whose physical lengths are related to the pitch as 3/4

3. One-half length, i.e., resonators whose

physical lengths are related to the pitch as 1/2

4. Three-eighth length, i.e., resonators whose physical lengths are related to the pitch as 3/8

Of the various possibilities listed, Praetorius much prefers resonators of three-quarter length, i.e., 12' resonator for 16' pitch; 6' resonator for 8' pitch; or 3' resonator for 4' pitch. These, he claims, develop a proud, resplendent, and substantial tone. The modern concept, concerning conical reeds as expressed by Mahrenholz, recommends the same ratio of physical length to pitch.[88]

With respect to the size of the shallots and the width of the corresponding reed tongues, Praetorius urges the adoption of long and narrow ones in preference to the short and wide examples formerly in general use. Mahrenholz records this tendency as follows:

> The evolution of the reed tongues with respect to their width and thickness pursues a single course up to the present. The Renaissance and Early Baroque favor very thin and extraordinarily wide tongues which functioned very nearly as membranes, thereby reinforcing the partial tones materially. However, already in the days of Praetorius a decided movement toward narrower tongues can be detected, which supposedly were capable of producing a "lovelier resonance."[89]

Praetorius' observations on temperature and its influence on the tuning of reed voices indicates an opposite effect between labial and lingual pipes. Whereas a falling temperature increases the density of the standing air in the

labial pipe, making it denser and thus lowering the pitch,
the same condition will shrink the reed tongue, reduce its
curvature, and diminish the size of the shallot opening,
causing the pipe to rise in pitch. A rising temperature produces a correspondingly opposite effect in both orders of
pipes, raising the pitch of the labial specimens, and lowering it in the lingual.

Proportionate Lengths for Resonators

In his discussion of resonator lengths, Praetorius
isolates three open conical reeds and relates their lengths
to each other in a direct proportion. The voices in question
are the Posaune, the Trumpet, and the Schalmei. His grouping
of these would indicate that he looks upon them as a set of
chorus reeds, or at least a group, no matter how dispersed,
which should stand in a certain relationship to each other.
The Posaune appears as a sub-aequal voice, the Trumpet as an
aequal voice, and the Schalmei as a super-aequal voice. He
allows various lengths for the resonators but carefully relates the three voices as shown in Table 104.

Praetorius carefully points out that once the dimension for the resonator has been adopted for one member of the
set, the corollary ratio of physical length to pitch must be
maintained for the other members. Thus, a three-quarter
length for the Trumpet requires, likewise a three-quarter
length for the Posaune and for the Schalmei.

TABLE 104

PROPORTIONATE LENGTHS OF RESONATORS
FOR OPEN CONICAL REEDS

Item	Pitch	Resonator Lengths			
		A[a]	B[b]	C[c]	D[d]
Posaune	16'	16'	12'	8'	6'
Trumpet	8'	8'	6'	4'	3'
Schalmei	4'	4'	3'	2'	1 1/2'

[a]Column A gives a full-length resonator for each member of the group.

[b]Column B gives the normal or three-quarter length resonator. The ratio of physical length to pitch is 3/4. Praetorius maintains that this is the proper length needed to secure a proud, resplendent, and substantial tone from open conical reeds.

[c]Column C shows a one-half length resonator for the several species. The ratio of physical length to pitch is 1/2. Praetorius points out that this ratio was commonly adopted in practice in his day.

[d]Column D shows a three-eighth length resonator. The ratio of physical length to pitch is 3/8.

Copies of the Trumpet and Schalmei as they appear in the _Theatrum Instrumentorum_[90] are reproduced on Plate XCII, 1 and 3. Actual measurements of the resonators for the same are shown in Table 105.

The Open Lingual Family

Praetorius does not propose to discuss all manner of open reeds, but merely selects a few noteworthy examples from the resource which had been developed and found application by his time. He claims that the practice of organ building varies so greatly in this respect, that it is impossible to handle the subject with any degree of definitude. His account follows:

Ob nun zwar sonsten auch allhier von allerley anderer Arten der Schnarrwercke auszfuehrliche meldung geschehen solte; So ist doch wegen der vielfaeltigen verenderung vnd mancherley Inventionen, solche alle zubeschreiben vnmoeglich / sonderlich weil derselben noch taeglich mehr / vnd viel frembder erfunden werden; Vnd solch ein Schnarrwerck nach einem andern Instrument, welches mit dem Munde geblasen wird / recht nach zu machen / vnd dessen Art vnd Resonantz recht zu treffen / sehr schwehr fellet; So wil ich nur etliche der fuernembsten Art zur nachrichtung allhier gedencken.

Although ordinarily, a full account ought be made here of other species of reed voices, it is impossible to describe all of them because of their great variety and the details of their construction, which are daily subject to many and unusual inventions. To prepare a reed voice which corresponds accurately in type and tone to its mouth-blown counterpart is a difficult task. Therefore, I shall recall and report here only some of the most important species.

Schalmeyen seynd
8. Fusz Thon:

Schalmei
of 8' pitch

Aber besser nicht / als mit rechten Schallmeyen Corporibus, jedoch etwas weiter / nachzumachen; Wie sie denn auch dieselbige Art gar fein mit dem rechten Schallmeyenklange vereiniget.

[. . .] cannot be constructed better than by adopting the proportions of the true [i.e., mouth-blown] Schallmey, but making [the resonator] somewhat wider [in its diameter]. This way the tone color [of the pipes] will [correspond very closely] to that of the mouth-blown Schallmey.

Krumbhorn ist allein
8. Fusz Thon:

Krummhorn is
only of 8' pitch

Vnd ob es auch wol mueg-

[. . .] and although it is

lich / disz Stimmwerck vff
16. Fusz Thon / darinnen es
doch gar selten gefunden
wird / zu bringen: So ists
doch / weil es etwas starck
lautet vnd so tieff gehet /
Manualiter nicht fast lieblich / sondern besser Pedaliter allein in solcher
tieffen zu gebrauchen.

Es ist aber derselben In-
vention mancherley: Denn
obwol etliche solchen klang
in einem rechten Regal Corpore (das oben mit eim dek-
kel zugemacht / vnd zwey /
drey oder mehr Loecherlein /
entweder oben im selbigen
deckel / oder vnten nebenst
dem Mundstuecke darein gebohret) oder sonsten durch
andere Arten mehr zu wegen
bringen wollen; Daher sie
dann wol vnter die Gedacte
Schnarrwercke auch koendten
referirt werden: So ist
doch diese Invention, dasz
die Corpora gleichaus weit /
oben offen / vnd an der lenge 4. Fusz haben / die beste
vnd gleicheste Art der
Krumbhoerner.

Sie wollen aber gleich anderen solchen lieblichen
Schnarrwercken durch guten
vnd rechten Verstand gewisz /
vnd nicht leichtlich von einem jedem gemacht vnd gefertiget seyn.

Grob Regal seynd
8. Fusz Thon:

Werden in Orgeln meistlich
von Messing / vnd 5. oder
6. Zoll hoch an der Mensur
gearbeitet: Wiewol man
biszweilen / sonderlich in
den Regallwercken / so zu

quite possible to develop
this voice at 16' pitch, it
is seldom found thus. At this
grave pitch, it is not, because
of its fairly loud tone and
low register, very lovely in
the Manual but more useful in
the Pedal.

[The Krummhorns] display
various realizations: although
some seek to develop its [char-
acteristic] tone by means of
true Regal resonators (which
are covered at the top and
pierced with two, three, or
more holes either above in
the lid or below near the
shallot or in some other way
reminiscent of the shaded reed
voices, the construction best
suited to reproduce the [8']
Krummhorn tone faithfully, requires cylindrical resonators,
open at the top, and of four-
foot length.

[The Krummhorns], like other
such delicate reed voices, can
be made and finished with con-
fidence [by those] who possess
the [necessary] understanding
and skill, but [certainly] not
so easily by everyone [else].

Grob Regal
of 8' pitch

In organs [the Grob Regal]
is most often fabricated of
brass with [a resonator] five
or six inches high. It occurs
that in Regal instruments like
those recently constructed in

Augspurg vnd Nuernberg bisz-
her gemacht worden / gar
kleine Corpora der Regal-
pfeifflin / die kaum ein
Zoll hoch seyn / findet /
vnd doch 8. Fusz am Thon haben: Wie hiervon im vorher-
gehenden II. Theil / Num.
43. weitlaeufftiger ist
erinnert worden.

Augsburg and Nuernberg, one
finds very small resonators
for Regal pipes; some are
hardly an inch high and yet
deliver an 8' pitch. We have
recalled this more fully in
the preceding section II,
chapter 45.

[Jungfrauregal
of 4' pitch]

JungfrawenRegal oder Basz
ist 4. Fusz Thon; An jhm
selbsten ein klein offen Regal mit einem kleinen gerin-
gen Corpore, etwan ein / o-
der vffs meiste zweene Zoll
hoch; Wird aber darumb also
geheissen / weil es / wenns
zu andern Stimmen vnd Floeitwercken im Pedal gebraucht
wird / gleich einer Jung-
frawenstimme / die einen
Basz singen wolte / gehoeret
wird.

The Jungfrauregal or [Jung-
frauregal-]bass is of 4' pitch.
By itself, it is a small open
Regal with a tiny and insigni-
ficant resonator about one,
or at most, two inches high.
It is so called because, when
used together with other voices
and registers in the Pedal,
[it gives the effect] of a
maiden trying to sing bass.

[Klein Regal or
Geigendregal
of 4' pitch]

Es wird auch solch klein
Regal vff 4. Fusz Thon von
etlichen Geigen- oder Gie-
gendRegal genennet; Vnd solches darumb / dasz es / wenn
die Quintadehna vff 8. fusz
Thon darzu gezogen / etli-
cher massen (sonderlich
wenns in der rechten Hand
zum Discant allein gebraucht
wird) einer Geigen gar ehnlich klinget.

Such a small Regal of 4'
pitch is sometimes called a
Geigen or Geigendregal, largely because when the 8' Quintade is drawn with it, the
combination resembles very
nearly the tone of a violin,
(especially when it is played
in the right hand for the discant).

Dieweil aber in jede Stimme fuer sich allein / ohne
anderer huelffe also klingen
sol / als sie wil / vnd sol
genennet werden / so kan man

However, since every voice
ought reproduce the [charac-
teristic] tone color suggested
by its name, without the help
of another voice, this voice

diese Stimme nicht billi-
cher / als klein Regal nennen.

cannot better be designated
than as Klein Regal.

Zincken 8. Fusz Thon:

Zink of 8' pitch

Werden allein durchs halbe
Clavir im Discant gebraucht /
haben gleichaus weitte Corpora, vnten etwas zugespitzet / oben offen; Darumb
werden sie am klang etwas
hol / als ein Floeitwerck /
vnd nicht also schnarrend /
denn jhnen wegen der stark-
ken bletter / vnd starcken
windes das schnarren ziem-
licher massen vergehet vnd
verboten wird.

[Zinks] are used only
through half of the compass
of the Manual; namely, in
the discant portion. They
have cylindrical resonators,
somewhat tapered [inward]
below, and open at the top.
For this reason their tone is
somewhat hollow as in the
case of [certain] labial
registers. Because of the
[relatively] heavy tongues
and considerable winding, the
usual rattling is effectively
prevented and practically
disappears.

[Kornett of 4' or 2' pitch]

Cornett wird meistentheils
im Basz allein gebraucht /
ist zwar Regal Mensur, aber
enger vnd lenger: Denn ob
es gleich nur von 4. oder
2. fusz Thon / so ist doch
das Corpus 9. Zoll hoch /
vnd also hoeher / als ein
Regal Corpus 8. fi. Thon:
Darumb es sich auch einer
Menschenstimm gantz vnd gar
vergleichen thut. Wiewol
etliche die Corpora im Cornett kaum 4. oder 5. Zoll
hoch machen: Denn hierinn
von den Orgelmachern gar
sehr variirt wird / vnd also nichts gewisses darvon
kan geschrieben werden.[91]

The Kornett is used mainly
in the Pedal and is indeed of
Regal proportions, but narrower and longer. For although
it is only of 4' or 2' pitch,
the resonator is 9 inches high,
thus even higher than that of
a Regal of 8' pitch. Its tone
resembles quite remarkably and
faithfully that of the human
voice. Some make the resonator of the Kornett hardly four
or five inches high, which indicates the variable practice
among organbuilders, and pre-
vents us from describing
[these voices] definitively.
[Translation by the present
author]

From Praetorius' opening remarks on open lingual

pipes it is evident that he looks upon the balance of the

reeds he intends to discuss as imitative voices of mouth-blown prototypes. The selected voices he discusses are dispersed at the following pitches:

1. At 16' pitch: the Krummhorn

2. At 8' pitch: the Schalmei, Krummhorn, Dulzian, Zink, and Grob Regal

3. At 4' pitch: the Jungfrau Regal, Geigendregal, and Kornett

4. At 2' pitch: the Kornett

In the Theatrum Instrumentorum[92] a number of open and shaded lingual pipes are pictured in scale. From these sketches the lengths and shapes of the several resonators can be determined. Table 105 gives these dimensions for certain open lingual pipes and may serve as a reference for the subsequent discussion. Exact copies of Praetorius' sketches for these pipes are reproduced on Plate XCII, 1-6.

The Schalmei Species

The Schalmei serves as Praetorius' representative species from the open conical family of resonators. Praetorius' sketch of the organ Schalmei from the Theatrum Instrumentorum[93] is reproduced on Plate XCII, 3 and shows a corpus which resembles that of the mouth-blown Schalmei,[94] a copy of which is reproduced on Plate XCI, 6. The corpus or resonator is conical; hence, in modern classifications, the voice is considered an open conical resonator. In comparison to other conical reeds, its scale is narrow. Praetorius'

TABLE 105

DIMENSIONS AND DISPOSITION OF SELECTED OPEN LINGUAL PIPES

Item	Reference to Theatrum....: Plate-Number	Reference to Present Atlas: Plate-Number	Raw Dimension from Praetorius in Mm.	Actual Dimension in Cm.^{a}	Equivalent Actual Dimension: British Units	Shape of Corpus	Ratio of Physical Length to Pitch	Qualitative Description of Resonator
8' Trumpet	38-8	XCII-1	145.5	168.3	5.5'	Conical	3/4	Normal
8' Krummhorn	38-9	XCII-2	106.0	122.6	4.0'	Cylindrical	1/2	Normal
[4'] Schalmei	38-10	XCII-3	72.0	83.3	2.75'	Conical	3/4	Normal
[8'] Zink: [c'] Kornett Discant	38-12	XCII-4	27.0	31.2	1.0'	Cylindrical	1/2	Normal
8' Messing Regal	38-14	XCII-5	11.0	12.7	5.0"	Conical	1/16	Fractional
[8'] Gedaempft Regal	38-15	XCII-6	11.5	13.3	5.25"	Conical	1/16	Fractional

^{a}See chapter xiv of the present study for the method employed by the present author to interpret the raw scale dimensions on Plate XXXVIII of Praetorius' _Theatrum Instrumentorum_, and to convert them into real and usable values.

example of the 4' organ Schalmei shows a conical resonator
of three-quarter length; hence, a normal corpus for this species. See Table 105 for the exact dimensions of this voice.

The Krummhorn-Zink-Dulzian Species

The Krummhorn is Praetorius' first example from the
open cylindrical family of resonators. He suggests the voice
for use at 16' pitch in the Pedal, and at 8' and 4' pitch for
the Manual. He describes many contemporary forms of the
Krummhorn including both open and shaded examples as well as
compound resonators; he prefers, however, a resonator of open
cylindrical disposition and of one-half length. This is the
form and length in which the Krummhorn is generally executed
in modern practice, although today the voice occurs most frequently at 8' pitch, occasionally at 4', and rarely at 16'.
A copy of the mouth-blown Krummhorn as pictured in the Theatrum Instrumentorum[95] is reproduced on Plate XCI, 7, where
a is the corpus pierced with holes and provided with an extension valve; b is the reed assembly including the mounting;
and c, a protective cover for the same. A careful inspection
of Praetorius' scale drawing for an 8' Krummhorn[96] as reproduced on Plate XCII, 2 and quantitatively delineated in
Table 105 reveals that the organ Krummhorn exhibits a cylindrical resonator of one-half length, which is the normal
length for resonators of the open cylindrical family.

The second example which Praetorius presents from

the open cylindrical family is the Zink. In his time, this
voice usually appeared as a half-voice, i.e., from c' to the
upper limit of the compass, and was designated as discant.
The resonator is open and cylindrical, and is attached to
the block by means of an inverted and truncated conical member. According to Praetorius, the reed tongue is of greater
mass than usual and is generously winded. Because of these
conditions the tone is somewhat hollow and less crass than
usual with reeds. His description points to open cylindrical construction, hence, requiring resonators of one-half
length. The scale was probably very wide, which effectively
prevented its execution below the middle of the compass. The
example pictured in the Theatrum Instrumentorum[97] and reproduced on Plate XCII, 4 exhibits a resonator 1' in length;
inasmuch as the legend calls it a Zink: Kornettdiscant, the
note given is probably c' of a 2' actual pitch. Accordingly,
the ratio of the physical length to the pitch is 1/2. See
Table 105 for the actual dimensions.

Between the Krummhorn and the Zink must be interpolated the open Dulzian to which Praetorius refers later under his discussion of shaded lingual pipes. He says:

Some leave it [i.e., the Dulzian] entirely open
at the top, for which reason it is not nearly as soft
[as the shaded example] and resembles the mouth-blown
instruments of the same name more closely.[98]

Praetorius does not illustrate either the open or

shaded Dulzian. It can be surmised, however, that the scale
lies between the Krummhorn and Zink (hence, moderate), that
the resonator is cylindrical and open (in this case); hence,
of normal one-half length. Of course, the Dulzian can also
be constructed with shaded resonators and in fractional corpora as a Regal.

The Regal Species

For the Regal species of lingual pipes, Praetorius
presents two open examples together with attendant variants
of the same. The first is the Regal of open conical, but
fractional resonators; the second is the Kornett with open
cylindrical, but fractional resonators.

The 8' Grob Regal, he describes as having fractional
open resonators of brass about five or six inches long; he
points out, however, that it can also be constructed of very
diminutive resonators hardly one inch high, yet giving an 8'
pitch. Copies of the examples of a Messing Regal[99] and a
Gedaempft Regal[100] from the Theatrum Instrumentorum are reproduced on Plate XCII, 5-6 and exhibit open conical resonators about five inches long; hence, fractional. Precise
dimensions are given in Table 105.

The Jungfrauregal, Praetorius maintains, is a diminutive form of the Grob Regal; its resonators are open and
very short, being only about one or two inches long. He describes its tone as reminiscent of "a virgin attempting to

sing bass."[101]

    From Praetorius' account it is evident that the 4'
Klein Regal is an octave form of the Grob Regal; hence, it
employs fractional open resonators of a conical shape. When
combined with an 8' Quintade and used as a solo registration,
the effect resembles the tone color of a solo violin, according to Praetorius. For this reason it is often called a
Geigendregal.

    Praetorius delineates the Kornett as the Regal deriv-
ative of the Zink. As such, it has an open cylindrical resonator of fractional length but of a narrow scale, and longer
than the usual Regal corpus. The length of the same for a
4' or 2' tone is no greater than 9 inches, and some builders
develop it from resonators only 4 or 5 inches long. The
voice is used chiefly in the Pedal at 4' or 2' pitch and its
tone, according to Praetorius, resembles that of the human
voice. It may, therefore, be considered an early form of
the Vox Humana.

    From the Universal Table[102] an additional variety of
Regal can be mustered, even though Praetorius does not include it in his dictionary of organ voices; this is the 1'
Zimbelregal. Mahrenholz[103] explains the voice as the only
rank of reed pipes that may be considered a "Mixture" for
the reed chorus.[104] He maintains that it was a high-pitched
Regal, which repeated in every octave, after the manner of
the I Zimbel (labial) in the Compenius organ at Frederiksborg

which is graphically represented on Chart 77. See Table 106 for a likely disposition of the Zimbelregal and Chart 84 for a possible graphic representation of it.

TABLE 106

POSSIBLE DISPOSITION OF
I ZIMBELREGAL 1'

Segment	Pitches of the Choirs
$\underline{C}$	1'
$\underline{c}$	2'
$\underline{c}$'	4'
$\underline{c}$''	8'

Among the entries in Praetorius' catalog of dispositions the Zimbelregal occurs only once; namely, in the Brust of the Grueningen, Schlosz organ, where it appears at 2' pitch.

Classifications of the Species

From the Universal Table,[105] the dictionary of organ voices,[106] and the Theatrum Instrumentorum[107] a summary can be submitted which will classify the open lingual voices as to their divisional function as well as to their physical characteristics. In the Universal Table Praetorius suggests the following voices as useful manual registers:

8' Trumpet   8' Zinkdiscant

8' Schalmei   4' Klein Geigendregal

8' Krummhorn	4' Jungfrauregal
8' Grob Regal	1' Zimbelregal

For use in the Pedal, Praetorius musters an even more extensive array:

16' Posaune	4' Klein Krummhorn
8' Trumpet	4' Klein Geigendregal
8' Schalmei	4' Jungfrauregal
4' Klein Schalmei	4' Kornett
16' Gross Krummhorn	2' Kornett
8' Krummhorn	

With respect to their physical characteristics the open lingual voices, according to Praetorius' delineations, assort as follows when arranged in a modern classification:[108]

A Brief of Praetorius' Open Lingual Voices

I.   Open Lingual Voices

    A.   Open Cylindrical Resonators

        . 1.   Normal Resonators (one-half length)

            a.   Krummhorn

            b.   Dulzian

            c.   Zink

        2.   Fractional Resonators (less than one-half length)

            a.   Kornett

    B.   Open Conical Resonators

        1.   Normal Resonators (three-quarter length)

a. Posaune

b. Trumpet

c. Schalmei

2. Fractional Resonators (less than three-
quarter length)

a. Grob Regal

b. Klein Regal

c. Jungfrauregal

d. Messing Regal

e. Gedaempft Regal

Lingual Pipes with Shaded Resonators

Inasmuch as all lingual voices function acoustically
as covered pipes, Praetorius' designation, "covered", means,
in reality, "shaded." The term refers to the visible portion of the resonator; some opening must always be provided
or else the pipe will fail to speak. The opening is often
a hole or a series of holes introduced at the upper end of
the resonator, near its base, or in the surmounted cap. In
some instances, the top of the resonator is only partly covered, or a slot or rectangular opening is provided. At times
the partial closure is effected by a high degree of conicity
in the upper member of the corpus.

Praetorius' Account

Praetorius' discussion of the Gedaeckte Schnarrwercke,
as he calls them, reveals again a certain insecurity as to

their classification and acoustical functions, so that his

account becomes largely descriptive and extremely difficult

to assort. He says:

VIII.	VIII
Gedaecte Schnarrwerck.	Shaded Reed Voices

Sordunen sind
16. Fusz Thon:

Sordun
of 16' pitch

Koennen auch wegen der Invention, dasz sie gedaeckt seyn muessen / vnnd in sich noch ein verborgen Corpus mit ziemlichen langen Rohren haben / nicht wol hoeher / wenn sie jhre rechte Art behalten sollen / intoniret werden: Jhr auszwendiges Corpus ist zwar ohngefehr zwey fusz hoch / vnd seine weite / als ein Nachthorn Corpus von 4. Fusz Thon. Es ist aber sehr lieblich vnd stille / wenn es seinen rechten Meister gehabt hat / vnd also zu Saeiten- oder Floeitwerck gar wol zu gebrauchen. Man musz aber dabey in guter acht haben / dasz es gleich wie ander grob Pfeiffwerck von oder vff 16. fusz / mit den Concordantiis, als tertien oder Quinten in der lincken Hand zu greiffen verschonet / vnd von solchen teiffem Thon nicht verderbet / vnd vbel anzuhoeren gemacht werde: Vornemlich aber ist es zierlich im Pedal zu vielen enderungen zu gebrauchen.	Because of their construction, which requires them to be shaded and to have an additional resonator of a fairly long and cylindrical shape hidden within them, they cannot, if they are to retain their true character, be voiced in any higher pitch. The external resonator is about two feet high and its diameter is comparable to that of a Nachthorn of 4' pitch.[109] When built by a skillful master, it has a very delicate and quiet [tone, admirably suited to accompany stringed instruments or flutes. However, one must be very careful that, as in the case of other grave pipes of 16' pitch, one avoid playing chords containing thirds and fifths in the left hand, since such low sounds spoil [the effect] and make it undesirable to hear. Above all it is an elegant voice in the Pedal, useful for many registrations.

Grosz Rancket sind auch
16. Fusz Thon:
Rancket ist
8. Fusz Thon:

Gross Rankett
of 16' pitch
Rankett
of 8' pitch

Sind auch auszbuendige
liebliche zugedaeckte Art
von Schnarrwercken / gantz
stille zu intoniren, vnd zu
vielen variationibus vnd
verenderungen gar bequem.

[These] are an exceedingly
lovely type of shaded reed
voice, very quietly voiced,
and convenient for many variations and registrations.

Es haben diese beyde Stimmen gleich kleine Corpora,
jhr groestes ist ohngefehr
einer guten Spannen / oder
neun Zoll lang / vnd haben
in sich noch ein verborgen
Corpus, gleich wie die Sordunen / derer vorher gedacht
worden ist.

Both of these voices have
equally small [double] resonators, the larger about a span
or nine inches long; inside
they have an additional hidden
resonator like the Sorduns mentioned before.

[Baerpfeife
of 16' and 8' pitch]

Baerpipen oder Baerpfeif-
fen sind auch 16. vnd 8.
fusz Thon / vnd nicht kleiner zu arbeiten / oder sie
verlieren jhren rechten namen vnd klang; Den sie vielleicht von eines Beeren
stillen brummen haben: Wie
sie denn auch gar in sich
klingen / vnd mit einer
brummenden intonation respondiren. Haben zwar nicht
hohe Corpora, doch ziemlich
weit / vnd als zweene zu-
sammen gestuelpte Troechter /
jedoch in der mitten einer
gleichen weite / vnd fast
gantz zugedaeckt. Von holtze aber werden sie etwas
anders gearbeitet / wie in
der Sciagraphia zu sehen.
Man kan sie vff mancherley
Art formiren / allein ist
disz jhr proprium, dasz sie
vnten eng / vnd alsobald gar
in die weite auszgestrecket
werden muessen.

Baerpfeifes are also of 16'
and 8' pitch and cannot be developed any smaller without
losing their true [and charac-
teristic] tone color, which
probably [is intended to] imitate the soft snoring of a
bear. The tone [of the pipes]
remains rather confined within
them and gives the effect of
a humming sound. The resonators are not very high but
quite wide, and resemble two
identical [truncated] cones
joined symmetrically at their
bases, the upper opening being
nearly closed. When constructed of wood, the [Baerpfeifes]
are developed somewhat differently, which can be observed
in the Sciagraphia. It is
possible to construct [these
pipes] in many different ways,
except that this principle
must be observed: they must
be of a narrow diameter at the
bottom, and then expand rapidly in width.

Zu Prag hab ich in der
Jesuiterkirchen ein Schnarr-

At Prague, in the Jesuit
church there, I saw a reed

werck gesehen / so Pater
Andreas erfunden / vnd gar
eines lieblichen Resonantzes / do das Corpus vier-
ecket neben einander hin vnd
herwider gefuehrt / vnd sich
allezeit auch in die weite
ergroesset hat: Wie in der
Sciagraphia zu sehen.

voice invented by Pater Andreas, which had a lovely tone.
The resonator was of a rectangular [shape] and was led
continuously back and forth
with a constant increase in
cross section, as can be observed in the Sciagraphia.

[Bombardon
of 16' and 8' pitch]

Pombarda: Jst fast der
Sordunen Invention gemesz /
ohne dasz die auszlassung
des Resonantzes durch die
Loecherlein geendert wird /
vnd groessere Mundstueck
vnd Zungen haben wil / daher sie denn auch sich lau-
terer vnd staercker hoeren
lesset; vnd ist vff 16. vnd
8. fusz Thon zu arbeiten.
Die Pombarden gehoeren vnd
schicken sich aber fueglich-
er vnd besser zum Pedal /
als zum Manual, denn sie
einen anmutigen vnnd mit-
telmessigen Klang im stark-
ken Laut geben.

[. . .] is almost identi-
cal to the Sordun with the exception, that the emission of
the sound through the small
holes is somewhat different,
and the shallots and tongues
are made larger; through this
[arrangement] they produce a
louder and stronger sonority.
They are to be constructed at
16' and 8' pitch. The Bom-
bardons belong into the Pedal,
since they are much more suitable there than in the Manual;
they deliver a charming and
moderate tone of considerable
intensity.

[Fagott
of 8' pitch]

Fagott ist 8. Fusz Thon:
Hat auch gleichaus weite vnd
enge Corpora, das groeste
von 4. fusz an der lenge /
vnd wird Manualiter geschlagen.

[. . .] has narrow-scaled
cylindrical resonators, the
largest being 4 feet in length.
It is a manual [register].

[Dulzian
of 8' pitch]

Dulcian ist nur 8. Fusz
Thon: Wird von etlichen
oben zugedaeckt / vnd durch
etliche loecherlein sein Resonantz vnten an der einen

The Dulzian is of 8' pitch
only. Some cover it at the
top, but permit the tone to
escape by means of several
small holes pierced below and

seiten auszgelassen / welche in denen Regalwercken / so zu Wien in Oesterreicht gemacht werden / zu finden. Etliche aber lassen es oben gantz offen / darumb sie auch gleichwol so stille nicht seyn / vnd sich dem blasenden Instrumenten, welches mit diesem Namen genennet wird / gleich artet; gehoeret auch billicher ins Pedal / dann zum Manual. Vnd weil derer Invention vff vnterschiedliche arten verendert wird / ist allhier mehr davon zu schreiben vnnoetig.

on one side. This [construction] can be observed in the Regal instruments fabricated at Vienna in Austria. Some, however, build [this voice] open at the top, thus causing its speech to be somewhat less retiring. [In this form] the voice resembles its orchestral prototype rather closely. It belongs more properly in the Pedal than in the Manual. Since so many variations exist in the shape and form of this voice, it is unnecessary to write more about it here.

Apfel oder Knopff Regal ist 8. Fusz Thon:

Apfel or Knopfregal of 8' pitch

Wird seiner Proportion halber / dasz es wie ein Apffel vffm Stiel stehet / also gennenet; Das groeste Corpus ist etwa 4. Zoll hoch / hat eine kleine Roehr / an der groesse wie sein Mundstueck / vnd vff derselben Roehren einen runden holen Knopff voller kleiner loecher / gleich einem Biesemknopff gebohret / da der Sonus wieder auszgehen musz: Jst auch nach Regal Art lieblicher vnd viel stiller / denn ein ander Regal anzuhoeren / dienet wol in Positiffen / so in Gemaechern gebraucht werden.

It is so called because of its appearance, which resembles an apple set upon its stem. The largest resonator is 4 inches high and has a small tube of the same size as the shallot, upon which is fastened a round and hollow button pierced full of small holes like a <u>Biesemknopf</u>, through which the tone escapes. Of the [various] types of Regal voices, this one is more delicate and much more quiet than usual, and serves well in Positives destined for use in chambers.

[Kopfregal of 4' pitch]

Koepfflin Regal sind 4. Fusz Thon / haben oben auch ein rund Knaeufflein / als ein Knopff / vnd ist derselbige in der mitten von ein-

[. . .] is surmounted at the top with a round knob similar to a button, which is divided in the middle like an open helmet. The tone is thereby

ander gethan / als ein offen Helm / also dasz es den
Resonantz gleich wieder ins
vnter Corpus einwendet / ist
gut vnnd lieblich.

deflected back down into the
resonator. It is a delicate
voice.

Vnd disz sey also von den
Stimmen in Orgeln vor dieses mal gnug.[110]

And let this be enough for
this time concerning the voices in organs. [Translation by
the present author]

The Shaded Lingual Family

The selection of shaded lingual voices which Praetorius discusses are dispersed at the following pitches:

1. At 16' pitch: the Sordun, Gross Rankett,
Baerpfeife, and Bombardon

2. At 8' pitch: the Rankett, Baerpfeife, Bombardon, Fagott, Dulzian, and Apfel or Knopfregal

3. At 4' pitch: the Kopfregal

The Fagott Species

Contrary to Praetorius' order of presentation, the
Fagott needs to be taken up first, since among the shaded
lingual voices he discusses, it is the only one of normal
length; all of the others apparently are species which exhibit fractional resonators and must, therefore, be adjudged,
Regals. Praetorius describes the voice as of cylindrical
resonators in narrow scale; he specifies a 4' resonator for
8' pitch. Accordingly, the voice is constructed of normal
length resonator for open cylindrical reeds; namely, a physical length equal to one-half the pitch. His description

points to a modern organ Clarinet with shaded resonators. In this regard, the voice classifies altogether differently than the modern Fagott, which is generally constructed of open conical pipes, albeit also of narrow scale. Whereas the modern Fagott relates to the Trumpet as an echo form of the same, Praetorius' Fagott seems to be an overlarge Krummhorn or Dulzian. He recommends it for use in the Manual at 8' pitch and records it similarly in his Universal Table[111] but does not exemplify it in the Theatrum Instrumentorum.

The Sordun-Rankett-Bombardon Species

These several species all seem to be fairly closely related in that they all are shaded, are of cylindrical resonators, and of fractional length. Praetorius devotes some discussion to each of the species separately, but also points out their kinship to the Sordun.

He takes up, first of all, the Sordun and Rankett. Copies of both of the examples from the Theatrum Instrumentorum are reproduced faithfully on Plate XCIII, 1 and 5. By interpretation of the scale rule appearing with these pipes in the Theatrum Instrumentorum[112] certain critical dimensions can be extracted from the sketches. These are given in Table 107.

Praetorius suggests the 16' Sordun as an admirable voice for the Pedal, since the tone is gentle and rather quiet. He claims that it combines well with stringed instruments

TABLE 107

DIMENSIONS AND DISPOSITION OF 16' SORDUN AND 16' OR 8' RANKETT

Item	Description	Raw Diameter of Resonator in Mm.[a]	Raw Length of Resonator in Mm.[a]	Reference to Present Atlas: Plate-Number	Reference to Theatrum....: Plate-Number[b]
16' Sordun	Cylindrical; five holes	6.0	43.0	XCIII-1	38-11
16' or 8' Rankett	Cylindrical; three holes	5.0	20.0	XCIII-5	38-13

Item	Classification of Resonator	Actual Diameter of Resonator in Mm.[b]	Ratio of Physical Length to Pitch	Equivalent Actual Length of Resonator in British Units	Actual Length of Resonator in Cm.[b]
16' Sordun	Fractional	69.4	1/10	1'-7 1/2"	49.7
16' or 8' Rankett	Fractional	57.8	1/20; 1/10	9"	23.0

[a] As measured directly from Praetorius' sketches on Plate XXXVIII of the Theatrum Instrumentorum.

[b] See chapter xiv of the present study for the method of interpreting the scale and converting into actual dimensions in metric measure.

and with woodwinds. A somewhat closer examination of the
Sordun as pictured in the Theatrum Instrumentorum, described
verbally by Praetorius, and sketched more accurately by
Supper[113] reveals a pair of telescoped resonators, an internal open one surmounted by a larger covered resonator provided with egress holes. Both resonators are cylindrical in
shape, the outer and visible one being joined to the block
by means of a conical connection. See Plate XCI, 8 for a
pictorial representation of Supper's Sordun. Since the Sordun as Praetorius describes it exhibits a fractional resonator whose ratio of physical length to pitch is 1/10, the
voice is properly considered a Regal.

Praetorius suggests the 16' Gross Rankett and the 8'
Rankett as useful lingual voices for the Manual and the Pedal
as shown in his Universal Table.[114] He describes the tone as
uncommonly lovely. A copy of an example of the voice from
the Theatrum Instrumentorum is reproduced on Plate XCIII, 5
and its critical dimensions are exhibited in Table 107. From
his legend in the Theatrum Instrumentorum, as well as the
title for the species in his dictionary of organ voices, and
his suggestion that both varieties have equally long resonators, one could easily be led to believe that the identical
measurements were considered suitable for either a 16' or an
8' variety of the species. His specification of a 9" length
for the resonator bespeaks the dimension given in his sketch
of the same and indicates an approximate ratio of physical

length to pitch of 1/20 for the 16', and 1/10 for the 8' variety of the Rankett. Both ratios indicate the voice as being a Regal, since the resonators are unquestionably of fractional length. A more exact reproduction of the voice is
given by Supper[115] where the double resonator is more clearly
indicated. A copy of Supper's sketch appears on Plate XCI,
9. The internal resonator is of extremely narrow scale and
open at the top; the external resonator is comparatively
larger in diameter, is closed at the top, is directly connected to the block, and is provided with three egress holes
near the base of the visible resonator. As Praetorius points
out, the voice is closely related to the Sordun, but differs
from it in certain physical respects:

1. It exhibits a somewhat narrower scale for the
external resonator

2. Its resonator is less than half as long as
that of the Sordun for an equivalent pitch

3. It is joined to the block directly and without a conical connector

4. It has fewer egress holes

For the Bombardon Praetorius suggests the pitches of
16' and 8'. He recommends it for the Pedal since it produces
a moderately voluminous tone, quite loud. In many respects
the voice supposedly resembles the structure of the Sordun
except for the following:

1. The tone egress holes are different

2. The pipe is equipped with larger shallots and heavier reed tongues

3. Its tone is considerably louder and stronger than that of the Sordun

Praetorius' description is quite insufficient to fix the family and genus of the Bombardon. The mouth-blown prototype for it seems to have been the Pommer which Praetorius pictures in the _Theatrum Instrumentorum_.[116] Adlung is the only theoretician who throws any light on the prevailing concept for the voice.[117] He classifies it as the appropriate bass for the Schalmei, which points to a three-quarter length, open conical resonator. Praetorius' suggestion that the voice is of a construction similar to the Sordun points to a fractional and cylindrical resonator, shaded, and provided with egress holes which he specifically mentions. It is, of course, quite possible that the concept for the Bombardon changed completely between Praetorius' and Adlung's time. The question remains, for the present, unsolved.

The Dulzian Species

For the _Dulzian_ Praetorius develops two distinct species. One is the open Dulzian, which has already been treated above under "Open Lingual Voices." The second species belongs properly under the concept of shaded lingual voices and provides Praetorius' reason for discussing it with other species in this family. He describes it as having resonators which

are covered at the top and provided with egress holes near
the base and on one side of the resonator. Neither of the
two species is represented in the Theatrum Instrumentorum,
so that only a guess can be made as to the general external
appearance of the shaded species. It is, in all probability,
a Regal voice with a covered or shaded fractional resonator
and egress holes in the same. A hypothetical sketch for the
shaded Dulzian appears in Plate XCI, 10. Praetorius points
out that the voice is well suited for the Pedal and that, in
his time, a number of variants were in use.

The Baerpfeife Species

Of the Baerpfeifes, Praetorius discusses only two in
his account, but includes sketches for seven, and possibly,
eight, in the Theatrum Instrumentorum.[118] Copies of all of
these are reproduced on Plate XCIII, 2[?], 3, 4, 6, and 7
and Plate XCIV, 1, 2, and 3 together with idealizations of
the latter three on Plate XCIV, 4, 5, and 6. The two specimens which he delineates to some extent in his account are
the ones reproduced on Plate XCIII, 6 and Plate XCIV, 1 and
4. Table 108 gives the dimensions for the two specimens as
extracted by careful measurement and interpretation of the
scale drawings.[119]

Praetorius maintains that the Baerpfeifes are suitable only at 16' and 8' pitch; smaller examples fail to produce the characteristic tone, which is somewhat veiled and

TABLE 108

DIMENSIONS FOR SPECIMENS OF THE 8' BAERPFEIFE

Item	Reference to Theatrum...: Plate-Number	Reference to Present Atlas: Plate-Number	Minimum Diameter		Maximum Diameter		Resonator: Full Length	
			Raw mm.[a]	Real mm.[b]	Raw mm.[a]	Real mm.[b]	Raw mm.[a]	Real mm.[b]
8' Baerpfeife in metal	38-17	XCIII-6	2.0	23.1	11.0	127.2	23.5	27.2
8' Baerpfeife in wood	38-19	XCIV-1	2.0	23.1	14.0	161.9	26.5	30.7

[a]As measured directly from Praetorius' sketches on Plate XXXVIII of the Theatrum Instrumentorum.

[b]See chapter xiv of the present study for the method of interpreting the scale and converting it into actual dimensions in metric measure.

reminiscent of the gentle snoring of a bear. The resonators are short but very wide; a critical feature is that although the diameter is narrow at the junction of block and resonator, it expands very rapidly. The first example of Table 108 is of metal and is described as two truncated cones joined at their greatest width which must, therefore, be equal. The rapid diminution of the diameter in the upper cone nearly covers the resonator.

The second example of Table 108 is of wood, but in all respects similar to the metal corollary, except that a

flare is added at the top of the resonator. Various other
forms occur, but the chief feature is the rapid increase of
the diameter or cross-sectional area from the junction of
block and resonator.

Praetorius' reference to a Baerpfeife which he saw
in the Barfuesser Kirche in Prague and which was supposedly
invented by Pater Andreas, indicates a wooden pyramidal resonator laid out like a labyrinth. Although he claims that
it is sketched in the Sciagraphia,[120] it is not to be found
there; there is, however, a similar form in metal,[121] of
which a copy is reproduced on Plate XCIII, 4.

All Baerpfeifes may be reckoned as Regals of fractional resonators.

Exceptional Regals

Finally, Praetorius takes up several Regals and
calls them by appropriate names. For 8' pitch, he suggests
the Apfel or Knopfregal; literally translated the terms mean
Apple or Buttonregal. The resonators are fractional; hence,
the voices are truly of the Regal family. Praetorius describes the tone as very lovely but also diminutive, suitable for a salon Positive. He compares the surmounting ball
to a Biesemknopf, which is, in all likelihood, a plant by
the name of Bisamkraut (L. Adaxa Moschatellina) which means,
"little holes."[122] Supper presents a Knopfregal[123] a reproduction of which appears on Plate XCI, 11 together with a

modification which bespeaks Praetorius' description a little
more closely in item 12 of the same Plate.

For 4' pitch, Praetorius suggests the Kopfregal,
which, having the appearance of a knob or button cloven as
an open helmet may be surmised to have looked somewhat like
the hypothetical reproduction shown on Plate XCI, 14; this,
in turn, is a modification of Supper's Kopfregal[124] as reproduced on the same Plate as item 13.

Classifications of the Species

From the Universal Table,[125] the dictionary of organ
voices,[126] and the Theatrum Instrumentorum[127] a summary can
be submitted which will classify the shaded lingual voices
as to their divisional function as well as to their physical
characteristics. In the Universal Table Praetorius suggests
the following voices as useful manual registers:

16' Sordun	8' Bombardon
16' Gross Rankett	8' Baerpfeife
16' Gross Bombardon	8' Apfel or Knopfregal
8' Rankett	4' Kopfregal
8' Fagott	

For Pedal use Praetorius musters the following:

16' Sordun	8' Rankett
16' Gross Rankett	8' Bombardon
16' Gross Bombardon	8' Dulzian
16' Gross Baerpfeife	8' Baerpfeife

With respect to their physical characteristics the shaded lingual voices, according to Praetorius' delineations, assort as follows when arranged in a modern classification:[128]

Brief of Praetorius' Shaded Lingual Voices

I. Shaded Lingual Voices

    A. Open Cylindrical Resonators

        1. Normal Resonators (one-half length)

            a. Fagott

        2. Fractional Resonators (less than one-half length)

            a. Sordun

            b. Rankett

            c. Bombardon [?]

            d. Dulzian [Regal]

    B. Open Conical Resonators

        1. Normal Resonators (three-quarter length)

            a. None

        2. Fractional Resonators (less than three-quarter length)

            a. Baerpfeife

    C. Exceptional Resonators

            a. Apfel or Knopfregal

            b. Kopfregal

Conclusions

From the wealth of information which Praetorius

presents concerning the Flute, Gedackt, and Reed voices of
the Early Baroque, it is profitable to extract certain basic
concepts which seem to have served as compelling forces in
the realization of the instruments of the time. In many respects his delineation and organization of the voices and
their relationship to each other in corporate association
bespeak a theory which has again become compelling for our
time. It is not presumptuous to maintain that many of his
convictions may prove helpful in developing a more articulate
discipline for the concept of organ tone and organ voices.
A few statements compressed from the extended discussions of
the present chapter may be postulated in the hope that they
may contribute significantly to a clear understanding of the
art of the organ, not only for the Early Baroque, but for
the present as well:

 1. Praetorius adheres to a fairly systematic
nomenclature for the several varieties of each species
of register. The unmodified appellation (as for example, Gemshorn, Quintade, Flachfloete, etc.) establishes the primary pitch function of the voice; all
extensions of the same into varieties at lower and
higher pitch levels are, thereupon, differentiated
by appropriate modifying terms, as Gross, Klein, and
Super. Those voices for which he indicates, by means
of his nomenclature, a primary function at 8' pitch
are:

a. The Gemshorn   d. The Gedackt

b. The Spitzgedackt   e. The Rohrfloete

c. The Quintade

Those, for which he indicates a primary function at

4' pitch are:

a. The Hohlfloete   f. The Flachfloete

b. The Koppelfloete   g. The Labial Dulzian

c. The Spillfloete   h. The Nachthorn-Gedackt

d. The Blockfloete   i. The Querfloete-Gedackt

e. The Spitzfloete

He does not indicate a primary function at 2' pitch

for any species. Those, for which he indicates a

primary function at 1' pitch (and chiefly in the Ped-

al) are:

a. The Siffloete   c. The Bauerrohrfloete

b. The Bauerfloete   d. The Rohrschelle

2. By relating Praetorius' qualifying terms of

Gross, Klein, Super, as well as the unmodified appel-

lations for the registers to the identical terms which

he uses to designate the Principalbases of the several

corpora, it is possible to extract unison, sub-octave,

double sub-octave, octave, and super octave functions

for each of the species, the limit being set by the

number of varieties which he delineates in each case.

Whether or not Praetorius expected such an interpre-

tation to be made, remains an open question; the idea,

however, is provocative and useful for a refined understanding of his principles for the incorporation of the tonal resource

3. Although difficult to prove in a quantitative way, it seems that Praetorius was conscious of the necessity for reducing the ratio of the mouth width when increasing the diameter of the corpus, from moderate dimensions, in order to maintain a proper balance between the extensity of the tone and its dynamic force

4. Praetorius classifies the range of diameter values used in his day into two simple genera; namely, the narrow-scaled and the wide-scaled. The former is equivalent to moderate and moderately narrow scales in modern theory, and the latter, to wide and very wide scales. Accordingly, most of the species in the modern narrow and very narrow genera found only sparse application in the work of Praetorius and his contemporaries, except in isolated experimental essays as, for example, in some of the avant-garde work of Esaias Compenius

5. Praetorius exhibits a fine sense of propriety in his recommendations for voices at aequal pitch. Evidence for this refined understanding of the possible and likely detrimental effect of an over-great extensity of tone at this level lies in the fact that

he recommends only moderate-scaled or moderately
narrow-scaled voices for this purpose, reserving the
wider scales for the higher pitches

6. A review of Praetorius' labial registers reveals that nearly all of them have survived or been
redeveloped in modern times. In a few instances alternate terms have been substituted for his appellations

7. Praetorius' concept of the Spitzfloete differs widely from the customary modern concept for the
same. Whereas modern theory considers this species
as of a moderate genus and narrower than the Gemshorn,
Praetorius places it into a rather wide-scaled genus
and specifies it as larger than the Gemshorn

8. With respect to the Nachthorn, Praetorius
recognizes two identifiable and contrasting species
for the same; one is the very wide-scaled open cylindrical species, the other, the narrow-scaled covered
cylindrical one. He much prefers the latter, while
modern practice favors the former

9. Praetorius recognizes the Waldfloete as a
high-pitched variety of the Hohlfloete; as such it is
of wide scale and open cylindrical construction. The
modern concept for this species envisions a wide-
scaled but open conical construction for the same at
moderate and high pitches

10. Praetorius classifies the Koppelfloete and Spillfloete among <u>open</u> <u>conical</u> pipes, whereas most modern classifications associate them with the <u>partly</u> <u>covered</u> family

11. It appears that in the Early Baroque the term <u>Hohlfloete</u> was commonly used to designate a <u>partly</u> <u>covered</u> species. Praetorius, however, establishes the term as a proper appellation for wide-scaled <u>open</u> <u>cylindrical</u> pipes, and the term <u>Rohrfloete</u> for the partly covered and moderate-scaled species

12. Praetorius conceives of the Rohrfloete as a <u>moderate-scaled</u> voice in contradistinction to modern theory which generally suggests construction in <u>wide</u> <u>scale</u>. Since he considers it primarily as an 8' register, his moderate scale for it indicates his sensitivity about using wide scales at this pitch level

13. In line with customary (but questionable) modern practice, Praetorius does not classify the Spitzgedackt as a member of any covered family, but includes it as a member of the open conical family of registers

14. The concept of overblown pipes was clearly understood by Praetorius and seems to have found application in instruments of the time. He understood that open pipes and conical covered pipes overblow into the octave, and fully covered pipes, into the

twelfth. He correctly specifies appropriate physical lengths for the various conditions

15. Praetorius records an isolated experiment by Esaias Compenius which explored the possibility of using double mouths for labial pipes. One can deduce that the concept was only an incipient one for his time and came into fruition much later

16. The concept of echo voices, i.e., of quiet and diminutive forms of the various species, embraced only a few selected items in the Early Baroque. Among these, Praetorius discusses only the Schwegel as an echo form of the Hohlfloete, the Conical Schwegel as one for the Gemshorn and related species, and the Barem as one for Gedackts

17. Praetorius recognizes mutation voices only at fifth-sounding pitches. Among these he identifies 5 1/3', 2 2/3', 1 1/3', and 2/3' pitches. Neither in his written account nor in his catalog of dispositions are any mutation voices to be found which represent more remote ingredients from the Harmonic Series. Third-sounding ingredients were admitted only as components in the very high pitch region of the Klingend Zimbel

18. The principle of discant voices, i.e., stops which exhibit pipes only in the upper half or so of the compass, found occasional application among lingual

as well as labial voices in the organs of the time.
The same principle, in variant implementation, finds
occasional application today

19. Praetorius' discussion of the entire fund
of lingual voices gives an impression of uncertainty
and lacks the tight organization which is evident for
the labial voices. Apparently a clear insight into
the determinant characteristics of reed pipes eluded
him as much as it has many subsequent theorists

20. Because of his frequent and quite consistent
reference to orchestral instruments, it seems that
Praetorius looked upon most, if not all, reed voices
as imitative counterparts of mouth-blown prototypes,
and expected the lingual voices of the organ to exhibit a certain degree of fidelity to the tone of their
orchestral corollaries

21. Praetorius firmly establishes the theoretically normal lengths for resonators in open conical
reed pipes which are still accepted in theory today,
but often violated in practice. He maintains also,
that a normal physical length for open cylindrical
reeds is 1/2 of the pitch length; for open conical
reeds, 3/4. He further understood the possibility of
providing sub-normal or fractional lengths for the
same

22. Praetorius carefully points out that if a

certain family of reeds should appear in tandem, they
should be constructed of proportionately long resonators. If, for example, a three-quarter length is
adopted for one, all others of the same family should
be constructed in the same ratio of physical length
to pitch

23. Contrary to the apparently prevailing practice of his time, Praetorius recommends the adoption
of narrower shallots and reed tongues, in order to develop a proud, resplendent, and substantial tone. It
seems, from his concern, that inordinately wide shallots and tongues were much in vogue at his time

24. Praetorius' classification of the lingual
order of pipes into open and shaded families departs
widely from modern theory, which generally classifies
them into cylindrical, conical, and fractional resonators

25. Pursuant to modern theory and practice,
Praetorius recommends reeds at unison, octave, and
sub-octave pitches only. He does, however, discuss
a type of reed "Mixture", which, by means of unison
ingredients, engages the principle of repetition.
The voice was known as a Zimbelregal

26. Whereas modern theory generally considers
the Fagott as a species of the open conical family
and of a narrow-scaled genus, Praetorius clearly

defines the voice as of <u>open</u> <u>cylindrical</u> resonators

27. Regals seem to have held a commanding respect in the Early Baroque. A large number of the
reed voices which Praetorius discusses are Regals in
the sense that they exhibit sub-normal or fractional
resonators. In fact, among the array he discusses
and pictorializes are many examples which are of elaborate construction and have long since fallen into
disuse. Some of the simpler forms bear renewed examination with a view toward their redevelopment and incorporation into the modern repertoire of Regal voices

28. The Baerpfeifes seem to have been in high
favor during the Early Baroque. Praetorius discusses
two models in some detail, but illustrates seven or
eight examples in the <u>Theatrum</u> <u>Instrumentorum</u>

29. Attempts to imitate the sound of the human
voice by means of Regal pipes are so recorded by Praetorius. He mentions the <u>Jungfrauregal</u> and the <u>Kornett-</u>
<u>regal</u> as species suitable for this purpose

CHAPTER XIV

PRAETORIUS' "CHORTON"

The Quest for Praetorius' Reference Pitch

In the late nineteenth and early twentieth centuries certain significant efforts were made by interested scholars to search for the reference pitch of Praetorius. The De Organographia[1] returns again and again to this problem, which Praetorius considered a very vexing one for his time, and exhibits a persistent effort on his part to define with some degree of exactitude a suitable and useful reference pitch for the organ. Inasmuch as he was unable to measure and record frequency of vibration, all of his presentations in this regard are more nearly qualitative approximations than quantitative definitions. In the historical quest to define the Chorton quantitatively two attempts stand out as worthy of examination and appraisal. These are the method and result postulated by Alexander J. Ellis in 1880 and those by Arthur Mendel in 1948.

Ellis' Solution

To the present author's knowledge, only Alexander J. Ellis of England sought to arrive at an acceptable value for

722

Praetorius' Chorton[2] through the careful construction of a
single organ pipe as represented in the De Organographia.[3]
Ellis describes his procedure in sufficiently careful detail
to permit an objective inspection of his method and evalua-
tion of his results. He says:[4]

MA 424.2 [JA 422.9, EA 426.7], C 507.3, S 2.37.
(Ellis.) 1619, Brunswick.[5] "Suitable" Church Organ
Pitch. Praetorius (Syntagma Musicum," vol. ii.,
p. 231-2) gives what he terms "a correct drawing of
the proper church-pipe measure for c''', or the
half-foot tone of the organ-builders;" that is, 1/2 C.
This figure gives the dimensions of the whole octave
from 1/2 C to 1/4 C. It is a rough woodcut, on very
bibulous paper, which must have shrunk much in drying.
At the back of the title of the "Theatrum Instrumentorum seu Sciagraphia," in the same volume, Praetorius
gives a scale of six Brunswick inches, which, on the
figure, measure 140.5 mm. in place of 142.68 mm.[6]
Dividing the latter by the former, we obtain 1.0155
as the multiplier of the dimensions of the drawing to
correct for shrinkage. The actual drawing on the
paper gives 133.8 mm. for the length, and 25.2 mm.
for double the side of the square pipe, corresponding
to 1/2 C. Multiplying by 1.0155, we find 135.87 and
25.59 respectively. Doubling the first to get the
1 C, we have 271.74 mm. for the length, and 25.29 mm.
for the side of the square of a wooden pipe giving
this recommended pitch. I had a wooden pipe constructed which was 272 mm. long and 25.5 mm. in the
side, and spoke 503.6, 507.25, and 511.86 under pressures of 2 3/4, 3 1/4, and 4 inches respectively.
Correcting this by rule p. 296 [which refers to pressure and temperature corrections], by multiplying by
323 = 272 + 2 x 25.5 and dividing by 322.92 = 271.4 +
2 x 25.59, we obtain C 503.7, 507.4 respectively;[7]
practically, the same as before (the errors in length
and side being in opposite directions), giving MA
421.1, 424.2 and 428.0 respectively.[8] As 3 1/4 in.
was, according to Herr Schmahl (see "Authorities")
almost precisely the force of wind used by Praetorius,
I assume the second as most correct, and hence obtain
the above figures. This is the "mean pitch," being
practically the same as Handel's A 422.5, and it is
the earliest example of it that I have found.[9] It

was not then the ordinary pitch, but it was, in Praetorius' mind, the most suitable. It was this pitch
to which Praetorius must have referred, when he said
that the Halberstadt organ, A 505.8, was a good Tone,
and nearly a Tone and a half sharper than the suitable church pitch (als die unsrige itzige Chormessige
Werke stehen).[10] The difference of pitch was S 3.04,
just an equal minor Third; and just less than S 3.103,
the meantone minor Third.[11] These two pitches, therefore, confirm each other. The lengths and sides of
the other pipes in the Octave were not engraved with
sufficient accuracy to draw out the exact temperament;
but, as Praetorius explains how to tune in the meantone temperament, and no other (perfect major Thirds,
and Fifths a quarter of a comma too small), there was
no necessity to attend to the pitch of any but the
lowest note, which had the longest pipe, and was,
therefore, in all probability, most accurately rendered in the woodcut.

Thus reads Ellis' account of the Pfeifflin zur Chormasz and his interpretation and use of the same, which the
present author has rendered here in full, in order to be
more adequately able to analyze Ellis' procedure and to eval-
uate his result.

What Ellis used as the point of departure in his
quest for Praetorius' reference pitch is the graphic scale
drawing called the Pfeifflin zur Chormasz.[12] It is apparent
from his measurements that he used an original copy of the
De Organographia of 1619 as is borne out by the present author's use of a similar original copy.[13] The engraving is
a conventional scale table, not a picture. The graph presents full values for the actual lengths and fractional (or
possibly multiple)[14] values for the widths (i.e., circumferences)[15] of thirteen consecutive chromatic pipes constituting

a full octave ranging in pitch from c to c' of a 1' stop;[16]

hence, an absolute pitch of 1/2' to 1/4', inclusive. See

Plate XCV, 1 for a reasonably equivalent reproduction (not to

scale) of the Pfeifflin zur Chormasz as found in the De

Organographia. The original legends found on the graph are

subjoined, together with a parallel translation of the same:

Pfeifflin zur Chormasz.	Pipes for a reference measure.
b. Die Lenge der Pfeiffen zum rechten Chorton.	b. [Represents] the lengths of the pipes for the correct reference pitch.
a: ist die Weite / zweymahl genommen.	a. Represents the width, taken twice.
In Holtz / gevierdt.	In wood; quartered.
In Metal / rund.	In metal; round. [Translation by the present author]

Praetorius' introductory remarks for the Pfeifflin

zur Chormasz establish the note c on the graph as the c'''

of an 8' stop; consequently, the note c' on the graph is

equivalent to a c'''' of an 8' stop. He says:[17]

Derowegen hiervnter einen richtigen Abrisz der rechten Chormasz setzen wollen; von dem c̿, so nach Orgelmacher Mensur ein halben Fusz Thon (wenn das grosse C von 8. Fussen ist) bringet	For this reason [I] have wanted to subjoin an accurate sketch of the correct reference measure; from c''' which, according to the organbuilders' measure produces a half-foot tone (when Great C is reckoned as of 8' pitch).

C 8 Fuesz /	C: 8 foot
c 4 Fuesz /	c: 4 foot

$\overline{c}$	2 Fuesz /		$\underline{c}$':	2 foot
$\overline{\overline{c}}$	1 Fuesz /		$\underline{c}$'':	1 foot
$\overline{\overline{\overline{c}}}$	1/2 Fuesz /		$\underline{c}$''':	1/2 foot

It is clear from this delineation that Praetorius'
graph gives the measurements for the fifth octave segment of
an 8' stop, which delivers an absolute pitch extending from
1/2' to 1/4'. See Plate XCV, 2, where segment x represents
the range of the pitch level for the pipes of the graph.

The graph, as reproduced on Plate XCV, 1, is a coordinate system whose point of origin is located at o; the X-axis
is represented by the horizontal line extending to the right
of o, and the Y-axis, by the vertical line extending upward
from o. The lengths of the various pipes are plotted on the
X-axis, while the widths (i.e., the circumferences) are
plotted on vertical lines lying parallel to the Y-axis. The
longest dimension on the X-axis (oq) gives the length of
c''', i.e., the 49th pipe of an 8' stop, or an absolute pitch
of 1/2'. The shortest dimension on the same axis (or) gives
the length for c'''', i.e., the 61st pipe of an 8' stop, or
an absolute pitch of 1/4'. The longest dimension parallel
to the Y-axis (qk) gives the fractional (or multiple) width
(i.e., the circumference) for c''', while the shortest dimension (rm) gives the same for c''''.

A step by step analysis of Ellis' interpretation of
Praetorius' graph, and his procedure for realizing his findings will help to reinforce or question his ultimate

conclusions concerning the reference pitch recommended by Praetorius.

Ellis' method of correcting the graphic values of the drawing by means of a calculated coefficient of shrinkage as derived from the full scale rule exhibited by Praetorius on the reverse side of the titlepage for the *Theatrum Instrumentorum*[18] is quite defensible and necessary. His adjustment of the values to a common reference temperature is equally important, when valid comparisons of frequencies are to be made. It must be observed that Ellis consistently used 59° Fahrenheit (*i.e.*, 15° Centigrade)[19] as his reference temperature for all of the pitch values which appear in his published writings.[20] His values for *a*' at 68° Fahrenheit (*i.e.*, 20° Centigrade) adjust[21] to proportionately higher values as shown in Table 109.

TABLE 109

ELLIS' VALUES FOR PRAETORIUS' REFERENCE
PITCH AT VARIOUS TEMPERATURES

Ellis' Values	At 15° Centigrade in Double Vibrations per Second	At 20° Centigrade in Double Vibrations per Second[a]
Meantone *a*'	424.2	427.98
Equal Tempered *a*'	426.7	430.50

[a]Reference temperature used by the present author for purposes of comparing frequencies.

Ellis' arbitrary adjustment of the value for the length of the pipe by doubling its graphic value (as corrected for shrinkage from the X-axis of the graph) is a procedure which is not indicated by Praetorius. The given graphic dimension on the X-axis for the example which Ellis chose to fabricate is for a pipe which will sound a 1/2' pitch or the equivalent c''' of an 8' stop. Ellis actually constructed a pipe of twice the graphic length which supposedly was expected to sound an octave lower; i.e., a 1' pitch or the equivalent c'' of an 8' stop. Praetorius' direction for the proper use of the graph specifies precisely that the horizontal dimensions of the graph (i.e., along the X-axis) are the exact lengths of the pipes to be realized, and may, consequently, be neither halved nor doubled. This operation constitutes, in the present author's opinion, Ellis' first aberration.

According to his own account, Ellis took the dimension for the width of the pipe, not from the Y-axis of the graph (which is necessary in order to correlate properly with the length which he derived from the X-axis), but rather from the sketch in plan of a supposedly square pipe pictured above the graph and, in all likelihood, not to the same scale used for the values plotted on the X and Y-axes of the coordinate system. In fact, the "square" is not square but actually rectangular, since it exhibits divergent dimensions for two adjacent sides. Since, then, he took one side dimension and doubled it to secure one-fourth of the perimeter of a wooden pipe, he probably felt that he had adjusted the width in accordance with Praetorius' legend which specifies that the _Y_-axis (width) dimensions from the graph must be doubled to arrive at the true dimension. This adjusted dimension (provided it had been taken from the _Y_-axis of the graph), however, gives the width (_i.e._, the circumference) for a pipe of 1/2' pitch, not for one of 1' pitch which is the pitch at which Ellis chose to fabricate his model pipe.

This double misinterpretation of the graph coordinates coupled with the questionable attempt to construct a model for which no dimensions at par are given either in the graph or in the accompanying plan sketches, provided a trap out of which acceptable frequencies are impossible to obtain. In the present author's opinion, only values derived from the coordinate system at par, corrected for shrinkage, and adjusted according to the directions provided in the associated legends by Praetorius, can provide an operative framework from which acceptable frequency values can be obtained.

Having constructed one pipe after the manner described and extracted frequency values from the same, Ellis gives no indication of having checked his findings against other models available from the graph coordinates, particularly the octave above and at least selected examples between the extremes; nor did he check it against any other pipe dimensions which appear on Plates XXXVII and XXXVIII of the

Theatrum Instrumentorum and are there developed out of different reference rules. His venture, therefore, stands as
an experiment in isolation and places his conclusion regarding the reference pitch of Praetorius in jeopardy.

Ellis' acceptance of Schmahl's dictum that 3 1/4
inches was precisely the pressure used by Praetorius is a
final arbitrary procedure which is belied by all of the a-
vailable evidence with respect to pressures used in the Early
Baroque. It is, by all odds, much too high. The adoption
of a 3 1/4 inch pressure throws still further doubt on the
validity of his conclusion.

Accordingly, Ellis' arbitrary adjustment of the
graphic value for the length to serve other purposes than
those specifically intended by Praetorius, his adoption of
an approximate pictorial dimension for the width, his use of
an apparently specious wind pressure, and his neglect to
verify his conclusions, would strongly indicate an aberration
in his outcome: Ellis' meantone a' of 424.2 double vibrations per second at 15° Centigrade or the equivalent 427.98
at 20° Centigrade lies very much in question; so do also, of
course, his equal tempered a' of 426.7 double vibrations per
second at 15° Centigrade or the equivalent 430.50 at 20° Centigrade.

Mendel's Solution

Mendel's research represents another major attempt

o arrive at an acceptable pitch value for Praetorius' Chor

nd Cammerton. His research followed entirely different

aths from those of Ellis. He sought the answer to the enig-

a by investigating the voice ranges which Praetorius gives

tenor and bass for mature male voices; discant and alto for

oys or castrati), determining a mean pitch for these, com-

aring this with other mean pitches established by classical

riters, and trying, painstakingly to be sure, to secure some

ntelligent information and directive from Praetorius' own

ery confusing discussion of the Chor and Cammerton. It must

e remembered, however, that Mendel's major concern deals

ore particularly with the Cammerton than with the Chorton.

Mendel's conclusions regarding the actual pitches of

he Chor and Cammerton are the following:[22]

> Praetorius' chamber pitch, commonly called, in
> Praetorius' own time, "choir pitch"[;] "a" would be
> approximately equivalent to our c' - c#'[;] i.e., the
> approximate difference from a'=440, expressed in semi-
> tones, would be +3 [to] 4. [The] pitch [which] Prae-
> torius considers more desirable for church organs and
> [the] actual pitch of [the] Frederiksborg organ,
> built 1610[:] "a" would be approximately equivalent
> to our bb - b [;] i.e., the approximate difference
> from a'=440, expressed in semitones, would be +1 [to]
> 2.[23]

From this discussion, it is apparent that Mendel pro-

oses a value lying somewhere between 466.16 and 493.88

ouble vibrations per second at a' as an acceptable one for

he reference pitch which Praetorius recommends.

Mendel's conclusions were reached by interpreting

Praetorius' qualitative descriptions given throughout the
De Organographia and shored up by an advance study of similarly qualitative descriptions interpreted from Schlick's
Spiegel der Orgelmacher und Organisten with respect to the
compasses of keyboards and the instructions for transpositions contained therein.

Having arrived at his conclusions, Mendel seeks to
reinforce the same by marshaling a further suggestion of
Praetorius for ascertaining the proper reference pitch; namely, the Nuernberg Posaune.[24] Praetorius' directive in this
connection presents the opportunity of pursuing the problem
in a quantitative way, but Mendel pursues the problem aca-
demically and again in a qualitative way. He says:[25]

> Praetorius also says (p. 232) that he knows of
> "no better instrument for ascertaining the proper
> pitch than a trombone, especially those that were
> formerly made in Nuernberg, and are still made there;
> for if the slide is drawn out the width of two fingers
> from the end, it produces correctly and exactly, in
> the true choir pitch, the tenor 'a': [music notation] ["]
>
> Now the trombone he refers to is clearly the
> "Gemeine oder rechte Posaun", depicted in his plate
> VIII, and this instrument is of about the same size
> as the present-day tenor trombone in B♭. To produce
> a=220 (a'=440) on such an instrument, the player must
> pull the slide out from the closed position some
> 3 1/4" to 3 1/2", so the tone produced by pulling it
> out only the width of two fingers (say, 1 1/2") would
> be closer to b♭ than to a. This would make Prae-
> torius' choir pitch nearly a half-tone higher than
> a'=440, and a whole tone below his chamber pitch; and
> that is exactly in accord with what he says about
> choir pitch.

If the present author were to accept Mendel's claim

that the _gemeine_ _rechte_ _Posaune_ as pictured on Plate VIII of
the _Theatrum_ _Instrumentorum_ is of exactly the same size and
disposition as our modern tenor trombone in $\underline{B}b$ ($\underline{a}$'=440),
then the withdrawal of the slide for one-half position would
indicate a pitch half-way between $\underline{a}$ and $\underline{b}b$ ($\underline{a}$'=440), certainly
neither $\underline{a}$ nor $\underline{b}b$. In fact, during a visit to Nuernberg on
April 6, 1956, the present author consulted Dr. Willi Woerth-
mueller, author of "Die Nuernberger Trompeten- und Posaunen-
macher des 17. und 18. Jahrhunderts",[26] concerning the pitch
levels of historic examples still in existence and reposing
in museums and private collections over Europe. He pointed
out that the surviving examples from the first and second
decades of the seventeenth century are almost all largely
dismembered and in unplayable condition, and also that the
trombone manufacturers of the time held to no firm reference
pitches but simply constructed the instruments to suit pitch
levels requested by the purchasers. This professional opinion ruled out any hope of discovering Praetorius' reference
pitch from possible surviving examples of Nuernberg Posaunes
of the time indicated by Praetorius.

Although Mendel does not use his interpretation of
Praetorius' Nuernberg Posaune as a compelling argument for
his conclusion concerning the Chorton, he does muster it in
support of his conclusions concerning both the Cammerton and
the Chorton as derived in another way.

The two classical attempts in the quest for

Praetorius' Chorton attack the problem from opposite directions:

    1. Ellis pursues it by using a quantitative,
scientific approach (albeit, somewhat cavalierly)

    2. Mendel pursues it by a qualitative, academic
approach, relying upon narrative descriptions to
supply the necessary premises

    As will be observed in the subsequent discussion,
the present author's solution lies between the values postulated by Ellis and by Mendel.

Contribution toward the Quest

    It is the writer's opinion that another avenue re-
mains open to the modern scholar in the search for an acceptable value for Praetorius' Chorton, for the revelation of
which the Kapellmeister left paragraph after paragraph and
sketch after sketch in the De Organographia and the accompanying Theatrum Instrumentorum. This avenue follows the quantitative and scientific method of Ellis but on a larger scale
and consistently at par values.

    In the Theatrum Instrumentorum Praetorius presents
two plates on which are drafted, in generous scale, twenty-
one labial organ pipes at various pitches, mostly grave and
moderate; each plate provides its own scale rule of reference.[27] In addition there appears also (in the De Organographia) a graphic scale table for the Pfeifflin zur

Chormasz;[28] this gives, in the traditional and still conventional technical manner, the length and width (i.e., circumference) dimensions for thirteen consecutive chromatic pipes
for the fifth octave segment of an 8' stop, which exhibit,
therefore, an absolute pitch ranging from 1/2' to 1/4'.

The present author proposes that by a careful realization of all of the pipes found on the plates and all of
the pipes suggested in the Pfeifflin zur Chormasz an acceptable Chorton can be developed. By fulfilling the entire
project, a large array of crosschecks will help to minimize
errors that may inadvertantly have crept into the presentation or realization through some neglect of Praetorius, his
draftsman, his printer, or the various people responsible
for the modern realization of Praetorius' Theater of Organ
Pipes, if we may so call them.[29]

The writer undertook this project with the sympathetic and skillful help of the Schlicker Organ Company of
Buffalo, New York, during the years 1957 to 1959. The purpose of the project was a single one; namely, to try to secure by careful scientific procedures and acceptable statistical methods, a fairly accurate and refined value for the
Chorton of Praetorius. Any other outcomes of the project
were, and had to be viewed as concomitant by-products. The
project involved the fabrication of thirty-four actual pipes
to the precise dimensions given by Praetorius in the sketches
and graph; in every instance the pipes were constructed to

dimensions at par value; every extension or reduction of these values was strictly avoided. The project itself fell into four phases of work:

1. The interpretation of the sketches and graph, resolution of the scale rules, and the preparation of all technical data required for fabrication in the shop; this phase was executed in its entirety by the present author

2. The construction of all of the pipes; this work was done by the professional craftsmen of the Schlicker Organ Company under the supervision of Herman Schlicker, president of the company

3. The voicing of the pipes and the recording of the frequencies; this phase was executed by Louis Rothenbueger, head voicer of the Schlicker firm, and Benjamin Woodward, licensed professional engineer of Remington Rand, Inc.

4. The equating of the raw scores and interpretation of the results; this phase was undertaken by the present author

All phases of the project were executed under the constant and direct observation and supervision of the writer, so that no detail of fabrication or interpretation could escape his personal attention. In addition, the project was pursued at a deliberate pace, and the work was frequently halted to permit careful checking.

Praetorius' Theater of Organ Pipes

Plate XXXVII of the "Theatrum Instrumentorum"

The first major source for quantitative information
with respect to the pipes is Plate XXXVII of the Theatrum
Instrumentorum. On this plate there appear, in scale, elevation drawings for fourteen labial pipes, as follows:

1. Principal 8. Fusz.	1. 8' Principal
2. Octava 4. Fusz.	2. 4' Octave
3. Quinta 3. Fusz.	3. 2 2/3' Quinte
4. Klein Octava 2. Fusz.	4. 2' Klein Octave
5. Nachthorn 4. Fusz offen	5. 4' Nachthorn; open
6. Quintadehna 16. Fusz	6. 16' Quintade
7. Quintadehna 8. Fusz.	7. 8' Quintade
8. Nachthorn 4. Fusz	8. 4' Nachthorn-Gedackt
9. Groszgedact lieblich 8. Fusz	9. 8' Grossgedackt lieblich
10. Gemszhorn: 8. Fusz.	10. 8' Gemshorn
11. Spillfloit: 4. Fusz.	11. 4' Spillfloete
12. Plockfloit: 2. Fusz.	12. 2' Blockfloete
13. Offen Querfloit 4. Fusz	13. 4' Querfloete; open
14. Gedacte Querfloit. 4. f.	14. 4' Querfloete-Gedackt

At the lower edge of Plate XXXVII of the Theatrum
Instrumentorum appears a scale rule calibrated in feet and
half-feet; a copy of the same is reproduced (not to scale)
on Plate XCVI, 1. Certain premises need to be established,
in order to extract actual dimensions from the scale drawings necessary for the fabrication of the pipes sketched on
the plate. The basic premises are as follows:

1. **The scale rule represents Brunswick feet.** On
the reverse side of the titlepage to the *Theatrum Instrumentorum* there appears a rule of six inches of
measure; the accompanying legend asserts: "This is
the proper length and measure for one-half shoe or
foot according to the rule which is one-fourth of a
Brunswick Ell; all subsequent sketches are related to
this by means of a little scale rule which consistently appears with the sketch."[30]   From this legend
it is clear that a Brunswick foot contains twelve
Brunswick inches, and that a Brunswick Ell contains
two Brunswick feet

2. **The scale rule represents a true scale measure in its first segment of three calibrated feet.**
The rule, as sketched, contains an error; the calibration between the third and fourth foot-designations
presents three instead of two half-feet. The present
author, therefore, considered the first three foot-
calibrations of the rule as the true representation of
the measure; the calibrations beyond the fourth foot-
designation are exactly the same as in the first
three. In effect, the interval between the third and
fourth foot-designation must be ignored, in order to
arrive at a usable scale. Accordingly, the total rule
represents nine-and-one-half rather than nine Brunswick feet. To test his interpretation the author had

the Offenfloete 4' from Plate XXXVIII constructed
first according to the scale rule found on that plate;
this rule does not show any inadvertant interpolations
as does the one on Plate XXXVII of the Theatrum Instrumentorum. The Octave 4' from Plate XXXVII was
constructed next according to its own scale rule as
interpreted by the present author. The two pipes are
practically identical in the shape of the corpus and
in the length of the pipe body; hence, the pitch of
the two pipes would be influenced by identical factors. It was felt that if the two pipes agreed in
pitch, the interpretation of the scale rule on Plate
XXXVII could be considered valid; if not, another interpretation would need to be sought. The resultant
frequencies of the two pipes effectively validated
the interpretation. The equated scores, corrected for
temperature and calculated to 8' C revealed that the
Offenfloete 4' (from Plate XXXVIII) responded at 65.0,
while the Octave 4' (from Plate XXXVII) responded at
66.2 double vibrations per second. The difference of
1.2 double vibrations per second is negligible. The
imperfect scale rule appearing on Plate XXXVII has
nettled many a writer on this subject by serving as an
effective block in most, if not all, previous efforts
to solve or realize the sketches on this plate

   3. The Brunswick foot is equivalent to 285.36

actual <u>millimeters</u>. For this equivalent measure the present author is indebted to Bessaraboff, who reconstructed several orchestral instruments from the <u>Theatrum Instrumentorum</u> and compared his models with original surviving examples of them available to him.[31] Appendix Q, 2 gives the metric equivalents for Brunswick measure as recorded by Bessaraboff and extended by the present author

4. <u>Praetorius' sketches are accurate enough to guarantee faithful reproductions</u>. Bessaraboff attests to their accuracy. He says, ". . . the artist who made Praetorius' woodcuts was an exceptionally skillful craftsman and some of his drawings are very accurate"[32]

5. <u>The facsimile edition of the</u> Theatrum Instrumentorum (<u>Barenreiter</u>, <u>1929</u>) <u>is a legitimate source for the measurements</u>. It is obvious that a facsimile derived by photographic processes and subject to the properties of its own paper will not reproduce dimensions in exact values; in this case, the problem is merely academic, since both the sketches and the accompanying scale rule appear on the same page and were subject to the same degree of augmentation or diminution

With the basic premises established and verified, the scale rule can be converted into actual dimensions. The first three foot-designations of the scale rule measure out, in sum, to 73.25 raw millimeters;[33] hence, the interval for one foot-designation equals 73.25 / 3 = 24.416 raw millimeters. A raw measurement of 24.416 millimeters from the sketches, therefore, equals one actual Brunswick foot. Since an actual Brunswick foot converts to 285.36 actual millimeters, the actual value for a raw measurement (M_r) from the sketch equals, therefore

$$\frac{M_r \times 285.36}{24.416}$$

From this formula a convenient conversion factor in the form of a multiplier can be extracted, thus:

$$\frac{285.36}{24.416} = 11.687$$

The actual values (in millimeters) of the raw measurements (also in millimeters), therefore, equal

$$M_r \times 11.687$$

Table 110, parts 1 and 2, gives the raw measurements of the pipe sketches from Plate XXXVII of the <u>Theatrum Instrumentorum</u> and converts them into actual equivalents in metric units.

A summary of the actual dimensions used in the shop to fabricate the model pipes from Plate XXXVII is given in Appendix U, 1, where the values have been appropriately rounded off for practical use by the workmen.

TABLE 110, PART 1

RAW AND ACTUAL DIMENSIONS FOR
ITEMS FROM PLATE XXXVII

Item	Length of Pipe Body[a]		Diameter of Pipe Body		Circum-ference	Foot Length[b]
(1) Plate XXXVII	(2) Raw[c] mm.	(3) Actual[d] cm.	(4) Raw[c] mm.	(5) Actual[d] mm.	(6) Actual[e] mm.	(7) Actual cm.
1. 8′ Principal	193.0	225.55	12.2	142.6	448.0	40.6
2. 4′ Octave	94.5	110.44	7.9	92.3	290.0	30.5
3. 2 2/3′ Quinte	64.4	75.3	6.0	70.1	220.3	30.5
4. 2′ Klein Octave	47.4	55.4	4.0	46.7	146.9	30.5
5. 4′ Nachthorn; open	85.0	99.34	12.5	146.1	459.0	30.5
6. 16′ Quintade	192.0	224.4	13.1	153.1	481.0	40.6
7. 8′ Quintade	91.0	106.4	9.0	105.2	330.5	30.5
8. 4′ Nachthorn-Gedackt	47.0	54.9	6.5	76.0	238.7	20.3
9. 8′ Grossgedackt	122.5	143.17	. . .	. . .	. . .	40.6
At Mouth	. . .	. . .	12.8	149.6	470.0	. . .
At Top	. . .	. . .	2.5	29.2	91.7	. . .

Continued on following page

[a]Includes the dimension from the languid to the top edge of the pipe or a unit section in the case of compound corpora.

[b]These lengths are approximate and have been only lightly adjusted to facilitate fabrication and eventual mounting.

[c]As measured directly from Plate XXXVII of the Theatrum Instrumentorum.

[d]Calculated as column (2) or (4) times 11.687, the conversion factor for translating raw measurements into actual measurements for items appearing on Plate XXXVII only.

[e]The circumferences as calculated from the actual diameters: column (5) times 3.1416.

TABLE 110, PART 1--Continued

Item	Length of Pipe Body		Diameter of Pipe Body		Circumference	Foot Length
(1) Plate XXXVII	(2) Raw mm.	(3) Actual cm.	(4) Raw mm.	(5) Actual mm.	(6) Actual mm.	(7) Actual cm.
10. 8' Gemshorn	178.5	208.6	. . .	. . .	. . .	40.6
At Mouth	. . .	. . .	16.4	191.7	602.2	. . .
At Top	. . .	. . .	5.3	61.9	194.5	. . .
11. 4' Spillfloete	41.5	48.5	8.0	93.5	293.7	30.5
Cone Length	51.0	59.6	. . .	. . .	. . .	. . .
Cone Base	. . .	. . .	8.0	93.5	293.7	. . .
Cone Apex	. . .	. . .	2.5	29.2	91.8	. . .
12. 2' Blockfloete	42.0	49.1	. . .	. . .	. . .	20.3
At Mouth	. . .	. . .	7.5	87.7	275.4	. . .
At Top	. . .	. . .	3.3	38.6	121.2	. . .
13. 4' Querfloete; open	203.0	237.2	8.5	99.3	312.0	40.6
14. 4' Querfloete-Gedackt	142.0	165.1	7.5	87.7	275.5	30.5

Plate XXXVIII of the "Theatrum Instrumentorum"

The second major source for quantitative information on organ pipes is Plate XXXVIII of the Theatrum Instrumentorum. On this plate there appear, in scale, elevation drawings for seven labial pipes, as follows:

1. Dolcan. 4. Fusz.
2. Coppelfloit. 4. Fusz.
3. Flachfloit. 4. Fusz.
4. Klein Barduen. 8. Fusz.
5. Offenfloit. 4. Fusz.

1. 4' [Labial] Dulzian
2. 4' Koppelfloete
3. 4' Flachfloete
4. 8' Klein Barduen
5. 4' Offenfloete

TABLE 110, PART 2

RAW AND ACTUAL DIMENSIONS FOR
ITEMS FROM PLATE XXXVII

Item (1) Plate XXXVII	Width of Mouth		Height of Mouth		Description
	(2) Raw mm.[a]	(3) Actual mm.[b]	(4) Raw mm.[a]	(5) Actual mm.[b]	(6)
1. 8' Principal[c]	7.4	90.2	2.25	26.3	Open Cylindrical
2. 4' Octave	5.0	58.4	1.3	15.2	Open Cylindrical
3. 2 2/3' Quinte	3.0	35.0	1.2	14.0	Open Cylindrical
4. 2' Klein Octave	2.5	29.2	1.0	11.7	Open Cylindrical
5. 4' Nachthorn; open	7.0	81.8	1.9	22.2	Open Cylindrical
6. 16' Quintade[d]	9.0	105.2	2.5	29.2	Covered Cylind.
7. 8' Quintade[e]	6.0	70.1	2.0	23.4	Covered Cylind.
8. 4' Nachthorn- Gedackt[f]	4.5	52.6	1.5	17.5	Covered Cylind.
9. 8' Grossgedackt	8.0	93.5	2.3	26.9	Covered Conical

Continued on following page

[a]As measured directly from Plate XXXVII of the _The-atrum Instrumentorum_.

[b]Calculated as column (2) or (4) times 11.687, the conversion factor for translating raw measurements into actual measurements for items appearing on Plate XXXVII only.

[c]Inasmuch as the mouth assembly of the 8' Principal appears in semi-perspective on Plate XXXVII, the actual width of its mouth cannot very well be developed from its raw measurement on the drawing; the present author derived it from the calculated circumference of the 8' Principal by applying the same ratio of circumference to width as exhibited by the 4' Octave.

[d]The ears (in actual values) are 86.5 x 36.2 mm.

[e]The ears (in actual values) are 58.4 x 35.0 mm.

[f]The ears (in actual values) are 47.0 x 23.4 mm.

TABLE 110, PART 2--<u>Continued</u>

Item	Width of Mouth		Height of Mouth		
(1) Plate XXXVII	(2) Raw mm.	(3) Actual mm.	(4) Raw mm.	(5) Actual mm.	(6) Description
10. 8' Gemshorn	12.0	140.3	3.0	35.0	Open Conical
11. 4' Spillfloete	5.0	58.4	1.5	17.5	Compound; Open
12. 2' Blockfloete	4.0	46.7	1.5	17.5	Open Conical
13. 4' Querfloete; open	4.6	53.8	2.0	23.4	Open Cylindrical; Overblown
14. 4' Querfloete-Gedackt	4.2	49.1	2.5	29.2	Covered Cylind. Overblown

6. Gedact. 8. Fusz.
7. Rohrfloit: oder Holfloit. 8. f.

6. 8' Gedackt
7. 8' Rohrfloete or Hohlfloete

On the center of the plate and positioned vertically appears a scale rule calibrated in feet and half-feet. A replica of the same (not to scale) is shown on Plate XCVI, 2.

The premises established for Plate XXXVII are equally valid for Plate XXXVIII of the <u>Theatrum Instrumentorum</u>; inasmuch as the scale rule does not exhibit any inadvertant interpolations, no interpretation or verification of its true length is needed. The rule represents six Brunswick feet. The scale rule must, however, be independently converted into actual dimensions. The first three foot-designations of the scale rule measure out, in sum, to 74.0 raw millimeters; hence, the interval for one foot-designation equals

74.0 / 3 = 24.67 raw millimeters. A raw measurement of 24.67 millimeters from the sketches, therefore, equals one Brunswick foot. Since an actual Brunswick foot converts to 285.36 actual millimeters, the actual value for a raw measurement (M_r) from the sketch equals, therefore

$$\frac{M_r \times 285.36}{24.67}$$

From this formula a convenient conversion factor in the form of a multiplier can be extracted, thus:

$$\frac{285.36}{24.67} = 11.567$$

The actual values (in millimeters) of the raw measurements (also in millimeters), therefore, equal

$$M_r \times 11.567$$

Table 111, parts 1 and 2, gives the raw measurements of the pipe sketches from Plate XXXVIII of the <u>Theatrum Instrumentorum</u> and converts them into actual equivalents in metric units.

A summary of the actual dimensions used in the shop to fabricate the model pipes from Plate XXXVIII is given in Appendix U, 2, where the values have been appropriately rounded off for practical use by the workmen.

Praetorius' "<u>Pfeifflin</u> <u>zur</u> <u>Chormasz</u>"

The third major, and probably most accurate source for quantitative information with respect to Praetorius'

TABLE 111, PART 1

RAW AND ACTUAL DIMENSIONS FOR
ITEMS FROM PLATE XXXVIII

Item	Length of Pipe Body[a]		Diameter of Pipe Body		Circum-ference	Foot Length[b]
(1) Plate XXXVIII	(2) Raw[c] mm.	(3) Actual[d] cm.	(4) Raw[c] mm.	(5) Actual[d] mm.	(6) Actual[e] mm.	(7) Actual cm.
1. 4' [Labial] Dulzian	93.0	107.6	. . .	. . .	. . .	30.5
At Mouth	. . .	. . .	8.5	98.3	308.8	. . .
At Top	. . .	. . .	16.0	185.0	581.2	. . .
2. 4' Koppelfloete	59.0	68.25	10.0	115.7	363.5	30.5
Cone Length	31.0	35.9	. . .	. . .	. . .	. . .
Cone Base	. . .	. . .	10.0	115.7	363.5	. . .
Cone Apex	. . .	. . .	4.5	52.0	163.4	. . .
3. 4' Flachfloete	94.5	109.3	. . .	. . .	. . .	30.5
At Mouth	. . .	. . .	9.0	104.1	327.0	. . .
At Top	. . .	. . .	5.0	57.8	181.6	. . .
4. 8' Klein Barduen	101.0	116.8	10.7	123.8	388.8	30.5
5. 4' Offenfloete	96.0	111.0	9.5	109.9	345.3	30.5
6. 8' Gedackt	98.0	113.36	11.5	133.0	417.8	30.5
7. 8' Rohrfloete or Hohlfloete	110.5	127.8	13.5	156.2	490.7	40.6
Chimney	20.0	23.1	3.5	40.5	127.2	. . .

[a]Includes the dimension from the languid to the top edge of the pipe or a unit section in compound corpora.

[b]These lengths are approximate and have been only slightly adjusted to facilitate fabrication and mounting.

[c]As measured directly from Plate XXXVIII of the Theatrum Instrumentorum.

[d]Calculated as column (2) or (4) times 11.567, the conversion factor for translating raw measurements into actual measurements for items appearing on Plate XXXVIII only.

[e]The circumferences as calculated from the actual diameters: column (5) times 3.1416.

TABLE 111, PART 2

RAW AND ACTUAL DIMENSIONS FOR
ITEMS FROM PLATE XXXVIII

Item	Width of Mouth		Height of Mouth		
(1)	(2)	(3)	(4)	(5)	(6)
Plate XXXVIII	Raw mm.[a]	Actual mm.[b]	Raw mm.[a]	Actual mm.[b]	Description
1. 4' [Labial] Dulzian	4.5	52.1	2.0	23.1	Invert Conical; open
2. 4' Koppelfloete	5.0	57.8	1.7	19.7	Compound
3. 4' Flachfloete	5.2	60.2	2.0	23.1	Open Conical
4. 8' Klein Barduen[c]	7.0	81.0	2.2	25.4	Covered Cylind.
5. 4' Offenfloete	6.0	69.4	2.2	25.4	Open Cylindrical
6. 8' Gedackt[d]	6.7	77.5	2.5	28.9	Covered Cylind.
7. 8' Rohrfloete or Hohlfloete[e]	8.5	98.3	2.5	28.9	Partly Covered

[a]As measured directly from Plate XXXVIII of the Theatrum Instrumentorum.

[b]Calculated as column (2) or (4) times 11.567, the conversion factor for translating raw measurements into actual measurements for items appearing on Plate XXXVIII only.

[c]The ears (in actual values) are 76.3 x 67.1 mm.

[d]The ears (in actual values) are 59.0 x 33.5 mm.

[e]The ears (in actual values) are 70.6 x 33.5 mm.

organ pipes is the famous scale graph entitled Pfeifflin zur Chormasz.[34] A reproduction of the same (not to exact scale) appears on Plate XCV, 1 in the accompanying Atlas to the present study. Although discussed in part above, a more precise investigation and analysis of the same is necessary to

show the present author's approach and interpretation, since
the validity of his conclusions rests in considerable part
upon premises and operational procedures derived from this
graph. The graph represents a conventional method used by
organ builders for centuries, and still in use in similar
form today, to derive accurate shop dimensions for cutting
metal plates from stock for purposes of fabricating pipes.
The lengths of the plates represent the lengths, while the
widths represent the circumferences of cylinders after the
plates have subsequently been rolled to assume the typical
shape of the corpus of the pipes.[35]

The graph is, in reality, a coordinate system an-
chored upon an X-axis (horizontal line) and a Y-axis (vertical line) which intersect at o, the point of origin. The
lengths of the metal plates are plotted on the X-axis, while
the widths of the plates (i.e., the circumferences of the
eventual cylinders) are plotted on, or parallel to, the
Y-axis. The horizontal line (and dimension) oq gives the
length (either true or in scale, as the case may emerge) for
the pipe corpus which is intended to sound c'''; the line or
gives the length similarly for the note c'''', an octave
higher in pitch.[36] All intermediate values for the chromatic
notes between the two extremes can be established by measuring from o to the point where the appropriate note intersects
line oq. The vertical line (and dimension) qk gives the
width of the plate (i.e., the circumference of the eventual

cylinder, either true or in scale as may be subsequently determined) for the pipe corpus which is intended to sound the note c'''; the line rm gives the width similarly for the note c'''', an octave higher in pitch. All intermediate values for the chromatic notes between the two extremes can be established by measuring vertically from line oq to the point where the appropriate line intersects line km.

On the plate appear three additional items which must be considered in time, to establish their relevance to the graphic presentation. These are the extension of line qk to point p (and constituting thereby line qp), the partial circle bisected by line qp and the rectangular figure above the same.

Praetorius' introductory remarks preceding the graph in the De Organographia are helpful in establishing the absolute octave segment for which the graph gives dimensions. He says:

NB.

DJeweil in diesem Tomo Secundo, zum offtern des rechten Chor-Thons erwehnet: vnd ich befunden / das an vielen oertern / auch wol in sehr grossen vnd vornehmen Staedten / vnd doselbst befindlichen herrlichen Orgelwercken / die rechte Chormasz / wornach sich die Menschen Stimmen / so wol als die Instrumenta richten muessen / nicht= sondern der Tonus derselben entwe-

N[ota] B[ene]

Since in this Tomus Secundus the right Chorton has often been mentioned, I have found that in many places, even in large and important cities and among the splendid organs found there, the right Chormasz according to which the human voices and the instruments must be regulated, does not [prevail]; the pitch is either too high or too low. This condition constitutes one of the chief defects of the

der zu hoch oder zu niedrig:
Vnd solches einer von den
fuernembsten Defecten der
Orgeln ist. So hab ich vff
allerley Mittel vnd Wege
gedacht / wie vnd welcher
gestalt solchem abzuhelf-
fen / vnd einem jeden / so
wol Orgelmachern als Organisten der rechte Tonus vnd
Chormasz bekandt wuerde:
Wornach ein Orgelmacher sich
richten / die Newe Orgeln
nach demselben intoniren,
die Alten aber Renoviren
vnnd Corrigiren koente.
Derowegen hiervnter einen
richtigen Abrisz der rechten Chormasz setzen wollen;
von dem $\overset{\approx}{c}$, so nach Orgelmacher Mensur ein halben
Fusz Thon (wenn das grosse
C von 8. Fussen ist) bringet.

organs. For this reason I
have pondered many ways and
means, how and in what manner
such [a condition] could be
alleviated, so that among organbuilders and organists the
correct pitch and Chormasz
could become known, and according to which an organbuilder could regulate himself,
tune new organs, and renovate
and correct old ones. For
this reason I have wanted to
subjoin an accurate sketch of
the correct reference measure
from c''', which, according
to the organbuilders' measure
produces a half-foot tone
(when Great C is reckoned as
of 8' pitch).

C	8 Fuesz /		C:	8 foot
c	4 Fuesz /		c:	4 foot
$\overline{c}$	2 Fuesz /		c':	2 foot
$\overset{\approx}{c}$	1 Fuesz /		c'':	1 foot
$\overset{\approx}{\underset{=}{c}}$	1/2 Fuesz /		c''':	1/2 foot

Nach welcher Mensur et-
liche Pfeifflin zur rech-
ten Chormasz / durch eine
gantze Octav, gar just vnd
rein koennen gearbeitet werden: Deren sich / neben den
Orgelmachern / auch die Organisten vnd Cantores zum
anstimmen zugebrauchen.[37]

According to this measure
several pipes for the right
Chormasz, comprising an entire octave, can be exactly
and neatly fabricated. These
can also be used by organists
and cantors as well as by organbuilders to give out the
pitch. [Translation by the
present author]

From these specifications it is clear that the graph
gives the dimensions for the fifth octave segment of an 8'
stop. Accordingly the note-designations on the graph

represent the following absolute pitch designations:

c	=	c'''	g	=	g'''
cs	=	c#'''	gs	=	g#'''
d	=	d'''	a	=	a'''
ds	=	d#'''	b	=	a#'''
e	=	e'''	h	=	b'''
f	=	f'''	c̄	=	c''''
fs	=	f#'''			

From Plate XCV, 2 it can be observed that the segment marked
x is the true pitch for these pipes as proposed by Praetorius. In an absolute sense, the octave reaches from 1/2' to
1/4' pitch.

The introductory remarks also establish the graph as
being in scale and not only a pictorial representation; he
says, in part, "For this reason I have wanted to subjoin an
accurate [italics, mine] sketch of the correct reference
measure from c''' which, according to the organbuilders'
measure produces a half-foot tone."[38] To determine the exact
values of the scale upon which the graph is predicated, recourse must be had to the accompanying legends on the graph.
The first legend deals with the interpretation of the X-axis
which Praetorius identifies by the letter b. See Plate XCV,
1. He says:

b. Die Lenge der Pfeiffen
zum rochten Chormasz.

b [represents] the length
of the pipes for the correct
reference measure. [Transla-
tion by the present author]

Accordingly, the X-axis must be interpreted as having been

reproduced in full scale, thus:

$$\frac{\text{Raw dimension}}{\text{Actual dimension}} = \frac{1}{1}$$

Hence, 1 millimeter on the X-axis of the graph equals 1 millimeter on the model. The second legend deals with the widths of the plates (i.e., the circumferences of the eventual cylinders); it interprets, in effect, the scale of the Y-axis, which Praetorius identifies with the letter a. See Plate XCV, 1. He says:

a: ist die Weite / zwey-   a represents the width,
mahl genommen.   taken twice.

Accordingly, the Y-axis is not in full scale; it is reproduced in either half-scale or double scale, since the elliptical expression of the legend does not make this immediately clear. The legend permits two interpretations; it could mean either one of the following:

1. The letter a represents the width (i.e., the circumference), which should be taken twice from the graph (hence, in half-scale on the graph)

2. The letter a represents the width (i.e., the circumference) which is already taken twice on the graph (hence, in double scale on the graph)

In case 1 the graphic value of the width would need to be doubled in order to realize the actual dimension, whereas in case 2 it would need to be halved. For the moment, the ambiguity must remain unresolved until the dimensions of the axes have been quantitatively established. However, scale graphs of this period, as pointed out by Mahrenholz,[39] do not give double dimensions, but often present the length or the width or both in half, quarter, or eighth values; this observation supports the interpretation suggested in case 1 above, and becomes the point of departure in the further pursuit of delineating the proper interpretation of the Y-axis.

The actual disposition of the graph entitled Pfeifflin zur Chormasz together with the quantitative dimensions for all of its parts as taken from an original copy (not a facsimile) of the De Organographia reposing in the treasure room of the Sibley Musical Library, Eastman School of Music, Rochester, New York, is reproduced on Plate XCVI, 3. The dimensions given there, are raw measurements directly from the page and are not usable for realization of the models, since the ravages of time, temperature, humidity, and aridity have interfered with their original values. The measurements are subject to further correction by means of an appropriate coefficient for shrinkage or expansion, as the case may emerge, in order to arrive at the true measurements intended by Praetorius and so recorded by him.

In the same original copy used for the measurements of the graph above, there appears, on the reverse side of the titlepage of the accompanying atlas known as the Theatrum

Instrumentorum, a rule of six Brunswick inches in full scale. The raw measure of the six-inch rule from the aforementioned copy is 140.4 millimeters; since the actual value of six Brunswick inches equals 142.68 millimeters,[40] it is clear that the paper of the original copy under discussion has shrunk a certain amount, so that the ratio of the actual measure to the raw measure is

$$\frac{142.68}{140.4} = 1.0162$$

This figure becomes the coefficient of shrinkage and must be used as a multiplier to correct the raw measurements of the scale graph, in order to arrive at the actual measure of the several dimensions exhibited in the graph. Table 112 gives the raw and actual measurements of all of the items plotted on the X and Y-axes of the graph.

The actual or corrected measurements exhibited in Table 112 are reproduced in scale on Plate XCVII, where the corrected measurements for accompanying items on the graph may also be found.

With actual and corrected quantitative values in hand, it is possible to consider further the interpretation of the graph legend concerning the widths of the plates and to resolve the apparent ambiguity caused by its elliptical construction. It will be recalled that the legend discussed above, permits of two interpretations:

1. That the corrected measurements on the Y-axis

TABLE 112

RAW AND ACTUAL MEASUREMENTS FOR THE
PFEIFFLIN ZUR CHORMASZ

Note Designation on Graph	Equivalent Note of 8' Stop	Length of Plate[a]		Width of Plate[b]	
(1)	(2)	(3) Raw mm.[c]	(4) Actual mm.[d]	(5) Raw mm.[c]	(6) Actual mm.[e]
c	c'''	134.2	136.4	25.8	26.2
cs	c#'''	127.8	129.9	24.3	24.7
d	d'''	120.0	121.9	22.8	23.2
ds	d#'''	113.6	115.4	21.9	22.3
e	e'''	105.9	107.6	20.3	20.6
f	f'''	100.0	101.6	19.3	19.6
fs	f#'''	94.6	96.1	18.5	18.8
g	g'''	89.1	90.5	17.8	18.1
gs	g#'''	84.9	86.3	17.2	17.5
a	a'''	80.2	81.5	16.5	16.8
b	a#'''	75.8	77.0	15.6	15.9
h	b'''	71.0	72.2	14.8	15.0
c	c''''	66.3	67.3	13.7	13.9

[a]Dimensions in columns (3) and (4) are derived from the X-axis of the graph.

[b]Dimensions in columns (5) and (6) are derived from the Y-axis of the graph and represent either half or double values (as the case may emerge) for the circumferences.

[c]Measurements taken directly from an original copy of the De Organographia.

[d]Column (4) equals column (3) times 1.0162, which is the coefficient to correct the raw measurements.

[e]Column (6) equals column (5) times 1.0162; these values, although supposedly actual, are not yet usable for shop construction, since they do not represent full values for the circumferences.

of the graph represent one-half of the true dimensions
for the widths of the plates

2. That the same represent twice the true dimensions

The first clue, mentioned earlier, is the time-honored
practice (already prevalent in the Early Baroque) of representing actual values for lengths, widths, or both in fractional dimensions on a graph rather than in multiple dimensions of the same. This practice would support the interpretation suggested in case 1 above.

The second clue is presented by the extension of the
vertical parallel to the Y-axis, qk (26.2 mm.) to exactly
twice its length (52.4 mm.) to form line qp. See Plate
XCVII. The condition may be coincidental, but on the other
hand, Praetorius may have felt that a subtle reminder such
as this might help to prevent a misinterpretation of the
items plotted parallel to the Y-axis. Again the interpretation in case 1 seems to be reinforced.

The third clue is the half-circle inscribed around
point k. This may have been intended to be merely a pictorial way of showing that the values of the graph could be
executed in metallic cylinders, but the fact that the circumference of the circle (54.35 mm.) as calculated from its own
diameter (17.3 mm.) is remarkably close to a circumference
derived as twice the value of line qk (52.4 mm.) suggests
that the figure is drawn almost exactly in full scale, and

that the interpretation proposed in case 1 is more reasonable than the one suggested in case 2.

The fourth clue is the rectangular figure attached to line kp. A difficulty arises here; whereas modern theorists would compare the rectangle to the circle by means of the areas which each one encloses (whereby, in this instance, no direct relationship can be detected), it is quite likely that Praetorius relates the perimeter of the rectangle to the circumference of the circle. By such a comparison the perimeter of the rectangle (54.0 mm.) approaches the circumference of the circle (54.35 mm.) very closely. Accordingly the interpretation proposed in case 1 above is further (although not definitely) reinforced.

In a majority of instances, however, the four clues presented compel the present author to submit that the dimensions of the graph lying parallel to the Y-axis are one-half values and must be doubled in order to secure true actual dimensions for the widths of the plates (i.e., the circumferences of the eventual cylinders). Therefore, the ratio of raw dimensions on the Y-axis relate to actual dimensions as 1/2. Hence, 1/2 millimeter on the graph (Y-axis only) equals 1 millimeter on the model.

On the basis of this proposition the actual widths of the plates (i.e., the circumferences of the eventual cylinders) assume usable shop values as recorded in Table 113, column (4).

TABLE 113

CORRECTED GRAPHIC AND ACTUAL DIMENSIONS
FOR THE WIDTHS OF THE PLATES

(1) Note Designation on Graph	(2) Equivalent Note of 8' Stop	(3) Corrected Graphic Width in mm.[a]	(4) Actual Circumference of Cylindrical Model in mm.[b]	(5) Actual Diameter of Cylindrical Model in mm.[c]
c	c'''	26.2	52.4	16.68
cs	c#'''	24.7	49.4	15.72
d	d'''	23.2	46.4	14.77
ds	d#'''	22.3	44.6	14.20
e	e'''	20.6	41.2	13.11
f	f'''	19.6	39.2	12.50
fs	f#'''	18.8	37.6	11.97
g	g'''	18.1	36.2	11.52
gs	g#'''	17.5	35.0	11.14
a	a'''	16.8	33.6	10.70
b	a#'''	15.9	31.8	10.12
h	b'''	15.0	30.0	9.55
c	c''''	13.9	27.8	8.84

[a] Carried forward from Table 112, column (6).

[b] Column (3) times 2 equals column (4); it represents the true and usable measure.

[c] Column (4) divided by 3.1416 equals column (5).

From the corrected dimensions for the lengths of the plates (from Table 112, column (4)) and the corrected and expanded dimensions for the widths of the same (from Table 113, column (4)) the whole series of thirteen pipes was carefully executed in metal. The width of the mouth, not given in the graph, was derived from the usual mouth widths which Praetorius shows for the Principal pipes on Plate XXXVII, where the ratio of the mouth width to the circumference approaches 1/5. It should be observed that in normal shop practice today, the derivation of length and circumference from a scale graph such as the one here used is considered the most accurate way of securing a faithful realization.

A summary of the actual dimensions used in the shop to fabricate the model pipes from the graph entitled <u>Pfeifflin</u> <u>zur</u> <u>Chormasz</u> is given in Appendix U, 3, where the values have been appropriately rounded off for practical use by the workmen.

Realization of the "Theater of Organ Pipes"

Having arrived at usable shop measurements for all of the labial pipes of Plates XXXVII and XXXVIII of the <u>Theatrum</u> <u>Instrumentorum</u> and for the <u>Pfeifflin</u> <u>zur</u> <u>Chormasz</u> of the <u>De</u> <u>Organographia</u>, the present author undertook to have the pipes constructed in the pipe shop of the Schlicker Organ Company of Buffalo, New York. The actual construction was done by skilled pipe makers, and the entire project was personally supervised by the present author. By this method, any technical questions with respect to measurements and their interpretation could be solved immediately. The pipes derived from the two plates of the _Theatrum Instrumentorum_ were built in alternate order, so that a progressive check could be kept on the validity of the scale rule interpretation adopted for Plate XXXVII. The last group of pipes to be made were the thirteen items from the scale graph. Reproductions of the model pipes as constructed for this project are shown on Plates XCVIII, XCIX, C, and CV.

After the pipes were completed they had to be voiced by establishing a wind pressure, trimming the upper lips, adjusting the positions of the languids, etc. For a usable and defensible wind, the pressure of the surviving Compenius-Praetorius organ at Frederiksborg in Denmark was adopted as representing an actual pressure from a musical monument of the time.[41] The pressure used was 55 millimeters of water measured as the difference of the surfaces in an open double column manometer. All of the pipes, thirty-four in number, were voiced at this pressure. The upper lips were trimmed as little as possible; as soon as a natural, unforced speech had developed, the pipe was considered voiced and was laid aside to await frequency readings. In no case did the trimming of the upper lips exceed the limits of the cutup as determined from the drawings. At this point the pipes were ready for the final phase of the project; namely, to secure from them a pitch in terms of frequency of vibration.

Method of Determining Frequencies

In order to secure a frequency reading from each of

the model pipes directly, without having to calculate it as
a deviation from a given pipe of known frequency, it was decided to call in a professional engineer to study the problem and develop a solution that would give accurate values
directly and absolutely. Mr. Benjamin W. Woodward, P. E.,
Registered No. 22385PE, undertook to devise an electronic
recording apparatus by means of which direct readings could
be taken. The recording apparatus is pictured on Plates CI
and CII and comprises the following members (right to left):

1. An electronic timer

2. An audio oscillator

3. A pulse shaper

4. A junction box

5. A binary counter

By means of this apparatus, the audio oscillator was
tuned to one of the partials of the speaking pipe; when precisely in tune, the timer was engaged to send the tuned oscillations through the pulse shaper and the binary counter
for exactly one second of time. On the recorder board of
the binary counter the number of oscillations representing
the frequency of the partial to which the audio oscillator
had been tuned could be read off directly up to one decimal
place. All of the environmental conditions that might have
affected the pitch of the pipe or the efficiency of the electronic recording apparatus were carefully controlled, as follows:

1. All of the frequencies were registered in one unbroken period of time

2. The wind pressure was frequently checked and held constant

3. The temperature of the room housing both the pipe and the recording apparatus was frequently recorded, so that adjustments for temperature could be made in the final calculations

4. The timer was frequently calibrated against a standard tuning fork, in order to assure a consistent efficiency in the operation of the apparatus

In order further to insure accurate tuning of the oscillator to the pipe, skilled and experienced organ tuners did the actual registering. Among these were Mr. Louis Rothenbueger, head voicer of the Schlicker firm, and Mr. James Rothenbueger, superintendent of the shop. All registrations were checked by the engineer and by the present author. In every instance the audio oscillator was tuned to that partial of the pipe which was easiest to hear and which maintained a firm consistency. The frequency of the partial was registered ten times and a mean reading recorded. Table 114, parts 1, 2, and 3 gives the raw frequencies of the various pipes, showing also the conditions under which each pipe was registered, and an ultimate frequency value for the fundamental partial useful as a basis for equating the raw scores in the subsequent discussion.

TABLE 114, PART 1

MEAN RAW FREQUENCIES OF ITEMS FROM PLATE XXXVII
OF THE THEATRUM INSTRUMENTORUM

(1) Reference [a]	(2) Name of Pipe	(3) Pressure in mm. of Water [b]	(4) Actual Temperature in °F---°C [c]	(5) Partial tuned [d]	(6) Mean Raw Frequency of Ten Registrations in Double Vibrations/Sec.	(7) Equivalent Frequency of Fundamental in Double Vibrations/Sec. [e]
37-1	8' Principal	55	86--30	4	274.8	68.7
37-2	4' Octave	55	86--30	2	269.5	134.7
37-3	2 2/3' Quinte	55	86--30	1	192.1	192.1
37-4	2' Klein Octave	55	86--30	1	272.8	272.8
37-5	4' Nachthorn; open	55	86--30	2	266.5	133.2

Continued on following page

[a] Reference to M. Praetorius, Theatrum Instrumentorum seu Sciagraphia . . . (Wolfenbuettel, 1620), Plate XXXVII. The first number identifies the plate, the second, the specific item on the plate.

[b] Wind pressure applied to the pipe while its frequency was being registered; measured as the difference in water levels in an open double column manometer.

[c] The temperature of the room in which the frequencies were registered.

[d] The partial of the acoustic spectrum to which audio oscillator was tuned.

[e] Column (6) divided by column (5) equals column (7).

TABLE 114, PART 1--Continued

(1) Reference	(2) Name of Pipe	(3) Pressure in mm. of Water	(4) Actual Temperature in °F--°C	(5) Partial tuned	(6) Mean Raw Frequency of Ten Registrations in Double Vibrations/Sec.	(7) Equivalent Frequency of Fundamental in Double Vibrations/Sec.
37-6	16' Quintade	55	86--30	4	140.4	35.1
37-7	8' Quintade	55	86--30	3	205.9	68.6
37-8	4' Nachthorn-Gedackt	55	86--30	2	253.6	126.8
37-9	8' Grossgedackt	55	86--30	1	83.9	85.1
	Same	55	86--30	2	171.5 }	
	Same	55	86--30	2	171.3 }	
37-10	8' Gemshorn	55	84--28.89	1	71.9	71.9
37-11	4' Spillfloete	55	84--28.89	1	116.2	116.2
37-12	2' Blockfloete	55	84--28.89	1/2	125.4 }	
	Same	55	84--28.89	1	251.7 }	251.2
	Same	55	84--28.89	1 1/2	376.6 }	
37-13	4' Querfloete; open	55	84--28.89	2	271.9 }	136.0
	Same	55	84--28.89	1	136.1 }	
37-14	4' Querfloete-Gedackt	55	84--28.89	2	238.4 }	119.1
	Same	55	84--28.89	1 1/2	178.7 }	

TABLE 114, PART 2

MEAN RAW FREQUENCIES OF ITEMS FROM PLATE XXXVIII
OF THE THEATRUM INSTRUMENTORUM

(1) Reference[a]	(2) Name of Pipe	(3) Pressure in mm. of Water[b]	(4) Actual Temperature in °F--°C[c]	(5) Partial tuned[d]	(6) Mean Raw Frequency of Ten Registrations in Double Vibrations/Sec.	(7) Equivalent Frequency of Fundamental in Double Vibrations/Sec.[e]
38-1	4' [Labial] Dulzian	55	84--28.89	1	136.1	136.1
38-2	4' Koppelfloete	55	84--28.89	2	227.2	
	Same	55	84--28.89	2	226.6 }	113.6
	Same	55	84--28.89	1	113.9 }	
38-3	4' Flachfloete	55	84--28.89	1	135.0	135.0

Continued on following page

[a]Reference to M. Praetorius, Theatrum Instrumentorum seu Sciagraphia ...
(Wolfenbuettel, 1620), Plate XXXVIII. The first number identifies the plate, the
second, the specific item on the plate.

[b]Wind pressure applied to the pipe while its frequency was being registered;
measured as the difference in water levels in an open double column manometer.

[c]The temperature of the room in which the frequencies were registered.

[d]The partial of the acoustic spectrum to which audio oscillator was tuned.

[e]Column (6) divided by column (5) equals column (7).

TABLE 114, PART 2--Continued

(1) Reference	(2) Name of Pipe	(3) Pressure in mm. of Water	(4) Actual Temperature in °F---°C	(5) Partial tuned	(6) Mean Raw Frequency of Ten Registrations in Double Vibrations/Sec.	(7) Equivalent Frequency of Fundamental in Double Vibrations/Sec.
38-4	8' Klein Barduen	55	84--28.89	4	250.1 }	62.5
	Same	55	84--28.89	2	125.1 }	
38-5	4' Offenfloete	55	84--28.89	1	132.5 }	
	Same	55	84--28.89	1	131.6 }	132.0
	Same	55	84--28.89	2	263.8 }	
38-6	8' Gedackt	55	84--28.89	2	124.6 }	62.1
	Same	55	84--28.89	3	185.6 }	
38-7	8' Rohrfloete or Hohlfloete	55	84--28.89	2	126.3 }	63.2
	Same	55	84--28.89	4	253.3 }	

TABLE 114, PART 3

MEAN RAW FREQUENCIES OF ITEMS FROM
THE PFEIFFLIN ZUR CHORMASZ

(1) Item	(2) Note on Graph	(3) Equivalent Note of 8' Stop	(4) Pressure in mm. of Water[a]	(5) Actual Temperature in °F-°C[b]	(6) Partial tuned[c]	(7) Mean Raw Frequency of 10 Registrations in Double Vibrations per Sec.	(8) Equivalent Frequency of Fundamental in Double Vibrations per Sec.[d]
	c	c'''	55	86–30	1	1056.3	1056.3
	cs	c#'''	55	86–30	1	1104.3	1104.3
	d	d'''	55	86–30	1	1176.9	1176.9
	ds	d#'''	55	86–30	1	1253.2	1253.2
	e	e'''	55	86–30	1	1334.0	1334.0
	f	f'''	55	86–30	1	1415.5	1415.5
	fs	f#'''	55	86–30	1	1496.7	1496.7
	g	g'''	55	86–30	1	1567.9	1567.9
	gs	g#'''	55	86–30	1	1646.5	1646.5
	a	a'''	55	86–30	1	1753.5	1753.5
	b	a#'''	55	86–30	1	1867.3	1867.3
	h	b'''	55	86–30	1	1993.7	1993.7
	c	c''''	55	86–30	1	2116.7	2116.7

(Row labels at left: Pfeifflin zur Chormasz)

[a] Wind pressure applied to the pipe while its frequency was being registered; measured as the difference in water levels in an open double column manometer.

[b] The temperature of the room in which the frequencies were registered.

[c] The partial of the acoustic spectrum to which audio oscillator was tuned.

[d] Column (7) divided by column (6) equals column (8).

Equation of the Raw Scores

After the average raw frequency of the fundamental partial of each pipe had been determined, an adjustment had to be made in the values to bring the scores to a comparative level of 20° Centigrade (or, the equivalent, 68° Fahrenheit). This temperature may be considered the average tuning temperature in the United States at the present time. In order to make such an accurate adjustment, a coefficient must be developed which will reflect the divergent velocities of sound in air exhibited between the temperatures used for registering the frequencies (namely, 28.89° Centigrade and 30° Centigrade) and the adopted reference temperature at which it is desired to compare them (namely, 20° Centigrade).[42] The coefficient useful for readings taken at 28.89° Centigrade is .985 and, when applied as a multiplier to such values, will adjust them to equivalent values at 20° Centigrade. The coefficient for 30° Centigrade is .983 and, when similarly applied to the appropriate raw values, will adjust them to the adopted reference temperature of 20° Centigrade. The average raw frequency of the fundamental (i.e., the first partial) of each of the pipes examined will, when adjusted to a common reference temperature of 20° Centigrade, reveal a frequency value as recorded in column (5) of Table 115, parts 1, 2, and 3.

The frequencies, after adjustment to a common reference temperature must be further adjusted to an agreeable

TABLE 115, PART 1

FREQUENCIES OF ITEMS FROM PLATE XXXVII ADJUSTED TO
REFERENCE TEMPERATURE AND COMMON PITCH LEVEL

(1) Reference[a]	(2) Name of Pipe	(3) Mean Raw Frequency of Fundamental[b]	(4) Coefficient for Adjusting to Reference Temperature[c]	(5) Adjusted Frequency of Fundamental at 20° C[d]	(6) Equivalent Frequency of 8' Pitch[e]	(7) Comparative Pitch Level in American Standard Pitch (a'=440)
37-1	8' Principal	68.7	.983	67.5	67.5	C - C#
37-2	4' Octave	134.7	.983	132.4	66.2	BB - C
37-3	2 2/3' Quinte	192.1	.983	188.8	62.9	BB - C

Continued on following page

[a]Reference to M. Praetorius, Theatrum Instrumentorum seu Sciagraphia . . . (Wolfenbuettel, 1620), Plate XXXVII. The first number identifies the plate, the second, the specific item on the plate.

[b]Carried forward from column (7) of Table 114, part 1.

[c]The coefficient serves as a multiplier for values recorded in column (3).

[d]Column (3) times column (4) equals column (5).

[e]Derived as follows: Fundamental frequency of 8' items times 1; of 16' items times 2; of 4' items times 1/2; of 2 2/3' items times 1/3; of 2' items times 1/4; all equal column (6).

TABLE 115, PART 1—Continued

(1) Reference	(2) Name of Pipe	(3) Mean Raw Frequency of Fundamental	(4) Coefficient for Adjusting to Reference Temperature	(5) Adjusted Frequency of Fundamental at 20° C	(6) Equivalent Frequency of 8' Pitch	(7) Comparative Pitch Level in American Standard Pitch ($a' = 440$)
37-4	2' Klein Octave	272.8	.983	268.2	67.0	C – C#
37-5	4' Nachthorn; open	133.2	.983	130.9	65.5	C – C#
37-6	16' Quintade	35.1	.983	34.5	69.0	C – C#
37-7	8' Quintade	68.6	.983	67.4	67.4	C – C#
37-8	4' Nachthorn-Gedackt	126.8	.983	124.6	62.3	BB – C
37-9	8' Grossgedackt	85.1	.983	83.7	83.7	E – F
37-10	8' Gemshorn	71.9	.983	70.8	70.8	C# – D
37-11	4' Spillfloete	116.2	.985	114.5	57.3	AA – AA#
37-12	2' Blockfloete	251.2	.985	247.4	61.8	BB – C
37-13	4' Querfloete; open	136.0	.985	133.9	66.9	C – C#
37-14	4' Querfloete-Gedackt	119.1	.985	117.3	58.7	AA# – BB

TABLE 115, PART 2

FREQUENCIES OF ITEMS FROM PLATE XXXVIII ADJUSTED TO
REFERENCE TEMPERATURE AND COMMON PITCH LEVEL

(1) Reference[a]	(2) Name of Pipe	(3) Mean Raw Frequency of Fundamental[b]	(4) Coefficient for Adjusting to Reference Temperature[c]	(5) Adjusted Frequency of Fundamental at 20° C[d]	(6) Equivalent Frequency of 8' Pitch[e]	(7) Comparative Pitch Level in American Standard Pitch (a'=440)
38-1	4' [Labial] Dulzian	136.1	.985	134.1	67.1	C – C#
38-2	4' Koppelfloete	113.6	.985	111.9	55.9	AA – AA#
38-3	4' Flachfloete	135.0	.985	133.0	66.5	C – C#
38-4	8' Klein Barduen	62.5	.985	61.6	61.6	AA# – B
38-5	4' Offenfloete	132.0	.985	130.0	65.0	BB – C
38-6	8' Gedackt	62.1	.985	61.2	61.2	AA# – B
38-7	8' Rohr- or Hohlfloete	63.2	.985	62.3	62.3	BB – C

[a]Reference to Praetorius, Theatrum . . .; Plate XXXVIII. The first number identifies the plate, the second, the specific item on the plate.

[b]Carried forward from column (7) of Table 114, part 2.

[c]The coefficient serves as a multiplier for values recorded in column (3).

[d]Column (3) times column (4) equals column (5).

[e]Derived as follows: Fundamental frequency of 8' items times 1; of 4' items times 1/2; all equal column (6).

TABLE 115, PART 3

FREQUENCIES OF ITEMS FROM THE PFEIFFLIN ZUR CHORMASZ ADJUSTED TO
REFERENCE TEMPERATURE AND COMMON PITCH LEVEL

(1) Reference[a] Pfeifflin zur Chormasz	(2) Note — On Graph	(2) Note — Equivalent of 8' Stop	(3) Mean Raw Frequency of Fundamental[b]	(4) Coefficient for Adjusting to Reference Temperature[c]	(5) Adjusted Frequency of Fundamental at 20° C[d]	(6) Equivalent Frequency of 8' Pitch[e]	(7) Comparative Pitch Level in American Standard Pitch ($\underline{a}'$=440)
	c	c''''	1065.3	.983	1038.3	64.9	BB – C
	cs	c#''''	1104.3	.983	1085.5	...	...
	d	d''''	1176.9	.983	1156.9	...	...

Continued on following page

[a] Reference to M. Praetorius, Syntagmatis Musici Tomus Secundus De Organographia . . . (Wolfenbuettel, 1619; facs. ed. by W. Gurlitt, Kassel, 1929), p. 231.

[b] Carried forward from column (8) of Table 114, part 3.

[c] The coefficient serves as a multiplier for values recorded in column (3).

[d] Column (3) times column (4) equals column (5).

[e] Derived as follows: Fundamental frequency of c'''' times 1/16; of c'''''
times 1/32; all equal column (6).

TABLE 115, PART 3--Continued

(1) Reference	(2) Note — On Graph	(2) Note — Equivalent of 8' Stop	(3) Mean Raw Frequency of Fundamental	(4) Coefficient for Adjusting to Reference Temperature	(5) Adjusted Frequency of Fundamental at 20° C	(6) Equivalent Frequency of 8' Pitch	(7) Comparative Pitch Level in American Standard Pitch ($\underline{a}' = 440$)
	d̲s̲	d̲#'''	1253.2	.983	1231.9	. . . .	. . .
	e̲	e̲'''	1334.0	.983	1311.3	. . . .	. . .
	f̲	f̲'''	1415.5	.983	1391.4	. . . .	. . .
Chormasz	f̲s̲	f̲#'''	1496.7	.983	1471.3	. . . .	. . .
	g̲	g̲'''	1567.9	.983	1541.2	. . . .	. . .
zur	g̲s̲	g̲#'''	1646.5	.983	1618.5	. . . .	. . .
	a̲	a̲'''	1753.5	.983	1723.7	. . . .	. . .
Pfeifflin	b̲	a̲#'''	1867.3	.983	1835.6	. . . .	. . .
	h̲	b̲'''	1993.7	.983	1959.8	. . . .	. . .
	c̲	c̲''''	2116.7	.983	2080.7	65.0	BB - C

pitch reference level, so that they can be directly compared
with each other and actual deviations noted. For this purpose all values were reduced, extended, or retained (as the
individual case required) to an 8' pitch level. The frequencies of the several pipes, when adjusted to a common pitch
reference level at 8', exhibit values as recorded in column
(6) of Table 115, parts 1, 2, and 3.

Summary of Investigation

With the raw frequencies of the pipe models adjusted
to a common reference temperature and a common pitch level,
it would seem desirable to extract some convenient frequency
figure from the entire investigation which would bespeak an
acceptable value for Praetorius' reference pitch. Such a
figure would prove useful in comparing Praetorius' Chorton
to any standard reference pitch in use today.

Assortment of the Equated Scores

To do this effectively the pipes had best be assorted
according to their respective families, such as open cylindrical, covered cylindrical, open conical, and compound corpora. From each family a mean frequency can be determined
and a standard deviation computed. The standard deviation
will reveal the consistency of the values within each family.
Table 116 presents summations of such an analysis for the
open cylindrical family.

It will be observed that the range of frequencies

TABLE 116

DEVIATIONS FROM MEAN FREQUENCY FOR MODELS
OF THE OPEN CYLINDRICAL FAMILY

(1) Ref- er- ence[a]	(2) Name of Pipe	(3) Frequency of 8' Pitch in Double Vibra- tions per Second[b]	(4) Mean Frequency of Present Table[c]	(5) Devia- tion ($\pm$) from Mean Fre- quency[d]
37-1	8' Principal	67.5	66.0	1.5
37-2	4' Octave	66.2	66.0	0.2
37-4	2' Klein Octave	67.0	66.0	1.0
37-5	4' Nachthorn; open	65.5	66.0	0.5
37-13	4' Querfloete; open	66.9	66.0	0.9
38-5	4' Offenfloete	65.0	66.0	1.0
Chor- masz	$\underline{c}$ / $\underline{c}$'''	64.9	66.0	1.1
Chor- masz	$\underline{\bar{c}}$ / $\underline{c}$''''	65.0	66.0	1.0

[a]Reference to Praetorius, Theatrum . . ., Plates
XXXVII and XXXVIII, and De Organographia . . ., p. 232.

[b]Carried forward from columns (6) of Table 115,
parts 1, 2, and 3.

[c]Calculated as $\dfrac{a + b + c + \ldots + n}{n}$

[d]Column (3) minus column (4) equals column (5)

represented in the table equals 2.6 double vibrations per
second which is the difference between the highest and lowest values appearing in column (3). The mean frequency for
all the pipes of the open cylindrical family equals 66.0

double vibrations per second. The standard deviation[43] from
the mean is equal to .995, which indicates a high degree of
consistency.

Six items among the model pipes represent the covered
cylindrical family. The mean frequency as well as deviations
and the standard deviation from the same are presented in
Table 117.

TABLE 117

DEVIATIONS FROM MEAN FREQUENCY FOR MODELS
OF THE COVERED CYLINDRICAL FAMILY

(1) Reference[a]	(2) Name of Pipe	(3) Frequency of 8' Pitch in Double Vibrations per Second[b]	(4) Mean Frequency of Present Table[c]	(5) Deviation ($\pm$) from Mean Frequency[d]
37-6	16' Quintade	69.0	63.4	5.6
37-7	8' Quintade	67.4	63.4	4.0
37-8	4' Nachthorn-Gedackt	62.3	63.4	1.1
37-14	4' Querfloete-Gedackt	58.7	63.4	4.7
38-4	8' Klein Barduen	61.6	63.4	1.8
38-6	8' Gedackt	61.2	63.4	2.2

[a]Reference to Praetorius, Theatrum . . ., Plates
XXXVII and XXXVIII.

[b]Carried forward from columns (6) of Table 115,
parts 1 and 2.

[c]Calculated as $\dfrac{a + b + c + \ldots + n}{n}$

[d]Column (3) minus column (4) equals column (5).

The range of frequencies represented in the table is far greater than in the preceding instance; it amounts to 10.3 double vibrations per second, being the difference between the highest and lowest values found in column (3). The mean frequency for all of the pipes of the covered cylindrical family equals 63.4 double vibrations per second. The standard deviation from the mean is equal to 3.623, which indicates a lesser degree of consistency than in the case of the open cylindrical family.

Four items among the model pipes represent the open conical family. The mean frequency as well as deviations and the standard deviation from the same are presented in Table 118.

In the case of the open conical family, the range of frequencies between the highest and lowest values of column (3) equals 9.0 double vibrations per second. The mean frequency for the group of four pipes equals 66.5 double vibrations per second. The standard deviation from the mean is equal to 3.2, which indicates a lesser degree of consistency than in the case of the open cylindrical family.

The remaining pipe models, three in number, represent compound corpora, i.e., corpora which are a combination of open cylindrical and open conical members, or of covered cylindrical and open cylindrical ones. A summation of the mean frequency as well as deviations and the standard deviations for the same are presented in Table 119.

TABLE 118

DEVIATIONS FROM MEAN FREQUENCY FOR MODELS
OF THE OPEN CONICAL FAMILY

(1) Ref- er-[a] ence	(2) Name of Pipe	(3) Frequency of 8' Pitch in Double Vibra- tions per Second[b]	(4) Mean Frequency of Present Table[c]	(5) Devia- tion ($\pm$) from Mean Fre- quency[d]
37-10	8' Gemshorn	70.8	66.5	4.3
37-12	2' Blockfloete	61.8	66.5	4.7
38-1	4' [Labial] Dulzian	67.1	66.5	0.6
38-3	4' Flachfloete	66.5	66.5	0.0

[a]Reference to Praetorius, Theatrum . . ., Plates XXXVII and XXXVIII.

[b]Carried forward from columns (6) of Table 115, parts 1 and 2.

[c]Calculated as $\dfrac{a + b + c + \ldots + n}{n}$

[d]Column (3) minus column (4) equals column (5).

Among the pipe models fabricated of several identifiable members, the range of frequencies between the highest and lowest values of column (3) equals 6.4 double vibrations per second. The mean frequency for the group is 58.5 double vibrations per second. The standard deviation from the mean is equal to 2.747, which indicates a moderate degree of consistency among members of the group.

TABLE 119

DEVIATIONS FROM MEAN FREQUENCY FOR MODELS
EXHIBITING COMPOUND CORPORA

(1) Reference[a]	(2) Name of Pipe	(3) Frequency of 8' Pitch in Double Vibrations per Second[b]	(4) Mean Frequency of Present Table[c]	(5) Deviation ($\pm$) from Mean Frequency[d]
37-11	4' Spillfloete	57.3	58.5	1.2
38-2	4' Koppelfloete	55.9	58.5	2.6
38-7	8' Rohr- or Hohlfloete	62.3	58.5	3.8

[a]Reference to Praetorius, Theatrum . . ., Plates
XXXVII and XXXVIII.

[b]Carried forward from columns (6) of Table 115,
parts 1 and 2.

[c]Calculated as $\dfrac{a + b + c + \ldots + n}{n}$

[d]Column (3) minus column (4) equals column (5).

Isolation of Praetorius' Reference Pitch

When assorted into families, adjusted to a common

reference temperature, and compared at a common pitch level,

the various species of model pipes from Plates XXXVII and

XXXVIII of the Theatrum Instrumentorum and from the graph,

Pfeifflin zur Chormasz of the De Organographia exhibit aver-

age frequencies as recorded in Table 120.

It is obvious that a simple mean frequency derived

TABLE 120

EQUATED MEAN FREQUENCIES OF THE MODEL
PIPES ASSORTED INTO FAMILIES

Family	Number of Items	Temperature in Centigrade	Pitch Level	Absolute Note	Mean Frequency in Double Vibrations per Second
Open Cylindrical	8	20°	8'	$\underline{c}$	66.0^a
Covered Cylindrical	6	20°	8'	$\underline{c}$	63.4^b
Open Conical	4	20°	8'	$\underline{c}$	66.5^c
Compound	3	20°	8'	$\underline{c}$	58.5^d

[a]Carried forward from column (4) of Table 116.

[b]Carried forward from column (4) of Table 117.

[c]Carried forward from column (4) of Table 118.

[d]Carried forward from column (4) of Table 119.

from all of the entries in Table 120 would not produce a very
acceptable value for Praetorius' Chorton; rather, the isolation of such a reference pitch should be accomplished from
one or, at most, two families which represent the most direct
and simple method of fabrication. In the present author's
opinion, the open cylindrical family is best suited for this
purpose:

    1. The pipes from this family are the most
simple and direct to construct; they are easiest for
the draftsman to reproduce in scale and the simplest
for the craftsman to fabricate in metal

2. The corpora are the longest of any family for
the resultant pitch; errors in scaling or in fabrication have the least influential effect on the pitch.
Among them also appear the double length, overblown
pipes and, at the opposite extreme, the diminutive
pipes of the Pfeifflin zur Chormasz

3. The Pfeifflin zur Chormasz graph represents
a very accurate and traditional method for drafting
organ pipes and assures a highly faithful realization

4. The largest number of items (8, in fact) find
representation in this family

5. The range of frequencies and the standard deviation are exceptionally low

Accordingly, a very acceptable value for Praetorius'
Chorton at 8' C and at 20° Centigrade is 66.0 double vibrations per second.

Should it be desired to include the influential effect of another family of pipes, the present author would
suggest the open conical group since they manifest similar
advantages as those proposed for the open cylindrical family.
By combining the two families, twelve separate pipes are engaged. The values for the open cylindrical, the open conical, and a combination of the two are shown in Table 121.

The values of 66.0, and 66.25 double vibrations at
8' C, 20° Centigrade may be taken as very acceptable figures
for Praetorius' reference pitch. At this pitch level, a

TABLE 121

REASONABLE APPROXIMATIONS OF PRAETORIUS' CHORTON
AS DERIVED FROM TWO FAMILIES OF PIPES

Category	Number of Items	Temperature in Centigrade	Pitch Level	Absolute Note	Mean Frequency in Double Vibrations per Second
Open Cylindrical	8	20°	8'	c	66.0
Open Conical	4	20°	8'	c	66.5
Mean of Both Families	12	20°	8'	c	66.25

comparison may be struck between these values and an equivalent value in American Standard pitch as shown in Table 122.

In order to show a more convenient comparison of the Praetorius reference pitch to the American Standard pitch, all values may be calculated to the usual reference level of a', where the relationships appear as shown in Table 123. The table reflects an equal-tempered a' for both cases.[44]

For purposes of preparing tables and making various calculations pertaining to Praetorius' Chorton, a reference pitch of a' = 445 double vibrations per second may prove more convenient and is sufficiently accurate to satisfy most requirements.

Therefore, Praetorius' Chorton or reference pitch as developed from his "Theater of Organ Pipes" is about 1/10 of a semitone higher than the American Standard reference

TABLE 122

COMPARISON BETWEEN ACCEPTABLE VALUES FOR PRAETORIUS'
CHORTON AND AMERICAN STANDARD PITCH AT 8'C

(1) Category	(2) Pitch Level	(3) Absolute Note	(4) Frequency of Praetorius' Reference Pitch in Double Vibrations per Second	(5) Frequency of American Standard Pitch in Double Vibrations per Second	(6) Difference in Double Vibrations per Second[a]
Open Cylindrical	8'	C	66.0	65.41[b]	+.59
Mean of Open Cylindrical and Open Conical	8'	C	66.25	65.41	+.84

[a]Column (4) minus column (5) equals column (6).

[b]From C. D. Hodgman and others, Handbook of Chemistry and Physics (38th ed.; Cleveland, 1956), p. 2319.

pitch.[45] It also falls within the area of Bessaraboff's Polydiapasonal scale of C.[46]

Conclusions

Upon the basis of the discussions in the present chapter dealing with the historical quest for Praetorius' reference pitch, it may be worthwhile to extract the chief

TABLE 123

COMPARISON BETWEEN ACCEPTABLE VALUES FOR PRAETORIUS'
CHORTON AND AMERICAN STANDARD PITCH AT a'

(1) Category	(2) Pitch Level	(3) Mean Frequen- cy of Praeto- rius	(4) Frequen- cy of American Standard Pitch	(5) Difference in Double Vibrations per Second[a]
Open Cylindrical	a'	444.0	440.0	+4.0
Mean of Open Cy- lindrical and Open Conical	a'	445.68	440.0	+5.68

[a]Column (3) minus column (4) equals column (5).

concerns and summarize them here in the form of tangible conclusions.

1. The search for acceptable values for the reference pitch of Praetorius is an extremely difficult
venture because Praetorius was unable to define his
concept in quantitative terms that are directly intelligible to the modern scientist and musician

2. The terms Chorton and Chormasz seem to be
used interchangeably by Praetorius. A careful translation defines the Chorton as being the "reference
pitch" and the term Chormasz, the "reference measure."
In a musical context the former term, while in a scientific discussion, the latter seems more appropriate

3. A determined effort to define Praetorius' reference pitch was made by Alexander J. Ellis and reported in 1880. His value of an equal tempered a' at 430.5 double vibrations per second at 68° Fahrenheit or 20° Centigrade was derived by registering the frequency of a single wooden pipe which he had constructed from dimensions supplied by Praetorius

4. Ellis' realization reveals certain inaccuracies in the interpretation and application of Praetorius' record and is not reinforced by supporting evidence. Accordingly, his proposed value lies in question

5. A second major effort to define Praetorius' reference pitch was made by Arthur Mendel and reported in 1948. His proposed value lies between 466.16 and 493.88 double vibrations per second, and was derived by an analysis of Praetorius' voice ranges, supported by indications gleaned from Arnold Schlick as well as by Praetorius' Nuernberg Posaune. The value, extracted from elastic qualitative descriptions and subjected to considerable personal interpretation lacks conviction and presents too wide a span to be sufficiently satisfactory to serve as a basis from which subsequent deductions can be successfully made

6. The present author's attempt to develop an acceptable value for Praetorius' reference pitch

addresses itself to a comprehensive examination of all of the quantitative information recorded by Praetorius. Through the careful pursuit of the same, he has applied a scientific approach as far as practicable and has subjected his findings to acceptable statistical methods. His value of <u>c</u>.445 double vibrations per second for <u>a</u>' is offered as a contribution to the historical quest in the hope that it may incite others to investigate further, in order to verify, refute, or adjust the finding

7. In an attempt to solve the vexing problem of the falsely calibrated scale rule of Plate XXXVII of the <u>Theatrum Instrumentorum</u>, it has been found that the first three-foot segment of the same may be accepted as a reliable measure

8. The present investigation proposes that the graph of the <u>Pfeifflin zur Chormasz</u> uses a full scale for dimensions plotted along the <u>X</u>-axis and a half-scale for the <u>Y</u>-axis. The accompanying circle and rectangle figures seem to be in approximate full scale

9. The high degree of correlation between values developed from Plates XXXVII, XXXVIII, and the <u>Pfeifflin zur Chormasz</u> graph, point to a high level of accuracy in the sketches, and command the respect of the modern scholar for the skill exhibited by Praetorius' draftsman

CHAPTER XV

DISPOSITION AND REALIZATION OF PRAETORIUS'
TEMPERAMENT AND LAYOUT OF CLAVIERS

In the third chapter of the fourth part of the second
volume of the Syntagma Musicum[1] Praetorius lays down with the
utmost care his several methods of tuning keyed instruments
and develops his views, as well as those of selected contemporaries, regarding a practical and useful disposition of the
temperament. His chapter is headed by an extensive and ram-
bling title somewhat unclear and confusing but very characteristic of the time:

Das III. Capitel.	Chapter III
Vnterricht / Wie man die Schnarrwercke in den Orgeln / so wol auch absonderlich die Regal Wercke vnd andere Instrumenta, als Clavicymbalen / Spinetten / vnd dergleichen vor sich selbsten recht vnd reine accordiren vnd einstimmen koenne: Jm gleichen welcher massen die andern Pfeiffen nachzustimmen / oder jhnen im Stimmen nach zuhelffen.[3]	Instruction as to how one can "draw in" the reeds in organs, and also tune Regals and other instruments, such as clavicembalos, spinets, and the like, independently to a true and accurate pitch; likewise, in what order the remaining pipes [in organs] may be tuned or, [rather,] adjusted [to bring them into pitch when tuning.][2] [Translation by the present author]

Before giving directions for establishing the pitch
and laying the temperament, Praetorius sets down certain

788

basic rules regarding the practice of tuning which may be abstracted and summarized as follows:[4]

Reed pipes can easily be tuned to labial pipes if the latter are in good tune by themselves

It is advantageous to tune a reed voice to another labial voice which lies an octave higher or lower in pitch. For example, a 16' reed voice should be tuned to an 8' Principal, Octave, or Flute; or, an 8' reed voice should be tuned to a 4' Octave; or, a 4' reed voice should be tuned to an 8' Principal, Gross Octave, or to a combination of labial voices composed of an 8' Quintade and a 4' Octave

Labial pipes of the same pitch level as the reed voice to be tuned are unstable and will tend to deceive the ear

The most accurate tuning of reeds or regal voices can be achieved by tuning a single note (as C or c) of it to an entire chord (as c-e-g-c') from a labial voice appearing on another keyboard. It must be observed, however, that a labial voice used for this purpose may not materially exceed the loudness level of the reed to be tuned

Reeds and regal voices are adjusted by means of the tuning wire which, when depressed, will decrease the size of the shallot opening and thereby raise the pitch; on the other hand, when raised, it will enlarge the size of the opening and thereby lower the pitch

Open labial pipes will rise in pitch if the end of the pipe is coned outward or if it is shortened; they will drop in pitch if the same is coned inward or partially closed

Covered labial pipes are tuned by means of the surmounting cap or stopper; when either of these are depressed, the pitch rises; when raised, the pitch falls

Labial pipes having a fixed closure are tuned by means of their ears; when these are brought more closely together they will lower the pitch of the pipe; when separated, they will raise the pitch

Foreign particles introduced into the windway of labial pipes or between the tongue and shallot of reed pipes will silence the pipe

Overly curved reed tongues will resist the wind and

fail to vibrate, while inadequately curved tongues will be
pressed against the shallot, effect a fixed closure, and silence the pipe

The Praetorius Temperament

Following his practical hints for tuning organ pipes,
Praetorius discusses the art of tempering the scale. His
whole discussion, however, handles this problem in a purely
qualitative way without any quantitative specifications by
means of which one could determine the exact degree of tempering he requires. His discussion at this point is of some
value to the practicing tuner but is quite insufficient for
the mathematician or acoustician who needs quantitative specifications in order to arrive at exact values by means of
which Praetorius' temperament can be compared and related to
other noteworthy historical solutions. Fortunately, in the
very ultimate paragraphs of his chapter on tuning, Praetorius
quotes his friend [Seth] Calvisius in support of his own
qualitative directions for establishing the temperament.[5]
From Calvisius' specifications it is possible to work out
Praetorius' temperament in a quantitative way, sufficient to
delineate it mathematically and develop a profile useful for
purposes of comparison.

Qualitative Description of the Temperament

Praetorius sets down three specific rules for laying
the bearing of the temperament; he says:

Wie man ein Regal, Clavi-
cymbel, Symphonien vnd dergleichen Instrument vor sich
selbst accordiren vnd rein
stimmen koenne.

Allhier musz vornehmlich
nachfolgends mit fleisz in
acht genommen werden.

1. Dasz man einen gewis-
sen Clavem vor sich neme /
von welchem man zu stimmen
anhebe / vnd nach welchem
die andern / doch allwege
je einer nach dem andern
einzuziehen.

2. Das alle Octaven vnd
Tertiae perfectae seu ma-
jores gar rein gestimmet
werden / so wol der niedrig-
ste Clavis nach dem hoech-
stem / als der hoechste nach
dem niedrigsten.

3. Dasz alle Quinten nicht
gerade vnd rein / sondern
gegen einander (doch vff
gewisse masz) niedrig schwebend gelassen werden (zu-
verstehen / der hoechste
Clavis musz gegen dem niedrigen etwas nachgelassen /
oder herunterwarts stehen:
so man aber die Quinten von
vntenwarts / oder den vntersten Clavem gegen dem obern
stimmen wil / musz derselbe
zu hoch stehen vnd schwe-
ben / vnd also etwas mehr /
denn gar rein stehen.

Wenn nu diese dreyerley
recht in acht genommen werden / so kan man im stim-
men nicht leichtlich irren:
doch ist das letzte die
Quinten (vorbeschriebener
art nach) recht einzuziehen

How one can accurately tune
a Regal, clavicembalo, symphonium, and the like, and
bring it into consonance with
itself.

In particular, the following
must be diligently and specifically observed:

1. That one choose a specific key [or note] as the point
of departure to which all subsequent ones must be tuned or
"drawn in", but always in the
proper order [or rotation].

2. That all octaves and major thirds be tuned entirely
pure--the lower key against
the higher as well as the
higher key against the lower.

3. That all fifths be tuned,
not square and true, but tempered narrow by a specific
amount, with the understanding
that the upper key must be
tempered flat in relation to
the lower. If, however, the
fifths are to be tuned inverted, so that the lower key
is to be tuned to the upper,
then it must be tempered sharp
in relation to the upper, and
so appear somewhat higher than
if it were tuned pure.

If these three points are
properly observed, the tuning
errors should be held to a
minimum. The adjustment of
the fifths (according to the
above prescription) is the
most difficult [operation],

das schwehrste / oder in
acht zu nemen das vornemste.
Denn nach Octaven vnd Quinten kan man ein gantz In-
strument einstimmen / nur
allein / dasz die Tertiae
majores, als zu Richtern
gebraucht werden / davon
weitlaeufftiger meldung
geschicht.[6]

but remains also the most important consideration. An
entire instrument can be tuned
by means of octaves and fifths.
The major thirds [on the other
hand] must [always] serve as
tests of the progress, of
which further note will be tak-
en. [Translation by the present author]

By these specifications Praetorius establishes the
foundations of his temperament, which require that all octaves and major thirds must be tuned pure and that all fifths
must be tempered narrow.[7] The necessary corollaries of these
premises propose that all unisons and minor sixths will appear pure, while all fourths will appear tempered wide.[8]

Praetorius continues to develop further implications
of his basic premises over the entire gamut of the scale in
a qualitative way. His deductions may be abstracted as follows:[9]

Some skillful tuners are able to tune perfectly by
means of octaves and fourths, which in turn are tempered
exactly like the fifths, except in the opposite direction

The octave must be tuned pure; therefore, since an
octave is composed of a fifth and a fourth, should the fifth
be diminished by a certain amount, the fourth must be augmented by an equal amount in order to maintain the purity of
the octave

Since the fifth is composed of a major third and a
minor third, should the major third be pure, the minor third
must be impure to the same degree that the fifth is impure

Out of the major third there arises, by inversion,
the minor sixth; should the major third be tuned pure, the
minor sixth will also appear pure

Out of the minor third there arises, by inversion, the major sixth; should the minor third be tempered, the major sixth will also appear tempered, but in the opposite direction. Since the minor third is somewhat diminished by the temperament, the major sixth must be augmented to the same degree if the purity of the octave is to be preserved

Since octaves, major thirds, and minor sixths must be pure, should any of these intervals be divided into two component parts, then both components must be pure, or both must be impure; if one component is tempered wide, the other must be tempered narrow; conversely, if one is tempered narrow, the other must be tempered wide. Should this principle be violated, so that one component of a pure interval is tuned pure and the other tempered, the composite interval will be false, as is clear from a principle of geometry which maintains:

If to a certain number is added an uncertain one, then that total will become uncertain; or, if to a definite quantity an indefinite one is added, then that total quantity will become indefinite . . . [Translation by Prof. T. Klammer][10]

In what manner the basic intervals are to be tempered can be more readily visualized from the following arrangement of the concepts:

When tuning { fifths [or] minor thirds, / fourths [or] major sixths, } the { upper / lower } key must be tempered low in relation to the { lower / upper }

by the same amount as the { lower / upper } key is tempered high in relation to the { upper / lower

Quantitative Delineation of the Temperament

Having established his basic premises and deduced certain further implications from them, Praetorius proceeds to delineate three methods of laying a tempered bearing and of tuning the balance of the compass to it. In order to derive accurate values and establish meaningful relationships from his discussions, it becomes necessary to pass over the tuning methods at this point in order to consider the quantitative disposition of the various intervals which he reveals at the very close of the chapter. Under the heading NB [Nota Bene] he quotes at length Calvisius' views on the temperament to support his own preceding discussions. The Calvisius quotation fortunately develops the necessary intervals in a mathematically quantitative way, so that exact values and relationships can be set up. Because of the importance of the quotation it is subjoined in full together with a parallel translation:

NB.

N[ota] B[ene]

Hierbey habe ich auch des Calvisij Meynung de Temperatura Instrumentorum vffzusetzen nicht vnterlassen wollen.

Herewith I should not like to neglect presenting the view of Calvisius with respect to the temperament of instruments:

Das ist gewisz (sagt er) wenn die Consonantiae sollen recht klingen / so muessen sie rein in jhren proportionibus stehen / vnd weder vberheufft noch geringert werden; Vnd dasselbige befindet sich also in voce

It is certain, (says he,) that if the consonances are expected to sound pure, they must be tuned true to their ratios and may be neither augmented nor diminished. This condition prevails in the human voice; also in trombones

humana, auch in Posaunen vnd in andern / welchen man mit menschlichem Athem etwas zugeben oder nemen kan. Denn vox humana lencket sich natuerlich zu der rechten Proportion der Intervallorum, vnd legets jhnen zu / wo etwas mangeln / oder nimpt weg / wo was vberley seyn solte.

and such other [instruments] which can be modified by the human breath; for the human voice adjusts itself naturally to the proper ratios of the intervals, augmenting them if they are lacking, or diminishing them if they are excessive.

Auff den Instrumenten aber vnd Orgeln hat es eine andere Meynung / do seynd der Clavier gar zu wenig / darumb musz man allda etlichen Consonantiis etwas nemen / auff dasz solches alles nicht auff einem Clave allein mangle.

However, on [keyed] instruments and organs a different condition prevails; here there are far too few keys; hence, the necessary diminution must be spread over several intervals, so that the total error may not be concentrated in one.

Die Claves seynd also:

The notes are [related to each other] as follows:[11]

c vnd d distant tono majore 9/8.
d vnd e Tono minore 10/9.

c-d: a major tone: 9/8

d-e: a minor tone: 10/9

e vnd f distant Semitonio Majore 16/15.
f vnd g Tono majore 9/8

e-f: a major semitone: 16/15

f-g: a major tone: 9/8

g vnd a distant Tono minoro 10/9.
a vnd h tono majore 9/8.

g-a: a minor tone: 10/9

a-b: a major tone: 9/8

h vnd c Semitonio Majore 16/15.

b-c: a major semitone: 16/15

Wenn nun die Instrumenta nach diesen proportionibus sollen gestimmet werden / so wuerde alsobald aus dem d ins f Semiditonus imperfectus; Denn es ist Tonos minor cum semitonio, vnd fehlet ein gantz Comma; Jtem / aus dem d ins a wuerde in der Quinta auch ein

Should the [keyed] instruments be tuned to these ratios, the d-f interval, [for example,] would appear as an imperfect semiditone [i.e., an imperfect minor third]; for it amounts to a minor tone plus a semitone, and lacks an entire comma [to make it a just minor third of the ratio of

796

Comma mangeln / welches dann gar zu viel / vnd die Ohren koennen solchen mangel nicht erdulden. Darumb solte man billich mehr Clavier haben / also / dasz man zwey d hette / die nur ein Comma von einander weren;

Aber weil solches auch in andern Clavibus geschicht / wuerden der Clavier, sonderlich wenn die geduppelte Semitonia auch noch darzu kemen / gar zu viel werden; Darumb musz man die temperatur brauchen / die ist also.

Dem Tono majori wird ein halb Comma genommen; Dem Tono minori hergegen wird ein halb Comma gegeben. Hinc manifestum, quod Tertiae majori, quae constat Tono majore & minore, nihil decedat, vnd bleibet rein; Vnd altera pars videlicet Sexta minor, (dasz die Octava erfuellet werde) bleibet auch rein. Dem Semitonio majori aber wird ein vierthel eines commatis gegeben; Daher koempts / dasz numehr eine Quarta / welche ein tonum majorem vnd minorem, vnd ein Semitonium majus hat / zu grob ist / weil dem Semitonio quarta pars commatis zugelegt ist.

Also die Quinta hat zween Tonos majores, einen minorem, vnd ein Semitonium; Weil allhier jederm tono majori ein halb comma, vnd also beyden / ein gantz Com-

6/5]. Item, the fifth, d-a, would also lack a comma [to make it a just fifth of the ratio of 3/2]. Such a discrepancy is too great for the ear to tolerate. Therefore, it would appear necessary to provide more keys, so that, for example, one would have two d's separated by a single comma.

However, since this discrepancy prevails in other keys as well, the clavier would become overloaded, especially if double semitones were also provided. Therefore, one must employ a temperament, which is as follows:

The major tone must be diminished by one-half comma; the minor tone, on the other hand, must be augmented by one-half comma. From this it is clear that from a major third, which consists of a major and a minor tone, nothing is taken away, so that it remains pure; on the other hand, the minor sixth obviously remains pure also, (so that the octave may be complemented). The major semitone, however, is augmented by one-fourth of a comma; for this reason the fourth, which comprises a major tone, a minor tone, and a major semitone is too large, because the semitone has already been augmented by one-fourth of a comma.

The fifth is composed of two major tones, one minor tone, and one semitone. Since each major tone is already diminished by one-half comma, and, thus, both together by a

ma genommen wird / vnd hergegen nur drey viertheil commotis gegeben werden / folget / dasz die Quinta in Instrumenten nicht vallkommen seyn kan.

Weil aber eine Quarta vnd eine Quinta, eine Octavam machen / welche nicht kan geendert werden / so folget nothwendig / wenn ein theil groesser wird / dasz das ander kleiner werde / vnd darff ferner keiner demonstration nicht. Divide grossum in duas partes, sunt utrobique sex nummi: Si jam alterutri parti dabis septem nummos, necesse est, altera pars habeat tantum quinque nummos, si grossus integritatem custodire debet, & non minui aut augeri.

Wenn aber die Orgelmacher sagen / die Quinta d g schwebt: Die Tertia minor g b schwebt auch: Ergo so ist die Sexta minor rein / etc. Das ist wol etwas nach jhrer Art / aber nicht recht secundum artem & demonstrationem geredet / sondern wenn ich demonstriren wil / dasz die Sexta minor rein sey / musz ich also sagen.

Tertia major & Sexta minor constituunt Octavam; Sed Tertia major in temperatura retinet suam veram proportionem; Ergo necesse est, ut & sexta minor suam retineat, & legitima sit. Sic Quinta & Quarta constituunt duplam, sive octavam; & Quinta in temperatura per Quartam partem Commatis minuitur: Ergo necesse est, ut Quarta, quae

whole comma, and since only three-fourths of a comma are being contributed toward augmentation, it follows that the fifth in [keyed] instruments cannot be perfect.

Since an octave, which is unalterable, is composed of a fourth and a fifth, it follows of necessity, that if one [of the constituent intervals] is augmented, the other must be [proportionately] diminished. [This proposition] requires no further proof. If the whole is divided into two parts there will be, [let us say,] six units to each; should one part be given seven units, the other must of necessity receive only five, if the whole is to be kept intact without diminution or augmentation.

When the organbuilders say that the fourth, d-g is tempered; the minor third g-bb is tempered; therefore, the minor sixth d-bb is pure, etc., they are speaking colloquially and not really in terms of art and science. Should I wish to demonstrate that the minor sixth is pure, I must express myself as follows:

The major third and the minor sixth constitute an octave; but the major third in a tempered [scale] retains its true ratio; therefore, it is necessary that also the minor sixth retain its [true ratio] and be pure. Thus a fifth and a fourth constitute a pair [of intervals] or an octave; the fifth in a tempered [scale] is diminished by one-fourth

conjungitur, quarta parte commatis augeatur: Et contra, sic de aliis. Necesse enim est, ut de partibus judicetur ex integro.[12]

comma: therefore, it is necessary that the fourth, which is joined to it, be augmented by one-fourth comma. And thus it is with the others: parts must be measured by the whole. [Translation by the present author; Latin segments by Prof. T. Klammer]

Calvisius begins with just intonation and develops his temperament by a precise adjustment of the intervals. He establishes three just intervals from which he derives all of the others. These are:

1. The just major tone in the ratio of 9/8 as exemplified by the intervals c-d, f-g, and a-b

2. The just minor tone in the ratio of 10/9 as exemplified by the intervals d-e and g-a

3. The just diatonic semitone (or hemitone) in the ratio of 16/15 as exemplified by the intervals e-f and b-c

He further recognizes a comma and employs it in whole or in part to describe an intervallic condition or to adjust a discrepancy. To establish the value of the comma Calvisius extracts the combination of a just minor tone plus a just diatonic semitone from the ratio of a just minor third and claims the lack to be that of the comma, thus:

$$\begin{pmatrix} \text{Just} \\ \text{minor} \\ \text{third} \end{pmatrix} - \begin{pmatrix} \text{Just} & & \text{Just} \\ \text{minor} & + & \text{diatonic} \\ \text{tone} & & \text{semitone} \end{pmatrix} = \text{Comma}$$

$$\frac{6}{5} \quad \text{x} \quad \frac{9}{10} \quad \text{x} \quad \frac{15}{16} \quad = \quad \frac{81}{80} \text{ or } 5.3952 \text{ savarts}$$

He claims further that the fifth when derived as a combination of a just major tone, two just minor tones, and a just diatonic semitone lacks one comma of achieving a just fifth, thus:

$$\left(\begin{matrix}\text{Just}\\\text{fifth}\end{matrix}\right)-\left(\begin{matrix}\text{Just}\\\text{major}\\\text{tone}\end{matrix}+\begin{matrix}\text{Just}\\\text{minor}\\\text{tone}\end{matrix}+\begin{matrix}\text{Just}\\\text{minor}\\\text{tone}\end{matrix}+\begin{matrix}\text{Just}\\\text{diatonic}\\\text{semitone}\end{matrix}\right)=\text{Comma}$$

$$\frac{3}{2}\ \times\ \frac{8}{9}\ \times\ \frac{9}{10}\ \times\ \frac{9}{10}\ \times\ \frac{15}{16}\ =\ \frac{81}{80}\ \text{or}\ 5.3952\ \text{savarts}$$

These two examples, therefore, clearly establish the syntonic comma (81/80) as the comma which operates in his subsequent adjustments. His distribution of the comma or of parts of it serves to establish the disposition of his temperament, as follows:

1. The just major tone (9/8) must be diminished by one-half comma, thus:

$$\frac{9}{8}\sqrt{\frac{80}{81}}\ =\ \sqrt{\frac{81\times80}{64\times81}}\ =\ \sqrt{\frac{5}{4}}\ =\ \frac{\sqrt{5}}{2}\ \text{or}\ 48.455\ \text{savarts}$$

2. The just minor tone (10/9) must be augmented by one-half comma, thus:

$$\frac{10}{9}\sqrt{\frac{81}{80}}\ =\ \sqrt{\frac{100\times81}{81\times80}}\ =\ \sqrt{\frac{5}{4}}\ =\ \frac{\sqrt{5}}{2}\ \text{or}\ 48.455\ \text{savarts}$$

3. The equalization of the just major and minor whole tones leaves the major third undisturbed and just, thus:

$$\frac{\sqrt{5}}{2}\frac{\sqrt{5}}{\times 2}\ =\ \frac{5}{4}\ \text{or}\ 96.91\ \text{savarts}$$

4. By extracting the major third from the octave, the minor sixth appears as a pure interval also,

thus:

$$\frac{2 \times 4}{1 \times 5} = \frac{8}{5} \text{ or } 204.12 \text{ savarts}$$

5. The just diatonic semitone (or hemitone) must be augmented by one-fourth comma, thus:

$$\frac{16}{15} \sqrt[4]{\frac{81}{80}} = \frac{8}{\sqrt[4]{5^5}} \text{ or } 29.3775 \text{ savarts}[13]$$

6. The fourth, if compounded from the previously adjusted intervals (i.e., two seconds as $\sqrt{5}/2$ plus a diatonic semitone as $8/\sqrt[4]{5^5}$) is too large by one-fourth of a comma, thus:

$$\frac{\sqrt{5} \times \sqrt{5} \times 8}{2 \times 2 \times \sqrt[4]{5^5}} = \frac{5 \times 2}{5 \sqrt[4]{5}} = \frac{2}{\sqrt[4]{5}} \text{ or } 126.2875 \text{ savarts}[14]$$

If the just fourth is extracted from the overlarge fourth, the discrepancy indicates an augmentation equal to the ratio of $3/2\sqrt[4]{5}$, thus:

$$\frac{2}{\sqrt[4]{5}} \times \frac{3}{4} = \frac{3}{2 \sqrt[4]{5}} \text{ or } 1.3488 \text{ savarts}$$

This ratio, in turn, is equal to the value of one-fourth syntonic comma, thus:

$$\sqrt[4]{\frac{81}{80}} = \frac{\sqrt[4]{81}}{\sqrt[4]{80}} = \frac{\sqrt[4]{3^4}}{\sqrt[4]{16 \times 5}} = \frac{3}{2 \sqrt[4]{5}} \text{ or } 1.3488 \text{ savarts}$$

7. The fifth, when compounded of the previously adjusted intervals (i.e., three seconds as $\sqrt{5}/2$ plus a diatonic semitone as $8/\sqrt[4]{5^5}$) will fail to reach perfection, thus:

$$\left(\frac{\sqrt{5}}{2}\right)^3 \times \frac{8}{\sqrt[4]{5^5}} = \frac{\sqrt[4]{5^6}}{\sqrt[4]{5^5}} = \frac{\sqrt[4]{5}}{1} \quad \text{or } 174.7425 \text{ savarts}^{15}$$

This reduced fifth, when extracted from a just fifth (3/2) exhibits the lack of one-fourth comma, thus:

$$\frac{3 \times 1}{2 \times \sqrt[4]{5}} = \frac{3}{2 \sqrt[4]{5}} \quad \text{or } 1.3488 \text{ savarts}$$

To summarize, Calvisius establishes the following values for the critical intervals of his temperament:

1. The fifth equals $\sqrt[4]{5}/1$ or 174.7425 savarts
2. The fourth equals $2/\sqrt[4]{5}$ or 126.2875 savarts
3. The major third equals 5/4 or 96.91 savarts
4. The major second equals $\sqrt{5}/2$ or 48.455 savarts
5. The minor second equals $8/\sqrt[4]{5^5}$ or 29.3775 savarts

From these ratios all other ratios of the compass can readily be computed. The intervallic relationships are clearly those of the meantone temperament. Table 124 presents a complete catalog of the intervals within an octave as developed from Calvisius' specifications and commonly accepted as a model form of the meantone temperament.

The Tuning Course: First Method

Praetorius presents three methods of tuning and deriving an acceptable temperament. His first method comprises seventeen tuning steps and is checked by five tests. Following is his cursive account together with a parallel version

TABLE 124

INTERVAL RATIOS OF THE NOTES
OF THE MEANTONE SCALE

Interval	Derivation	Ratio	Savart Value
Chromatic Semitone	M3+M3−P5	$\sqrt[4]{5^7}$ / 16	19.0775
Diatonic Semitone	Calvisius	8 / $\sqrt[4]{5^5}$	29.3775
Major Second	Calvisius	$\sqrt{5}$ / 2	48.4550
Augmented Second	M3−Diatonic Semitone	$\sqrt[4]{5^9}$ / 32	67.5325
Minor Third	P5−M3	4 / $\sqrt[4]{5^3}$	77.8325
Major Third	Calvisius	5 / 4	96.9100
Perfect Fourth	Calvisius	2 / $\sqrt[4]{5}$	126.2875
Augmented Fourth	M2+M3	$\sqrt{5^3}$ / 8	145.3650
Diminished Fifth	P8−(M2+M3)	16 / $\sqrt{5^3}$	155.6650
Perfect Fifth	Calvisius	$\sqrt[4]{5}$ / 1	174.7425
Augmented Fifth	M3+M3	5^2 / 4^2	193.8200
Minor Sixth	Calvisius	8 / 5	204.1200
Major Sixth	P4+M3	$\sqrt[4]{5^3}$ / 2	223.1975
Augmented Sixth	M2+M3+M3	$\sqrt{5^5}$ / 32	242.2750
Minor Seventh	P4+P4	4 / $\sqrt{5}$	252.5750
Major Seventh	P5+M3	$\sqrt[4]{5^5}$ / 4	271.6525
Octave	P5+P4	2 / 1	301.0300

in English:

Vnd ob nun zwar nicht grosz (sonderlich deme der des Stimmens laeufftig) daran gelegen / von welchem Clave man den anfang mache / so ists doch bequemlich am f̄ / wenn dasselbe erstlich Chormaessig intoniret wird / anzufangen / vnd folget demnach die richtige Ordnung der Concordanten, also:

[The First Method]

Although it is a matter of indifference (especially to those who are skilled in tuning) with which key one might begin, it is convenient to begin at f', which must first be tuned true to the reference pitch, after which the intervals should be tuned in the following order:

Diese Claves vff dieser Seiten werden reine / vnd muessen die vff der andern Seiten gegen vber / allezeit nach diesen gestimmet / vnd eingezogen werden.

1.	f	
2.	f	c̄
3.	f	a
4.	c̄	c
5.	c	g
6.	c	e
7.	g	d̄
8.	g	h
9.	d̄	d
	d	a Prob. 1
10.	d	fs
11.	a	ē
	c̄	ē Prob. 2
12.	a	c̄s
13.	c̄s	cs
14.	cs	gs
	e	gs Prob. 3
15.	f̄	b
	b	d̄ Prob. 4
16.	b	ds
	ds	g Prob. 5
17.	ds	d̄s

The keys on this side, [i.e., the left hand column,] represent tuned notes, while those on the opposite side, [i.e., the right hand column,] represent notes which are to be tuned to those in the left column

1.	f	[f']
2.	f	c'
3.	f	a
4.	c'	c
5.	c	g
6.	c	e
7.	g	d'
8.	g	b
9.	d'	d
	d	a Test 1
10.	d	f#
11.	a	e'
	c'	e' Test 2
12.	a	c#'
13.	c#'	c#
14.	c#	g#
	e	g# Test 3
15.	f'	bb
	bb	d' Test 4
16.	bb	d#
	d#	g Test 5
17.	d#	d#'

[f] Chormessiger oder rechter Thon / nach deme sich das Instrument leiden wil / darein wird f rein eingezogen.

[f is the] reference or correct pitch according to which the instrument is to be tuned. The f' must be tuned to it directly.

Proba.

Wenn die vorhergehende Concordanten vnnd Quinten, nach vorschriebener Art recht eingezogen seyn / so muessen diese fuenff Proben auch recht seyn. Als wo in der 1. Proba die Quinta, d gegen dem gestimpten a nicht recht schwebet / oder etwas falsch stehet / So musz den vorigen Concordanten allen (weil sie entweder in den Quinten zu rein oder zu falsch gemacht seyn) nachgeholffen werden / bisz das d vnd a auch seine rechte schwebung erlangt. Wann dann diese Proba also justificiret ist / So ist kuehnlich mit den folgenden fort zufahren / vnd sich druff zuvorlassen.

Test

When the preceding consonances and fifths are drawn in according to the prescribed manner, the five tests will prove to be true. If, however, at the first test, the d does not undulate properly against the tuned a, or appears otherwise false, (because the component fifths exhibit too high a degree of purity or impurity), all the previous fifths must be readjusted until the d and a are properly tempered. If, [on the other hand,] the test proves valid, one may proceed boldly with the succeeding [steps] and be confident of the result.

Allhier aber / wenn man zum 15. mal stimmen wil / ist in acht zu nehmen / dasz alsdenn die Quinten vom vnterm Clave gegen dem oebersten / vff andere weise rueckwarts eingezogen werden. Als wenn der vnterste Clavis erstlich gar reine in die Quinten eintritt / so musz er ferner hochschwebend gebracht oder gestimmet werden: Jnmassen davon in voriger Tabell bericht geschehen.[16]

At the fifteenth tuning step, it is important to observe that from this [point] onward, the fifths must be drawn in, so that the lower note undulates with the upper on the opposite side of pure intonation. After the lower note enters the fifth true, it must be tempered somewhat sharp, as was reported in the previous outline. [Translation by the present author]

Realization and Analysis of the First Method

Praetorius' first method of tuning requires the

octaves and major thirds to be pure (_i.e._, in just intonation) and the fifths to be tempered. The tempered fifth is
equal to the meantone fifth as established quantitatively by
Calvisius. Since the just fifth (3/2) exhibits a savart value of 176.0913, the tempered fifth which is a just fifth
(3/2) diminished by one-fourth comma ($\sqrt[4]{81}$ / $\sqrt[4]{80}$ or 1.3488
savarts) equals 174.7425 savarts.

Appendix V, 1 gives a notational representation of
the various steps and tests which Praetorius prescribes as
the proper order of tuning by the first method. He uses five
octaves, seven fifths, and five thirds to establish the compass.

The tuning course establishes the following notes as
the compass of the bearing according to Praetorius:

c   c♯   d   d♯   e   f   f♯   g   g♯
a   b♭   b   c'   c♯'   d'   d♯'   e'   f'

In order to be able to present the entire scale in
a quantitative form useful for purposes of comparison with
other model forms of the meantone temperament, a savart value must be developed for each note of the bearing which will
relate that note to the note of origin by revealing its intervallic relationship to _f_. By adopting 301.03 savarts as
the interval of the pure octave, 96.91, as the interval of
the pure third, and 174.7425, as the interval of the tempered
fifth, a step-by-step pursuit of the tuning course develops

the savart values for each of the notes of the tuning compass and relates them to f. See Table 125.

A summary of the savart values as shown in Table 126
may prove helpful in visualizing the disposition of the notes
of the octave according to Praetorius' temperament; the initial note f exhibits a value of 0.0 as the point of origin.

It should be observed that although Praetorius claims
that his tuning compass reaches from B♭ to D♯, it actually
comprises the range from E♭ to G♯, thus:

```
                ┌─────────────────────────────────────┐
                │  Compass Indicated by Praetorius     │
  G♭ D♭ A♭ E♭ B♭ F  C  G  D  A  E  B  F♯ C♯ G♯ D♯ A♯
                │      Actual Compass Achieved         │
                └─────────────────────────────────────┘
```

Proof for this contention lies in the fact that Praetorius tunes the purported d♯ (actually e♭) as a fifth below
b♭ rather than as a fifth above g♯. Accordingly, the compass
exhibits two flats and three sharps rather than one flat and
four sharps as a cursory inspection of Praetorius' tuning
method would lead one to believe.

The "wolf" fifth occurs at the extremes of the compass, g♯ / e♭ (actually notated as a diminished sixth); the
interval exceeds the tempered fifth by the great or enharmonic diesis. In fact, all intervals involving a false spelling exhibit the great diesis as an imperfection by augmentation or diminution:

TABLE 125

DERIVATION OF SAVART VALUES FOR THE TUNING COMPASS,
FIRST METHOD

(1) Tuning Course	(2) Note to be Tuned	(3) Reference Note	(4) Interval	(5) Savart Value of Note in Column (3)[a]	(6) Savart Value of Interval in Column (4)[b]	(7) Resultant Savart Value of Note in Column (2) as Related to f[c]
Origin	f	Chorton	Pure Unison	......	......	0.0000
Step 1	f'	f	Pure Octave	0.0000	+301.0300	+301.0300
Step 2	c'	f	Tempered Fifth	0.0000	+174.7425	+174.7425
Step 3	a	f	Pure Third	0.0000	+ 96.9100	+ 96.9100
Step 4	c	c'	Pure Octave	+174.7425	-301.0300	-126.2875
Step 5	g	c	Tempered Fifth	-126.2875	+174.7425	+ 48.4550
Step 6	e	c	Pure Third	-126.2875	+ 96.9100	- 29.3775
Step 7	d'	g	Tempered Fifth	+ 48.4550	+174.7425	+223.1975

Continued on following page

[a]Plus (+) values represent notes lying above the point of origin, while minus (-) values represent those lying below.

[b]Plus (+) values represent an interval lying above the reference note; minus (-) values, one lying below.

[c]Algebraic sum of columns (5) and (6) equals column (7).

TABLE 125--Continued

(1) Tuning Course	(2) Note to be Tuned	(3) Reference Note	(4) Interval	(5) Savart Value of Note in Column (3)	(6) Savart Value of Interval in Column (4)	(7) Resultant Savart Value of Note in Column (2) as Related to f
Step 8	b	g	Pure Third	+ 48.4550	+ 96.9100	+145.3650
Step 9	d	d'	Pure Octave	+223.1975	-301.0300	- 77.8325
Step 10	f#	d	Pure Third	- 77.8325	+ 96.9100	+ 19.0775
Step 11	e'	a	Tempered Fifth	+ 96.9100	+174.7425	+271.6525
Step 12	c#'	a	Pure Third	+ 96.9100	+ 96.9100	+193.8200
Step 13	c#	c#'	Pure Octave	+193.8200	-301.0300	-107.2100
Step 14	g#	c#	Tempered Fifth	-107.2100	+174.7425	+ 67.5325
Step 15	bb	f'	Tempered Fifth	+301.0300	-174.7425	+126.2875
Step 16	d#	bb	Tempered Fifth	+126.2875	-174.7425	- 48.4550
Step 17	d#'	d#	Pure Octave	- 48.4550	+301.0300	+252.5750

TABLE 126

SUMMARY OF SAVART AND EQUIVALENT CENTS
VALUES FOR THE NOTES OF THE OCTAVE
AS DERIVED BY THE FIRST METHOD

Note	Savart Value[a]	Equivalent Cents Value
f	0.0000	0.0000
f♯	19.0775	76.0495
g	48.4550	193.1570
g♯	67.5325	269.2065
a	96.9100	386.3140
b♭	126.2875	503.4215
b	145.3650	579.4710
c'	174.7425	696.5785
c♯'	193.8200	772.6280
d'	223.1975	859.7355
e♭'[b]	252.5750	1006.8430
e'	271.6525	1082.8925
f'	301.0300	1200.0000

[a] The values reflect the interval ratio of the various notes to the point of origin, f.

[b] Although Praetorius designates this note as d♯, he tunes it as an e♭, i.e., a tempered fifth below b♭.

1. Fifths: g♯-e♭ (1)

2. Major Thirds: c♯-f; f♯-b♭; b-e♭; g♯-c (4)

3. Minor Thirds: f-g♯; e♭-f♯; b♭-c♯ (3)

4. Major Seconds: c♯-e♭; g♯-b♭ (2)

Praetorius' temperament as developed from his first

method of tuning agrees perfectly with Aron's Meantone

Temperament (1/4 comma) as developed and presented by Barbour.[17] The apparent difference between Aron's fourth note
(310 cents) and Praetorius' fourth note (269 cents) can be
resolved by shifting Aron's compass down a tempered fifth
(i.e., 697 cents) or Praetorius' up a similar amount, in order to achieve parallel notes and values.

The Tuning Course: Second Method

The second method divides the tuning course into two
phases; the first phase deals with the "white" keys, the second, with the "black." Praetorius' directions require nineteen tuning steps and four tests to complete the compass.
Following is the cursive account accompanied by a parallel
translation:

	Die 2. Art			The Second Method		
1.	f	f̄	Allhier musz	1.	f	f'	Here the same
2.	f	c̄	mit den Quin- ten vnd Oc-	2.	f	c'	conditions with respect to the
3.	c̄	ḡ	taven eben	3.	c'	g'	fifths and oc-
4.	ḡ	g	disz / was	4.	g'	g	taves must, to be sure, be ob-
5.	g	d̄	im vorigen erinnertt al-	5.	g	d'	served as in
6.	d̄	ā	lerdings auch in acht ge-	6.	d'	a'	the preceding.
Prob. 1	f̄	ā	nommen wer- den.	Test 1	f'	a'	
7.	ā	a		7.	a'	a	
8.	a	ē	Diese tertia	8.	a	e'	The major third,
9.	ē	h̄	major f a (wie auch al-	9.	e'	h'	f'-a', (as also all major
Prob. 2	h̄	ḡ	le andere per-	Test 2	b'	g'	thirds) must be
Prob. 3	ē	c̄	fectae terti- ae) oder Ter- tia majores	Test 3	e'	c'	quite pure. It is much easier to hear, dif-

musz gar rein seyn: Es kan   ferentiate, and draw in the
aber die Tertia viel besser   third accurately by using the

in der Decima, Als nemblich
f a̅ gehoeret vnd vnterschie-
den / auch gar rein eingezogen werden; Aber doch also / dasz die Quinta a̅ d̅
nicht zu sehr falsch / oder
zu rein werde.

interval of a tenth, as f̲-a̲';
but only in such a way, that
the fifth, a̲'-d̲', does not appear either too pure or too
impure.

Diese beyde Proben, [i.e.,
Probe 2 und 3,] muessen e-
ben also / wie jetzt vom f̅
a̅ angedeutet worden / vorge-
nommen werden.

The two tests, [i.e., tests
2 and 3] must now be undertak-
en precisely as indicated for
f̲'-a̲'.

Wann nun diese obgesetzte
Claves (dann die Octaven,
so wol die Tertiae perfectae
muessen gar perfect vnd
rein / vnd die Quarten noch
mehr als rein eingezogen vnd
gestimmet seyn; Die Quinten
aber / wie oben angedeutet /
etwas schweben) Alsdann
werden hernach nur die Octaven auff= vnd niederwerts
im gantzen Clavir, ohne die
Semitonia, gegen vnd nach
einander rein fortgestim-
met.

When the above prescribed
keys [are tuned,] (wherein
the octaves as well as the
major thirds are perfect and
pure, the fourths drawn in
ɔeyond their true intonation,
[i.e., wide,] and the fifths
tempered as indicated, [i.e.,
narrow,] then all the rest
of the "white" notes both upward and downward [from the
bearing] are tuned pure by
means of octave intervals.

Was aber die Semitonia be-
langen thut / musz man erstlich das b zu dem f̅ / (welches allbereit rein ist)
schwebend / wie alle andere
Quinten einziehen / vnd das
b alsdenn gegen der Tertia
majore d̅ auch probieren vnd
rein einziehen / welches b /
wie hiebevor gesagt / gegen
der Decima d̅ besser vernom-
men werden kan; Darauff die
Octav b b̅ vnd B b: Vnd die
Quint ds b / doch schwebend.
Alsdann musz das ds gegen
der Decima g̅ probieret /
vnd gar rein nachgezogen
werden: Folgends die Oc-
tava d̅s vnd [ds]: Diese drey
Claves aber c̅s f̅s g̅s sollen

As far as the semitones are
concerned, one must first relate b♭ as a tempered interval to f̲' (which has already
been tuned true) in the same
manner as the other fifths.
Thereupon, the b♭ must be
tested against its major
third, d̲' and appear pure. As
was pointed out before, the
b♭ can be more readily discerned when tested against
the tenth, d̲''. Then follow
the octaves, b♭-b♭' and B♭-
b♭, and the fifth, d♯-b♭, albeit, tempered. The d♯ must
then be tested against the
tenth, g̲' and appear pure.
Following this, the octave
d♯'-d♯ [must be drawn into

gegen jhren Tertien als a d̄ e̅ gar rein einstimmen: Wiewol solches gegen jhren Decimis (wie jetzt offt gedacht) allezeit eigendlicher zu vernehmen: Vnd hernach jhre Octaven vollends auch einzuziehen seyn.[18]

tune]. The three keys, c#', f#', and g#', however, should be tuned pure to their underlying thirds, a, d', and e'. As mentioned a number of times, the third relationship is more readily discerned through the use of tenths. After that, the corresponding octaves can be drawn in pure. [Translation by the present author]

Realization and Analysis of

the Second Method

The second method of tuning, although following a different course from the first, achieves precisely the same results and exhibits identical aberrations. The same premises prevail; namely, that the octaves and major thirds must be tuned pure, while the fifths must be tempered narrow by one-fourth comma. Accordingly, they should exhibit a savart value of 174.7425.

In the second method Praetorius runs the tuning course in two phases. In the first phase, only the "white" notes are tuned and exclusively by means of octaves and fifths, the major thirds being employed only to check the progress of the tuning. In the second phase, only the "black" notes are tuned, and these chiefly as pure major thirds to the already established "white" notes. Only occasionally is the octave or fifth used for this purpose.

Appendix V, 2 gives a notational representation of the various steps and tests which Praetorius prescribes as the proper order of tuning. He uses nine octaves, eight fifths, and three thirds to establish the bearing.

The entire tuning course establishes the following notes as the compass of the bearing according to Praetorius:

B♭   c♯   d♯   f   f♯   g   g♯   a   b♭   c'

c♯'   d'   e'   f'   f♯'   g'   g♯'   a'   b♭'   b'

Quantitative savart values for each of the notes tuned can be developed similarly as in the first method (exhibited in Table 125). The note f must be considered the point of origin, 301.03 savarts, the interval of the pure octave, 96.91 savarts, the interval of the pure third, and 174.7425 savarts, the interval of the tempered fifth. A summary of the savart values for the notes of the octave reveal an intervallic disposition in precise accord with that of the first method. See Table 126.

Although Praetorius leaves the impression that his tuning compass ranges from B♭ to D♯, it actually reaches from E♭ to G♯ and is useful for keys not exceeding two flats or three sharps. Since his D♯ is derived as a fifth below B♭ it gives a value equal to E♭, and must be so considered in making any further deductions. All deductions and implications enumerated for the first method apply to the second method as well, and need not be repeated here.

The Tuning Course: Third Method

The third method is a single course which requires seventeen tuning steps and is checked by nine tests. The following cursive account by Praetorius is accompanied by a

parallel translation:

	Die 3. Art.			The Third Method

Etliche haben im c̄ anzu-
stimmen / vnd sagen disz sey
Musicalisch / vnd ex Fundamento. Dann gleich wie die
Instrumenta vnd Orgeln vom
C (nach dessen Art fuessen
Thon sie denn genennet werden) mehrentheils anfangen /
vnnd denselben Clavem pro
fundamento, nicht alleine
vnten / besondern auch oben
haben / also sey es auch am
besten vnd fueglichsten in
der mitten von mehrgedach-
tem Clave den anfang zu
machen / deren Ordnung a-
ber ist also:

Some begin tuning at c̲',
and maintain that this is musical and scientific. For
since most instruments and organs begin at C̲, (deriving
their pitch designation there-
from,) and exhibit this fundamental key not only at the
lower [limit of the compass,]
but also at the upper, it is
best and most appropriate to
begin [tuning] in the middle
of the compass at this same
key. The order [of the tuning steps] is as follows:

1.	c̄	c		1.	c̲'	c̲	
2.	c	g		2.	c̲	g̲	
3.	c	e		3.	c̲	e̲	
4.	g	d̄		4.	g̲	d̲'	
5.	g	h		5.	g̲	b̲	
	e	h	1. Prob.		e̲	b̲	1st Test
6.	e	ē		6.	e̲	e̲'	
	c	ē	2. Prob.		c̲	e̲'	2nd Test
7.	d̄	d		7.	d̲'	d̲	
8.	d	a		8.	d̲	a̲	
	ē	a	3. Prob.		e̲'	a̲	3rd Test
9.	d̄	f̄s		9.	d̲'	f̲#'	
	h	f̄s	4. Prob.		b̲	f̲#'	4th Test
10.	f̄s	fs		10.	f̲#'	f̲#	
11.	fs	c̄s		11.	f̲#	c̲#'	
	a	c̄s	5. Prob.		a̲	c̲#'	5th Test
12.	c̄s	cs		12.	c̲#'	c̲#	

13.	cs	gs		13.	c♯	g♯	
	e	gs	6. Prob.		e	g♯	6th Test
14.	c̄	f		14.	c'	f	
	a	f	7. Prob.		a	f	7th Test
15.	f	f̄		15.	f	f'	
16.	f̄	b		16.	f'	b♭	
	d̄	b	8. Prob.		d'	b♭	8th Test
17.	b	ds		17.	b♭	d♯	
	g	ds	9. Prob.		g	d♯	9th Test

Zu mercken:
Vom anfange bisz vff Numero 14. werden die Quinten niedrig schwebend oder sinkkend / Nachmals aber muessen dieselben hochschwebend gestimmet werden / denn alsdenn musz sich der vnterste Clavis nach dem obersten richten.[19]

[Please] observe:
From the beginning until Number 14, the fifths are tempered flat; after that they must be tempered sharp, because from this point the lower key must be adjusted to the upper. [Translation by the present author]

Realization and Analysis of the Third Method

The third method of tuning differs from the previous methods in that it begins at a different point of origin (i.e., c' instead of the previous f) and employs six octaves, eight fifths, and three thirds to establish the bearing. The ultimate outcome achieves identical results and exhibits the same aberrations as the first and second methods. The same premises prevail; namely, that the octaves and thirds must be tuned pure, while the fifths must be tempered narrow by one-fourth comma, receiving thereby a savart value of exactly 174.7425. The resultant temperament is precisely that of Aron's meantone temperament as presented by Barbour.[20]

In the third method the tuning steps pursue one continuous course. Appendix V, 3 gives a notational representation of the various steps and tests which Praetorius prescribes as the proper order for tuning. The entire tuning
course establishes eighteen notes as the bearing according
to Praetorius:

c   c#   d   d#   e   f   f#   g   g#

a   bb   b   c'   c#'   d'   e'   f'   f#'

Quantitative savart values for each of the notes
tuned can be developed exactly as for the first method (exhibited in Table 125). However, the note c' rather than f
must be considered as the point of origin. As before, the
octaves must be assigned a savart value of 301.03, the thirds,
96.91, and the tempered fifths, 174.7425. A summary of the
savart values for all notes of the octave is shown in Table
127, where the initial note c is assigned a value of 0.0 as
a convenient point of origin.

As in the first and second methods, the tuning compass of the third method actually ranges from Eb to G# rather than from Bb to D# as a cursory inspection of the tuning
course would indicate. As such it is useful for keys not
exceeding two flats or three sharps. As in the previous
methods, the D# is derived as a fifth below Bb rather than
as a fifth above G#, and becomes, for this reason, a legitimate Eb.

All deductions and implications enumerated for the

TABLE 127

SUMMARY OF SAVART AND EQUIVALENT CENTS
VALUES FOR THE NOTES OF THE OCTAVE
AS DERIVED BY THE THIRD METHOD

Note	Savart Value[a]	Equivalent Cents Value
c	0.0000	0.0000
c♯	19.0775	76.0495
d	48.4550	193.1570
e♭ [b]	77.8325	310.2645
e	96.9100	386.3140
f	126.2875	503.4215
f♯	145.3650	579.4710
g	174.7425	696.5785
g♯	193.8200	772.6280
a	223.1975	889.7355
b♭	252.5750	1006.8430
b	271.6525	1082.8925
c'	301.0300	1200.0000

[a]The values reflect the intervals of the various
notes to the point of origin, c.

[b]Praetorius uses the designation, d♯, to identify
this note; however, he tunes it as an e♭, i.e., a tempered
fifth below b♭.

first method apply to the third method as well, and need not

be repeated, except that no transposition is necessary, in

order to compare the Praetorius temperament with Aron's mean-

tone as presented by Barbour.[21] They agree perfectly in all

respects, since both begin the tuning course at the same

point of origin.

Praetorius' Criticism and Adjustment

of the Temperament

Following his presentation for the second method of
tuning, Praetorius describes certain customs with respect to
an arbitrary adjustment of the temperament which seem to have
been undertaken by his forebears to overcome certain problems
encountered in connection with the "wolf." It is apparent
that the note $G\sharp$ as derived by a strict application of the
customary meantone temperament produced intolerable imperfections in the construction of certain intervals which lay outside the normal tuning compass. It is also apparent from his
discussion that certain key transpositions demanded a greater
compass than the meantone octave would permit without the annoyance of duplicate keys for certain notes. The theoretical
compass which arose out of the methods of tuning used by
Praetorius and his contemporaries reached from $E\flat$ to $G\sharp$ as
previously demonstrated. Such a compass presents acceptable
notes for keys not exceeding two flats or three sharps. If,
however, a transposition required an $A\flat$ rather than a $G\sharp$,
the traditional "wolf" (equal to the great diesis) would be
very much in evidence. Such a transposition obviously required a compass at least from $A\flat$ to $C\sharp$, which would present
acceptable values for keys not exceeding three flats or two
sharps.

Adjustment of the G-sharp

Since a compass from $A\flat$ to $G\sharp$ appeared compelling, and since there had already developed a great desire to avoid split or duplicate keys, the only solution to the problem was to split the difference between G♯ and A♭ (i.e., to equalize the same), in order to realize a compromise value at this point which would exhibit a tolerable discrepancy in both directions rather than an intolerable concentration in one. It represents an attempt, arbitrary to be sure, to "equalize" the temperament at this point. The following abstract will serve to trace Praetorius' argument with respect to the meantone value of G♯ and his proposals for arbitrary adjustment of the same:[22]

The fifths c♯-g♯ and f♯-c♯: may be neither too impure nor too pure. They should not be permitted to undulate as much as other fifths, so that if one is required to play in a remote key, or if chromatic notes occur, the dissonance will not be intolerable

Our forefathers called the interval f-g♯, the "wolf", because these two notes constitute a very false minor third (when at times Mode II is transposed to f [hence, requiring three flats] or otherwise *musica ficta* or a chromatic progression is used)

In order to overcome this difficulty our forefathers adjusted the other notes and made the major third e-g♯ not pure but somewhat augmented. This was effected by adjusting the g♯ somewhat higher and nearer to the a; this procedure widened the interval between f and g♯, and even though no real effective minor third was achieved, it could serve in case of need

Although Praetorius does not give an exact value for such an adjustment, it might prove provocative and help to visualize the resultant disposition if the g♯ were elevated so as to err one-fourth comma beyond its just value rather

than below it when associated with its underlying c♯. Such
an adjustment would give the note g♯ a savart value of
196.5176 instead of 193.82 to represent its ratio to c, the
point of origin.[23] The results of an examination of the intervals which could be associated with such an adjusted g♯
are shown in Table 128, which also exhibits the degree of
aberration from just intonation which such intervals would
develop.

By such adjustment of the g♯, (i.e., by elevating it
one-fourth comma above a just fifth over c♯), all intervals
that might be associated with it become aurally tolerable,
not any approaching the discrepancy of the great diesis, although about half of them still exceed the discrepancy of
the syntonic comma. Furthermore, the compromise exacts its
toll by removing all pure intervals from the possible combinations.

Inadequacy of the Compass

An additional paragraph by Praetorius sheds some
light on his dissatisfaction with the limitations of the
compass he had developed in his three methods of tuning.[24]
It is evident that he desires a much more comprehensive compass, particularly on the sharp side, for purposes of transposition, for musica ficta, and for chromatic progressions.
He decries the limitations imposed upon the composer, or more
particularly, upon the performer by the limitations of the

TABLE 128

SAVART VALUES OF THE INTERVALS ASSOCIATED WITH AN
ADJUSTED G#↑ EXCEEDING THE JUST VALUE BY
ONE-FOURTH COMMA

(1) Intervals Using Adjusted G#↑ as a Component[a]	(2) Quality of Interval	(3) Savart Value of Interval[b]	(4) Savart Value of Equivalent Just Interval	(5) Quantitative Aberration from Just Interval[c]	(6) Qualitative Evaluation of the Aberration[d]
c#↑ - g#↑/ab	Perfect Fifth	177.4401	176.0913 (3/2)	+1.3488	+1/4K
eb - g#↑/ab	Perfect Fourth	118.6851	124.9387 (4/3)	-6.2536	-(GD-3/4K)
e| - g#↑/ab	Major Third	99.6076	96.9100 (5/4)	+2.6976	+1/2K
f| - g#↑/ab	Minor Third	70.2301	79.1813 (6/5)	-8.9512	-(GD-1/4K)
f#↑ - g#↑/ab	Major Second	51.1526	48.4550 $\left(\frac{9\times10}{8\times9}\right)$	+2.6976	+1/2K
g - g#↑/ab	Minor Second	21.7751	28.0287 (16/15)	-6.2536	-(GD-3/4K)

Continued on following page

[a] The g#↑/ab lies one-fourth syntonic comma above the just fifth, c#↑-g#↑.

[b] Derived from values exhibited in Table 127 with the G#↑ adjusted to a savart value of 196.5176.

[c] Column (3) minus column (4) equals column (5).

[d] GD represents the great or enharmonic diesis (10.3 savarts); K represents the syntonic comma (5.3952 savarts).

TABLE 128--Continued

(1) Intervals Using Adjusted G#/ab as a Component	(2) Quality of Interval	(3) Savart Value of Interval	(4) Savart Value of Equivalent Just Interval	(5) Quantitative Aberration from Just Interval	(6) Qualitative Evaluation of the Aberration
g#/ab - a	Minor Second	26.6799	28.0287 (16/15)	-1.3488	-1/4K
g#/ab - bb	Major Second	56.0574	48.4550 $\left\{\sqrt{\frac{9 \times 10}{8 \times 9}}\right\}$	+7.6024	+(GD-1/2K)
g#/ab - b	Minor Third	75.1349	79.1813 (6/5)	-4.0464	-3/4K
g#/ab - c'	Major Third	104.5124	96.9100 (5/4)	+7.6024	+(GD-1/2K)
g#/ab - c#'	Perfect Fourth	123.5899	124.9387 (4/3)	-1.3488	-1/4K
g#/ab - eb'	Perfect Fifth	182.3449	176.0913 (3/2)	+6.2536	+(GD-3/4K)

meantone temperament. Praetorius, who so carefully developed
and expounded practical methods for realizing a meantone temperament in tuning keyboard instruments, already by 1619
raised objections to the meantone temperament which, in time
led to its abandonment in favor of a full compromise, the
equal temperament. He does not, however, propose equalization of all aberrations; he resorts to the usual solutions
of the time by proposing arbitrary equalization of the worst
aberrations or by providing double keys in order to enlarge
the compass.

He says, in effect, that the reason why f#, g#, and
c# must be adjusted is, among other things, the formation of
cadences which may occur on such semitones. Without adjustment, he maintains, no la-fa or mi-fa effect can be achieved
at f - f#, g - g#, or c - c# as is possible at a - bb or at
d - eb. The reason lies in the fact that in the layout of
the temperament bb and eb pre-empt a# and d#. However, if
the black keys are divided and appear in duplicate, one can
overcome the problem

Praetorius' reasoning seems, on the surface, to be
somewhat unclear or obscure. In the present author's opinion, Praetorius is pointing up the inadequacy of the meantone f#, g#, and c# when these notes serve as tonics in the
formation of either or both harmonic and melodic cadences.
His reference to the relatively unsatisfactory la-fa and
mi-fa effects to be obtained on the notes f#, g#, and c# is
probably a colloquial way of expressing certain melodic and
harmonic functions which are associated with various cadences
on these notes. He says that the cadences f - f#, g - g#,

and c - c# do not present as acceptable la-fa or mi-fa effects as do the cadences a - bb and d - d# [actually tuned
as eb; hence d - eb] since, in the former cadences the necessary a# and d# are not available since the normal 12-note
meantone compass tunes these two notes as bb and eb.

If one interprets Praetorius' la-fa effect to denote
a plagal cadence (i.e., subdominant to tonic, in the modern
sense), then such cadence, when transposed to close on f#,
g#, or c# involves the aberrant d# and a# in a critical way.
Table 129 presents the conditions that are likely to occur
and isolates the aberrant notes which would tend to despoil
the aural effect.

TABLE 129

ABERRANT NOTES INVOLVED IN PLAGAL CADENCES ON
F#, G#, and C# IN A MEANTONE TEMPERAMENT

Transposed Cadence Point	Subdominant Function	Tonic Function	Aberrant Notes
f#	b - d# - f#	f# - a# - c#	d#, a#
g#	c# - e# - g#	g# - b# - d#	e#, b#, d#
c#	f# - a# - c#	c# - e# - g#	a#, e#
bb	eb - g - bb	bb - d - f	. . . . . .
eb	ab - c - eb	eb - g - bb	ab

It will be observed from the table that in the first
three cadences the aural effect is considerably imperfected

not only by the d♯ and a♯ as Praetorius indicates, but also by e♯ and b♯. The last two cadences are almost entirely free of such imperfect effects; in any case, they exhibit far less aberration than do the first three.

If one interprets the mi-fa effect to denote a melodic movement from the leading tone to the tonic, then the cadences enumerated by Praetorius will exhibit an aberrant note in either the penultimate or ultimate note of the cadence depending upon the actual transposition realized. His cadence f - f♯ will actually be either e♯ - f♯ or f - g♭, where e♯ and g♭ will be out of tune; the cadence g - g♯ will be fx - g♯ or g - a♭, where fx and a♭ will be out of tune; and the cadence c - c♯ is actually b♯ - c♯ or c - d♭, where b♯ and d♭ will be out of tune.

Harmonically considered as a progression from a dominant to a tonic function, the mi-fa effect exhibits similar imperfections as does the fa-la effect discussed above. Table 130 presents the likely conditions and isolates the imperfect notes.

The table shows that in the first three cadences the aural effect is strongly imperfected by the d♯ and a♯, as Praetorius points out, and by e♯, fx, and b♯ as well. The last two cadences can be realized without imperfections.

A summary of these cadences demands, then, a comprehensive supply of semitones, so that the keyboard may exhibit

TABLE 130

ABERRANT NOTES INVOLVED IN AUTHENTIC CADENCES ON
F#, G#, AND C# IN A MEANTONE TEMPERAMENT

Transposed Cadence Point	Dominant Function	Tonic Function	Aberrant Notes
f#	c# – e# – g#	f# – a# – c#	e#, a#
g#	d# – fx – a#	g# – b# – d#	d#, fx, a#, b#
c#	g# – b# – d#	c# – e# – g#	b#, d#, e#
bb	f – a – c	bb – d – f	. . . . .
eb	bb – d – f	eb – g – bb	. . . . .

at least eight sharps plus two flats, which the meantone
temperament, when relying upon twelve keys to the octave is
woefully inadequate to supply.

The Early Baroque Keyboards

Inasmuch as the efforts to overcome the limitations
of the meantone temperament had an influential effect upon
the disposition and layout of the manual and pedal claviers,
it would seem worthwhile to explore the various dispositions
of the keyboards employed by the early baroque organbuilders.
Praetorius is one of the very few writers of the time who,
in some instances, gives clear information not only as to the
layout of the keyboards in general but also of the several
octave segments contained within them.

From among the instruments presented in his catalog

of dispositions[25] and from a surviving instrument of the
time, Praetorius clearly delineates the manual claviers of
five noteworthy instruments:

1. The Bueckeburg [Stadtkirche] instrument of
1615 by E. Compenius[26]

2. The Dresden, Schlosskirche instrument of 1614
by G. Fritzsche[27]

3. The Schoeningen, Schlosskapelle instrument of
c. 1616 by G. Fritzsche[28]

4. The Bayreuth instrument of c. 1618 by G.
Fritzsche[29]

5. The Frederiksborg, Schloss instrument of c.
1612 by E. Compenius[30]

Six instruments from the same sources reveal the layout of their pedal claviers; these are the same as those mentioned above plus the Riddagshausen, Kloster instrument of
c. 1610 by H. Compenius.[31]

In a number of other instances Praetorius gives the
extreme limits of the compass, but the accompanying information is insufficient to draw useful conclusions from it concerning the disposition of the layout.

General Layout of the Claviers

Of the examples clearly defined by Praetorius, the
manual keyboards engage all or parts of five octaves (i.e.,
the great, small, one-line, two-line, and three-line octaves),

while the pedal keyboards involve elements of three octaves
(i.e., the great, small, and one-line octaves). The concept
operating at the time seems to divide the manual claviers
into three segments, each of which exhibits consistent characteristics. The segments comprise the following:

1. The bass octave, whose extremes are defined
by notes C and B, but whose content varies from eight
to twelve notes

2. The internal octaves, whose extremes are defined by notes c and b'', and which cover a range of
three octaves, each of which contains from twelve to
fourteen notes

3. The treble octave, whose initial note is
c''', whose final note varies from instance to instance, and whose range exhibits anywhere from one to
six notes

The pedal claviers reflect the concept but differ in
certain respects:

1. The bass octave reaches from note C to B,
but contains only from eight to eleven notes

2. The internal octave (one only) reaches from
note c to b and contains from twelve to fourteen notes

3. The treble octave begins at note c' and appears only in part, exhibiting either three or four
notes

Variant Forms of the Bass Octave

From the examples cited, three different dispositions
of the bass octave in manual claviers can be identified:

    1. The 8-note Guidonian bass octave[32]

    2. The 10-note chromatic bass octave

    3. The 12-note chromatic-enharmonic bass octave

All of these forms are generally referred to in the
literature as _short_ or _broken_ octaves, but since these terms
are too inclusive, an attempt will be made here to assort
the concepts more accurately and definitively.

The Guidonian bass octave exhibits the contents and
limits set by the Guidonian hexachords. It contains no more
and no less notes than the required ones; namely, C, D, E, F,
G, A, B♭, and B. Of these, C, D, E, F, G, and A realize the
hexachordum naturelle; G, A, B, C, D, and E, the hexachordum
durum; and F, G, A, B♭, C, and D, the hexachordum molle. The
physical layout of these notes on manual keys consistently
follows the pattern shown on Plate CIII, 1, where the eight
keys are laid out as specified by Praetorius. The octave
contains seven diatonic and one chromatic note distributed
over five "white" and three "black" keys. The 8-note Guidonian bass octave appears in the manual claviers of Dresden,
Schlosskirche; Schoeningen, Schlosskapelle; and Frederiksborg, Schloss.

The 10-note chromatic bass octave resembles the 8-note
Guidonian, except that two additional "black" half-keys are

inserted to control the added notes $F\sharp\sharp$ and $G\sharp\sharp$, which give the octave a much more, albeit yet incomplete, chromatic character. The missing chromatic notes are $C\sharp\sharp$ and $E\flat$. In order, the octave contains the notes $\underline{C}$, $\underline{D}$, $\underline{E}$, $\underline{F}$, $\underline{F\sharp\sharp}$, $\underline{G}$, $\underline{G\sharp\sharp}$, $\underline{A}$, $\underline{B\flat}$, and $\underline{B}$, which are physically laid out on manual keys as shown on Plate CIII, 2. The octave contains seven diatonic and three chromatic notes distributed over five "white", three "black" keys, and two "black" half-keys. The 10-note chromatic bass octave appears in the manual claviers of <u>Bayreuth</u>.

The 12-note chromatic-enharmonic bass octave as realized by the early baroque builders resembles the modern standard octave with the exception that the $C\sharp\sharp$ is left out and a "black" half-key is added to control $A\flat$ instead. For the time, this represented a luxurious disposition of the bass octave and appears only on important or <u>de luxe</u> instruments. The addition of the $A\flat$ beside the $G\sharp\sharp$ lends a slight enharmonic character to the octave and serves to identify it from the other varieties listed above. In order, the octave contains the notes $\underline{C}$, $\underline{D}$, $\underline{D\sharp\sharp}$ (probably tuned as $E\flat$), $\underline{E}$, $\underline{F}$, $\underline{F\sharp\sharp}$, $\underline{G}$, $\underline{G\sharp\sharp}$, $\underline{A\flat}$, $\underline{A}$, $\underline{B\flat}$, and $\underline{B}$, and is physically laid out on manual keys as shown on Plate CIII, 3. The octave contains seven diatonic, four chromatic, and one enharmonic note distributed over seven "white", four "black" keys, and one "black" half-key. The 12-note chromatic-enharmonic bass octave appears on the manual claviers of <u>Bueckeburg</u>.

The bass octave of the pedal clavier displays in some

respects similar, but in others, divergent dispositions from those encountered in the manual claviers. From the examples defined by Praetorius, three forms can be identified:

1. The 8-note Guidonian bass octave

2. The 10-note chromatic bass octave

3. The 11-note chromatic bass octave

As in the case of the manual claviers, the 8-note Guidonian bass octave contains the notes C, D, E, F, G, A, Bb, and B physically laid out on the pedal clavier as shown on Plate CIII, 4. It is in all respects a reflection of the corresponding bass octave used for the manual claviers. The 8-note Guidonian bass octave appears on the pedal claviers of Dresden, Schlosskirche; Schoeningen, Schlosskapelle; and Frederiksborg, Schloss.

The 10-note chromatic bass octave again reflects the corresponding manual bass octave in all particulars. A physical layout for the same appears on Plate CIII, 5. Examples of this form are to be found in the pedal claviers of Bueckeburg and Riddagshausen, Kloster. It seems that the 10-note chromatic bass octave served as the norm for the time, the 8-note Guidonian representing a sparse disposition, and the 11-note chromatic, a luxurious one.

The 11-note chromatic bass octave represents the most comprehensive form delineated by Praetorius for pedal claviers. It resembles the standard modern form of the octave except that the C♯ is omitted. It contains, therefore, the notes $\underline{C}$, $\underline{D}$, $\underline{D}\sharp$ (probably tuned as $\underline{E}\flat$), $\underline{E}$, $\underline{F}$, $\underline{F}\sharp$, $\underline{G}$, $\underline{G}\sharp$, $\underline{A}$, $\underline{B}\flat$, and $\underline{B}$ physically laid out on the pedal clavier as shown on Plate CIII, 6. The octave contains seven diatonic and four chromatic notes distributed over seven "white", and four "black" keys. The 11-note chromatic bass octave appears in the pedal clavier of Bayreuth.

Variant Forms of the Internal Octaves

In all cases cited by Praetorius, the form developed for the small octave is consistently carried through the remaining internal octaves of the claviers; in almost all instances as well, the internal octaves of the manual claviers are faithfully reflected in the corresponding octaves of the pedal clavier in the same instrument.[33] This condition makes it possible to consider both manual and pedal realizations together. Three forms of the internal octaves are identifiable from Praetorius' descriptions:

1. The 12-note chromatic internal octave

2. The 13-note chromatic-enharmonic internal octave

3. The 14-note chromatic-enharmonic internal octave

The 12-note chromatic internal octave resembles the standard modern disposition in every respect. It contains the notes $\underline{c}$, $\underline{c}\sharp$, $\underline{d}$, $\underline{d}\sharp$ (probably tuned as $\underline{e}\flat$), $\underline{e}$, $\underline{f}$, $\underline{f}\sharp$, $\underline{g}$, $\underline{g}\sharp$, $\underline{a}$, $\underline{b}\flat$, and $\underline{b}$ and is laid out on the manual and pedal claviers as shown on Plate CIII, 7 and 8 respectively. It is quite reasonable to assume that in the usual manner of setting a meantone temperament, the d♯ was likely tuned as an e♭. The octave contains seven diatonic notes and five chromatic ones distributed over seven "white" and five "black" keys. The 12-note form constitutes the internal octave(s) for the pedal clavier of Riddagshausen, for which no manual disposition is given; for the pedal clavier of Bayreuth, for which the manual clavier exhibits a divergent form;[34] and for the manual and pedal claviers of Frederiksborg, Schloss.

The 13-note chromatic-enharmonic form for internal octaves resembles the standard modern form except that an additional "black" half-key appears between the keys d♯ and e in order to control a separate e♭ note. Through the appearance of d♯ and e♭ as separate keys the octave assumes a slightly enharmonic character which serves to distinguish it from other dispositions and appears in its appellation. Its complement of notes comprises c, c♯, d, d♯, e♭, e, f, f♯, g, g♯, a, b♭, and b and is similarly laid out on manual and pedal claviers as shown on Plate CIV, 1 and 2 respectively. The octave contains seven diatonic, five chromatic, and one enharmonic note distributed over seven "white", five "black" keys, and one "black" half-key. It finds application in the internal octaves of the manual and pedal claviers of Schoeningen, Schlosskapelle and in the manual clavier only of Bayreuth, where the pedal clavier shows a different layout.[35]

It should be observed that the normal tuning for the time, as described by Praetorius, reaches from $E\flat$ to $G\sharp$ (thus being eminently suitable for keys not exceeding two flats and three sharps), so that the additional note is really a $d\sharp$, which enlarges the compass to absorb successfully a four-sharp key as well, enriches the number of acceptable plagal and authentic cadences, and permits more transpositions than are possible on the 12-note chromatic octave.

The 14-note chromatic-enharmonic internal octave represents a very rich disposition for the time and seems to have been applied to large and important church instruments or to palace chapel instruments. In addition to the standard modern layout it exhibits an extra $e\flat$ (probably tuned as $d\sharp$) and an $a\flat$ beside the normal $g\sharp$, achieving thereby a moderately enharmonic character from which it derives its name. The octave contains the notes c, $c\sharp$, d, $d\sharp$, $e\flat$, e, f, $f\sharp$, g, $g\sharp$, $a\flat$, a, $b\flat$, and b and is physically laid out in manual and pedal keys as shown on Plate CIV, 3 and 4 respectively. The octave contains seven diatonic, five chromatic, and two enharmonic notes distributed over seven "white", five "black" keys, and two "black" half-keys. The disposition as outlined appears as internal octaves in the manual and pedal claviers of Bueckeburg, and likewise in Dresden, Schlosskirche. As in the previous instance, the addition of the seemingly enharmonic notes enriches the compass of the tuning to include $a\flat$

on the one side and $\underline{d}\sharp$ on the other side of the normal tuning compass of $\underline{E}\flat$ to $\underline{G}\sharp$, thereby making the instrument eminently suitable for keys not exceeding three flats or four
sharps. Additional by-products are the greater number of
plagal and authentic cadences available, and the larger number of transpositions possible for the player.

Variant Forms of the Treble Octave

In the early baroque instruments for which Praetorius
gives precise specifications, the treble octave of the manual claviers lies within the range of the three-line octave,
while that of the pedal claviers lies within the range of the
one-line octave. In both cases the treble octave is very incomplete, being represented by only a few notes. In the manual claviers, three or four dispositions are reasonably well
delineated by Praetorius:

1. The 1-note treble octave

2. The 3-note treble octave

3. The 5-note or 6-note treble octave

The 1-note treble octave for manual claviers represents the most economical disposition and appears only in one
defined example; namely, the Frederiksborg, Schloss, where
$\underline{c}$''' marks the upper limit.

The 3-note disposition seems to have been the norm
for manual claviers of the time and exhibits the notes and
keys for $\underline{c}$''', $\underline{c}\sharp$''', and $\underline{d}$''', laid out on the keyboard as

in standard modern practice. Such a treble octave is exemplified in the manual claviers of <u>Dresden</u>, <u>Schlosskirche</u>;
<u>Schoeningen</u>, <u>Schlosskapelle</u>; and possibly <u>Bayreuth</u>.[36]

The 5-note or 6-note treble octave represents a rich
layout for the time and exhibits the notes <u>c</u>''', <u>c</u>$\sharp$''', <u>d</u>''',
<u>e</u>''', and <u>f</u>''' or <u>c</u>''', <u>c</u>$\sharp$''', <u>d</u>''', <u>d</u>$\sharp$''', <u>e</u>''', and <u>f</u>''',
neither of which dispositions can be differentiated with cer-
tainty from Praetorius' over-meager delineations. He generally defines the upper limit of the compass by one note (as
<u>f</u>''') or by two notes (as <u>e</u>''', <u>f</u>'''), leaving the chromatic
notes and keys undefined. However, in corresponding pedal
claviers (in which he defines the treble octave more fully),
the <u>d</u>$\sharp$ is consistently omitted. In any case, the upper limit
in either of these dispositions is <u>f</u>'''. The octave contains,
therefore, four diatonic and one or two chromatic notes and
is probably laid out in manual keys as shown on Plate CIV, 5
and 6. Praetorius cites manual claviers of <u>Bueckeburg</u> and
<u>Bayreuth</u> as examples exhibiting 5-note or 6-note treble oc-
taves.

In pedal claviers Praetorius clearly defines two dispositions of the treble octave, of which the first represents
the more common application:

    1. The 3-note treble octave

    2. The 4-note treble octave

The 3-note treble octave of the pedal clavier consistently exhibits two diatonic and one chromatic note as <u>c</u>',

$c\sharp'$, and $\underline{d}'$ and is always distributed over two "white" and one "black" key in the standard modern manner. This disposition is exemplified by <u>Dresden, Schlosskirche</u>; <u>Schoeningen, Schlosskapelle</u>; and <u>Frederiksborg, Schloss</u>.

The 4-note treble octave of the pedal clavier exhibits three diatonic and one chromatic note as $\underline{c}'$, $\underline{c\sharp}'$, $\underline{d}'$, and $\underline{e}'$ and is distributed over three "white" and one "black" key as shown on Plate CIV, 7. Praetorius clearly delineates such treble octaves for the pedal claviers of <u>Bueckeburg</u>; <u>Riddagshausen, Kloster</u>; and <u>Bayreuth</u>.

Undefined Compasses

Lest the impression be given that all early baroque manual claviers comprise all or parts of five octaves, and the pedal claviers, three octaves, an inspection of undefined claviers becomes necessary. For these, Praetorius gives only the extreme limits, which will suggest a somewhat more restricted disposition in certain cases. From the catalog of dispositions the following overall but undefined compasses can be extracted:

1. <u>Luebeck, St. Peters</u>:[37] Manuals from $\underline{C}$ to $\underline{a}''$; Pedal from $\underline{C}$ together with $\underline{F\sharp}$ and $\underline{G\sharp}$ to $\underline{d}'$. Here the manual clavier engages all or parts of four octaves, and the pedal clavier, three octaves

2. <u>Luebeck, Lieben Frauen</u>:[38] Manuals from $\underline{C}$ to $\underline{a}''$ and $\underline{D}$ to $\underline{a}''$ (engaging four octaves); Pedal from

C to d' (engaging three octaves)

3. Luebeck, Thumb:[39] Manuals from F to a'' (engaging four octaves); Pedal from C to c' (engaging three octaves)

4. Magdeburg, Thumb:[40] Manuals from C to c''' (engaging five octaves); Pedal from g [more probably, C] to d' (engaging three octaves)[41]

5. Bernau in der Marckt:[42] Manuals from C to c''' (engaging five octaves); Pedal from C to d' (engaging three octaves)

6. Braunschweig, St. Blasius:[43] Manuals from C together with D#, F#, and G# to c''' together with g#'' and bb'' (engaging five octaves);[44] Pedal from C together with D#, F# and G# to d' together with c#' (engaging three octaves)

7. Model Disposition 4:[45] Manuals from C to c''' or d''' (engaging five octaves); Pedal from C to d' (engaging three octaves)

8. Sondershausen:[46] Manuals from C to f''' with double semitones at d# (engaging five octaves)

From the entire array of defined and undefined manual claviers it is evident that in the Early Baroque the compass reaches upward at least to a'', frequently to c''', occasionally to d''', and rarely to f'''. The pedal claviers reach at least to c', frequently to d', and occasionally to e'. In all instances, save two, the lower limit of both manual and pedal claviers is C; the exception being the Magdeburg, Thumb instrument where the manual claviers reach down only to F, and Luebeck, Lieben Frauen where D constitutes the lower limit of one manual clavier. Both of these examples may be looked upon as vestiges of earlier times.

Conclusions

Praetorius' minute directions for three methods of tuning keyboard instruments and his quotations from authoritative theoreticians to support his practical suggestions make it possible not only to reconstruct the tuning procedures but also to define the theoretical premises which underlie the setting of the temperament and the rather exact mathematical disposition of the same. He provides also sufficient information to realize with a considerable degree of certainty various dispositions of the manual and pedal claviers of the time. A few succinct statements sublimated from the discussions of the present chapter may be helpful to throw the compelling concepts of the time and in this regard into somewhat sharper relief:

1. Praetorius' entire discussion on the disposition of the temperament and tuning of the keyboard reveals a fine pedagogical mind, thoroughly versed in higher mathematics, and acquainted with the contemporary geometric axioms which he applies effectively to

support his various theses. His theoretical conclusions and propositions served the musical confrater-
nity for many years beyond his time and occur in re-
spectful references time and again in the writings of
his successors

2. His temperament is of the one-fourth comma
meantone variety. It agrees in all respects with the
model form of the same as proposed by Aron

3. Calvisius, whom Praetorius musters in support of his proposed temperament, derives the quantitative definition of his intervals by appropriate adjustments of the classical ratios of just intonation
through distribution of fractions of the syntonic comma. His meantone ratios are $8 \ / \ \sqrt[4]{5^5}$ for the diatonic
semitone, $\sqrt{5} \ / \ 2$ for the major second, $5 \ / \ 4$ for the
major third, $2 \ / \ \sqrt[4]{5}$ for the perfect fourth, $\sqrt[4]{5} \ / \ 1$
for the perfect fifth, and $8 \ / \ 5$ for the minor sixth

4. Praetorius' three methods of tuning a keyboard instrument achieve identical outcomes in all
respects; they differ from each other only in the layout of the tuning course and in the point of origin.
Two of them begin the course at _f_ and one at _c_'

5. His tuning methods are predicated upon pure
octaves, pure major thirds, and fifths tempered by
one-fourth comma. In general, he relies chiefly upon
octaves and tempered fifths to achieve the actual

tuning, and uses pure major thirds or tenths to check
the progress of the course

6. His tuning compass actually embraces a range
from E♭ to G♯, despite the fact that his description
suggests a compass from B♭ to D♯. As such, the temperament is eminently suitable for diatonic keys not
exceeding two flats or three sharps

7. Praetorius already considered the meantone
temperament as inadequate for the musical practices
of his time. He deplores its limitations with respect to transpositions which required more than two
flats or three sharps, its inability to denote certain musica ficta conditions effectively, its fail-
ure to reproduce plagal and authentic cadences satisfactorily, and its shortcomings in realizing a number
of desirable transpositions

8. He proposes an arbitrary and approximate
equalization of G♯ and A♭ in order to ameliorate the
dissonance of the "wolf" which consistently appears
at the extremes of the tuning compass in meantone
temperament

9. He appreciates the necessity for providing
additional pipes and "black" half-keys, particularly
at E♭ and at G♯ in order to extend the useful compass
of the temperament, but he considers all such devices

as intolerable annoyances for the performer

10. Although Praetorius sought primarily to im-
prove the intervallic aberrations caused by the G♯,
the contemporary builders inserted a separate D♯ beside the E♭ before they introduced a separate A♭ beside G♯

11. For the Early Baroque the normal 12-note
meantone octave embraces a compass from E♭ to G♯ and
is useful for diatonic keys lying within two flats
and three sharps; the 13-note octave adds D♯ and permits effective use of four-sharp keys; the 14-note
and most comprehensive octave extends the compass to
include an A♭ and enlarges its usefulness to include
diatonic keys of three flats

12. The early baroque builders constructed their
manual claviers in three segments, each of which conforms to certain typical specifications. The bass
octave or first segment operates within the confines
of the great octave; the internal octaves, within the
limits of the small, the one-line, and often the two-
line octave together; and the treble octave engages
either a large portion of the two-line, or a small
portion of the three-line octave, depending upon the
extreme upper limit adopted for the compass

13. Instruments of the time exhibit manual bass
octaves of three varieties. The most parsimonious

disposition is the 8-note Guidonian bass octave; the most common seems to have been the 10-note chromatic form; the most luxurious disposition is represented by the 12-note chromatic bass octave

14. Three varieties of internal octave disposition are evident in the manual and pedal claviers of the time. The simplest form is the 12-note chromatic internal octave; a seemingly favored layout is the 13-note chromatic-enharmonic form; a luxurious disposition exhibits two "split" keys in the form of the 14-note chromatic-enharmonic internal octave

15. Four varieties of the treble octave are identifiable on the manual claviers of the period. Undefined are those where the compass does not exceed the two-line octave; these generally culminate at a'' and seem to be from surviving earlier examples. The builders of the time seem to favor culmination of the compass in the three-line octave where three or, possibly, four dispositions are evident. The 1-note treble octave represents a sparse layout for the time and culminates on c'''. The 3-note form reaches to d''' and seems to represent the norm for the period. The 5-note or 6-note form ends at f''' but seems consistently to omit d#'''. It is the most luxurious disposition found in the De Organographia

16. A division of the pedal clavier into three

segments similar to that encountered in the manual claviers prevails in the instruments of the period. The bass octave is derived from notes of the great octave; the internal octave (one only) comprises the small octave; the treble octave engages a few notes of the one-line octave

17. Three varieties of the bass octave appear in pedal claviers of the time. A sparse disposition is represented by the 8-note Guidonian bass octave; a normal and seemingly common layout is the 10-note chromatic form; a rich clavier exhibits the 11-note chromatic bass octave which generally omits the C#

18. The treble octave of the pedal claviers of the period exhibits generally two dispositions. The 3-note treble octave culminates at d' whereas the 4-note form reaches up to f' but omits d#'. Occasionally a culmination at c' is found which probably bespeaks an earlier practice surviving on older instruments

19. For the lower limit of the manual compass C appears quite consistently in the instruments of the Early Baroque. A few isolated examples, probably from an earlier time, exhibit D or F as the lower limit. The pedal claviers begin consistently at C

NOTES AND REFERENCES

PART III

Chapter XII: Notes and References

1 Not to be confused with <u>Chorton</u>, which describes a reference pitch.

2 <u>Dictionary of organ voices</u> is a convenient reference expression by the present author to identify chapter ii of Part IV of M. Praetorius, <u>Syntagmatis Musici Tomus Secundus De Organographia</u> . . . (Wolfenbuettel, 1619; facs. ed. by W. Gurlitt, Kassel, 1929), pp. 124-48, which is, in effect, a topical dictionary of the various families, genera, and species of organ voices.

3 <u>Catalog of dispositions</u> is also a convenient reference expression by the present author to identify Part V of M. Praetorius, <u>De Organographia</u> . . ., pp. 161-195; 197-203; 233-234; wherein are presented the stoplists of existing organs of the time, of instruments under construction at the time of the preparation of Praetorius' manuscript, and of real and theoretical prospectuses, which Praetorius had gathered by personal inspection, by letter, and by hearsay. They represent a cross section of the organ builder's art in the Early Baroque and are supposedly the more significant or noteworthy instruments of the period. Praetorius' record of these instruments is, in many respects, incomplete and often erroneous, as subsequent research has revealed.

4 See Praetorius, <u>De Organographia</u> . . ., p. 130, where he states, "Here belong also the Quintes of 6', 3', and 1 1/2' tone."

5 Praetorius, <u>De Organographia</u> . . ., p. 165.

6 Praetorius, <u>De Organographia</u> . . ., p. 169.

7 Praetorius, <u>De Organographia</u> . . ., p. 170.

8 Praetorius, <u>De Organographia</u> . . ., pp. 172-73.

9 Praetorius, <u>De Organographia</u> . . ., p. 168.

10 The complexity of the Mixture is recorded as of eight ranks by P. Smets, <u>Die Dresdener Handschrift Orgeldispositionen</u> (Kassel, 1931), p. 58.

11 The complexity of the Scharf is recorded as of three ranks in Smets, <u>Dresdener</u> . . ., p. 58.

12 Praetorius, <u>De Organographia</u> . . ., p. 169.

Chapter XII: Notes and References—Continued

13 The confusion was compounded in practice by a cavalier
   and indiscriminate use of the two terms plus the additional derivative corruptions which appeared from time to
   time and were, most likely, the result of misunderstand-
   ing. Thus, one finds Quindetz or Quinttetz 1 1/2'; Sedecima or Sedetz 1' or 4'; Decem 4'; Sedetzen-quint
   1 1/2'; etc., among the stoplists of Praetorius' catalog
   of dispositions.

14 Praetorius, De Organographia . . ., pp. 121–22.

15 The inclusion of a reference to the Pedal, when it seems
   that the discussion is concerned with divisions rather
   than with entire instruments suggests the common practice
   of the Early Baroque whereby the pedal keyboard was often
   permanently coupled to a manual division, so that its
   keys would necessarily sound corresponding notes of voices
   which were drawn on the Manual. For a detailed discussion see chapter ix of the present study.

16 Praetorius, De Organographia . . ., p. 191.

17 Praetorius, De Organographia . . ., pp. 122–23. Abstracts
   prepared by the present author.

18 Praetorius, De Organographia . . ., p. 123; abstracted by
   the present author.

19 Praetorius, De Organographia . . ., p. 124. The reference
   is to chapter ii of Part IV.

20 Praetorius, De Organographia . . ., pp. 124–25; abstracted
   by the present author.

21 Praetorius, De Organographia . . ., pp. 125–26.

22 Praetorius, De Organographia . . ., opposite p. 126.

23 I.e., exhibiting a constant diameter throughout the length
   of the pipe corpus, in contrast to conical or invert conical pipes which exhibit a graduated diameter.

24 As seems to have been customary for the time, Praetorius
   frequently delineates scale (i.e., Mensur) as a function
   of the length of a pipe corpus rather than of the diameter
   or cross-sectional area. Thus, he speaks of short scale
   (i.e., kurze Mensur) or long scale (i.e., lange Mensur)
   which, in modern terminology are equivalent to wide scale
   or narrow scale, respectively.

Chapter XII: Notes and References--Continued

25 Praetorius, De Organographia . . ., p. 126.

26 I.e., in the exterior casework or facade of the instrument.

27 See above for a discussion concerning the designation of corpora and of entire instruments by means of the Principalbases which they exhibit.

28 One can only speculate as to the meaning of this obscure passage. It is possible that Praetorius was aware of partial tones in the tonal structure of the Principal pipes, and that he was alluding here to the blending quality of Principal pipes when registrated with pipes of higher pitch in the same species.

29 The term discant indicates a register whose compass lies in the upper portion of a keyboard, beginning usually at c'.

30 The true pitch is 4'. A voice of this pitch, constructed of open cylindrical pipes, and beginning on the eighteenth half-step of its normal compass would need to be about 1 1/3 feet long to deliver 4' pitch.

31 Praetorius, De Organographia . . ., pp. 126-28.

32 See chapter v of the present study for an explanation of the Principalbasis concept.

33 M. Praetorius, Theatrum Instrumentorum seu Sciagraphia . . . (Wolfenbuettel, 1620; facs. ed. by W. Gurlitt, Kassel, 1929), Plate XXXVII, 1.

34 See Appendix S for the method used to establish a Praetorius Norm and for a full table of values for the same. Diameter value for the 8' Principal has been extracted from chapter xiv of the present study, q.v.

35 I.e., of the open cylindrical family in moderate scale.

36 A reference to the orchestral prototype of the Schweizerpfeife.

37 Ears: shields attached to the sides of the mouths of pipes to help guide the windsheet emanating from the windway and prevent its dissipation. Beards: shields attached below the mouth for a similar purpose.

Chapter XII: Notes and References--Continued

38 I.e., made somewhat "fatter" than an appropriate mathematical ratio of diminution would require.

39 I.e., somewhat wider in diameter than the Schweizerpfeifes
just discussed.

40 Praetorius' complete description of the two varieties of
Schweizerpfeifes (i.e., the open and the covered), is
somewhat unclear. C. Mahrenholz in Die Orgelregister,
ihre Geschichte und ihr Bau (2nd ed.; Kassel, 1942), p. 59
maintains that Praetorius' discussion of the open Schweizerpfeife presupposes and clearly points to an overblown
species; hence, 8' length for 4' pitch. The covered species, then, would need to be 6' long to give 4' pitch
since, being covered, the pipe could not overblow into
the octave but rather into the twelfth. An overblown
covered pipe of 8' length would sound a 5 1/3' pitch; one
of 4' length, 2 2/3' pitch; one of 3' length, 2' pitch,
etc.

41 Praetorius, De Organographia . . ., pp. 128-29.

42 Praetorius, De Organographia . . ., pp. 138-39.

43 Praetorius, Theatrum . . ., Plate XXXVII, 13.

44 The term Principal, accordingly, is used by Praetorius in
two different senses: a) to denote the basic Principal
voice of a division or instrument, and b) to denote a
voice mounted visibly in the facade of the organ; his subsequent use of the term allows such a facade Principal to
be any appropriate species of voice; such as, Principal,
Trompete, Schalmei, and the like.

45 I.e., the mean pitch of the collective registers of the
organ. Of the pitches (32'), 16', 8', 4', 2', 1', (1/2'),
the 4' pitch occupies the middle position.

46 Praetorius' discussion bears evidence of his concern for
developing a meaningful and consistent nomenclature.

47 Praetorius does not care to allow the term Positive to be
used for any instrument or division which has a Principal
voice lower than 2' in pitch.

48 Quinta decima is the Latin ordinal for "fifteenth" and
denotes, in correct usage, a super octave pitch; such as
2' in an 8' series, 1' in a 4' series, or 4' in a 16'

Chapter XII: Notes and References—Continued

series. See also above and note 13 of the present chapter.

49 See chapter vi of the present study for an accurate delineation of the mixed voice concept.

50 Praetorius, De Organographia . . ., pp. 129-30.

51 Praetorius, Theatrum . . ., Plate XXXVII, 1, 2, and 4.

52 Praetorius, Theatrum . . ., Plate XXXVII, 3.

53 In the sense: unison voices, including also the basic
Principal voice.

54 The passage is somewhat obscure; in the present author's
opinion, Praetorius wishes to indicate that neither the
Mixture nor the Zimbel are useful without the admixture
of supporting unison and quint voices of the same or similar species.

55 It should be understood that in the archaic Gross Mixture,
all the ranks of pipes in the instrument played as a mixture; there were no separately playable registers since
the full organ played whenever the keys were depressed.

56 I.e., the initial bass choir is pitched at the 2' or 1'
level.

57 A careful inspection of two original copies of the De Organographia at the Sibley Musical Library of the University of Rochester, Rochester, N. Y., reveals the following
(p. 131): f̄, f̄, c̄, f̄. It is quite possible and very
likely that the c and the final f are intended to have
double lines over them which failed to reproduce. A previous one-line c on the same page has the line very close
over the c. The last f has its line so much higher than
the first two, that a double line can readily be suspected. Applying these contentions to the letters, the
composition of the voice can be interpreted as having
probably been f̄, f̄, c̄, f̄, as given in the translation.

58 Namely, because these dispositions show a preponderance
of unison ingredients and are predicated upon a rather
acutely-pitched bass choir.

59 Praetorius, De Organographia . . ., pp. 130-31.

60 See chapter vii of the present study for delineation of

Chapter XII: Notes and References--Continued

concepts and terms relating to various types of tonal crowns.

61 A. Werckmeister, Erweiterte und verbesserte Orgel-Probe (Quedlinburg, 1698; facs. ed. by Baerenreiter Verlag, Kassel, 1927), p. 35.

62 Mahrenholz, Orgelregister . . ., p. 218.

63 By personal visit at Hannover on May 13, 1956.

64 As for example at Hamburg, St. Jacob (Praetorius, De Organographia . . ., p. 168) or at Hamburg, St. Peter (p. 169).

65 Praetorius, De Organographia . . ., p. 131.

66 The specification suggests that all of the Zimbelbasses are of unison and quint ingredients which, by necessity, will exhibit superposed intervals of fourths and fifths.

67 Praetorius, De Organographia . . ., p. 131.

68 The complexity of the Zimbelbass is not defined by Praetorius, but surmised by the present author.

69 The complexity of the Zimbelbass is not defined by Praetorius, but surmised by the present author.

70 I.e., in 1621.

71 Werckmeister, Orgelprobe . . ., p. 73.

72 Praetorius, De Organographia . . ., p. 189.

73 P. Andersen, Orgelbogen (København, 1955), p. 72. The disposition of the I Zimbel 1/6' in the Frederiksborg organ was confirmed by an exchange of letters between Poul-Gerhardt Andersen and the present author in 1965.

74 From a copy made in Denmark by Miss Joanne Curnutt and kindly put at the present author's disposal.

75 Praetorius, De Organographia . . ., p. 168.

76 Mahrenholz, Orgelregister . . ., p. 252.

Chapter XIII: Notes and References

1 Praetorius' frequent way of indicating a wide diameter. The shorter the pipe, the wider it must be to produce the same pitch as a parallel reference pipe; conversely, the longer a pipe, the narrower it must be to produce the same pitch effect.

2 I.e., Gedackts of the same physical length, not pitch; thus, the comparison is reasonably valid if a Gedackt of 8' pitch is related to a Hohlfloete of 4' pitch. In this case both pipes exhibit bodies of approximately equal physical length.

3 M. Praetorius, Syntagmatis Musici Tomus Secundus De Organographia . . . (Wolfenbuettel, 1619; facs. ed. by W. Gurlitt, Kassel, 1929), p. 131.

4 Such qualifying nomenclature consists in appending modifying adjectives to the basic appellation for a given species; thus, Gross indicates a sub-octave variety; Klein, an octave variety; and Super, a double-octave variety.

5 I.e., for making Nachthorns. It will be noted that Praetorius prefers covered and narrow-scaled pipes for the Nachthorn rather than the wide open cylindrical pipes of the Hohlfloete group.

6 The term chorale, in all likelihood, refers here to Choralbass registrations.

7 The 1 1/3' pitch designation may be questioned for the following reasons: a) Praetorius already has identified a Quintfloete at this pitch in the Hohlfloete group; b) the Universal Table designates this voice at 1/2' (i.e., 2/3') pitch; c) the compulsion for several repetitions, which Praetorius specifically points out, is provided by a 2/3' pitch but hardly necessary for the 1 1/3' pitch in view of the limited compass which the instruments of the time generally exhibited. The present author will adopt the 2/3' pitch as Praetorius' intention and adhere to it in future references to this voice.

8 The repetition here indicated occurred, in all likelihood, in the upper octaves of the compass, where the difficulty of constructing such diminutive pipes demanded recourse to larger pipes in lower pitches than the normal course of the voice would require.

9 Praetorius, De Organographia . . ., pp. 132-33.

Chapter XIII: Notes and References--Continued

10 M. Praetorius, _Theatrum Instrumentorum seu Sciagraphia_
. . . (Wolfenbuettel, 1620; facs. ed. by W. Gurlitt,
Kassel, 1929), Plate XXXVIII, 7.

11 C. Mahrenholz, _Die Orgelregister, ihre Geschichte und ihr
Bau_ (2nd ed.; Kassel, 1942), p. 115.

12 Praetorius, _Theatrum_ . . ., Plates XXXVII, 5 and XXXVIII,
5.

13 _Dictionary of organ voices_ is a convenient reference expression by the present author to identify chapter ii of
Part IV of Praetorius, _De Organographia_ . . ., pp. 124-48,
which is, in effect, a topical dictionary of the various
families, genera, and species of organ voices. See also
chapter xii of the present study for a discussion of the
Principalbasis.

14 Praetorius points out that the term _Nachthorn_ is sometimes
used to designate the 2' Klein Hohlfloete; he advises
against this practice, however, since he prefers the term
Nachthorn to be used for narrow-scaled and covered pipes,
such as the Nachthorn-Gedackt.

15 The 2/3' pitch designation is a substitution for 1 1/3' by
the present author; see note 7 of the present chapter for
the compelling reasons for this change.

16 A Choralbass registration is a combination of pedal voices
based upon a 4' Choralbass and useful for presenting a
pedal _cantus firmus._ In the present instance the registration would likely consist of 4' Choralbass and 2' Klein
Floetebass.

17 The 1' Bauerfloete seems to have been a very popular pedal
voice at the time; subsequent discussion will show how the
1' Bauerfloete was constructed of various species of registers; noteworthy among these were the Hohlfloete species,
the Gedackt species, and the Rohrfloete species.

18 Praetorius, _De Organographia_ . . ., opposite p. 126.

19 The reference is to S. Virdung, _Musica getutscht und aus-
gezogen_ . . ., 1511. A facsimile of the same has been
issued by Baeremeiter Verlag, Kassel, in 1931, under the
editorship of Leo Schrade.

20 Praetorius' specifications point to an echo form of the
Spillfloete, which would require a corpus partly

Chapter XIII: Notes and References--Continued

cylindrical and partly conical in shape (i.e., "bevelled inward at the top"). This form associated with a narrow mouth and light winding would produce an interesting Schwegel.

21 Praetorius, De Organographia . . ., p. 133.

22 Praetorius, De Organographia . . ., opposite p. 126.

23 "Equally proportioned bodies" may be interpreted to mean pipe bodies which maintain a consistent diameter or cross-sectional area throughout their length; hence, cylindrical.

24 Praetorius, De Organographia . . ., pp. 133-35.

25 See chapter iv of the present study for interpretation of the various ratios.

26 Praetorius, Theatrum . . ., Plate XXXVII, 10.

27 There is sufficient internal evidence in Praetorius' account to lead the present author to suspect an error in the legend for this voice as found on Plate XXXVII, 10 of the Theatrum Instrumentorum, where the model is labelled as Gemszhorn: 8. Fusz. Praetorius' specification that the Gemshorn resembles the orchestral Viola da Gamba strongly suggests a moderate if not narrow scale. One would expect a voice which is to deliver a broad String tone to exhibit a diameter which is less, if not considerably less, than a Principal voice; it should, accordingly, show a negative deviation from the Norm. Furthermore, his specification that the corpus of the Gemshorn should have one-half as great a diameter at the top as at the mouth does not bespeak the dimensions of his model; here the relationship of the respective diameters is actually less than 1/3. On the other hand, his subsequent comparison of the Gemshorn to the Spitzfloete calls for a larger scale and a greater degree of conicity in the latter. There is, therefore, considerable evidence to support the hypothesis that the model of the purported Gemshorn found in the Theatrum Instrumentorum could have been inadvertantly misnamed and that it reflects, in reality, the general specifications which Praetorius lays down for the Spitzfloete. So considered, his entire discussion of the two species and their relation to each other falls more perfectly into place. Of course, it is impossible to prove such a hypothesis, but its postulation may prove provocative and help to remove the recurring

Chapter XIII: Notes and References--Continued

stumbling blocks caused by the apparent lack of correlation between Praetorius' cursive account and the model he presents pictorially.

28 Praetorius, De Organographia . . ., opposite p. 126.

29 Praetorius' contention that the 8' Aequal Gemshorn resembles the tone of the orchestral Viola da Gamba is a stumbling block for the accurate delineation of the voice. Certainly, the effect is not the result of the scale he recommends for this voice, because the same is relatively generous. The considerable conicity of the corpus may, however, help to produce a tone which is not a pure Flute tone, but reminiscent of the Viola da Gamba. See also note 27 of the present chapter for a hypothetical solution of this apparent paradox.

30 Praetorius, Theatrum . . ., Plates XXXVII, 11 and XXXVIII, 2.

31 Mahrenholz, Orgelregister . . ., p. 121.

32 Praetorius, Theatrum . . ., Plate XXXVIII, 2.

33 Praetorius, De Organographia . . ., opposite p. 126.

34 Praetorius, Theatrum . . ., Plate XXXVII, 12.

35 Praetorius, De Organographia . . ., opposite p. 126.

36 Praetorius, Theatrum . . ., Plate XXXVII, 9.

37 Mahrenholz, Orgelregister . . ., p. 109.

38 H. Jahnn, "Registernamen und ihr Inhalt," Beitraege zur Organistentagung Hamburg-Luebeck / 6. bis 8. Juli 1925 (Klecken, 1925), p. 11.

39 More than likely, a typographical error occurs here; it seems that a "k" has been substituted for an "h", so that the word should read gedachte (i.e., afore-mentioned) instead of gedackte (i.e., covered).

40 Praetorius, De Organographia . . ., p. 135.

41 Praetorius, De Organographia . . ., opposite p. 126.

42 Perhaps it does, after all. See note 27 of the present chapter.

Chapter XIII: Notes and References--Continued

43 Praetorius, De Organographia . . ., p. 136.

44 Praetorius, Theatrum . . ., Plate XXXVIII, 3.

45 Jahnn, "Registernamen . . .," p. 9.

46 Praetorius, De Organographia . . ., p. 139.

47 Praetorius, De Organographia . . ., opposite p. 126.

48 The voice is labelled Dolcan in Praetorius, Theatrum . . .,
   Plate XXXVIII, 1.

49 Praetorius, De Organographia . . ., pp. 136-37.

50 Praetorius, Theatrum . . ., Plate XXXVIII, 1.

51 Praetorius, De Organographia . . ., opposite p. 126.

52 Praetorius, De Organographia . . ., p. 137.

53 Praetorius, Theatrum . . ., Plate XXXVII, 7.   A 16' example of the Quintade appears on the same plate as item 6.

54 Praetorius, De Organographia . . ., opposite p. 126.

55 Praetorius, De Organographia . . ., p. 138.

56 Praetorius, Theatrum . . ., Plate XXXVII, 8.

57 Mahrenholz, Orgelregister . . ., p. 106.

58 To state the case more simply, Praetorius wishes to point
   out that, in order to overblow into the desirable pitch,
   the corpus of the pipe needs to be somewhere between 2
   and 2 1/2 times as long as it has to be to produce the
   same pitch without being overblown.   Actually 3 times the
   normal physical length is required to achieve this effect.

59 The reference is to a surviving musical monument in the
   form of a de luxe instrument constructed by Esaias Compenius under the supervision of M. Praetorius for the
   Hessen, Schlosz in 1612 and removed to Frederiksborg,
   Schlosz in Denmark shortly thereafter.   For a fuller description of the instrument see chapter ix of the present
   study.   Notes 14-18 of the same chapter provide some historical information concerning the same.

60 Praetorius, De Organographia . . ., pp. 138-39.

Chapter XIII: Notes and References—Continued

61 Praetorius, Theatrum . . ., Plate XXXVII, 14.

62 Praetorius, De Organographia . . ., opposite p. 126.

63 The Duifloete recalls the modern Doppelfloete.

64 Praetorius, De Organographia . . ., pp. 139-40.

65 Praetorius, De Organographia . . ., opposite p. 126.

66 Praetorius, Theatrum . . ., Plate XXXVIII, 4 and 6.

67 Praetorius, De Organographia . . ., opposite p. 126.

68 Praetorius, De Organographia . . ., pp. 140-41.

69 Praetorius, Theatrum . . ., Plate XXXVIII, 7.

70 Praetorius, De Organographia . . ., opposite p. 126.

71 Mahrenholz, Orgelregister . . ., p. 115.

72 I.e., on Plates XXXVII and XXXVIII of the same.

73 See note 59 of the present chapter.

74 Compenius did, in fact, prepare and issue such a report
   in manuscript form. It is referred to in the literature
   today as M. Praetorius and E. Compenius, Orgeln Verdingnis. For further information see chapter xi, note 16.

75 Praetorius, De Organographia . . ., pp. 141-42.

76 Praetorius, De Organographia . . ., opposite p. 126.

77 Praetorius, De Organographia . . ., pp. 124-48.

78 Praetorius, Theatrum . . ., Plates XXXVII and XXXVIII.

79 The present author suspects, but is not ready to claim,
   that the Gedackt Schweizerpfeife and the Querfloete-
   Gedackt might be alternate names for identical registers.

80 See chapter xii of the present study.

81 I.e., Plates XXXVII and XXXVIII.

82 The manufacturing project is more fully discussed in chapter xiv of the present study.

Chapter XIII: Notes and References--Continued

83 See Appendix S for derivation and values of the Praetorius Norm.

84 See Appendix S for derivation of the Praetorius Norm.

85 See chapter v of the present study for several catalogs of modern registers.

86 Regalia mobilia suggests that Regals move or wander out of tune and into tune; they tend to be more mobile and less static than labial voices.

87 Praetorius, De Organographia . . ., pp. 142-44.

88 See Mahrenholz, Orgelregister . . ., p. 18.

89 Mahrenholz, Orgelregister . . ., p. 131.

90 Praetorius, Theatrum . . ., Plate XXXVIII, 8 and 10.

91 Praetorius, De Organographia . . ., pp. 144-46.

92 Praetorius, Theatrum . . ., Plate XXXVIII.

93 Praetorius, Theatrum . . ., Plate XXXVIII, 10.

94 Praetorius, Theatrum . . ., Plate XI, 4 and 5.

95 Praetorius, Theatrum . . ., Plate XIII, 2.

96 Praetorius, Theatrum . . ., Plate XXXVIII, 9.

97 Praetorius, Theatrum . . ., Plate XXXVIII, 12.

98 Praetorius, De Organographia . . ., p. 147.

99 Praetorius, Theatrum . . ., Plate XXXVIII, 14.

100 Praetorius, Theatrum . . ., Plate XXXVIII, 15.

101 Praetorius, De Organographia . . ., p. 145.

102 Praetorius, De Organographia . . ., opposite p. 126.

103 Mahrenholz, Orgelregister . . ., pp. 253-54.

104 A Mixture in the sense that it exhibits breaks, segmental courses, the principle of repetition, and displays a generally static progression.

Chapter XIII: Notes and References--Continued

105 Praetorius, De Organographia . . ., opposite p. 126.

106 Praetorius, De Organographia . . ., pp. 124-48.

107 Praetorius, Theatrum . . ., Plate XXXVIII.

108 Which identifies the species by coordinating the families and genera.

109 I.e., a Nachthorn-Gedackt, of which a model appears on Plate XXXVII, 8 of the Theatrum Instrumentorum which has an actual diameter of 76 mm.

110 Praetorius, De Organographia . . ., pp. 146-48.

111 Praetorius, De Organographia . . ., opposite p. 126.

112 Praetorius, Theatrum . . ., Plate XXXVIII, 11 and 13

113 W. Supper, Die Orgeldisposition (Grossausgabe; Kassel, 1950), p. 268, item 160.

114 Praetorius, De Organographia . . ., opposite p. 126.

115 Supper, Orgeldisposition, p. 268, item 155.

116 Praetorius, Theatrum . . ., Plate XI, 1, 2, and 3.

117 J. Adlung, Anleitung zu der musikalischen Gelahrtheit (Erfurt, 1758; facs. ed. by Baerenreiter Verlag, Kassel, 1953), p. 398.

118 Praetorius, Theatrum . . ., Plate XXXVIII, 8-23. It is quite apparent that items 17 and 18 which are labelled as Krumbhorn should have been included with the Baerpfeifes, since they precisely exemplify Praetorius' written description of the same.

119 The derivation and conversion of the measurements for Plate XXXVIII of the Theatrum Instrumentorum are fully explained in chapter xiv of the present study.

120 Sciagraphia is Praetorius' alternate or subtitle for the Theatrum Instrumentorum.

121 Praetorius, Theatrum . . ., Plate XXXVIII, 21.

122 For this interpretation of the "Biesemknopf" the present author is indebted to Dr. C. Mahrenholz at the occasion

Chapter XIII: Notes and References--Continued

of a personal interview at Hannover, May 13, 1956.

123 Supper, Orgeldisposition, p. 267, item 130.

124 Supper, Orgeldisposition, p. 267, item 131.

125 Praetorius, De Organographia . . ., opposite p. 126.

126 Praetorius, De Organographia . . ., pp. 124-48.

127 Praetorius, Theatrum . . ., Plate XXXVIII.

128 Which identifies the species by coordinating the families and genera.

Chapter XIV: Notes and References

1 M. Praetorius, Syntagmatis Musici Tomus Secundus De Organographia . . . (Wolfenbuettel, 1619; facs. ed. by W. Gurlitt, Kassel, 1929).

2 The terms Chorton and Chormasz appear but vaguely differentiated in Praetorius' writings. The former may be interpreted as "reference pitch" and is useful in conversations with musicians, while the latter suggests "reference measure" and is more useful in discussions with organbuilders and related technicians.

3 Ellis chose to adapt dimensions from the largest pipe represented in the graph entitled Pfeifflin zur Chormasz in Praetorius, De Organographia . . ., p. 232.

4 A. J. Ellis, "On the History of Musical Pitch" (Reprinted with corrections and an appendix from the Journal of the Society of Arts for 5 March and 2 April; London, 1880), pp. 320-21. (The actual edition used by the present author is a further offprint put out by Frits A. M. Knuf, Amsterdam, 1963).

5 MA denotes frequency of a' in meantone temperament; JA denotes frequency of a' in just intonation; EA denotes frequency of a' in equal temperament; C denotes frequency of c''; S denotes deviation in semitones from a zero point which, in turn, is defined by Ellis as 370 double vibrations per second; (Ellis) indicates that the problem was investigated by Ellis personally; 1619 gives the date of the source used, namely the De Organographia.

6 Metric and British equivalents for Brunswick measure are given in Appendix Q, 2.

7 C 503.7, 507.4 are values for the frequency of c'' (i.e. 1' c).

8 MA 421.1, 424.2, and 428.0 are the calculated frequencies in double vibrations per second of a' (meantone temperament) at pressures of 2 3/4", 3 1/4", and 4" respectively.

9 A 422.5 denotes frequency of a'.

10 A 505.8 denotes frequency of a'.

11 S denotes deviation in semitones from theoretical zero point of 370 double vibrations per second.

12 Praetorius, De Organographia . . ., p. 232.

Chapter XIV: Notes and References--Continued

13 An original copy reposing in the treasure room of the Sibley Musical Library, Eastman School of Music, Rochester, New York.

14 It is evident from the legend accompanying the graph that the values along the Y-axis and representing the widths are not in full scale. The ambiguity of the legend will be resolved in the subsequent discussion.

15 The term "width" refers to the width of the rectangular metal plate when cut from stock and before being rolled into the shape of a cylinder.

16 Or C to c of a 1/2' stop; c' to c'' of a 2' stop; c'' to c''' of a 4' stop; c''' to c'''' of an 8' stop. It is extremely important that the exact pitch level of the range be clearly understood.

17 Praetorius, De Organographia . . ., p. 231.

18 M. Praetorius, Syntagmatis Musici Theatrum Instrumentorum seu Sciagraphia . . . (Wolfenbuettel, 1620; facs. ed. by W. Gurlitt, Kassel, 1929).

19 The conversion from Fahrenheit to Centigrade scales is subject to the relationships expressed in the formula $F = 32 + \frac{9C}{5}$, where F denotes degrees Fahrenheit and C degrees Centigrade. Accordingly $C = \frac{5(F-32)}{9}$. By solving the equation numerically, $C = \frac{5(59-32)}{9} = 15°$.

20 See H. Helmholtz, On the Sensations of Tone as a Physiological Basis for the Theory of Music (translated and rendered conformable to the fourth [and last] German edition of 1877 by A. Ellis; New York, 1954), p. 494, Article 2 and 5.

21 Since the ratio of velocity to frequency at one temperature is directly proportional to that at another, the following equation balances: $\frac{V_a}{F_a} = \frac{V_b}{F_b}$; hence $F_b = \frac{V_b \times F_a}{V_a}$. The velocity of sound at 0° Centigrade (V_0) is equal to 331.9 meters per second; the increase in velocity for every degree rise in Centigrade equals .607 meters per second. Therefore, $V_t = V_0 + .607t$,

Chapter XIV: Notes and References--Continued

where V_t equals the velocity at temperature t, and V_o, the velocity at 0° Centigrade. Expressed numerically, V_{15} = 331.9 + 15(.607) = 341.005 meters per second; V_{20} = 331.9 + 20(.607) = 344.04 meters per second. To convert 424.2 double vibrations per second at 15° Centigrade to an unknown frequency at 20° Centigrade, when

$$F_{20} = \frac{V_{20} \times F_{15}}{V_{15}} \text{ , then } F_{20} = \frac{344.04 \times 424.2}{341.005} = 427.982$$

double vibrations per second. Ellis' value of the equal tempered $\underline{a}$' converts similarly to 430.502 double vibrations per second at 20° Centigrade.

22 A. Mendel, "Pitch in the 16th and Early 17th Centuries--Part II", The Musical Quarterly, XXXIV (1948), 221.

23 The quotation is rendered in tabular form by Mendel; the punctuation enclosed in brackets has been added by the present author to clarify the cursive rendering here employed.

24 Praetorius, De Organographia . . ., p. 232.

25 Mendel, "Pitch . . .," p. 201, footnote 40.

26 Published in Nuernberg, 1955 as Part II of a Sonderdruck aus den Mitteilungen des Vereins fuer Geschichte der Stadt Nuernberg, Band 46.

27 Praetorius, Theatrum . . ., Plates XXXVII and XXXVIII.

28 Praetorius, De Organographia . . ., p. 232.

29 The expression, "Theater of Organ Pipes" provides a convenient appellation for all of the pipes that are quantitatively defined by Praetorius; namely, the sketches on Plates XXXVII and XXXVIII of the Theatrum Instrumentorum and the graph Pfeifflin zur Chormasz on p. 232 of the De Organographia.

30 Praetorius, Theatrum . . ., reverse side (unnumbered) of the titlepage.

31 N. Bessaraboff, Ancient European Musical Instruments, An Organological Study of the Musical Instruments . . . at the Museum of Fine Arts Boston (Boston, 1941), p. 356.

Chapter XIV: Notes and References--Continued

32 Bessaraboff, Ancient . . ., p. 353.

33 The term "raw" will be consistently used in the present
   treatise to identify measurements taken directly from
   Praetorius' sketches and graphs, before adjustment into
   actual or real dimensions.

34 Praetorius, De Organographia . . ., p. 232.

35 The term "width" as used by Praetorius can easily be misleading; on the graph, the term must be interpreted as
   "circumference," since the metal plates have a rectangular
   shape before being rolled into cylinders; hence, their
   dimensions appear as lengths and widths.

36 Line oq represents the length of the note c as designated
   on the graph, but which must be reckoned at c''' of an 8'
   stop; line or represents the same for the note c on the
   graph, or c'''' of an 8' stop.

37 Praetorius, De Organographia . . ., p. 231.

38 Praetorius, De Organographia . . ., p. 231.

39 C. Mahrenholz, Die Berechnung der Orgelpfeifenmensuren
   (Kassel, 1938), p. 39.

40 See Appendix Q, 2 for metric and British equivalents of
   Brunswick measure.

41 J. Woersching, Die Compenius-Orgel auf Schlosz Frederiksborg (Mainz, 1946), p. 10.

42 The formulas developed in note 21 of the present chapter
   are applicable. Since $V_t = V_o + .607t$, the velocities
   at 20°, 28.89°, and 30° Centigrade can be computed as
   follows:

   $V_{20} = 331.9 + 20(.607) = 344.04$ meters per second;

   $V_{28.89} = 331.9 + 28.89(.607) = 349.44$ meters per second;

   $V_{30} = 331.9 + 30(.607) = 350.11$ meters per second.

   Since the ratio of velocity to frequency at one temperature is directly proportional to that at another, the
   equation balances as follows: $\dfrac{V_a}{F_a} = \dfrac{V_b}{F_b}$. To reduce the
   raw frequencies at 28.89° Centigrade to equivalent values

Chapter XIV: Notes and References--Continued

at 20° Centigrade, the following equation must be realized numerically: $\dfrac{V_{28.89}}{F_{28.89}} = \dfrac{V_{20}}{F_{20}}$. By solving for F_{20}, the equation balances thus: $F_{20} = \dfrac{V_{20} \times F_{28.89}}{V_{28.89}}$; by substituting appropriate values: $F_{20} = \dfrac{344.04 \times F_{28.89}}{349.44}$. By simplifying the numerical factors, a coefficient (in the form of a multiplier) can be extracted: $F_{20} = F_{28.89} \times .985$; hence, the coefficient to reduce raw values taken at 28.89° Centigrade to an equivalent value at 20° Centigrade is .985. By similar calculation the coefficient to reduce raw values taken at 30° Centigrade to equivalent values at 20° Centigrade is .983.

43 The standard deviation is derived as follows:

$$\sigma = \sqrt{\frac{a^2 + b^2 + c^2 + \ldots + n^2}{n}} \quad \text{or} \quad \sigma = \sqrt{\frac{\Sigma(x^2)}{n}} \ .$$

44 The frequency of American Standard pitch at a' equals 440 double vibrations per second. To compare Praetorius' reference pitch at the same level an equal tempered a' must be sought for it; if F_C represents Praetorius' reference pitch at Great C, then a' $= F_C \times 4 \sqrt[4]{2^3}$; in numerical values, a' $= 66.0 \times 4 \sqrt[4]{2^3} = 444.0$ double vibrations per second. Similarly a' $= 66.25 \times 4 \sqrt[4]{2^3} = 445.68$ double vibrations per second.

45 The method of calculating the interval of difference is as follows: Since the ratio of the octave is $\dfrac{2}{1}$, the ratio for a whole tone or a whole step (i.e., 1/6 of an octave) may be expressed as $\dfrac{\sqrt[6]{2}}{1}$. If F represents the frequency of Praetorius' reference pitch at a', and f, that of American Standard pitch at the same level, then the intervallic difference between the two values will be that part of a whole tone expressed by n in the equation: $\dfrac{F}{f} = \dfrac{\sqrt[n]{\sqrt[6]{2}}}{1}$; by solving for n,

$n = \dfrac{\log 2}{6(\log F + \text{colog } f)}$; by substituting numerical

Chapter XIV: Notes and References--Continued

values, n = $\dfrac{\log 2}{6(\log 445 + \text{colog } 440)}$ = 10.224.   Accord-

ingly, $\dfrac{F}{f} = \dfrac{10.224\sqrt{\sqrt[6]{2}}}{1}$; hence, the intervallic dif-

ference between the two reference pitches is equal to

$\dfrac{1}{10.224}$ or approximately 1/10 of a whole tone.

46 N. Bessaraboff, Ancient . . ., pp. 377-78 (Appendix D).
He delineates the polydiapasonal scales as follows:

"The Polydiapasonal Scale

Tonality of Musical System:	A	B♭	B	C	C♯	D	E♭
Diapason (a'):	370.0	392.0	415.3	440	466.2	494.9	523.3

The number of cycles is given here to the first decimal point. The tolerance is plus or minus one-quarter of a
tone (50 cents); that is, a pitch either flatter or sharper
by not more than that interval with respect to any of these
points of reference is regarded as belonging to a tonality
chosen as the point of reference."

Chapter XV: Notes and References

1 M. Praetorius, Syntagmatis Musici Tomus Secundus De Organographia . . . (Wolfenbuettel, 1619; facs. ed. by W. Gurlitt, Kassel, 1929), pp. 148-58.

2 The passage is exceptionally obscure in the original German; the translation submitted is a possible one, which
seeks to present the thoughts in an intelligible fashion.

3 Praetorius, De Organographia . . ., p. 148.

4 The abstractions summarize the significant concepts developed in Praetorius, De Organographia . . ., pp. 148-50.

5 Praetorius, De Organographia . . ., pp. 156-58. Calvisius
(1556-1615) was Praetorius' senior by 16 years.

6 Praetorius, De Organographia . . ., pp. 150-51.

7 In the present treatise the expression "tempered narrow"
is used to designate an interval somewhat diminished from
its just value. Ordinarily, the term "flat" is used to
describe tempering; however, in the present context the
tempered fifth requires a "flat" upper note or a "sharp"
lower note to achieve the desired result. Accordingly,
the expression "tempered narrow" describes the condition
more accurately.

8 Similarly, the expression "tempered wide" is used herein
to describe an interval which is somewhat augmented beyond its just value, so that the upper note appears
"sharp", and the lower note, "flat."

9 The abstractions summarize the most important aspects of
Praetorius, De Organographia . . ., pp. 151-52.

10 Praetorius, De Organographia . . ., p. 152. The present
author is indebted to the kindness of Prof. T. Klammer of
the faculty of Concordia College, Ann Arbor, Michigan for
the translation of the Latin passage quoted here.

11 Although a parallel translation requires the intervals
and ratios to be presented as shown, the relationships
are more accurately equated thus: d/c = 9/8; e/d = 10/9;
f/e = 16/15; g/f = 9/8; a/g = 10/9; b/a = 9/8; c/b = 16/15.

12 Praetorius, De Organographia . . ., pp. 156-58.

Chapter XV: Notes and References--Continued

13 Simplify as follows: $\dfrac{16}{15}\sqrt[4]{\dfrac{81}{80}} = \dfrac{16\sqrt[4]{81}}{15\sqrt[4]{80}} = \dfrac{16 \times 3}{15\sqrt[4]{80}} =$

$\dfrac{16}{5\sqrt[4]{16}\sqrt[4]{5}} = \dfrac{16}{5 \times 2\sqrt[4]{5}} = \dfrac{8}{5\sqrt[4]{5}} = \dfrac{8}{5^{4/4} \times 5^{1/4}} =$

$\dfrac{8}{\sqrt[4]{5^5}}$.

14 Simplify as follows: $\dfrac{\sqrt{5}\sqrt{5} \times 8}{2 \times 2 \times \sqrt[4]{5^5}} = \dfrac{5 \times 8}{4\sqrt[4]{5^5}} = \dfrac{5 \times 2}{\sqrt[4]{5^5}} =$

$\dfrac{5 \times 2}{5\sqrt[4]{5}} = \dfrac{2}{\sqrt[4]{5}}$.

15 Simplify as follows: $\left(\dfrac{\sqrt{5}}{2}\right)^3 \times \dfrac{8}{\sqrt[4]{5^5}} = \dfrac{5^{3/2} \times 8}{8 \times \sqrt[4]{5^5}} =$

$\dfrac{5^{3/2}}{5^{5/4}} = \dfrac{5^{6/4}}{5^{5/4}} = \dfrac{5^{1/4}}{1} = \dfrac{\sqrt[4]{5}}{1}$.

16 Praetorius, De Organographia . . ., p. 153.

17 J. Barbour, Tuning and Temperament (Lansing, 1953), p. 26.

18 Praetorius, De Organographia . . ., pp. 154-55.

19 Praetorius, De Organographia . . ., p. 156.

20 Barbour, Tuning . . ., p. 26.

21 Barbour, Tuning . . ., p. 26.

22 Praetorius, De Organographia . . ., p. 155.

23 Derivation of the value for $g\sharp$ to represent a note lying one-fourth comma above the just fifth, $c\sharp-g\sharp$, summates the values of $c\sharp$ (19.0775 savarts) plus a just fifth (176.0913 savarts) plus one-fourth comma (1.3488 savarts). The sum equals 196.5176 savarts and represents the ratio of $g\sharp$ to c within the framework of Praetorius' bearing.

Chapter XV: Notes and References--Continued

24 Praetorius, De Organographia . . ., p. 155, paragraph 4.

25 Catalog of dispositions is a convenient reference expression used herein to identify Part V of Praetorius, De Organographia . . ., pp. 161-95; 197-203; and 233-34 wherein are presented stoplists of instruments of the Early Baroque.

26 Praetorius, De Organographia . . ., pp. 185-86.

27 Praetorius, De Organographia . . ., pp. 186-88.

28 Praetorius, De Organographia . . ., pp. 189-90.

29 Praetorius, De Organographia . . ., pp. 200-02.

30 J. Woersching, Die Compenius-Orgel auf Schlosz Frederiksborg (Mainz, 1946), p. 10.

31 Praetorius, De Organographia . . ., pp. 199-200.

32 The term Guidonian bass octave is original with the present author; it describes very accurately the disposition of the bass octave under discussion and is submitted as a useful appellation for the same.

33 An exception occurs at Bayreuth, where the internal octaves of the manual claviers exhibit 13-note chromatic-enharmonic forms, whereas the pedal clavier exhibits what appears to be a 12-note chromatic one. Praetorius' delineation seems a little haphazard here, since he fails to mention a c♯ for the internal octave but does indicate a c♯' in the treble octave.

34 Including a half-key for e♭.

35 The pedal clavier does not include any half-keys; the omission of c♯ seems to be an inadvertant error on the part of Praetorius.

36 Praetorius records the upper limit of the manual clavier as either d''' or f'''.

37 Praetorius, De Organographia . . ., p. 164.

38 Praetorius, De Organographia . . ., p. 165.

39 Praetorius, De Organographia . . ., p. 166.

Chapter XV: Notes and References--Continued

40 Praetorius, De Organographia . . ., p. 172.

41 A lower limit for the pedal at g seems an inadvertant error; it is reasonable to assume that C was intended even though it cannot be proven.

42 Praetorius, De Organographia . . ., p. 176.

43 Praetorius, De Organographia . . ., p. 178.

44 Praetorius gives "c̿ sampt g̿s vnd b̅," i.e., "c''' together with g♯''' and b♭'' "; it is more than likely that g♯''' is a typographical error for g♯''.

45 Praetorius, De Organographia . . ., p. 193.

46 Praetorius, De Organographia . . ., p. 197.

PART IV

ATLAS: APPENDICES, BIBLIOGRAPHIES,

CHARTS, AND PLATES

SECTION A

APPENDICES

LIST OF APPENDICES

874

LIST OF APPENDICES--Continued

LIST OF APPENDICES--<u>Continued</u>

APPENDIX A

FREQUENCIES IN EQUAL TEMPERAMENT[a]

Note	16'	8'	4'	2'	1'	1/2'	1/4'	1/8'
C	32.70	65.41	130.81	261.63	523.25	1046.50	2093.00	4186.00
C♯	34.65	69.30	138.59	277.18	554.37	1108.73	2217.46	4434.92
D	36.71	73.42	146.83	293.66	587.33	1174.66	2349.32	4698.64
D♯	38.89	77.78	155.56	311.13	622.25	1244.51	2489.02	4978.04
E	41.20	82.41	164.81	329.63	659.26	1318.51	2637.02	5274.04
F	43.65	87.31	174.61	349.23	698.46	1396.91	2793.83	5587.66
F♯	46.25	92.50	185.00	369.99	739.99	1479.98	2959.96	5919.92
G	49.00	98.00	196.00	392.00	783.99	1567.98	3135.96	6271.92
G♯	51.91	103.83	207.65	415.30	830.61	1161.22	3322.44	6644.88
A	55.00	110.00	220.00	440.00	880.00	1760.00	3520.00	7040.00
A♯	58.27	116.54	233.08	466.16	932.33	1864.66	3729.31	7458.62
B	61.74	123.47	246.94	493.88	987.77	1975.53	3951.07	7902.14

[a]The table is predicated upon a reference pitch of a' = 440 cycles per second, American Standard. Values from C. D. Hodgman and others, Handbook of Chemistry and Physics (38th ed.; Cleveland, 1956) p. 2319.

APPENDIX B

FREQUENCIES IN JUST INTONATION[a]

Note	Ratio to C	16'	8'	4'	2'	1'	1/2'	1/4'	1/8'
C	1/1	32.00	64.00	128.00	256.00	512.00	1024.00	2048.00	4096.00
C♯	25/24	33.33	66.66	133.33	266.67	533.33	1066.67	2133.33	4266.67
Db	16/15	34.13	68.27	136.53	273.07	546.13	1092.27	2184.53	4369.07
D	9/8	36.00	72.00	144.00	288.00	576.00	1152.00	2304.00	4608.00
D♯	75/64	37.50	75.00	150.00	300.00	600.00	1200.00	2400.00	4800.00
Eb	6/5	38.40	76.80	153.60	307.20	614.40	1228.80	2457.60	4915.20
E	5/4	40.00	80.00	160.00	320.00	640.00	1280.00	2560.00	5120.00
F	4/3	42.66	85.33	170.66	341.33	682.66	1365.33	2730.66	5461.33
F♯	25/18	44.44	88.88	177.77	355.55	711.11	1422.22	2844.44	5688.88
Gb	64/45	45.51	91.02	182.04	364.09	728.18	1456.36	2912.71	5825.42
G	3/2	48.00	96.00	192.00	384.00	768.00	1536.00	3072.00	6144.00
G♯	25/16	50.00	100.00	200.00	400.00	800.00	1600.00	3200.00	6400.00
Ab	8/5	51.20	102.40	204.80	409.60	819.20	1638.40	3276.80	6553.60
A	5/3	53.33	106.66	213.33	426.66	853.33	1706.66	3413.33	6826.66
A♯	125/72	55.55	111.11	222.22	444.44	888.88	1777.77	3555.55	7111.11
Bb	16/9	57.60	115.20	230.40	460.80	921.60	1843.20	3686.40	7372.80
B	15/8	60.00	120.00	240.00	480.00	960.00	1920.00	3840.00	7680.00

[a]The table is developed from a reference pitch of C 8' = 64 cycles per second.

APPENDIX C

ENGLISH AND ITALIAN PITCH DESIGNATIONS RECKONED FROM VARIOUS BASES

Par-tial	Foot Designation			English Terms	Italian Terms
	16' Basis	8' Basis	4' Basis		
1st	16'	8'	4'	Unison	Principale
2nd	8'	4'	2'	Octave	Ottava
3rd	5 1/3'	2 2/3'	1 1/3'	Twelfth	Duodocima
4th	4'	2'	1'	Fifteenth	Decimaquinta
5th	3 1/5'	1 3/5'	4/5'	Seventeenth	Decimasettima
6th	2 2/3'	1 1/3'	2/3'	Nineteenth	Decimanona
7th	2 2/7'	1 1/7'	4/7'	Twenty-first	Vigesimaprima
8th	2'	1'	1/2'	Twenty-second	Vigesimaseconda
9th	1 7/9'	8/9'	4/9'	Twenty-third	Vigesimaterza
10th	1 3/5'	4/5'	2/5'	Twenty-fourth	Vigesimaquarta
11th	1 5/11'	8/11'	4/11'	Twenty-fifth	Vigesimaquinta
12th	1 1/3'	2/3'	1/3'	Twenty-sixth	Vigesimasesta
13th	1 3/13'	8/13'	4/13'	Twenty-seventh	Vigesimasettima
16th	1'	1/2'	1/4'	Twenty-ninth	Vigesimanona
20th	4/5'	2/5'	1/5'	Thirty-first	Trigesimaprima
24th	2/3'	1/3'	1/6'	Thirty-third	Trigesimaterza

APPENDIX C--Continued

Par-tial	Foot Designation			English Terms	Italian Terms
	16' Basis	8' Basis	4' Basis		
32nd	1/2'	1/4'	1/8'	Thirty-sixth	Trigesimasesta
40th	2/5'	1/5'	1/10'	Thirty-eighth	Trigesimaottava
48th	1/3'	1/6'	1/12'	Fortieth	Quadragesima
64th	1/4'	1/8'	1/16'	Forty-third	Quadragesimaterza

APPENDIX D

1. VALUES FOR THE DIAMETERS OF THE FREIBERG NORMPRINCIPAL[a]
(VALUES IN MILLIMETERS)

Note	32'	16'	8'	4'	2'	1'	1/2'	1/4'	1/8'	1/16'
C	439.7	261.5	155.5	92.4	54.9	32.6	19.3	11.5	6.8	4.0
C♯	421.2	250.4	148.9	88.5	52.6	31.3	18.6	11.0	6.5	3.9
D	403.2	239.8	142.6	84.7	50.4	29.9	17.8	10.5	6.3	3.7
D♯	386.2	229.6	136.5	81.1	48.2	28.7	16.9	10.1	6.0	3.6
E	369.9	219.9	130.7	77.7	46.2	27.4	16.3	9.7	5.7	3.4
F	354.1	210.6	125.2	74.4	44.2	26.3	15.6	9.3	5.5	3.3
F♯	339.1	201.6	119.9	71.3	42.3	25.2	14.9	8.8	5.2	3.1
G	324.7	193.1	114.8	68.2	40.5	24.1	14.3	8.5	5.0	3.0
G♯	311.0	184.9	109.9	65.3	38.8	23.1	13.7	8.1	4.8	2.8
A	297.8	177.1	105.3	62.6	37.2	22.1	13.1	7.8	4.6	2.7
A♯	285.2	169.5	100.8	59.9	35.6	21.1	12.6	7.4	4.4	2.6
B	273.1	162.3	96.5	57.4	34.1	20.2	12.0	7.1	4.2	2.5

[a]The table is predicated upon International Pitch (a' = 435 cycles per second), a base value of 155.5 mm. for C 8', and an octave ratio of diminution of 1:$\sqrt{8}$ for the cross-sectional areas or 1:$\sqrt[4]{8}$ for the diameters.

APPENDIX D--Continued

2. THE FREIBERG NORMPRINCIPAL ADJUSTED
TO AMERICAN STANDARD PITCH OF
$\underline{a}'$ = 440 CYCLES PER SECOND

In order to make it possible to compare modern American scales with those in use in Europe today, it is necessary to have available in tabular form the diameter dimensions of the Freiberg Normprincipal adjusted to represent equivalent values for American Standard Pitch. This pitch establishes a reference frequency of $\underline{a}'$ = 440 cycles per second. Since the values for the Normprincipal were developed and proposed by the Freiberger Orgelkommission in 1927-28, they are predicated upon International Pitch ($\underline{a}'$ = 435 cycles per second) and require appropriate adjustment in order to secure equivalent values at other reference pitches. The method for converting these values from International to American Standard Pitch follows the subjoined mathematical propositions.

Since the difference in frequency between the American Standard and the International Pitch are known, and since the values for the frequencies in both systems relate the octaves as 2/1, while those for the diameters relate the same as $1/\sqrt[4]{8}$, it will be necessary, first of all, to determine what geometric portion of an octave the difference in frequency of the reference notes represents, and then apply the resultant coefficient to the known diameter of a reference pipe in International Pitch in order to secure

APPENDIX D--Continued

a numerical value for the unknown diameter of a parallel

pipe in American Standard Pitch.

The interval of the octave relates the frequencies

of its components by the ratio of 2/1; in equation form,

the relationship appears as a proportion: $f/F = 2/1$, where

F is the frequency of a given note, and f, that of its super

octave. In order to determine which geometric portion of

an octave the actual difference in frequency between paral-

lel notes of the two systems comprises, an unknown root (x)

will need to be extracted from the octave ratio, thus:

$$\frac{f_x}{F} = \sqrt[x]{\frac{2}{1}} \quad \text{or} \quad \frac{\sqrt[x]{2}}{1} \quad ,$$

where f_x represents the frequency of

a given note in American Standard Pitch (a' = 440 cycles per

second), and F, the frequency of an equivalent note in In-

ternational Pitch (a' = 435 cycles per second). According-

ly, $\frac{440}{435} = \frac{\sqrt[x]{2}}{1}$; solving for x: $\frac{\log 2}{x} = \log 440 -$

log 435, or $x = \dfrac{\log 2}{\log 440 + \text{colog } 435}$ or $x = 60.65.$

Therefore, the difference in frequency of identical notes

in American Standard and International Pitch is equal to

the 60.65th root of the octave, or $f_x / F = \dfrac{\sqrt[60.65]{2}}{1}$.

The interval of the octave further relates the

diameters of its components as $1/\sqrt[4]{8}$; in equation form,

APPENDIX D--Continued

thus: $\dfrac{d}{D} = \dfrac{1}{\sqrt[4]{8}}$, where $\underline{D}$ is the diameter of a given pipe,

and $\underline{d}$, that of its super octave. In order to determine the

equivalent diameter for a reference pipe when tuned to Amer-

ican Standard rather than to International Pitch, the equa-

tion will need to be influenced by the coefficient which

represents that geometric portion of the octave reflected

by the frequency difference of parallel notes in the two

systems, thus: $\dfrac{d_x}{D} = \dfrac{60.65}{\sqrt{\dfrac{1}{\sqrt[4]{8}}}}$ or $\dfrac{1}{60.65\sqrt{\dfrac{1}{\sqrt[4]{8}}}}$, where

$\underline{D}$ represents the diameter of a reference pipe in Interna-

tional, and $\underline{d_x}$, that of a parallel pipe in American Stand-

ard Pitch. If 155.5 mm. is taken as the diameter for $\underline{C}$ 8'

in International Pitch, then $\dfrac{d_x}{155.5} = \dfrac{1}{60.65\sqrt{\dfrac{4}{\sqrt{8}}}}$ or $d_x =$

$\dfrac{155.5}{242.6\sqrt{8}}$ or 154.173 mm. Therefore, the diameter of $\underline{C}$ 8'

in American Standard Pitch needs to be 154.173 mm. in order

to represent an equivalence for $\underline{C}$ 8' in International Pitch.

With the numerical value thus defined, it is possible to

compute the diameter dimensions for the remaining and suc-

cessively ascending half-steps by multiplying the directly

underlying value by $1 / \sqrt[16]{2}$. The actual values for all

notes in the table bespeak equivalences for parallel notes

of the Freiberg Normprincipal. A table showing values for

all notes of the usable compass follows.

APPENDIX D—Continued

2. VALUES FOR THE DIAMETERS OF THE AMERICAN EQUIVALENT OF THE FREIBERG NORMPRINCIPAL[a]
(VALUES IN MILLIMETERS)

Note	32'	16'	8'	4'	2'	1'	1/2'	1/4'	1/8'
C	436.06	259.28	154.17[b]	91.67	54.51	32.41	19.27	11.46	6.81
C#	417.57	248.29	147.63	87.78	52.20	31.04	18.45	10.97	6.52
D	399.87	237.76	141.36	84.06	49.98	29.72	17.67	10.51	6.25
D#	382.91	227.68	135.38	80.50	47.86	28.46	16.92	10.06	5.98
E	366.68	218.03	129.64	77.09	45.83	27.25	16.21	9.64	5.73
F	351.13	208.78	124.14	73.82	43.89	26.10	15.52	9.23	5.49
F#	336.25	199.93	118.88	70.68	42.03	24.99	14.86	8.84	5.25
G	322.00	191.46	113.84	67.69	40.25	23.93	14.23	8.46	5.03
G#	308.35	183.34	109.01	64.82	38.54	22.92	13.63	8.10	4.82
A	295.27	175.57	104.39	62.07	36.91	21.95	13.05	7.76	4.61
A#	282.73	168.12	99.97	59.44	35.34	21.02	12.50	7.43	4.42
B	270.76	160.99	95.73	56.92	33.84	20.12	11.97	7.12	4.23

[a]The table is predicated upon American Standard Pitch (a' = 440 cycles per second), a base value of 154.17 mm. for C 8', and an octave ratio of diminution of $1:\sqrt{8}$ for the cross-sectional areas or $1:\sqrt[4]{8}$ for the diameters.

[b]This value is derived by conversion from the Freiberg Normprincipal table currently in use in Europe. It bespeaks the American equivalent of the 155.5 mm. C 8' generally found in modern European tables.

APPENDIX D--Continued

3. THE FREIBERG NORMPRINCIPAL ADJUSTED
TO THE PRAETORIUS CHORTON OF
a' = 445 CYCLES PER SECOND

In order to make it possible to compare Praetorius'
scales with those in use today, it is similarly necessary
to have available in tabular form the diameter dimensions
of the Freiberg Normprincipal adjusted to represent equivalent values for Praetorius' reference pitch or Chorton.
The present study proposes and accepts a reference pitch
of a' = 445 cycles per second as an acceptable value for
Praetorius' Chorton. The reasons for adopting this value
are fully set forth in chapter xiv of the present study.
The method of conversion follows the mathematical propositions set forth in item 2 of the present appendix, except
that the pertinent numerical values reflecting the Chorton
must be substituted.

The geometric portion of the octave represented by
the difference in frequency between the Praetorius Chorton
and the International Pitch can be established by the equa-

tion: $\dfrac{f_x}{F} = \sqrt[x]{\dfrac{2}{1}}$ or $\dfrac{\sqrt[x]{2}}{1}$, where f_x is Praetorius' Chor-

ton (a' = 445 cycles per second), and F is International
Pitch (a' = 435 cycles per second). Accordingly, by insert-

ing the numerical values, $\dfrac{445}{435} = \dfrac{\sqrt[x]{2}}{1}$; by solving for x,

$\dfrac{\log 2}{x} = \log 445 - \log 435,$ or x $= \dfrac{\log 2}{\log 445 + \text{colog } 440}$

APPENDIX D—Continued

or $x = 30.5$. Therefore, the difference in frequency between parallel notes in Praetorius' Chorton and in International Pitch is equal to the 30.5th root of the octave, or

$$\frac{f_x}{F} = \frac{\sqrt[30.5]{2}}{1}.$$

The numerical value for the diameter dimension of a given note in Praetorius' Chorton can be derived from the value of a parallel note in International Pitch by applying the above coefficient to the octave ratio of the diameters of the two systems, as follows: $\dfrac{d_x}{D} = \sqrt[30.5]{\dfrac{1}{\sqrt[4]{8}}}$ or

$\dfrac{1}{\sqrt[30.5]{\sqrt[4]{8}}}$, where $\underline{D}$ represents the diameter of a reference pipe in International Pitch, and $\underline{d}_x$, that of a parallel pipe in Praetorius' Chorton. If 155.5 mm. is taken as the diameter dimension for $\underline{C}$ 8' in International Pitch, then

$$\frac{d_x}{155.5} = \frac{1}{\sqrt[30.5]{\sqrt[4]{8}}} \quad \text{or} \quad d_x = \frac{155.5}{\sqrt[122]{8}} \quad \text{or} \quad d_x = 152.872 \text{ mm.}$$

Therefore, the diameter dimension of $\underline{C}$ 8' in Praetorius' Chorton needs to be 152.872 mm. in order to represent an equivalent value for the $\underline{C}$ 8' of 155.5 mm. in International Pitch. A table showing the values for all notes of the usable compass follows.

APPENDIX D--Continued

3. VALUES FOR THE DIAMETERS OF THE PRAETORIUS EQUIVALENT
OF THE FREIBERG NORMPRINCIPAL[a]
(VALUES IN MILLIMETERS)

Note	32'	16'	8'	4'	2'	1'	1/2'	1/4'	1/8'
C	432.38	257.10	152.87[b]	90.90	54.05	32.14	19.11	11.36	6.76
C♯	414.06	246.20	146.39	87.04	51.76	30.78	18.30	10.88	6.47
D	396.50	235.76	140.51	83.35	49.56	29.47	17.56	10.42	6.20
D♯	379.69	225.76	134.27	79.82	47.46	28.22	16.78	9.98	5.93
E	363.59	216.19	128.55	76.44	45.45	27.02	16.07	9.55	5.68
F	348.18	207.03	123.10	73.20	43.52	25.88	15.39	9.15	5.44
F♯	333.41	198.25	117.88	70.25	41.68	24.78	14.74	8.78	5.21
G	319.28	189.84	112.88	67.14	39.91	23.73	14.11	8.39	4.99
G♯	305.74	181.80	108.10	64.27	38.22	22.72	13.51	8.03	4.78
A	292.78	174.09	103.51	61.55	36.60	21.76	12.94	7.69	4.57
A♯	281.01	166.71	99.12	58.94	35.13	20.84	12.39	7.37	4.39
B	268.54	159.64	94.92	56.44	33.57	19.95	11.87	7.06	4.20

[a]The table is predicated upon Praetorius' Chorton (a' = 445 cycles per second), a base value of 152.872 mm. for C 8', and an octave ratio of diminution of
1:√8 for the cross-sectional areas or 1:⁴√8 for the diameters.

[b]This value is derived by conversion from the Freiberg Normprincipal table
currently in use in Europe. It bespeaks the Praetorius equivalent of the 155.5 mm.
C 8' generally found in modern European tables.

APPENDIX E

THEORETICAL LENGTHS OF OPEN CYLINDRICAL PIPES[a]
(VALUES IN CENTIMETERS)

Note	16'	8'	4'	2'	1'	1/2'	1/4'	1/8'
C	525.55	262.78	131.39	65.69	32.85	16.42	8.21	4.11
C♯	495.98	247.99	124.00	62.00	31.00	15.50	7.75	3.87
D	468.14	234.07	117.04	58.52	29.26	14.63	7.31	3.66
D♯	441.90	220.95	110.48	55.24	27.62	13.81	6.90	3.45
E	417.12	208.56	104.28	52.14	26.07	13.04	6.52	3.26
F	393.71	196.86	98.43	49.21	24.61	12.30	6.15	3.08
F♯	371.58	185.79	92.90	46.45	23.22	11.61	5.81	2.90
G	350.72	175.36	87.68	43.84	21.92	10.96	5.48	2.74
G♯	331.06	165.53	82.77	41.38	20.69	10.35	5.17	2.59
A	312.47	156.24	78.12	39.06	19.53	9.76	4.88	2.44
A♯	294.93	147.47	73.73	36.87	18.43	9.22	4.61	2.30
B	278.35	139.18	69.59	34.79	17.40	8.70	4.35	2.17

[a]Valid only for a reference pitch of a' = 440 cycles per second (American Standard Pitch) at 20° Centigrade or 68° Fahrenheit.

APPENDIX F

THEORETICAL LENGTHS OF COVERED CYLINDRICAL PIPES[a]
(VALUES IN CENTIMETERS)

Note	16'	8'	4'	2'	1'	1/2'	1/4'	1/8'
C	262.78	131.39	65.69	32.85	16.42	8.21	4.11	2.06
C♯	247.99	124.00	62.00	31.00	15.50	7.75	3.87	1.98
D	234.07	117.04	58.52	29.26	14.63	7.31	3.66	1.83
D♯	220.95	110.48	55.24	27.62	13.81	6.90	3.45	1.73
E	208.56	104.28	52.14	26.07	13.04	6.52	3.26	1.63
F	196.86	98.43	49.21	24.61	12.30	6.15	3.08	1.54
F♯	185.79	92.90	46.45	23.22	11.61	5.81	2.90	1.45
G	175.36	87.68	43.84	21.92	10.96	5.48	2.74	1.37
G♯	165.53	82.77	41.38	20.69	10.35	5.17	2.59	1.29
A	156.24	78.12	39.06	19.53	9.76	4.88	2.44	1.22
A♯	147.47	73.73	36.87	18.43	9.22	4.61	2.30	1.15
B	139.18	69.59	34.79	17.40	8.70	4.35	2.17	1.08

[a]Valid only for a reference pitch of a' = 440 cycles per second (American Standard Pitch) at 20° Centigrade or 68° Fahrenheit.

APPENDIX G

THEORETICAL LENGTHS FOR COVERED CONICAL PIPES[a]
(VALUES IN CENTIMETERS)

Note	16'	8'	4'	2'	1'	1/2'	1/4'	1/8'
C	371.62	185.81	92.91	46.45	23.23	11.61	5.80	2.90
C#	350.72	175.36	87.68	43.84	21.92	10.96	5.48	2.74
D	331.00	165.50	82.75	41.38	20.69	10.34	5.17	2.59
D#	312.48	156.24	78.12	39.06	19.53	9.77	4.88	2.44
E	294.96	147.48	73.74	36.87	18.44	9.22	4.61	2.30
F	278.39	139.19	69.60	34.80	17.40	8.70	4.35	2.17
F#	262.76	131.38	65.69	32.85	16.42	8.21	4.11	2.05
G	248.00	124.00	62.00	31.00	15.50	7.75	3.87	1.94
G#	234.08	117.04	58.52	29.26	14.63	7.32	3.66	1.83
A	220.96	110.48	55.24	27.62	13.81	6.90	3.45	1.72
A#	208.55	104.28	52.14	26.07	13.03	6.52	3.26	1.63
B	196.82	98.41	49.20	24.60	12.30	6.15	3.07	1.54

[a]Valid only for a reference pitch of $a' = 440$ cycles per second (American Standard Pitch) at 20° Centigrade or 68° Fahrenheit.

APPENDIX H

OCTAVE RATIOS OF DIMINUTION
FOR THE DIAMETERS

| Half Measure on | | Octave Ratios | | Alternate Form of Ratio | Symbolization |
Step (1)	Pipe (2)	Raw (3)	Reduced (4)	(5)	(6)
12	13	$1/\ 2^{12/12}$	$1/\ 2$	$1/\ 2$	$\diagup\diagdown$
13	14	$1/\ 2^{12/13}$	$1/\ 2^{12/13}$	$1/\ \sqrt[13]{2^{12}}$	$\diagup\diagdown$
14	15	$1/\ 2^{12/14}$	$1/\ 2^{6/7}$	$1/\ \sqrt[7]{64}$	$\diagup\diagdown$
15	16	$1/\ 2^{12/15}$	$1/\ 2^{4/5}$	$1/\ \sqrt[5]{16}$	$\diagup\diagdown$
16	17	$1/\ 2^{12/16}$	$1/\ 2^{3/4}$	$1/\ \sqrt[4]{8}$	$=$
17	18	$1/\ 2^{12/17}$	$1/\ 2^{12/17}$	$1/\ \sqrt[17]{2^{12}}$	$\diagdown\diagup$
18	19	$1/\ 2^{12/18}$	$1/\ 2^{2/3}$	$1/\ \sqrt[3]{4}$	$\diagdown\diagup$
19	20	$1/\ 2^{12/19}$	$1/\ 2^{12/19}$	$1/\ \sqrt[19]{2^{12}}$	$\diagdown\diagup$
20	21	$1/\ 2^{12/20}$	$1/\ 2^{3/5}$	$1/\ \sqrt[5]{8}$	$\diagdown\diagup$
21	22	$1/\ 2^{12/21}$	$1/\ 2^{4/7}$	$1/\ \sqrt[7]{16}$	$\diagdown\diagup$
22	23	$1/\ 2^{12/22}$	$1/\ 2^{6/11}$	$1/\ \sqrt[11]{64}$	$\diagdown\diagup$

APPENDIX I

VALUES FOR THE MOUTH WIDTHS OF THE AMERICAN EQUIVALENT
OF THE FREIBERG NORMPRINCIPAL[a]
(VALUES IN MILLIMETERS)

Note	32'	16'	8'	4'	2'	1'	1/2'	1/4'	1/8'
C	342.47	203.64	121.09	72.00	42.81	25.45	15.14	9.00	5.35
C#	327.95	195.00	115.95	68.94	40.99	24.37	14.49	8.62	5.12
D	314.07	186.74	111.02	66.02	39.26	23.34	13.88	8.25	4.91
D#	300.75	178.82	106.33	63.22	37.59	22.35	13.29	7.90	4.70
E	288.00	171.23	101.82	60.54	36.00	21.40	12.73	7.57	4.50
F	275.77	163.98	97.50	57.97	34.47	20.50	12.19	7.25	4.31
F#	264.08	157.03	93.37	55.51	33.01	19.63	11.67	6.94	4.13
G	252.90	150.37	89.41	53.16	31.61	18.80	11.18	6.65	3.95
G#	242.17	144.00	85.62	50.91	30.27	18.00	10.70	6.36	3.78
A	231.90	137.88	81.99	48.75	28.99	17.24	10.25	6.09	3.62
A#	222.05	132.04	78.52	46.68	27.76	16.51	9.81	5.84	3.47
B	212.65	126.45	75.19	44.70	26.58	15.81	9.40	5.59	3.32

[a] The table is predicated upon a reference pitch of $\underline{a}'$ = 440 cycles per second (American Standard Pitch). All of the values represent 1/4 of the circumference values of the Normprincipal (R_m = 1/4).

APPENDIX J

VALUES FOR THE DIAMETERS AND CORRESPONDING MOUTH WIDTHS OF THE AMERICAN EQUIVALENT OF THE FREIBERG NORMPRINCIPAL[a]
(VALUES IN MILLIMETERS)

Note	32' Diameter	32' Mouth Width	16' Diameter	16' Mouth Width	8' Diameter	8' Mouth Width	4' Diameter	4' Mouth Width
C	436.06	342.47	259.28	203.64	154.17	121.09	91.67	72.00
C#	417.57	327.95	248.29	195.00	147.63	115.95	87.78	68.94
D	399.87	314.07	237.76	186.74	141.36	111.02	84.06	66.02
D#	382.91	300.75	227.68	178.82	135.38	106.33	80.50	63.22
E	366.68	288.00	218.03	171.23	129.64	101.82	77.09	60.54
F	351.13	275.77	208.78	163.98	124.14	97.50	73.82	57.97
F#	336.25	264.08	199.93	157.03	118.88	93.37	70.68	55.51
G	322.00	252.90	191.46	150.37	113.84	89.41	67.69	53.16
G#	308.35	242.17	183.34	144.00	109.01	85.62	64.82	50.91
A	295.27	231.90	175.57	137.88	104.39	81.99	62.07	48.75
A#	282.73	222.05	168.12	132.04	99.97	78.52	59.44	46.68
B	270.76	212.65	160.99	126.45	95.73	75.19	56.92	44.70

Continued on following page

[a]The table is predicated upon American Standard Pitch (a' = 440 cycles per second); temperature at 20° Centigrade or 68° Fahrenheit; diameters of the Normprincipal; mouth widths are 1/4 of the circumferences; octave ratio of diminution for all values equals 1:$\sqrt[4]{8}$.

APPENDIX J—Continued

Note	2' Diameter	2' Mouth Width	1' Diameter	1' Mouth Width	1/2' Diameter	1/2' Mouth Width	1/4' Diameter	1/4' Mouth Width	1/8' Diameter	1/8' Mouth Width
C	54.51	42.81	32.41	25.45	19.27	15.14	11.46	9.00	6.81	5.35
C#	52.20	40.99	31.04	24.37	18.45	14.49	10.97	8.62	6.52	5.12
D	49.98	39.26	29.72	23.34	17.67	13.88	10.51	8.25	6.25	4.91
D#	47.86	37.59	28.46	22.35	16.92	13.29	10.06	7.90	5.98	4.70
E	45.83	36.00	27.25	21.40	16.21	12.73	9.64	7.57	5.73	4.50
F	43.89	34.47	26.10	20.50	15.52	12.19	9.23	7.25	5.49	4.31
F#	42.03	33.01	24.99	19.63	14.86	11.67	8.84	6.94	5.25	4.13
G	40.25	31.61	23.93	18.80	14.23	11.18	8.46	6.65	5.03	3.95
G#	38.54	30.27	22.92	18.00	13.63	10.70	8.10	6.36	4.82	3.78
A	36.91	28.99	21.95	17.24	13.05	10.25	7.76	6.09	4.61	3.62
A#	35.34	27.76	21.02	16.51	12.50	9.81	7.43	5.84	4.42	3.47
B	33.84	26.58	20.12	15.81	11.97	9.40	7.12	5.59	4.23	3.32

APPENDIX K

1. RATIOS OF MOUTH WIDTHS: A COMPOSITE OF VARIOUS DIVISIONS OF THE RATIOS[a]

<u>Diminishing, Left to Right</u>:

[1/3]	5/16	4/13	3/10	5/17
[2/7]	5/18	3/11	4/15	5/19
[1/4]	5/21	4/17	3/13	5/22
[2/9]	5/23	3/14	4/19	5/24
[1/5]	5/26	4/21	3/16	5/27
[2/11]	5/28	3/17	4/23	5/29
[1/6]	5/31	4/25	3/19	5/32
[2/13]	5/33	3/20	4/27	5/34

[a]The values most commonly used, are bracketed. The spacing between the successive values is non-equidistant.

APPENDIX K--Continued

2. RATIOS OF MOUTH WIDTHS: A TEN-POINT
DIVISION OF THE RATIOS[a]

Diminishing, Left to Right:

[1/3]	10/31	5/16	10/33	5/17
[2/7]	5/18	10/37	5/19	10/39
[1/4]	10/41	5/21	10/43	5/22
[2/9]	5/23	10/47	5/24	10/49
[1/5]	10/51	5/26	10/53	5/27
[2/11]	5/28	10/57	5/29	10/59
[1/6]	10/61	5/31	10/63	5/32
[2/13]	5/33	10/67	5/34	10/69

[a]The values most commonly used, are bracketed.
The spacing between the successive values is equidistant.

APPENDIX L

QUANTITATIVE INTERPRETATION OF THE QUALITATIVE
DESCRIPTIONS OF THE MOUTH WIDTHS[a]

Qualitative Description	Approximate Range (Diminishing, Left to Right)				
Very Wide	. .	. .	[1/3]	5/16	4/13
Wide	3/10	5/17	[2/7]	5/18	3/11
Normal	4/15	5/19	[1/4]	5/21	4/17
Medium	3/13	5/22	[2/9]	5/23	3/14
Moderately Narrow	4/19	5/24	[1/5]	5/26	4/21
Narrow	3/16	5/27	[2/11]	5/28	3/17
Very Narrow . . .	4/23	5/29	[1/6]	5/31	4/25
Minimum	3/19	5/32	[2/13]	5/33	1/7

[a]The values most commonly used, are bracketed.

APPENDIX M

RATIOS OF MOUTH WIDTHS AS INFLUENCED
BY TABULAR DIFFERENCE

Tabular Difference $(T_w - T_d)$	Exact Ratio $(W/D\pi)$	Approximate Ratio	Tabular Difference $(T_w - T_d)$	Exact Ratio $(W/D\pi)$	Approximate Ratio
-13 HT	1/7.025	1/7	-3 HT	1/4.555	5/23
-12 HT	1/6.728	10/67	-2 HT	1/4.362	5/22
-11 HT	1/6.442	5/32	-1 HT	1/4.177	5/21
-10 HT	1/6.169	5/31	0 HT	1/4.000	1/4
-9 HT	1/5.908	10/59	+1 HT	1/3.831	5/19
-8 HT	1/5.656	10/57	+2 HT	1/3.668	10/37
-7 HT	1/5.417	5/27	+3 HT	1/3.513	2/7
-6 HT	1/5.187	5/26	+4 HT	1/3.363	5/19
-5 HT	1/4.968	1/5	+5 HT	1/3.221	5/16
-4 HT	1/4.757	5/24	+6 HT	1/3.085	10/31

APPENDIX N

TABULAR DIFFERENCES AS INFLUENCED BY DEPENDENT RATIOS OF MOUTH WIDTHS

Dependent Ratio $(W/D\pi)$	Approximate Tabular Difference between W and D $(T_w - T_d)$	Dependent Ratio $(W/D\pi)$	Approximate Tabular Difference between W and D $(T_w - T_d)$
1/3	+7 HT	10/51	−5 2/3 HT
10/31	+6 HT	5/26	−6 HT
5/16	+5 HT	10/53	−6 1/2 HT
10/33	+4 1/3 HT	5/27	−7 HT
5/17	+3 2/3 HT	2/11	−7 1/3 HT
2/7	+3 HT	5/28	−7 2/3 HT
5/18	+2 1/3 HT	10/57	−8 1/6 HT
10/37	+1 2/3 HT	5/29	−8 2/3 HT
5/19	+1 1/6 HT	10/59	−9 HT
10/39	+1/2 HT	1/6	−9 1/3 HT
1/4	0 HT	10/61	−9 2/3 HT
10/41	−2/3 HT	5/31	−10 1/6 HT
5/21	−1 1/6 HT	10/63	−10 1/2 HT
10/43	−1 2/3 HT	5/32	−10 5/6 HT
5/22	−2 1/6 HT	2/13	−11 1/6 HT
2/9	−2 2/3 HT	5/33	−11 1/2 HT
5/23	−3 1/6 HT	10/67	−12 HT
10/47	−3 2/3 HT	5/34	−12 1/3 HT
5/24	−4 1/6 HT	10/69	−12 2/3 HT
10/49	−4 2/3 HT	1/7	−13 HT
1/5	−5 1/6 HT		

APPENDIX O

1. RATIOS OF THE CUTUP: COMMONLY USED
DIVISIONS OF THE RATIOS[a]

Diminishing, Left to Right:

[1/3]	5/16	4/13	3/10	5/17
[2/7]	5/18	3/11	4/15	5/19
[1/4]	5/21	4/17	3/13	5/22
[2/9]	5/23	3/14	4/19	5/24
[1/5]	5/26	4/21	3/16	5/27
[2/11]	5/28	3/17	4/23	5/29

[a]The values most commonly used, are bracketed.

APPENDIX O—Continued

2. QUANTITATIVE INTERPRETATION OF THE QUALITATIVE
DESCRIPTIONS OF THE CUTUPS[a]

Qualitative Description	Approximate Range (Diminishing, Left to Right)						
Very High	. .	1/3	10/31	[5/16]	4/13	. .	. .
High	. .	3/10	5/17	[2/7]	5/18	3/11	. .
Normal	4/15	5/19	10/39	[1/4]	10/41	5/21	4/17
Medium	. .	3/13	5/22	[2/9]	5/23	3/14	. .
Low	4/19	5/24	10/49	[1/5]	10/51	5/26	4/21
Very Low	. .	3/16	5/27	[2/11]	5/28	3/17	. .
Minimum	4/23	5/29	10/59	[1/6]	10/61	. .	. .

[a]The values most commonly used, are bracketed.

APPENDIX P

APPROXIMATE NOTATION OF THE FIRST SIXTEEN PARTIALS OF THE HARMONIC SERIES

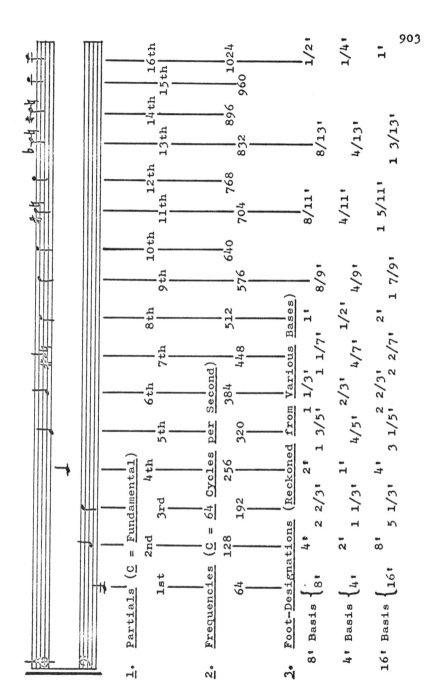

APPENDIX Q

EQUIVALENT LINEAR MEASURES

1. Rhenish Measure

Rhenish Inches	Degrees	Millimeters	British Inches	Rhenish Inches	Degrees	Millimeters	British Inches
1.0	10	26.15[a]	1.03[b]	3.1	31	81.08	3.19
1.1	11	28.77	1.13	3.2	32	83.69	3.29
1.2	12	31.38	1.23	3.3	33	86.31	3.40
1.3	13	34.00	1.34	3.4	34	88.92	3.50
1.4	14	36.62	1.44	3.5	35	91.54	3.60
1.5	15	39.23	1.54	3.6	36	94.15	3.70
1.6	16	41.85	1.65	3.7	37	96.77	3.81
1.7	17	44.46	1.75	3.8	38	99.39	3.91
1.8	18	47.08	1.85	3.9	39	102.00	4.01
1.9	19	49.69	1.96	4.0	40	104.62	4.12
2.0	20	52.31	2.06	4.1	41	107.23	4.22
2.1	21	54.92	2.16	4.2	42	109.85	4.32
2.2	22	57.54	2.26	4.3	43	112.46	4.42
2.3	23	60.15	2.37	4.4	44	115.07	4.53
2.4	24	62.77	2.47	4.5	45	117.69	4.63
2.5	25	65.38	2.57	4.6	46	120.31	4.73
2.6	26	68.00	2.68	4.7	47	122.92	4.84
2.7	27	70.62	2.78	4.8	48	125.54	4.94
2.8	28	73.23	2.88	4.9	49	128.15	5.04
2.9	29	75.85	2.98	5.0	50	130.76	5.15
3.0	30	78.46	3.09				

[a]Derived from Meyer, Universal-Lexikon (1864), VII, 227, which establishes the Rhenish foot of 12 inches as 0.31385 meter. Accordingly, the Rhenish inch equals 313.85 / 12 or 26.1542 millimeters.

[b]Derived as 26.15 / 25.4 = 1.029 British inches.

APPENDIX Q--Continued

2. Brunswick Measure

Brunswick Inches	Millimeters	British Inches	Brunswick Inches	Millimeters	British Inches
0.1	2.38	.093	1.0	23.78	.936
1/8	2.97	.117	2.0	47.56	1.870
0.2	4.76	.190	3.0	71.34	2.809
1/4	5.94	.234	4.0	95.12	3.745
0.3	7.13	.280	5.0	118.90	4.670
3/8	8.92	.351	6.0	142.68	5.620
0.4	9.51	.375	7.0	166.46	6.550
0.5	11.89	.468	8.0	190.24	7.490
0.6	14.27	.562	9.0	214.02	8.426
5/8	14.86	.585	10.0	237.80	9.362
0.7	16.65	.655	11.0	261.58	10.298
3/4	17.83	.702	12.0	285.36[a]	11.235[b]
0.8	19.02	.749	24.0	570.72	22.469
7/8	20.81	.818	36.0	856.08	33.704
0.9	21.40	.843	48.0	1141.44	44.940

[a]Key reference from N. Bessaraboff, Ancient European Musical Instruments (Boston, 1941), p. 356, Appendix A.

[b]Derived as 285.36 / 25.4 = 11.235 British inches.

APPENDIX R

STOP NOMENCLATURE

Inasmuch as Praetorius' descriptions of the various species of pipes are extremely important in developing a clear and true concept of his viewpoints concerning the stops and their classification, a comparative presentation of the stop nomenclature becomes highly necessary. It is evident that Praetorius sought not only to report what he had observed in instruments known to him, but also to organize and classify contemporary knowledge and practice related to this subject, and in some cases to propose modifications. Praetorius' personal friendship and association with Esaias Compenius, one of the great organ builders of the time, was invaluable to him for this presentation, and lends a degree of authenticity to his conclusions which could not so easily have been achieved without such association.

Certain problems constantly stalk the scholar who seeks to translate the names of Praetorius' registers. His spellings are archaic and largely obsolete; his qualifying adjectives follow inconsistent methods of declension and often make the designations long and cumbersome; parallel terms in modern German often denote registers which differ widely from the ones which Praetorius describes.

Since Mahrenholz in his Die Orgelregister, ihre Geschichte und ihr Bau (2nd ed.; Kassel, 1942) proposes a uniform nomenclature in modern German, it would be appropriate

APPENDIX R—Continued

to follow his suggestions, but to subject them to the following modifications, in order to arrive at an acceptable and
practical American usage:

    1. The spelling of the nouns might well follow
Mahrenholz' practice

    2. Qualifying adjectives (as aequal, grosz,
grob, klein, etc.,) had best be rendered without declension, since they have often been used in this
way in American organ building practice; furthermore,
a shorter designation is thereby possible

Praetorius' Designation	Adaptation for Present Study
Apffel Regal	Apfelregal

Baerpipen, Baerpfeiffen
  Baerpipen Bass
  Grosz Baerpipen
	Baerpfeife
	  Baerpfeifebass
	  Gross Baerpfeife

Bawerfloeit, Bawerfloeitlein
  Bawerfloeit Basz, Paeurlin
  Bawer Rohrfloetlin Basz
	Bauerfloete
	  Bauerfloetebass
	  Bauer Rohrfloetebass

Blockfloeiten, Plockpfeiffen	Blockfloete

Bombart, Pombarda
  Grosz Bombart
  Bombart Basz
	Bombardon
	  Gross Bombardon
	  Bombardonbass

Cornett
  Cornett Basz
	Kornett
	  Kornettbass

Dulcian
  Dulcian Basz
  Dulzian
	Dulzian
	  Dulzianbass
	  Dulzian

Dulzaen
  Dulzain
	Labial Dulzian
	  Labial Dulzian

APPENDIX R--Continued

Fagott

Fagott

Flachfloeit, Flachfloeiten
   Flachfloeiten Basz
   Grosse Flachfloeit
   Grosse Flachfloeit Basz
   Klein Flachfloeit
   Klein Flachfloeit Basz
   Klein Flachfloeit Discant

Flachfloete
   Flachfloetebass
   Gross Flachfloete
   Gross Flachfloetebass
   Klein Flachfloete
   Klein Flachfloetebass
   Klein Flachfloetediscant

Floeit
   Klein Floeitlin Basz

Floete
   Klein Floetebass

Gedact, Gedacten
   Gedact Basz
   Gedacte Quinta
   Gedact Vntersatz
   Grosz Gedact
   Grosz Gedact Basz
   Grosz Gedacter Sub Basz
   Klein Gedact
   Klein Gedact Basz
   Supergedaectlin

Gedackt
   Gedacktbass
   Gedacktquinte
   Gedacktuntersatz
   Gross Gedackt
   Gross Gedacktbass
   Gross Gedacktsubbass
   Klein Gedackt
   Klein Gedacktbass
   Super Gedackt

Geigend Regal
   Kleingeigend Regal

Geigendregal
   Klein Geigendregal

Gemszhorn, Gembszhoerner
   Gembs Quinta
   Gemszhorn Basz
   Grosz Gembszhorn
   Grosz Gembszhorn Basz
   Klein Gembszhoernlin
   Klein Gembszhoernlin Basz
   Klein Gembszhorn Quinta
   Octaven Gembszhorn
   Octaven Gembszhorn Basz
   Super Gembszhoernlin
   Super Gembszhoernlin Basz

Gemshorn
   Gemsquinte, Gemshornquinte
   Gemshornbass
   Gross Gemshorn
   Gross Gemshornbass
   Klein Gemshorn
   Klein Gemshornbass
   Klein Gemshornquinte
   Octave Gemshorn
   Octave Gemshornbass
   Super Gemshorn
   Super Gemshornbass

Holfloeit, Holfloeiten
   Grosz Holfloeiten
   Grosz Holfloeiten Basz
   Holfloeiten Basz
   Hol Quint
   Kleine Holfloeit
   Kleine Holfloeit Basz

Hohlfloete
   Gross Hohlfloete
   Gross Hohlfloetebass
   Hohlfloetebass
   Hohlquinte
   Klein Hohlfloete
   Klein Hohlfloetebass

Holpfeiff
   Holpfeiffen Discant

Hohlpfeiffe
   Hohlpfeifediscant

Hol Quint, Holquinten	Hohlquinte
Hol Quint Basz	Hohlquintebass
Klein Hol Quinta	Klein Hohlquinte
Jungfraw Regal	Jungfrauregal
Knopff Regal	Knopfregal
Koepfflin Regal	Kopfregal
Krumbhorn, Krumbhoerner	Krummhorn
Grosz Krumbhorn Basz	Gross Krummhornbass
Klein Krumbhorn Basz	Klein Krummhornbass
Krumbhoerner Basz	Krummhornbass
Mixtur	Mixture
Grosse Mixtur	Gross Mixture
Grosse Mixtur Basz	Gross Mixturebass
Klein Mixtur	Klein Mixture
Klein Mixtur Basz	Klein Mixturebass
Mixtur Basz	Mixturebass
Nachthorn	Nachthorn
Klein Nachthorn Basz	Klein Nachthornbass
Nachthorn Basz	Nachthornbass
Nasat, Nasath	Nasat
Octava, Octaven Principal	Octave
Grosz Octava	Gross Octave
Grosz Octava Basz	Gross Octavebass
Klein Octava	Klein Octave
Klein Octava Basz	Klein Octavebass
Octava Basz	Octavebass
Superoctaevlin	Super Octave
Plockpfeiffen, Blockfloeiten	Blockpfeife
Posaune, Posaunen	Posaune
'Posaunen Basz	Posaunebass
Prestant	Praestant
Prestant Basz	Praestantbass
Principal, Principaln	Principal
Grosz Principal	Gross Principal
Grosz Principal Vntersatz	Gross Principaluntersatz
Grosz Sub Principal Basz	Gross Subprincipalbass

Klein Principal	Klein Principal
Klein Principal Basz	Klein Principalbass
Klein Principal Discant	Klein Principaldiscant
Principal Basz	Principalbass
Querfloeit	Querfloete
Grosz Querfloeit	Gross Querfloete
Grosz Querfloeit Basz	Gross Querfloetebass
Quintadeen, Quintadehna	Quintade
Grosz Quintadeen	Gross Quintade
Grosz Quintadeen Basz	Gross Quintadebass
Klein Quintadeen	Klein Quintade
Klein Quintadeen Basz	Klein Quintadebass
Quintadeen Basz	Quintadebass
Quinta	Quinte
Grosz Quinta	Gross Quinte
Grosz Quinta Basz	Gross Quintebass
Klein Quinta	Klein Quinte
Quinta Basz	Quintebass
Quint Floeit	Quintfloete
Rancket	Rankett
Grosz Rancket	Gross Rankett
Grosz Rancket Basz	Gross Rankettbass
Rancket Basz	Rankettbass
Rauschpfeiff	Rauschpfeife
Rauschpfeiffen Basz	Rauschpfeifebass
Rausch Quint	Rauschquinte
Rauschquinten Basz	Rauschquintebass
Regal	Regal
Grob Regal	Grob Regal
Grosz Regal	Gross Regal
Rohrfloeit, Rohrfloeiten	Rohrfloete
Bawer Rohrfloeitlin Basz	Bauer Rohrfloetebass
Grosse Rohrfloeiten	Gross Rohrfloete
Grosse Rohrfloeiten Basz	Gross Rohrfloetebass
Kleine Rohrfloeite	Klein Rohrfloete
Kleine Rohrfloeite Basz	Klein Rohrfloetebass
Rohrschell	Rohrschelle
Super Rohrfloeitlin	Super Rohrfloete
Schallmeyen, Schalmeyen	Schalmei
Klein Schallmeyen	Klein Schalmei
Schallmeyen Basz	Schalmeibass

APPENDIX R--<u>Continued</u>

Scharp	Scharf
Scharp Basz	Scharfbass
Sch..ztzerpfeiff	Schweizerpfeife
Grosz Schweitzerpfeiff	Gross Schweizerpfeife
Grosz Schweitzerpfeiff Basz	Gross Schweizerpfeifebass
Klein Schweitzer Pfeiff	Klein Schweizerpfeife
Klein Schw. Pf. Basz	Klein Schweizerpfeifebass
Klein Schw. Pfei. Disc.	Klein Schweizerpfeifediscant
Schwiegel, Schwiegell	Schwegel
Grosz Schwiegel	Gross Schwegel
Grosz Schwiegel Basz	Gross Schwegelbass
Klein Schwiegel	Klein Schwegel
Klein Schwiegel Basz	Klein Schwegelbass
Sedetz	Sedecima
Siefflit	Siffloete
Sorduen, Sordunen	Sordun
Sorduen Basz	Sordunbass
Spillfloeite, Spillfloeiten	Spillfloete
Spitzfloeit, Spitzfloeiten	Spitzfloete
Klein Spitzfloeit	Klein Spitzfloete
Klein Spitzfloeit Basz	Klein Spitzfloetebass
Spitz Quintlein	Spitzquinte
Suiffloeit, Suiffloeitlin	Siffloete
Trommeten	Trompete, Trumpet
Trommeten Basz	Trompetebass, Trumpetbass
Waldfloeitlin	Waldfloete
Zimbel, Zimbeln	Zimbel
Grober Zimbel	Grob Zimbel
Grober Zimbel Basz	Grob Zimbelbass
Kleiner Zimbel	Klein Zimbel
Klingende Zimbel	Klingend Zimbel
Klingend Zimbel Basz	Klingend Zimbelbass
Repetirende Zimbel	Repetierend Zimbel
Zimbel Basz	Zimbelbass
Zimbel Regal	Zimbelregal
Zincken	Zink
Zincken Discant	Zinkdiscant

APPENDIX S

THE PRAETORIUS NORM

In order to be able to judge the relative scales of
Praetorius' registers, it is necessary to compare them to
some basic norm which was, either consciously or unconscious-
ly, operative at the time of their development and execution.
It would be inappropriate to compare their actual diameter
dimensions to those exhibited in modern Normprincipal tables,
since the base values upon which such tables are predicated
are not necessarily the same. Historically, at least two
base values have been quantitatively defined in theory and
used in practice by general agreement. Toepfer submitted
a diameter dimension of 148.9 mm. for C 8', while the Freiberger Orgelkommission submitted 155.5 mm. for the same.
See Appendix D, 1.

Accordingly, it becomes necessary to seek a hypothetical value which may represent a norm for mensuration
operative among the Praetorius registers, which could appropriately be called, The Praetorius Norm (not to be confused with the Praetorius equivalent of the Freiberg Normprincipal as shown in Appendix D, 3). The present author
proposes that an acceptable base value for C 8' can be extracted from the actual dimensions which Praetorius specifies for the 8' Principal and the 4' Octave. By striking
a geometric mean between these two diameter dimensions, a

useful base value can be established to which the various
species which he defines in a quantitative way can be compared and the deviations noted in positive or negative half-
tones ($\pm$ HT). Such deviations will more nearly approximate
the relative position of these registers in the mensuration
palette of the time than would deviations derived by comparing these registers directly with the Toepfer Norm or the
Freiberg Norm. Inasmuch as each of these norms is predicated
upon a different base value, cross comparisons between them
will fail to reveal how the registers within each system are
related to each other.

Since the diameter dimension for C of the 8' Principal, as shown on Plate XXXVII, 1 of the Theatrum Instrumentorum, equals 142.58 mm., and that for C of the 4' Octave,
as shown on item 2 of the same plate, equals 92.3 mm., the
geometric mean of the two values is equal to $\sqrt{C \times c\sqrt[4]{8}}$ or
$\sqrt{142.58 \times 92.3 \sqrt[4]{8}}$ or 148.77 mm. This dimension, then,
becomes the base value for the Praetorius Norm and is proposed herewith as a useful and practical value for purposes
of comparing the various species of Praetorius registers
with each other and with a hypothetical Principal derived
as shown. The diameters of the remainder of the compass can
be computed, as usually, by relating the octaves to each other as 1: $\sqrt[4]{8}$, or the half-steps, as 1: $\sqrt[16]{2}$.

APPENDIX S--Continued

VALUES FOR THE DIAMETERS OF THE PRAETORIUS NORM[a]

(VALUES IN MILLIMETERS)

Note	32'	16'	8'	4'	2'	1'	1/2'	1/4'	1/8'
C	420.80	250.20	148.77[b]	88.46	52.60	31.27	18.59	11.06	6.57
C♯	403.88	239.60	142.46	84.71	50.48	29.95	17.81	10.59	6.31
D	385.84	229.44	136.42	81.12	48.23	28.68	17.05	10.14	6.03
D♯	369.48	219.70	130.64	77.68	46.18	27.46	16.33	9.71	5.77
E	353.84	210.40	125.10	74.39	44.23	26.30	15.64	9.29	5.53
F	338.84	201.94	119.80	71.23	42.35	25.24	14.97	8.90	5.29
F♯	324.48	192.92	114.72	68.21	40.56	24.11	14.34	8.53	5.07
G	310.72	184.74	109.85	65.32	38.84	23.09	13.73	8.16	4.85
G♯	297.54	176.92	105.20	62.55	37.19	22.11	13.15	7.82	4.65
A	284.92	169.42	100.97	59.90	35.61	21.18	12.62	7.49	4.45
A♯	272.84	162.24	96.46	57.36	34.10	20.28	12.06	7.17	4.26
B	261.28	155.36	92.37	54.92	32.66	19.42	11.55	6.86	4.08

[a]The table is predicated upon a proposed base value of 148.77 mm. for C 8', and an octave ratio of diminution equal to 1:√8 for the cross-sectional areas or 1:⁴√8 for the diameters.

[b]The base value for C 8' is derived as the geometric mean of Praetorius' 8' Principal and 4' Octave as shown on Plate XXXVII, 1 and 2 of the Theatrum Instrumentorum.

APPENDIX T

SUMMARY OF RELATIVE SCALES
OF LABIAL PIPES

Item	Reference to Thea-trum ...: Plate-No.	Reference to Present Atlas: Plate-No.	Diam-eter at Mouth in Mm.	Deviation from Prae-torius Norm
[8' Praetorius Norm	. . .	LXXXVII-1	148.77	. . . .]
16' Quintade	37-6	LXXXVII-5	153.1	-11.5 HT
8' Principal	37-1	LXXXVII-2	142.6	-1.0 HT
8' Gemshorn	37-10	LXXXVII-3	191.7	+6.0 HT
8' Grossgedackt	37-9	LXXXVII-4	149.6	0.0 HT
8' Quintade	37-7	LXXXVIII-2	105.2	-8.0 HT
8' Klein Barduen	38-4	LXXXVIII-3	123.8	-4.5 HT
8' Gedackt	38-6	LXXXVIII-4	133.0	-2.5 HT
8' Rohrfloete	38-7	LXXXVIII-5	156.2	+1.0 HT
[4' Praetorius Norm	. . .	LXXXIX-1	88.46	. . . .]
4' Octave	37-2	LXXXIX-2	92.3	+1.0 HT
4' Offenfloete	38-5	LXXXIX-3	109.9	+5.0 HT
4' Nachthorn, open	37-5	LXXXIX-4	146.1	+11.5 HT
4' Flachfloete	38-3	LXXXIX-6	104.1	+4.0 HT
4' Spillfloete	37-11	LXXXIX-7	93.5	+1.0 HT
4' Koppelfloete	38-2	LXXXIX-8	115.7	+6.0 HT
4' Labial Dulzian	38-1	XC-2	98.3	+2.5 HT
4' Nachthorn-Gedackt	37-8	XC-3	76.0	-3.5 HT
4' Querfloete, open	37-13	XC-4	99.3	+3.0 HT
4' Querfloete-Gedackt	37-14	XC-5	87.7	0.0 HT
[2 2/3' Praetor. Norm	. . .	XCI-1	65.32	. . . .]
2 2/3' Quinte	37-3	XCI-2	70.1	+2.0 HT
[2' Praetorius Norm	. . .	XCI-3	52.6	. . . .]
2' Klein Octave	37-4	XCI-4	46.7	-3.0 HT
2' Blockfloete	37-12	XCI-5	87.7	+12.0 HT

APPENDIX U

1. USABLE SHOP DIMENSIONS FOR THE MODEL PIPES OF
PLATE XXXVII OF THE THEATRUM INSTRUMENTORUM[a]

Item from Plate XXXVII of the Theatrum Instrumentorum	Actual Length of Pipe Body in Cm.	Actual Circumference of Pipe Body in Cm.	Actual Width of Mouth in Mm.
1. 8' Principal	225.6	44.8	90.2
2. 4' Octave	110.4	29.0	58.4
3. 2 2/3' Quint	75.3	22.0	35.0
4. 2' Klein Octave	55.4	14.7	29.2
5. 4' Nachthorn; open	99.3	45.9	81.8
6. 16' Quintade	224.4	48.1	105.2
7. 8' Quintade	106.4	33.1	70.1
8. 4' Nachthorn-Gedackt	54.9	23.9	52.6
9. 8' Grossgedackt	143.2	. . .	93.5
At Mouth	. . .	47.0	. . .
At Top	. . .	9.2	. . .
10. 8' Gemshorn	208.6	. . .	140.3
At Mouth	. . .	60.2	. . .
At Top	. . .	19.5	. . .
11. 4' Spillfloete	48.5	29.4	58.4
Cone Length	59.6	. . .	. . .
Cone Base	. . .	29.4	. . .
Cone Apex	. . .	9.2	. . .
12. 2' Blockfloete	49.1	. . .	46.7
At Mouth	. . .	27.6	. . .
At Top	. . .	12.1	. . .
13. 4' Querfloete; open	237.2	31.2	53.8
14. 4' Querfloete-Gedackt	165.1	27.6	49.1

[a]The present author had the model pipes fabricated according to the dimensions given in this table.

APPENDIX U--Continued

2. USABLE SHOP DIMENSIONS FOR THE MODEL PIPES OF
PLATE XXXVIII OF THE THEATRUM INSTRUMENTORUM[a]

Item from Plate XXXVIII of the Theatrum Instrumentorum	Actual Length of Pipe Body in Cm.	Actual Circumference of Pipe Body in Cm.	Actual Width of Mouth in Mm.
1. 4' [Labial] Dulzian	107.6	. . .	52.1
At Mouth	. . .	30.9	. . .
At Top	. . .	58.1	. . .
2. 4' Koppelfloete	68.3	36.4	57.8
Cone Length	35.9	. . .	. . .
Cone Base	. . .	36.4	. . .
Cone Apex	. . .	16.3	. . .
3. 4' Flachfloete	109.3	. . .	60.2
At Mouth	. . .	32.7	. . .
At Top	. . .	18.2	. . .
4. 4' Klein Barduen	116.8	38.9	81.0
5. 4' Offenfloete	111.0	34.5	69.4
6. 8' Gedackt	113.4	41.8	77.5
7. 8' Rohrfloete or Hohlfloete	127.8	49.1	98.3
Chimney	23.1	12.7	. . .

[a]The present author had the model pipes fabricated
according to the dimensions given in this table.

3. USABLE SHOP DIMENSIONS FOR THE MODEL
PIPES OF THE PFEIFFLIN ZUR CHORMASZ
OF THE DE ORGANOGRAPHIA[a]

Note Designation on Graph	Equivalent Note of 8' Stop	Actual Length of Plate or Pipe Body in Mm.	Actual Width of Plate or Circumference of Pipe Body in Mm.
c	c'''	136.4	52.4
cs	c#'''	129.9	49.4
d	d'''	121.9	46.4
ds	d#'''	115.4	44.6
e	e'''	107.6	41.2
f	f'''	101.6	39.2
fs	f#'''	96.1	37.6
g	g'''	90.5	36.2
gs	g#'''	86.3	35.0
a	a'''	81.5	33.6
b	a#'''	77.0	31.8
h	b'''	72.2	30.0
c̄	c''''	67.3	27.8

[a]The present author had the model
pipes fabricated according to the dimensions
given in this table.

APPENDIX V

Praetorius proposes three methods of laying a bearing in the meantone temperament and tuning the remainder of the compass to it.

1. PROGRESSIVE STEPS AND TESTS FOR TUNING BY MEANS OF THE FIRST METHOD[a]

[a]The black noteheads represent the notes to be tuned, while the white noteheads, either oval or diamond-shaped, represent notes tuned earlier in the course.

APPENDIX V--Continued

2. PROGRESSIVE STEPS AND TESTS FOR TUNING BY MEANS OF THE SECOND METHOD[a]

[a]The black noteheads represent the notes to be tuned, while the white noteheads, either oval or diamond-shaped, represent notes tuned earlier in the course.

APPENDIX V--Continued

3. PROGRESSIVE STEPS AND TESTS FOR
TUNING BY MEANS OF THE
THIRD METHOD[a]

[a]The black noteheads represent the notes to be tuned, while the white noteheads, either oval or diamond-shaped, represent notes tuned earlier in the course.

SECTION   B

BIBLIOGRAPHIES

BIBLIOGRAPHY
PART I

Adelung, Wolfgang. Einfuehrung in den Orgelbau. Leipzig:
Breitkopf & Haertel, 1955.

Audsley, G. Ashdown. The Art of Organ Building. 2 vols.
New York: Dodd, Mead, and Company, 1905.

Bartholomew, W. Acoustics of Music. New York: Prentice
Hall, 1946.

Bedos de Celles, Dom Francois. L'Art du Facteur d'Orgues.
4 vols. in 3 cases. Bordeaux [?]: 1766-1778; facsimile in 2/3 size by C. Mahrenholz, Kassel: Baerenreiter, 1936.

Bericht ueber die dritte Tagung fuer deutsche Orgelkunst in
Freiberg i. Sa. vom 2. bis 7. Oktober 1927. Edited
by C. Mahrenholz. Kassel: Baerenreiter, 1928.

Bericht ueber die Freiburger Tagung fuer deutsche Orgelkunst
vom 27. bis 30. Juli 1926. Edited by W. Gurlitt.
Augsburg: Baerenreiter, 1926.

Boner, C. P. "Acoustic Spectra of Organ Pipes," Journal of
the Acoustical Society of America X (1929), 39.

Buck, Percy. Acoustics for Musicians. Oxford: Clarendon
Press, 1917.

Ellerhorst, W. Handbuch der Orgelkunde. Einsiedeln: Benziger, 1936.

Frotscher, G. Die Orgel. Leipzig: J. J. Weber, 1927.

Hodgman, C. and others. Handbook of Chemistry and Physics.
38th ed.; Cleveland: Chemical Rubber Publishing
Co., 1956.

Jahnn, Hans Henny. "Registernamen und ihr Inhalt," Beitraege zur Organistentagung Hamburg-Luebeck / 6. bis 8.
Juli 1925. Klecken: Ugrino, 1925. Pp. 5-25.

Klotz, Hans. Das Buch von der Orgel. 5th ed.; Kassel:
Baerenreiter, 1955.

Lange, M. Kleine Orgelkunde. Kassel: Baerenreiter, 1954.

Mahrenholz, C. Die Berechnung der Orgelpfeifenmensuren.
Kassel: Baerenreiter, 1938.

_____. Die neue Orgel in der St. Marienkirche zu Goet-
tingen. 2nd ed.; Kassel: Baerenreiter, 1931.

_____. Die Orgelregister, ihre Geschichte und ihr Bau.
2nd ed.; Kassel: Baerenreiter, 1942.

Olson, Harry F. Musical Engineering. New York: McGraw-
Hill Book Co., 1952.

Oosterhof, A. P. and A. Bouman. Orgelbouwkunde. Leiden:
Spruyt, van Mantgem & de Does, 1956.

Praetorius, M. Michael Praetorius' Syntagma, II Teil: Von
den Instrumenten. Wolfenbuettel 1618. Newprint by
R. Eitner. Berlin: Trautwein, 1884. 13. Band der
Publikationen aelterer praktischer und theoretischer
Musikwerke herausgegeben von der Gesellschaft fuer
Musikforschung.

_____. Syntagma musicum Tomus Secundus De Organographia.
Wolfenbuettel: Elias Holwein, 1619.

_____. Syntagmatis Musici Theatrum Instrumontorum seu
Sciagraphia . . . . Wolfenbuettel: 1620; facsimile
by W. Gurlitt, Kassel: Baerenreiter, 1929.

_____. Syntagmatis Musici Tomus Secundus De Organographia
. . . . Wolfenbuettel: Holwein, 1619; facsimile by
W. Gurlitt, Kassel: Baerenreiter, 1929.

Roessler, E. Klangfunktion und Registrierung. Kassel:
Baerenreiter, 1952.

Rupp, E. Die Entwicklungsgeschichte der Orgelbaukunst.
Einsiedeln: Benziger & Co., 1929.

Schlick, Arnold. Spiegel der Orgelmacher und Organisten.
1511; newprint by E. Flade, Kassel: Baerenreiter,
1951.

Schneider, Thekla. Die Namen der Orgelregister. Kassel:
Baerenreiter, 1958.

Smets, Paul. Die Orgelregister, ihr Klang und Gebrauch. 3rd and 4th ed.; Mainz: Rheingold Verlag, 1943.

_____. Neuzeitlicher Orgelbau. 5th and 6th ed.; Mainz: Rheingold Verlag, 1944.

Sumner, William L. The Organ, its Evolution, Principles of Construction and Use. 2nd ed.; London: MacDonald, 1955.

Supper, Walter. Die Orgeldisposition, eine Heranfuehrung. Grossausgabe. Kassel: Baerenreiter, 1950.

_____. Fibel der Orgeldisposition. Kassel: Baerenreiter, 1946.

Toepfer, J. G. and Max Allihn. Die Theorie und Praxis des Orgelbaues. 2 vols. Weimar: Voigt, 1888.

_____ and Paul Smets. Lehrbuch der Orgelbaukunst. 4 vols. 4th and 5th ed.; Mainz: Rheingold Verlag, 1955-60.

Virdung, Sebastian. Musica getutscht . . . . Basel, 1511; facsimile by L. Schrade, Kassel: Baerenreiter, 1931.

BIBLIOGRAPHY
PART II

Adelung, Wolfgang. Einfuehrung in den Orgelbau. Leipzig:
Breitkopf & Haertel, 1955.

Adlung, J. Anleitung zu der musikalischen Gelahrtheit. Erfurt: Jungnicol, 1758; facsimile by H. J. Moser,
Kassel: Baerenreiter, 1953.

_____. Musica mechanica organoedi. Edited by J. L. Al-
brecht. Berlin: Birnstiel, 1768; facsimile by C.
Mahrenholz, Kassel: Baerenreiter, 1931.

Anderson, P. Orgelbogen Klangteknik, Arkitektur og Historie.
København, 1955.

Audsley, G. Ashdown. The Art of Organ Building. 2 vols.
New York: Dodd, Mead, and Company, 1905.

Bedos de Celles, Dom Francois. L'Art du Facteur d'Orgues.
4 vols. in 3 cases. Bordeaux [?]: 1766-1778; facsimile in 2/3 size by C. Mahrenholz, Kassel: Baerenreiter, 1936.

Biermann, J. Organographia Hildesiensis Specialis . . . .
Hildesheim: Schlegel, 1738; facsimile by Ernst Palandt, Kassel: Baerenreiter Verlag, 1930.

Blume, F. "Das Werk des Michael Praetorius," Zeitschrift
fuer Musikwissenschaft XVII (1935), 321-32; 482-502.

_____. Michael Praetorius Creuzburgensis. Wolfenbuettel-
Berlin: G. Kallmeyer, 1929.

Burgemeister, Ludwig. Der Orgelbau in Schlesien. Strass-
burg: J. H. Ed. Heitz, 1925.

Daehnert, Ulrich. Der Orgel- und Instrumentenbauer Zacharias Hildebrandt. Leipzig: Breitkopf & Haertel,
1960.

Distler, H. and E. Thienhaus. Die beiden Orgeln in St. Ja-
kobi zu Luebeck nach dem Umbau 1935. Luebeck:
Rahtgen, 1935.

926

Elis, Carl. Orgelwoerterbuch. 3rd ed.; Mainz: Rheingold
    Verlag, 1949.

Erpf, H. "Eine Orgel nach Michael Praetorius," Neue Musik-
    zeitung XLIII (1922), 122.

Fellerer, K. Orgel und Orgelmusik, ihre Geschichte. Augs-
    burg: Dr. Benno Filser Verlag, 1929.

Flade, Ernst. Gottfried Silbermann. Leipzig: Breitkopf &
    Haertel, 1953.

Fock, G. "Hamburgs Anteil am Orgelbau im niederdeutschen
    Kulturgebiet," Zeitschrift des Vereins fuer Hambur-
    gische Geschichte. 1939, 306-53.

Frotscher, G. Deutsche Orgeldispositionen aus fuenf Jahr-
    hunderten. Wolfenbuettel-Berlin: G. Kallmeyer Ver-
    lag, 1939.

Gurlitt, W. "Der Kursaechsische Hoforgelmacher Gottfried
    Fritzsche," Festschrift Arnold Schering 1937, 106-24.

_____. Michael Praetorius (Creuzbergensis), sein Leben
    und seine Werke. Leipzig: Breitkopf & Haertel,
    1915.

_____. "Zum Schuelerkreis des Kursaechsischen Hoforgel-
    machers Gottfried Fritzsche," Musik und Kirche X
    (1938), 158-69.

Haacke, W. Die Entwicklungsgeschichte des Orgelbaus im
    Lande Mecklenburg-Schwerin. Wolfenbuettel-Berlin:
    Kallmeyer Verlag, 1935.

Hammerich, A. "Eine historische Orgel auf Frederiksborg
    Schlosz bei Kopenhagen," Bulletin de la Société
    Union Musicologique II (1922), 65-78.

Harms, G. "Umfang und Anordnung der Pedalklaviatur," Bei-
    traege zur Organistentagung Hamburg-Luebeck / 6. bis
    8. Juli 1925. Klecken: Ugrino, 1925. Pp. 26-33.

Hopkins, E. J. The Organ, its History and Construction.
    London: Robert Cocks and Co., 1855.

Kade, O. "Gottfried Fritsche," Monatshefte fuer Musikge-
    schichte III (1871), 90-94.

Kaufmann, W. Der Orgelprospekt in stilgeschichtlicher Ent-
    wicklung. 2nd ed.; Mainz: Rheingold Verlag, 1939.

Klotz, Hans. Das Buch von der Orgel. 5th ed.; Kassel:
Baerenreiter, 1955.

_____. Ueber die Orgelkunst der Gotik, der Renaissance,
und des Barock. Kassel: Baerenreiter, 1934.

"Leichensermone auf Musiker des 17. Jahrhunderts--Michael
Praetorius," Monatshefte fuer Musikgeschichte VII
(1875), 177-78.

Mahrenholz, C. "Der gegenwaertige Stand der Orgelfrage im
Lichte der Orgelgeschichte," Bericht ueber die
dritte Tagung fuer deutsche Orgelkunst in Freiberg
i. Sa. vom 2. bis 7. Oktober 1927. Kassel: Baerenreiter, 1928. Pp. 13-37.

_____. Die Orgelregister, ihre Geschichte und ihr Bau.
2nd ed.; Kassel: Baerenreiter, 1942.

Mattheson, J. Friedrich Erhard Niedtens Musicalischer Handleitung Anderer Theil von der Variation des General-
Basses . . . . Hamburg: Schiller u. Kiszner, 1721.

Oosterhof, A. P. and A. Bouman. Orgelbouwkunde. Leiden:
Spruyt, van Mantgem & de Does, 1956.

Pfeiffer-Duerkop, Hilde. Die Geschichte der Gottfried
Fritzsche-Orgel in St. Katharinen zu Braunschweig.
Mainz: Rheingold Verlag, 1955.

Praetorius, M. Michael Praetorius' Syntagma, II Teil: Von
den Instrumenten. Wolfenbuettel 1618. Newprint by
R. Eitner, Berlin: Trautwein, 1884. 13. Band der
Publikationen aelterer praktischer und theoretischer
Musikwerke herausgegeben von der Gesellschaft fuer
Musikforschung.

_____. Syntagma musicum Tomus Secundus De Organographia.
Wolfenbuettel: Elias Holwein, 1619.

_____. Syntagmatis Musici Theatrum Instrumentorum seu
Sciagraphia . . . . Wolfenbuettel: 1620; facsimile
by W. Gurlitt, Kassel: Baerenreiter, 1929.

_____. Syntagmatis Musici Tomus Secundus De Organogra-
phia . . . . Wolfenbuettel: Holwein, 1619; facsimile by W. Gurlitt, Kassel: Baerenreiter, 1929.

_____ and E. Compenius. Orgeln Verdingnis . . . . Edited by F. Blume in Kieler Beitraege zur Musikwissenschaft IV. Wolfenbuettel-Berlin: G. Kallmeyer,
1936.

Rubardt, P. "Einige Nachrichten ueber die Orgelbauerfamilie Scherer und die Orgel zu St. Marien in Bernau Mark sowie ueber deren Erweiterung durch Paul Lindemann und Arp Schnitger," Musik u. Kirche II (1930), 111-26.

Sammlung einiger Nachrichten von beruehmten Orgel-Wercken in Teutschland mit vieler Muehe aufgesetzt von einem Liebhaber der Musik. Breszlau: Carl Gottfried Meyer, 1757.

Schneider, Thekla. "Die Orgelbauerfamilie Compenius," Archiv fuer Musikforschung II (1937), 8-76.

Seidel, Johann J. Die Orgel und ihr Bau. Breslau, 1843; reprint at Amsterdam: Knuf, 1962.

Smets, Paul. Die Dresdener Handschrift Orgeldispositionen. Kassel: Baerenreiter, 1931.

Sponsel, Johann Ulrich. Orgelhistorie. Nuernberg: George Peter Monath, 1771; newprint by P. Smets; Kassel: Baerenreiter, 1931.

Stahl, W. "Geistliche Musik," Musikgeschichte Luebecks. Band II. Kassel: Baerenreiter, 1952.

Strube, W. "Beruehmte Orgelbauer und ihre Werke," Musik und Kirche I (1929), 115-25.

Sumner, William L. The Organ, its Evolution, Principles of Construction and Use. 2nd ed.; London: MacDonald, 1955.

Supper, W., Wolfgang Adelung, Walter Schindler, Guenter Seggermann, and Henry Weman. Orgelbewegung und Historismus. Berlin: Merseburger, cop. 1958.

Toepfer, J. G. and Max Allihn. Die Theorie und Praxis des Orgelbaues. 2 vols. Weimar: Voigt, 1888.

Vente, M. A. Die Brabanter Orgel. Amsterdam: H. J. Paris, 1958.

Viderø, F. "Compenius Organ Album," Gramophone Shop Celebrities. New York, [n.d.].

Walcker, O. Erinnerungen eines Orgelbauers. Kassel: Baerenreiter Verlag, 1948.

Walther, J. G. Musikalisches Lexikon . . . . Leipzig:
        Wolfgang Deer, 1732; facsimile by R. Schaal, Kassel:
        Baerenreiter, 1953.

Werckmeister, A. Erweiterte und verbesserte Orgelprobe.
        Quedlinburg: T. P. Calvisius, 1698; facsimilie at
        Kassel: Baerenreiter, 1927.

_____. Musicalische paradoxal-discourse . . . . Qued-
        linburg: T. P. Calvisius, 1707.

_____. Organum Gruningense redivivum. Quedlinburg and
        Aschersleben: Struntz, 1705; newprint by P. Smets,
        Mainz: Rheingold Verlag, 1932.

Woersching, J. Die Compenius-Orgel auf Schlosz Frederiks-
        borg (Kopenhagen). Mainz: Rheingold Verlag, 1946.

BIBLIOGRAPHY
PART III

Adlung, J. Anleitung zu der musikalischen Gelahrtheit. Erfurt: Jungnicol, 1758; facsimile by H. J. Moser,
Kassel: Baerenreiter, 1953.

Arkin, H. and R. Colton. Statistical Methods. 4th ed.;
New York: Barnes and Noble, Inc., 1939.

Barbour, J. "Irregular Systems of Temperament," Journal of
the American Musicological Society I (1948), 20-26.

_____. Tuning and Temperament. East Lansing: Michigan
State College Press, 1953.

Bartholomew, W. Acoustics of Music. New York: Prentice
Hall, 1946.

Bessaraboff, N. Ancient European Musical Instruments, An
Organological Study of the Musical Instruments . . .
at the Museum of Fine Arts Boston. Boston: Harvard
University Press, 1941.

Blume, F. "Das Werk des Michael Praetorius," Zeitschrift
fuer Musikwissenschaft XVII (1935), 321-32; 482-502.

_____. Michael Praetorius Creuzburgensis. Wolfenbuettel-
Berlin: G. Kallmeyer, 1929.

Buck, Percy. Acoustics for Musicians. Oxford: Clarendon
Press, 1917.

Clowes, D. Michael Praetorius and the organ: his concep-
tion of the instrument and his music for it. Unpub-
lished Master's thesis, Eastman School of Music,
1950.

Dupont, W. Geschichte der musikalischen Temperatur. Kassel: Baerenreiter, 1935.

Elis, Carl. Orgelwoerterbuch. 3rd ed.; Mainz: Rheingold
Verlag, 1949.

931

Ellis, A. "On the History of Musical Pitch," reprinted with corrections and an appendix from the Journal of the Society of Arts (March 5 and April 2), London, 1880.

Erpf, H. "Eine Orgel nach Michael Praetorius," Neue Musikzeitung XLIII (1922), 122.

Gurlitt, W. "Ueber Prinzipien und zur Geschichte der Registrierkunst in der alten Orgelmusik," Bericht ueber den I. Musikwissenschaftlichen Kongresz der deutschen Musikgesellschaft (Leipzig 1926), 232-36.

Helmholtz, H. On the Sensations of Tone as a Physiological Basis for the Theory of Music. Transl. and rendered conformable to the fourth (and last) German edition of 1877, by A. Ellis; New York: Dover Publications, 1954.

Jahnn, Hans Henny. "Registernamen und ihr Inhalt," Beitraege zur Organistentagung Hamburg-Luebeck / 6. bis 8. Juli 1925. Klecken: Ugrino, 1925. Pp. 5-25.

"Leichensermone auf Musiker des 17. Jahrhunderts—Michael Praetorius," Monatshefte fuer Musikgeschichte VII (1875), 177-78.

Mahrenholz, C. "Der gegenwaertige Stand der Orgelfrage im Lichte der Orgelgeschichte," Bericht ueber die dritte Tagung fuer deutsche Orgelkunst in Freiberg i. Sa. vom 2. bis 7. Oktober 1927. Kassel: Baerenreiter, 1928. Pp. 13-37.

_____. Die Berechnung der Orgelpfeifenmensuren. Kassel: Baerenreiter, 1938.

_____. Die Orgelregister, ihre Geschichte und ihr Bau. 2nd ed.; Kassel: Baerenreiter, 1942.

Mattheson, J. Der vollkommene Kapellmeister. Hamburg: Christian Herold, 1739.

Mendel, A. "Pitch in the 16th and early 17th Centuries," The Musical Quarterly XXXIV (1948), 28-45; 199-221; 336-57; 575-93.

Olson, Harry F. Musical Engineering. New York: McGraw-Hill Book Co., 1952.

Praetorius, M. Michael Praetorius' Syntagma, II Teil: Von den Instrumenten. Wolfenbuettel 1618. Newprint by R. Eitner. Berlin: Trautwein, 1884. 13. Band der

Publikationen aelterer praktischer und theoretischer Musikwerke herausgegeben von der Gesellschaft fuer Musikforschung.

_____. Syntagma musicum Tomus Secundus De Organographia. Wolfenbuettel: Elias Holwein, 1619.

_____. Syntagmatis Musici Theatrum Instrumentorum seu Sciagraphia . . . . Wolfenbuettel: 1620; facsimile by W. Gurlitt, Kassel: Baerenreiter, 1929.

_____. Syntagmatis Musici Tomus Secundus De Organographia . . . . Wolfenbuettel: Holwein, 1619; facsimile by W. Gurlitt, Kassel: Baerenreiter, 1929.

_____ and E. Compenius. Orgeln Verdingnis . . . . Edited by F. Blume in Kieler Beitraege zur Musikwissenschaft IV. Wolfenbuettel-Berlin: G. Kallmeyer, 1936.

Schleifer, K. "Die Klanggeschichte der Orgel in den Haupt-zeitraeumen der Musikgeschichte," Musik u. Kirche I (1929), 61-79; 125-31.

Schneider, Thekla. Die Namen der Orgelregister. Kassel: Baerenreiter, 1958.

Smets, Paul. Die Dresdener Handschrift Orgeldispositionen. Kassel: Baerenreiter, 1931.

Supper, Walter. Die Orgeldisposition, eine Heranfuehrung. Grossausgabe. Kassel: Baerenreiter, 1950.

Virdung, Sebastian. Musica getutscht . . . . Basel, 1511; facsimile by L. Schrade, Kassel: Baerenreiter, 1931.

Werckmeister, A. Erweiterte und verbesserte Orgelprobe. Quedlinburg: T. P. Calvisius, 1698; facsimile at Kassel: Baerenreiter, 1927.

Woersching, J. Die Compenius-Orgel auf Schlosz Frederiks-borg (Kopenhagen). Mainz: Rheingold Verlag, 1946.

Woerthmueller, Willi. Die Nuernberger Trompeten- und Posau-nenmacher des 17. und 18. Jahrhunderts. Teil II. Nuernberg, 1955.

SECTION C

CHARTS

LIST OF CHARTS

935

LIST OF CHARTS--Continued

LIST OF CHARTS--Continued

LIST OF CHARTS--Continued

LIST OF CHARTS--<u>Continued</u>

LIST OF CHARTS--<u>Continued</u>

CHART 1

ACOUSTIC SPECTRUM OF c' OF THE
GEIGENDPRINCIPAL[a]

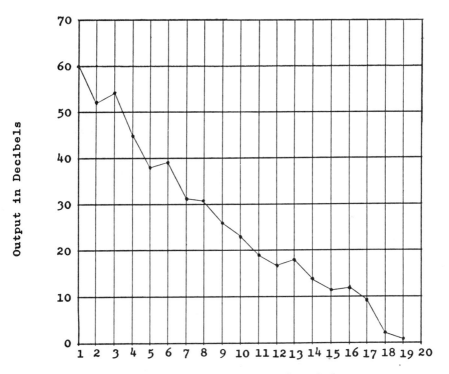

Serial Number of Partial

[a]C. P. Boner, "Acoustic Spectra of Organ Pipes,"
Journal of the Acoustical Society of America, X (1929), 39.
The note c' represents a frequency of 261.6 cycles per second.

CHART 2

GRAPHIC COURSE OF THE NORMPRINCIPAL
CONSTANT SCALE: ══════

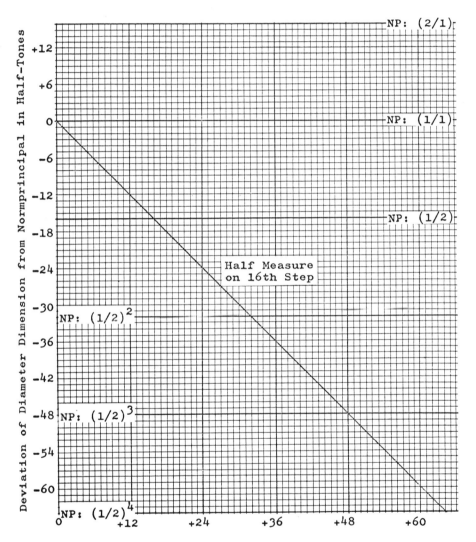

Deviation of Pitch from Great C in Half-Steps

CHART 3

GRAPHIC COURSES FOR TWO CONSTANT SCALES
CASE 1a: ═══════, 1b: ═══════

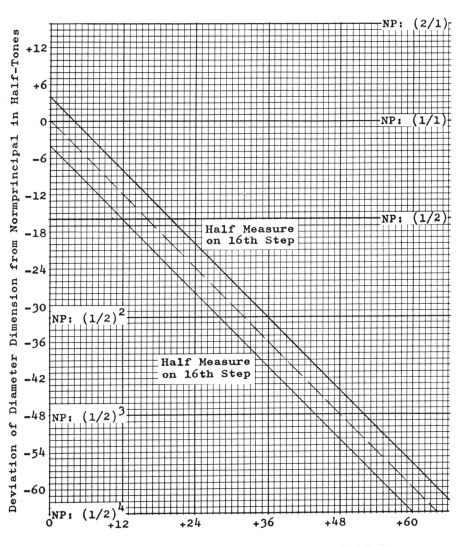

Deviation of Pitch from Great C in Half-Steps

CHART 4

GRAPHIC COURSES FOR DECREASING AND INCREASING CONSTANT SCALES
CASE 2a: ⟩⟩⟩ , 2b: ⟨⟨⟨

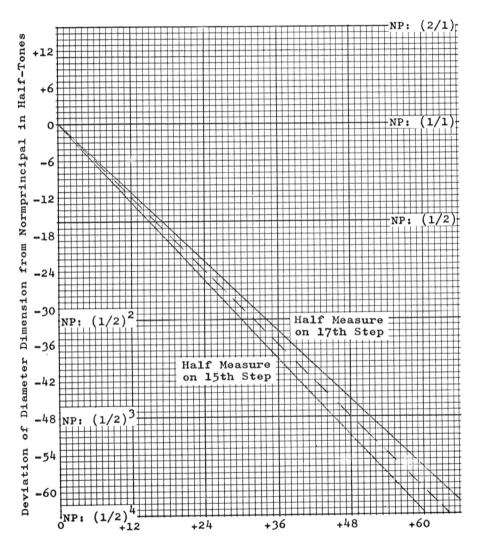

Deviation of Diameter Dimension from Normprincipal in Half-Tones

Deviation of Pitch from Great $\underline{C}$ in Half-Steps

CHART 5

GRAPHIC COURSES FOR DECREASING AND
INCREASING CONSTANT SCALES
CASE 3a: ⟩, 3b: ⟨

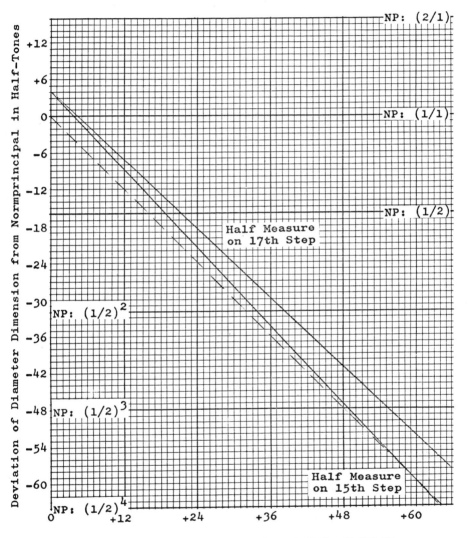

Deviation of Diameter Dimension from Normprincipal in Half-Tones

Deviation of Pitch from Great C in Half-Steps

CHART 6

GRAPHIC COURSES FOR DECREASING AND INCREASING CONSTANT SCALES
CASE 4a: ⟋ , 4b: ⟍

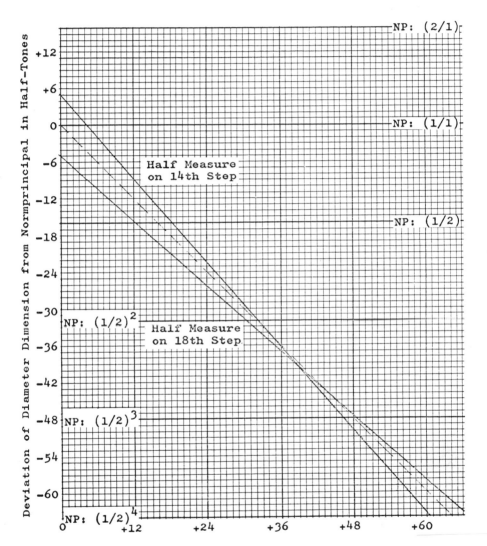

Deviation of Diameter Dimension from Normprincipal in Half-Tones

Deviation of Pitch from Great $\underline{C}$ in Half-Steps

CHART 7

GRAPHIC COURSE FOR A CONTINUOUS SEGMENTAL SCALE
CASE 1a: ═══ g♯' ◁ (BIPARTITE)

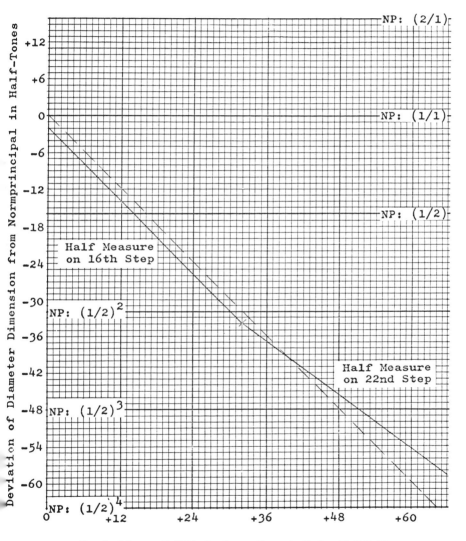

Deviation of Pitch from Great C in Half-Steps

CHART 8

GRAPHIC COURSE FOR A CONTINUOUS SEGMENTAL SCALE
CASE 1b: ══════g⧣' ▷ (BIPARTITE)

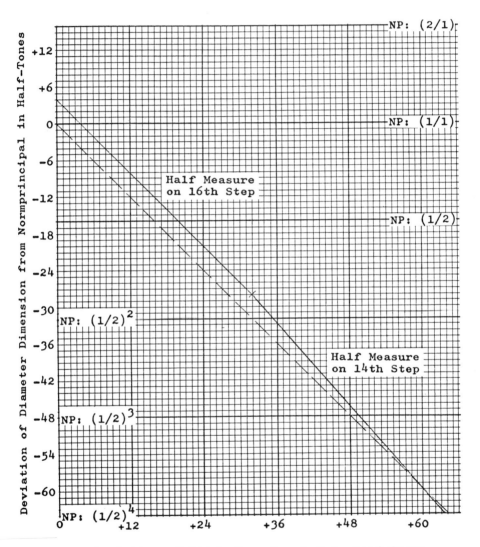

Deviation of Pitch from Great <u>C</u> in Half-Steps

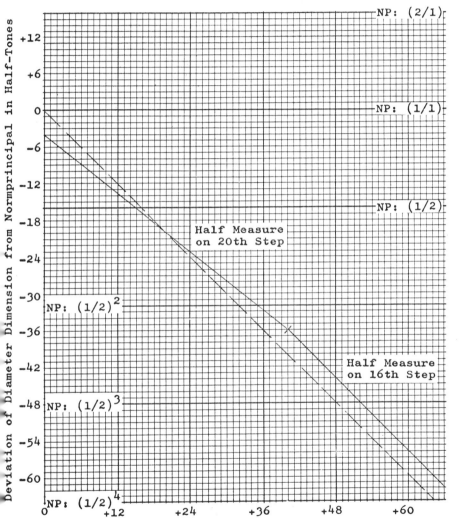

950

CHART 10

GRAPHIC COURSE FOR A CONTINUOUS SEGMENTAL SCALE
CASE 1d: ⟶ e' ═══ (BIPARTITE)

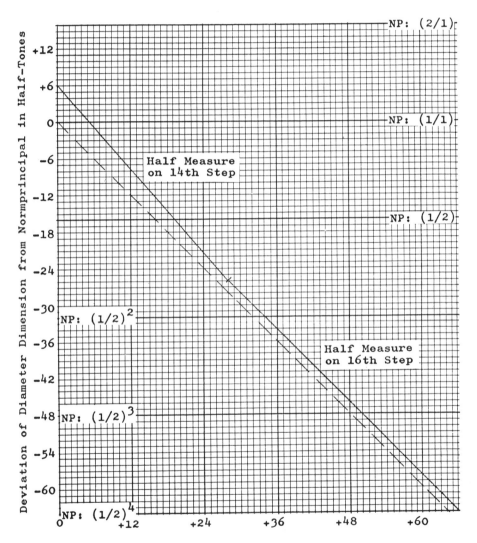

Deviation of Pitch from Great C in Half-Steps

CHART 11

GRAPHIC COURSE FOR A CONTINUOUS SEGMENTAL SCALE
CASE 2a: e' g♯'' (TRIPARTITE)

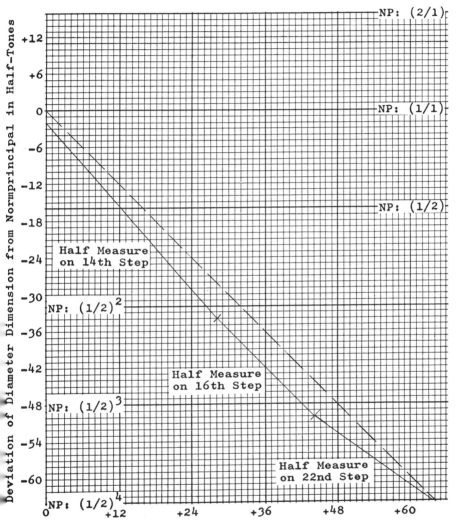

Deviation of Pitch from Great C in Half-Steps

CHART 12

GRAPHIC COURSE FOR A CONTINUOUS SEGMENTAL SCALE
CASE 2b: ══════ e ══> e' ═══ (TRIPARTITE)

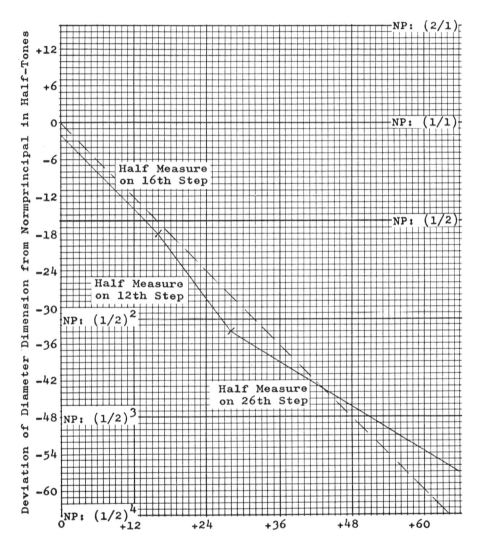

CHART 13

GRAPHIC COURSE FOR A BROKEN SEGMENTAL SCALE
CASE 3a: ◁ f♯' .... e'' ◁ (TRIPARTITE)

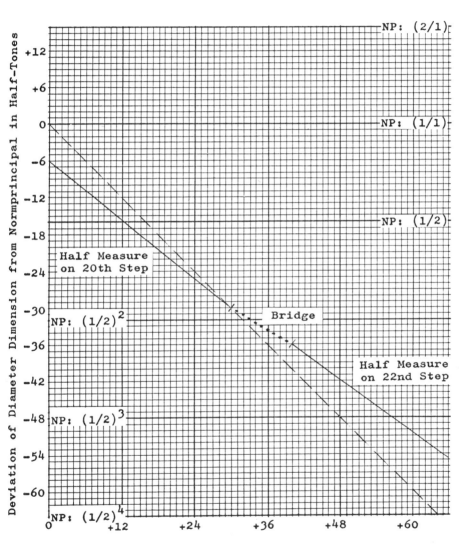

Deviation of Pitch from Great C in Half-Steps

CHART 14

GRAPHIC COURSE FOR A VARIABLE SCALE
CASE 1a: POSITIVE CURVE

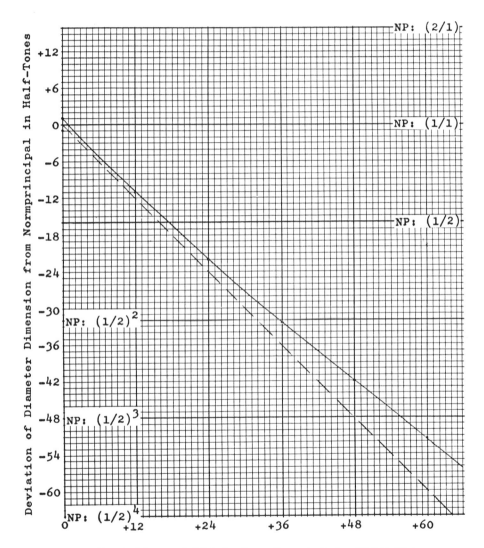

Deviation of Pitch from Great C in Half-Steps

CHART 15

GRAPHIC COURSE FOR A VARIABLE SCALE
CASE 1b: NEGATIVE CURVE

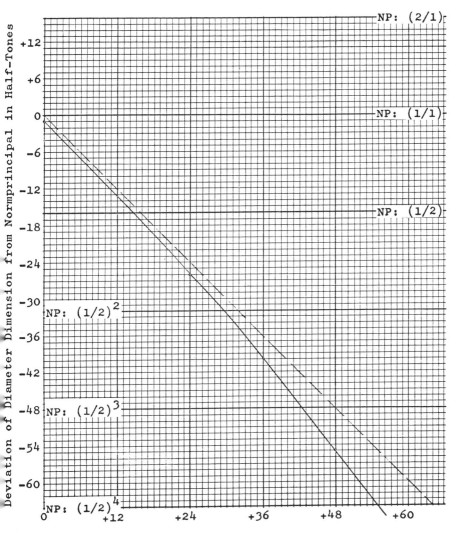

Deviation of Pitch from Great C in Half-Steps

CHART 16

CORRELATION OF TABULAR DIFFERENCE AND
DEPENDENT RATIOS OF MOUTH WIDTHS

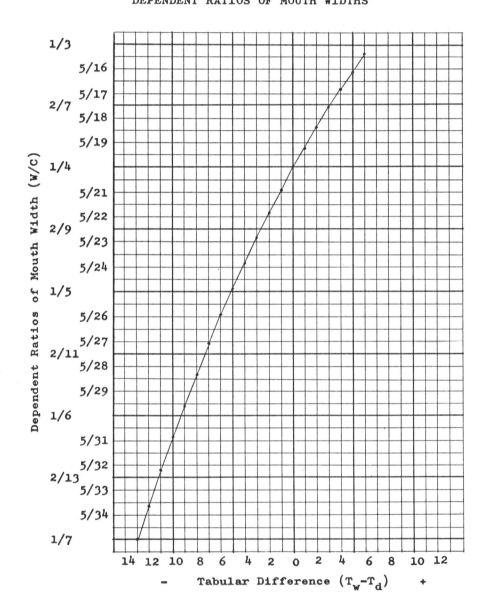

CHART 17

GRAPHIC COURSES FOR INDEPENDENT RATIOS
OF DIAMETER AND MOUTH WIDTH
CASE 1a: D ════ , W ════

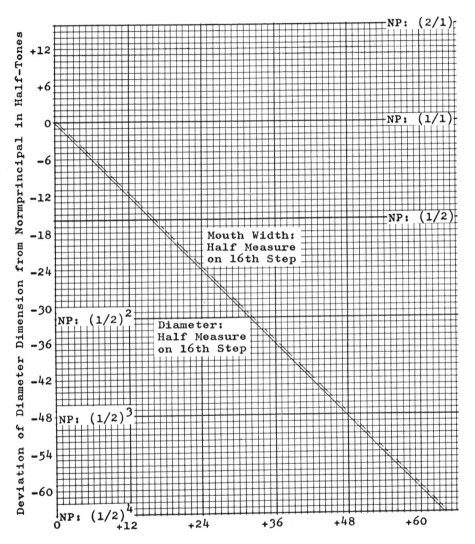

Deviation of Pitch from Great C in Half-Steps

CHART 18

GRAPHIC COURSES FOR INDEPENDENT RATIOS
OF DIAMETER AND MOUTH WIDTH
CASE 1b: D ⟩⟩⟩ , W ⟩⟩⟩

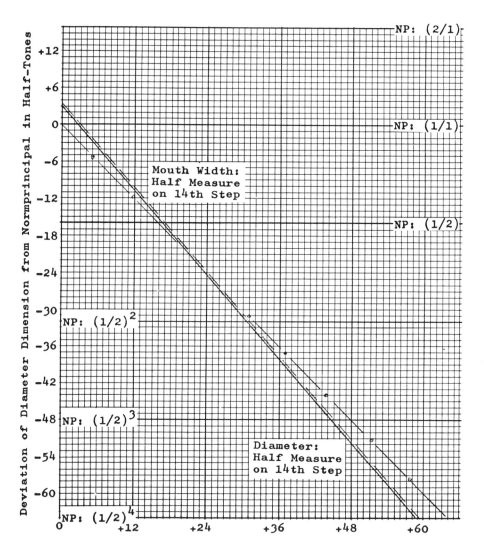

Deviation of Pitch from Great C in Half-Steps

CHART 19

GRAPHIC COURSES FOR INDEPENDENT RATIOS
OF DIAMETER AND MOUTH WIDTH
CASE 1c: D ⪤ , W ⪤

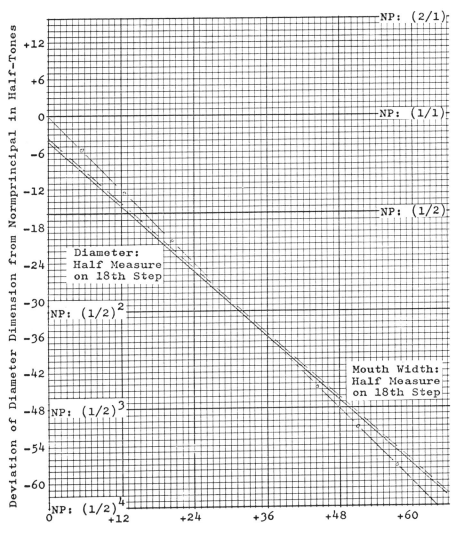

Deviation of Pitch from Great C̲ in Half-Steps

CHART 20

GRAPHIC COURSES FOR INDEPENDENT RATIOS
OF DIAMETER AND MOUTH WIDTH
CASE 2a: D ═══, W ▷

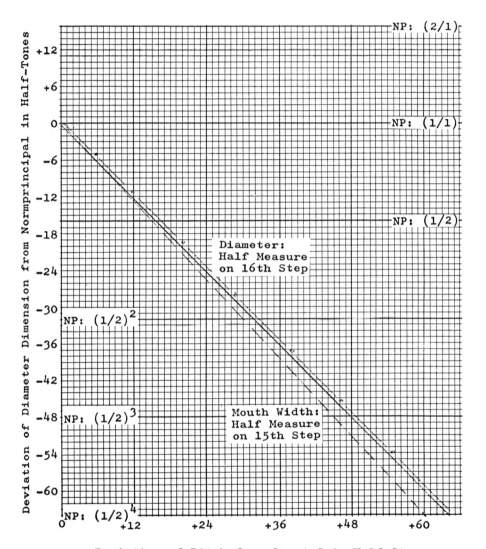

Deviation of Pitch from Great C in Half-Steps

CHART 21

GRAPHIC COURSES FOR INDEPENDENT RATIOS
OF DIAMETER AND MOUTH WIDTH
CASE 2b: D ⟩⟩, W ⟹

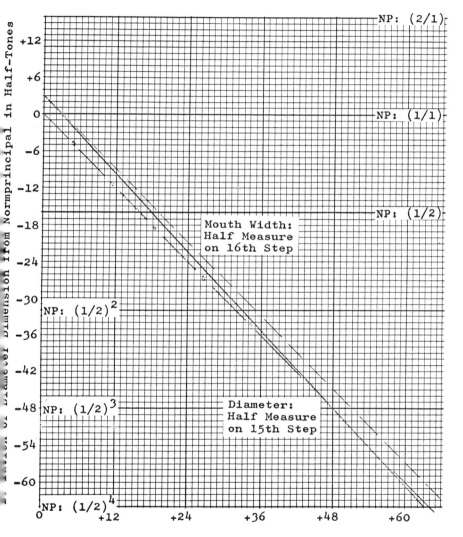

Deviation of Pitch from Great C in Half-Steps

CHART 22

GRAPHIC COURSES FOR INDEPENDENT RATIOS
OF DIAMETER AND MOUTH WIDTH
CASE 3a: D ═══ , W ═══

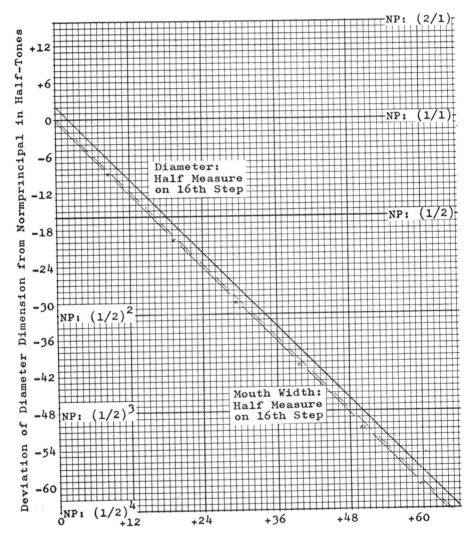

Deviation of Pitch from Great <u>C</u> in Half-Steps

CHART 23

GRAPHIC COURSES FOR INDEPENDENT RATIOS
OF DIAMETER AND MOUTH WIDTH
CASE 3b: D ⟩⟩ , W ⟩⟩

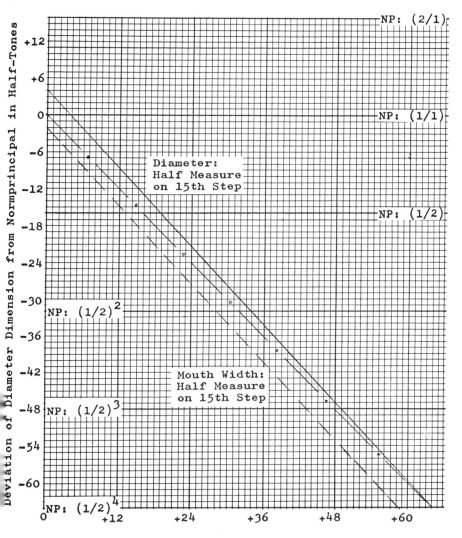

Deviation of Pitch from Great C in Half-Steps

CHART 24

GRAPHIC COURSES FOR INDEPENDENT RATIOS
OF DIAMETER AND MOUTH WIDTH
CASE 4a: D ▷ , W ◁

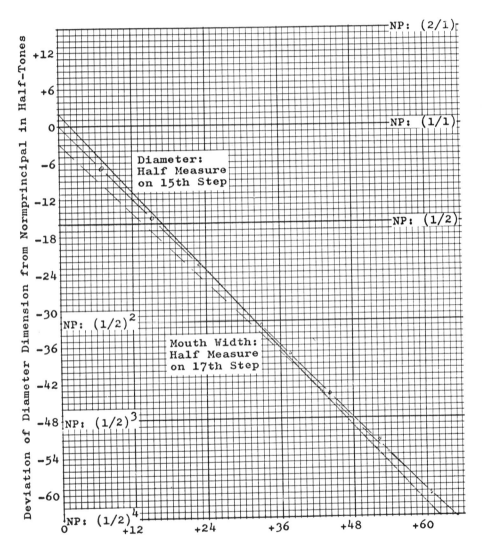

Deviation of Pitch from Great <u>C</u> in Half-Steps

CHART 25

GRAPHIC COURSES FOR INDEPENDENT RATIOS
OF DIAMETER AND MOUTH WIDTH
CASE 4b: D ◀ , W ═══

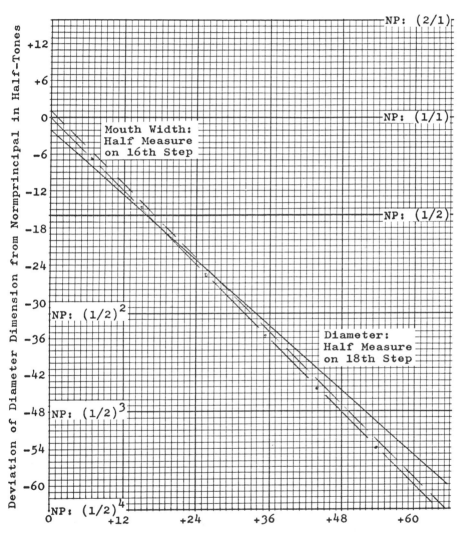

Deviation of Pitch from Great C̲ in Half-Steps

CHART 26

THEORETICAL COURSE FOR TWO MUTATION
VOICES (2 2/3' AND 1 1/3')

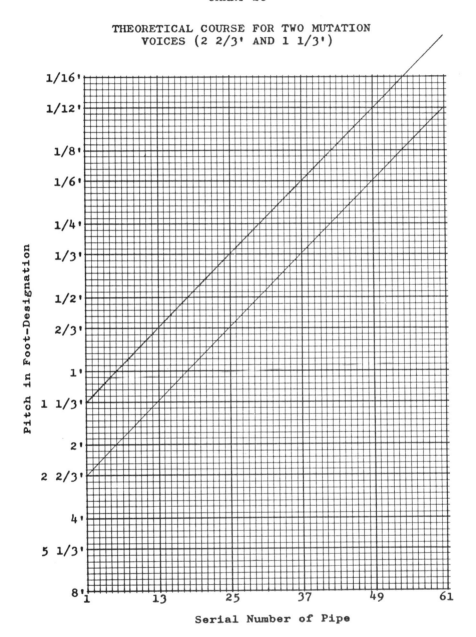

Serial Number of Pipe

CHART 27

MUTATION VOICE MODIFIED
BY REPETITION

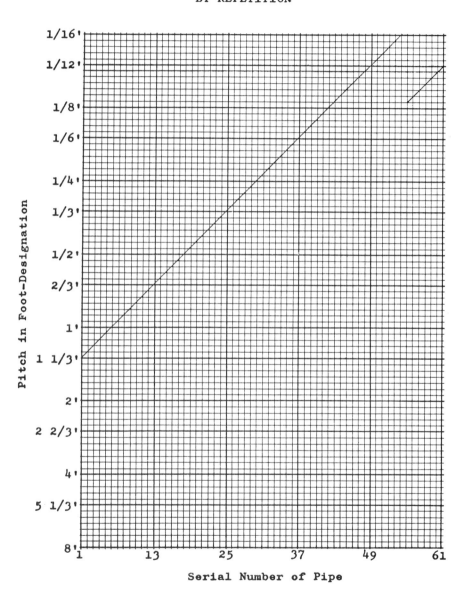

Serial Number of Pipe

CHART 28

MUTATION VOICE MODIFIED
BY REDUCTION

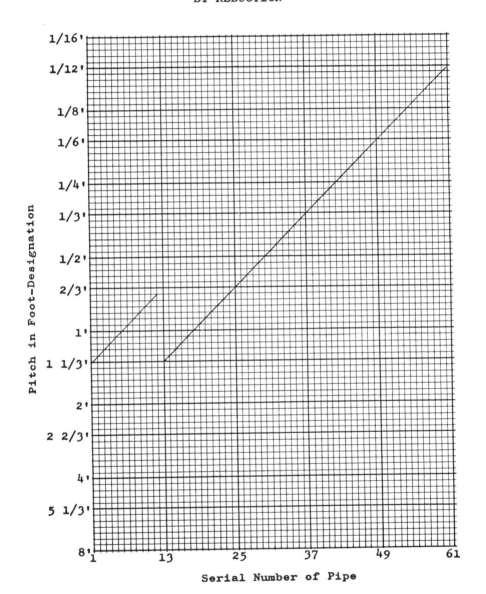

Serial Number of Pipe

CHART 29

LAYOUT OF A DIVISION SHOWING REDUCTION
AND REPETITION OF A MUTATION VOICE

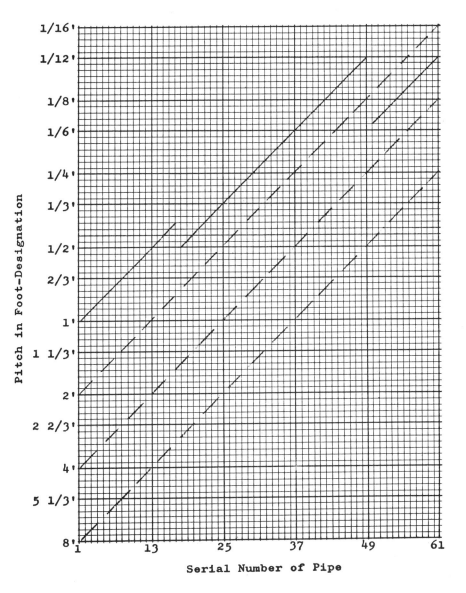

Serial Number of Pipe

CHART 30

POSSIBLE COURSE FOR A 1 3/5' TIERCE MODIFIED
BY REDUCTION AND REPETITION

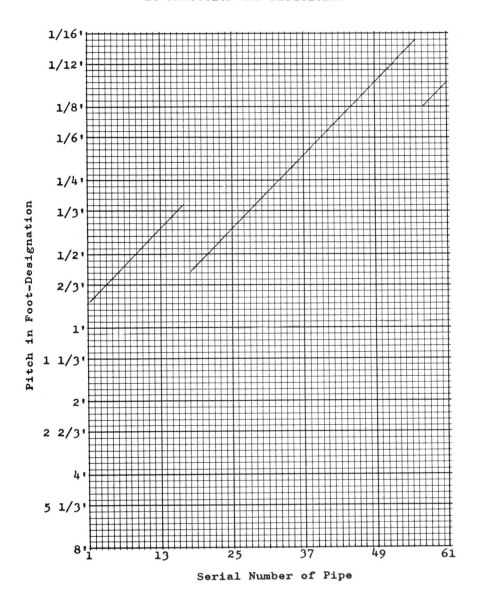

CHART 31

POSSIBLE COURSE FOR A 1 1/7' SEPTIME
MODIFIED BY SUPPRESSION

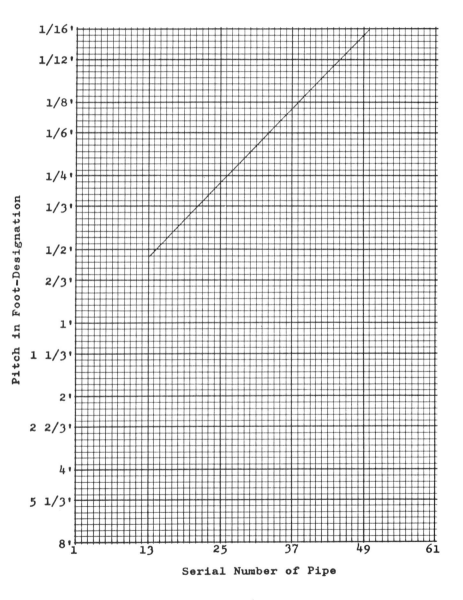

Serial Number of Pipe

CHART 32

COURSE OF THE TONUS FABRI OR
GLOECKLEINTON 2' AND 1'

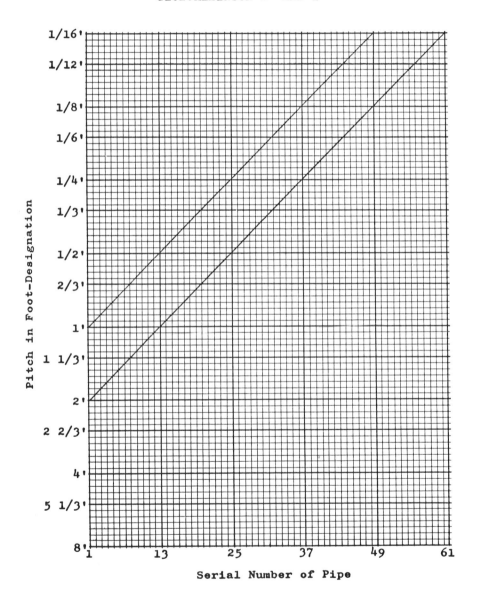

Pitch in Foot-Designation

Serial Number of Pipe

CHART 33

COURSE FOR THE CHORALBASS
4' AND 2'

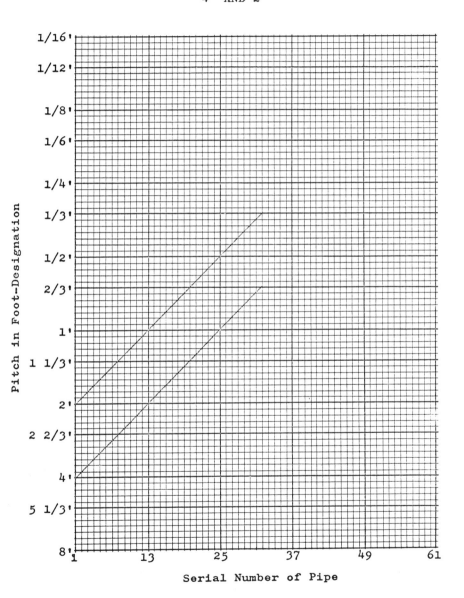

CHART 34

COURSE OF THE JAUCHZENDPFEIFE
1' AND 1/2'

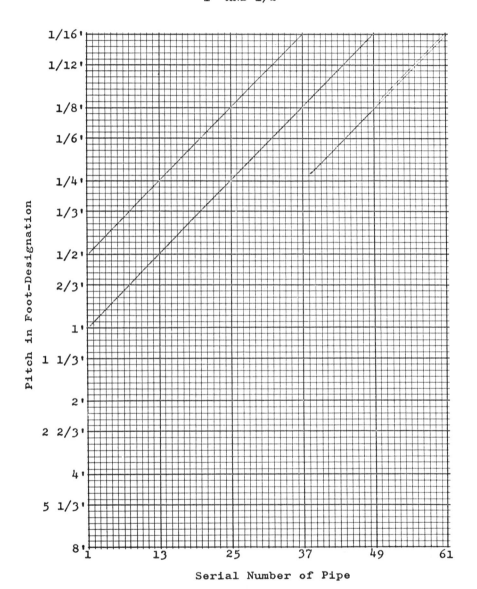

Serial Number of Pipe

CHART 35

COURSE OF THE II RAUSCHPFEIFE
2 2/3' AND 2'

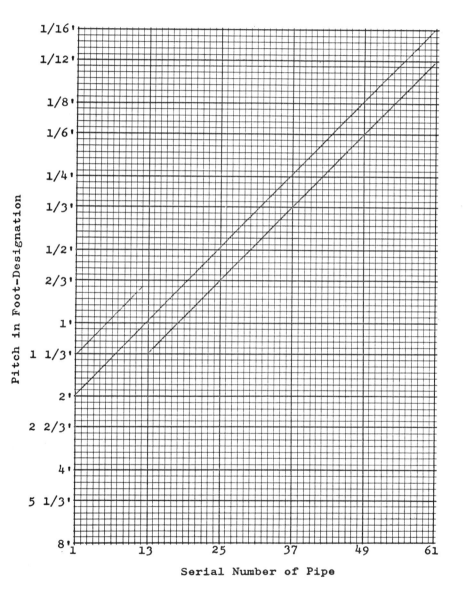

Serial Number of Pipe

CHART 36

FULL COURSE FOR A
V KORNETT 8'

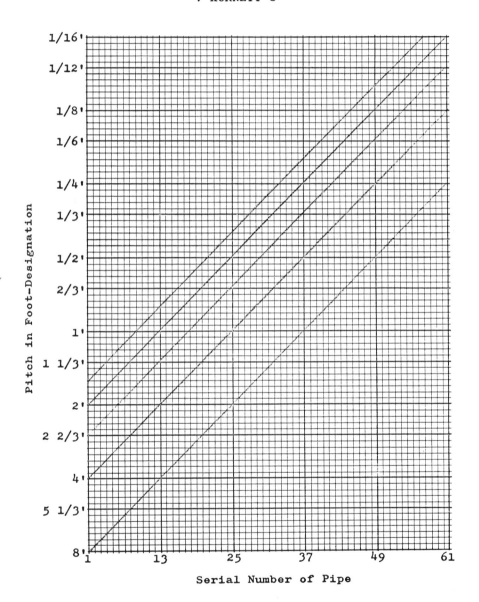

CHART 37

COURSE FOR A III-V KORNETT 8'
MODIFIED BY SUPPRESSION

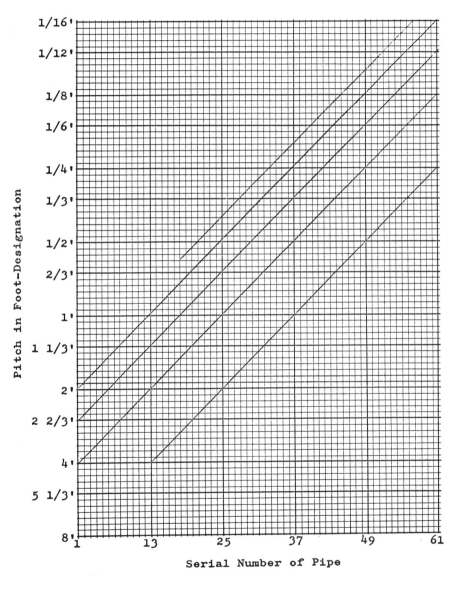

Pitch in Foot-Designation

Serial Number of Pipe

CHART 38

COURSE OF A II SESQUIALTERA
MODIFIED BY SUPPRESSION

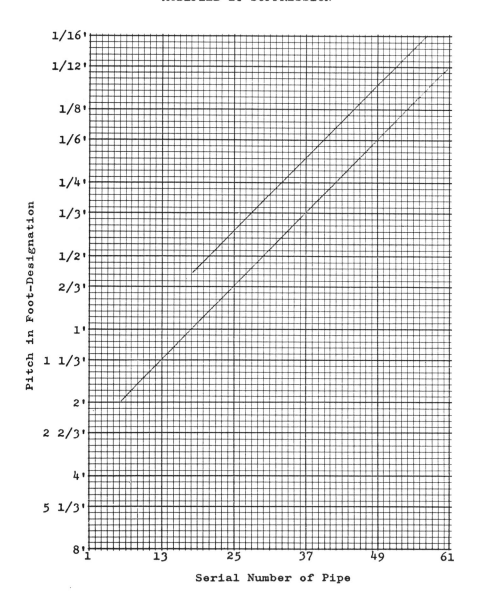

Pitch in Foot-Designation

Serial Number of Pipe

CHART 39

POSSIBLE COURSE FOR A III SCHREIPFEIFE MODIFIED
BY REPETITION AND SUPPRESSION

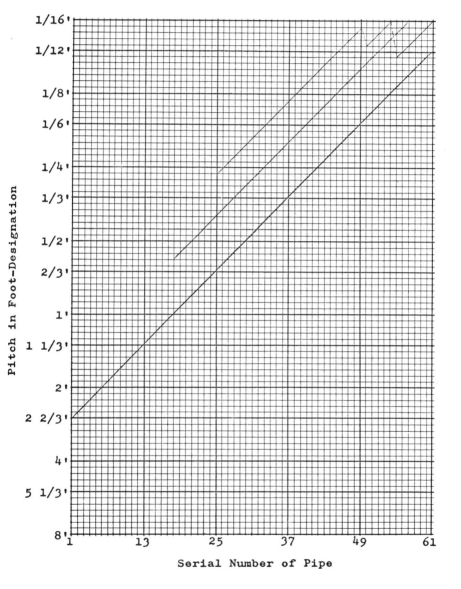

Serial Number of Pipe

CHART 40

HYPOTHETICAL DISPOSITION OF
III MIXTURE 1'

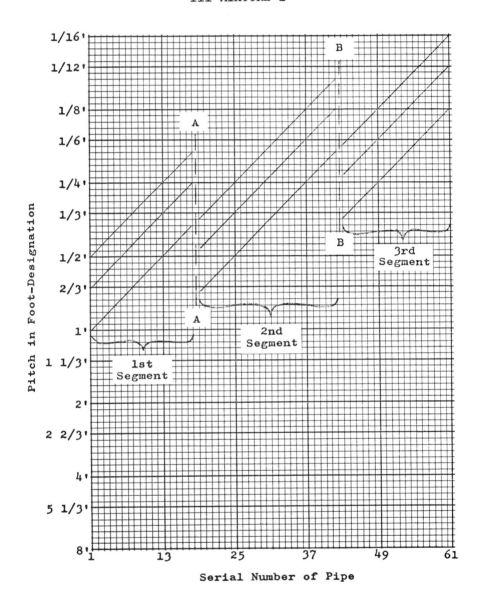

CHART 41

HYPOTHETICAL DISPOSITION OF
III MIXTURE 2'

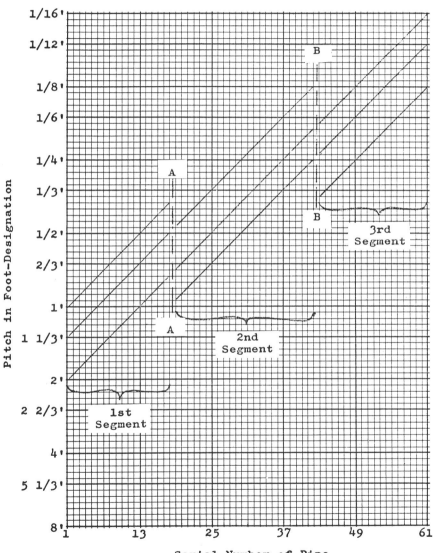

Pitch in Foot-Designation

Serial Number of Pipe

CHART 42

HYPOTHETICAL DISPOSITION OF
III MIXTURE 1'

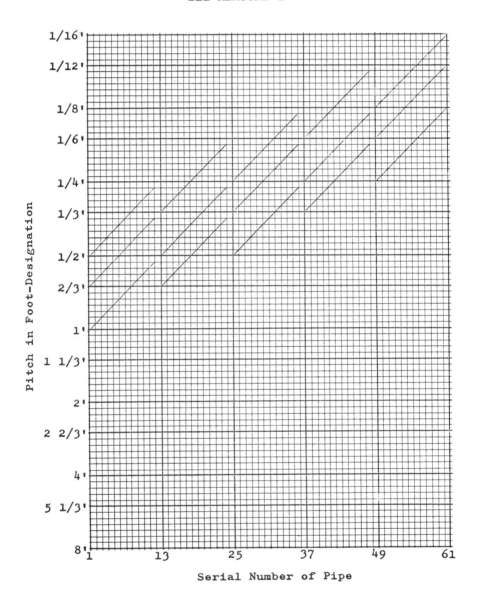

Serial Number of Pipe

CHART 43

HYPOTHETICAL DISPOSITION OF
IV MIXTURE 2'

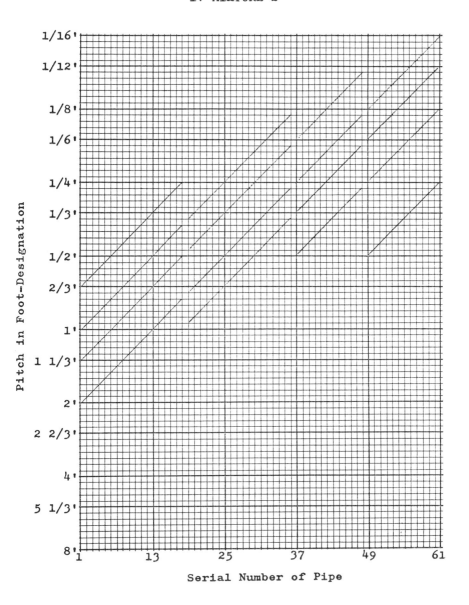

CHART 44

HYPOTHETICAL DISPOSITION OF
IV MIXTURE 1'

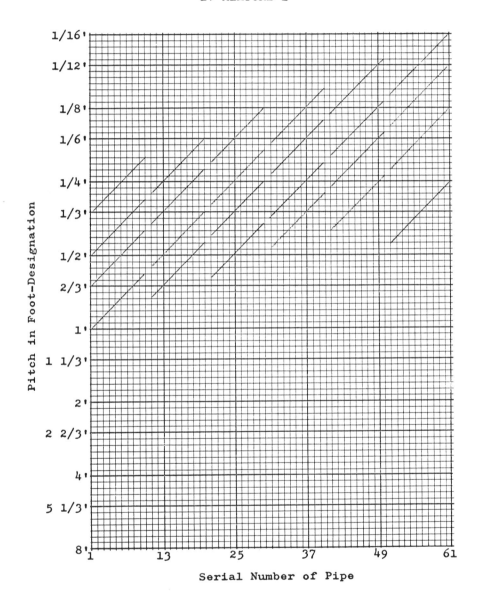

Serial Number of Pipe

CHART 45

THEORETICAL DISTRIBUTION OF RANKS
IN A FULL CROWN

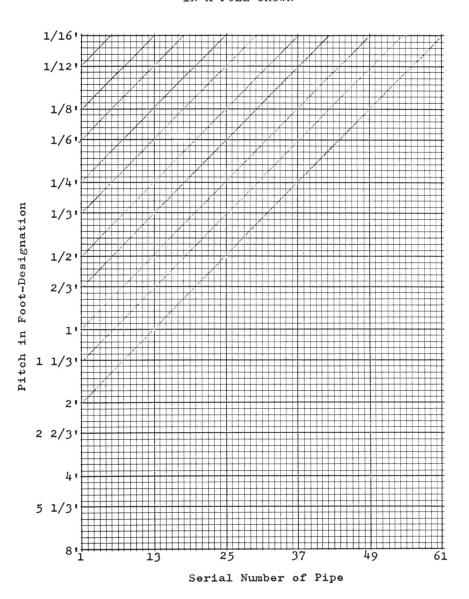

CHART 46

POSSIBLE HYPOTHETICAL DISPOSITION
OF LOWER CROWN

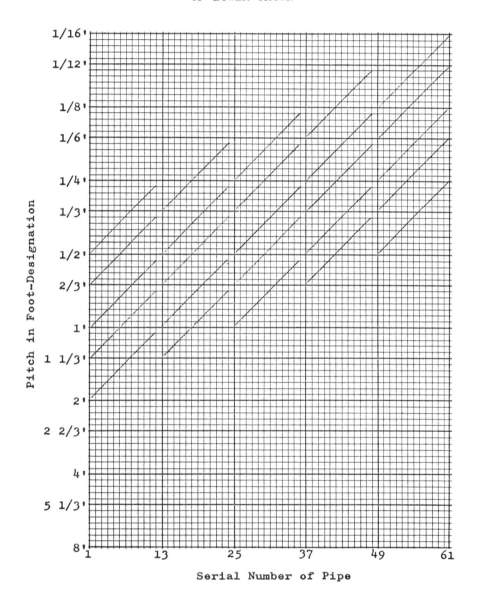

Pitch in Foot-Designation

Serial Number of Pipe

CHART 47

POSSIBLE HYPOTHETICAL DISPOSITION
OF HIGHER CROWN

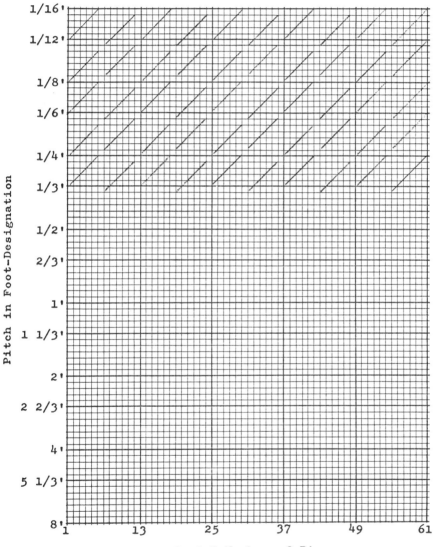

CHART 48

HYPOTHETICAL COMBINATION OF
LOWER AND HIGHER CROWNS

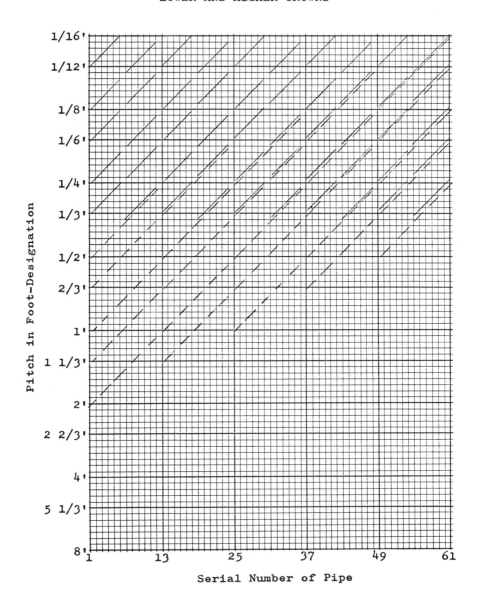

Serial Number of Pipe

CHART 49

ACTUAL DISPOSITION OF V FOURNITURE 2'
(DOM BEDOS-MAHRENHOLZ)

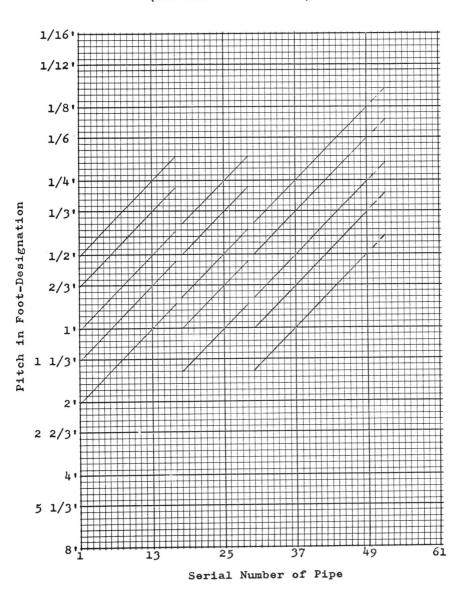

Serial Number of Pipe

CHART 50

ACTUAL DISPOSITION OF IV MIXTURE 2'
(GOTTFRIED SILBERMANN-MAHRENHOLZ)

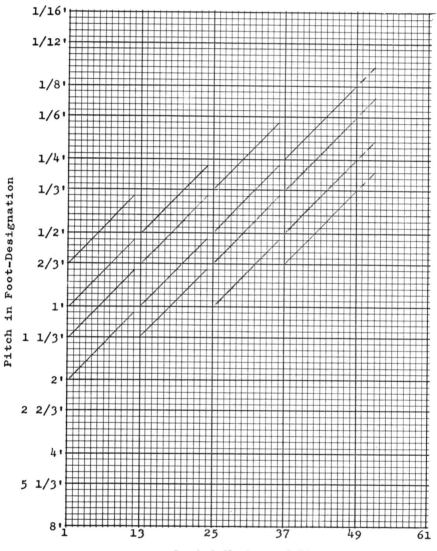

Pitch in Foot-Designation

Serial Number of Pipe

CHART 51

ACTUAL DISPOSITION OF III-V MIXTURE 2'
(WINFRED ELLERHORST)

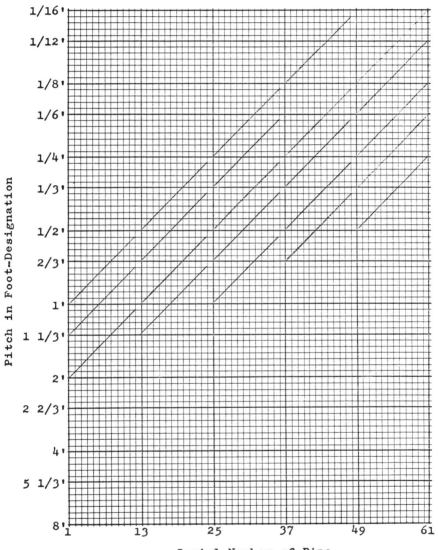

Serial Number of Pipe

CHART 52

ACTUAL DISPOSITION OF IV-VI MIXTURE 1 1/3'
(DR. ELIS-ELLERHORST)

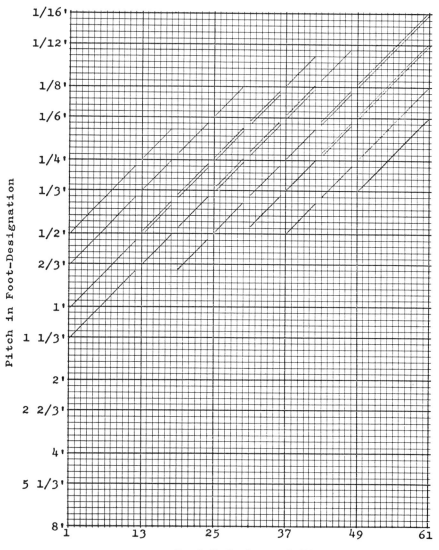

Serial Number of Pipe

CHART 53

HYPOTHETICAL DISPOSITION OF IV SCHARF 1'
(FIRST SEGMENT BY SMETS)

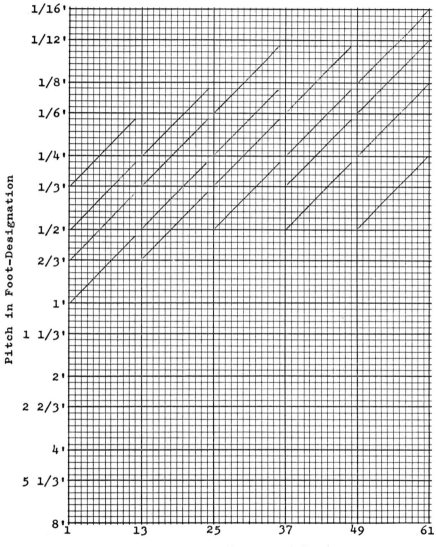

Serial Number of Pipe

CHART 54

ACTUAL DISPOSITION OF IV SCHARF 2/3'
(1619. QUOTED BY MAHRENHOLZ)

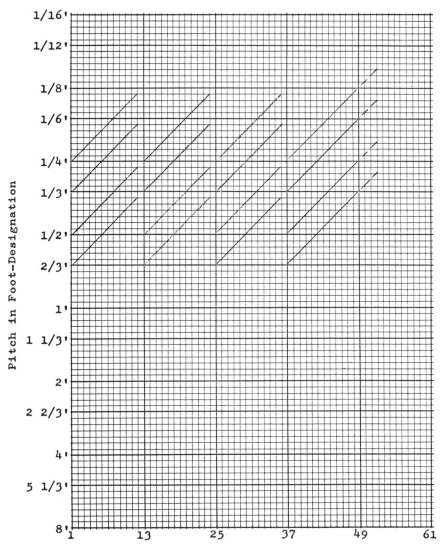

Serial Number of Pipe

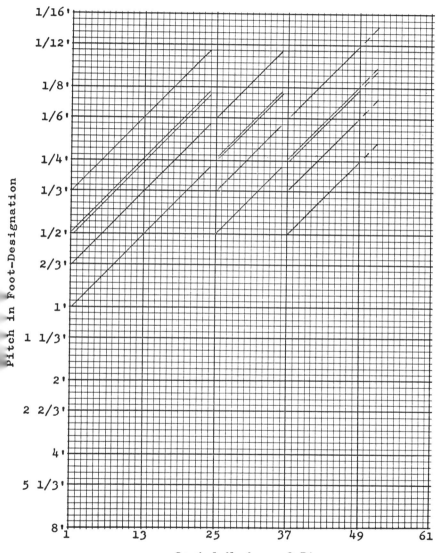

CHART 55

ACTUAL DISPOSITION OF V SCHARF 1'
(1682.   QUOTED BY MAHRENHOLZ)

Serial Number of Pipe

CHART 56

ACTUAL DISPOSITION OF VI-VIII SCHARF 1 1/3'
(ARP SCHNITGER, ST. JACOBI, HAMBURG)

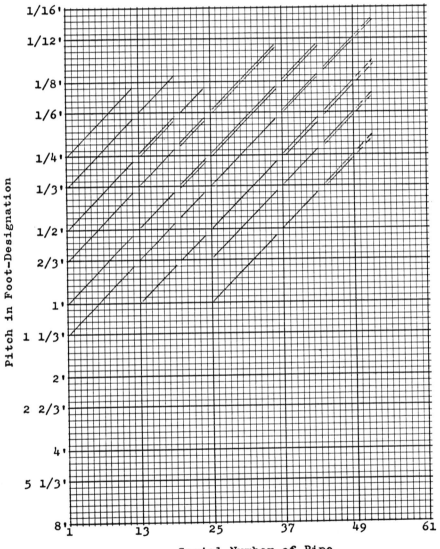

CHART 57

ACTUAL DISPOSITION OF III SCHARF 1/2'
(BAROQUE. QUOTED BY MAHRENHOLZ)

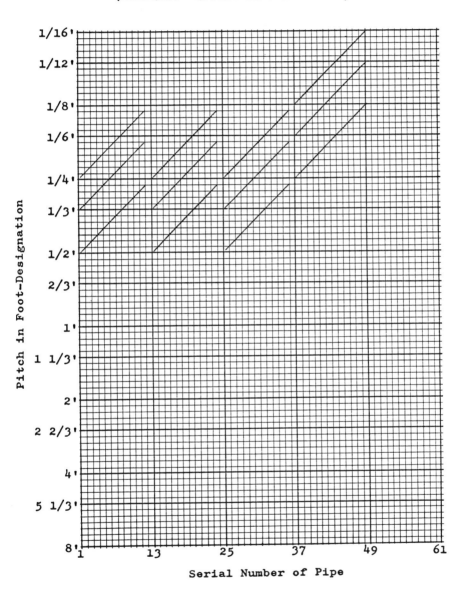

Serial Number of Pipe

CHART 58

HYPOTHETICAL DISPOSITION OF IV SCHARF 1'
(FIRST SEGMENT BY SMETS)

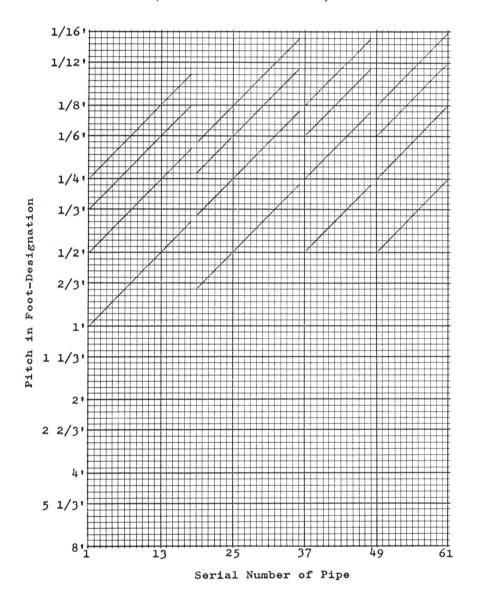

CHART 59

ACTUAL DISPOSITION OF III SCHARF 1'
(ELLERHORST)

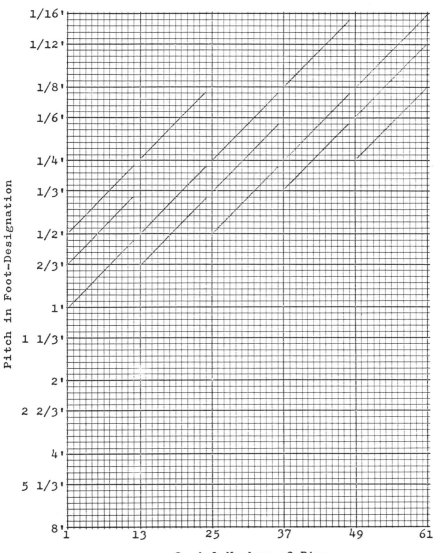

Serial Number of Pipe

CHART 60

HYPOTHETICAL REALIZATION OF V TERZSCHARF 1 1/3'
(J. WAGNER. FIRST AND LAST SEGMENTS
QUOTED BY MAHRENHOLZ)

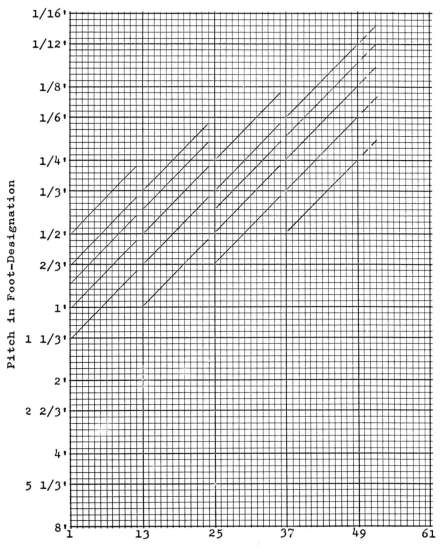

Serial Number of Pipe

CHART 61

HYPOTHETICAL REALIZATION OF III OCTAVEZIMBEL 1/4'
(FIRST SEGMENT AND METHOD OF
REPETITION BY MAHRENHOLZ)

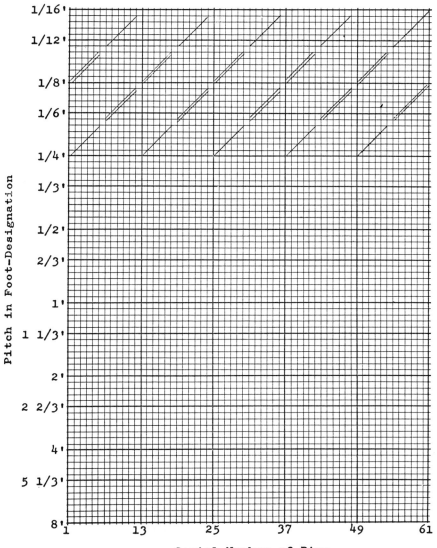

Serial Number of Pipe

CHART 62

ACTUAL DISPOSITION OF II QUINTZIMBEL 1/6'
(EARLY GERMAN. QUOTED BY MAHRENHOLZ)

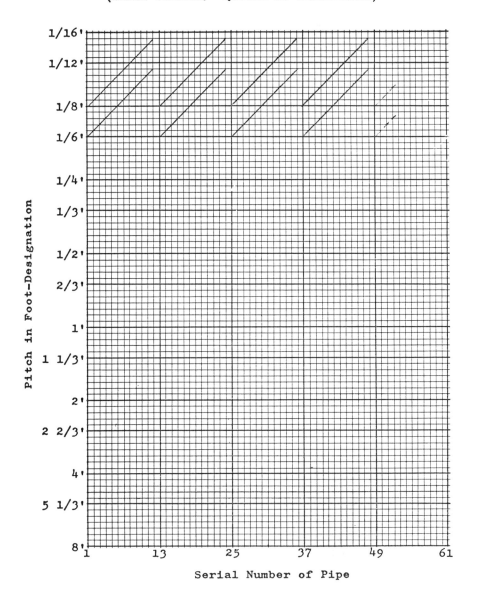

Serial Number of Pipe

CHART 63

ACTUAL DISPOSITION OF III QUINTZIMBEL 1/4'
(EARLY GERMAN.   QUOTED BY MAHRENHOLZ)

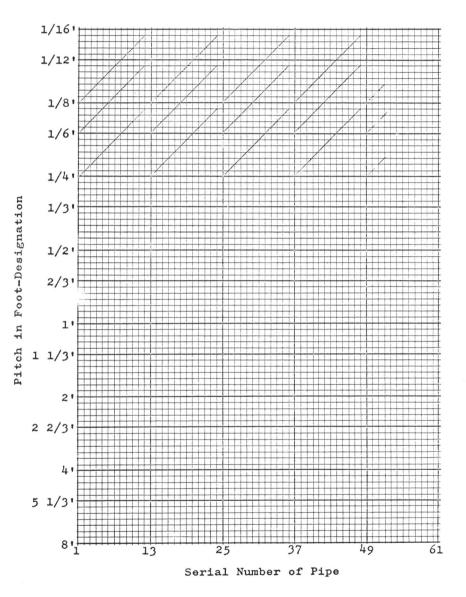

Serial Number of Pipe

CHART 64

ACTUAL DISPOSITION OF III TERZZIMBEL 1/6'
(ARP SCHNITGER, ST. JACOBI, HAMBURG)

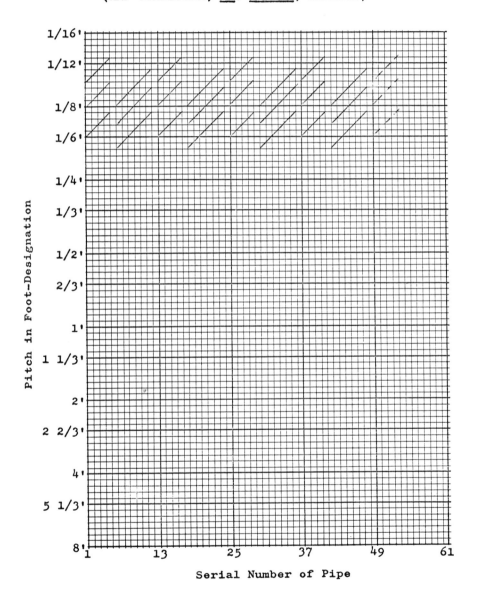

Serial Number of Pipe

CHART 65

ACTUAL DISPOSITION OF III TERZZIMBEL 1/5'
(DR. ELIS. QUOTED BY ELLERHORST)

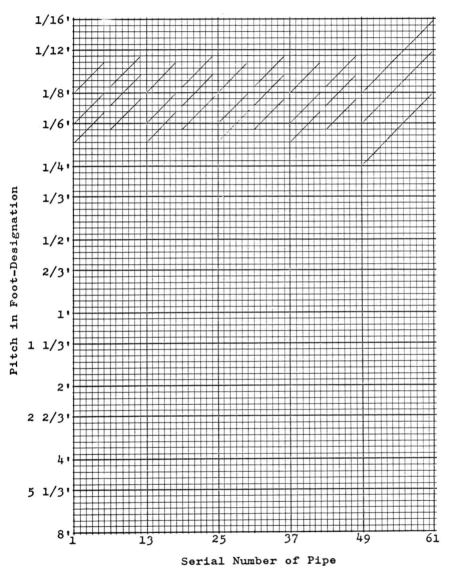

Pitch in Foot-Designation

Serial Number of Pipe

CHART 66

ACTUAL DISPOSITION OF III TERZZIMBEL 2/5'
(DR. ELIS. QUOTED BY ELLERHORST)

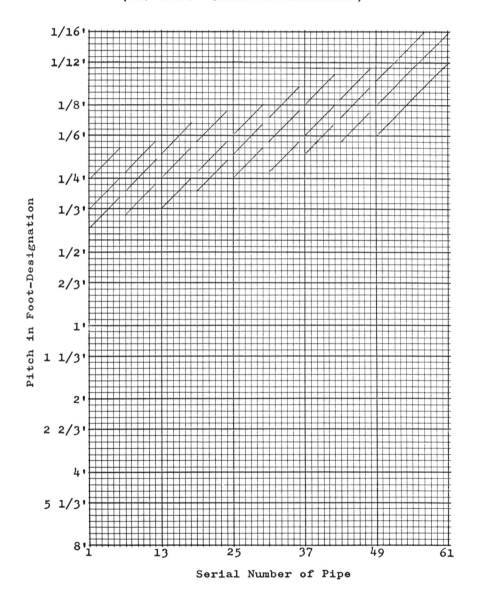

CHART 67

ACTUAL DISPOSITION OF III TERZZIMBEL 1/5'
(SCHLICKER, <u>GRACE LUTHERAN</u>, RIVER FOREST)

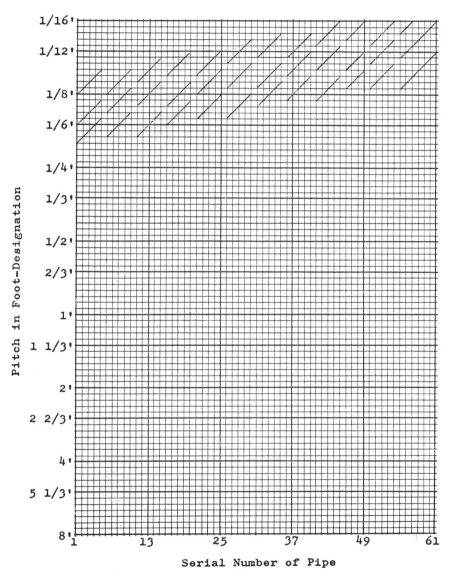

Serial Number of Pipe

CHART 68

ACTUAL DISPOSITION OF IV MIXTURE 2/3'
(1619. QUOTED BY MAHRENHOLZ)

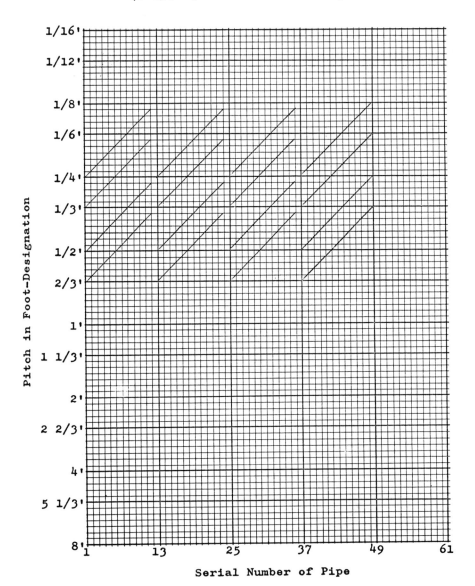

Pitch in Foot-Designation

Serial Number of Pipe

CHART 69

POSSIBLE DISPOSITION OF IV MIXTURE 1'
(HYPOTHETICAL PROJECTION)

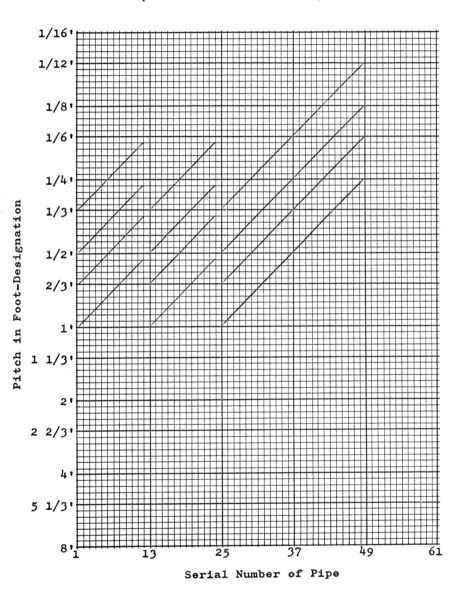

CHART 70

POSSIBLE DISPOSITION OF IV MIXTURE 2'
(HYPOTHETICAL PROJECTION)

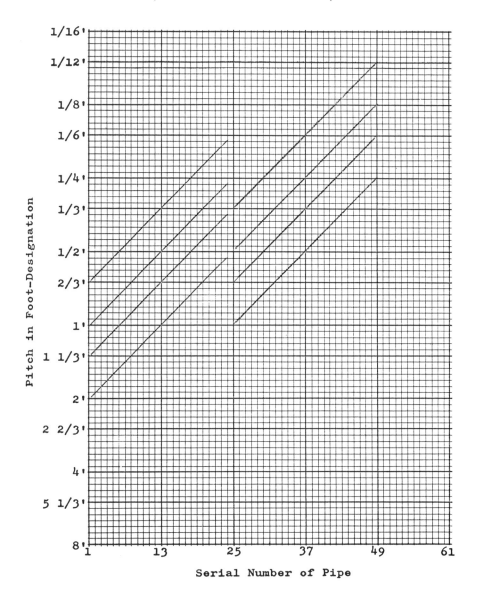

Serial Number of Pipe

CHART 71

POSSIBLE DISPOSITION OF X GROSS MIXTURE 4'
(HYPOTHETICAL PROJECTION)

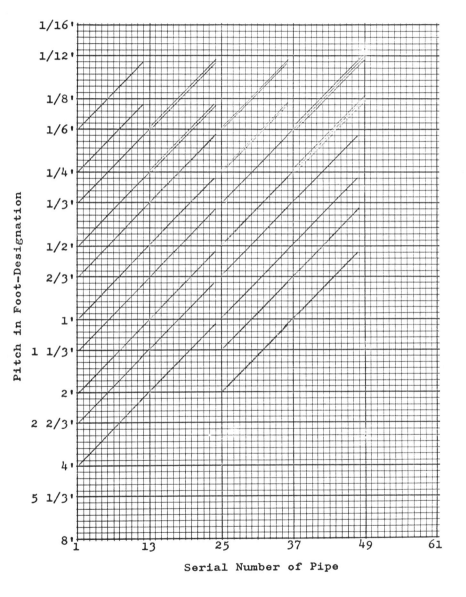

Serial Number of Pipe

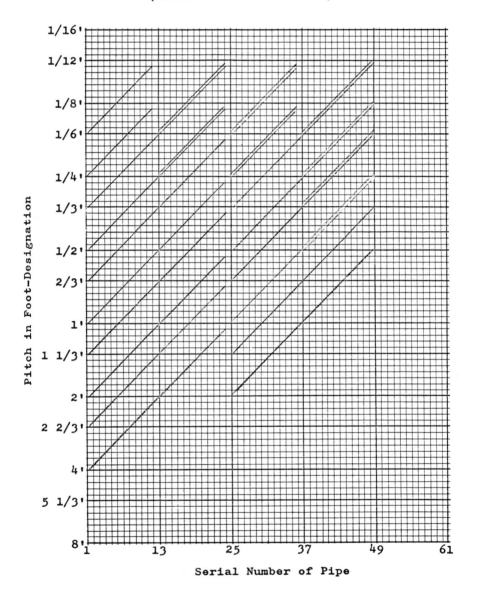

CHART 72

ALTERNATE POSSIBLE DISPOSITION OF X GROSS MIXTURE 4'
(HYPOTHETICAL PROJECTION)

Pitch in Foot-Designation

Serial Number of Pipe

CHART 73

POSSIBLE DISPOSITION OF KLEIN MIXTURE OR SCHARF
(CASE 1)

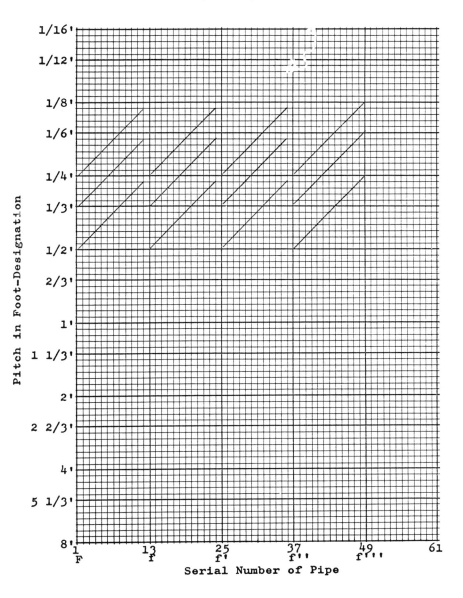

CHART 74

POSSIBLE DISPOSITION OF KLEIN MIXTURE OR SCHARF
(CASE 2)

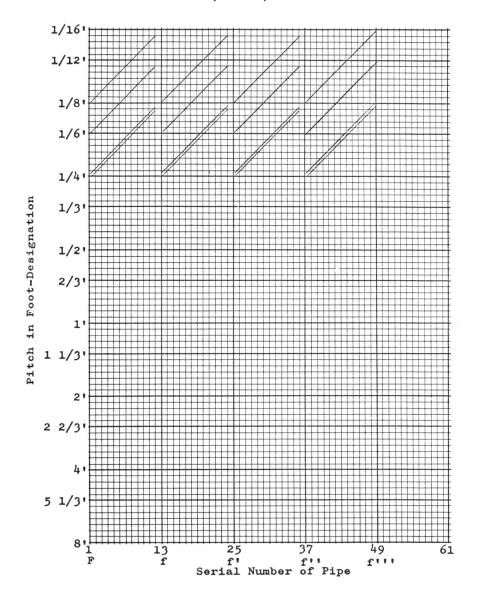

Serial Number of Pipe

CHART 75

POSSIBLE DISPOSITION OF KLEIN MIXTURE OR SCHARF
(CASE 3)

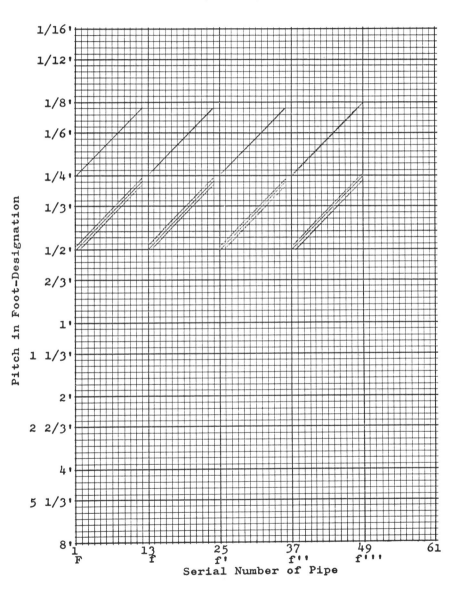

CHART 76

POSSIBLE DISPOSITION OF KLEIN MIXTURE OR SCHARF
(CASE 4)

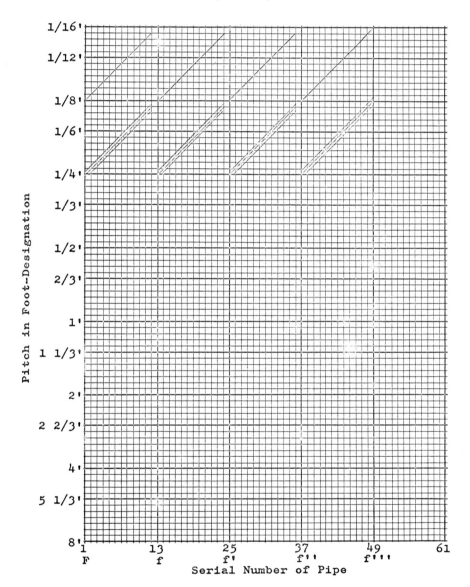

CHART 77

ACTUAL DISPOSITION OF I ZIMBEL 1/6'
(COMPENIUS, FREDERIKSBORG, DENMARK)

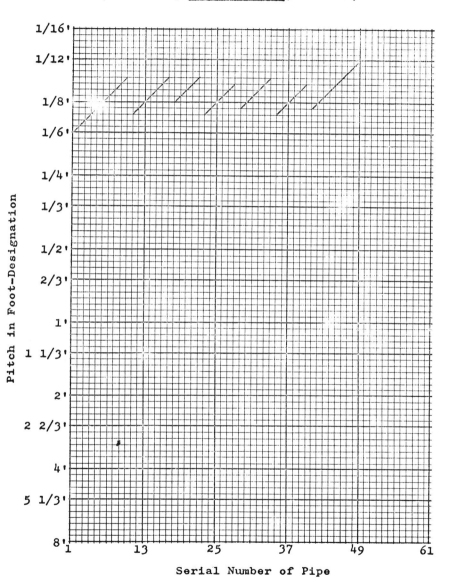

Pitch in Foot-Designation

Serial Number of Pipe

CHART 78

ACTUAL DISPOSITION OF III KLINGEND ZIMBEL 1/6'
(HANS SCHERER, ST. JACOBI, HAMBURG)

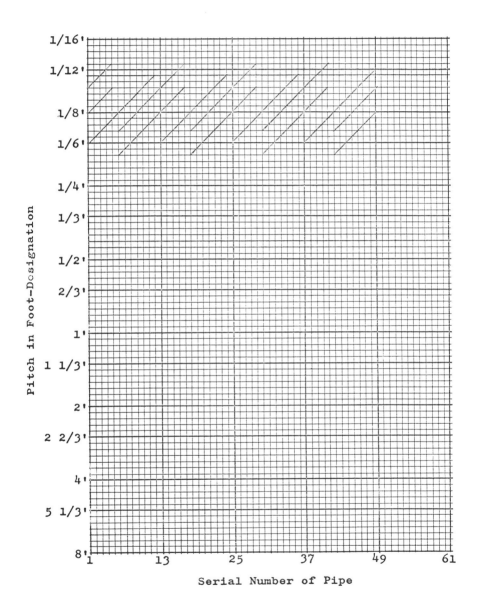

Serial Number of Pipe

CHART 79

POSSIBLE DISPOSITION OF III ZIMBELBASS 1/2'
(PEDAL)

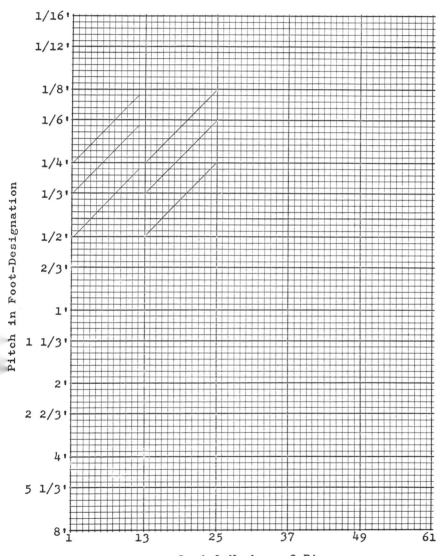

Serial Number of Pipe

CHART 80

POSSIBLE DISPOSITION OF III ZIMBELBASS 1/3'
(PEDAL)

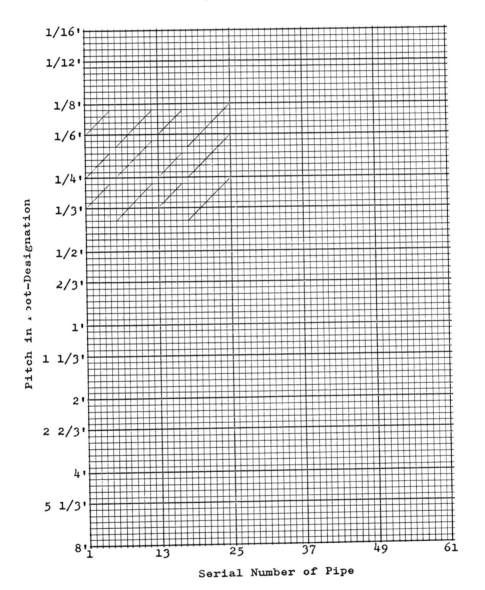

Pitch in Foot-Designation

Serial Number of Pipe

CHART 81

POSSIBLE DISPOSITION OF
III GROB ZIMBEL 1/4'

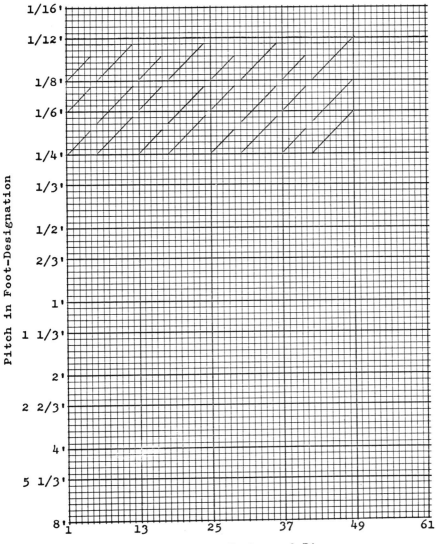

Pitch in Foot-Designation

Serial Number of Pipe

CHART 82

POSSIBLE DISPOSITION OF
II ZIMBEL 1/6'

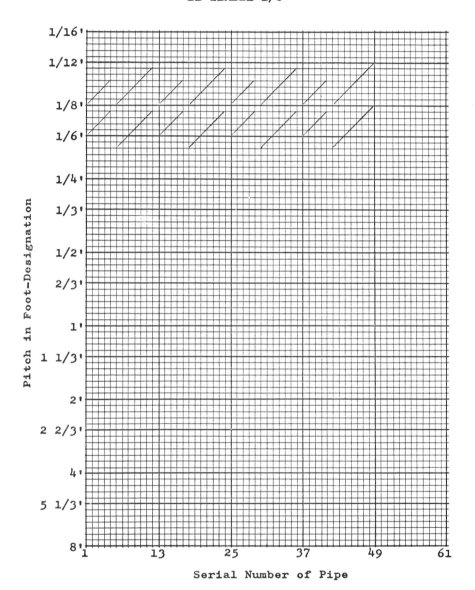

Serial Number of Pipe

CHART 83

POSSIBLE DISPOSITION OF II-I
REPETIEREND ZIMBEL 1/6'

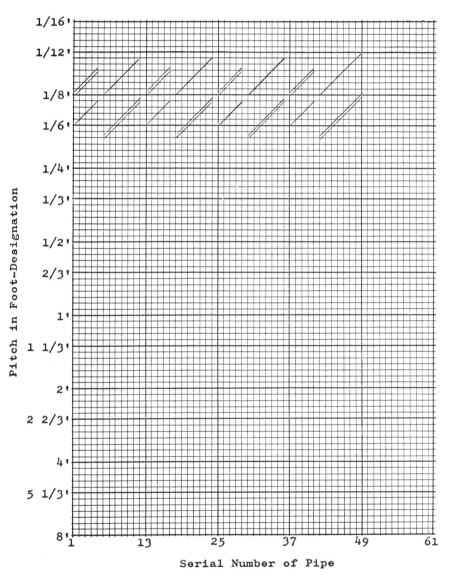

CHART 84

POSSIBLE DISPOSITION OF
I ZIMBELREGAL 1'

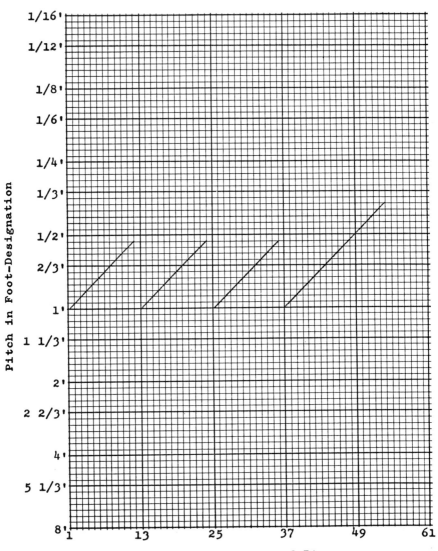

SECTION   D

PLATES

PLATE I

THE SLIDER CHEST
Side View in Section

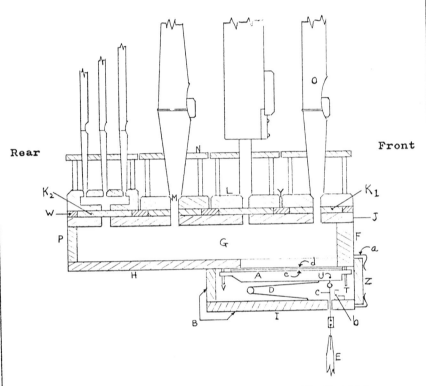

Rear   Front

A. Pallet	J. Table	U. Eyelet
B. Pallet Box	K_1. Slider, "on"	V. Guide
C. Pull-down	K_2. Slider, "off"	W. Bearer
D. Spring	L. Upper Board	Y. Space
E. Tracker	M. Pipehole, Bore	Z. Bung
F. Front Cheek	N. Rackboard	a. L-screw
G. Channel	O. Pipe	b. Thumping Rail
H. Bottom Board	P. Chest, Rear	c. Felt Packing
I. Bottom Board	T. Guide	d. Leather

PLATE II

THE SLIDER CHEST

Bottom View in Plan

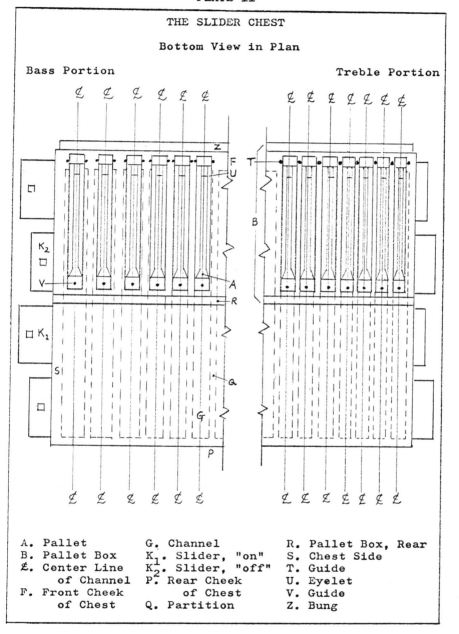

Bass Portion

Treble Portion

A. Pallet	G. Channel	R. Pallet Box, Rear
B. Pallet Box	K_1. Slider, "on"	S. Chest Side
₵. Center Line	K_2. Slider, "off"	T. Guide
of Channel	P. Rear Cheek	U. Eyelet
F. Front Cheek	of Chest	V. Guide
of Chest	Q. Partition	Z. Bung

PLATE III

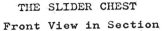

THE SLIDER CHEST
Front View in Section

Bass Portion   Treble Portion

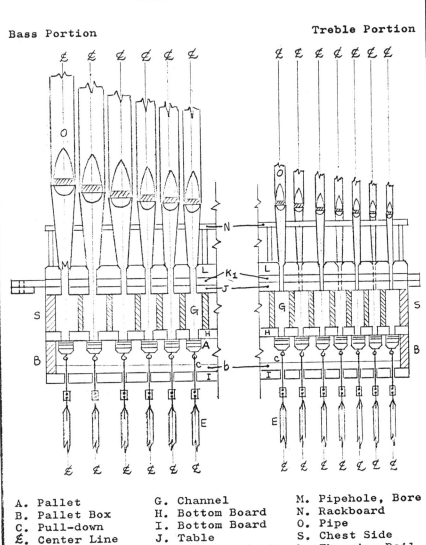

A. Pallet	G. Channel	M. Pipehole, Bore
B. Pallet Box	H. Bottom Board	N. Rackboard
C. Pull-down	I. Bottom Board	O. Pipe
$\mathcal{E}$. Center Line	J. Table	S. Chest Side
of Channel	K_1. Slider, "on"	b. Thumping Rail
E. Tracker	L. Upper Board	

PLATE IV

THE SLIDER CHEST

Top View of Table with Bearers in Place

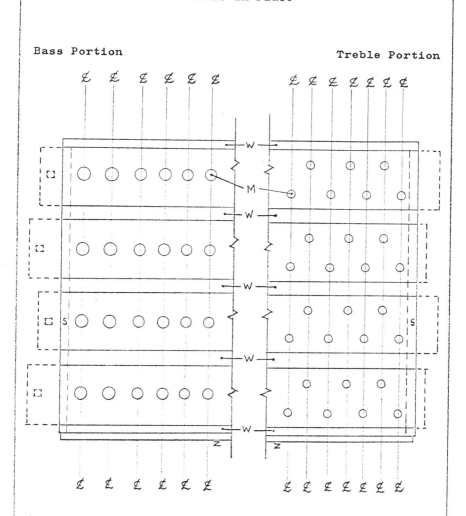

Bass Portion

Treble Portion

₡. Center Line
    of Channel
M. Bore

S. Chest Side
W. Bearer
Z. Bung

PLATE V

THE SLIDER CHEST

Top View of Bearers and Sliders

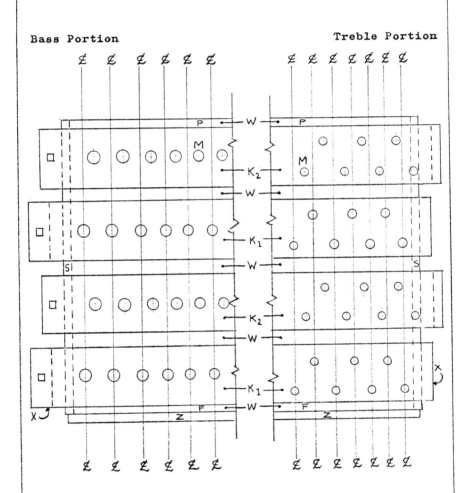

£. Center Line of Channel
F. Front Cheek
K_1. Slider, "on"
K_2. Slider, "off"
M. Bore

P. Rear Cheek
S. Chest Side
W. Bearer
X. Bumper
Z. Bung

PLATE VI

THE SLIDER CHEST
Top View of Upper Boards

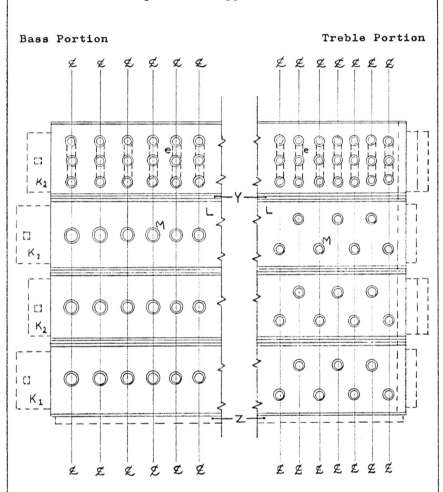

Bass Portion

Treble Portion

¢. Center Line
    of Channel
K_1. Slider, "on"
K_2. Slider, "off"
L. Upper Board

M. Pipehole, Bore
Y. Space between
    Upper Boards
Z. Bung
e. Groove in Groove Board

PLATE VII

THE SLIDER CHEST

View in Perspective

Bass Portion

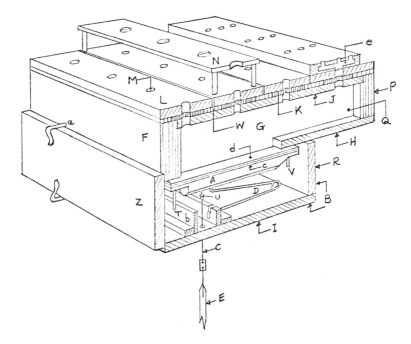

A. Pallet	J. Table	U. Eyelet
B. Pallet Box	K. Slider	V. Guide
C. Pull-down	L. Upper Board	W. Bearer
D. Spring	M. Pipehole, Bore	Z. Bung
E. Tracker	N. Rackboard	a. L-screw
F. Front Cheek	P. Rear Cheek	b. Thumping Rail
G. Channel	Q. Partition	c. Felt Packing
H. Bottom Board	R. Pallet Box, Rear	d. Leather
I. Bottom Board	T. Guide	e. Groove

PLATE VIII

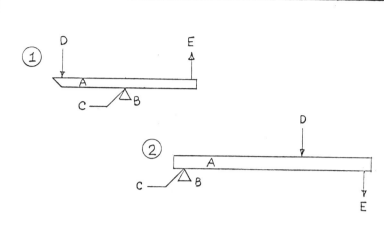

A. Key
B. Rail
C. Fulcrum

D. Impact
E. Resultant Force

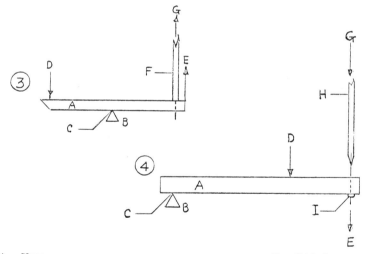

A. Key
B. Rail
C. Fulcrum
D. Impact
E. Resultant Force

F. Sticker
G. Transmitted
   Force
H. Tracker
I. Button

PLATE IX

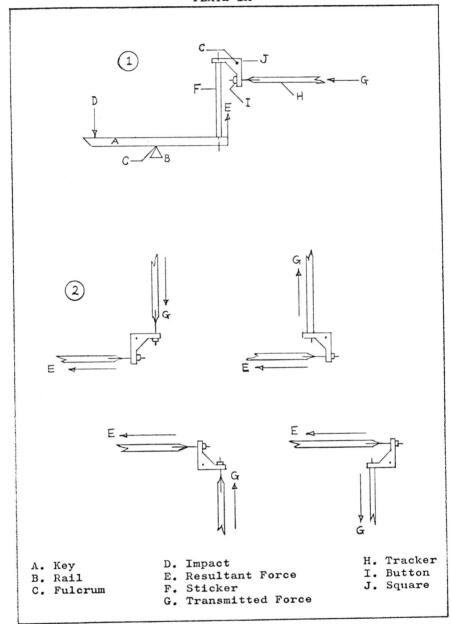

A. Key
B. Rail
C. Fulcrum
D. Impact
E. Resultant Force
F. Sticker
G. Transmitted Force
H. Tracker
I. Button
J. Square

PLATE X

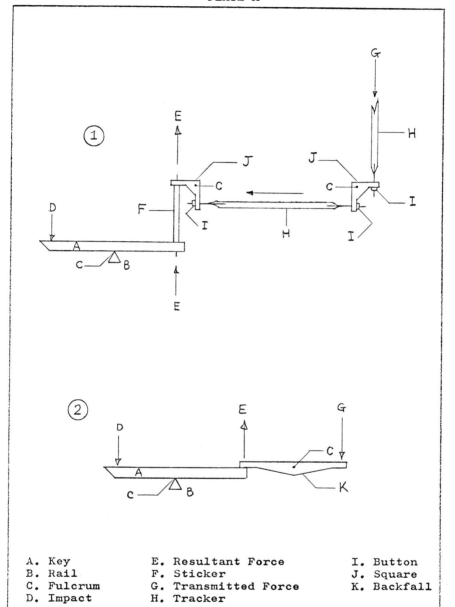

A. Key   E. Resultant Force   I. Button
B. Rail   F. Sticker   J. Square
C. Fulcrum   G. Transmitted Force   K. Backfall
D. Impact   H. Tracker

PLATE XI

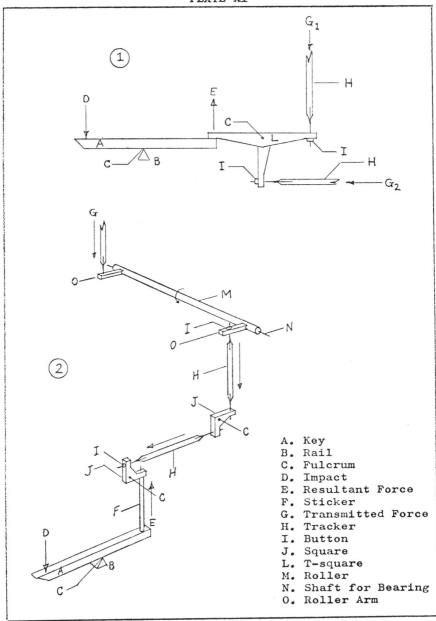

A. Key
B. Rail
C. Fulcrum
D. Impact
E. Resultant Force
F. Sticker
G. Transmitted Force
H. Tracker
I. Button
J. Square
L. T-square
M. Roller
N. Shaft for Bearing
O. Roller Arm

PLATE XII

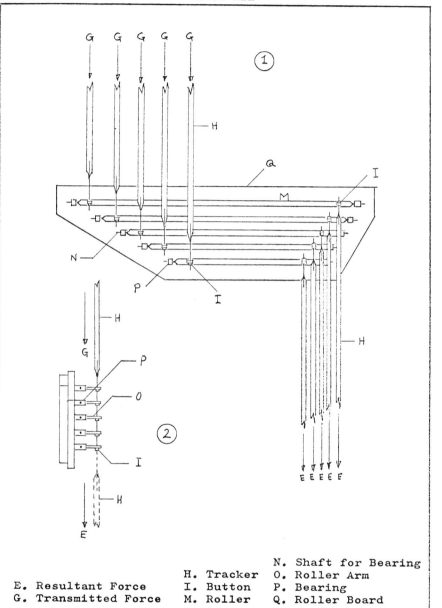

E. Resultant Force   H. Tracker   N. Shaft for Bearing
G. Transmitted Force   I. Button   O. Roller Arm
   M. Roller   P. Bearing
   Q. Roller Board

PLATE XIII

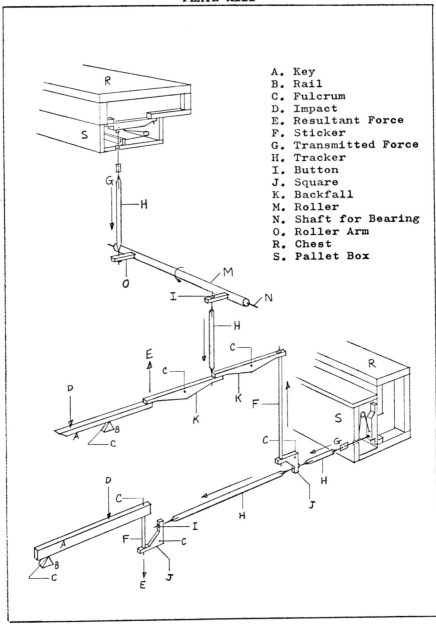

A. Key
B. Rail
C. Fulcrum
D. Impact
E. Resultant Force
F. Sticker
G. Transmitted Force
H. Tracker
I. Button
J. Square
K. Backfall
M. Roller
N. Shaft for Bearing
O. Roller Arm
R. Chest
S. Pallet Box

PLATE XIV

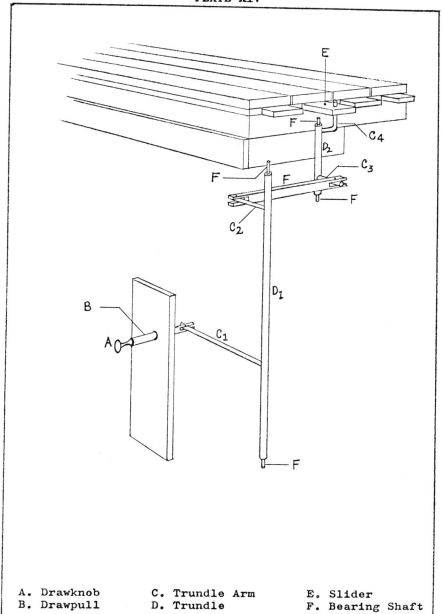

A. Drawknob   C. Trundle Arm   E. Slider
B. Drawpull   D. Trundle   F. Bearing Shaft

PLATE **XV**

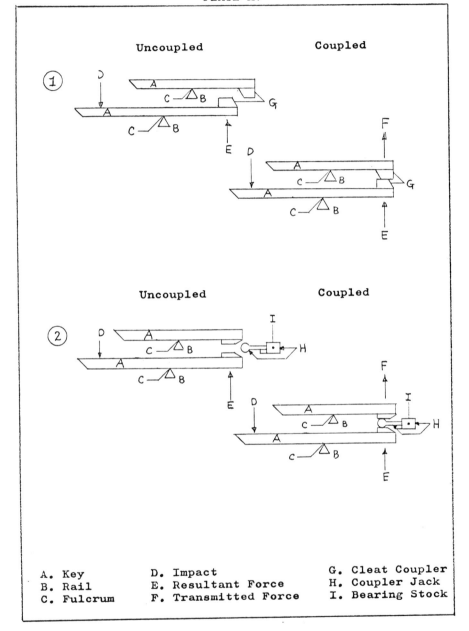

A. Key   D. Impact   G. Cleat Coupler
B. Rail   E. Resultant Force   H. Coupler Jack
C. Fulcrum   F. Transmitted Force   I. Bearing Stock

PLATE XVI

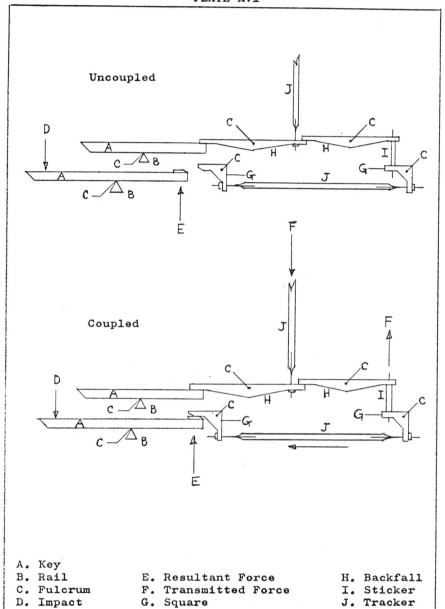

Uncoupled

Coupled

A. Key
B. Rail
C. Fulcrum   E. Resultant Force   H. Backfall
D. Impact   F. Transmitted Force   I. Sticker
                    G. Square   J. Tracker

PLATE XVII

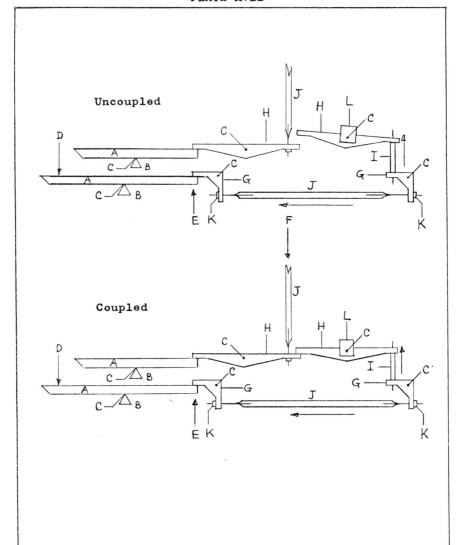

A. Key
B. Rail
C. Fulcrum
D. Impact

E. Resultant Force
F. Transmitted Force
G. Square
H. Backfall

I. Sticker
J. Tracker
K. Button
L. Bearing Stock

PLATE XVIII

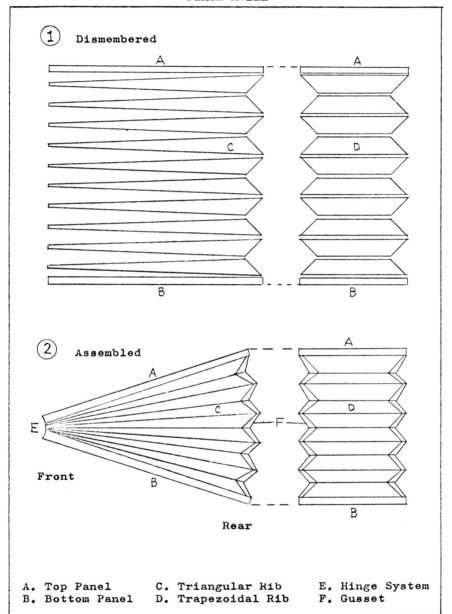

① Dismembered

② Assembled

Front

Rear

A. Top Panel   C. Triangular Rib   E. Hinge System
B. Bottom Panel   D. Trapezoidal Rib   F. Gusset

PLATE XIX

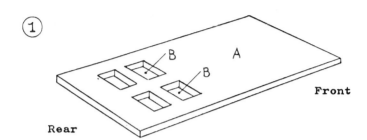

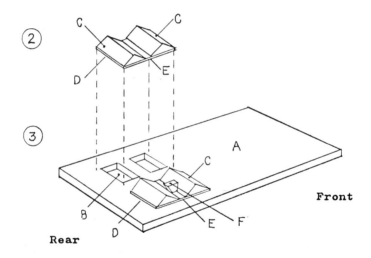

A. Bottom Panel   C. Intake Valve   E. Leather Hinge
B. Intake Opening D. Leather Packing F. Bumper

PLATE XX

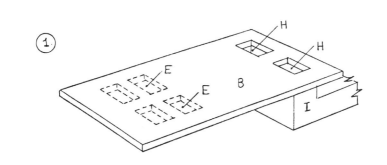

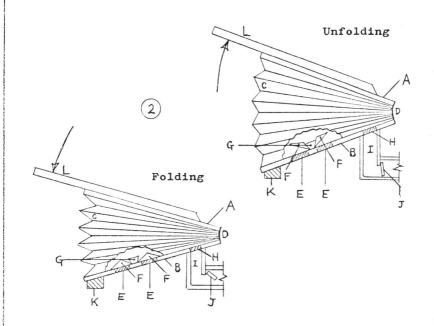

A. Top Panel	E. Intake Opening	I. Throat
B. Bottom Panel	F. Intake Valve	J. Exhaust Valve
C. Rib	G. Bumper	K. Support Beam
D. Hinge	H. Exhaust Opening	L. Handle

PLATE XXI

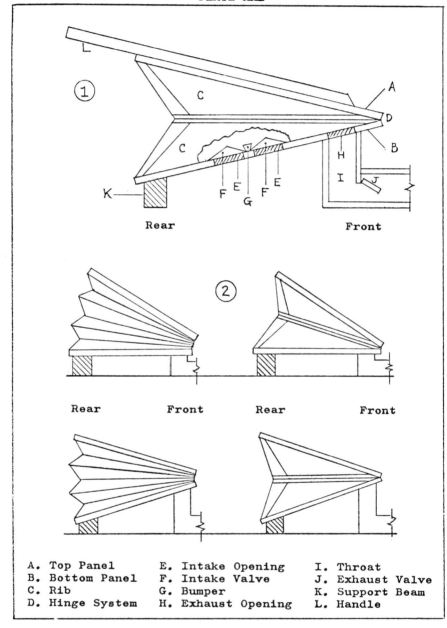

A. Top Panel   E. Intake Opening   I. Throat
B. Bottom Panel   F. Intake Valve   J. Exhaust Valve
C. Rib   G. Bumper   K. Support Beam
D. Hinge System   H. Exhaust Opening   L. Handle

PLATE XXII

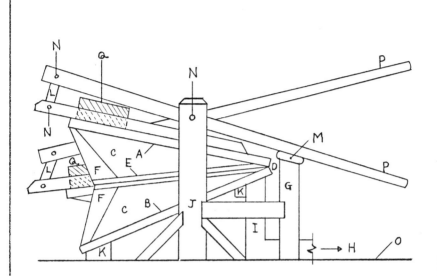

Rear   Front

A. Top Panel
B. Bottom Panel
C. Rib
D. Hinge System
E. Leather Strip
F. Gusset

G. Bumper
H. Canal
I. Throat
J. Cradle
K. Support Beam

L. Trace
M. Padding
N. Pivot
O. Floor
P. Lever
Q. Weight

PLATE XXIII

A FORM OF COMPOUND BELLOWS[a]

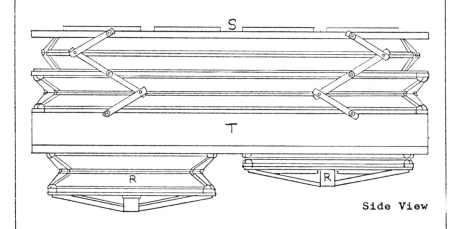

Side View

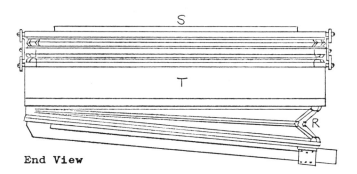

End View

R. Feeder   S. Receiver   T. Trunk Band

[a]From G. A. Audsley, The Art of Organ Building
(New York, 1905) II, Plate XIV, opposite p. 694.

PLATE XXIV

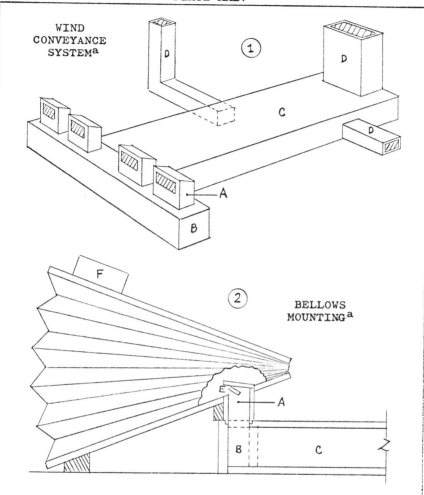

WIND
CONVEYANCE
SYSTEM[a]

1

D

D

C

D

A

B

2

BELLOWS
MOUNTING[a]

F

E

A

B

C

A. Throat   C. Wind Trunk   E. Exhaust Valve
B. Canal   D. Wind Conductor   F. Inert Weight

[a]Adapted from Dom Bedos, L'Art du Facteur
d'Orgues (Bordeaux [?], 1766-1778; facs. ed. by C.
Mahrenholz, Kassel, 1934) I, Plate XLVIII.

PLATE XXV

BELLOWS MOUNTING[a]

(1)

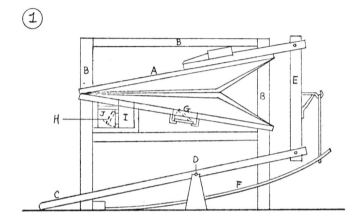

WIND TRUNK VENTIL

(2)

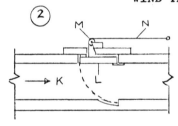 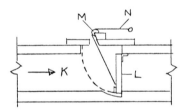

A. Bellows
B. Bellows Cradle
C. Handle
D. Fulcrum
E. Trace

F. Spring
G. Intake Valve
H. Exhaust Valve
I. Throat
J. Canal

K. Wind Trunk
L. Wind Trunk
   Ventil
M. Pulley
N. Cable

[a]From A. Oosterhof and A. Bouman, Orgelbouw-kunde (Leiden, 1956), p. 58.

PLATE XXVI

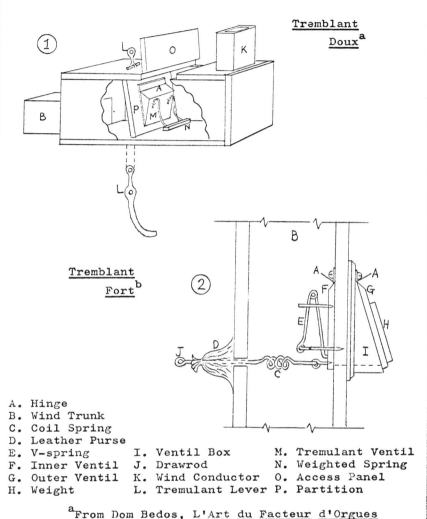

Tremblant
Doux[a]

Tremblant
Fort[b]

A. Hinge
B. Wind Trunk
C. Coil Spring
D. Leather Purse
E. V-spring
F. Inner Ventil
G. Outer Ventil
H. Weight

I. Ventil Box
J. Drawrod
K. Wind Conductor
L. Tremulant Lever

M. Tremulant Ventil
N. Weighted Spring
O. Access Panel
P. Partition

[a]From Dom Bedos, L'Art du Facteur d'Orgues
(Bordeaux [?], 1766-1778; facs. ed. by C. Mahrenholz,
Kassel, 1934) I, Plate XLIX.

[b]From Dom Bedos, L'Art . . . I, Plate XLVI,
figures 5 and 7-13.

PLATE XXVII

SINGLE COLUMN
MANOMETER[a]

DOUBLE COLUMN
MANOMETER[b]

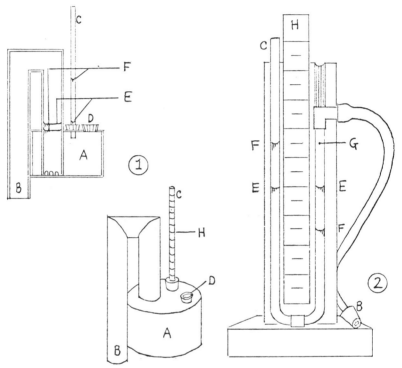

A. Canister	E. Initial Water Level
B. Intake Nozzle	F. Final Water Level
C. Glass Tube--Secondary	G. Glass Tube--Primary
D. Bung	H. Calibrated Gauge

[a]From Dom Bedos, L'Art du Facteur d'Orgues (Bordeaux [?], 1766-1778; facs. ed. by C. Mahrenholz, Kassel, 1934) I, Plate XII, figures 99-100.

[b]Adapted from J. Toepfer and M. Allihn, Theorie und Praxis des Orgelbaues (2nd ed.; Weimar, 1888) Atlas, Tafel I, Figur 42.

PLATE XXVIII

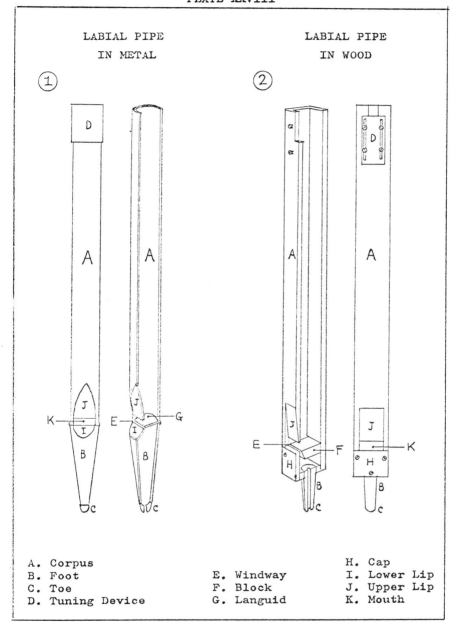

LABIAL PIPE
IN METAL

LABIAL PIPE
IN WOOD

A. Corpus
B. Foot
C. Toe
D. Tuning Device

E. Windway
F. Block
G. Languid

H. Cap
I. Lower Lip
J. Upper Lip
K. Mouth

PLATE XXIX

LINGUAL PIPE

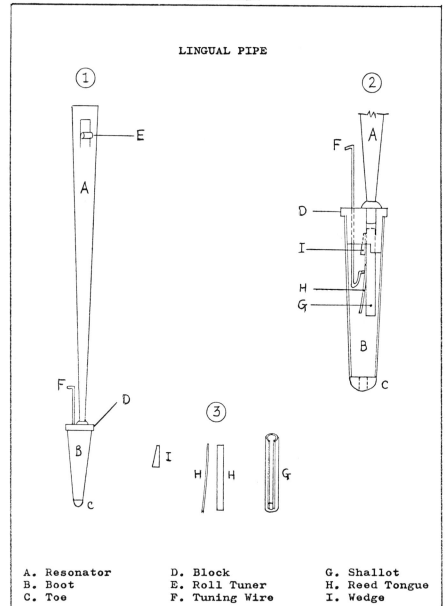

A. Resonator   D. Block   G. Shallot
B. Boot   E. Roll Tuner H. Reed Tongue
C. Toe   F. Tuning Wire I. Wedge

PLATE XXX

MODELS OF OPEN CYLINDRICAL PIPES

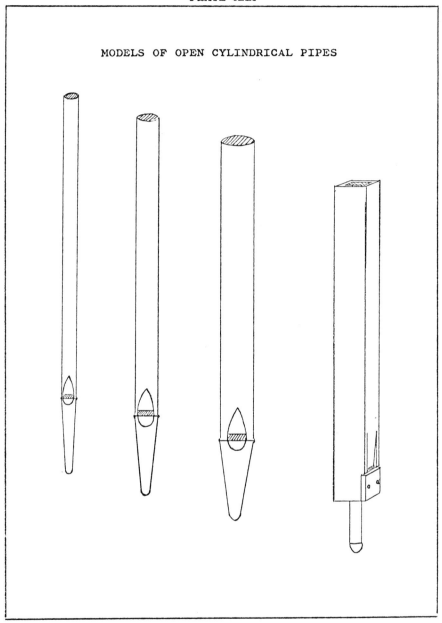

PLATE XXXI

MODELS OF OPEN CONICAL PIPES

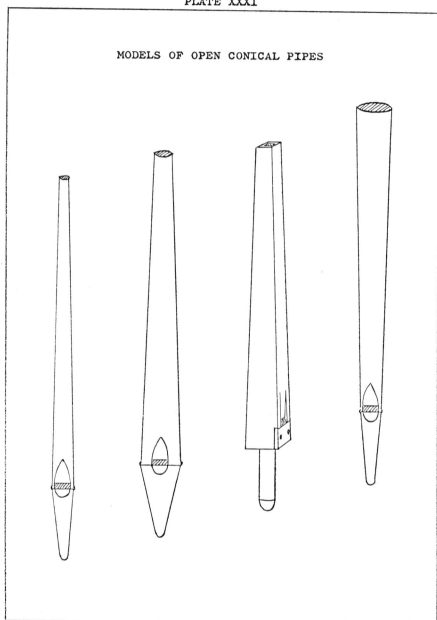

PLATE XXXII

MODELS OF FULLY COVERED PIPES

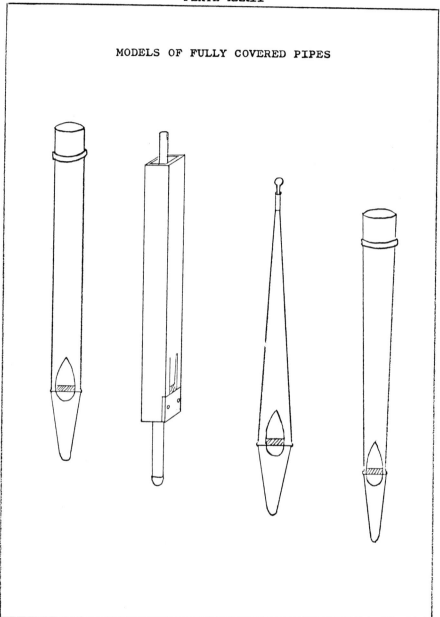

PLATE XXXIII

MODELS OF PARTLY COVERED PIPES

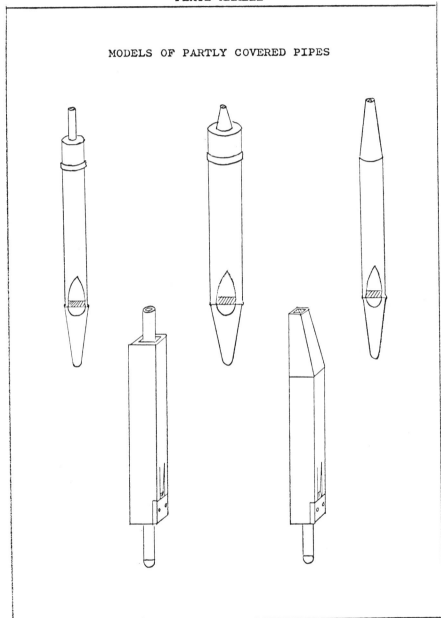

PLATE XXXIV

MODELS OF REEDS WITH CYLINDRICAL RESONATORS

PLATE XXXV

MODELS OF REEDS WITH CONICAL RESONATORS

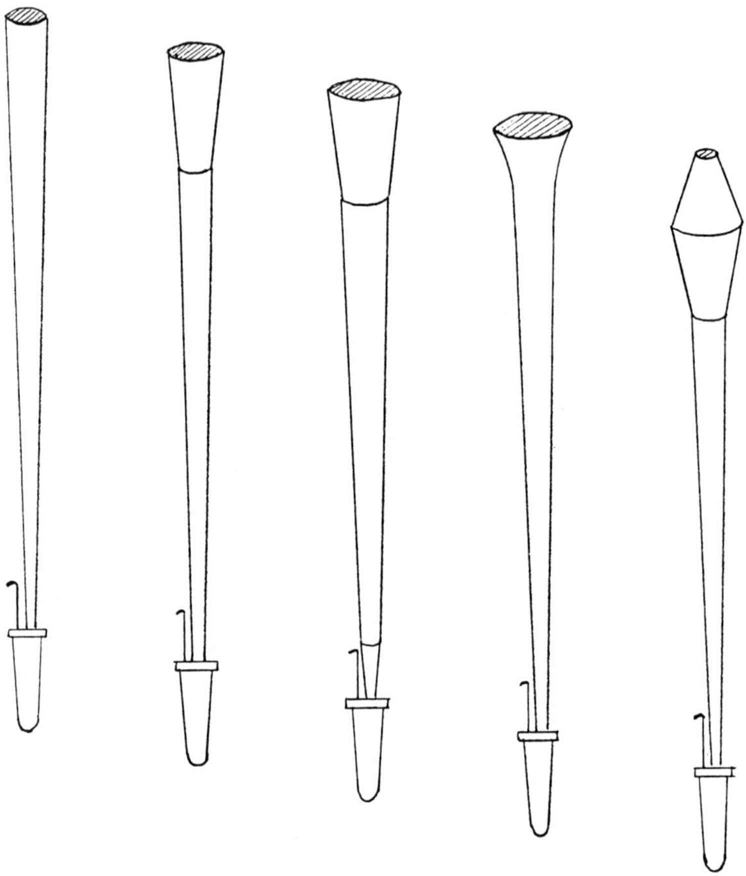

PLATE **XXXVI**

MODELS OF REGALS WITH PREPONDERANTLY
CYLINDRICAL RESONATORS

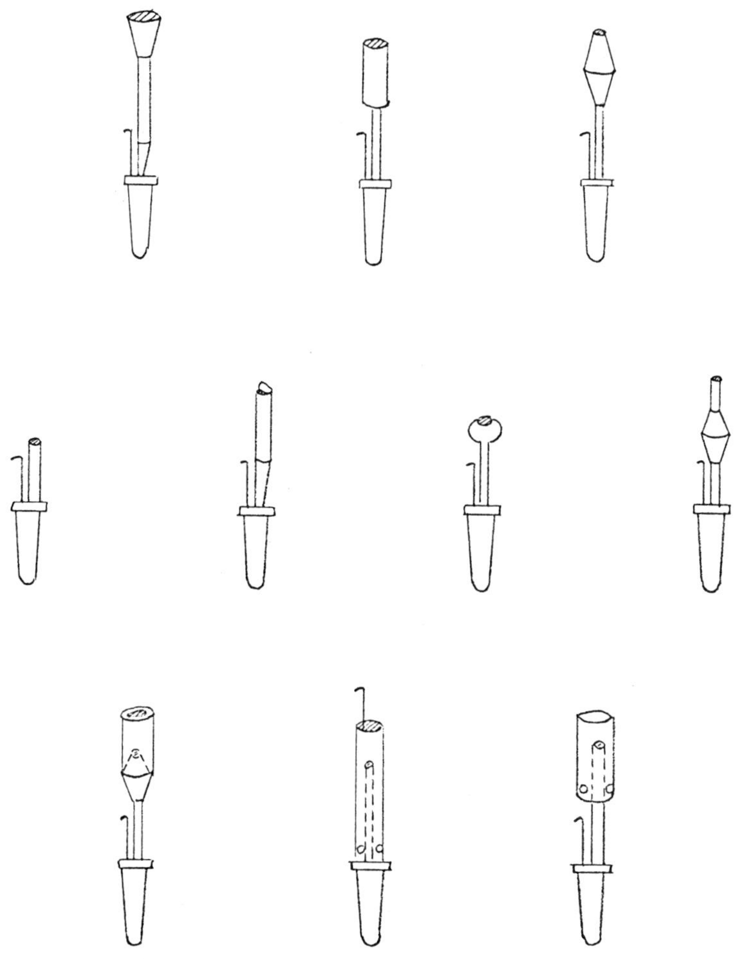

PLATE XXXVII

MODELS OF REGALS WITH PREPONDERANTLY
CONICAL RESONATORS

PLATE XXXVIII

MODELS OF REGALS WITH
VARIOUS RESONATORS

PLATE XXXIX

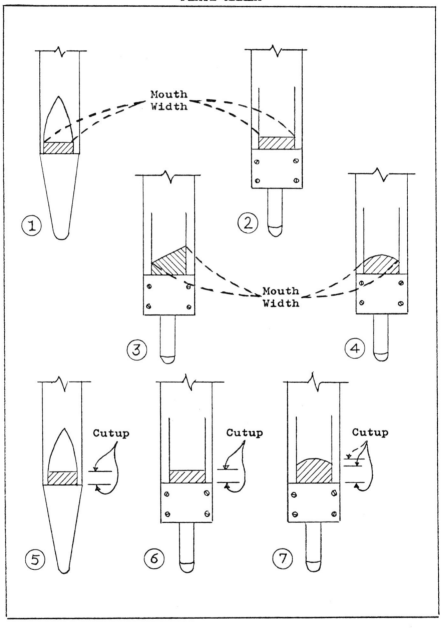

PLATE XL

SCALE MODEL OF 8' SALICIONAL

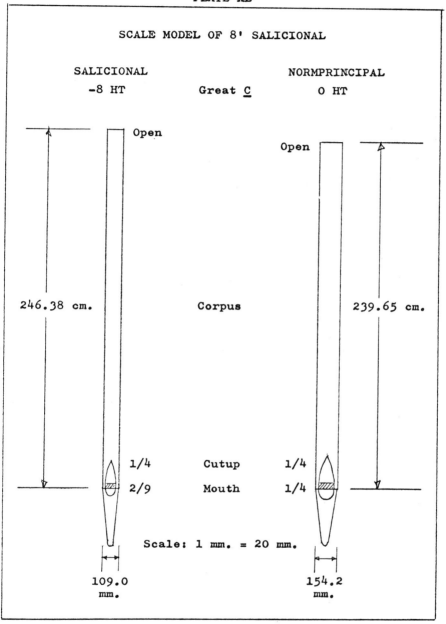

SALICIONAL		NORMPRINCIPAL
-8 HT	Great C	0 HT

Open

246.38 cm.

Corpus

239.65 cm.

Open

| 1/4 | Cutup | 1/4 |
| 2/9 | Mouth | 1/4 |

Scale: 1 mm. = 20 mm.

109.0
mm.

154.2
mm.

PLATE XLI

SCALE MODEL OF 8' QUINTADENA

QUINTADENA   Great <u>C</u>   NORMPRINCIPAL

-12 HT   0 HT

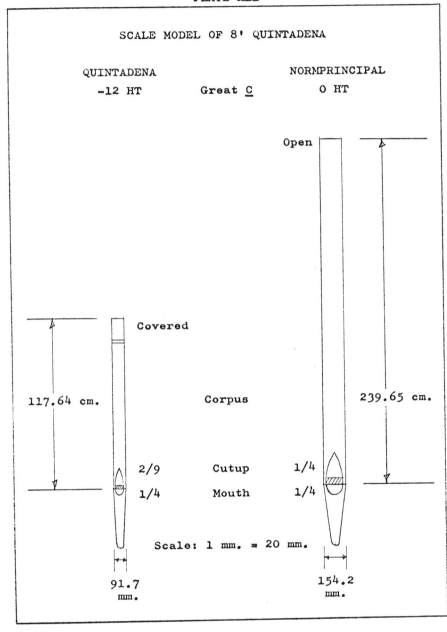

Open

Covered

117.64 cm.   Corpus   239.65 cm.

2/9   Cutup   1/4

1/4   Mouth   1/4

Scale: 1 mm. = 20 mm.

91.7   154.2
mm.   mm.

PLATE XLII

SCALE MODEL OF 8' ZARTGEIGE

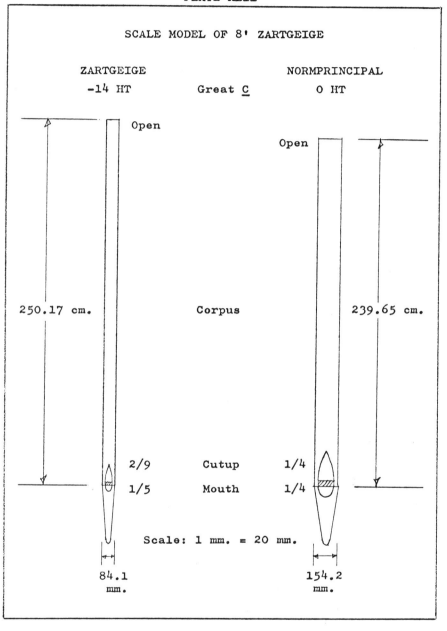

ZARTGEIGE		NORMPRINCIPAL
-14 HT	Great <u>C</u>	0 HT

Open

Open

250.17 cm.   Corpus   239.65 cm.

| 2/9 | Cutup | 1/4 |
| 1/5 | Mouth | 1/4 |

Scale: 1 mm. = 20 mm.

84.1
mm.

154.2
mm.

PLATE XLIII

SCALE MODEL OF 8' GEIGENDPRINCIPAL

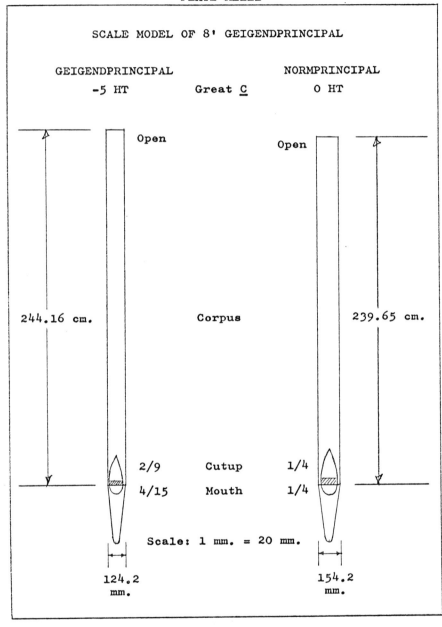

GEIGENDPRINCIPAL

NORMPRINCIPAL

-5 HT   Great C̲   0 HT

Open

Open

244.16 cm.

Corpus

239.65 cm.

2/9   Cutup   1/4

4/15   Mouth   1/4

Scale: 1 mm. = 20 mm.

124.2
mm.

154.2
mm.

PLATE XLIV

SCALE MODEL OF 8' SPITZGAMBE

SPITZGAMBE

−6 HT; d/D = 2/5   Great C̲

NORMPRINCIPAL

0 HT

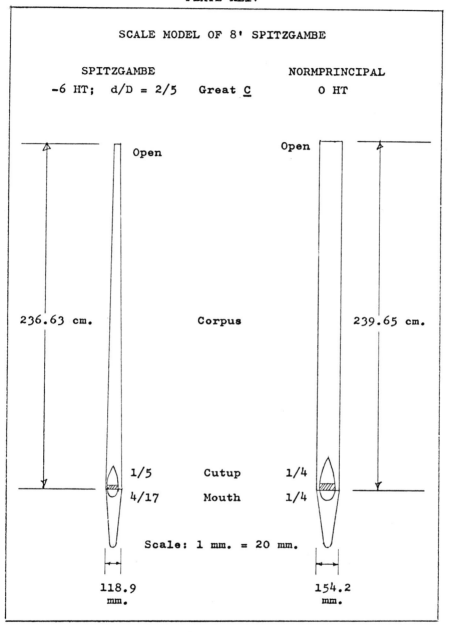

236.63 cm.

Open

Corpus

1/5   Cutup   1/4
4/17   Mouth   1/4

Scale: 1 mm. = 20 mm.

118.9
mm.

Open

239.65 cm.

154.2
mm.

PLATE XLV

SCALE MODEL OF 8' GEDACKTPOMMER

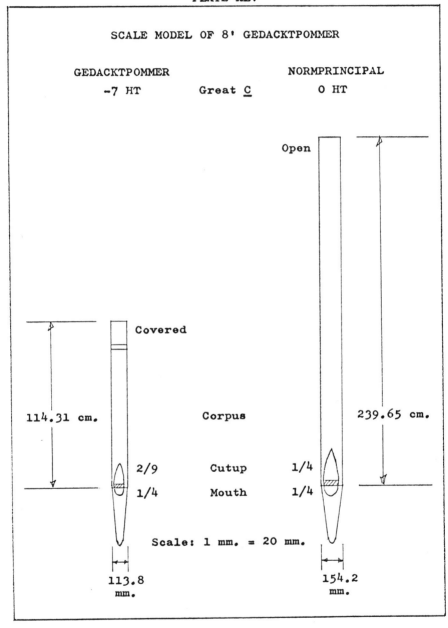

GEDACKTPOMMER		NORMPRINCIPAL
-7 HT	Great <u>C</u>	0 HT

Open

Covered

114.31 cm.

239.65 cm.

Corpus

| 2/9 | Cutup | 1/4 |
| 1/4 | Mouth | 1/4 |

Scale: 1 mm. = 20 mm.

113.8
mm.

154.2
mm.

PLATE XLVI

SCALE MODEL OF 8' SPILLPFEIFE

SPILLPFEIFE	NORMPRINCIPAL
−2 HT; d/D = 1/2 Great C	0 HT

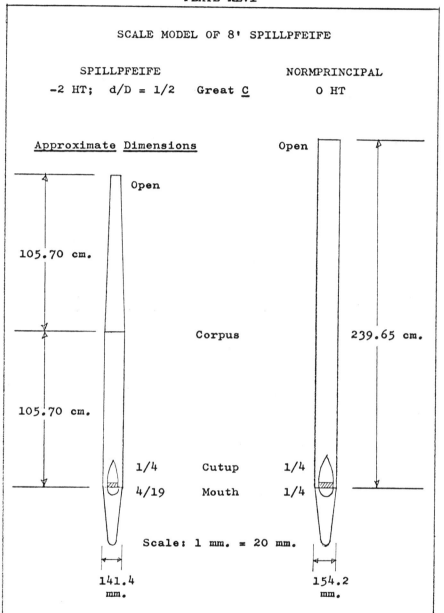

Approximate Dimensions

Open

Open

105.70 cm.

Corpus

239.65 cm.

105.70 cm.

1/4   Cutup   1/4

4/19   Mouth   1/4

Scale: 1 mm. = 20 mm.

141.4
mm.

154.2
mm.

PLATE XLVII

SCALE MODELS OF NARROW-SCALED ECHOFORMS
AT 8' PITCH

STREICH-
FLOETE

Great <u>C</u>

NORM-
PRINCIPAL

-8 HT; d/D = 1/2

0 HT

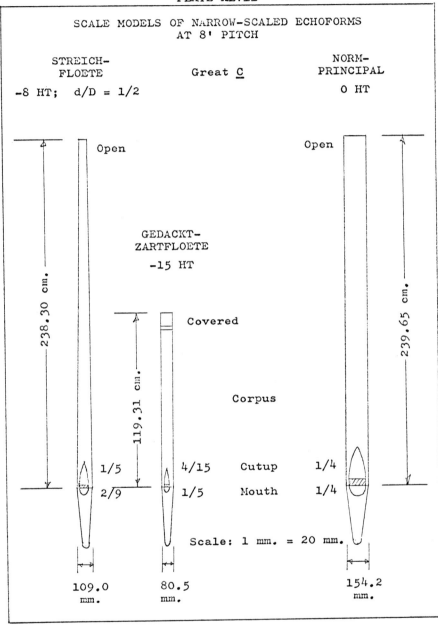

Open

Open

GEDACKT-
ZARTFLOETE

-15 HT

238.30 cm.

Covered

119.31 cm.

239.65 cm.

Corpus

1/5   4/15   Cutup   1/4

2/9   1/5   Mouth   1/4

Scale: 1 mm. = 20 mm.

109.0
mm.

80.5
mm.

154.2
mm.

PLATE XLVIII

SCALE MODEL OF 8' PRINCIPAL

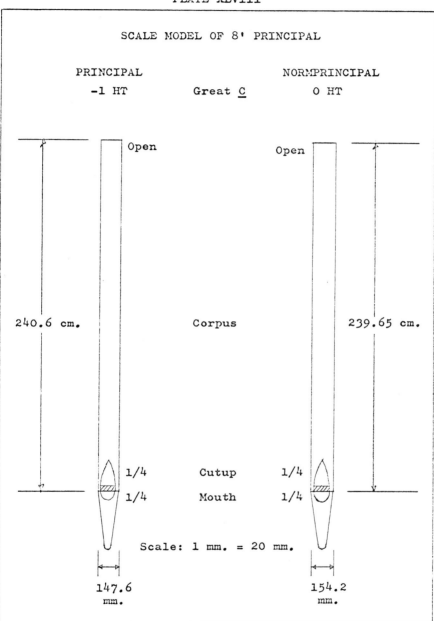

PRINCIPAL   NORMPRINCIPAL

-1 HT Great <u>C</u> 0 HT

Open   Open

240.6 cm.   Corpus   239.65 cm.

1/4 Cutup 1/4

1/4 Mouth 1/4

Scale: 1 mm. = 20 mm.

147.6   154.2
mm.   mm.

PLATE IL

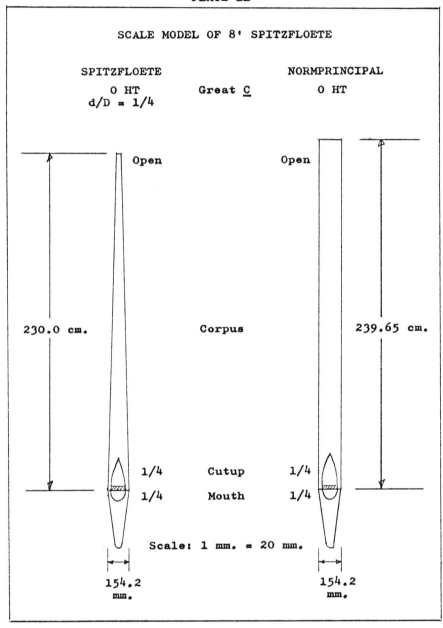

SCALE MODEL OF 8' SPITZFLOETE

SPITZFLOETE   NORMPRINCIPAL

O HT   Great C   O HT

d/D = 1/4

Open   Open

230.0 cm.   Corpus   239.65 cm.

1/4   Cutup   1/4

1/4   Mouth   1/4

Scale: 1 mm. = 20 mm.

154.2   154.2
mm.   mm.

PLATE L

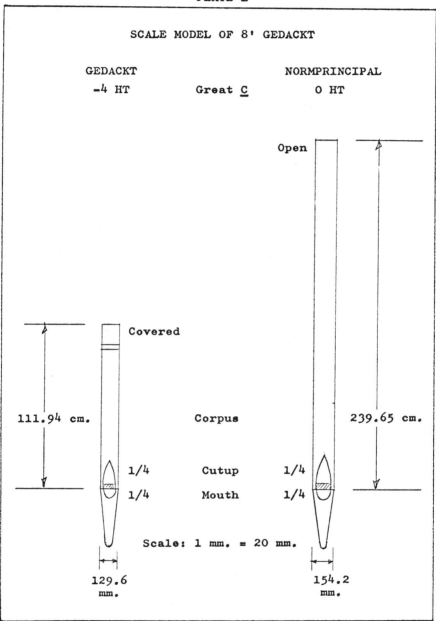

SCALE MODEL OF 8' GEDACKT

GEDACKT   NORMPRINCIPAL

-4 HT   Great C   0 HT

Open

Covered

111.94 cm.   Corpus   239.65 cm.

1/4   Cutup   1/4

1/4   Mouth   1/4

Scale: 1 mm. = 20 mm.

129.6   154.2
mm.   mm.

PLATE LI

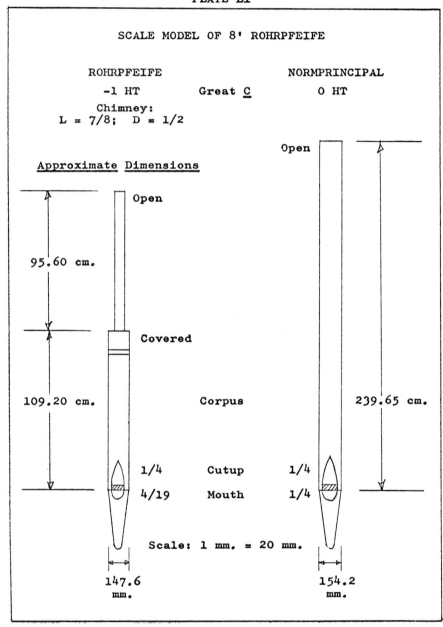

SCALE MODEL OF 8' ROHRPFEIFE

ROHRPFEIFE   NORMPRINCIPAL

-1 HT   Great C̲   0 HT

Chimney:
L = 7/8; D = 1/2

Approximate Dimensions

Open

95.60 cm.

Covered

109.20 cm.   Corpus

Open

239.65 cm.

1/4   Cutup   1/4

4/19   Mouth   1/4

Scale: 1 mm. = 20 mm.

147.6
mm.

154.2
mm.

PLATE LII

SCALE MODELS OF VARIOUS ECHOFORMS
AT 8' PITCH

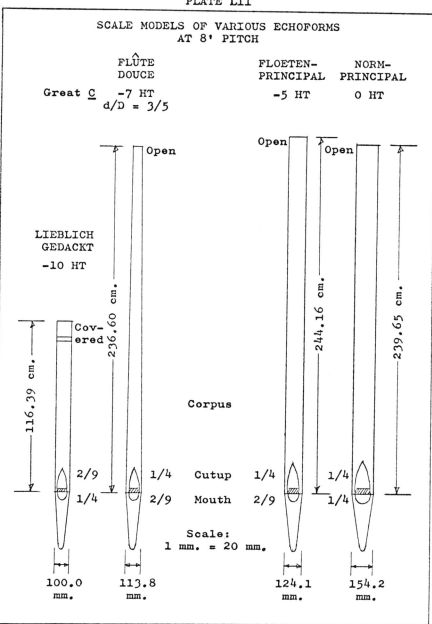

PLATE LIII

SCALE MODEL OF 8' NACHTHORN

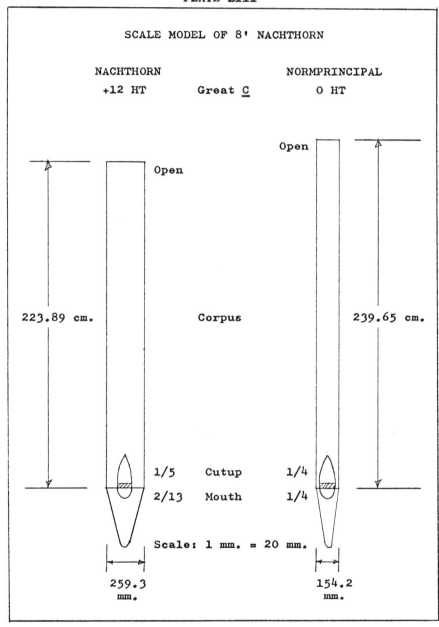

| NACHTHORN | | NORMPRINCIPAL |
| +12 HT | Great C | 0 HT |

Open

Open

223.89 cm.   Corpus   239.65 cm.

| 1/5 | Cutup | 1/4 |
| 2/13 | Mouth | 1/4 |

Scale: 1 mm. = 20 mm.

259.3
mm.

154.2
mm.

PLATE LIV

SCALE MODEL OF 8' GEMSHORN

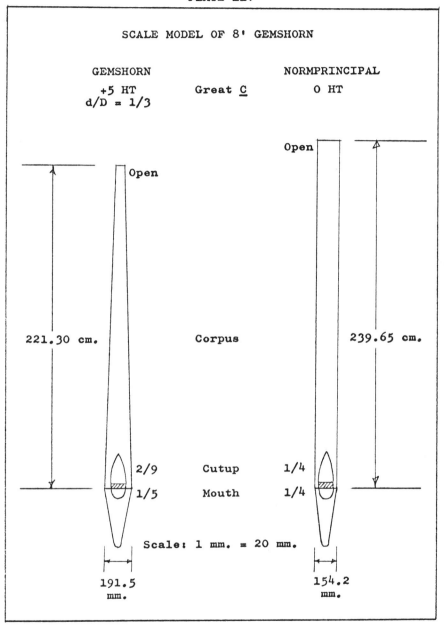

GEMSHORN   Great <u>C</u>   NORMPRINCIPAL

+5 HT   0 HT
d/D = 1/3

Open   Open

221.30 cm.   Corpus   239.65 cm.

2/9   Cutup   1/4

1/5   Mouth   1/4

Scale: 1 mm. = 20 mm.

191.5   154.2
mm.   mm.

PLATE LV

SCALE MODEL OF 8' GEDACKTFLOETE

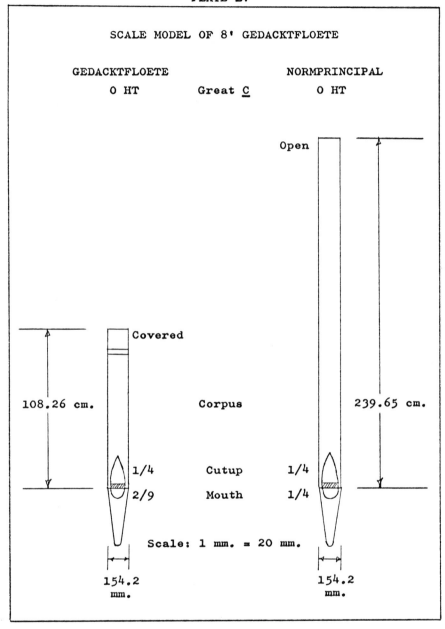

GEDACKTFLOETE   NORMPRINCIPAL
0 HT   Great <u>C</u>   0 HT

Open

Covered

Corpus

108.26 cm.   239.65 cm.

1/4   Cutup   1/4
2/9   Mouth   1/4

Scale: 1 mm. = 20 mm.

154.2   154.2
mm.   mm.

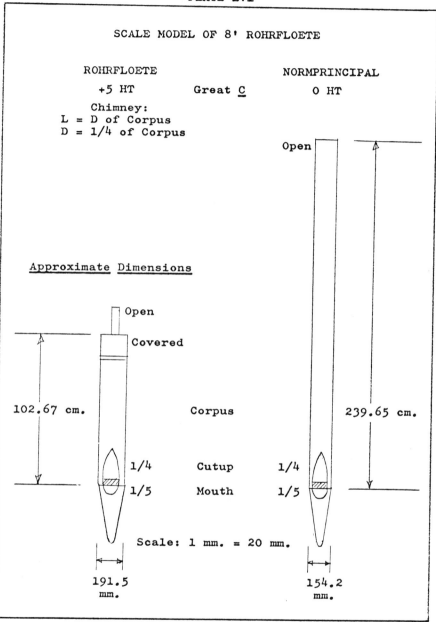

PLATE LVI

SCALE MODEL OF 8' ROHRFLOETE

ROHRFLOETE   NORMPRINCIPAL

+5 HT   Great C   0 HT

Chimney:
L = D of Corpus
D = 1/4 of Corpus

Approximate Dimensions

PLATE LVII

SCALE MODEL OF WIDE-SCALED ECHOFORM

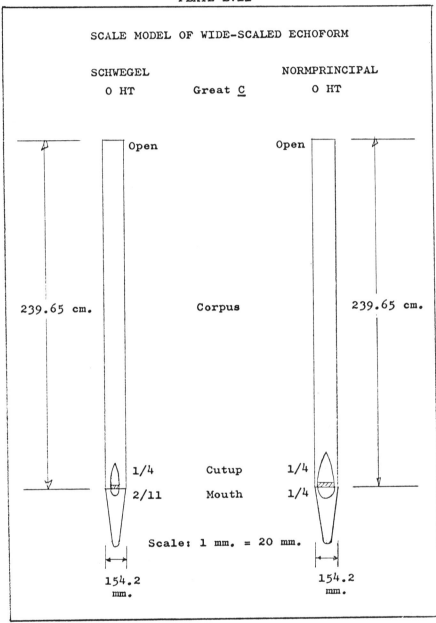

SCHWEGEL   NORMPRINCIPAL

O HT   Great <u>C</u>   O HT

Open   Open

239.65 cm.   Corpus   239.65 cm.

1/4   Cutup   1/4

2/11   Mouth   1/4

Scale: 1 mm. = 20 mm.

154.2 mm.   154.2 mm.

PLATE LVIII

THE SPRING CHEST[a]

Transverse Section

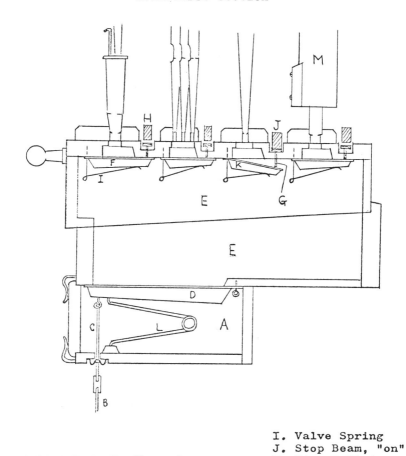

A. Pallet Box
B. Tracker
C. Pull-down
D. Key Pallet
    Valve

E. Channel
F. Stop Pallet
    Valve, "closed"
G. Sticker
H. Stop Beam, "off"

I. Valve Spring
J. Stop Beam, "on"
K. Stop Pallet
    Valve, "open"
L. Key Pallet
    Valve Spring
M. Pipe

[a]From W. Supper and others, _Orgelbewegung und Historismus_ (Berlin, 1958), p. 50.

PLATE LIX

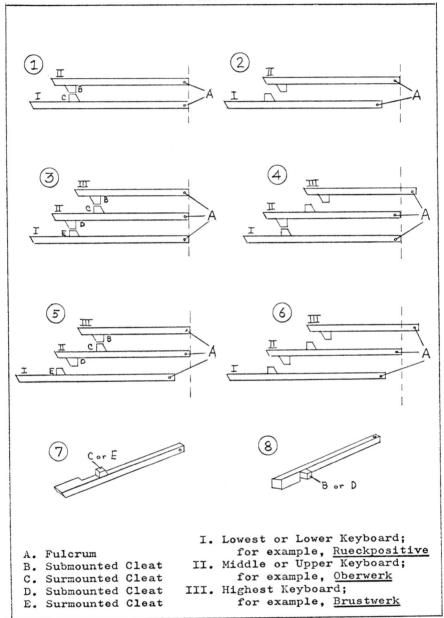

A. Fulcrum
B. Submounted Cleat
C. Surmounted Cleat
D. Submounted Cleat
E. Surmounted Cleat

I. Lowest or Lower Keyboard;
   for example, <u>Rueckpositive</u>
II. Middle or Upper Keyboard;
   for example, <u>Oberwerk</u>
III. Highest Keyboard;
   for example, <u>Brustwerk</u>

PLATE LX

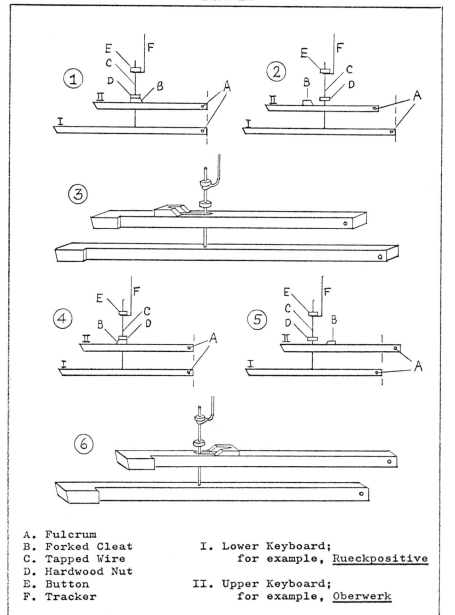

A. Fulcrum
B. Forked Cleat
C. Tapped Wire
D. Hardwood Nut
E. Button
F. Tracker

I. Lower Keyboard;
   for example, _Rueckpositive_

II. Upper Keyboard;
   for example, _Oberwerk_

PLATE LXI

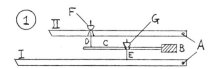

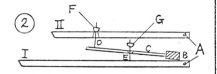

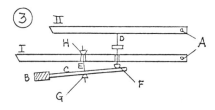

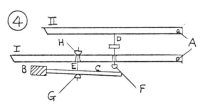

A. Fulcrum
B. Bearing Stock
C. Lever Arm
D. Tapped Wire   I. Lower Keyboard;
E. Tapped Wire   for example, <u>Rueckpositive</u>
F. Leather Button
G. Leather Button   II. Upper Keyboard;
H. Leather Button   for example, <u>Oberwerk</u>

PLATE LXII

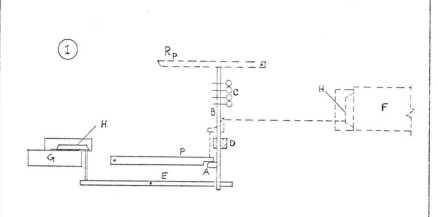

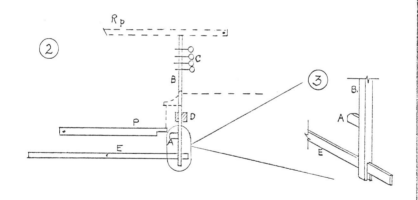

A. Bevelled Cleat
B. Sticker
C. Roller System
D. Movable Register
E. Backfall

F. Pedal Chest
G. Rueckpositive Chest
H. Pallet
P. Pedal Key
Rp. Rueckpositive Manual

PLATE LXIII

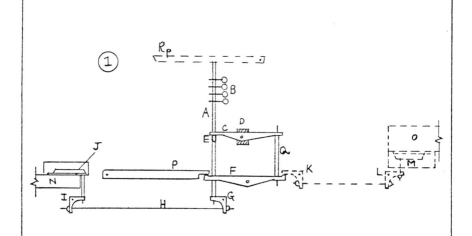

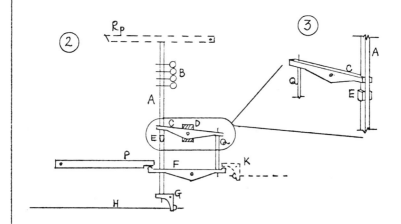

A. Sticker
B. Roller System
C. Backfall
D. Bearing Stock
E. Attached Cleats
F. Backfall

G. Square
H. Tracker
I. Square
J. Pallet
K. Square
L. Square

M. Pallet
N. Rueckpositive Chest
O. Pedal Chest
P. Pedal Key
Q. Sticker
Rp. Rueckpositive Manual

PLATE LXIV

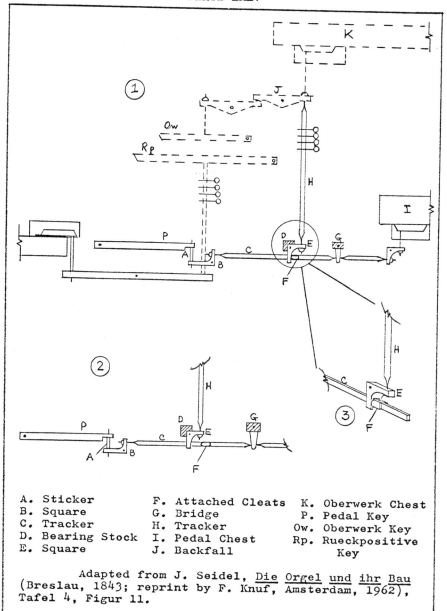

A. Sticker
B. Square
C. Tracker
D. Bearing Stock
E. Square

F. Attached Cleats
G. Bridge
H. Tracker
I. Pedal Chest
J. Backfall

K. Oberwerk Chest
P. Pedal Key
Ow. Oberwerk Key
Rp. Rueckpositive
    Key

Adapted from J. Seidel, *Die Orgel und ihr Bau* (Breslau, 1843; reprint by F. Knuf, Amsterdam, 1962), Tafel 4, Figur 11.

PLATE LXV

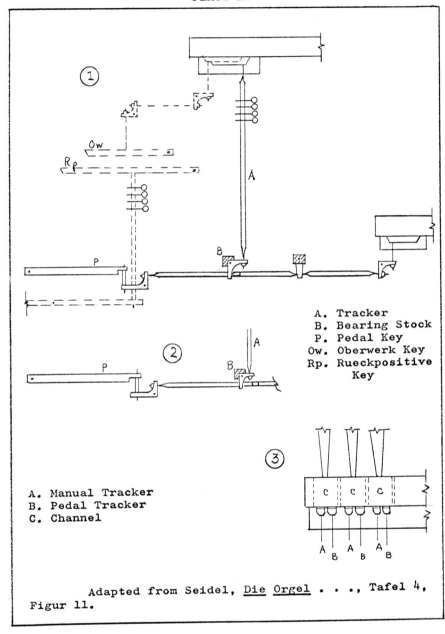

A. Tracker
B. Bearing Stock
P. Pedal Key
Ow. Oberwerk Key
Rp. Rueckpositive
    Key

A. Manual Tracker
B. Pedal Tracker
C. Channel

Adapted from Seidel, Die Orgel . . ., Tafel 4, Figur 11.

PLATE LXVI

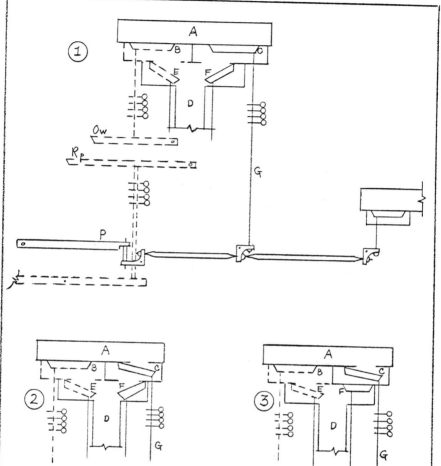

A. Oberwerk Chest
B. Oberwerk Key Pallet
C. Pedal Key Pallet
D. Wind Conductor
E. Oberwerk Ventil

F. Pedal Ventil
G. Tracker
Ow. Oberwerk Key
P. Pedal Key
Rp. Rueckpositive Key

Adapted from Seidel, Die Orgel . . ., Tafel 4, Figur 11.

PLATE LXVII

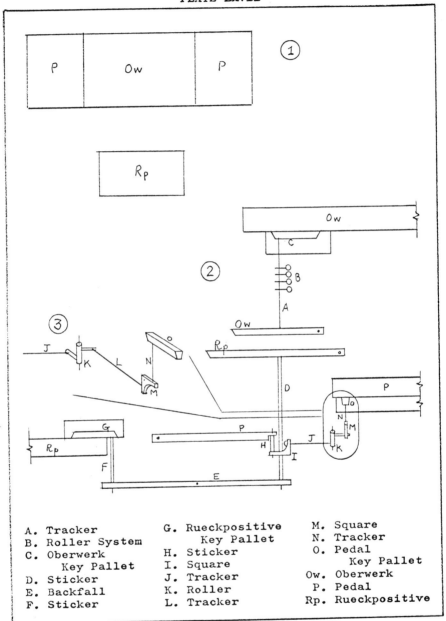

A. Tracker
B. Roller System
C. Oberwerk
   Key Pallet
D. Sticker
E. Backfall
F. Sticker

G. Rueckpositive
   Key Pallet
H. Sticker
I. Square
J. Tracker
K. Roller
L. Tracker

M. Square
N. Tracker
O. Pedal
   Key Pallet
Ow. Oberwerk
P. Pedal
Rp. Rueckpositive

PLATE LXVIII

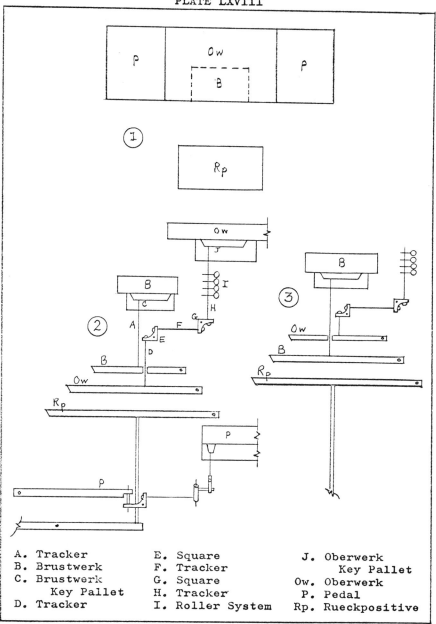

A. Tracker
B. Brustwerk
C. Brustwerk
   Key Pallet
D. Tracker

E. Square
F. Tracker
G. Square
H. Tracker
I. Roller System

J. Oberwerk
   Key Pallet
Ow. Oberwerk
P. Pedal
Rp. Rueckpositive

PLATE LXIX

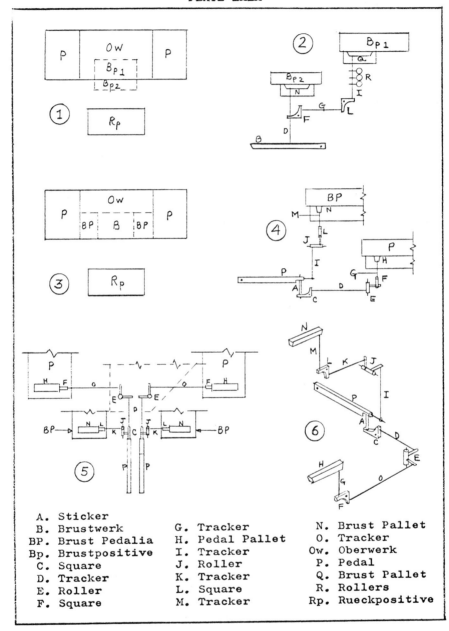

A. Sticker
B. Brustwerk
BP. Brust Pedalia
Bp. Brustpositive
C. Square
D. Tracker
E. Roller
F. Square

G. Tracker
H. Pedal Pallet
I. Tracker
J. Roller
K. Tracker
L. Square
M. Tracker

N. Brust Pallet
O. Tracker
Ow. Oberwerk
P. Pedal
Q. Brust Pallet
R. Rollers
Rp. Rueckpositive

PLATE LXX

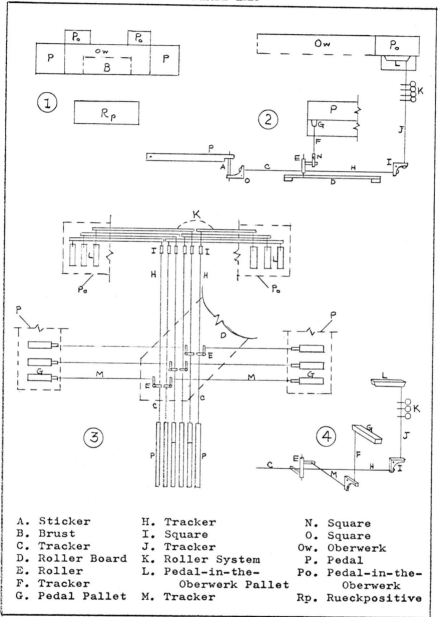

A. Sticker
B. Brust
C. Tracker
D. Roller Board
E. Roller
F. Tracker
G. Pedal Pallet

H. Tracker
I. Square
J. Tracker
K. Roller System
L. Pedal-in-the-
    Oberwerk Pallet
M. Tracker

N. Square
O. Square
Ow. Oberwerk
P. Pedal
Po. Pedal-in-the-
    Oberwerk
Rp. Rueckpositive

PLATE LXXI

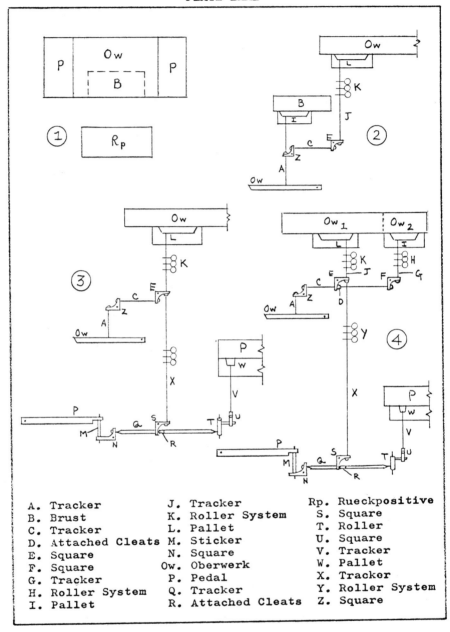

A. Tracker
B. Brust
C. Tracker
D. Attached Cleats
E. Square
F. Square
G. Tracker
H. Roller System
I. Pallet

J. Tracker
K. Roller System
L. Pallet
M. Sticker
N. Square
Ow. Oberwerk
P. Pedal
Q. Tracker
R. Attached Cleats

Rp. Rueckpositive
S. Square
T. Roller
U. Square
V. Tracker
W. Pallet
X. Tracker
Y. Roller System
Z. Square

PLATE LXXII

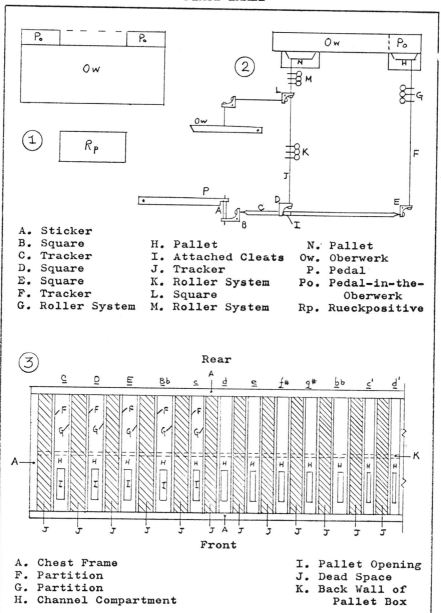

A. Sticker

B. Square

C. Tracker

D. Square

E. Square

F. Tracker

G. Roller System

H. Pallet

I. Attached Cleats

J. Tracker

K. Roller System

L. Square

M. Roller System

N. Pallet

Ow. Oberwerk

P. Pedal

Po. Pedal-in-the-Oberwerk

Rp. Rueckpositive

A. Chest Frame

F. Partition

G. Partition

H. Channel Compartment

I. Pallet Opening

J. Dead Space

K. Back Wall of Pallet Box

PLATE LXXIII

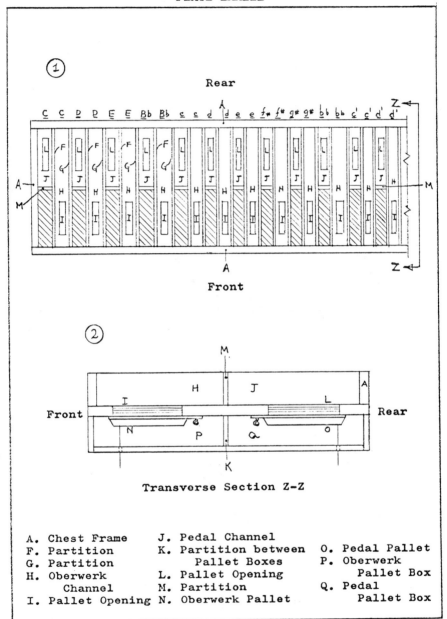

Transverse Section Z-Z

A. Chest Frame
F. Partition
G. Partition
H. Oberwerk
     Channel
I. Pallet Opening

J. Pedal Channel
K. Partition between
     Pallet Boxes
L. Pallet Opening
M. Partition
N. Oberwerk Pallet

O. Pedal Pallet
P. Oberwerk
     Pallet Box
Q. Pedal
     Pallet Box

PLATE LXXIV

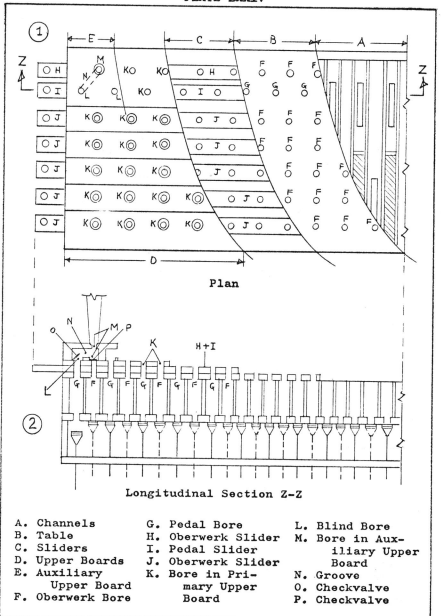

Plan

Longitudinal Section Z-Z

A. Channels
B. Table
C. Sliders
D. Upper Boards
E. Auxiliary
   Upper Board
F. Oberwerk Bore

G. Pedal Bore
H. Oberwerk Slider
I. Pedal Slider
J. Oberwerk Slider
K. Bore in Pri-
   mary Upper
   Board

L. Blind Bore
M. Bore in Aux-
   iliary Upper
   Board
N. Groove
O. Checkvalve
P. Checkvalve

PLATE LXXV

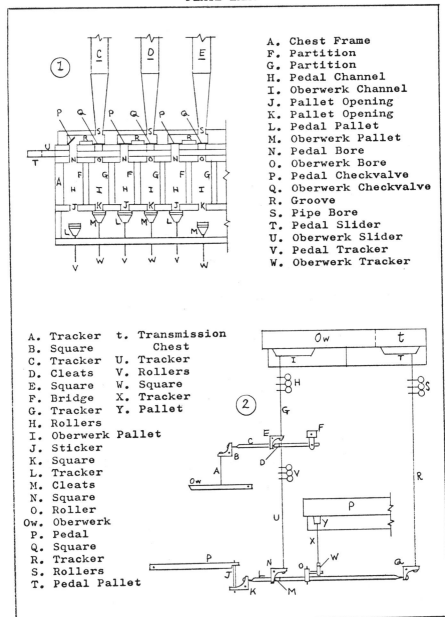

Figure 1 labels:

A. Chest Frame
F. Partition
G. Partition
H. Pedal Channel
I. Oberwerk Channel
J. Pallet Opening
K. Pallet Opening
L. Pedal Pallet
M. Oberwerk Pallet
N. Pedal Bore
O. Oberwerk Bore
P. Pedal Checkvalve
Q. Oberwerk Checkvalve
R. Groove
S. Pipe Bore
T. Pedal Slider
U. Oberwerk Slider
V. Pedal Tracker
W. Oberwerk Tracker

Figure 2 labels:

A. Tracker
B. Square
C. Tracker
D. Cleats
E. Square
F. Bridge
G. Tracker
H. Rollers
I. Oberwerk Pallet
J. Sticker
K. Square
L. Tracker
M. Cleats
N. Square
O. Roller
Ow. Oberwerk
P. Pedal
Q. Square
R. Tracker
S. Rollers
T. Pedal Pallet
t. Transmission Chest
U. Tracker
V. Rollers
W. Square
X. Tracker
Y. Pallet

PLATE LXXVI

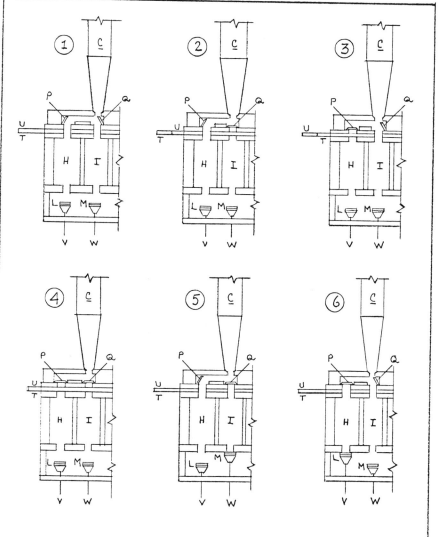

H. Pedal Channel
I. Oberwerk
    Channel
L. Pedal Pallet

M. Oberwerk Pallet
P. Pedal
    Checkvalve
Q. Oberwerk
    Checkvalve

T. Pedal Slider
U. Oberwerk Slider
V. Pedal Tracker
W. Oberwerk Tracker

PLATE LXXVII

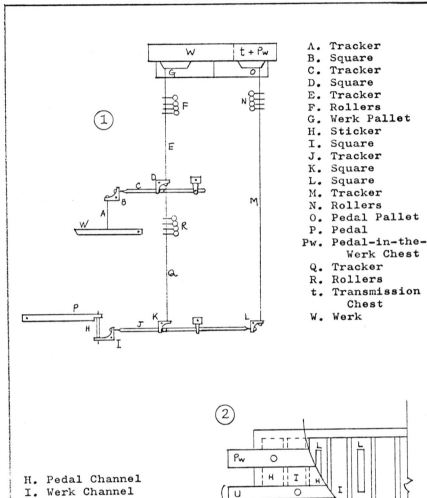

A. Tracker
B. Square
C. Tracker
D. Square
E. Tracker
F. Rollers
G. Werk Pallet
H. Sticker
I. Square
J. Tracker
K. Square
L. Square
M. Tracker
N. Rollers
O. Pedal Pallet
P. Pedal
Pw. Pedal-in-the-
    Werk Chest
Q. Tracker
R. Rollers
t. Transmission
   Chest
W. Werk

H. Pedal Channel
I. Werk Channel
L. Pedal Pallet Opening
Pw. Pedal-in-the-
    Werk Slider
T. Pedal Slider
U. Werk Slider
X. Werk Slider

PLATE LXXVI

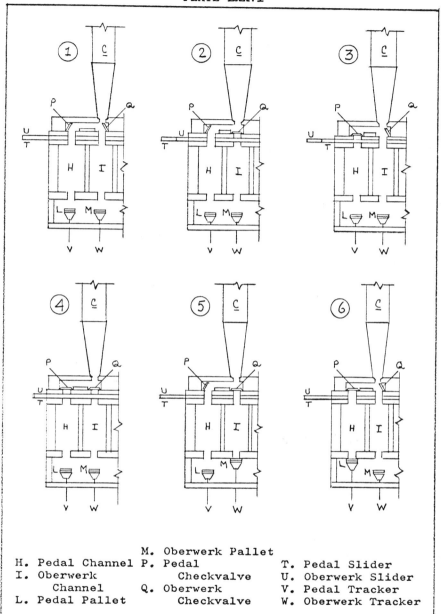

H. Pedal Channel
I. Oberwerk
    Channel
L. Pedal Pallet

M. Oberwerk Pallet
P. Pedal
    Checkvalve
Q. Oberwerk
    Checkvalve

T. Pedal Slider
U. Oberwerk Slider
V. Pedal Tracker
W. Oberwerk Tracker

PLATE LXXVII

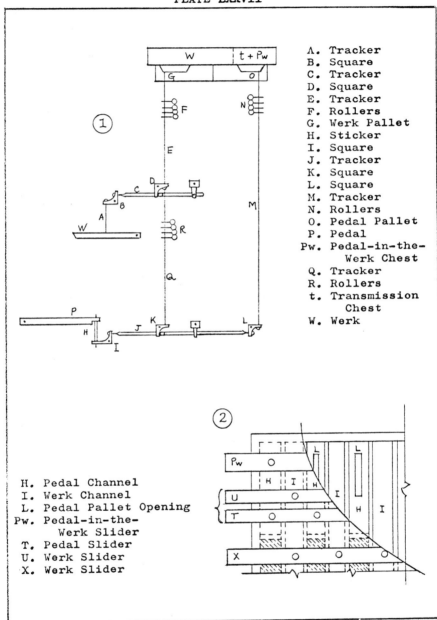

A. Tracker
B. Square
C. Tracker
D. Square
E. Tracker
F. Rollers
G. Werk Pallet
H. Sticker
I. Square
J. Tracker
K. Square
L. Square
M. Tracker
N. Rollers
O. Pedal Pallet
P. Pedal
Pw. Pedal-in-the-
      Werk Chest
Q. Tracker
R. Rollers
t. Transmission
      Chest
W. Werk

H. Pedal Channel
I. Werk Channel
L. Pedal Pallet Opening
Pw. Pedal-in-the-
      Werk Slider
T. Pedal Slider
U. Werk Slider
X. Werk Slider

PLATE LXXVIII

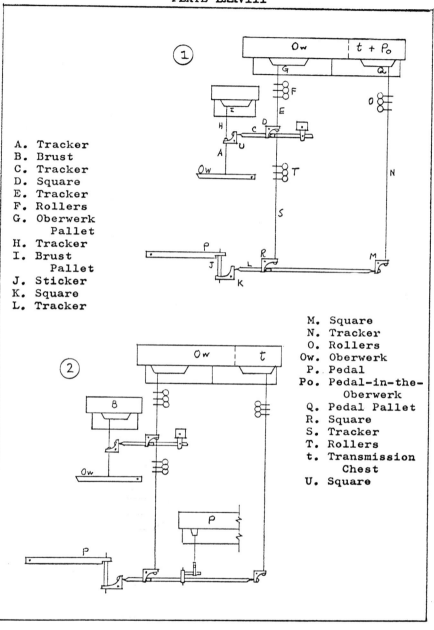

A. Tracker
B. Brust
C. Tracker
D. Square
E. Tracker
F. Rollers
G. Oberwerk
   Pallet
H. Tracker
I. Brust
   Pallet
J. Sticker
K. Square
L. Tracker

M. Square
N. Tracker
O. Rollers
Ow. Oberwerk
P. Pedal
Po. Pedal-in-the-
   Oberwerk
Q. Pedal Pallet
R. Square
S. Tracker
T. Rollers
t. Transmission
   Chest
U. Square

PLATE LXXIX

A. Tracker
B. Brust
BP. Brust
     Pedalia
C. Square
D. Tracker
E. Square
F. Tracker
G. Pallet
H. Sticker
I. Square
J. Tracker
K. Square
L. Tracker
M. Rollers
N. Square
O. Tracker

Ow. Oberwerk
P. Pedal
Po. Pedal-in-the-
     Oberwerk
Q. Pallet
R. Roller
S. Square
T. Tracker
t. Transmission
U. Pallet
V. Square
W. Tracker
X. Rollers
Y. Rollers
Z. Pallet
a. Tracker
b. Roller
d. Square
e. Tracker
f. Pallet
g. Pallet

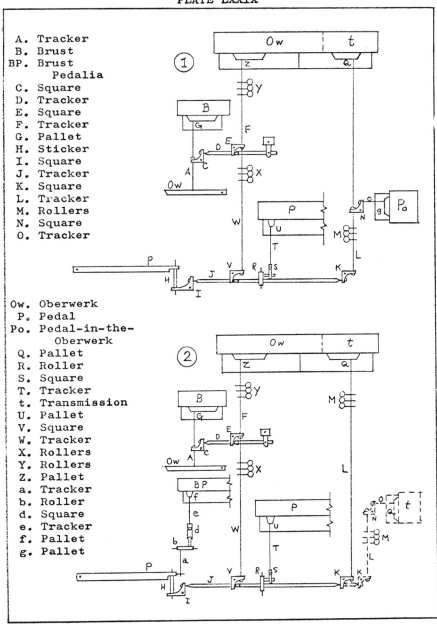

PLATE LXXX

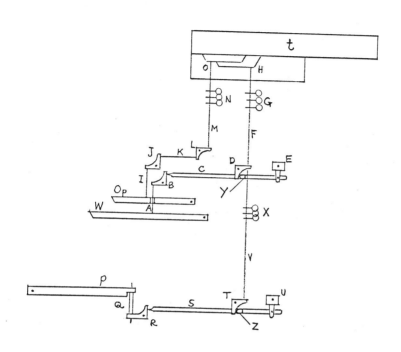

A. Tracker
B. Square
C. Tracker
D. Square
E. Bridge
F. Tracker
G. Rollers
H. Werk Pallet
I. Tracker
J. Square

K. Tracker
L. Square
M. Tracker
N. Rollers
O. Oberpositive
    Pallet
Op. Oberpositive
P. Pedal
Q. Sticker

R. Square
S. Tracker
T. Square
t. Transmission
U. Bridge
V. Tracker
W. Werk
X. Rollers
Y. Cleats
Z. Cleats

PLATE LXXXI

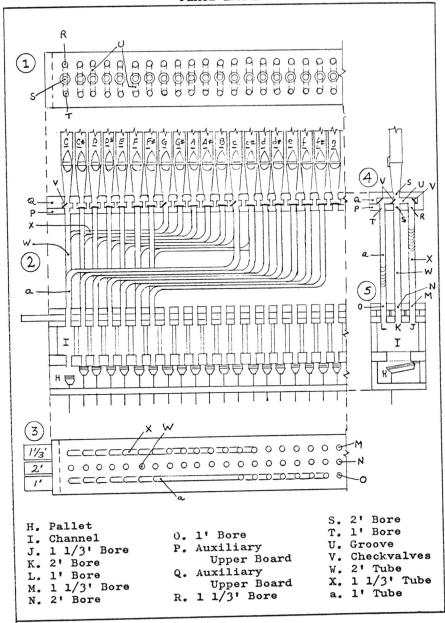

H. Pallet
I. Channel
J. 1 1/3' Bore
K. 2' Bore
L. 1' Bore
M. 1 1/3' Bore
N. 2' Bore

O. 1' Bore
P. Auxiliary
   Upper Board
Q. Auxiliary
   Upper Board
R. 1 1/3' Bore

S. 2' Bore
T. 1' Bore
U. Groove
V. Checkvalves
W. 2' Tube
X. 1 1/3' Tube
a. 1' Tube

PLATE LXXXII

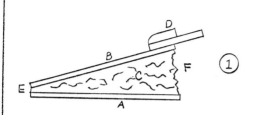

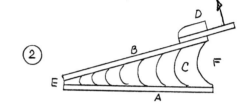

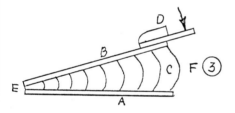

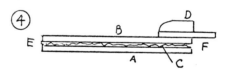

A. Bottom Panel   C. Leather Apron   E. Front Hinge
B. Top Panel   D. Stirrup   F. Rear

PLATE LXXXIII

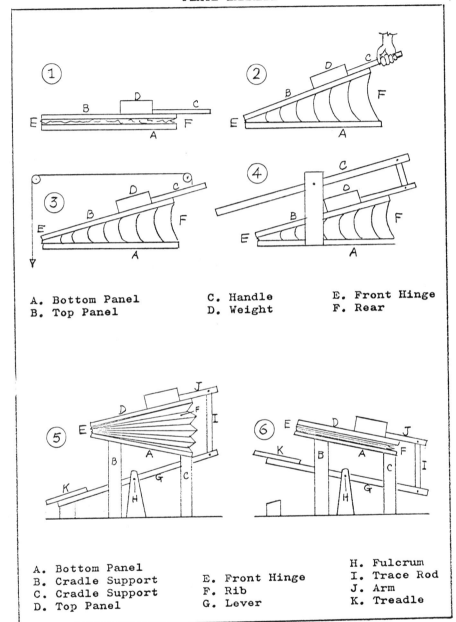

A. Bottom Panel   C. Handle   E. Front Hinge
B. Top Panel   D. Weight   F. Rear

A. Bottom Panel   H. Fulcrum
B. Cradle Support   E. Front Hinge   I. Trace Rod
C. Cradle Support   F. Rib   J. Arm
D. Top Panel   G. Lever   K. Treadle

PLATE LXXXIV

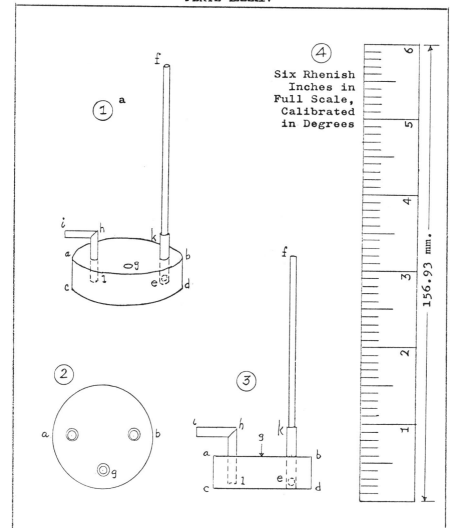

Six Rhenish
Inches in
Full Scale,
Calibrated
in Degrees

156.93 mm.

[a]Fig. 1 is a reproduction of the Foerner Wind-probe as presented in J. Adlung, Anleitung zu der musi-kalischen Gelahrtheit (Erfurt, 1758; facs. ed. by H. Moser, Kassel, 1953), Tab. III opposite p. 542, and identified there as Fig. 23.

PLATE LXXXV

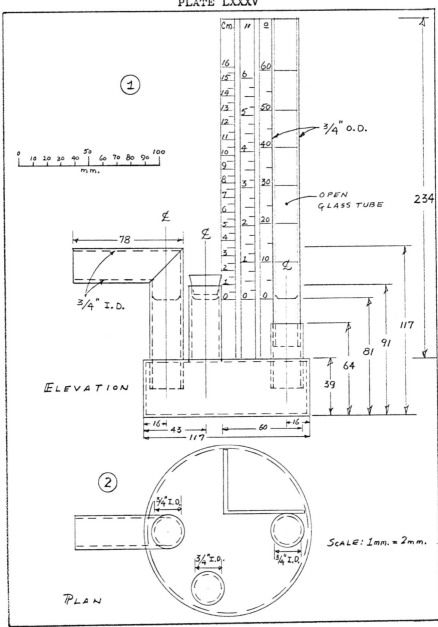

PLATE LXXXVI

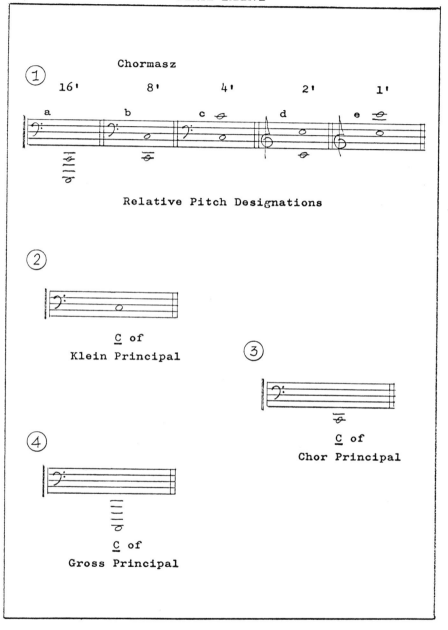

Chormasz

Relative Pitch Designations

C of
Klein Principal

C of
Chor Principal

C of
Gross Principal

PLATE LXXXVII

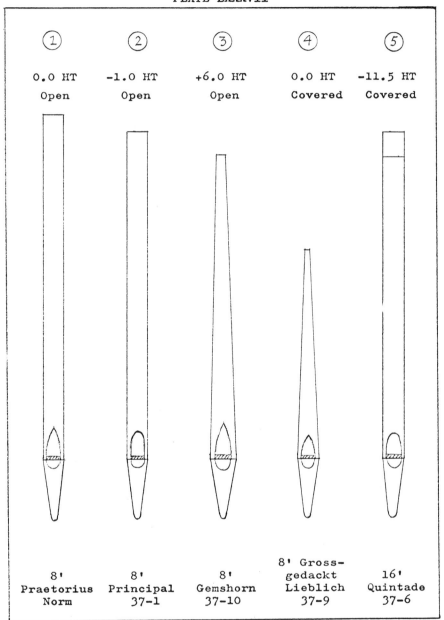

PLATE LXXXVIII

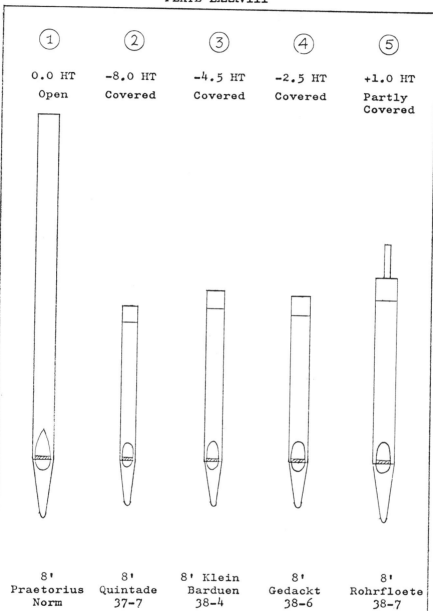

PLATE LXXXIX

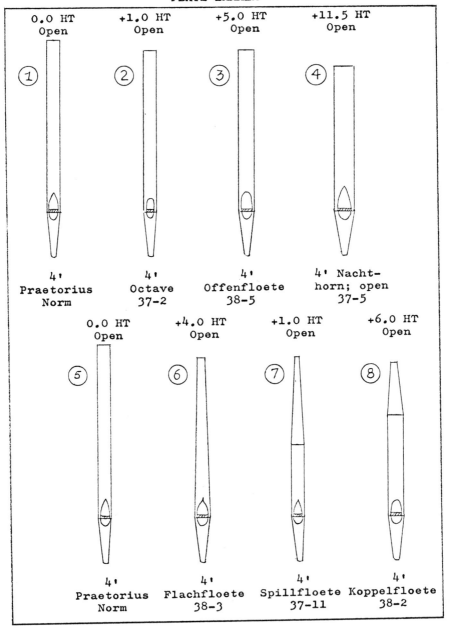

PLATE XC

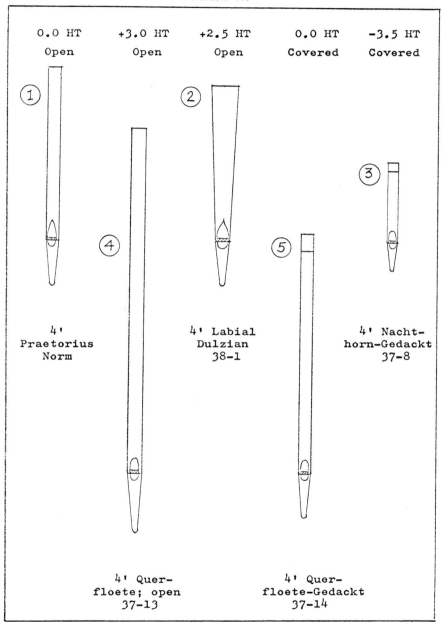

0.0 HT
Open

+3.0 HT
Open

+2.5 HT
Open

0.0 HT
Covered

-3.5 HT
Covered

4'
Praetorius
Norm

4' Labial
Dulzian
38-1

4' Nacht-
horn-Gedackt
37-8

4' Quer-
floete; open
37-13

4' Quer-
floete-Gedackt
37-14

PLATE XCI

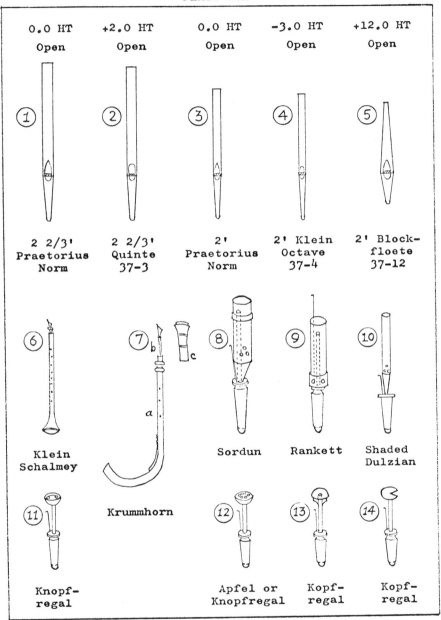

0.0 HT   +2.0 HT   0.0 HT   -3.0 HT   +12.0 HT

Open   Open   Open   Open   Open

① ② ③ ④ ⑤

2 2/3'   2 2/3'   2'   2' Klein   2' Block-
Praetorius   Quinte   Praetorius   Octave   floete
Norm   37-3   Norm   37-4   37-12

⑥ ⑦ ⑧ ⑨ ⑩

Klein   Sordun   Rankett   Shaded
Schalmey   Dulzian

Krummhorn

⑪ ⑫ ⑬ ⑭

Knopf-   Apfel or   Kopf-   Kopfregal   Knopfregal   regal   regal

PLATE XCII

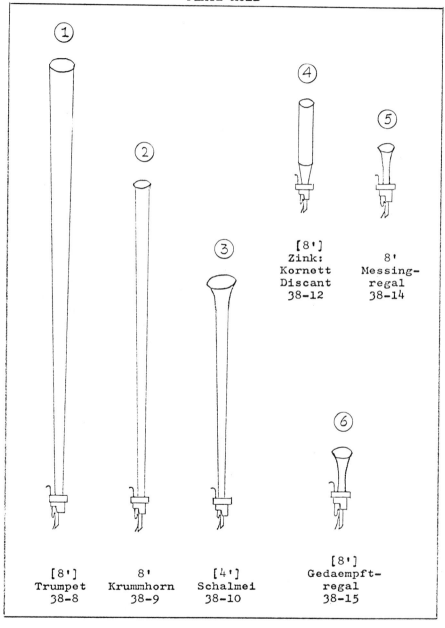

[8']
Zink:
Kornett
Discant
38-12

8'
Messing-
regal
38-14

[8']
Trumpet
38-8

8'
Krummhorn
38-9

[4']
Schalmei
38-10

[8']
Gedaempft-
regal
38-15

PLATE XCIII

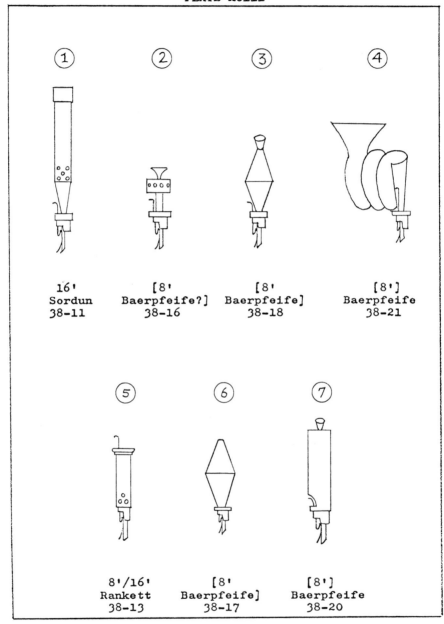

① 16'
Sordun
38-11

② [8'
Baerpfeife?]
38-16

③ [8'
Baerpfeife]
38-18

④ [8']
Baerpfeife
38-21

⑤ 8'/16'
Rankett
38-13

⑥ [8'
Baerpfeife]
38-17

⑦ [8']
Baerpfeife
38-20

PLATE XCIV

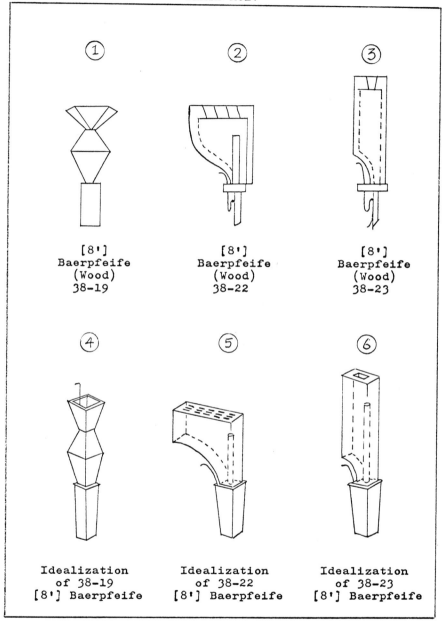

①

[8']
Baerpfeife
(Wood)
38-19

②

[8']
Baerpfeife
(Wood)
38-22

③

[8']
Baerpfeife
(Wood)
38-23

④

Idealization
of 38-19
[8'] Baerpfeife

⑤

Idealization
of 38-22
[8'] Baerpfeife

⑥

Idealization
of 38-23
[8'] Baerpfeife

PLATE XCV

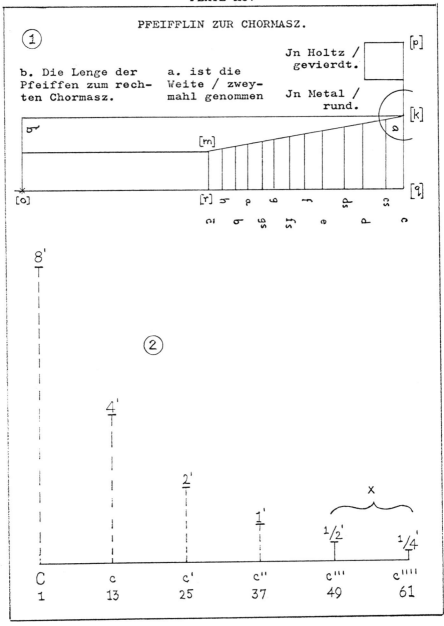

PFEIFFLIN ZUR CHORMASZ.

① [p] Jn Holtz / gevierdt.

b. Die Lenge der Pfeiffen zum rechten Chormasz.

a. ist die Weite / zweymahl genommen

Jn Metal / rund. [k]

[m] [o] [r] [q]

② 8' 4' 2' 1' ½' ¼' x

C	c	c'	c''	c'''	c''''
1	13	25	37	49	61

PLATE XCVI

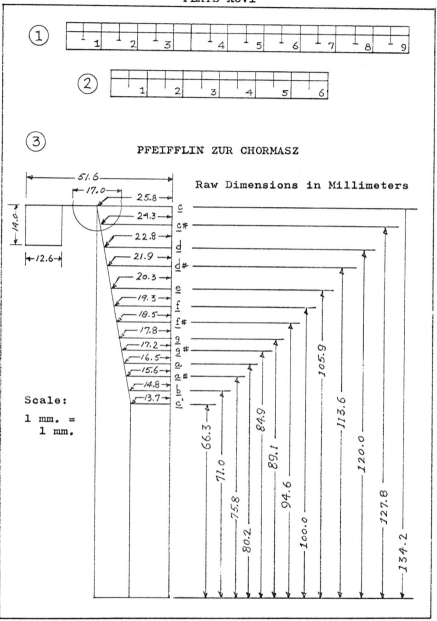

PFEIFFLIN ZUR CHORMASZ

Raw Dimensions in Millimeters

Scale:

1 mm. =
   1 mm.

PLATE XCVII

PFEIFFLIN ZUR CHORMASZ

Corrected Dimensions in Millimeters

Scale: 1 mm. = 1 mm.

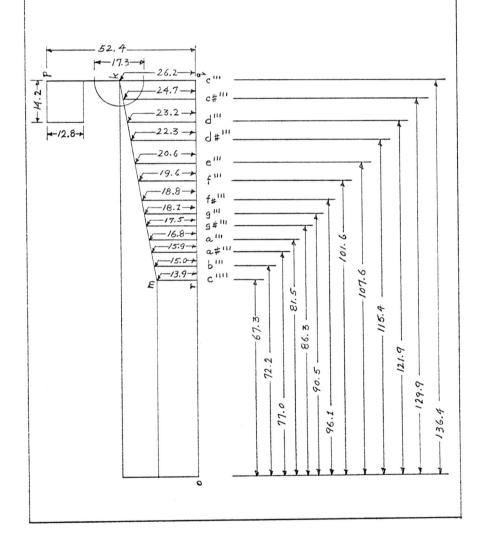

PLATE XCVIII

REALIZATIONS FROM PLATE XXXVII OF THE
THEATRUM INSTRUMENTORUM (PART 1)

Actual Dimensions in Metric Units

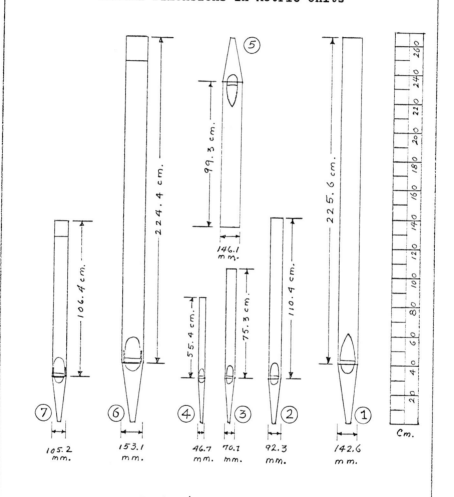

1. 8' Principal
2. 4' Octave
3. 2 2/3' Quinte
4. 2' Klein Octave
5. 4' Nachthorn; open
6. 16' Quintade
7. 8' Quintade

PLATE XCIX

REALIZATIONS FROM PLATE XXXVII OF THE THEATRUM INSTRUMENTORUM (PART 2)

Actual Dimensions in Metric Units

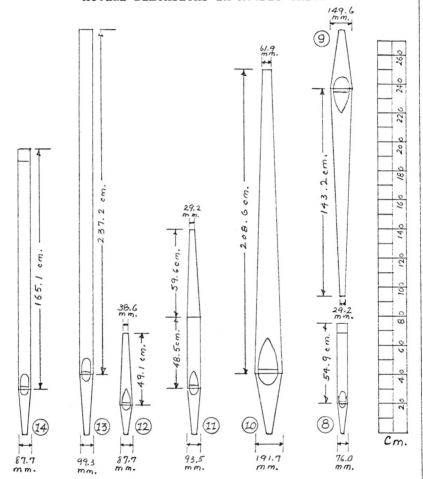

8. 4' Nachthorn-Gedackt
9. 8' Grossgedackt
10. 8' Gemshorn
11. 4' Spillfloete
12. 2' Blockfloete
13. 4' Querfloete; open
14. 4' Querfloete-Gedackt

PLATE C

REALIZATIONS FROM PLATE XXXVIII
OF THE THEATRUM INSTRUMENTORUM

Actual Dimensions in Metric Units

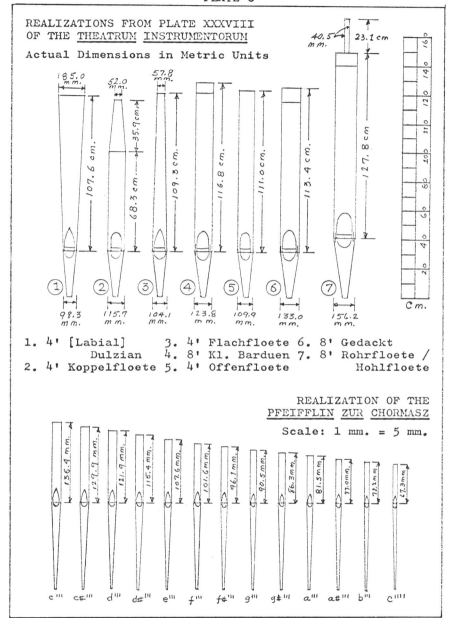

1. 4' [Labial]   3. 4' Flachfloete   6. 8' Gedackt
         Dulzian   4. 8' Kl. Barduen   7. 8' Rohrfloete /
2. 4' Koppelfloete   5. 4' Offenfloete   Hohlfloete

REALIZATION OF THE
PFEIFFLIN ZUR CHORMASZ

Scale: 1 mm. = 5 mm.

PLATE CI

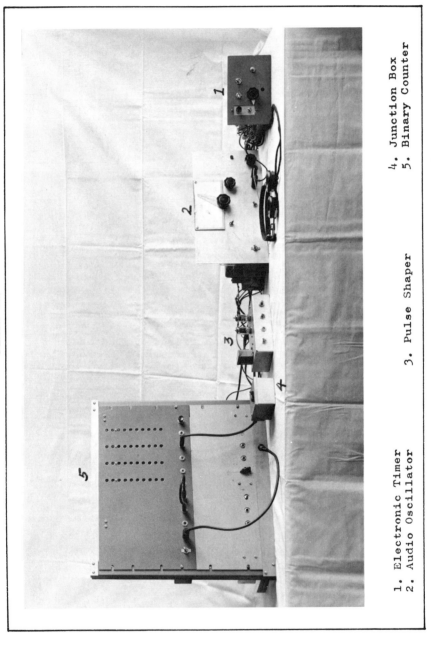

1. Electronic Timer   3. Pulse Shaper   4. Junction Box
2. Audio Oscillator   5. Binary Counter

PLATE CII

1. Electronic Timer   3. Pulse Shaper   4. Junction Box
2. Audio Oscillator   5. Binary Counter

PLATE CIII

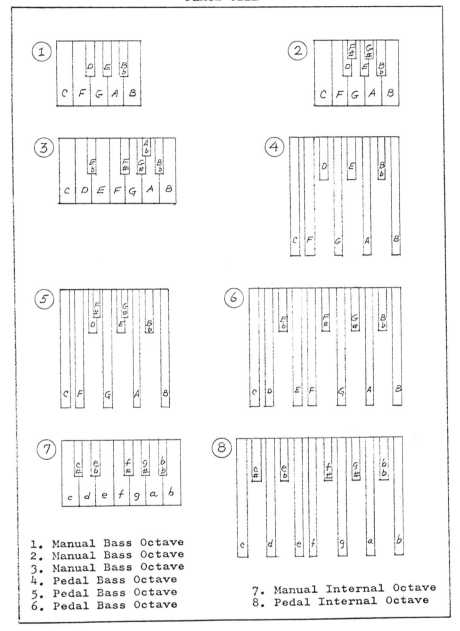

1. Manual Bass Octave
2. Manual Bass Octave
3. Manual Bass Octave
4. Pedal Bass Octave
5. Pedal Bass Octave
6. Pedal Bass Octave

7. Manual Internal Octave
8. Pedal Internal Octave

PLATE **CIV**

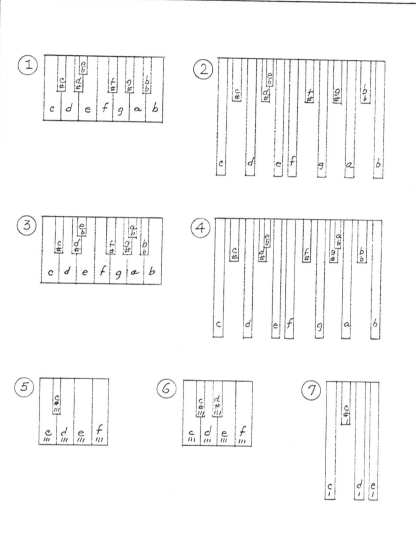

1. Manual Internal Octave
2. Pedal Internal Octave
3. Manual Internal Octave
4. Pedal Internal Octave
5. Manual Treble Octave

6. Manual Treble Octave
7. Pedal Treble Octave

PLATE CV

PRAETORIUS' "THEATER OF ORGAN PIPES" [a]

1. 4' Querfloete; 8. 4' Nachthorn- 15. 8' Gedackt
   open   Gedackt   16. 4' Octave
2. 16' Quintade   9. 2 2/3' Quinte 17. 4' Spillfloete
3. 4' Querfloete- 10. 4' Koppel-   18. 8' Quintade
   Gedackt   floete   19. 4' Nachthorn;
4. 8' Gross-   11. 4' [Labial]   open
   gedackt   Dulzian   20. 2' Klein
5. 8' Rohrfloete / 12. 4' Flachfloete   Octave
   Hohlfloete   13. 4' Offenfloete 21. 2' Blockfloete
6. 8' Gemshorn   14. 8' Klein   22. Pfeifflin zur
7. 8' Principal   Barduen   Chormasz

[a]The pipes were fabricated from scale models
and graphs of the same as presented in M. Praetorius,
Theatrum Instrumentorum seu Sciagraphia . . . (Wolfenbuettel, 1620), Plates XXXVII and XXXVIII, and in M.
Praetorius, Syntagmatis Musici Tomus Secundus De Organographia . . . (Wolfenbuettel, 1619), p. 232; both titles
in facsimile edition by W. Gurlitt (Kassel, 1929).